Last Chance for Victory

Robert E. Lee and
the Gettysburg Campaign

Scott Bowden
& Bill Ward

Da Capo Press

Maps by George Skoch
Unless otherwise indicated, artwork courtesy of Gallon Historical Art, Gettysburg, Pennsylvania

Cataloging-in-Publication data for this book is available from the Library of Congress.

First Da Capo Press edition 2001
Originally published by Savas Publishing Company in 2001.
ISBN 1-882810-65-1

Published by Da Capo Press
A Member of the Perseus Books Group
http://www.dacapopress.com

Da Capo Press books are available at special discounts for bulk purchases in the U.S. by corporations, institutions, and other organizations. For more information, please contact the Special Markets Department at the Perseus Books Group, 11 Cambridge Center, Cambridge, MA 02142, or call (617) 252-5298.

2 3 4 5 6 7 8 9—05 04 03 02 01

General Robert Edward Lee
(1807 - 1870)

TABLE OF CONTENTS

continued . . .

TABLE OF CONTENTS (continued)

MAPS AND TABLES

ILLUSTRATIONS AND PHOTOGRAPHS

continued . . .

ILLUSTRATIONS AND PHOTOGRAPHS

(continued)

continued . . .

ILLUSTRATIONS AND PHOTOGRAPHS

(continued)

Preface

ore has been written about Gettysburg than any other battle in American military history. Tens of hundreds of books and articles had been printed on the subject. Even bits and pieces of the fighting have received book-length treatment. For example, a large monograph appeared recently covering in minute detail the fighting for Culp's Hill and Cemetery Hill; another and even larger volume by the same author examined the fighting on the southern end of the field on July 2. Even the skirmishing around the Bliss Farm, a small complex of buildings improbably situated between two low ridges that would feel the tramp of thousands of feet marching in one of the greatest assaults in military history, has received lengthy attention.

We were thus not surprised when students of the War for Southern Independence reacted, at least initially, with some skepticism to the news that we were intending to add to this deluge of ink. "Do we really need another book about Gettysburg and Pickett's Charge?" they often asked. The short answer to that question is yes, another book is necessary. And the following paragraphs explain why.

Many generations have passed since the great armies clashed in southeastern Pennsylvania and almost 50,000 men in blue and gray were killed, wounded or captured in a supreme display of conviction and courage on both sides. Efforts to interpret exactly what had happened and why began almost immediately. Men in the ranks discussed the great events comprising the three days in July; letters found their way home praising heroic efforts and lamenting lost opportunities. And the seeds of discord—spread initially in whispered conversation, hinted at in battle reports—were sown for later generations to harvest. Murmurs of misconduct (and worse) commenced soon after the fighting stopped, but after General Lee died in 1870, Southern mischief makers like Jubal Early and William Nelson Pendleton kicked their slander and libel efforts into high gear. Many of their fabrications, printed in one form or another and delivered in speeches across succeeding generations, have braided themselves into the original fabric of the battle. Variations of their vitriol have emerged as accepted reality. Other mistakes, some great and others less so, have been repeated so often they are now looked upon as gospel. Modern historians, steeped in Gettysburg "tradition," have continued perpetrating these accepted "facts" of the battle without subjecting them to the cold and often unforgiving light of logic, reason, and objectivity. Consequently, significant misunderstandings exist and continue to be perpetuated about the generalship of Robert E. Lee during the invasion of Pennsylvania.

Many writers and most students of the Civil War today believe that Gettysburg was the nadir of Lee's career; that his performance in Adams County during the first few days of July 1863 evidenced an overly combative and headstrong general who could not stem his impulse to throw his men away by the thousands in frontal attacks against George Meade's Army of the Potomac. Lee, it is often said, issued discretionary orders to his key subordinates at critical moments—and lost control of his army; once engaged, the ailing commanding general displayed a "passive" form of personal generalship while asking of his men the impossible. Longstreet, tradition holds, ran roughshod over Lee, who allowed his corps leader to drag his recalcitrant heels in the Pennsylvania dirt as the hours ticked by on July 2 that could have been better used crushing the enemy's left flank. Lee's decisions doomed his legions to defeat. Most of this is simply *assumed* to be true.

But is any of this *really* true? What are the facts behind these assertions? Did Jeb Stuart have the authority to conduct a raid as the Confederate army moved north, and how did his absence affect the campaign? How does Lee's generalship look when his decisions are judged within their proper historical context? What was Lee trying to accomplish in Pennsylvania? What were his goals on July 1? July 2? July 3? How did his key corps, division, and brigade subordinates perform?

The Gettysburg Campaign was a complex series of events and is now a celebrated part of our national heritage. Questioning its core dogma will be seen as heresy by many. But repeating stories because others continue to assert them as true is not good history, and does nothing to further the study of the campaign or honor the men who waged it. To illustrate this point, consider the criticism writers often heap upon Lee for committing the Army of Northern Virginia to the offensive on the second day at Gettysburg. After flaying him for his rashness, Lee is further condemned for the manner in which he attacked late on the afternoon of July 2, when (so tradition largely holds) Longstreet dripped his men into action in a piecemeal and largely frontal attack against Meade's southern flank. As readers of *Last Chance for Victory* will discover, Lee had very good reasons for renewing the offensive that day, considerations rarely if ever seen in print. In fact, resuming the offensive was in accord with every sound military principle of the age and displayed in Lee a moral courage commensurate to the task at hand. Lee also carefully modified his original plan of attack that afternoon from a more standard flanking assault into an *en échelon* attack to take advantage of the changed tactical dispositions of his enemy. And we demonstrate conclusively that, contrary to popular belief, it was George Gordon Meade who was piecemealing his army toward destruction on the afternoon of July 2, 1863—not Robert E. Lee.

But none of what transpired in Pennsylvania can ever be fully understood or appreciated unless the events that spawned the campaign are carefully considered. Accordingly, we explore fully the strategic and political state of the Confederacy in the weeks leading up to the Pennsylvania invasion and the decisions and options President Jefferson Davis and Lee faced in May 1863. This examination includes an evaluation of President Davis' important (and often overlooked) role in shaping the composition of the Southern army that forded the Potomac in the middle of June 1863. Davis' policies impacted the campaign far more than most people believe.

Because all men are but reflections of their upbringing, education, and experiences, we also expend considerable effort scrutinizing both the man and the general who led the Army of Northern Virginia north that summer. Robert E. Lee was trained as an engineer at West Point, studied extensively the campaigns of the Great Captains of military history, and learned the art of command and maneuver at the elbow of General Winfield Scott during the Mexican War. The aggregate of these experiences had a profound and demonstrable influence on his generalship. It is against this backdrop of education and experience that Lee's decisions during the Gettysburg Campaign must be examined, understood, and judged.

*   *   *

Our approach and method of presentation is also radically different from traditional fare. For example, the complex series of decisions, movements, and fighting on July 2 are always—*always*—broken apart and tendered to readers in separate chunks. The fighting around Devil's Den and Little Round Top is usually handled in one chapter, the Peach Orchard salient in another section, Cemetery Ridge in yet another chapter, and so on. The consequence of this customary method of presentation compartmentalizes these phases of the engagement into mini-battles comprising separate actions. And that is how most students of Gettysburg have come to view them. But they were not unrelated sequestered endeavors. Rather, they were part of one overall interlocking strategy of attack that came much closer to breaking apart and decisively defeating Meade's army than anyone heretofore has fully explained. Thus, Chapter 7—all 137 pages of it—is presented as a single fluid event so that readers may fully comprehend what Lee intended to accomplish with his echelon attack, how the attack was progressing, where it broke down, and who was responsible—and just how close Lee came to realizing his bid for victory on Northern soil.

Most modern military studies lump strings of sources together, which makes it difficult for readers to locate an original quote or source relied upon by the author. We have employed a more traditional note methodology and have endeavored to identify each source as it is used within each respective sentence and paragraph. We are extremely grateful to the publisher for agreeing to accommodate us in this regard.

Many chapters conclude with a recapitulation of their primary events, decisions, and results. While this inevitably leads to some redundancy, we believe it is both helpful and worthwhile—especially since several of the chapters are quite lengthy. Further, each summation includes commentary refuting assertions made by other prominent historians on several major issues of import. Our intent is nothing more than an attempt to correct the historical record, and we hope readers understand and appreciate our efforts in that light.

Finally, it should be obvious to anyone who has read this far that *Last Chance for Victory* is a critical examination of General Lee and *Southern* leadership during the campaign. Therefore, it does not examine equally the role played by General Meade and his top subordinates; that task we leave to others.

Acknowledgments

No work of this magnitude could have been produced without the kind assistance of many others too numerous to mention. However, we would like to take this opportunity to offer our gratitude to several individuals and institutions who went above and beyond the call of duty. We are greatly indebted to the Dean and staff of the Harold B. Simpson History Complex at Hill College, Hillsboro, Texas, who oversee the valuable Confederate Research Center. Dr. B. D. Patterson, Dean, was always accessible and answered all of our questions patiently and fully. Dr. Patterson embodies what we consider to be the finest traits of a true Southern gentleman. As the research center's director, Peggy Fox fielded from us what must have seemed like a never-ending barrage of questions about source material. When she was not available, Sandra Rich was always gracious with her time and assistance. At the Library of Congress, we were ably assisted by Mary Isom, who saved us much time and trouble, while the staff of the Museum of the Confederacy always treated us with courtesy and handled our requests on a timely basis. Earl

Upchurch and Lynn Totten read and commented on early versions of the manuscript and offered valuable suggestions on how to make it better. Matt DeLaMater used his expertise in military history to read and comment on a draft of our manuscript and was also kind enough to help us obtain valuable documents from several different institutions of higher learning. We are appreciative of Jesse Lewis' efforts in securing documents from the Library of Congress. Thanks also to Larry Slayton, Peter W. Orlebeke, and Fred Stovall for taking time to read and comment on various aspects of Southern military operations. Mark Cichock also provided notable assistance. We are further indebted to Charles Tarbox who, during our many trips to Gettysburg, was always willing to walk the ground and discuss terrain features and artillery-related aspects of the battle. Few people know more about artillery and Gettysburg than Charlie. Timothy H. Smith provided insight and answers concerning different structures in Gettysburg. James Kralik, a licensed battlefield guide at Gettysburg, extended considerable time during our visits to that sacred field.

Additional thanks are due Dale and Anne Gallon of Gallon Historical Art in Gettysburg. The inclusion of Dale's magnificent pieces breathes life and spirit into *Last Chance for Victory*.

Accomplished cartographer George Skoch ably prepared the maps in record time. His work is excellent and we are grateful for his efforts.

Finally, we wish to thank our publisher and editor, Theodore P. Savas, for his faith in this sizable project. Ted read the manuscript countless times and offered insightful recommendations that in the end made this a much better book. It was a pleasure working with him.

Scott Bowden
Arlington, Texas

Bill Ward
Arlington, Texas

*"The Confederate Army's fight against overwhelming odds,
is one of the most glorious moments in Anglo-Saxon history."*

—Sir Winston Churchill

Chapter 1

"There is Nothing to be Gained by This Army
Remaining Quietly on the Defensive"

Robert E. Lee and Jefferson Davis

*"Unless it [the Federal Army] can be drawn out in a position to be assailed,
it will take its own time to prepare and strengthen itself to renew its advance
upon Richmond, and force this army back within the intrenchments of that
city. . . . I think it is worth a trial to prevent such a catastrophe."*
—Robert E. Lee[1]

On May 14, 1863, General Robert E. Lee, President Jefferson Davis, and members of Davis' cabinet began an arduous four-day conference in a small oblong room on the second floor of the Confederacy's White House in Richmond, Virginia. The purpose of the lengthy discussions, held in the wake of Lee's stunning victory at Chancellorsville earlier in the month over the Army of the Potomac, was to determine Confederate strategy for the upcoming summer months. Momentous consequences hung in the balance.

The Clerk and the General

Lee's latest victory and the end, at least for the moment, of the Federal threat in Virginia gave birth yet again to the issue of transferring troops from Lee's army west. After being bombarded with Lee's requests for reinforcements, President

The White House of the Confederacy

Robert E. Lee attended the strategy conference with President Davis and his cabinet here in May 1863. Built in 1818 and now a National Historic Landmark, the John Brockenbrough House was used by Davis as both an office and living space for his family. The home now serves as part of the complex of the Museum of the Confederacy. *Library of Congress*

Davis summoned the esteemed commander of the Army of Northern Virginia to Richmond to discuss not only the course of the war in Virginia, but Southern strategy in other parts of the South as well. Departing from his headquarters along Davis' mandated defensive line on the Rappahannock River in Virginia, Lee knew that the conference would be perhaps the most important summit of his career. He was also aware that Davis, with whom he enjoyed a cordial working relationship, was under intense pressure from cabinet members, generals, politicians, and influential civilians to do something about the dire strategic situation in the Western Theater of operations. Davis and his cabinet were going to seek help from Lee and his army, and having worked closely with Davis in the past, Lee knew he would be asked for his opinion on what should be done.

In his modest headquarters on the windblown plain near Hamilton's Crossing on the Rappahannock, and during his journey into Richmond to meet with Davis, Lee thought long and hard about the status of the Southern war effort and his role in it. Bloody battles in every theater had drained away tens of thousands of men the South could ill-afford to lose. Holding Kentucky was a dream long past, most of Tennessee and large portions of the Trans-Mississippi states were now occupied by Federal forces, and all but a short swath of the Mississippi River was patrolled by

Yankee war ships. Major southern cities, one by one, had fallen to the invading enemy, including New Orleans, Nashville, and Memphis. Federal enclaves peppered the long and meandering Southern coastline, threatening more railroads and cities than the South could afford to defend. Even now, Federal forces were moving to capture Vicksburg, a key Southern logistical point on the Mississippi River, and drive Southern defenders out of the critical rail junction and industrial city of Chattanooga, Tennessee. Only in Virginia had the Confederates enjoyed sustained success. And President Davis and his cabinet members knew the reason was largely due to the brilliance of Robert E. Lee and his magnificent Army of Northern Virginia.

There were a number of factors Lee had to consider in order to prepare a response to the questions he would face in Richmond. His army faced acute shortages of sustenance for both men and animals, and the pools of available manpower from which his army drank were steadily shrinking. Where would this food, forage, and manpower be found in the weeks and months ahead? President Davis' conceptions about how the Confederacy should wage its war for independence were often at odds with his own opinions. Would Lee be able to formulate a strategic plan for victory consistent with Davis' determination to defend every inch of Southern soil?

Other issues came into play. How could Lee maximize the formidable combat power and soaring morale of his troops? Where would he find qualified lieutenants to replace his combat-stricken officers? What were the resources, condition, and intentions of the Federal Army of the Potomac, currently recuperating from its Chancellorsville wounds across the Rappahannock River? The general was also keenly aware that military operations and politics were intertwined; one necessarily affected the other. How, exactly, would the politics of the hour play into the decision making process about to unfold in Richmond?

Food and Fodder

Lee had always feared the consequences of a long war. Unlike the North, the Southern states did not have the population, industry, or natural resources required for a protracted conflict. When he assumed command of what later became known as the Army of Northern Virginia in the spring of 1862, Lee knew the odds were stacked against victory. After another year of the hard hand of war, the Confederacy's resources were being exhausted at an alarming rate. Unable to keep his force concentrated and properly supplied, he was forced into the unenviable position of dispersing his numerically inferior Army of Northern Virginia in order to feed it.

The primary reason for scattering his divisions was the acute shortage of forage for the army's animals and food for his men. The hard winter of 1862-63 had exposed the Confederate railroad and supply systems for the failures they were, and the Southern armies were on the verge of starvation. "Virginia no longer had enough supplies to support the army," wrote supply historian Richard Goff. "Fresh beef was almost exhausted," a situation brought about in part by a drought in the deep South that had "extinguished the surplus meat supply."[2]

The lack of sufficient food was particularly devastating for the army's animals. Forage had always been one of Lee's major concerns, and its scarcity affected the numbers of animals that could be sustained, as well as their health and activity. "By February the situation had reached crisis proportions," explained Goff, "and Lee had to scatter his cavalry so widely to subsist the animals as to render it almost useless."[3]

On February 13, 1863, Lee wrote to his cavalry commander, James Ewell Brown "Jeb" Stuart, about a combined scouting and raiding mission into the Shenandoah Valley. "Particular attention must be given to the comfort of your men & horses," admonished Lee, "& should circumstances now unforeseen render it inexpedient in your judgment with a due regard to their future usefulness & service, upon your reaching the Valley, to carry out the object of the expedition, you are desired to limit or abandon it at your discretion."[4] Three days later, Lee advised President Davis about the alarming physical state of the animals responsible for moving the army. "Our horses and mules are in that reduced state that the labor & exposure incident to an attack would result in their destruction, & leave us destitute of the means of transportation."[5] The same sentiment was echoed by Robert Garlick Hill Kean, an official in the Confederate War Department in Richmond, who noted, "The most alarming feature of our condition by far is the failure of means of subsistence."[6]

On February 18, Lee dispatched a letter to the commander of his First Corps, Lieutenant General James Longstreet, ordering him to move the divisions of George Pickett and John Bell Hood, together with two battalions of artillery—and possibly one corps artillery reserve battalion—away from the rest of the army and towards the James River. Although the move was originally intended to counter what looked like a Federal threat against Richmond or Petersburg from the east, it would also make it easier for Longstreet to find provender for his weakened animals. "The horses are in such a reduced state, & the country so saturated with water," explained Lee, "that it will be almost impossible for them to drag the guns."[7]

The horses and men remaining with Lee along the Rappahannock River relied on forage that was supposed to be railed in from Richmond on a daily basis. Unfortunately, these supplies did not always arrive. On February 23, Lee wrote to his wife that "our short rations for man & horse will have to be curtailed . . . our animals suffer terribly."[8] The difficulty in the supply department obtaining proper food for the animals of Lee's army prompted the general to advise Davis on February 26 that "it is impossible to procure sufficient forage."[9] Without enough animals to properly service his army and lacking sufficient subsistence for those that were present, Lee was forced on March 21 to issue General Orders No. 43: "It will be necessary to reduce the transportation of the army to the lowest limit. This necessity arises from the difficulty of procuring animals and forage, and from the increased demand for transportation of subsistence when the army shall be removed from the vicinity of railroads."[10]

Bureaucratic and technological inefficiency were not the only reasons behind the army's lack of sufficient forage. Weather had also been a cruel adversary. The hard winter of 1862-63 and late arriving spring had delayed the growth of grass, upon which Lee's animals fed.[11] All of this prompted Lee to instruct the chief of the army's artillery reserve, Brigadier General William N. Pendleton, that "to bring [more horses] up now would but add to our difficulties and might destroy the animals."[12] Two days later on April 3, Lee wrote his wife that the army was "without forage & provisions, & could not remain long together if united for want of food."[13] A few days later, the horses which had been recently forwarded to the army were already beginning to deteriorate. "I am very fearful," the commanding general wrote Pendleton on April 6, "that you may be increasing your horses faster than you can forage them."[14]

On April 19, the issue of healthy horses still weighed heavily on Lee's mind. His letter to Jeb Stuart concluded with these telling words: "I will see [Chief Quartermaster] Colonel [James L.] Corley about the horses for your artillery, but fear he can do nothing [about finding more forage], there is such a demand on him. Save your horses all you can."[15] The following day, Lee wrote President Davis about information he had received about forage and supplies from an artillery officer who had just returned to his command following a recruiting trip in Georgia and Florida. Davis, Lee urged, should authorize the purchase of badly needed foodstuffs for the army from the deep South.[16]

The decaying strength and shortages of horseflesh caused Lee to issue General Orders No. 58 on April 20, 1863. This measure, intended to preserve the serviceable animals still present with the army, effectively reduced the army's transportation capabilities to a dangerously low level.[17] "The difficulty of procuring horses renders it necessary to reduce the transportation as low as possible," Lee wrote Pendleton a few days later. "The destruction of horses in the army [for lack of forage] is so great that I fear it will be impossible to supply our wants."[18]

Forage supply levels were directly tied to the number of animals in Lee's army. After the conclusion of the Chancellorsville Campaign in early May, the number of horses in the Army of Northern Virginia numbered 20,000. In addition to equal amounts of hay that were to be obtained locally, each horse required at least seven to 10 pounds of corn per day (oats was the preferred grain for horses and mules, but corn was the usual staple). This meant that the minimum monthly corn requirement for Lee's army was 140,000 bushels, which was about the supply expected to be delivered to the army in May. This amounted to a daily supply requirement of almost

5,000 bushels of corn, and there was rarely more than a single day's supply on hand.[19] The outlook for improving this situation was bleak.

Lee had been advised that no more than 120,000 bushels could be found and forwarded to the army in the month of June.[20] Other Virginia cavalry commands were similarly suffering. During the Chancellorsville Campaign, Lee noted that John Imboden's horses had "been much reduced by hard work, bad roads, and scant forage."[21] Unable to procure sufficient future supplies of grain, and requiring thousands of additional horses and mules for the summer campaign to augment those already with the Army of Northern Virginia in order to fully mobilize, Lee's fears about being able to supply his army while in Virginia rose to a new level.

Finding enough grain and forage for the army's animals was not the only major logistical concern confronting Lee. Food for the men in the ranks was also in shockingly short supply, and the prices of available food were skyrocketing. In addition, the civilians in Richmond and most of the combat-ravaged counties in Virginia were also suffering. "Some idea may be formed of the scarcity of food in this city [Richmond]," clerk John B. Jones wrote on February 11, 1863, "while my youngest daughter was in the kitchen today, a young rat came out of its hole and seemed to beg for something to eat; she held out some bread, which it ate from her hand, and seemed grateful. Several others soon appeared, and were as tame as kittens. Perhaps we shall have to eat them!"[22] Such was typical of the South's plight for food. In response to this desperate situation, "the government seized the flour in the mills and warehouses" in Richmond on March 5 and the prices rose "from $30 to $40 per barrel."[23] Five days later, Jones admitted that "the great fear is famine."[24] That anxiety was realized on April 2, when an early morning crowd of several hundred women and boys met at Capitol Square in Richmond, "saying that they were hungry, and must have food."[25] The critical shortages in Richmond were but a reflection of the serious lack of proper subsistence for the men and horses in the Army of Northern Virginia. The subject dominated much of Lee's correspondence in the first few months of 1863.[26]

Many people serving in the Confederate government in Richmond understood Lee's plight and the deleterious effects of food shortages on his army. One of those was Robert Kean. The shortages of food were so critical, penned the Richmond war department official on March 7, 1863, that "the army will be starved, and famine will ensue."[27] Only three weeks earlier on February 18, another government official saw "one or two regiments of Gen. Lee's army" in Richmond, noting that "the men were pale and haggard. They have but a quarter of a pound of meat per day."[28]

Lee knew only too well the plight of his starving men, and had spent the first several months of 1863 writing a continuous stream of pleas for relief to officials in Richmond. The situation was deemed so critical that when the Federal threat to Richmond did not materialize, General Longstreet and his two divisions were dispatched south and east of Petersburg beyond the Black River in an attempt to gather foodstuffs for the army from the enemy-held territory around Suffolk, Virginia. Lee's March 27, 1863, letter to Seddon discussed the situation:

> I have endeavored during the past campaign to draw subsistence from the country occupied by the troops, wherever it was possible, and I believe by that means much relief has been afforded to the Commissary Department. At this time but few supplies can be procured from the country we now occupy.
>
> Genl Longstreet has been directed to employ the troops south of the James River [Pickett and Hood], when not required for military operations, to collect supplies in that quarter, and penetrate, if practicable, the district held by the enemy.
>
> The troops of this portion of the army have for some time been confined to reduced rations . . . and I fear they will be unable to endure the hardships of the approaching campaign. Symptoms of scurvy are appearing among them [and] for so large an army the supply obtained is very small.[29]

This supply theme was continued in Lee's April 9 letter to Seddon outlining the general's views of the strategic situation facing the South, and why two of his best divisions—Hood's and Pickett's—continued to be detached from the army. "Genl Longstreet is now engaged on an extended line," explained Lee, "endeavoring to withdraw supplies from the invaded districts south of the James River."[30] Kean echoed these sentiments in his diary when he explained that "The object of [General Longstreet's] expedition is to forage for his army in the unexhausted and productive country between the James and the [Albemarle] Sound, especially on the Chowan."[31]

And Longstreet's foraging mission had to date been very successful. Lee's corps commander had driven Federal forces inside Suffolk's defensive network and his wagons were searching far and wide for food and forage. The fruits of his mission, however, had not yet reached the hungry men and animals along the Rappahannock River. On April 16, Lee again notified Davis about the dire consequences of the army's improper subsistence. This time, Lee broached with Davis his desire for another advance north across the Potomac River. Such a move, he contended, would break the existing stalemate in northern Virginia and aid other areas of the embattled Confederacy:

> My only anxiety arises from the present immobility of the army, owing to the condition of the horses and the scarcity of forage and provisions . . . If we could be placed in a condition to make a vigorous advance . . . I think the Valley could be swept of Milroy and the army opposite me be thrown north of the Potomac. I believe greater relief would in this way be afforded to the armies in middle Tennessee and on the Carolina coast than by any other method. I had hoped by Genl Longstreet's operations in [Virginia and] North Carolina to obtain sufficient subsistence to commence the [invasion] movement, and by the operations in north west Virginia to continue the supplies. It must depend

therefore upon the success of these operations unless other means can be devised for procuring subsistence. I therefore submit the matter to Your Excellency for consideration in the hope that some plan may be formed to attain this object. At present we are very much scattered and I am unable to bring the army together for want of proper subsistence & forage.[32]

The following day, Lee continued his pleas for Richmond to provide his army with some relief. With his troops already on one-third rations, the commanding general wrote Secretary Seddon:

I am informed by the chief commissary of the army that he has been unable to issue the sugar ration to the troops for the last ten days. Their ration, consequently, consists of one-fourth pound of bacon, 18 ounces of flour, 10 pounds of rice to each 100 men about every third day, with some few peas and a small amount of dried fruit occasionally, as they can be obtained. This may give existence to the troops while idle, but will certainly cause them to break down when called upon for exertion . . .

I beg that you will take the necessary measures to cause the supplies to be forwarded promptly and regularly. The time has come when it is necessary the men should have full rations. Their health is failing, scurvy and typhus fever are making their appearance . . . .[33]

Seddon's response did little to comfort Lee. "Your letter of the 17th instant causes concern and anxiety respecting the sanitary condition of your army, and stimulates the efforts I am earnestly making to increase your supplies of subsistence," replied the secretary on April 19. "I have made arrangements [for supplies to] be drawn from the reserve stores of the commissariat at Atlanta, Ga. In addition, considerable amounts may be expected from the operations of Generals Longstreet and Hill, and from the action of the people in response to the President's proclamation." Seddon also noted that Richmond had "contracts for large supplies from external sources, which should begin to be delivered by May 1." These arrangements, cautioned Seddon, "must be precarious, and I do not, consequently, count too strongly upon them."[34]

When Major General Joseph Hooker and his Federal Army of the Potomac began operations in late April culminating in the Battle of Chancellorsville, Lee was heavily outnumbered and his men and horses low on food. "Our scattered condition [because of want of food and forage] favors their operations," Lee telegraphed Davis on April 29.[35] "Please order the forwarding of our supplies."[36]

Although supply problems had weakened his army and much of Longstreet's First Corps was absent, Lee refused to remain on the defensive or withdraw south. When it became clear that the Federals opposite Fredericksburg did not pose an immediate threat, Lee moved quickly west with the bulk of his divisions to confront Hooker and the majority of the Army of the Potomac in the heavily wooded terrain around Chancellorsville. Shocked by Lee's audacious move, Hooker pulled up and began entrenching, relinquishing the tactical initiative over to Lee. When he learned that the Federal right flank was exposed and subject to a flank attack, the Confederate commander divided his army a third time in the face of a superior enemy. While Lee remained with a token force in front of Hooker, Lieutenant General Thomas J. "Stonewall" Jackson and his corps embarked on a flank march around Hooker's exposed right wing. Jackson's subsequent assault rolled up the Federal flank, threw the enemy in a panic, and allowed Lee to join together the two primary wings of his army. Unfortunately for the Confederates, Jackson was severely wounded by his men during a nighttime reconnaissance. With the befuddled Hooker firmly on the defensive, Lee turned and struck a blow at the Federals who had crossed the Rappahannock at Fredericksburg and were now threatening his rear, driving them back across the river. It was one of the most remarkable victories in the history of warfare. This impressive feat of arms not withstanding, Lee recognized that Chancellorsville could have been a far more decisive victory had the divisions of John Bell Hood and George Pickett been with the army rather than off gathering subsistence. "Had I had the whole army with me," Lee lamented to Hood, "General Hooker would have been demolished."[37]

As convinced as Lee was about the fate that would have befallen the Federal army if the absent divisions of Hood and Pickett had been present at Chancellorsville—Longstreet arrived shortly after the battle ended—his efforts to rectify the supply situation remained tentative at best. Lee either did not feel familiar enough with the supply service to step in and institute any real change, or he believed that the responsibility for implementing substantive corrections lay outside his command authority. "Admirable as was the training of Lee it was not complete," explained his biographer, Douglas Southall Freeman. "Most of all was he lacking in any detailed knowledge of the service of supply. Belonging to the élite corps of the army [engineers], he had never performed lengthy duty as quartermaster or as commissary."[38]

Although he may not have enjoyed formal training in supply logistics, Lee's correspondence during this period reveals his appreciation of the problems confronting both his army and the South's deteriorating supply system. No one was more aware of the critical situation facing his army and the need for Virginia to have a respite from war than Lee. While he may not have known how to solve the vexing problem, he did comprehend the necessity of formulating a strategic policy to address it. Thus, the pressing problems of food and forage figured prominently in his decision as to what his army should do in the wake of his victory at Chancellorsville.

Lee drew little comfort from his recent triumph. Although the larger Army of the Potomac had been thrown back across the Rappahannock, Hooker was still as much of a threat as before, firmly entrenched on the north side of the river at Falmouth. In addition, Lee's own infantry losses had been heavy, and Stonewall Jackson had finally succumbed to his wounds a week after the battle ended. With the same situation confronting his army, Lee knew it was unwise to simply remain in place and wait for his enemy to dictate the time and place of the next encounter. "At Chancellorsville we gained another victory; our people were wild with delight," he wrote later that summer. "I, on the contrary, was more depressed than after Fredericksburg; our loss was severe, and again we had gained not an inch of ground and the enemy could not be pursued."[39]

Each engagement resulted in the loss of irreplaceable soldiers, and the summer of 1863 was shaping up to be the decisive campaigning season of the war. With Major General Ulysses S. Grant's Federals tightening their grip on Vicksburg, Mississippi, both Lee and Davis were under pressure to dispatch reinforcements west to alleviate the situation. If he did so, Lee's weakened army would be forced to remain on the defensive in Virginia. To Lee's way of thinking, however, keeping the Confederate army chained to a defensive line in Virginia was a fatally bad idea. If the South was going to win her independence, the next campaign might well be the last real opportunity for the Confederacy to actively influence the outcome. Whatever course President Davis chose to implement, Lee knew that every veteran in uniform was needed for service with the army.

"I have the honor to represent to you the absolute necessity that exists, in my opinion, to increase our armies," Lee wrote in an emotional plea to Secretary of War James Seddon on January 10, 1863:

> While the spirit of our soldiers is unabated, their ranks have been greatly thinned by casualties of battle and the diseases of the camp. Losses in battle are rendered much heavier by reason of our being compelled to encounter the enemy with inferior numbers . . . the great increase of the enemy's forces will augment the disparity of numbers to such a degree that victory, if attained, can only be achieved by a terrible expenditure of the most precious blood of the country . . .
>
> The country has yet to learn how advantages, secured at the expense of many valuable lives, have failed to produce their legitimate results by reason of our inability to prosecute them against the reinforcements which the superior numbers of the enemy enabled him to interpose between the defeat of an army and its ruin.
>
> More than once have most promising opportunities been lost for want of men to take advantage of them, and victory itself has been made to put on the appearance of defeat, because our diminished and exhausted troops have been unable to renew a successful struggle against fresh numbers of the enemy . . .
>
> In view of the vast increase of the forces of the enemy, of the savage and brutal policy he has proclaimed, which leaves us no alternative but success or degradation worse than death, if we would save the honor of our families from pollution, our social system from destruction, let every effort be made, every means be employed, to fill and maintain the ranks of our armies, until God, in His Mercy, shall bless us with the establishment of our independence.[40]

Lee wrote Davis on April 20, and again after the battle on May 7, asking that more cavalry be forwarded to the Army of Northern Virginia.[41] Even more important was the need for infantry—especially veteran formations led by skilled officers. "I am particularly anxious to get back [Robert] Ransom's [Jr.] division," Lee told Davis on April 27.[42] By May 10, rumblings that Richmond officials were seriously contemplating sending Pickett and his men to Mississippi instead of back to Lee alarmed the general. "If you determine to send Pickett's division to General Pemberton [in Mississippi], I presume it could not reach him until the last of this month," argued Lee to Secretary Seddon. "The uncertainty of its arrival and the uncertainty of its application cause me to doubt the policy of sending it. Its removal from this army will be sensibly felt." If we remain on the defensive, contended Lee, the army "may be obliged to withdraw into defenses around Richmond. We are greatly outnumbered by the enemy now . . . General Hooker's army . . . amounts to more than 159,000."[43]

While Lee recognized the difficulty in transporting large bodies of troops over the dilapidated rail system of the South, he may have *underestimated* the difficulty in moving Pickett's Division, or any troops for that matter, from Virginia to Mississippi. The root of the problem rested with the Confederacy's 113 different railroads and eight different gauges. The trip via railroad from Virginia to Mississippi included numerous time consuming transfers. Once in Montgomery, Alabama, Pickett's men would ride on to Tensas, where they, their equipment, and animals would have to detrain and continue on foot to Mobile, Alabama. There, the entire entourage had to reboard and continue to Meridian, Mississippi, before transferring again onto the Southern Railroad of Mississippi for the final leg into Jackson. The tedious process—which would require a minimum of 14 different rail lines and transfers from Richmond, Virginia, to Jackson, Mississippi—would have consumed three weeks under the most favorable circumstances.[44]

To Lee's way of thinking, dispatching proven troops from the Army of Northern Virginia to serve under undistinguished commanders in the Vicksburg theater—with no guarantee they would even arrive in time to affect the outcome of the ongoing campaign—made little strategic sense. Instead, he sought to strengthen his army to either meet Hooker's next advance or assume the offensive himself. Lee's letter campaign continued. The thrust of his May 11 communiqué to Davis was to request the return of Robert Ransom's troops, together with the remainder of Pickett's Division, which included the splendid brigade of South Carolinians under Brigadier General Micah Jenkins.[45] These requests for reinforcements would continue, in one vein or another, well into June.[46]

As it became clear within the army's high command that a move north was being contemplated, James Longstreet, Lee's stalwart First Corps commander, endorsed the plan and supported Lee's entreaties to reinforce the army in Virginia with every Confederate formation possible. On May 13, 1863—the day before Lee met with Davis and his cabinet in Richmond—Longstreet wrote to Texas Senator

Louis Trezevant Wigfall. Wigfall, one of Longstreet's confidants in the Confederate government, was a "Western Solutionist," meaning that he favored pulling forces from Lee's army and shipping them west to relieve Vicksburg. According to Longstreet, Lee "can spare nothing from this army to re-enforce in the West. On the contrary, we should have the use of our own [troops from the west]. In fact, we should make a grand effort against the Yankees this summer [in the east], every available man and means should be brought to bear against them."[47] Lee also sought to augment his strength by increasing the numbers within existing regiments. In a letter written on February 28, Lee told his son Custis that the Army of Northern Virginia "must try & defeat it [the Federal army]. To do this, will require our regiments to be filled up."[48]

Jefferson Davis and the Strategy of Defense

In addition to manpower concerns and issues of forage and supply, perhaps the most crucial problem facing the South in May of 1863 was how and where to employ the Confederacy's outnumbered soldiers. Many of the battlefield disasters suffered by the South had been brought on, or greatly exacerbated by, President Davis' defensive policy. Responding in part to pleas from often churlish and narrow-minded Southern governors, Davis decided to implement a static perimeter defense. In other words, he decided to defend every square mile of the vast geographic expanse of the Confederacy in order to validate his government's position that the Confederacy was an autonomous nation fighting off an outside aggressor. To Davis' way of thinking, abandoning *any* territory was unthinkable. He equated the loss of ground with military weakness, and he was not about to let the Yankees possess any part of the new Confederacy. This explains why he insisted so mightily that Lee hold the line of the Rappahannock River. Both Lee and Jackson, however, had recognized that the Army of Northern Virginia, just 50 miles north of Richmond, could be easily turned from that position, a fact confirmed by Hooker's early maneuvers during the Chancellorsville Campaign.

The adoption of a "strategy of defense by dispersal,"[49] to Davis' way of thinking, would force the Federals to dedicate an enormous amount of manpower, resources, and time—hopefully more than they were willing to spend—in an attempt to conquer the Confederacy. By defending everywhere, Davis reasoned, the Federals would have to subjugate the entire South. Davis hoped that playing for time in this manner, as earlier Americans had done in the American Revolution, assistance would eventually reach Southern shores from Europe. By 1863, however, few in the Confederate government believed that European recognition would lead to French, British, or Spanish forces coming to the South's aid. Still, some hoped that European recognition in almost *any* form would lead to mediation and an end to

Jefferson Finis Davis (1808-1889)

As president of the Confederate States of America, no one was more committed to the cause for Southern independence. Unfortunately, Davis' personality often hindered the Confederacy's efforts. His inability to admit that he could be wrong about anything created lasting animosity between him and many generals and politicians. Even more fatal was his flawed "strategy of defense by dispersal." As a result, Davis failed to see the need to fully support the one successful commander and army of the Confederacy during the crucial Gettysburg Campaign. *Library of Congress*

hostilities. Unfortunately, wrote historian William C. Davis, this belief that European countries would somehow intervene on the side of the Confederacy was fantasy based on "false logic, and a willingness to which all too many of us are prone simply to accept what we have always heard without examining it further."[50]

The fatal flaw in Davis' strategy was as simple as basic arithmetic. The Confederacy had fewer men upon which to draw than did the Union. Thus, Davis' decision to disperse troops across the South in order to contest every enemy incursion surrendered the strategic initiative to Abraham Lincoln's generals. This allowed the Federals to select where and when to attack. It also virtually guaranteed that when they did move, they did so with more soldiers, supplied over a better railroad system, and often supported by a navy. Thus, the Federals invariably outnumbered the Confederates at the point of attack, and Southern defeat habitually followed.

Furthermore, deploying sorely needed frontline organizations into static garrison roles, or into *ad hoc* commands of observation opposite numerous Federal enclaves of troops, insured that the full potential of these veteran troops would not be realized. Davis could have employed militia units in these static roles (he occasionally did so), thereby releasing more valuable units for service with the primary Confederate armies.

The Southern president's strategic plan for survival was implemented through a series of semi-autonomous bureaucratic military departments. Each was under the command of a general officer endowed with the responsibility for both defensive and offensive movements within its boundaries.

Because of poor communications, Davis generally allowed his departmental commanders substantial discretion in their operation, and their opinions carried great weight with the president. At first blush, carving up the South in this manner seemed a reasonable way to wage war. In reality, the compartmentalization of authority spawned petty empire building and all but prevented cooperation between geographic departments. This side effect of dissecting the Confederacy into mini-fiefdoms was especially injurious to the Confederate war effort when it came to the distribution and allocation of troops and resources. Troops entering one department were often hijacked by local commanders who were often reluctant to release veteran organizations passing through or temporarily stationed in their departments—even when they were desperately needed elsewhere. Precious resources, such as gunpowder, iron, lead, guns, and uniforms, and food were hoarded to the detriment of the soldiers for whom they were intended.[51]

Unfortunately, President Davis was not the kind of man to reevaluate his policies or admit that he was wrong—even when it was obvious that his departmental organization had serious problems. Nor were those around him likely to remind the chief executive of his shortcomings. In a land where a feudal society and the age of chivalry were perpetuated, there were precious few Southern aristocrats willing to openly question the leadership of the president. These members of the ruling class knew Davis' devotion to the cause for Southern independence. Additionally, they were aware of Davis' military background.

Ironically, the first and only president of the Confederacy did not want the job. The Kentucky native who grew up in Mississippi had developed an impressive resume by the time Fort Sumter opened fire in April 1861. After graduating from West Point in 1828, he was commissioned a second lieutenant of infantry and served at a variety of frontier posts. Eventually tiring of garrison duty, Davis resigned to become a successful planter and Mississippi politician. When the Mexican War broke out, he was elected colonel of a volunteer regiment from Vicksburg. He served honorably and his actions at the battles of Monterrey and Buena Vista earned him a lasting reputation as a soldier of some merit. Thereafter Davis was appointed to an unexpired senate seat, was reelected in 1850, and enjoyed his position in Washington as one of the government's most influential politicians. He served as secretary of war under President Franklin Pierce from 1853-1857.

Contemporaries both North and South had faith in Davis in the years leading up to the Civil War, and respected his generally moderate positions and thoughtful oratory. Following Abraham Lincoln's election Davis, however, resigned his senate seat on January 21, 1861, and returned to Mississippi, where he was commissioned a major general of state troops. The organizers of the Confederacy, reasoning that the Mississippian could better serve the young nation as president because of his experience in politics and military matters, elected him to that position. The disappointed Davis, who craved a field command, knew full well that the position of chief of state would be a difficult one requiring endless hours of work—he suffered from ill health, which only worsened with long hours of work—but accepted it out of a sense of duty. He also believed he was eminently qualified for it. Long after the end of the Civil War, Davis bragged to a contemporary, "By early education, by years of service in the army, by other years spent in administering the U.S. War Dept., I had learned the usages of war."[52]

Once the war began, however, serious deficiencies that had long existed in Davis' mental makeup began to surface that directly affected the Confederate war effort. He believed every decision he made was the right one; calling them into question was, in Davis' mind, a personal attack upon his character. The combination of his immodest personality and military and political experiences, coupled with his social status, contributed to his inflated opinion of his abilities.[53]

Davis seems to have forgotten his West Point lessons on the Great Captains of history. If he had remembered, he would not have adopted a policy of dispersing his manpower to hold every point in the South, a course of action that went against the advice of both Napoleon and Frederick the Great. "Little minds try to defend everything at once," wrote the Prussian king, who had warred successfully against numerically superior allied powers during wars of the mid-18th century. "If you try to hold everything, you hold nothing."[54] Frederick the Great, for example, would have never approved of Davis' fixation of defending the Rappahannock River line by ordering Lee to keep the river *in front* of the Army of Northern Virginia. "Never base your defense on rivers," Frederick wrote, "the only way to defend a river is to keep it *behind* you."[55] Napoleon agreed with Frederick. The French emperor maintained that an army should never be forced to defend a river by deploying behind it, and like Frederick, Napoleon believed that the enemy should be intercepted in an intermediate place.[56] According to Napoleon, with a river between his army and that of the enemy, the river would serve as an obstacle to his goal of outmaneuvering his opponent, which, in turn, made possible decisive confrontations. Finally, and as Frederick the Great correctly observed, intelligent generals could simply outflank any defended river position. "The defense of a river crossing is the worst of all assignments," he wrote. "[It] is impracticable."[57]

Davis' strategy of defense by dispersal also unintentionally hamstrung the field commanders of the two major mobile armies of the Confederacy—the Army of Tennessee in the West and the Army of Northern Virginia in the East—in their ability to concentrate as many troops as possible in order to maneuver with the intent of retaining the operational initiative. More flexibility in this regard would likely have produced additional engagements on Northern soil, where Federal defeats would have proven far more damaging in political terms than setbacks suffered in either Virginia or Tennessee.

An additional example of Davis' egocentric personality surfaced during the Seven Days Battles. Accompanying Lee into the field, the president witnessed portions of several battles, but did not correct reporters of the *Richmond Examiner*, who wrote that the president assisted in the victorious campaign. This vainglorious vision of himself only exacerbated Davis' impression of himself and his insatiable need to always be right. As one historian put it, he possessed an "almost unbearable need to be appreciated."[58] All of this combined to feed his delusions of genius. Davis' second wife, Varina, painted a succinct picture of her husband. He was, she wrote, "a nervous dyspeptic by habit," and when he ate while upset or excited, remained ill for days. This exacerbated his already "super-sensitive temperament" that in the eyes of his wife, "was abnormally sensitive to disapprobation" and "even a child's disapproval discomposed him."[59]

Another limitation of this self-aware man was his resistance to intellectual growth. Davis' success in efficiently managing the paper work of the peace-time army during the Pierce Administration no doubt fed his delusions that he was qualified to command the Confederate armies in the field, and as such, could set policy and plan campaigns. This self-assurance, in turn, reinforced Davis' vision of himself as the one person who could lead the South to victory, which, in turn, gave birth to his departmental approach to managing war that was an unmistakable hallmark of Davis' accustomed bureaucratic methods of management while Pierce's secretary of war.

Certainly Davis faced an extremely difficult challenge as Confederate president, and he may have been the best man for the job, given the paucity of candidates from which to choose. The young nation he was asked to lead was on a wartime footing from beginning to end. The Old South had a limited industrial base and an archaic railroad network that made it ill-suited to deal with pressing logistical demands for producing the implements of war and distributing materiel and food. Like other nations founded through revolution, the Confederacy was never financially solvent, and runaway inflation undermined the economy. Thus, the longer the war dragged on, the greater its financial difficulties.

Fredericksburg and the Rappahannock River

Defending a river line by stationing forces *behind it* was not a course of action recommended by such notable Great Captains as Gustavus Adolphus, Frederick the Great, and Napoleon. Despite the lessons of history, Jefferson Davis mandated the Rappahannock River as a defensive line to be held. Both Robert E. Lee and Stonewall Jackson recognized this position offered little or no advantage for the Confederates. *Library of Congress*

The Confederacy was founded upon "states rights," a concept that only made it more difficult for Davis to govern effectively while conducting a war of survival. Many governors were lukewarm at best to Davis and the idea of a strong central government. Chief among these state leaders were Joseph E. Brown of Georgia, and Zebulon Vance of North Carolina, both of whom created enormous difficulties for Davis, often by utilizing Davis' departmental system against his efforts and to their personal advantage.

Unfortunately for the Confederacy, Davis' leadership only worsened as the war turned against the South. Even in the face of steady defeat in the West he refused to reassess his strategy, choosing instead to concentrate on bureaucratic details as a means of providing a feeling of accomplishment. Davis became increasingly compulsive and obsessive, which only made it more difficult for anyone outside the president himself to assume the responsibility of moving troops. In the words of a contemporary, Davis "managed the [Confederate] War Department, in all its various details," taking great pains to pay attention to "its minutiae . . . and the very disbursement of its appropriations."[60] There can be little doubt that by delving into such military minutiae and micro-management, Davis afforded his harried brain "a sense of adequacy in the press of events beyond his capacity to direct," explained one historian. "The consequences of this mania, and the policy behind it,"[61] had the net effect of finally forcing Davis to deal with the crisis that he had created by beckoning General Lee to Richmond for a meeting in the spring of 1863 that would ultimately have a profound effect on the course of the war.

Robert E. Lee and Confederate Strategy in the Summer of 1863

General Lee's vision of how the Confederacy should spend its limited resources differed substantially from Davis' vision. And Lee's ideas were based on more than the previously mentioned factors of food and manpower shortages. Like every successful general, Lee appreciated the necessity of maintaining the initiative, something he and his men had wrested from the enemy during the hard-fought Chancellorsville Campaign. This factor, coupled with the army's institutional memory of victories won, established a deep-seated conviction from private to commanding general of invincibility. Lee's dilemma was how to allocate the South's limited numbers in a way that would maximize these intangibles on the next battlefield and turn them into a decisive Confederate victory.

Unlike Davis, Lee did not subscribe to the theory of dispersing valuable troops to defend every point of the compass. And, unlike Davis, who had to concern himself with every Federal incursion into Confederate territory, Lee enjoyed the luxury of dealing only with his army and events in the Eastern Theater. "Partial encroachments by the enemy we must expect," Lee wrote to Virginia Governor Gustavus W. Smith on January 4, 1863, "but they can always be recovered, and any defeat of their large army will reinstate everything."[62] In a letter to Davis on January 13, 1863, Lee warned of drawing valuable manpower away from his army in response to Federal movements. "As far as I have been able to judge," wrote the general, "I have apprehended the [Federal] movements in North Carolina were intended more as a feint to withdraw troops from this point [near Fredericksburg], when Genl Burnside could move at once upon Richmond."[63] A few months later on April 16, Lee detailed his ideas to Samuel Cooper, the adjutant and inspector general, about reinforcing other departments—such as Mississippi—at the expense of jeopardizing the Virginia front.[64] On May 11, only days before Lee traveled to Richmond to meet with Davis, he wrote the president with his estimates of the considerable Federal reinforcements destined for Hooker's army in the wake of Chancellorsville, and as a result every man was needed for duty with the Army of Northern Virginia.[65]

One of the most important things Lee had won at Chancellorsville was also one of the most difficult achievements in war for a defending army to accomplish—

seizing the initiative from an attacking foe. Now that he had it, Lee had no intention of letting this elusive ally slip through his fingers. The question was, how could he use it to best advantage? Lee had already demonstrated his understanding of the value of acquiring and maintaining the initiative. He had wrested it away from George McClellan in the Seven Days Battles, and preserved it through the Second Manassas and Maryland campaigns. With his army utterly exhausted by months of marching and fighting, Lee reluctantly relinquished the strategic initiative to the Federals by withdrawing from Maryland and taking up residence in northern Virginia behind the Rappahannock River. Although he scored a stunning defensive success at Fredericksburg in December 1862, circumstances beyond his control made it largely impossible for him to follow up on the victory. Now, after Chancellorsville, Lee and his triumphant army were once again in a position to possibly dictate the next move in Virginia. And he was not about to relinquish it.

Lee knew that if he simply waited behind the Rappahannock River, the Army of the Potomac would replace its losses suffered at Chancellorsville and resume the offensive, forcing the Confederates to repeat the miracle of Chancellorsville or fall back in the direction of Richmond. Neither option was palatable to Lee, nor were they in the best overall interests of the South. The general knew all too well that his hungry army would starve itself into inefficiency and immobility if forced to fight another major campaign in northern Virginia in the summer of 1863, or be ruined if forced into siege lines around Richmond, where attrition would dictate inevitable defeat. The Army of Northern Virginia, therefore, had to march north and carry the war beyond the Potomac River.

Lee's strategic beliefs were grounded in the lessons of history and his own experience. Unlike Davis, he had not forgotten his West Point studies, which dictated that a smaller force had to maintain its maneuverability in order to keep the initiative away from a stronger adversary. Lee also understood the importance of Napoleon's maxims. "The strength of an army," wrote the Great Captain, "like the power in mechanics, is estimated by multiplying the mass by the rapidity; a rapid march augments the morale of an army, and increases all the chances of victory."[66] Equally important, Lee knew that Napoleon was correct in assessing what an outnumbered force had to do: "When an army is inferior in number," wrote the French general, "[this] deficiency should be supplied by rapidity of movement . . . In such circumstances the morale of the soldier does much."[67]

And it was the morale of the troops in the Army of Northern Virginia that Lee considered one of the most important issues in formulating his plans for the next campaign. Perhaps more than any other soldier in Confederate uniform, Lee understood the *élan* and perceived superiority that his troops had over the Federals—as well as the corresponding combat power and morale of the men in the Army of Northern Virginia. During the Suffolk Campaign, Lee advised General Longstreet to seek out and strike the enemy, knowing full well his men believed they would win whenever they engaged their opponents. "If . . . you see an opportunity of dealing a damaging blow," Lee wrote on March 21, 1863, "or of driving him [the enemy] from any important positions, do not be idle, but act promptly."[68] Six days later, Lee wrote Longstreet of his own desire to strike out at an exposed enemy once he had crossed below the Rappahannock: "I deem it advantageous to keep the enemy at a distance & trust to striking him on his line of advance."[69] The victory that followed at Chancellorsville only deepened the commanding general's considerable respect for his men, their impressive fighting power, and ability to achieve anything—regardless of the difficulty or the odds. Following the battle, Lee told John Bell Hood that "there never were such men in an army before. They will go anywhere and do anything if properly led."[70]

And this view was shared by most of the men within the army. Colonel Risden T. Bennett of the 14th North Carolina looked on the Army of Northern Virginia and considered it "as tough and efficient as any army of the same number ever marshaled on this planet."[71] William Daniel of the 2nd South Carolina Infantry agreed. Writing immediately after Chancellorsville, he opined that the Southern cause "is brighter than ever."[72] William A. Johnson of the same regiment had an even stronger opinion of the capabilities of Lee's army. "The Confederate army," claimed the South Carolinian, "felt that omnipotence had endowed it with the power to conquer a universe."[73]

Carolinians were not the only ones who believed their army invincible. "Never was the Army of Northern Virginia in better condition. The troops had unbounded confidence in themselves and in their leaders," wrote James Francis Crocker, adjutant of the 9th Virginia Infantry. "They were full of the fervor of patriotism—had abiding faith in their cause . . . the spirit and elan of our soldiers was beyond description [and] had the courage and dash to accomplish anything."[74]

"So high-wrought was the pride and self-reliance of the troops," wrote John Bell Hood after the war, "that they could carve their way through almost any number of the enemy's lines, formed in the open field in their front."[75] The officers and men of Hood's Division agreed. Captain George T. Todd, Company A, 1st Texas Infantry, believed that "Hood's old brigade was never in finer fighting trim . . . the Army of Northern Virginia was the most enthusiastic and irresistible fighting machine on the face of the earth . . . thoroughly trained and inured to every hardship and danger."[76] Sergeant D. H. Hamilton, Company M, 1st Texas Infantry, exuded a similar confidence. Hamilton wrote that the men of the 1st Texas "had the most implicit confidence in their ability to whip the enemy whenever and wherever we met them on equal terms, even when outnumbered."[77] Lieutenant Watson D. Williams, acting commander of Company F, 5th Texas Infantry, in a letter dated June 23, 1863, may well have summarized the feeling of so many in the army:

> That we will be successful in our advance I cannot doubt. My confidence in the skill and ability of Gen'l Lee is so great that I believe he can accomplish almost anything he undertakes. He has a large and powerful army under his control and

are much better fighting men than the enemy have ever been; and to be victorious we have only to meet him in battle.[78]

Chancellorsville had not only fortified the redoubtable spirit of the Army of Northern Virginia, but deepened the new nation's faith in Robert E. Lee to carry them to ultimate victory. Lee's biographer, Douglas Southall Freeman, observed that "the victory over Hooker raised enthusiasm in the South above anything that had been known even after Second Manassas or Fredericksburg. It was felt that a single direct blow, aimed at the vitals of the North, might end the war and bring peace."[79] According to one observer, "Genl R. E. Lee . . . [is] the idol of his soldiers & the Hope of His Country. . . . The prestige which surrounds his person & the almost fanatical belief in his judgment & capacity . . . is the one idea of an entire people."[80] Major Walter H. Taylor, a member of Lee's staff, attributed the army's latest victory to both Lee's genius and divine assistance. "When I consider our numerical weakness, our limited resources and the great strength & equipments of the enemy," Taylor wrote, "I am astonished at the result. Surely the hand of God was on our side."[81]

The high spirit and confidence that flowed through the veins of the Army of Northern Virginia contrasted sharply with the psychological makeup of the Army of the Potomac. This factor was something Lee had continually monitored since taking command of the army. Time and again Lee had seen his men defeat armies larger than his own, and Chancellorsville only served to heighten his expectations of what his army could accomplish. These same Confederate successes had the opposite effect on the Army of the Potomac. Reflecting on the defeat at Chancellorsville, Hooker admitted in a dinner conversation with Lincoln's secretary, John Hay, that the Army of the Potomac—which had been dubbed "the finest on the planet"—was "far superior to the Southern army in everything but . . . vigor of attack." In Hooker's mind, the fault rested with George McClellan's limitless timidity that had molded the Army of the Potomac "into a mass of languid inertness destitute of either dash or cohesion."[82] Coming on the heels of the disastrous Fredericksburg defeat, Chancellorsville convinced many Northerners that the Army of the Potomac was simply unable to defeat Lee's Army of Northern Virginia. "Experience should have taught us," John Sherman wrote after Chancellorsville, "not to hope much from this army . . . It is gloomy."[83] Colonel Philip Régis Dénis de Keredern de Trobriand, a brigade commander in the Third Corps of the Army of the Potomac, summed up the state of the army's morale in his memoirs when he wrote, "Our soldiers, humiliated by defeat, [were] shaken in their confidence in themselves and in the commander."[84]

Lee, who enthusiastically devoured Northern newspapers for information about his enemy, understood that an inferiority complex of sorts was spreading through the Federal ranks. It was yet another reason for him to take advantage of the initiative and morale superiority of his Southern troops to strike what he hoped would be a decisive blow north of the Potomac River.

Staffs and Strategy

In the press of events following Chancellorsville, Lee chose not to address what was arguably the gravest weakness of the army (and one that most historians have routinely minimized): the small size of his staff and the staffs of those officers commanding the army's corps.[85] Lee's feeling about staff size was revealed in his letter to Jefferson Davis before Chancellorsville on March 21:

> Upon an examination of the Senate bill presented by Genl Sparrow for the organization of the staff of the army, I think some changes might be made to advantage... I think it important & indeed necessary to simplify the mechanism of our army as much as possible, yet still to give it sufficient power to move & regulate the whole body... This is accomplished in the French Service by their staff corps, educated instructed & practiced for the purpose. The same circumstances that produced that corps exist in our own army. Can you not shape & form the staff of our army to produce equally good results? Although the staff of the French army is larger than that proposed by Senate bill, *I am in favour of keeping ours down* [emphasis added], as it is so much easier to build up than to reduce, if experience renders it necessary.[86]

The staff that existed during the American Civil War—and indeed, much of the modern staff system—was first modeled in French service before being slowly adopted by American armies.[87] Before the mid-18th century, European staffs employed by such notable warriors as Oliver Cromwell, Marlborough, and some of Louis XIV's marshals, had been efficient enough for their time but were temporary organizations designed for a specific campaign of limited duration and distance. This concept changed forever with the developments introduced by the father of the modern military staff, Pierre-Joseph Bourcet (1700-1780). A true pioneer and expert on staff procedures, Bourcet was deeply impressed with the military efficiency of Frederick the Great's headquarters staff and saw many ways to improve on the Prussian model. Putting pen to paper, Bourcet's *Mémories Historiques su la Guerre que les François Ont Soutenue en Allemagne 1757 Jusqu'en 1762* advocated a permanent corps of educated and trained staff officers. Among other qualifications, these men would be experts in topography, intelligence, geography, reconnaissance, and the science of the art of war as waged by the Great Captains. Equally important, Bourcet's work also stressed careful planning and the many advantages of the offensive. Napoleon was deeply impressed by Bourcet's writings, and the French Imperial staff created by Napoleon not only incorporated Bourcet's ideas, but also significantly broadened and improved upon its mission.[88]

The staff of Napoleon's various armies were used to help efficiently coordinate the movements of the various corps. These army staffers, along with the corps headquarters staff, made sure that major commands, such as divisions, carried out their mission. The size of a Napoleonic staff was impressive. For example, at the

Battle of Austerlitz in 1805, Napoleon's *Grande Armée* numbered 74,595. These combatants were organized into 18 major commands, of which nine divisions were infantry, eight divisions were cavalry, and the Imperial Guard. For an army of this size Napoleon employed an army headquarters staff of almost 200 men, all of whom were used throughout the famous battle in various roles of order conveyance and compliance. This number takes on particular importance when divided by the number of major commands within the army: the *Grande Armée* at Austerlitz had 11 personnel at the army staff level for every major command in the army.[89]

Napoleonic corps commanders also utilized large staffs. Using Austerlitz again as an example, the typical Napoleonic marshal (who was a French corps commander in 1805 and throughout the early years of the Empire) had a corps staff of 30 or more personnel to oversee the three or four divisions of the corps—a ratio of more than seven officers at the corps level for every major command.[90]

Even Napoleonic division commanders had large staffs. Typically, 20 or more officers were on hand to run two or three infantry brigades, while a fewer number of staff officers were present with cavalry divisions. If one was to count all the staff officers available at army, corps, and division level, each major command element in Napoleon's army at Austerlitz had an average of 50 staff officers. The emergence of an active, large staff at the army, corps, and division levels was just one of many reasons why Napoleon's *Grande Armée* was history's first modern army.[91]

Prior to 1861, American armies had never come close to approaching the number of combatants fielded by Napoleonic armies. Accordingly, American military leaders had no practical experience with the movement and coordination of Napoleonic-sized armies that consistently numbered tens of thousands of men.[92] And even though Lee studied Napoleon, as well as the other Great Captains, the Confederate general—like other officers on both sides—simply had no point of practical reference either during the Mexican War or afterwards in building his staff to that described by Bourcet and crafted by Napoleon. It was while Napoleon was engaged in the campaign for Germany in 1813 that America began recognizing the advantages of a permanent staff. That year, Congress created a General Staff at the War Department in Washington City (as the seat of government was called at that time). The purpose for the General Staff was the attending of various housekeeping functions of the American military. The staffs in the field were assumed to exist only for limited reasons. As such, the size of the American staffs was kept small. Napoleon's staff not only embraced the administrative functions of the army, but also housed experts in every branch of service who actively assisted the commander in chief in the implementation and execution of orders. Because of this difference, the staff of American armies during the American Civil War could barely be considered a distant relative to the staff of Napoleonic France.

When Robert E. Lee was thrust into the command of the Confederate forces confronting George McClellan's large Federal host only seven miles from Richmond on June 1, 1862, he inherited Joseph Eggleston Johnston's general staff.

This completely unorganized gaggle of hangers-on already, according to historian Clifford Dowdey, "had proven to be worse than useless."[93] Without sufficient time to put his own stamp on the staff, Lee had to deal with the crisis at hand in turning back McClellan's Army of the Potomac with those staff personnel already in place, along with the few and capable staff officers already assigned to him. According to Walter Taylor, for the battles comprising the Seven Days, Lee's staff "consisted of an assistant adjutant general [the equivalent of chief of staff], a military secretary, five aides, five clerks, and a handful of couriers."[94]

In the months that followed, Lee improved his army staff by selecting new officers based on merit, but he did not attempt to broaden the scope or function of the general staff to approach the Napoleonic model. To Lee's way of thinking, officers capable of field command were more valuable at the head of line formations than they were at army headquarters.[95] In size alone, the staffs at army, corps, and division levels for Napoleon's *Grande Armée* of 1805 dwarfed those of Lee's 1863 Army of Northern Virginia. Perhaps the most telling statistic is that the typical Napoleonic infantry division commander, who was at the head of about 9,000 combatants or less, had a larger staff than Robert E. Lee had at his headquarters to run his 70,000-man army. And, where the Napoleonic army had 50 staff officers at all levels for every major command, Lee's Army of Northern Virginia had only five.

The American inexperience with large staffs was also reflected in the Federal armies, which were only marginally better off vis-à-vis the numbers of staff personnel present. The Army of the Potomac had a larger army headquarters staff than Lee, but it was still very small compared to the Napoleonic example. Not surprisingly, more staff officers at the army level were needed for a Federal force that was not only much larger than Lee's, but which was also operating in Virginia, where few Federal officers were intimately knowledgeable about the terrain. In contrast, Lee could rely upon the knowledge of his Virginia officers and their familiarity with their native state to compensate for the lack of staff officers. However, once Lee moved out of Virginia and into hostile territory, the consequences of the diminutive size of his army staff became evident. His excursion into Maryland in 1862 exposed this problem, a dilemma which would again be graphically illustrated during the Gettysburg Campaign. As things stood in mid-May 1863, pressing concerns other than increasing the size or introducing new concepts to his diminutive staff occupied Lee's mind as he traveled to Richmond to meet with Davis and other government officials.

Virginia vs. Mississippi: Lee and the Strategic Situation in the Western and Trans-Mississippi Theaters

The strategic picture facing not only Lee's beloved Virginia, but the entire South, was grim. Arguably, the course of events was the result of President Davis' system of scattering troops everywhere to defend everything. In the Trans-Mississippi theater, where some 47,000 Confederates were under arms and widely dispersed from Louisiana through Arkansas and Texas, General Kirby Smith was struggling to carry out Davis' order to defend all Confederate-held territory along the Mississippi River. Another 56,000 soldiers were scattered up and down the long Southern coast line, tied down watching a number of small Federal enclaves in Florida, the Carolinas, and Virginia. These Federal forces, especially those in and around Suffolk, Virginia, and on the coast of the Tar Heel State, had the potential of threatening both Richmond and the vital blockade-running port of Wilmington, North Carolina. Federal presence in these isolated pockets alarmed not only the local populace, but their political representatives as well. Lee was also aware that these Federal threats greatly agitated the generals on the scene, most notably Gustavus W. Smith, Harvey Hill, W. H. C. Whiting, and North Carolina's governor, Zebulon Vance. All four men had spent weeks pressuring Richmond to send detachments from Lee's army to deal with the invaders.

As grim as the situation was beyond the Mississippi River and along the coast, matters were much more serious in the Western Theater. There, Major General Williams S. Rosecrans and his 84,000-man Federal Army of the Cumberland were poised in middle Tennessee to drive Braxton Bragg's 45,000-man Army of Tennessee out of the southeastern portion of the state and capture the vital rail center of Chattanooga. Bragg's record as the head of the Army of Tennessee offered little encouragement to military and government officials in Richmond that he had the wherewithal to stop Rosecrans.

As real as the unpleasant possibility was of losing Tennessee and the vital rail junction of Chattanooga, Lee recognized that what most concerned President Davis and other top officials in Richmond were events unfolding along the Mississippi River at Vicksburg. The city, located on the east bank of the river midway between Memphis, Tennessee, and New Orleans, Louisiana, was an important defensive point and a key link between the eastern states and the Trans-Mississippi region. It was also the focus of Major General Ulysses S. Grant's relentless efforts. From October 1862, Grant had unsuccessfully poked and pried at the Southern stronghold. In early 1863, Grant decided to march his army down the Louisiana bank of the Mississippi River below Vicksburg, ferry his men to the opposite shore, and move against the city and its rail lines from the east. It was a brilliant and daring plan the Southerners were ill-equipped to counter. The threat also placed considerable pressure on Davis to detach men from other armies in an attempt to rescue the deteriorating situation.

The Confederate commander at Vicksburg, Lieutenant General John C. Pemberton, was particularly unsuited to meet the crisis at hand. The recently promoted general was in reality a bureaucrat, not a field commander. He already had some 40,000 men assigned to his region, but thousands of them were dispersed on fruitless missions chasing enemy cavalry or tied down defending fixed locations.

Only about 23,000 were with him in or around Vicksburg. Pemberton's calls for reinforcements from Kirby Smith's army west of the river, unfortunately for the South, achieved nothing. (Indeed, Smith's inability or unwillingness to cooperate was just another in a string of examples of President Davis' rigid bureaucratic system in action.)

In early May, Grant landed at Bruinsburg with 23,000 men and defeated a small Confederate force at Port Gibson and Grand Gulf. Thereafter he struck out north and east, simultaneously threatening both Vicksburg and the state capital at Jackson. The first serious inland attempt to defeat the Federal invasion ended in disaster on May 12 at the Battle of Raymond, just 14 miles southwest of Jackson. Utilizing his central location between his primary objective (Vicksburg) and the state capital, Grant ordered two of his three corps to destroy railroads and move toward Jackson, while the third kept an eye on Pemberton. On the same day the Federal corps moved out, Confederate General Joe Johnston arrived in Jackson.

Joseph Eggleston Johnston was the South's principal hope for saving Pemberton and Vicksburg. His wartime performance, however, did not engender confidence that he would succeed. He had enjoyed a strong reputation early in the war, largely as a result of his pre-war service. His image began to tarnish with his steady retreats in the face of George McClellan's advance up the peninsula of Virginia, which carried his army to the very gates of Richmond. Finally forced to act, Johnston launched a disjointed offensive at Battle of Seven Pines and was badly wounded on May 30, 1862. After the battle, command of the army was turned over to Robert E. Lee, whose outstanding performance thereafter precluded Johnston's return to Virginia. When he recovered from his wounds, Johnston was appointed by Davis in November 1862 to assume the leadership of the vast Department of the West, where unified command was needed to allocate scarce resources and maximize Southern use of interior lines.[96] The important post included authority over all Confederate forces west of the Allegheny range and east of the Mississippi River—including Braxton Bragg's Army of Tennessee and John C. Pemberton's Army of Vicksburg. Johnston, however, who had been conducting a running feud with Davis over a host of issues for more than a year (and who was still fuming over the loss of his position with the Virginia army), viewed his new situation as one of little authority encumbered with tremendous responsibility. As a result, Bragg and Pemberton continued to exercise the prerogatives they enjoyed prior to Johnston's appointment, including direct correspondence with the Confederate War Department. This fractured command presence in the West was nothing short of a recipe for Southern disaster.

Unable to get Johnston to properly supervise the threatened Mississippi region from his headquarters in Tullahoma, Tennessee, Secretary of War Seddon ordered him on May 9 to "proceed at once to Mississippi and take chief command of the forces" in the field.[97] Johnston reached Jackson on the 13th, where about 6,000 Confederate troops were waiting for him, with another 6,000 expected by the

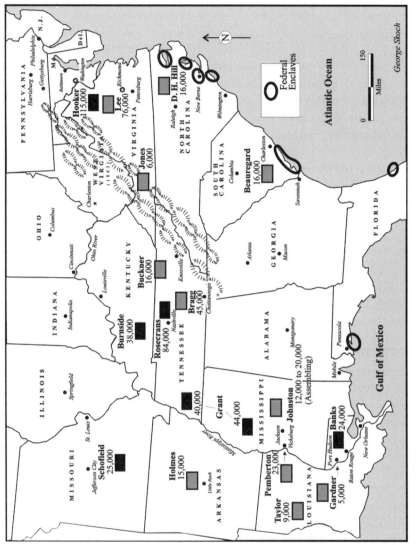

Strategic Situation Facing the Confederacy, Mid-May 1863

morning of the 15th.[98] His first telegram to Richmond revealed the basic character fabric imbued within his personality: "I arrived this evening, finding the enemy's force between this place and General Pemberton, cutting off communication. I am too late."[99] A despondent Pemberton seemed to feel the same way. "I think . . . but little reliance can be placed on the kind of assistance you refer to [receiving reinforcements]," he wrote Davis the same day. "My forces are very inadequate."[100]

Johnston's previous record in Virginia demonstrated his preference for avoiding combat at all costs. With a new field command in Mississippi, "Retreatin' Joe," as historian Clifford Dowdey called him, once again displayed his curious skill in evasion unaccompanied by any purpose to inflict injury upon the enemy. There were glimpses of brief exceptions to this rule, some of which were framed by the specter of an anxious president demanding battle, such as Johnston's May 13 message to Pemberton urging a joint attack upon the enemy.[101]

Despite his call to Pemberton for action, Johnston arrived in Jackson, Mississippi, just in time to do what came natural for him in the face of an aggressive enemy—retreat. After urging Pemberton, who was only 50 miles away, to act with celerity and concentration to effect a junction of their forces, Johnston committed what some historians believe was one of the more egregious blunders of the war. Within hours of his arrival in Jackson, he issued orders at 3:00 a.m. on May 14 to abandon the capital and its vital rail hub and manufacturing facilities, without which the relief of Vicksburg could not take place. In the words of distinguished historian Stephen E. Ambrose, "Johnston's pessimism was so great that he decided to retreat before any pressure was exerted and before he could possibly be certain that the Federal concentration was aimed at Jackson."[102] Johnston ordered his men to move away from the beleaguered Pemberton by falling back to the northeast. He retreated more than six miles the first day and another ten miles the next, even though the Federals were not in pursuit. Pemberton, meanwhile, had notified Johnston by courier that the majority of the Vicksburg army would, in accordance with Johnston's message of May 13, march eastward to engage the Federals on May 15.[103] Instead of Pemberton's forces hitting the Federals from the west while Johnston's men occupied their attention from the east, Johnston simply counted numbers and retreated, leaving Pemberton and his men to their fate.

Johnston's generalship, regardless of the theater of war in which he was employed, was perhaps best described by one of the war's most renowned writers. Johnston, wrote Clifford Dowdey, "directed his army as if engaged in a contest without stakes."[104] Indeed, the effect of Johnston's decision to evacuate Jackson was not lost on those trapped in Vicksburg. Captain Samuel H. Lockett, an engineer with the Vicksburg army, lamented that "Pemberton moved out from Edwards Depot in obedience to General Johnston, ordering him to attack in the rear a force he supposed General Johnston was going to engage in front. Instead of this, he encountered Grant's victorious army returning, exultant from the capture of Jackson."[105]

Joseph Eggleston Johnston
(1807-1891)

He was fourth in seniority among the full generals of the Confederacy, and in the summer of 1863 was in charge of the important and large Department of the West, which included Vicksburg. Unfortunately, he had a penchant for counting numbers and falling back in the face of the enemy. The result for Confederate forces was predictable— retreat and defeat.

Library of Congress

As Johnston retreated, he wired Davis on May 16 about his withdrawal to Calhoun Station 17 miles northeast of Jackson and seven miles south of Canton, Mississippi. In complete contradiction to his actions, Johnston ended the message claiming his object "is to unite all the troops."[106] To an outraged Davis, himself a Mississippian, Johnston's action was unthinkable and tantamount to deserting the Army of Vicksburg in its greatest hour of need.[107]

Ironically, Davis, Lee, and the Confederate cabinet were discussing whether or not to reinforce Johnston with elements of the Army of Northern Virginia when Johnston's breathtaking dispatch arrived. Johnston's misuse of troops and abandonment of Jackson provided Davis with the opportunity to rebuff the call of the "Western Solutionists" for a transfer of troops from Virginia. Johnston, as Davis had long suspected and now realized, was simply incapable of saving Vicksburg. What the South required was an officer imbued with strategic imagination and celerity of action, qualities that Johnston had never demonstrated in the field regardless of what was at stake. What the Confederates needed in Mississippi in the spring of 1863 was someone who had the intestinal fortitude to match General Grant blow-for-blow and fight him to a standstill or defeat him in the field. Unfortunately for the South, there was only one senior Confederate officer in possession of these qualities, and he commanded the Army of Northern Virginia. President Davis could have ordered Lee to personally assume command in Mississippi, a choice that was for a time considered. Untold problems, beginning with Lee's utter unfamiliarity with Johnston subordinates, would have made such a move sheer folly. In addition, word of such a transfer would have leaked quickly and the powerful Army of the Potomac would have advanced on Richmond. Who was ready to lead the Eastern army in Lee's absence? The plain truth was that Robert E. Lee could only be at one place at one time, a situation that underscored Davis' fundamental problem: he did not have enough qualified generals to lead his armies, and none of them came close to matching Lee's abilities.

Although many historians and students of the war criticize Davis for not sending troops from Virginia to relieve Vicksburg, Davis' decision was indeed the correct one. For all of his faults, Davis displayed keen strategic insight by not stripping Lee's army of men in May 1863. First, whatever one thinks of Johnston's abilities, his favored Fabian approach to war did not hold any promise that reinforcements would be promptly and properly utilized as Davis desired—even though Johnston clearly understood the gravity of the situation before him. Second, the logistical difficulties that would face any reinforcing troops would have been staggering—especially given Johnston's decision to evacuate the critical Jackson rail junction. Even if George Pickett's Division or some other body of troops had been stripped from Lee's already outnumbered army and sent west, it would not have had the wagons and transport animals necessary to move away from Mississippi's railroads for more than a few days at a time.[108] And Johnston's logistical situation would only worsen. Once existing rail lines were torn up by the Federals, Confederates would have to rely on wagons to forward supplies to the front, which would have further restricted Johnston's cross-country capabilities. How, then, could he have ever linked up with Pemberton or seriously threatened Grant?

All of these problems were compounded by the bitter hatred Johnston and Davis felt for one another, and Johnston's unwillingness to deal squarely with his superiors in Richmond. "He treats the Department [of War] as an enemy with whom he holds no communication which he can avoid and against which he only complains and finds fault," complained Robert Garlick Hill Kean to his diary pages. "He is a *very little man*, has achieved nothing, full of himself, [and] above all other things, eaten up with morbid jealousy of Lee and all his superiors in position, rank, or glory."[109]

Although Davis knew the Vicksburg area personally and was a native of Mississippi, both he and Lee knew that Richmond and the region east of the Alleghenies, including Virginia, the Carolinas, and parts of Georgia, possessed the vast majority of the industrial heartland of the Confederacy. Its safety had to take priority over all other considerations. After all, what implements of war to sustain the Confederate cause poured forth from the Trans-Mississippi region? Where were the cattle drives from Texas that fed the principal armies of the Confederacy?[110] Where were the long columns of replacement troops from west of the Mississippi River choking the roads on their way to regiments in either the Army of Tennessee or Army of Northern Virginia? Any imports coming through Texas by way of Mexico had to be transported more than 1,000 miles to reach even Bragg's army in Tennessee. Not a single rail line connected either Texas or Arkansas directly to Mississippi. Therefore, in the truest sense, the Trans-Mississippi was a backwater region that supplied some much-valued infantry and artillery units to the two principal Confederate armies, but precious little else that could sustain the war effort. In spite of the gains made by Federals in the Trans-Mississippi, along the Mississippi River, or even in Tennessee, Lee appreciated that the Federals would focus their attention in Virginia, the only place where he and his army had a chance to influence the war's outcome.

Ultimately, Davis' decision not to strip men from Lee's army was the result of the general's cogent arguments against such a move. In addition to voicing concerns dealing with the allocation of resources and the difficulty of getting men from Virginia to Mississippi in time to be of service, Lee asserted four other important points justifying why his army should be reinforced and mount an invasion of the North.

First, for over a year the Army of Northern Virginia had brought unparalleled success and hope to the Southern nation with a string of remarkable victories; no other army or general had come close to delivering what he and his men had achieved.

Second, much of the army's battlefield prowess lay in the synergy between its commanding general and its proven combat veterans. Why, therefore, would any general, much less Lee, advocate a plan of action that denied to his side the best prospects for his country's long term goal?

Third, the Army of Northern Virginia operated in the one theater that could do the most damage to the Northern war effort. Despite what a few members of the Confederate cabinet thought—namely Postmaster-General Reagan from Texas—and what a legion of other "Western Solutionists" have argued to this day, the strategically sensitive points of the North were virtually all in the Eastern Theater of operations. Lee understood that relieving the siege of Vicksburg in May-June 1863, desirable as that nearly-impossible goal was for the psychological well being of the South, paled in comparison to the political, psychological, and military ramifications a major victory north of the Potomac River would generate. A victory on the scale of Second Manassas in Pennsylvania, for example, would create more political opportunities than a string of successes in Mississippi or Tennessee—or even Virginia. This was largely because the major psychological trigger points for the North—which included the capital and other major cities, leading press outlets, and the foreign diplomatic corps—were concentrated in the eastern corridor between the Potomac and New England. Lee had always known this. "The lives of our soldiers are too precious to be sacrificed in the attainment of successes that inflict no loss upon the enemy beyond the actual loss in battle," he had written Secretary of War Seddon on January 10, 1863. "Every victory should bring us nearer to the great end which it is the object of this war to reach."[111] This attitude was echoed by Colonel Josiah Gorgas, chief of the Confederate Ordnance Department, who wrote after Chancellorsville that, "all our sacrifices of life and all our successes [must lead to a] decisive result."[112]

Fourth, Lee was aware that the continued success of his army was key in forcing some sort of political solution upon the North. "Nothing can arrest during the present [Lincoln] administration," Lee expressed to Seddon, "the most desolating war that was ever practiced, except by a revolution among their people. Nothing can produce a revolution except systematic success on our part."[113] And Lee knew the Northern populace was growing weary of the war. This disaffection in various parts of the North was reported in newspapers and forwarded by spies for Lee's consideration. The growing fatigue north of the Mason-Dixon Line energized some Southerners, especially when coupled with word that the Lincoln administration was taking steps to ratchet up their war effort as their own people grew tired of the conflict. Robert Kean noted that in passing the conscription, bank, and *habeas corpus* bills, Lincoln and those in power in Washington were exhibiting "a truculent determination to crush us at every hazard, which has not been without effect here."[114] The growing unrest in the North and firm Southern resolve to the cause of independence animated Lee, who realized the political possibilities these circumstances created. "If successful this year, next fall there will be a great change in public opinion at the North," the general predicted to his wife on April 19, 1863. "The Republicans will be destroyed & I think the friends of peace will become so strong as that the next administration will go in on that basis."[115] Government officials in Richmond echoed similar sentiments. "Everything depends upon the issues of the present campaign," reads clerk John B. Jones' entry of March 28, 1863. "Our men must prevail in combat, or lose their property, country, freedom, everything—at least this is their conviction."[116]

The political implications brought about by Lee's bloody and miraculous victory of Chancellorsville are perhaps best summarized by Douglas Southall Freeman:

> Hooker's defeat was an extremely heavy blow to the North not so much in the actual loss, serious as though they were, as in confirmation it gave the widespread belief that the South could not be subdued. Never had the spirit of the North sunk so low as when Hooker's broken corps limped back to safety across the Rappahannock. Many who had frantically proposed opposition to peaceable secession in 1861 were willing, in June, 1863, to let the 'erring sisters' of Scott's figure, 'go in peace.'[117]

But before Lee could add to his victories, he had to increase his numbers while he still had a decent cadre of officers to lead them. But the pool for qualified officers—and men to swell the ranks—was evaporating. The consecutive victories at Fredericksburg and Chancellorsville, even as they were damaging Northern morale, demonstrated to Lee that the Army of Northern Virginia could ill afford to win another victory without furthering the political imperative of the South, i.e., winning its independence. To Lee, his army's fighting power would only wane as time passed.

All of this boiled down to one central and recurring theme: while the South could very well lose the war in the West, it could *never* win it there. In order for the South to have any chance of victory, its actions had to bring the political imperative into play, and this could best—and *only*—be accomplished in the East. This is why throughout the war the largest Federal army was located there, defending its capital, and why Lincoln spent countless hours devoted to the operations of the Army of the Potomac, as well as seeking the best Federal officer to command it.

Lee understood all of this better than anyone else. His determination to keep the Army of Northern Virginia intact and to reinforce it with its valuable missing brigades of proven troops, demonstrates a sound strategic vision based upon a realistic understanding of the tightly interwoven military and political situation that existed in the spring of 1863. Reinforcing Joe Johnston with formations from the Army of Northern Virginia offered virtually no possibility for victory and endless possibilities for retreat and defeat in both theaters of operation. That is why before the Chancellorsville Campaign, Lee, knowing that a numerically inferior force had to retain its freedom of maneuver, wrote: "There is no better way of defending a long line than by moving into the enemy's country."[118]

Just a few days before he met with Davis and his cabinet in Richmond, Lee became convinced that the Army of the Potomac was going to be reinforced in the wake of its Chancellorsville defeat before another renewed offensive began. "I judge from the tone of the Northern papers that it is the intention of the administration at Washington to reinforce the army of Genl Hooker," Lee wrote Davis. "The *Chronicle,* the *Herald*, and the *World* state this positively ... It would seem therefore that Virginia is to be the theater of action, and this army, if possible, ought to be strengthened. If I could get in a position to advance beyond the Rappahannock I should certainly draw their troops from the Southern coasts and give some respite in that quarter."[119] He became further convinced as to Federal intentions to renew the offensive in Virginia when he read the publication of Hooker's congratulatory order to his troops following the Chancellorsville Campaign.[120] Lee had every reason to know that once the Federal losses from the May fighting were replenished, the Army of the Potomac would once again move south toward Richmond. Would his army be intact and strong enough to withstand the assault?

Lee hoped so. In response, he wrote to D. H. Hill on May 16 requesting that the commander of the Department of North Carolina and Southern Virginia (also called the Department South of James River) send to the Army of Northern Virginia as many troops as Hill could spare. Because of Davis' clumsy departmental structure, the language of the request was as strong as Lee could effect:

> As far as I am able to judge, the plan of the enemy is to concentrate as large a force as possible to operate in Virginia. Whether he will unite the whole under

General H[ooker] on the Rappahannock or operate with different columns I cannot say, but from the information I receive he is withdrawing troops from South Carolina & the country south of James River. It is of course our best policy to do the same & to endeavor to repel his advance into Virginia. If he weakens his force in North Carolina I think you will be able, by using all your local troops, such portion of your regular cavalry & regular brigades as may be necessary, to repulse & restrain his marauding expeditions, protect the railroads & farming interests of the country you now hold. Every man not required for this purpose I desire you to send to me & rely upon your good judgment to proportion the means to the object in view.[121]

Strengthening his army and carrying the war into Northern territory was something Lee had been contemplating even before Joe Hooker advanced across the Rappahannock to begin the Chancellorsville Campaign. Writing to Secretary Seddon on April 9, 1863, Lee outlined his thinking on the strategic picture facing his country, and the best way to help struggling Confederate forces in the Western Theater. "Should Genl Hooker's army assume the defensive, the readiest method of relieving the pressure upon Genl Johnston & Genl Beauregard would be for this army to cross into Maryland," submitted Lee. "This cannot be done, however, in the present condition of the roads, nor unless I can obtain a certain amount of provisions and suitable transportation. But this is what I would recommend if practicable." The victory at Chancellorsville only reinforced his beliefs.[122]

Hard facts and political realities were the bedrock upon which Lee's calculations rested. Considerations of intangibles such as initiative, fighting spirit, morale and the institutional memory of the Army of Northern Virginia, combined with physical want, such as lack of sufficient forage for his army's animals and food for the men, dwindling pools of manpower and officers, the deepening financial crisis across the South that "became worse almost daily,"[123] pointed Lee to the only possible course to give the Confederacy a *chance* for victory. That course was another incursion into Yankee territory, boldly undertaken to outmaneuver the numerically superior foe and bring politics into play. Then, somewhere north of the Potomac River, a series of engagements culminating in a resounding Southern victory might prove so politically damaging to the Lincoln administration that Confederate independence would be substantially closer or realized. At the very least, shifting the fight to Pennsylvania would relocate the defense of Richmond from war-torn Virginia into the fertile regions of the enemy, allowing Lee's army to subsist easier and better than it would chained to the defensive line that had been mandated by President Davis.

And it was with this frame of mind that Lee arrived in Richmond on May 14 to meet with Davis and his cabinet to determine the South's course of action.

Decisions

Though still a handsome and robust man, as he walked up the steps and into the Confederate White House, General Lee appeared to some in Richmond to be aging rapidly. John B. Jones noted that Lee "looked thinner, and a little pale."[124] The appearance of the 56-year-old general was probably affected to some degree by the early stages of hypertension and a cardiac condition. The endless duties and constant stress of his position were clearly taking their toll.[125]

Lee's most pressing aggravation was the immediate conference at hand. For four days Lee, Davis, and the Confederate cabinet officials were consumed with how to address the military situation facing their country. Eventually the choice boiled down to either dispatching reinforcements from the Army of Northern Virginia to Johnston in Mississippi, or strengthening Lee for a new strike north. Although Lee's strategic sagacity was decidedly superior to either Davis' or Seddon's, he exhibited an almost limitless tact dealing with officials in Richmond. This verbal diplomacy put him in good stead with his president, but yielded intricate circumlocutions during the Richmond conference. Still, his theme and goals remained clear and consistent, and can be summarized as follows:

> 1. Taking troops away from the Army of Northern Virginia by sending them to help raise Vicksburg during a time when the Federal Army of the Potomac would again resume the offensive would leave Lee little choice but to retire to the works around Richmond, thereby resulting in two sieges instead of one;

> 2. Remaining on the defensive line of the Rappahannock River was tantamount, given the lack of sufficient food and forage, to a middle Virginia siege and, with the logic of simple arithmetic, a stalemate. Like a siege, stalemate doomed the Confederacy to an agonizing, irrevocable defeat—"a mere question of time" as Lee would later describe it, and;

> 3. In order to accomplish the political imperative of the South and *win* independence, a major military victory on Northern soil was needed that would severely damage Lincoln's political stock, for which every possible veteran brigade and division were needed for duty with the Army of Northern Virginia.

By the time the laborious conference ended on May 17, every participant except Postmaster-General Reagan favored reinforcing Lee as the best remedy available. For his part, President Davis understood that the invasion would at the least disrupt Federal plans for a summer campaign in Virginia. It would also, as one historian has noted, "satisfy the clamor that pervaded the South for an invasion of the North to make the Yankees feel more sensibly the disastrous effects of the war they had inaugurated."[126] Accordingly, Davis sanctioned the movement, especially in light of what had already transpired in Mississippi with Johnston's abandonment of Jackson and the resulting lurch in which he had left Pemberton and his army.

Lee, Davis, and the Missing Brigades

One of the first things the president authorized was that three brigades of George Pickett's Virginia division currently in Richmond (those of James Kemper, Richard Garnett, and Lewis Armistead) move north to rejoin the Army of Northern Virginia. However, Lee did not know that the inflexible Davis was unwilling to modify his bureaucratic and self-fulfilling strategy of defense by dispersal. Although he agreed to the invasion, Davis simultaneously denied Lee the wholehearted support he so desperately needed for such a bold undertaking. Lee repeatedly and urgently asked for the return of the last two of Pickett's brigades, those of Micah Jenkins and Montgomery Corse, as well as Brigadier General Robert Ransom's detached division in North Carolina, which consisted of Ransom's own brigade and those of John R. Cooke and Nathan "Shanks" Evans. Instead of showing unfeigned support of the invasion by pledging the return of these five proven brigades led by capable officers—especially the talented young Micah Jenkins—Lee was allowed to begin planning the invasion while Davis continued his preference for maintaining defensive garrisons over Lee's requests to return all possible *veteran* formations to his army.[127] In analyzing the Gettysburg Campaign, it is important to understand that Davis *never* announced this decision to Lee during their Richmond meeting. Instead, wrote one historian, he "simply refused to cooperate in returning detached units and, in effect, countermanded Lee's orders for bringing up his troops to the army."[128]

Davis' unbending rigidity in support of his intellectually bankrupt and unworkable bureaucratic departmental structure is well illustrated by his actions in mid-May 1863. On May 16, when it became evident to the president and other Richmond officials that Joe Johnston was going to do nothing more than act like himself, Davis remained mired within his own dogma. He was too inflexible and too proud to admit that his departmental command structure was failing, and too wrapped up in his own micro-management style to realize that, as Frederick the Great said, "He who defends everything defends nothing." Thus, instead of reinforcing Lee to the hilt, Davis insisted that the Confederacy would continue to wage war his way. The result was that thousands of men were withheld from the Army of Northern Virginia even as its general planned his bold northern gambit upon which the continued existence of the South likely depended.

Part of the problem at the root of Davis' self-defeating strategy, which has in turn become rooted in the mentality of modern-day Lee detractors, was an almost unthinking perception that Lee and the Army of Northern Virginia were a constant sum. To Davis, Lee's army would always be the shield that protected Richmond. It could be argued that following Lee's two consecutive victories at Fredericksburg and Chancellorsville, Davis himself became trapped by the institutional memory of Lee's seemingly invincible army. Perhaps that is why a military dilettante such as Davis did not appreciate, or fully understand, the importance of Lee's undeviating and urgent requests for the return of every experienced brigade to the Army of Northern Virginia before embarking on an invasion of the North. Instead, Davis believed that the return of three of Pickett's brigades, followed later by two untested brigades led by his nephew, Brigadier General Joseph Davis, and Brigadier General James Johnston Pettigrew, were enough troops for Lee. In his rigid mind, Davis *thought* he was supporting Lee by allowing these formations to go and serve in the mobile Army of Northern Virginia.

Davis' ostensible support of Lee's plan to move north does not suggest that Davis maintained his strategic views or authorized Lee's invasion without furious opposition from those advocates who believed the correct course was to send troops from Virginia to Mississippi to relieve Vicksburg. Indeed, he was bombarded with letters from military and civilian personnel alike, urging him to draw troops from the Army of Northern Virginia and send them to Mississippi. If letters weren't enough, additional pressure was supplied by a delegation of influential Mississippians, including Bishop Paine and former Governor James Whitfield, who had recently traveled to Richmond to confer with Davis about the defense of that state. To Davis, the necessity of holding Vicksburg and Port Hudson, along with the 200 miles of meandering river between those points, was of prime importance. Like many others, Davis placed significant value on this meager supply and communications line into Louisiana, Arkansas, and Texas. More important to the president was that Vicksburg symbolized to the Trans-Mississippi Confederates their connection to the rest of the young nation; its loss, he sensed, would hopelessly demoralize them.[129]

What those who made entreaties to Davis assumed—as do many historians working today—was that the formations drawn from the Army of Northern Virginia would be as effective in Mississippi under John Pemberton or Joe Johnston as they had been in Virginia under Robert E. Lee. This line of thinking fails to consider every other major consideration, military and political, shaping the Confederate war effort. If Davis had decided to embrace success and fully reinforce it, he would have not only returned to Lee all his missing brigades, but would have reversed the logic advanced by the "Western Solutionists" and detached a division of troops from Braxton Bragg's army—such as the excellent command under John C. Breckinridge—for duty with Lee.

However, Davis was not a man to change his course or his mind. Rather than alter his thinking he simply held his strategic course. His strategy of defense by dispersal was maintained by procuring reinforcements for Mississippi from Bragg's Army of Tennessee. Perhaps more important was Davis' decision to leave valuable veteran troops in static coastal defenses in the Carolinas and Virginia, instead of garrisoning these points with inexperienced or militia units and sending the others on to Lee.

Jefferson Davis' unwillingness to reassess his views at the time of his country's greatest crisis would have serious consequences for Robert E. Lee and his army.

General Lee's "Lost Brigades"
(Strengths as of May 31, 1863)

Robert Ransom, Jr's Brigade
24th North Carolina
25th North Carolina
35th North Carolina
49th North Carolina
8th North Carolina Battalion

Present & under arms: 3,067

John R. Cooke's Brigade
15th North Carolina
27th North Carolina
46th North Carolina
48th North Carolina

Present & under arms: 2,332

Micah Jenkins' Brigade
1st South Carolina (Hagood's)
2nd South Carolina (Rifles)
5th South Carolina
6th South Carolina
Hampton S.C. Legion
Palmetto S.C. Sharpshooters

Present & under arms: 2,644

Montgomery D. Corse's Brigade
15th Virginia
17th Virginia
30th Virginia
32nd Virginia

Present & under arms: 1,100

N. G. "Shanks" Evans' Brigade
17th South Carolina
22nd South Carolina
23rd South Carolina
61st North Carolina
Holcombe South Carolina Legion

Present & under arms: 2,000

These five brigades amounted to more than 11,000 experienced infantry in 20 regiments and four smaller battalions (the Hampton Legion, Holcombe Legion, 8th North Carolina Battalion, and Palmetto Sharpshooters). The strengths listed above are found in *OR* 18, pp. 929, 1086. Figures for Evans and Corse are estimates based on prior returns. According to Corse (*OR* 27, pt. 3, p. 893), on June 15, 1863, his command did not number "over 1,200 effective men." Cooke reported on June 20, 1863 (*OR* 27, pt. 3, p. 909) that the number of officers and other ranks present in his brigade was 2,486. See also returns for June 30, 1863 (*OR* 27, pt. 3, pp. 946-947).

Reassessment and Reorganization

Following his meeting with Davis, Lee returned to his headquarters near Hamilton's Crossing outside Fredericksburg on May 18. He had no illusions about the difficulties and uncertainties facing him. More men and animals and the means to provide for them had to be found, Hooker's army had to be carefully watched, and the army's day-to-day concerns occupied his time. Before his army could take a single step in the direction of the Potomac, however, the question of reshuffling commands had to be addressed. Every major engagement required some degree of reorganization within the army's ranks, but the attrition of officers suffered during the Chancellorsville fighting, and especially Stonewall Jackson's demise, required that Lee overhaul the basic structure of his army. The small staffs employed by both Lee and his generals, coupled with the short amount of time within which the reorganization had to be accomplished before the Federals could reclaim the initiative and resume the offensive, made the entire complex undertaking doubly demanding.

The growing difficulty of finding qualified subordinates to replace killed and wounded officers was one of Lee's chief concerns. Each battle cost the army dozens of veteran officers, and the pool from which they were drawn was steadily shrinking. If a hard and decisive blow was going to be delivered, it had to be accomplished before the flower of the army's officer corps was used up. This point is well illustrated by the demise of Stonewall Jackson and the heavy attrition in line officers at Chancellorsville—losses that would directly shape the Battle of Gettysburg.

More than anything else, the death of Jackson weighed heavily on Lee. No other officer in Confederate uniform had better understood Lee's bold vision for waging war than his former commander of the Second Corps. And like Lee, Jackson appreciated the military value inherent in rapid flanking movements and sudden, powerful strikes against an unwary foe. These hallmarks of Jackson's leadership, coupled with the Southern soldier's ability to endure the hardships of rigorous campaigning while ill-fed and indifferently shod, augmented the morale of the Army of Northern Virginia. The audacious and aristocratic Lee, and the tenacious western Virginia-born Jackson, had forged a near-perfect collaboration. Both men understood and agreed what was required for the Confederacy to have a chance to gain independence: the war had to be taken to the enemy in order to convince the Federals of the futility of its continued prosecution. To sit idle and surrender the operational initiative to a numerically superior enemy, who could then choose the time and place to attack, was more than just unthinkable to both Lee and Jackson; it was tantamount to national suicide.

The meshing of Lee's and Jackson's intuitive agreement on operational policy allowed Lee to use "Jackson's Foot Cavalry" for bold offensive maneuvers intended to mystify, mislead, and surprise the Federals. Jackson's wide ranging strategic strike in John Pope's rear during the Second Manassas Campaign, for example, allowed the hero of the Shenandoah Valley Campaign to do what he did best, i.e., maneuver and strike within a semi-independent command environment. The magnificent and astonishingly risky flank march at Chancellorsville, perhaps Jackson's crowning wartime achievement, only lifted audacity to new heights. "I had such implicit confidence in Jackson's skill and energy," Lee later said, "that I never troubled myself to give him detailed instructions. The most general suggestions were all that he needed."[130] With the exception of Jackson's lethargic performance during the Seven Days Battles, the results proved Lee right. Jackson had also developed a successful battlefield relationship with Jeb Stuart that coordinated infantry and cavalry operations vital to every successful operation. And now, the great Jackson was no more. Facing the future without Jackson, and with a deep sense of mingled perplexity and stoicism, Lee confessed to his wife on May 11 that: "I know not how to replace him. God's will be done. I trust He will raise up someone in his place."[131] Whether he would or not remained to be seen.

Deprived forever of Jackson's daring energy, Lee knew that he could no longer retain the same large two-corps organization of his army. In fact, he had believed for some time that his dual corps structure was unwieldy even for such accomplished generals as Jackson and Longstreet. "I have for the past year felt that the corps of this army were too large for one commander," Lee explained to Davis on May 20, just ten days after Jackson's death. "Nothing prevented my proposing to you to reduce their size & increase their number, but my inability to recommend commanders. . . . The loss of Jackson from the command of one half the army seems to me a good opportunity to remedy this evil."[132] The Army of Northern Virginia's infantry was about to be reorganized into three corps.

James Longstreet, Lee's capable lieutenant and second in command of the army, would continue to lead First Corps. At Lee's recommendation, a pair of major generals were promoted and elevated to corps level command. Richard Stoddert Ewell, who formerly led a division under Jackson until a severe leg wound at Groveton necessitated amputation, was tapped to lead Second Corps; Ambrose Powell Hill, an impetuous, aggressive division commander who had served under both Longstreet and Jackson, would command a newly created Third Corps.

Lee presented the subject of reorganization and his recommendations in a lengthy letter to Jefferson Davis:

> If therefore you think [Richard] Ewell is able to do field duty, I submit to your better judgment whether the most advantageous arrangement would not be to put him in command of three divisions of Jackson's corps. To take one of Longstreet's divisions [R. H. Anderson's], [and] A. P. Hill's division, & form a division of [Robert] Ransom's, [John] Cooke's, & [James] Pettigrew's brigades, & give the corps thus formed to A. P. Hill. This would make three corps of three divisions each, under Longstreet, Ewell & A. P. Hill. The former is an honest, brave soldier, who has always done his duty well. The latter I think upon the whole is the best soldier of his grade with me. Inasmuch as this army

has done hard work, & there is still harder before it, I wish to take advantage of every circumstance to inspire & encourage them, & induce the officers & men to believe that their labours are appreciated, & when vacancies occur that they will receive the advantages of promotion if they deserve it. I believe the efficiency of the corps would be promoted by being commanded by lt genls, & I do not know where to get better men than those I have named.[133]

Davis approved Lee's recommendations. On May 23, the president authorized the necessary promotions for both Richard Ewell and Powell Hill. The following day, Hill was summoned to army headquarters on the Rappahannock, where he was informed of his promotion. Lee, in his genteel and congenial style, described to Hill that a reorganization of the army had been determined, and that the president had agreed to the establishment of a Third Corps. On May 25, the Adjutant and Inspector General's Office in Richmond ordered Ewell, who had finally recovered from his leg amputation, to report to Lee at Fredericksburg "for assignment to duty."[134]

These new appointments brought about command changes throughout the army's upper ranks. In both reconfiguration and personnel, the least affected outfit in the reorganization was Longstreet's First Corps, which reorganized and prepared for the new campaign without the divisions of Richard Anderson and Robert Ransom. Lee planned to use both formations to help create Hill's new Third Corps. The remaining three divisions comprising First Corps were those of John Bell Hood, George Pickett, and Lafayette McLaws. The first two had missed the severe fighting at Chancellorsville because of their foraging operation around Suffolk. Each of the officers holding the 17 positions from corps to brigade command in First Corps remained in place. This stability was reinforced by the quality of the commanders of First Corps' artillery reserve, Edward Porter Alexander and James Walton, two of the best artillery officers in the army. With such a solid core of division and brigade officers at the head of many élite troops, it is little wonder Lee sought to take full advantage of what he called the "intrinsic" value of "tried troops under experienced officers"[135] by having Pickett's missing two brigades—Micah Jenkins' and Montgomery Corse's—returned to their parent division.

If First Corps was the army's "heavy infantry," then Jackson's old Second Corps might be funnily considered Lee's "light infantry." Old Jack's brigades had been often utilized as a fast moving flanking and striking force. The appointment of "Old Baldy" Dick Ewell as their new corps chief provided the veterans with every reason to believe they would continue in that role. Indeed, few questioned Ewell's ability to lead the organization. While serving under the strict Jackson, Ewell, the army's ranking major general, developed a reputation as a fierce fighter and superb horseman. Before the loss of his leg at Groveton, which required nine months to heal, the widely-respected Ewell had carved out a reputation as one of the army's best division commanders. The respect he had garnered was tempered somewhat by the impression that he lacked initiative. According to one prominent historian, he needed the "confirmation of another officer's judgment before putting his own ideas into operation."[136] Whether Ewell truly lacked the initiative a corps commander required in Lee's army remained to be seen. Although the cheering soldiers were glad to see him back, it was nothing short of a lack of qualified officers that forced the Confederacy to press this amputee into service. It did not take long for the officers who knew and had served under Ewell before his wounding to detect that the newly minted lieutenant general was not the firebrand he once was.[137]

Just as Ewell was new in his role, so too were several Second Corps division and brigade commanders.[138] Since Powell Hill and his outstanding "Light Division" had been pulled from Jackson's old corps to form the nucleus of the newly-created Third Corps, Ewell's most experienced division leader was now Jubal Anderson Early. A sharp-tongued native of Virginia and West Point graduate, Early had led Ewell's Division competently since Groveton. An overdue promotion in April 1863 officially made the division his own. Two of Early's four brigades were led by Harry Hays and John Brown Gordon, both experienced brigadiers. A third, Robert Hoke's outfit, was in the hands of the capable Colonel Isaac Avery, since Hoke was absent nursing a severe arm wound. The fourth brigade, however, would require extra attention. Formerly Early's own, the all-Virginia brigade was now in the hands of 65-year-old William "Extra Billy" Smith, a valiant soldier and former Virginia governor. Smith, who had only recently been appointed to brigadier general and knew next to nothing of military affairs, was, to use Lee's term, an "uninstructed" officer.[139]

The remaining two Second Corps divisions had suffered severely at Chancellorsville, with Jackson's old organization the hardest hit. To fill command vacancies, Lee had to find a new division commander as well as four new brigadiers. Not surprisingly, Lee's first choice to lead Jackson's old division was the surly and tenacious fighter Isaac Trimble. Unfortunately for Lee and the members of that command, Trimble could not take the reins of the division that Jackson had so long saved for him. Although the spirit of the 63-year-old Trimble was in the field with the army, his body was racked by osteomyelitis that kept him prisoner in an administrative role.[140] Instead, Jackson's old division was entrusted to Major General Edward "Allegheny" Johnson, an 1845 graduate of West Point and one of Jackson's Shenandoah Valley veterans. Stonewall held Johnson in high regard and had originally asked that he command his division earlier in the spring, but "Old Clubby" had not yet fully recovered from his McDowell wound. Lee himself had hoped he would have been promoted the previous October, despite the fact that Johnson had never served under him.[141]

Finding qualified brigadiers for Johnson's Division was more difficult. West Pointer George H. Steuart, a native of Maryland and another Shenandoah Valley veteran, was placed in command of Raleigh Colston's troublesome brigade after the latter officer proved himself incapable of field command during the Chancellorsville fighting (Colston had led Jackson's Division at Chancellorsville while a colonel took his brigade into action). James A. Walker, a veteran officer and former student of Jackson's at VMI, was tapped as the new commander of the legendary Stonewall Brigade, replacing the fallen Elisha Franklin Paxton. Walker's appointment outraged the unit's regimental commanders because he came from outside the sacred band. When they threatened to resign, General Lee had to intervene to quell the mini-rebellion. Another interesting choice for brigade command was John M. Jones, who was placed in charge of John R. Jones' Brigade after that officer exhibited cowardice on several fields of battle. The new Jones was an experienced staff officer and recovered alcoholic with absolutely no Civil War combat experience. His new assignment only highlights the fact that Lee was running out of experienced officers to lead his brigades. Since Francis Nicholls' grievous foot wound would not allow him to return to the field, his 2nd Louisiana Brigade was left to the direction of its senior colonel, Jesse Milton Williams. The fact that Lee had unsuccessfully sought a different replacement for Nicholls indicates the commanding general was not entirely comfortable leaving Williams in charge.[142]

The remaining Second Corps division, formerly Daniel Harvey Hill's, was permanently assigned to Robert Rodes, who had led it successfully at Chancellorsville as its senior brigadier. Jackson had recommended from his deathbed that Rodes be promoted for his valiant service. The young North Carolinian was one of the armies true rising stars. Only two of the division's five brigades, Stephen Ramseur's North Carolinians and George Doles' Georgians, were guided by experienced hands. Two more included the unbloodied North Carolinians under the equally untested Brigadier General Junius Daniel, and the inexperienced Colonel Edward A. O'Neal, who ran Rodes' distinguished brigade of five Alabama regiments. Rodes' remaining brigade was in the hands of Brigadier General Alfred Iverson, who would soon prove his incompetence in that high position. By the time General Lee completed the reorganization of the Second Corps, it had as many infantry brigades as Longstreet's First Corps—13—even after losing Hill's six-brigade "Light Division."[143]

As earlier indicated, Powell Hill's crack former division constituted the nucleus of the army's new Third Corps. This corps initially was intended to be, at least in Lee original organizational plans, the largest in the army. The commanding general planned for the Third Corps to consist of 15 or 16 infantry brigades allocated as follows: six brigades with the Light Division, five brigades with Richard Anderson's Division, and four, or possibly five, brigades with Robert Ransom's Division. The brigades comprising Anderson's and Hill's divisions were part of proven veteran commands, although the superb brigade of South Carolinians in the Light Division had temporarily lost their outstanding brigadier, Samuel McGowan, to a severe wound at Chancellorsville (Colonel Abner Perrin replaced him). Lee intended to augment Ransom's three-brigade division with two additional and largely untested brigades led by Johnston Pettigrew and Joseph Davis. Thus, with the exception of

Ransom's untested new material, every Third Corps brigade was supposed to be a battle-hardened command.

However, the largely veteran army that Lee envisioned reunited and reorganized for the invasion was not the army President Davis had in mind. As Lee prepared for the invasion, increasing the number of infantry, explained Douglas Southall Freeman, "though it seemed so imperative, was almost a forlorn hope."[144] Although the superb First Corps divisions under John Bell Hood and Lafayette McLaws remained intact, Longstreet's third division under George Pickett lingered in its under strength condition. Pickett's three brigades bivouacked at Hanover Junction (Kemper, Garnett, and Armistead) were going north with the army. But, wrote Freeman, "all of Lee's powers of persuasion had not sufficed to prevail upon President Davis to release" the balance of the division.[145] The missing formations consisted of the two brigades under Micah Jenkins and Montgomery Corse, some 3,700 tested veterans.

Nor would the experienced regiments in the brigades of John Cooke, Nathan Evans, or Robert Ransom, all serving Ransom's divisional command, be joining Lee's army any time soon. Davis' decision to withhold Ransom's Division forced Lee to rearrange brigades in order to scrape together a makeshift third division for Hill's new corps. After considering the situation, Hill suggested to Lee what the army commander had already reluctantly decided to do—reduce the size of the splendid Light Division. Thus, the brigade of Tennesseans and Alabamians under James Archer, and the Virginians of Henry Heth's old brigade under Colonel John Brockenbrough, were removed from Hill's former division and combined with the two new brigades of Pettigrew and Davis, both of which were originally intended to have been part of Ransom's expanded division.[146]

Choosing a leader for this new division proved to be somewhat of a challenge. Eventually, both Hill and Lee agreed Henry "Harry" Heth was the best available choice. Heth, a native Virginian and graduate of West Point, had already been nominated for promotion to major general by the president in October of 1862 after but scant service in Kentucky. The senate, however, refused to confirm him.[147] Thereafter Heth was given the command of a brigade of Virginians in Hill's Light Division. That assignment meant that Heth was now the division's senior officer, a circumstance that did not sit well with the organization's more experienced and battle-tested brigadiers. Lee, who always practiced meticulous care in selecting officers for elevated rank and responsibilities, hesitated to submit Heth's name to the Senate a second time. Still, Davis' refusal to release Robert Ransom and his division for service with Lee meant that a new ninth infantry division, and a new major general to command it, was required. Lee took the chance and put Heth's name before the government. This time the Senate acted with celerity and confirmed his appointment.[148]

Both Hill and Lee concurred that Dorsey Pender would succeed Hill to the command of the reduced Light Division. The North Carolinian was an outstanding brigade commander with a solid resume of combat service. Unlike Heth, who was a virtual stranger to the Army of Northern Virginia, Pender possessed "the unbounded confidence" of the men.[149]

The effects of the massive reorganization of the army from two corps into three necessarily spilled into the artillery arm. In addition to the artillery battalion that supported each division of infantry, Lee directed that each infantry corps should also have two additional battalions of guns to act as a corps artillery reserve. Under this new arrangement, the army was to have 15 battalions of artillery with the three infantry corps, each corps with five battalions of ordnance. The corps artillery reserve battalions were established on June 2, and two days later the army artillery reserve was broken up in order for those officers to be reassigned to the corps reserve battalions.[150]

The "corresponding adjustment" of Lee's "long arm," as William N. Pendleton called it, left that officer without any general artillery reserve to command. As a result, he reverted to his old title of chief of artillery and remained a brigadier general. The selection of officers to head the three corps artillery chiefs was smoothly undertaken. Colonel James Walton, who had been acting head of Longstreet's First Corps guns for months, remained in that position. To Ewell's Second Corps was assigned the senior battalion commander, Colonel J. Thompson Brown. The guns of the new Third Corps were given to Colonel R. Lindsay Walker, an officer of some distinction who had served much of the war with Hill's Light Division.[151]

Lee also sought to increase the size of his cavalry for the upcoming campaign. The movement north would require significantly more horsemen than the two brigades he had at his disposal during the Chancellorsville operations. In addition to matching the ever-increasing numbers of Federal cavalry operating in Virginia, Lee required a strong cavalry arm to screen and scout for the army as it moved into enemy territory. Major General Jeb Stuart, who had performed so brilliantly thus far, was given an expanded command of five brigades, including William Edmondson "Grumble" Jones' from the Valley and Beverly Robertson's from North Carolina. His remaining three brigades were led by Brigadier Generals Wade Hampton and Fitzhugh Lee, and Colonel John Chambliss. When assembled, the five *regular cavalry* brigades, plus supporting horse artillery companies, numbered 9,536 enlisted troopers (a total of 10,292 including officers). These brigades were organized into a single division under Stuart, the largest mounted outfit he had ever, or was ever, to command. Rounding out the mounted contingent for the army were two additional brigades of poorly disciplined raiders under John Daniel Imboden (who had his own horse artillery battery) and Albert Gallatin Jenkins, both of which would operate independent of Stuart. Stuart's cavalry division's élite horse artillery, nurtured by the late John Pelham, was organized into a single battalion of six batteries under the command Major Robert Franklin Beckham.[152]

Lee's massive reorganization was, for the most part, smoothly handled, but such large-scale retooling efforts on the eve of a new campaign carried with it significant risk—even if the subjects were the magnificent fighting men of the Army of Northern Virginia. Although the army's divisional commands were being filled with competent, and sometimes brilliant, officers, both Richard Ewell and Powell Hill were new to corps level command. Only Longstreet had experience—and it was extensive—leading tens of thousands of troops in battle. What the army suffered from most, however, was a glaring shortage of qualified brigadiers. Far too many untested generals were about to lead collections of regiments during what promised to be one of the most demanding and decisive campaigns the Army of Northern Virginia had ever undertaken—and Lee knew it. Unfortunately, the war had yet to toss up others better suited to take their places.

While Lee may have harbored doubts about certain officers or organization, these reservations did not extend to the fighting men of the Army of Northern Virginia. His unshakeable confidence in their physical toughness and fighting qualities buoyed his hopes and confidence that he would defeat the enemy whenever and wherever he found them. This understanding sustained the general's conviction that his army, which had been molded under the most trying circumstances, could triumph over any conditions. "The troops," explained Douglas Southall Freeman, "were the same magnificent fighting men, but the groupings, in large part, were new."[153] And just how these "groupings" would perform together in battle remained to be seen.

As the army spasmed through reorganization, Lee sought to improve its mobility through the procurement of additional horses. In this, he met with almost no luck. On May 20, Chief Quartermaster Lieutenant Colonel James L. Corley reported that there were no more animals to be found in the South.[154] Those horses already with the Army of Northern Virginia were slowly gaining weight and strength due to the rich spring grass, but they were still seriously undernourished. In fact, Lee's conglomeration of scrawny horses had appeared to one Federal officer during the Chancellorsville Campaign like a "congregation of all the crippled Chicago emigrant trains that ever escaped off the desert."[155] Worse still, the prospects of fattening the animals were bleak since Southern grain supplies for June were projected to be inadequate. Lee realized that if he remained in Virginia through the summer months, the army would become seriously immobilized. Once that happened, inevitable defeat would follow. The inability to provide for his thousands of animals was but another reason Lee was anxious to move the area of operations across the Blue Ridge Mountains, into the agriculturally rich Shenandoah Valley, and over the Potomac River, where his hungry animals could get proper forage and where his purchasing agents could flesh out the army's requirements by obtaining healthy animals that had been grazing on the lush Cumberland Valley.

Before his army could reach the fertile country north of the Potomac, however, Lee had to make sure he had sufficient food and forage for his men and animals to get there. Longstreet's foraging efforts during the Suffolk Campaign had gathered tons of pork, bacon, corn, and other foodstuffs. Much of this booty was stored along the railroads west of Suffolk below Petersburg until wagons and rail cars could be found to shuttle it north to the Rappahannock line. Unfortunately, little had yet been forwarded to advance bases from which the army could draw its subsistence for any prolonged period of time once it pulled away from middle Virginia. Additional supplies were garnered from an expedition conducted by Major John W. Mitchell, commissary of the Department of Southwestern Virginia, along with a raid by Brigadier General John D. Imboden that secured more than 4,200 head of cattle from the mountainous regions of southwestern and western Virginia.[156] Lee advised Seddon that he planned to drive a large majority of these beefs with the army so that the men had sufficient food until they reached the plentiful farmlands of the enemy.[157]

As Lee labored at Hamilton's Crossing, disastrous news reached Richmond from Mississippi: John Pemberton's Army of Vicksburg had been beaten outside the city and forced to fall back within its defenses. The defeats at Champion Hill and Big Black River Bridge, combined with Joe Johnston's lethargic actions following his retreat from Jackson, prompted Davis to call another meeting of the Confederate cabinet on May 26; Lee, busy on the Rappahannock line in preparation for his move north, was unable to attend. The result of this second meeting was the same as the first: the cabinet upheld the earlier decision to allow Lee to move northward, while reinforcements for Johnston would be pulled from other commands. Only the Texas Postmaster General John H. Reagan, as he had before, disagreed with this policy.[158]

While those in Richmond debated a military situation in Mississippi already lost, Lee renewed his efforts to reclaim those brigades that had still not yet been returned to his army. To that end he mounted a letter writing campaign during the last week of May. He had earlier written Harvey Hill, commander of the Department of North Carolina, on May 16 requesting the immediate return of the veteran brigades that had been temporarily detached from the army. "Ransom & Cooke," Lee informed Harvey Hill, "I consider as belonging to the Army of Northern Virginia & *have relied* [emphasis added] upon their return."[159] Unfortunately for Lee, in Jefferson Davis' departmentalized Confederacy possession was nine-tenths of the law. Hill had no intention of relinquishing control of eight veteran regiments. His unwillingness to cooperate with Lee only confirmed what Lee had suspected for some time: Hill was an excellent combat officer but not reliable enough to exercise the discretionary powers Lee demanded in a major general. As a result, he was unsuited for service in the Army of Northern Virginia.

Lee turned to Davis for help in getting his detached brigades back.[160] However, instead of supporting Lee and ordering Hill to return the brigades in question—as well as ordering the return of other formations needed and requested by Lee—Davis allowed a curiously long and cumbersome series of negotiations to take place between himself, Lee, Hill, and Governor Vance of North Carolina.[161] These letters, thought Douglas Southall Freeman, left the impression that the correspondence was between "jealously cautious allies [rather] than among the officials of a Confederacy engaged in a life-and-death revolution."[162]

A close inspection of this correspondence shows that Lee was reduced to begging for the return of his men because of Davis' refusal to alter his departmental jurisdiction and his inability to take charge of what was in reality a critical situation. Meanwhile, Governor Vance and Harvey Hill were doing everything they could to hold on to as many of the 22,822 largely idle troops assigned to their local department as possible. So focused were they on local concerns—Hill went so far as to claim that a rising level of "Toryism" threatened the state—that neither man was able to see the national strategic picture unfolding before them.[163] Davis either already believed Hill's claims or swallowed their bogus tales of woe in order to validate his strategy of defense by dispersal. "To withdraw Ransom's, Cooke's, and Jenkins' brigades is to abandon the country to the enemy," the president wired Lee, "if last [Hill's] information be correct."[164]

General Lee's was not the only voice calling for the return of the brigades to the Army of Northern Virginia before the Battle of Gettysburg. When Federal troops were withdrawn from the coastal area southeast of Petersburg in early and mid-June, Micah Jenkins took up his pen on June 20 to plead with Hill to release him for active duty. "If their forces from this department are withdrawn in consequence of General Lee's movements," wrote the young brigadier, whose men were suffering discipline and morale problems because of non-action in North Carolina, "I beg as a personal and great favor that you will arrange . . . to send my brigade, if any is sent, to Lee's army."[165] Hill declined. The frustrated Jenkins took the unusual step of petitioning Richmond directly to request his return to Lee's army. In his attempt to convince President Davis of the futility of wasting the fighting power of his brigade, every commissioned officer in the organization signed Jenkins' request, to no avail.[166] The South Carolinians remained in North Carolina.

Lee's weeks of discussion, pleading, and bargaining added to the army only the brigades of Pettigrew, Davis, and Junius Daniel, three organizations with untested leaders and troops with little or no combat experience. Lee, in his consummate *savoir faire,* charitably described these leaders as "uninstructed."[167] Neither Davis nor Harvey Hill nor Governor Vance appreciated Lee's eloquent logic: it made no sense to leave thousands of veterans detached from the Army of Northern Virginia on what many considered the eve of the most critical campaign in the nation's history, only to partially replace them with inferior men and officers. Such a decision, Lee wrote to Harvey Hill on May 16, 1863, weakened the army "intrinsically by taking away tried troops under experienced officers and replacing them with fresh men and uninstructed commanders. I should therefore have more to feed but less to depend on."[168]

Viewed in this light, President Davis' failure to order Lee's brigades back to his army indicates that the chief executive did not fully appreciate the stakes involved in

Lee's desperate attempt to score a decisive victory on enemy soil, as opposed to continuing the chronic debilitating stalemate along the Rappahannock River. This northern Virginia deadlock had already cost the South the services of some of her finest soldiers, including the irreplaceable Stonewall Jackson, while doing little or nothing to achieve the political goals the Confederacy so desperately sought.

Final Preparations for Invasion

As the process of reorganizing continued, Lee began collecting topographical maps depicting the terrain extending from the Rappahannock northward to the Susquehanna River in Pennsylvania. On June 1, the commanding general summoned his corps commanders for a meeting. The most important piece of information brought to that conference was the map drawn by Jedediah Hotchkiss, who had joined Stonewall Jackson's staff as a topographical engineer on March 26, 1862, three days after the Battle of Kernstown. Following Jackson's death, Hotchkiss had remained on the staff of Second Corps, and his map of the area over which the proposed invasion would take place impressed Lee. Not only did Hotchkiss have an excellent eye for terrain and detail, but the self-taught map maker was also familiar with large portions of Pennsylvania, including the anthracite region north of Harrisburg and the Cumberland Valley and its extensions southward into Virginia, where Hotchkiss had taught school following his graduation in 1846 from Windsor Academy in New York. Armed with Hotchkiss' detailed map, Lee saw a host of opportunities before him to conduct a series of maneuvers from which he expected to garner the fruits of a successful campaign. He immediately ordered copies of the Hotchkiss map for all his corps commanders.[169]

Throughout these preparations, Lee appreciated the fact that Davis, much like Abraham Lincoln in the North, was anxious, perhaps overly so, about the safety of his capital city. As far as Davis was concerned, Richmond's defensive garrison had to be composed, at least in part, of brigades from the Army of Northern Virginia. Lee, of course, never intended to expose Richmond unnecessarily. Given the risks and possible rewards involved in the campaign about to begin, he had suggested that local militia units be raised to help temporarily guarantee the security of the capital. Neither Secretary Seddon nor President Davis seems to have taken his suggestion seriously.[170]

Lee also predicted that serious Federal activity along the coasts was going to be minimal that summer. (As it turned out, he was correct.) That fact, he argued in a rather clever attempt to both get back his errant brigades and satisfy Davis' concerns, provided an unique opportunity to draw formations from the Departments of South Carolina, Georgia, and Florida, as well as others from the James to the Cape Fear Rivers, and place them before Richmond. This army in effigy, augmented with local militia, would be more than enough to provide the security for the capital Davis demanded. But Davis did not share Lee's vision. Once again, instead of following Lee's suggestions Davis refused to reevaluate his policies and continued to withhold Lee's valuable veteran brigades. His intransigence on this issue is even more remarkable given the situation developing east of Richmond: Federal troops previously believed to be threatening the city from West Point on the York River, supported by a force at Gloucester Point and Yorktown, had evacuated West Point for points north. All of this meant that there would not be a Federal advance on Richmond from the east in the foreseeable future.[171] Davis himself summed up the situation accurately in a dispatch to Lee on May 31. "I had never fairly comprehended your views and purposes until the receipt of your letter of yesterday," the president admitted, "and now have to regret that I did not earlier know all that you had communicated to others."[172]

On the morning of June 3, one month after Chancellorsville, Lee finally decided it was time to move. Richmond was out of immediate danger, and there was little or no Federal activity along the Rappahannock line. Ewell's and Longstreet's corps would lead the way, screened by Stuart's cavalry. Hill's men, meanwhile, would remain behind at Fredericksburg to keep an eye on Hooker and his army and deceive the Federals into believing that Lee's men were still at bay behind the Rappahannock. Lee's divisions broke camp and started for Culpeper Courthouse: Lafayette McLaws's brigades departed on the 3rd, Robert Rodes' on the 4th, and Jubal Early's and Edward Johnson's on the 5th. On the following day, June 6, Lee was convinced Hooker was remaining static, despite the Federal pontoon bridge that had been laid over the Rappahannock the day before and subsequent demonstrations by a small force of Federal infantry. Hill's Third Corps was ordered to move out and screen the army's westward movement.[173]

Lee broke up his headquarters at Hamilton's Crossing on June 6 and joined the army on the march. He arrived at Culpeper Courthouse on the morning of June 7, where he met up with the divisions that had gone before him, plus John Bell Hood's First Corps division. His belief that his army was under strength for the task at hand continued to gnaw away at him, as did the thought of leaving experienced troops scattered from Hanover Junction in Virginia to South Carolina.[174] Knowing full well the president's tendency to micro-manage everything, Lee dispatched a report to Davis on June 7 detailing the events underway. It also included specific directions which, if Davis followed, would result in the return of additional troops for the army. "I desire to bring up the remaining division of Longstreet (Pickett's), and . . . request that J. R. Cooke should be advanced to his place, and that [M.] Jenkins should be brought from the Blackwater to replace Cooke." If it is true that the enemy is reduced in that quarter, explained Lee, "Ransom's brigade will be more than sufficient for that line." Then Lee drove his point home: "West Point being evacuated, and the force at Yorktown reduced, there is nothing to be apprehended from that quarter, and Cooke and Jenkins should be directed to follow me as soon as you think it is safe for them to do so." Lee also suggested that reinforcements should be immediately drawn from General P. G. T. Beauregard's Department of South Carolina for service with either Joe Johnston in Mississippi or "to reinforce this army." Nothing came of these requests.[175]

After a grand review of Jeb Stuart's cavalry at Culpeper[176] on Monday, June 8, Lee took valuable time to respond yet again to complaints emanating from North Carolina. The latest round of dire predictions of disaster from that quarter claimed the Confederates there were vastly outnumbered by an aggressive enemy. As Lee was well aware, this constant carping was largely predicated on his decision to withdraw troops from that region to bolster the Army of Northern Virginia for its northward strike. The first half of Lee's judicious reply to Secretary Seddon's June 5 letter dealt with these matters. "I can understand the anxiety felt by General [W. H. C.] Whiting for the safety of Wilmington and its railroad connections," was Lee's politic response. But, he reasoned, "I think if the force of the enemy was a strong as supposed by Generals D. H. Hill and Whiting, at least more would have been attempted. There is always hazard in military movements," Lee gently chided, "but we must decide between the positive loss of inactivity and the risk of action."[177]

The second half of Lee's communiqué ostensibly sought final permission to commence the invasion, on his terms, that was already underway. It was also a cogent explanation of why he was undertaking the movement and the stakes involved:

> As far as I can judge, there is nothing to be gained by this army remaining quietly on the defensive, which it must do unless it can be re-enforced. I am aware that there is difficulty and hazard in taking the aggressive with so large an army in its front, intrenched behind a river, where it cannot be advantageously attacked. Unless it can be drawn out in a position to be assailed, it will take its own time to prepare and strengthen itself to renew its advance upon Richmond, and force this army back within the intrenchments of that city. This may be the result in any event; still, I think it is worth a trial to prevent such a catastrophe. Still, if the Department thinks it better to remain on the defensive, and guard as far as possible all the avenues of approach, and await the time of the enemy, I am ready to adopt this course. You have, therefore, only to inform me.
>
> I think our southern coast might be held during the sickly [summer] season by local troops, aided by a small organized force, and the predatory excursions of the enemy be repressed. This would give us an active force in the field with which we might hope to make some impression on the enemy, both on our northern and western frontiers. Unless this can be done, I see little hope of accomplishing anything of importance. All our military preparations and organizations should now be pressed forward with the greatest vigor, and every exertion made to obtain some material advantage in this campaign.[178]

Noted Gettysburg historian Edwin Coddington, writing more than 100 years after the close of the epic campaign, summarized in support of Lee's missive to

Secretary Seddon. "Never again," Coddington held, "would General Lee have as good an opportunity to defeat his old foe under conditions which might bring about the decisive military and political results he so eagerly sought."[179]

Notes for Chapter 1

1. *The War of the Rebellion: A Compilation of the Official Records of the Union and Confederate Armies* (130 vols.; Washington, D.C., 1880-1901), Series I, vol. 27, part 3, pp. 868-869. Hereinafter cited as *OR*. Unless otherwise indicated, all citations are to Series I.

2. Richard D. Goff, *Confederate Supply* (Durham, 1969), pp. 78-79.

3. Goff, *Confederate Supply*, p. 74.

4. Clifford Dowdey and Louis H. Manarin, eds., *The Wartime Papers of R. E. Lee* (New York, 1961), number 374. This is an example of a true "discretionary order," as opposed to an "order with discretion." While the subject of the differences between "discretionary orders" and "orders with discretion" will be developed and discussed at length in future chapters, General Lee knew the difference between the two, as is shown in his written and verbal orders.

5. *OR* 25, pt. 2, p. 627; Dowdey and Manarin, *The Wartime Papers of R. E. Lee,* number 376.

6. Robert Garlick Hill Kean, *Inside the Confederate Government,* edited by Edward Younger (New York, 1957), p. 40.

7. Dowdey and Manarin, *The Wartime Papers of R. E. Lee,* number 378.

8. Dowdey and Manarin, *The Wartime Papers of R. E. Lee,* number 380.

9. Dowdey and Manarin, *The Wartime Papers of R. E. Lee,* number 381.

10. *OR* 25, pt. 2, pp. 681-682.

11. *OR* 25, pt. 2, p. 750.

12. *OR* 25, pt. 2, p. 697.

13. *OR* 25, pt. 2, pp. 686-687; Dowdey and Manarin, *The Wartime Papers of R. E. Lee,* number 393.

14. *OR* 25, pt. 2, p. 709.

15. *OR* 25, pt. 2, p. 737.

16. *OR* 25, pt. 2, pp. 737-738.

17. *OR* 25, pt. 2, pp. 739-740.

18. *OR* 25, pt. 2, p. 749.

19. John B. Jones, *A Rebel War Clerk's Diary*, Earl Schenck Miers, ed. (New York, 1958), p. 229. The grain was supposed to be supplemented by at least the same amount of hay or grass, and ideally about 14 pounds of hay per day, which was supposed to be secured locally. As with the men, the Confederates rarely achieved constant, desired food levels for their horses.

20. Jones, *A Rebel War Clerk's Diary*, p. 222.

21. Dowdey and Manarin, *The Wartime Papers of R. E. Lee,* number 422.

22. Jones, *A Rebel War Clerk's Diary*, p. 164.

23. Jones, *A Rebel War Clerk's Diary*, p. 170.

24. Jones, *A Rebel War Clerk's Diary*, p. 174.

25. Jones, *A Rebel War Clerk's Diary*, p. 183.

26. *OR* 25, pt. 2, Lee to Seddon on p. 612 and Northrop's response on 612-613; Lee to Davis on pp. 631-632; Lee to Davis on p. 643; Lee to Trimble on p. 658; Lee to Stuart on p. 664; Lee to Pendleton on p. 680; Lee to W. E. Jones on p. 685; Lee to Seddon on pp. 686-687; Lee to Seddon on p. 713; Lee to Seddon on p. 726; Lee to Seddon on p. 730; Also see "Inspection Report of Artillery of Second Army Corps" in same volume and pt., pp. 634-638; Sam Jones' letter to A. G. Jenkins on p. 662; Northrop's report on the meat ration reduction on pp. 687-688; Pendleton's letter to Cole, p. 695; Jones' letter to Seddon, pp. 701-702; Jones' letter to Imboden on pp. 716-717; Jerrold Northrop Moore, *Confederate Commissary General: Lucius Bellinger Northrop and the Subsistence Bureau of the Southern Army* (Shippensburg, 1996), pp. 186-197.

27. Kean, *Inside the Confederate Government*, p. 41. One example of how a prolonged exposure to undernourishment is vividly illustrated by the plight of Captain George T. Todd, Company A., 1st Texas Infantry. Todd, who stood 6'3" wrote that his weight was down to 150 pounds. See details in George T. Todd, *Sketch of History: The First Texas Regiment, Hood's Brigade, A. N. Va.* (Waco, 1963 reprint of original, which is undated, believed to be 1909), p. ix, located in the Confederate Research Center, Harold B. Simpson History Complex, Hill College, Hillsboro, Texas.

28. Jones, *A Rebel War Clerk's Diary*, p. 166.

29. Dowdey and Manarin, *The Wartime Papers of R. E. Lee*, number 390. For Seddon's response, see *OR* 25, pt. 2, pp. 693-94.

30. *OR* 25, pt. 2, pp. 713-714; Dowdey and Manarin, *The Wartime Papers of R. E. Lee*, number 396.

31. Kean, *Inside the Confederate Government*, p. 52.

32. *OR* 25, pt. 2, pp. 724-725; Dowdey and Manarin, *The Wartime Papers of R. E. Lee*, number 400.

33. *OR* 25, pt. 2, p. 730. The starving Confederate soldiers could only manage to stretch their meager rations over two days. The resulting hunger made it all the more difficult for the men to apportion their food when rations were distributed. See the quotes in Stephen W. Sears, *Chancellorsville* (New York, 1996), including that by Sergeant W. R. Montgomery of Georgia's Phillips Legion on p. 36: "We generally draw rations for three days at a time & eat them up in two, & do without until we draw again."

34. *OR* 25, pt. 2, pp. 725-736.

35. *OR* 25, pt. 2, p. 757.

36. Dowdey and Manarin, *The Wartime Papers of R. E. Lee*, number 411.

37. Dowdey and Manarin, *The Wartime Papers of R. E. Lee*, number 447.

38. Douglas Southall Freeman, *R. E. Lee* (New York, 1935), 4 volumes, vol. 1, p. 458.

39. Henry Heth, "Causes of Lee's Defeat at Gettysburg," *Southern Historical Society Papers*, 52 vols. (Reprint: Wilmington, 1991), vol. 4, pp. 153-154.

40. Dowdey and Manarin, *The Wartime Papers of R. E. Lee*, number 362.

41. *OR* 25, pt. 2, pp. 740-741 and 782-783.

42. *OR* 25, pt. 2, p. 752. See Seddon's telegraph message to D. H. Hill of May 6 in *OR* 25, pt. 2, p. 780.

43. *OR* 25, pt. 2, p. 790. In addition to battlefield losses and illness, Lee's manpower crisis in early 1863 was the result of President Davis' policy of detaching organizations from the Army of Northern Virginia and his failure to return them promptly.

44. Robert C. Black, *The Railroads of the Confederacy* (Chapel Hill, 1952), pp. 141, 189 and large fold-out map.

45. *OR* 25, pt. 2, p. 791.

46. *OR* 27, pt. 2, p. 293. On June 7, after the start of the movement toward Pennsylvania, Lee, desperate for more men, telegraphed Davis yet again. "I require all troops that can be spared. Pickett has been ordered to Culpeper. I advise Cook's brigade be sent immdy to the [Hanover] Junction [on the Virginia Central Railroad] and [Micah] Jenkins take its place." Lee wanted as many troops as possible shifted northward so that it would be easier, if necessary, to fold them into the army. His pleas fell on deaf ears.

47. Letter from James Longstreet to Louis T. Wigfall, May 13, 1863. Library of Congress, Louis T. Wigfall Papers. This contemporary letter by Longstreet runs contrary to his subsequent writings penned many years after the campaign, when he was trying to counter unfair and baseless accusations leveled against him by certain Confederate veterans in order to make him the scapegoat for the Confederate defeat. Please see Chapters 7 and 9 for further discussion of this issue.

48. Dowdey and Manarin, *The Wartime Papers of R. E. Lee,* number 382.

49. Clifford Dowdey, *Death of a Nation: The Story of Lee and His Men at Gettysburg* (New York, 1958), p. 16.

50. William C. Davis, *The Cause Lost: Myths and Realities of the Confederacy* (Lawrence, 1996), p. 138.

51. William Glenn Robertson, "Army Departments," in Richard N. Current, ed., *Encyclopedia of the Confederacy,* 4 vols. (New York, 1994), vol. 1, p. 71. A good example of the failure of Davis' departmentalization is found in the ostensibly reasonable decision to divide the Department of the Trans-Mississippi and the Departments No. 2 and Mississippi and East Louisiana by the Mississippi River. The practical effect left the defense of that important waterway in the hands of several squabbling generals instead of under the unified authority of a single commander.

52. Davis's biographical material is drawn from Frank E. Vandiver, "Jefferson Davis," in Current, ed., *Encyclopedia of the Confederacy,* 2, pp. 448-453; Letter from Jefferson Davis to C. J. Wright, February 12, 1876, Jefferson Davis MSS, Library of Congress, Jefferson Davis Papers.

53. William C. Davis, *Jefferson Davis: The Man and His Hour* (Baton Rouge, 1991), pp. 72-75 and 83-86; Davis, *The Cause Lost*, pp. 9-11, illustrate these points.

54. Frederick the Great, as quoted in Hermann Foertsch, *The Art of Modern Warfare* (New York, 1940).

55. *Frederick the Great on the Art of War,* translated and edited by Jay Luvaas (New York, 1966), pp. 328-329.

56. *The Military Maxims of Napoleon* (London, 1901), Maxim 38.

57. Frederick the Great, *Instructions to His Generals, 1747*. Edited by T. R. Phillips, *Roots of Strategy*, Book 1 (Harrisburg, 1985).

58. Alf J. Mapp, Jr., *Frock Coats and Epaulets: Psychological Portraits of Confederate Military and Political Leaders* (Landham, 1990), p. 96.

59. Varina Howell Davis, as quoted in Davis, *Jefferson Davis: The Man and His Hour*, p. 448.

60. Thomas C. DeLeon, *Four Years in Rebel Capitals: An Inside View of Life in the Southern Confederacy from Birth to Death* (New York, 1962), p. 54.

61. Dowdey, *Death of a Nation*, p. 16.

62. Dowdey and Manarin, *The Wartime Papers of R. E. Lee,* number 356.

63. Dowdey and Manarin, *The Wartime Papers of R. E. Lee,* number 362.

64. Dowdey and Manarin, *The Wartime Papers of R. E. Lee,* number 399.

65. *OR* 25, pt. 2, pp. 791-792.

66. *The Military Maxims of Napoleon*, Maxim 9.

67. *The Military Maxims of Napoleon*, Maxim 10.

68. Dowdey and Manarin, *The Wartime Papers of R. E. Lee,* number 387.

69. Dowdey and Manarin, *The Wartime Papers of R. E. Lee,* number 389.

70. Dowdey and Manarin, *The Wartime Papers of R. E. Lee,* number 447.

71. Dowdey and Manarin, *North Carolina Regiments*, vol. 1, p. 717.

72. Mac Wyckoff, *A History of the 2nd South Carolina Infantry: 1861-65* (Fredericksburg, 1994), p. 74.

73. Wyckoff, *2nd South Carolina Infantry*, pp. 73-74.

74. James F. Crocker, "Gettysburg—Pickett's Charge," *Southern Historical Society Papers*, vol. 33, p. 120.

75. John Bell Hood, *Advance and Retreat* (New Orleans, 1880), p. 54.

76. Todd, *The First Texas Regiment, Hood's Brigade*, p. 14.

77. D. H. Hamilton, *History of Company M, First Texas Volunteer Infantry, Hood's Brigade, Longstreet's Corps, Army of the Confederate States of America* (Waco, 1925), p. 30; a typed manuscript copy is in the Confederate Research Center, Harold B. Simpson History Complex, Hill College, Hillsboro, Texas.

78. Watson D. Williams, "The Letters of Watson D. Williams, Company F, 5th Texas Infantry," June 23, 1863, Camp 5th Texas, Near Milwood. Typed manuscript is located in the Confederate Research Center, Harold B. Simpson History Complex, Hill College, Hillsboro, Texas.

79. *Lee's Dispatches; Unpublished Letters of General Robert E. Lee, C.S.A., to Jefferson Davis and the War Department of the Confederate States of America 1862-65*, edited with an Introduction and Notes by Douglas Southall Freeman (New York, 1957), p. 104.

80. Thomas Conolly, *An Irishman in Dixie: Thomas Conolly's Diary of the Fall of the Confederacy*, edited by Nelson D. Lankford (Columbia, 1988), p. 52.

81. Walter Herron Taylor, *Lee's Adjutant; The Wartime Letters of Colonel Walter Herron Taylor, 1862-1865*, edited by R. Lockwood Tower (Columbia, 1995), p. 53.

82. John Hay, "Letters of John Hay and Extracts from Diary" (Printed but not published, 1908), diary entry for September 9, 1863, pp. 95-96, copy in the Confederate Research Center, Harold B. Simpson History Complex, Hill College, Hillsboro, Texas.

83. John Sherman and William Tecumseh Sherman, *The Sherman Letters: Correspondence between General and Senator Sherman from 1837 to 1891*, edited by Rachel Sherman Thorndike (New York, 1894), letter of May 7, 1863, pp. 203-205.

84. Philip Régis de Trobriand, *Four Years With the Army of the Potomac*, translated by George K. Dauchy (Boston, 1889), pp. 471 and 480.

85. For a list of Lee's staff officers, see Joseph Crute, *Confederate Staff Officers, 1861-1865* (Powhatan, VA, 1982), pp. 114-117.

86. *OR,* Series IV, vol. 2, pp. 447-448.

87. Although the conflict is most accurately described as the "War Between the States," or the "War for Southern Independence," for the sake of clarity we have used American Civil War, or simply Civil War.

88. Pierre-Joseph Bourcet, *Mémories Historiques su la Guerre que les François Ont Soutenue en Allemagne 1757 Jusqu'en 1762* (Paris, 1792).

89. Scott Bowden, *Napoleon and Austerlitz* (Chicago, 1997), Appendix H. Compare the size of the 1805 staff to those of later years by consulting Scott Bowden, *Napoleon's Grande Armée of 1813* (Chicago, 1990), Scott Bowden and Charles Tarbox, *Armies on the Danube*, 2nd edition (Chicago, 1989) and Scott Bowden, *Armies at Waterloo* (Arlington, 1983).

90. Scott Bowden, *Napoleon and Austerlitz,* Appendix H.

91. Scott Bowden, *Napoleon and Austerlitz,* Chapter 1.

92. For an excellent document dealing with the development and changing makeup of the army corps during the Civil War, consult Robert M. Epstein, "The Creation and Evolution of the Army Corps in the American Civil War," *Journal of Military History,* Lexington, Volume 55, January, 1991, pp. 21-46.

93. Clifford Dowdey, *The Seven Days: The Emergence of Lee* (Boston, 1964), p. 143. See specifically Dowdey's description and discussion of Lee's staff on pp. 142-147.

94. Walter H. Taylor, *Four Years With General Lee,* edited and with a New Introduction by James I. Robertson, Jr. (Bloomington, 1996), p. 2.

95. Dowdey and Manarin, *The Wartime Papers of R. E. Lee,* number 98.

96. Clifford Dowdey, *The Land They Fought For: The story of the South as the Confederacy, 1832-1865* (Garden City, 1955), p. 131. This work by Dowdey was reprinted and retitled *The History of the Confederacy 1832-1865* (New York, 1992).

97. *OR* 24, pt. 1, p. 215.

98. *OR* 24, pt. 3, p. 925. These forces numbered about 12,000 in mid-May.

99. Hudson Strode, *Jefferson Davis: Confederate President* (New York, 1959), p. 401.

100. *OR* 24, pt. 3, p. 870.

101. *OR* 24, pt. 3, p. 870. Johnston's message to Pemberton reads as follows: "I have lately arrived, and learn that Major-General Sherman is between us, with four divisions, at Clinton. It is important to re-establish communications, that you may be reinforced. If practicable, come up on his rear at once. To beat such a detachment, would be of immense value. The troops here could cooperate. All the strength you can quickly assemble should be brought. Time is all-important."

102. Stephen E. Ambrose, *Americans at War* (New York, 1997), p. 27.

103. *OR* 24, pt. 3, p. 877.

104. Dowdey, *The Seven Days*, p. 143.

105. Strode, *Jefferson Davis: Confederate President,* p. 401.

106. *OR* 24, pt. 1, pp. 215-216.

107. *OR* 24, pt. 1, p. 216. President Davis' endorsement to Secretary Seddon on Johnston's dispatch evidenced his frustration with the general's inconceivable actions: "Do not perceive why a junction was not attempted, which would have made our force nearly equal in number to the estimated strength of the enemy, and might have resulted in his total defeat under circumstances which rendered retreat or reinforcement to him scarcely practicable."

108. *OR* 24, pt. 1, pp. 289-290, 307 and 309; *OR* 24, pt. 3, p. 625.

109. Kean, *Inside the Confederate Government,* p. 50.

110. Lucius Bellinger Northrop, "Report of Commissary General Northrop," *Southern Historical Society Papers*, vol. 2, p. 99. Northrop specifically draws attention to the failed attempts to drive cattle from Texas to either Tennessee or Virginia during 1862 and 1863.

111. Dowdey and Manarin, *The Wartime Papers of R. E. Lee,* number 356.

112. Josiah Gorgas, as quoted in Frank E. Vandiver, *Ploughshares into Swords: Josiah Gorgas and Confederate Ordnance* (College Station, 1994 edition of 1952 original publication), p. 185.

113. Dowdey and Manarin, *The Wartime Papers of R. E. Lee,* number 361.

114. Kean, *Inside the Confederate Government,* p. 42.

115. Dowdey and Manarin, *The Wartime Papers of R. E. Lee,* number 403.

116. Jones, *A Rebel War Clerk's Diary*, p. 181.

117. Freeman, *Lee's Dispatches,* p. 104.

118. Barron Deaderick, *Strategy in the Civil War* (Harrisburg, 1946), p. 82.

119. Dowdey and Manarin, *The Wartime Papers of R. E. Lee,* number 440.

120. Lee mentions this in a letter to his wife dated May 20, 1863, Dowdey and Manarin, *The Wartime Papers of R. E. Lee,* number 444.

121. Dowdey and Manarin, *The Wartime Papers of R. E. Lee,* number 443.

122. *OR* 25, pt. 2, pp. 713-714; *The Wartime Papers of R. E. Lee,* number 396.

123. A. L. Long, *Memoirs of Robert E. Lee* (London, 1886), p. 266.

124. Jones, *A Rebel War Clerk's Diary*, p. 209.

125. Dowdey, *Death of a Nation,* p. 19. According to Dowdey, "the early stages of hypertension that was, with a cardiac condition . . . cause[d] his death in his sixty-third year."

126. Terry Jones, ed., *The Civil War Memoirs of Captain William J. Seymour: Reminiscensces of a Louisiana Tiger* (Baton Rouge, 1991), p. 58. Freeman, *R. E. Lee,* vol. 3, p. 19, provides a brief description of the conference. Postmaster-General Reagan's account can be found in John H. Reagan, *Memoirs; With Special Reference to Secession and the Civil War* (New York, 1906), pp. 121-122.

127. *OR* 25, pt. 2, p. 827; pp. 832-833; p. 849; vol. 27, pt. 2, p. 293. Dowdey and Manarin, *The Wartime Papers of R. E. Lee*, numbers 450, 452, 453, 457, 461, 494, 496 and 500. Davis sent Lee the two untried brigades of Pettigrew and Joseph Davis. The latter was led by the President's nephew who had no battle experience whatsoever. Therefore, instead of five experienced brigades—the equivalent of another division—with the army as it headed north, Lee was saddled with two brigades with several untried regiments under the command of inexperienced men. All of this would have profound effects at Gettysburg, because veteran units were more important to Lee than ever before due to the loss of Jackson.

128. Dowdey and Manarin, *The Wartime Papers of R. E. Lee*, comments on p. 476. Also see Dunbar Rowland, ed., *Jefferson Davis: Constitutionalist; His Letters, Papers and Speeches* (Jackson, 1923), vol. 5, pp. 500-502.

129. Strode, *Jefferson Davis: Confederate President*, p. 403.

130. R. E. Lee, Jr., *Recollections and Letters of General Robert E. Lee* (New York, 1904), p. 94.

131. Fitzhugh Lee, *General Lee: A Biography of Robert E. Lee* (New York, 1994 reprint of the 1989 and 1894 editions), p. 257. On May 23, Lee reiterated the same thoughts, this time to Stuart. See *OR* 25, pt. 2, p. 821.

132. Dowdey and Manarin, *The Wartime Papers of R. E. Lee*, number 445.

133. Dowdey and Manarin, *The Wartime Papers of R. E. Lee*, number 445.

134. Freeman, *Lee's Dispatches*, p. 91; *OR* 25, pt. 2, pp. 824-25.

135. *OR* 18, p. 1063.

136. Glenn Tucker, *High Tide at Gettysburg* (Dayton, 1973), p. 9.

137. Randolph H. McKim, *A Soldier's Recollections* (New York, 1910), p. 134.

138. For a complete and detailed look at the commanders of the reorganized Army of Northern Virginia, please see Douglas Southall Freeman, *Lee's Lieutenants*, 3 vols. (New York, 1942-1944), vol. 2, pp. 689-714.

139. Larry Tagg, *The Generals of Gettysburg: The Leaders of America's Greatest Battle* (Savas, 1998), pp. 256-268. Tagg's study provides a fascinating examination of these men; *OR* 25, pt. 2, p. 809. The "uninstructed" quote is found in *OR* 18, p. 1063.

140. *OR* 25, pt. 2, pp. 801-802. See also, Jack D. Welsh, *Medical Histories of Confederate Generals* (Kent, 1995), pp. 216-218. Welsh's study is indispensable on this topic.

141. *OR* 19, pt. 2, p. 677; Tagg, *The Generals of Gettysburg*, p. 269; Freeman, *Lee's Lieutenants*, 2, pp. 702-703.

142. Tagg, *The Generals of Gettysburg*, pp. 269-283; Freeman, *Lee's Lieutenants*, 2, pp. 703-705.

143. Tagg, *The Generals of Gettysburg*, pp. 283-300; Freeman, *Lee's Lieutenants*, 2, pp. 700-701.

144. Freeman, *R. E. Lee*, 3, p. 23.

145. Freeman, *R. E. Lee*, 3, p. 23.

146. Freeman, *Lee's Lieutenants*, 2, p. 699. Robert Ransom's brother, Colonel Matthew Whitaker Ransom, was promoted to brigadier general and took over command of Robert's brigade.

147. Robert K. Krick, "Henry Heth," in William C. Davis, ed., *The Confederate General*, 6 vols. (National Historical Society, 1991), vol. 3, p. 89.

148. *OR* 25, pt. 2, p. 811. Heth's was commissioned major general on May 23, 1863, to rank from the following day. Krick, "Henry Heth," p. 89.

149. Powell Hill's quote and assessments of both Heth and Pender are found in Freeman, *Lee's Lieutenants*, 2, p. 698.

150. *OR* 25, pt. 2, pp. 850-851; *OR* 51, pt. 2, pp. 720-721.

151. *OR* 25, pt. 2, pp. 850-851; vol. 27, pt. 3, p. 859; Freeman, *Lee's Lieutenants*, 2, p. 707.

152. The strengths of Stuart's various brigades increased rapidly in late May 1863. There are incomplete returns for May 20 and 25, the latter being found in *OR* 25, pt. 2, p. 825. The

strengths cited here are those of May 31, 1863, as mentioned by Fitzhugh Lee in his "A Review of the First Two Days' Operations at Gettysburg and a Reply to General Longstreet," *Southern Historical Society Papers*, 5, pp. 165-166, and in Walter Herron Taylor's "Numerical Strength of the Armies at Gettysburg," *Southern Historical Society Papers*, 5, pp. 239-241. Finally, Edward G. Longacre, *The Cavalry at Gettysburg* (Lincoln, 1993), provides a good account of Stuart's command for the Gettysburg campaign on pp. 27-33.

153. Freeman, *R. E. Lee,* vol. 3, p. 28.

154. *OR* 25, pt. 2, pp. 846-847. For an excellent examination of Longstreet's first semi-independent campaign, see generally, Steven A. Cormier, *The Siege of Suffolk: The Forgotten Campaign, April 11- May 4, 1863* (Lynchburg, 1990), and pp. 287-295 for Cormier's conclusions and how Longstreet's efforts assisted the Gettysburg Campaign.

155. *OR* 25, pt. 2, p. 847. James Power Smith, in "General Lee at Gettysburg," *Southern Historical Society Papers*, 33, p. 135, claimed that after Chancellorsville, Commissary General Northrop in Richmond concluded, "If General Lee wants rations let him seek them in Pennsylvania." And Lee intended to do so. He told Harry Heth that a movement north of the Potomac River "breaks up all his preconceived plans, relieves our country of his presence, and we subsist while there on his resources. The question of food for this army gives me more trouble than everything else combined." Henry Heth, "Causes of Lee's Defeat at Gettysburg," *Southern Historical Society Papers*, 4, p. 153. Heth agreed with his commander. The desperate want for subsistence, he maintained, made it "very difficult for anyone not connected with the Army of Northern Virginia to realize how strained we were for supplies of all kinds, especially food." Heth, "Causes of Lee's Defeat at Gettysburg," *Southern Historical Society Papers*, 4, p. 153.

156. *OR* 25, pt. 2, pp. 812-813.

157. *Marginalia,* p. 48, as quoted in Douglas Southall Freeman, *R. E. Lee,* 3, p. 23.

158. Reagan, *Memoirs*, pp. 151-153.

159. Dowdey and Manarin, *The Wartime Papers of R. E. Lee,* number 443.

160. *OR* 25, pt. 2, pp. 832-833; Dowdey and Manarin, *The Wartime Papers of R. E. Lee,* number 453.

161. *OR* 18, p. 1062, 1063, 1066, 1067, 1071-1073, 1076-1080, 1082-1084, 1092; *OR* 25, pt. 2, p. 798, 811 and 813.

162. Freeman, *Lee's Lieutenants,* 2, p. 710.

163. *OR* 18, p. 1092; *OR* 27, pt. 3, pp. 946-947; "The Correspondence of Gen. Robt. E. Lee: Chancellorsville to Gettysburg—March to August, 1863," *Southern Historical Society Papers*, 28, p. 155.

164. *OR* 25, pt. 2, p. 831.

165. *OR* 27, pt. 3, p. 908.

166. James Lide Coker, *History of Company G, 9th S.C. Regiment, Infantry, and of Company E, 6th Regiment, Infantry, S.C. Army* (Greenwood, 1979), p. 124.

167. *OR* 18, p. 1063.

168. *OR* 18, p. 1063.

169. Jedediah Hotchkiss, *Make Me a Map of the Valley: The Civil War Journal of Stonewall Jackson's Topographer,* edited by Archie P. McDonald (Dallas, 1973), p. 146; Jedediah Hotchkiss, *Confederate Military History,* Vol. 3, *Virginia* (Atlanta 1899), p. 396.

170. *OR* 25, pt. 2, p. 827, 832-834, 839 and 844; Dowdey and Manarin, *The Wartime Papers of R. E. Lee,* number 455.

171. *OR* 25, pt. 2, p. 847.

172. *OR* 25, pt. 2, p. 842.

173. Freeman, *Lee's Lieutenants,* 2, p. 714; Lee's detailed instructions to Hill are in *OR* 27, pt. 3, p. 859. Hooker was aware Lee was on the move, but did not know his intentions.

174. *OR* 27, pt. 2, p. 293; Freeman, *R. E. Lee,* 3, p. 29.

175. *OR* 27, pt. 2, pp. 293-294; *The Wartime Papers of R. E. Lee,* number 461.

176. Although the cavalry review was rather spectacular and many in attendance wrote of the event, Lee was not so taken with the spectacle that he did not notice the poor quality saddles and defective carbines. *OR* 27, pt. 3, pp. 872-873; Dowdey and Manarin, *The Wartime Papers of R. E. Lee,* number 462.

177. *OR* 27, pt. 3, pp. 868-869; Dowdey and Manarin, *The Wartime Papers of R. E. Lee,* number 463. An outstanding engineer, William Henry Chase Whiting had served under Lee during the Seven Days Battles. Recognizing his inability to get along with others and general pessimistic nature, Lee arranged for his transfer to command the military district of Wilmington, N.C., where his engineering skills could, and were, put to good use.

178. *OR* 27, pt. 3, pp. 868-869; Dowdey and Manarin, *The Wartime Papers of R. E. Lee,* number 463. Other Confederate general officers saw the same opportunities Lee did for achieving the South's political imperative. Jubal Early, a staunch defender of Lee during the postwar period, was one of those who believed that an incursion into Yankee country was the surest way to do "more to produce a financial crisis in the North and secure our independence than a succession of victories on the soil of Virginia." Jubal A. Early, "Causes of Lee's Defeat at Gettysburg," *Southern Historical Society Papers*, 4, p. 52.

179. Edwin B. Coddington, *The Gettysburg Campaign: A Study in Command* (New York, 1968), p. 259.

Chapter 2

"The Very Best Soldier I Ever Saw in the Field"

Robert E. Lee and His Art of War

"Stop, Stop! If you go to ciphering we are whipped beforehand."
—Robert E. Lee to Brig. Gen. W. H. C. Whiting, on the day Lee
took command of the Virginia army[1]

*"If we can defeat or drive the armies of the enemy from the field, we shall
have peace. All our efforts & energies should be devoted to that object."*
— Robert E. Lee to Jefferson Davis[2]

"The very best soldier I ever saw in the field."
—Gen. Winfield Scott, when asked to give his assessment of Robert E. Lee[3]

e was not Jefferson Davis' first choice to command what would soon be known as the Army of Northern Virginia. In fact, his elevation to that position was the result of a stray artillery shell. The unusual set of circumstances unfolded within the smokey thickets of Seven Pines on May 31, 1862, just a handful of miles outside Richmond. There, a pair of riders watched with growing alarm as General Joseph E. Johnston's offensive to destroy one of George McClellan's corps unraveled in confusion. Darkness arrived with an errant round from an unidentified battery that arched its way into the history books when it unsaddled and seriously wounded Johnston. An unexpected meeting on the field with General Gustavus Smith, Johnston's second in command, left one of the riders less than satisfied that Smith was up for the job.

Little is known of what transpired between the two mounted men as they rode the seven miles to the Southern capital. But by the time they arrived there, Jefferson Davis had informed General Robert E. Lee, his 55-year-old military advisor, that he would assume the mantle of command the following day. There was ample evidence that the new commander possessed outstanding qualities as a soldier, but few would have prophesied that over the next three years Lee would carve out his place as one of the greatest military commanders in American history.[4]

Reveille

Robert Edward Lee was born on January 19, 1807, at "Stratford," Westmoreland County, in the Tidewater region of northern Virginia. He was the third son and fourth of five children born to Ann Hill Carter Lee and Henry "Light-Horse Harry" Lee. His father had been a hero of the Revolutionary War and a governor of Virginia. Unfortunately, the elder Lee's irresponsible personal habits, which included a number of hair-brained financial schemes, burdened his family with debt and finally drove "Light-Horse Harry" out of the country in 1813. Homesick and terminally ill, he died on his journey home from the West Indies at Cumberland Island, Georgia, in 1818. Young Robert, only six years old when his father fled his creditors, never saw him again. Without the benefit of a father figure, Robert was raised by his mother, who impressed upon the youth her devout Episcopalian faith and characteristics of duty, honor, courage and self-discipline.[5]

In his early teens, Robert completed a course of study at the Alexandria Academy, where he revealed a considerable aptitude for Latin and mathematics. At the age of 17, Lee applied for and received an appointment to the United States Military Academy at West Point. He matriculated in 1825 and was an exemplary cadet. As a third classman (sophomore) he served as a staff sergeant, a cadet rank usually reserved for second classmen (juniors). During both his third and second class years, Lee's prowess in math earned him an appointment as an acting assistant professor of mathematics. Lee garnered the most coveted and important rank open to a cadet, that of Corps Adjutant, during his final year at West Point. The Corps Adjutant was selected by the post's superintendent from those first classmen (seniors) demonstrating outstanding scholarship, exceptional military bearing, and the best record on the drill grounds. He devoured works on the Great Captains and took a keen interest in Napoleonic history, which perhaps helped him make perfect scores in his final exams in both artillery and tactics. Lee graduated at the top of the corps in those topics, and second in overall scholastic average. More remarkably, during his entire four-year tenure as a cadet he did not earn a single demerit for misconduct, a stunning achievement and proud reflection of the characteristics instilled in him by his mother at an early age. When he graduated in 1829, Lee applied for and received an assignment to the army's élite Corps of Engineers.[6]

After graduating from West Point, Lee did something atypical of a man who had just received a diploma: he continued to vigorously apply himself in a self-study program of military history and theory. In particular, the Napoleonic wars captured his imagination, and he became especially interested in the writings of the prominent, though self-aggrandizing, Swiss-born military theorist Baron Antoine Henri Jomini.[7]

The new second lieutenant's initial assignment was in Georgia on Cockspur Island in the Savannah River, where he helped design and construct Fort Pulaski. Lee labored there until the middle of the 1830s, when a summer hiatus was called because of the intense Georgia heat, humidity, and increased dangers from disease-carrying mosquitoes. Until Lee's return to coastal Georgia, the young officer spent his leisure time visiting friends in the Washington area. While there, he was introduced to Mary Randolph Custis, an eligible young lady who lived with her parents at "Arlington," the magnificent family estate in northern Virginia overlooking Washington City and the Potomac River. Rising from the south bank of the majestic Potomac, the hill on which the stately mansion rested offered panoramic vistas of the nation's capital and surrounding countryside that were, and continue to be, breathtaking. Mary was the only child of George Washington Parke Custis, the step-grandson of George Washington, and Mary Lee Fitzhugh Custis, a cousin of Robert's mother.

The women relatives encouraged the courtship between the young people, although neither seemed to need much prodding. Robert and Mary were attracted to each other, and he enjoyed visiting Arlington, where the Custis family maintained an extensive collection of George Washington's former possessions. Robert had a special appreciation for the former general and president, who not only was a fellow Virginian but the most revered man in the young country's history. That fact, coupled with the Custis family's social status and wealth, certainly did not inhibit Lee in his pursuit of Mary. Fortunately for the young suitor, the following year he was transferred from Fort Pulaski to Fort Monroe at Old Point Comfort, Virginia, where the opportunities to visit the Custis household became more frequent. On June 30, 1831, the couple were wed in a ceremony at Arlington.

Lee's marriage was one of the most important events in his life, for it brought him into one of the most extensive, influential, and well-to-do families of Virginia. It also made him George Washington's great-grandson-in-law. In fact, a list of Lee's extended family reads like a who's who of the Old Dominion state and of the South. James Madison, Jr., the fourth president of the United States, was a first cousin-in-law, while Zachary Taylor, Jr., who would be elected the twelfth president of the United States in 1848, was a third cousin. John Marshall, one of the most famous jurists in the nation's history and chief justice of the United States Supreme Court, was a third cousin-in-law. Numerous prominent future Confederates were included in Lee's extended family. Jefferson Davis, who would one day assume the presidency of the Confederate States, was a fourth cousin-in-law, while future cavalry generals Fitzhugh Lee and James Ewell Brown Stuart were, respectively, Lee's nephew and third cousin-in-law. Samuel Cooper, the Confederacy's future adjutant and inspector general, was Lee's brother-in-law. Many other prominent personages, including generals and politicians—John C. Breckinridge, a vice president of the United States, George Davis, the future Confederate States attorney general, John Brown Gordon, Wade Hampton III, William Henry Harrison, the ninth president of the United States, Eppa Hunton, Sr., Thomas Jonathan "Stonewall" Jackson, Albert Sidney Johnston, Joseph Eggleston Johnston, Robert Garlick Hill Kean, William Nelson Pendleton, James K. Polk, the eleventh president of the United States, George W. Randolph, one of the Confederacy's secretaries for war, Edmund Kirby Smith, Richard Taylor II, and Martin Van Buren, the eighth president of the United States—were relatives. Through a combination of his own family ties and those of his new wife, Lee was also part of the extended family of other immortal Virginia sons. Five of the seven signers of the Declaration of Independence hailing from the Old Dominion were Lee's relatives, including Patrick Henry and Thomas Jefferson, the third president of the United States. Seven times his kinsmen, including his father, had held office in Virginia as governor or acting governor. A number of Lee's ancestors and immediate family were former members and speakers of the House of Burgesses, as well as Virginia state legislators. Lee's marriage, combined with his own distinguished ties, produced an enormous breadth and composition of friends and family that would play a major role in the formulation of his decision to stay and serve Virginia when the state seceded from the Union.[8]

Robert E. Lee, ca. 1850-1852

This photograph was taken by Matthew Brady about 10 years before Lee was picked to command what would become the Army of Northern Virginia. He sat for this photograph prior to his superintendency of West Point.

Eleanor S. Brockenbrough Library.
The Museum of the Confederacy. Richmond

Following his marriage and for the next 15 years, Lee's career continued in the grueling work of designing, building, and repairing coastal fortifications and channeling rivers for navigation. Throughout, Lee demonstrated his ability as an engineer. His efforts helped save the important port of St. Louis, Missouri, from the flooding Mississippi River, build Fort Carroll in Baltimore harbor, and strengthen the fortifications guarding New York harbor. It was in 1844, while involved in the work at New York, that Lee received two appointments that were to enhance his prestige and expand his career horizons. One was to the board of engineers for the Atlantic coastal defenses; the second was for the final examinations of the seniors at West Point. It was in connection with the second appointment that Lee came in contact with the man who served as the chief examiner for the graduating West Point cadets: the commanding general of the army, Winfield Scott. Scott's exploits would soon make him the most influential American soldier of the first half of the 19th century. As one prominent historian described it, this intercourse with General Scott marked the beginning of Lee's association with the man who would play a "decisive role in the shaping of Lee's career as a soldier."[9]

War With Mexico

Robert E. Lee was still engaged with his assignment in New York when important news came: war had broken out with Mexico. In August of 1846, Lee received orders to report to Brigadier General John C. Wool in San Antonio, Texas, for service destined to take Lee across the Rio Grande River into Mexico. Although Lee did not see combat during the ensuing months of 1846, his skills were put to good use in the construction of roads and bridges for Wool's march southwestward from San Antonio.[10] Lee's talents were soon better employed. In January of 1847 he was ordered to report to General Scott, who was preparing a campaign against Mexican forces holding the Gulf of Mexico city of Vera Cruz, one of the most powerful fortresses in the Western hemisphere. Lee, by this time a captain, had made a favorable impression on the demanding Scott in their earlier association, and the general was anxious to utilize his talents. Assigned to the general's staff, Lee assisted Scott in planning the assault on Vera Cruz, an audacious plan that called for the first sizable amphibious operation in United States military history. After an unopposed landing south of the fortress city, Scott directed Lee to oversee the placement and direction of the investment of the stronghold with a battery of heavy naval guns. A sustained two-day bombardment followed, and the garrison capitulated. The successful operation provided Lee with his first experience in combat. He was 40 years old.[11]

Following the capture of Vera Cruz, General Scott readied his army for a land campaign designed to defeat the numerically superior Mexican Army under Santa

General Winfield Scott
(1786-1866)

The most influential American military man of the first-half of the 19th century. Winfield Scott was brave, resourceful, energetic, audacious, and perceptive—the consummate soldier. He was also a meticulous organizer, gifted tactician and strategist, and capable diplomat. After working extensively with Robert E. Lee during the Mexican War, Scott claimed Lee was "the greatest soldier he ever saw."

National Archives

Anna and take Mexico City. By the middle of April 1847, Scott's army of 8,500 men arrived in front of Cerro Gordo, a heavily fortified mountain position some 150 miles east of Mexico City held by 12,000 Mexicans. It was here that Lee received his first hands-on lesson in how a smaller but better-trained force should deal with a numerically superior foe deployed on favorable terrain. Scott, who was also a student of the Great Captains of history, knew better than to revert to the defensive and wait for Santa Anna to strike him. A direct attack, however, was out of the question. To Lee he assigned the task of scouting the terrain in order to find a way to flank the Mexican lines. Lee's reconnaissance missions were fraught with peril. During one scout, he was working his way around the Mexican position and only avoided capture by lying motionless for hours behind a log while enemy soldiers circled around him. After his narrow escape, he returned the next day to make a more thorough examination of the topography. The Americans, he concluded, could move around the enemy's left flank and cut their communications, forcing the larger enemy out of their strong position. The result was the victorious Battle of Cerro Gordo, which was fought according to Lee's strategy.[12]

But Lee did more than just provide invaluable reconnaissance for Scott and the army. While a portion of the American army demonstrated against the enemy's front, Lee personally guided the flanking force around the face of the Mexican position. Although the plan was excellent, its execution was less so. When the left wing of the enemy finally retreated, Lee took part in the pursuit that captured about 3,000 of Santa Anna's men. His accomplishments in his first land battle were significant. He had provided the accurate reconnaissance of the enemy positions upon which Scott based his daring offensive strike, coolly led the van of one of the flanking columns into the enemy's fire, and assumed a prominent role in the final pursuit that finished off the Mexicans holding Cerro Gordo. Equally important was the fact that Lee had been party to an impressive victory authored by a bold army commander willing to implement a daring plan in the face of a numerically superior enemy. With a better led but numerically inferior force, Scott had maneuvered, attacked, and routed a dangerous enemy deployed in a formidable defensive position. Lee witnessed firsthand General Scott's method of conducting war: he provided his subordinates with his general plan of battle and trusted them with the discretion to carry out their instructions to the best of their abilities. The fighting at Cerro Gordo left an indelible mark on Lee, and served to fortify General Scott's opinion that his fellow Virginian was one of the army's finest officers. His superiors praised his brilliant conduct at Cerro Gordo, with Scott making special mention of his staffer's tireless and bold operations. A brevet promotion to major was part of Lee's reward.[13]

After scattering Santa Anna's army, Scott continued his march toward Mexico City. A lengthening supply line and insufficient numbers of transport created a whole new set of problems for the American army. Scott again turned to Lee for assistance, this time in finding the best possible march route to Mexico City, which Lee accomplished with consummate skill. By the middle of August 1847, the American army was within nine miles of the capital of Mexico, approaching the city from the south along the line of march scouted by Lee. There, Scott's army was confronted with another barrier of formidable Mexican works consisting of the fortified hacienda at San Antonio (Mexico) backed up by additional fortifications at Churubusco. The strength of the enemy's position led to a collective agreement among many of the officers at Scott's headquarters that a direct advance against the fortified positions was not desirable (although many officers advocated direct attack along the causeways leading to the southern part of the city). Lee once again offered Scott an alternative plan of operation.[14] He had scouted a rugged and virtually undefended tract of land south and west of San Antonio known locally as the Pedregal—an immense field of lava more than five miles across on an east-west axis and three miles long from north to south. Lee argued for a flanking movement through the volcanic scoria as a means of bypassing the fortified hacienda at San Antonio. If successful, the move would allow the Americans to strike directly for the Churubusco River.[15]

Lee's scouting efforts and subsequent recommendation to Scott impressed Raphael Semmes, a navy lieutenant at Scott's headquarters who would later achieve distinction as a Confederate admiral and high seas raider. Lee's contributions during this phase of the campaign "were invaluable" to Scott. "Endowed with a mind which has no superior in his corps, and possessing great energy of character," wrote Semmes years later, "he examined, counseled and advised with a judgment, tact and discretion worthy of all praise. His talent for topography was peculiar, and he seemed to receive impressions intuitively, which it cost other men much labor to acquire."[16]

Remarkably, Lee duplicated his feat at Cerro Gordo. After finding a route across the Pedregal, he guided and fought with the columns as Scott's army flanked the Mexican position at San Antonio and participated in the defeat of the enemy forces at Padierna and Churubusco. His actions required extraordinary feats of stamina. According one of his biographers, Lee "had been on his feet or in the saddle almost continuously for thirty-six hours, had thrice crossed the Pedregal, and had been in all three actions, that of the 19th in the Pedregal, that of Padierna, and that of Churubusco."[17] General Scott's narrative of the Mexican campaigns, written years after the war, characterized Lee's nocturnal excursions across the Pedregal as "the greatest feat of physical and moral courage" exhibited during the entire campaign for Mexico.[18] For his heroics at the Pedregal, Lee was breveted lieutenant colonel.[19]

Lee followed up his heroics at the Pedregal by reconnoitering for the American army as it approached Mexico City, keeping General Scott informed about the movements of the enemy forces during the action at Molina del Ray on September 8, and performing various and often vital engineering and scouting duties in preparation for the September 13 storming of Chapultepec, Santa Anna's main defense of Mexico City. In another example of his impressive physical endurance and supreme effort of will, Lee's Chapultepec exertions came at the end of a 30-hour

Attack on Chapultepec Castle

The formidable stone fortress and castle of the Mexican national military academy, the *Colegio Militar*, were on el Cerro de Chapultepec just outside Mexico City. Undaunted by the apparent strength of the position and believing in the leadership qualities of his officers and the élan of his men, Winfield Scott attacked Chapultepec on September 13, 1847. This painting shows American forces storming the southeast side of the hill. *Library of Congress*

Chapultepec Castle (viewed from the west)

The Americans assaulted Chapultepec from two directions—southeast and west. This
view shows the western face of the hill and castle. *Library of Congress*

period during which he had been continuously on the move without rest.
Immediately after the capture of Chapultepec, Lee watched as General Scott dealt
with the disorganized and retreating foe. Unwilling to grant the enemy any respite,
Scott immediately ordered the American forces to pursue; Lee was directed to once
again scout the effort. While reconnoitering the approaches to the San Cosme Gate
of Mexico City, Lee received a slight wound which, combined with fatigue and
sleeplessness, explained Douglas Southall Freeman, caused him to faint "for the first
and only time in his life."[20] His actions in the operations of the 13th, including the
successful storming of the Chapultepec stronghold, won Lee the rank of
colonel—his third brevet promotion of the war.[21]

Twenty months of service in Mexico ended in June 1848, when Lee returned
home to Virginia. He departed with the satisfaction of knowing that he had earned
the highest admiration of General Scott, the only American of the 19th century to
serve as a general officer in three major wars, and who was associated with every
president from Thomas Jefferson to Abraham Lincoln. The Reverend J. William
Jones remembered one of many tributes paid by Scott to Lee: "When, soon after
Scott's return from Mexico, a committee from Richmond waited on him to tender
him a public reception in the Capitol of his native State, he said: 'You seek to honor
the wrong man. Capt. R. E. Lee is the Virginian who deserves the credit for that
brilliant campaign.'"[22]

Having witnessed so much of the young country's history, and after having served with so many outstanding Americans, it is of no little importance that in an official letter in 1858, Scott proclaimed Lee "the very best soldier that I ever saw in the field."[23] In a conversation with Kentucky Congressman William Preston, Scott declared Robert E. Lee to be "the greatest living soldier in America."[24] "I tell you that if I were on my death bed to-morrow," the aging general eloquently informed Preston, "and the President of the United States should tell me that a great battle was to be fought for the liberty or slavery of the country, and asked my judgment as to the ability of a commander, I would say with my dying breath, let it be Robert E. Lee."[25] In a confidential interview just before the Civil War, Scott told a close friend, "I tell you, sir, that Robert E, Lee is the greatest soldier now living, and if he ever gets the opportunity, he will prove himself the greatest captain of history."[26]

Lee had, indeed, repeatedly displayed a remarkable capacity for endurance, courage, and sangfroid under fire. Equally important, he had learned many valuable lessons in Mexico at the elbow of America's foremost soldier— lessons that left a lasting impression.

The Formation of Lee's Philosophy of War

Lee's experiences in the war with Mexico played a major role in the formation of his philosophy of war—a philosophy inextricably linked to his mentor, General Winfield Scott. As the most important and influential soldier of his time, Winfield Scott had a significant impact on the military thought of the entire American officer corps. One of Scott's leading biographers, Timothy Johnson, explained the general's influence this way: "[Scott] learned to be bold without being impetuous. He wanted to dictate the course of military operation, which meant taking the initiative through offensive action. Consequently, his influence helped set the tone for an offensive-minded officer corps in the 1860's."[27] As a member of what Winfield Scott called his "Little Cabinet," and from the landing at Vera Cruz to the capture of Mexico City, Lee was positioned to benefit from Scott's tutoring. Lee was a superior student, but lessons learned can have either a positive or negative impact on one's future conduct. It is therefore instructive to examine the types of lessons Lee absorbed from Scott and his experiences in Mexico, and their impact on his philosophy of war. This, in turn, helps us understand and better appreciate Lee's performance as a field commander in the Civil War.

Under the tutelage of the bold General Scott, Lee learned and had reinforced in his mind time and again some of the cardinal principles of warfare. One of the primary lessons Lee absorbed was that a numerically inferior force could consistently engage and defeat a larger force—even if the enemy was on the defensive. Four things were required to accomplish this feat.

Robert E. Lee, circa 1861

Based on the Brady photo taken about 1850-1852, this image of Lee was widely circulated early in the war. It is a reworked engraving; the uniform was painted on in an attempt to portray Lee as a major general of Virginia militia.

Library of Congress

First, all the information possible about the enemy and the countryside had to be gathered and analyzed. As he would later demonstrate, Lee became so proficient at analyzing information during the Civil War that it is often forgotten, explains one historian, that "he brought highly developed deductive powers to balancing those indications of the enemy's intentions against a background of known factors."[28]

Second, the commanding general of the inferior force had to be willing to take risks—but not blind risks. In other words, the fruits of a thorough reconnaissance had to be effectively utilized in order to calculate the potential cost and benefits of battle. This method, properly applied, allowed for the development of a plan that could be both audacious and sound at the same time.

Third, Lee learned that the commanding general of an army had to be able to make a decision and then *act* upon that decision, even if subordinate commanders were not favorably disposed to the idea. "Nothing is more difficult, and therefore more precious, than to be able to decide," wrote Napoleon. Lee saw the value of this Maxim in action through the generalship of Winfield Scott.

Fourth, and perhaps most important, the commanding general of a numerically inferior force had to dictate as much as possible the flow of military operations. In other words, seizing the initiative and the resulting freedom of maneuver attached to that initiative, were of vital importance.

During the Mexican War campaigns from Vera Cruz to Mexico City, Lee saw firsthand that each time the smaller American army paused, for whatever reason, the respite allowed the Mexican forces to recover their strength and balance. The enemy utilized this recess to strengthen their position at the eventual cost of additional American blood. While some of the interruptions were unavoidable because of supply or transport concerns, the American army, as the smaller force, had to maintain the initiative through maneuver, which it was able to do most of the time.

Like other officers serving under Scott in Mexico, Lee observed that flanking movements were preferable to direct attack. Scott's repeated employment of flanking operations demonstrated the relationship between cause and effect in both strategy and tactics—and Lee was an integral part of these maneuvers. Scott's staffer not only provided important insight into planning these flanking maneuvers, but scouted or led many of them while the enemy's attention was distracted with frontal demonstrations.[29]

In addition to these vital military lessons, Lee absorbed other important guidance from Scott's leadership. During the long overland march to Mexico City, Scott enforced tough discipline on his troops and combined this with political skill to insure that the American forces conducted themselves with restraint towards the local populace, as well as towards the institutions held dear to the Mexican people, such as the Catholic Church. These efforts helped minimize the frequency and severity of possible acts of sabotage by the local populace against American troop detachments or supply lines. It is reasonable to surmise that Lee remembered this, and that it played some role in his decision to order his troops during the Sharpsburg and Gettysburg campaigns to act with similar restraint and respect, and to pay for any supplies they obtained from local citizens. Lee's Mexican service also provided him with the opportunity to witness how politics could, and often did, exert influences on military strategy and operations. While all these lessons were certainly positive ones, were there others which may not have been so beneficial?[30]

In his excellent biography of Robert E. Lee, historian Emory Thomas claims that Lee learned a number of positive lessons from Mexico—and at least one that was not. The most valuable, argues Thomas, was that Lee learned "he was much more than a capable, conscientious engineer; he was a warrior of uncommon ability."[31] Lee's unwavering confidence in himself was tempered by humility and deep respect for others—a combination that is as rare today as it was then. Indeed, much of Lee's confidence developed as a result of his many daring reconnaissance missions, during which he developed the capability to *read* terrain beyond the level expected of an ordinary engineer. His successful scouting of the Pedregal lava fields provides an excellent example: Lee studied the terrain carefully and recommended to Scott that it could be traversed to envelop Churubusco and San Antonio, while other engineers on Scott's staff thought the area unsuitable for such movement. The second beneficial lesson Thomas claims Lee grasped was the value of maneuver and the attentive advantages of striking an opponent's flank.

Nonetheless, Thomas contends, Lee absorbed at least one harmful lesson from his Mexican War ordeal. This adverse lesson, in Thomas' opinion, was the unchecked belief in the value of offensive action. "Lee and many of his contemporaries accepted their experience of offensive success in Mexico as universally valid," writes Thomas. "The Mexican experience confirmed Napoleonic teaching and rendered reliance upon offense as an article of faith in the military mind. What veterans of the Mexican War forgot or failed to emphasize were the factors which allowed attackers to succeed in Mexico—the poor state of Santa Anna's army and the use of muskets as primary infantry weapons."[32]

Thomas's assertion is interesting and, to a degree, even compelling. The Mexican army was indeed beset with a host of problems, all of which are detailed in such noteworthy works as John S. D. Eisenhower's *So Far From God: The U. S. War With Mexico 1846-1848*, and William A. DePalo, Jr.'s *The Mexican National Army, 1822-1852*. But it has long been an article of faith, and history has shown over and over, that soldiers fight with more tenacity defending their homeland, as the Mexican army was doing, rather than invading another. Despite their lack of training, sometimes shoddy equipment, and uneven leadership, Mexican soldiers fought with courage and bravery—especially in the battles around Mexico City. It must also be remembered that the American forces had to contend with numerous supply and other problems of their own, which were only overcome by the outstanding leadership of Scott, and the courage and resourcefulness of subordinates like Robert E. Lee.

Thomas' idea that Lee may not have "forgot" the difference between the smoothbore muskets employed during the Mexican War and the more common rifled muskets of the American Civil War era, however, is of particular interest. Thomas is apparently arguing that because of the limited accurate range of smoothbore muskets, troops on the defensive equipped with such weapons enjoyed little if any tactical advantage over attacking troops, whereas troops on the defensive armed with *rifled* muskets held a significantly greater advantage. This might be true only if two factors were in play: the attacker relied solely on frontal assaults, and the quality of the opposing troops was relatively equal. What is lost in this argument are three central facts.

First, during the Mexican War, General Scott rarely employed full frontal attacks as the sole means of engaging the enemy. Instead, Scott sought to increase the numeric strength of his smaller army through maneuver and strikes against the flank and/or rear of enemy positions.[33] The crucial issue relating to this first fact, therefore, is whether Lee absorbed Scott's offensive methodology and encapsulated it into his own philosophy of war as a central principle. By virtue of his position on Scott's staff, Lee was able to observe and participate in these flanking maneuvers as preludes to attacks. Indeed, some were Lee's own suggestions. Lee learned many things in Mexico, but he did not come away with the understanding that direct frontal attacks were the preferred method of defeating the enemy. A review Lee's early battles as commander of the Army of Northern Virginia provides evidence that he understood the vital lessons of maneuver and flanking attacks. During the Seven Days Battles, Second Manassas, and Chancellorsville, Lee repeatedly sought to strike the Federals on one of their exposed flanks. Indeed, even the Maryland Campaign was a large-scale turning movement. It is irrelevant whether or not a particular attempt was successful; the important lesson is that Lee planned and intended to deliver most of his principal attacks against the enemy's flanks.[34]

Second, the introduction of the rifled musket did not undermine the concept of maneuver and striking the flank or rear of an enemy force. Wrapped tightly around this core issue is the notion that immutable principles of war remain valid throughout military history. In other words, advances in technology merely modify how the principles are tactically applied. The concept of pinning an enemy in place with part of an army while maneuvering another portion in order to strike the opponent's flank or rear is more than 2,300 years old. (Examples may be found in the wars of Alexander the Great, Hannibal, Julius Caesar, Frederick the Great, Napoleon and many others.) In the American military establishment, this concept is directly connected in spirit to the tactics employed by Continental Army officers during the American Revolution; Winfield Scott refined and applied these tactics in Mexico, passing these theories on to Robert E. Lee.

Many historians ignore or only pay lip service to the nature of the hilly and wooded American terrain and its effects on the rifled musket and tactics. On the North American continent, soldiers rarely engaged in long range rifle fire. In order to gain decisive results, the compact formations of infantry had to press forward with *élan* and deliver firepower at close range against their opponents. Some writers have maintained that it was nearly impossible for similarly equipped and organized armies in the modern era to win decisive victories, and use the battles of the Civil War as evidence of support for this contention. The validity of this holding is open to serious debate. What is not is that most of the engagements of the Civil War (largely because of terrain factors) were conducted within restricted ranges, and troops on the defensive equipped with rifled muskets enjoyed an advantage over their attacking enemy. As many battles demonstrated, however, the defensive rifled musket advantage was not absolute. Even if we assume for the sake of argument that it was, such an advantage would not, in and of itself, invalidate the longstanding principle of war of an offensive force trying to maneuver around and strike the flank or rear of the defending opponent. Accordingly, the tactics favored by Scott in the Mexican War and emulated so well by Lee in the Civil War were not invalidated by the advent of the rifled musket.

The third central issue in the smoothbore versus rifled musket argument is perhaps the most often overlooked aspect of warfare during this period in history: the quality of the units involved and their respective regimental leadership. Units with better officers, *élan*, and training, produced greater volumes of fire. That is why during the Civil War, units with good or excellent leadership and corresponding high morale were able to attack and inflict more damage on the defenders than they suffered in return.[35]

Lee and Initiative and Opportunity

According to historian Stephen W. Sears, "nothing in Robert E. Lee's military character was more fixed than his determination to seize the initiative; to his mind, gaining the initiative strategically and tactically was the essential first step to gaining the victory."[36] Sears accurately describes what Lee intuitively understood—that gaining the initiative was especially important for a numerically smaller force. When combined with the lesson of audacity in action absorbed during the Mexican War, and reinforced by his study of Napoleon and other Great Captains, this seizing of the initiative translated into what Robert E. Lee constantly referred to as "opportunity."

Unlike so many army commanders throughout history, Lee did not simply look for "opportunity" but sought to *create* it and then *profit* from it. This was Lee's version of Napoleon's unmistakable command style. Napoleon employed an enormous staff that made it possible to conduct a centralized command in order to react swiftly to changing circumstances. Lee, however, who recognized that this was not possible with his much smaller staff, extended wide discretion and flexibility to his subordinate officers in order to take advantage of any opportunity created by operational maneuver, or to profit from enemy mistakes at the tactical level once the battle was joined. Thus a consistent pattern of Lee's generalship emerges— regardless of the battlefield, be it the Seven Days Battles, Second Manassas, Sharpsburg, Chancellorsville, Gettysburg, or the bloody engagements from the Wilderness to Petersburg: he would calculate the potential cost and benefits of battle, and implement a plan usually designed to seize the initiative to create or take advantage of "opportunity." Like all Great Captains of history Lee sought openings for decisive action and then attempted to exploit them. This constant search by Lee to conceptualize, create, and then exploit what he called "opportunity" helps explain the flexibility he extended to his subordinates, as well as Lee's own ability to adapt to unexpected circumstances. On those occasions when his plan of battle miscarried, it was at least due, in large part, to an error on the side of action rather than inaction. If the "opportunity" necessitated an offensive thrust, Lee possessed the moral courage to attempt to exploit it.

Lee's appreciation of the value in seeking and exploiting initiative leads some critics to claim he was overly wedded to offensive action. His experiences in Mexico and his extensive study of Napoleon, Frederick the Great, and other Great Captains, however, taught him that it was only through bold offensive strokes that any side would prevail in war. This was, and continues to be, especially true in the case of an army fielding inferior numbers of men. Abundant examples from history demonstrate that when a smaller army simply counts numbers and remains on the defensive in the face of a resourceful and larger enemy, ultimate defeat follows.

Robert E. Lee understood this during his tenure with the Army of Northern Virginia. Remaining on the defensive would have extended to the Federals the incalculable benefit of initiative, while reinforcing their already significant advantages of industry, logistical capabilities, and superior numbers. With both more and better supplied troops *and* the strategic initiative, the North would have been able to fully employ its vast logistical capabilities and powerful navy to bring its armies into the field wherever and whenever desired. Eventually, indeed inevitably, the Confederacy's cities would have fallen one by one, lines of communication would have been broken, and her armies ground down to defeat. This is why the principle of war that a smaller force had to maneuver in order to seize the initiative and dictate the course of events through offensive action—which has the effect of a force multiplier—has been proven to be consistently true through much of recorded military history regardless of the level of technology involved. For the numerically and industrially inferior Confederates, the key to victory was *how* to undertake offensive actions designed to keep the Federals off-balance and unable to fully employ the weight of their numbers and the power of their industry. This concept included the use of proper tactics, both defensive and offensive, along with the all-important element of leadership. All of these salient principles of war were clearly formulated in Lee's mind prior to the outbreak of the Civil War; his experiences on the field of battle prior to Gettysburg merely validated them.

In addition to Scott's profound influence, Lee's 1852-1855 tenure as the superintendent at the United States Military Academy also helped shape his thinking about military conflict. Lee took advantage of his sojourn in the Hudson Valley of New York to expand his professional knowledge of military history with an exhaustive study of Napoleon's numerous campaigns and ideas. "Lee tended to read French military histories, treatises, and manuals, and to study the campaigns of Napoleon as interpreted by Baron Henri Jomini and then reinterpreted by Napoleon himself," writes recent biographer Emory Thomas. "The Superintendent made good use of the Academy library, and his contact with the faculty and various visitors broadened his professional vision."[37]

Thus, by the time Lee stepped onto the stage of the American Civil War, he had learned most of the important lessons of the Great Captains. Even the manner in which Lee marched his separate corps in the Gettysburg Campaign mirrors Napoleon's principle of corps formations moving by different routes while still remaining within supporting distance of one another. Lee's constant quest for "opportunity" was classically Napoleonic in concept. Maneuvering—whether operationally or tactically—was the only way to create conditions that would allow a smaller army to catch a larger and better equipped foe off guard and defeat it piecemeal. And, like Napoleon's philosophy of war, Lee's genius was essentially of a practical rather than theoretical nature; he never really formulated a system or theory of war on paper.

Instead, researcher's desiring to mine Lee's philosophy of war are forced to rely on his letters, orders, official reports and an interpretation of his battles. This methodology allows us to analyze Lee's actions as an army commander which in turn provides insight to his true genius.

Analysis of Lee's Philosophy of War

Anyone embarking upon an analysis of Robert E. Lee's philosophy of war as expressed through his generalship is confronted with an interesting dichotomy. One school of thought asserts that Lee utilized his outstanding military skills and daring to frustrate the designs of successive Federal commanders for almost three years of war, but was finally overwhelmed by the North's vastly superior military resources. The other posits that Lee pursued a plan of action as a commanding general that contributed mightily to the ultimate defeat of the Southern Confederacy by engaging in costly operational and tactical offensive actions that bled his army, when he should have waged a largely defensive effort to preserve manpower and other resources. Yet, most historians, regardless of which view they support, agree that Lee was a formidable general. Thus the question persists: was Lee a military genius who led the Confederacy to the cusp of victory through skill and daring, only to be finally overwhelmed by superior resources, or did his generalship recklessly bleed his army and contribute to the South's ultimate defeat?

The fact that this question is still hotly debated today attests to the continuing interest in differing interpretations of Lee's generalship, plus a number of other factors. First, was it even possible for the Confederacy to win its war against the North? War, in large part, is the generation and application of force, but there is no guarantee that the side with the most force at its disposal will always emerge victorious. Second, waging war requires the commitment of collective resources, and vividly illustrates the distinguishing features of the societies engaged in it. The Confederacy provides a good example. As a collection of independent states concerned with their rights and privileges, it was often difficult for the central government in Richmond to effect concerted action. Third, the view of Lee's generalship held by many Southerners borders on the verge of uncritical devotion. Many have embraced Lee's uncompromising sense of duty and noble dignity as a salve to ease wounded pride and the harshness visited upon the population of the Old South during the war and afterward. Historians Douglas Southall Freeman, Charles Roland, Cyril Falls, Gamaliel Bradford, Colonel G. F. R. Henderson and others consider Lee a great soldier. Virginian Clifford Dowdey evaluated the general as *the* greatest soldier of the American Civil War, a traditional view held by many historians and students of the conflict.

Any analysis of Lee's philosophy of war (i.e., his generalship) must begin with an examination of whether or not he understood the nature of the war in its proper context. Historian Gary Gallagher argues that Lee "predicted from the beginning a long war that would demand tremendous sacrifice in the Confederacy. He called for a national draft, the concentration of manpower in the principal Southern field armies, the subordination of state interests to the goal of national independence, and, near the end, the arming of blacks."[38] Stephen Sears maintains that one of Lee's greatest talents "was a cool unsparing appraisal of military reality."[39] Lee, it seems understood the nature of the war: it would be a long and bitter conflict. Yet, critics such as John Keegan claim the Confederate general was a man of "limited imagination" who hurt his cause with sustained offensives, prompting Gallagher to ask in a recent essay, "What about Lee's supposed over-reliance on the offensive?"[40]

From his own deep studies of military history and extensive experiences during the Mexican War, Lee knew that wars were won through bold offensive action. That fact was tempered by his realization that the South stood virtually no chance of victory in a war of attrition with the North. The Confederacy simply lacked the resources, particularly manpower, to engage in sustained offensive action. The very nature of the war dictated that the South would fight on the strategic defensive. The North had to subjugate the Confederacy in order to win, and that meant invading its territory, seizing its resources, defeating its armies, and occupying its cities. Waging a strategically defensive war, however, did not chain Lee—or any Southern general—to solely defensive strategies and tactics. Lee's solution, therefore, was to win a strategically defensive war by implementing an operational and tactical offensive.

He did this by relying on speed, maneuver, and the fog of war to augment the size of his numerically smaller force and create opportunities. When opportunities presented themselves, Lee sought to take advantage of them by attempting to deliver overwhelming attacks against selected portions of the enemy. His plans for action during the Seven Days Battles, Second Manassas, and Chancellorsville are prime examples of this principle. And in each of these campaigns, Lee planned to maneuver and strike an enemy flank or an exposed segment of the Federal line of battle. Thus, when Lee attacked, he did so with the dual purpose of destroying major elements of the enemy army and psychologically damaging the enemy's will to resist.

Historian Gary Gallagher, for example, argues forcefully that:

> many critics fail to give Lee credit for what he accomplished through aggressive generalship. At the Seven Days he blunted a Federal offensive that seemed destined to pin defending Confederates in Richmond; his counter punch in the campaign of Second Manassas pushed the eastern military frontier back to the Potomac and confronted Lincoln with a major crisis at home and abroad. The tactical masterpiece at Chancellorsville, coming as it did on the

heels of a defensive win at Fredericksburg, again sent tremors through the North. Lee failed to follow up either pair of victories with a third win at [Sharpsburg] or Gettysburg; however, in September 1862 and June 1863 it was not at all clear that the Army of Northern Virginia would suffer defeat in Maryland and Pennsylvania. A victory in either circumstance might have altered the course of the conflict.[41]

Gallagher's cogent analysis reinforces a fact many critics of Lee's "supposed over-reliance on the offensive" seem either to have overlooked or ignored altogether. From the time of First Manassas until the Battle of Seven Pines, approximately one year, the principal Confederate army in Virginia, under the command of Joseph E. Johnston, had remained entirely on the defensive—and yet the Federal army had advanced to the very outskirts of Richmond. There, Johnston was wounded and Lee assumed command. During the next twelve months, from the Seven Days Battles through Chancellorsville, Lee acted primarily on the operational and/or tactical offensive. His succession of victories created the real possibility that the Confederate nation might achieve its political goal—independence. Indeed, following Lee's victory at Second Manassas, at least two foreign powers were seriously contemplating some form of intervention. The fruits of Joe Johnston's defensive approach to war, contrarily, had produced nothing but the near-collapse of the Confederate effort in the Eastern Theater. Historian Richard M. McMurry aptly summarized these points when he wrote, "The Confederates had only one army commander (full general) who ever exhibited an ability to devise and execute the bold and daring yet rational plans that were necessary if the smaller Rebel armies were to defeat their more numerous opponents. That general was Lee."[42]

Despite his successes, Lee's willingness to employ the operational and tactical offensive has been heavily criticized, especially by a new wave of revisionist writers. It is not the intention of this work to detail every critical view of Lee's conduct of operations. However, a review of several of these critiques is necessary in order for readers to understand and appreciate Lee's conduct in the Gettysburg Campaign.

In his recent book *Robert E. Lee's Civil War*, historian Bevin Alexander argues that Lee was "a bellicose, direct soldier" who did not "truly understand offensive warfare."[43] It was during the Seven Days Battles, he avers, that Lee revealed his idea of offensive warfare that set the pattern for the campaigns that followed: "assaults by massed bodies of infantry against a waiting enemy."[44] Certainly such attacks took place, Gaines' Mill and Malvern Hill being two prime examples. Unfortunately, Alexander ignores the fact that Lee *planned* time and again during the Seven Days Battles to maneuver and strike the enemy's *flanks*. The resulting battles, however, were very different tactical affairs than what Lee had envisioned. This was because few officers at that early stage of the war had ever maneuvered large bodies of troops under any circumstances, much less under combat conditions. The failure of Lee's offensive plans were usually shortcomings of execution on the part of subordinates, rather than Lee's penchant for frontal attacks. Lee's own report of the Seven Days confirms this. "Under ordinary circumstances," he lamented to President Davis "the Federal Army should have been destroyed."[45] In his next campaign, Lee employed at Second Manassas the same offensive operational and tactical philosophy in an effort to position his divisions for a strike against the enemy's flanks. This time, his subordinates swept the opposing army from the field. Lee's following campaign in Maryland was also designed as a strategic turning movement. What sets Second Manassas and the Maryland Campaign apart from the Seven Days Battles is that Lee and his subordinates had learned how to maneuver large bodies of troops, coordinate their actions, and execute orders on the battlefield. These campaigns were hardly the product of "a bellicose, direct soldier" who did not "truly understand offensive warfare."[46]

Alexander also castigates Lee for ignoring advice proffered by James Longstreet and Thomas "Stonewall" Jackson to fight primarily on the tactical defensive. Lee, this line of reasoning maintains, should have adopted a defensive posture in the works ringing the Confederate capital, waited for his enemy's attacks, repulsed them, and only then counterattacked. This line of reasoning is seriously flawed. In war, each belligerent possesses independent will. As such, each commander attempts to gain his own objectives while denying his opponent the ability to gain theirs. In war if a particular plan of battle succeeds, the chances of repeating that success decreases. The logic of war is thus *paradoxical*, not linear. Therefore, even if Lee had been able to place his army in a formidable defensive position, McClellan would have had to launch direct and sustained frontal assaults—tactics contrary to his nature. Assuming Lee could have repulsed them, there is little likelihood the Federal general would have repeated the same mistake, or that Lee's counterattacks would have succeeded without heavy losses. Alexander ignores the fact that the Federals possessed a numerically superior force and enjoyed superior movement and logistical capabilities via both rail and sea unavailable to the Confederates. "Little Mac" could just as easily have chosen some form of maneuver—his preferred method of conducting war—over direct assault. Alexander's theory of how Lee should have conducted his battles would have resulted in a protracted siege and inevitable defeat.

Michael A. Palmer attacks Lee on another front. In his recent study *Lee Moves North: Robert E. Lee on the Offensive from Antietam, to Gettysburg, to Bristow's Station*, Palmer denigrates the general's decentralized method of command and control when on the offensive. One needs "well motivated and confident subordinates . . . [who] understand the primary goals of a campaign," argues Palmer.[47] When Lee undertook offensive action, Palmer argues, his decentralized command system worked against the very success he was seeking. Palmer, however, fails to grasp that the only way army-sized formations operating in a horse-drawn society could be controlled within a centralized command was if Lee had employed an enormous professional and thoroughly specialized staff such as Napoleon's. Of course, no North American armies of this era utilized Napoleonic size, specially trained, staffs. And no one was more aware of the smallish size of his staff than Lee, which is one of the reasons he always encouraged his subordinates to use their initiative in order to adapt to changing situations without having to wait for instructions from army headquarters. Lee's encouragement that his subordinates exercise the discretion and initiative inherent in a decentralized system of command demonstrates that he understood something Michael Palmer does not: that success in war is impossible unless you are able to take into account uncertainty (i.e., the fog of war), make allowances for it, and find a way to make it work to your advantage. Lee's chief subordinates were professionally trained soldiers operating with diminutive staffs leading tens of thousands of citizen soldiers, all of which made centralization in the pre-wireless military campaign environment impossible. Therefore, it is illogical to criticize General Lee for going on the offensive with a decentralized style of command. Given the military environment within which Lee had to operate, his adoption of a decentralized command structure not only fit his personality, but made perfect military sense.[48]

Was General Lee, wonders critic John D. McKenzie, "the high quality strategist and tactician that was required to win a war?"[49] Apparently not, he argues, since Lee's leadership ultimately failed the Confederacy in its bid for independence. McKenzie offers five grounds to support his conclusion: 1) Lee could not overcome the Confederate bureaucracy sufficiently to counter the defects imposed by his political superiors' failure to mobilize all available resources for the war; 2) Lee had an insufficient grasp of logistics and failed to employ an accomplished logistician on his staff; 3) Lee failed to realize his early successes were won against inferior Federal commanders which, in turn, led him to believe his men could achieve anything asked of them; 4) Lee was devoted to outdated offensive tactics; and 5) Lee did not understand himself, namely, that his skill rested in defensive warfare.[50] McKenzie's assertions merit further examination.

As outlined in some detail in the first chapter of this study, General Lee felt keenly the failure of Confederate political leaders to mobilize all available resources to wage war. The constitutional fabric of American culture, however, is predicated on the fact that military leaders are subordinate to political officials. What else could Lee have done to overcome these political shortcomings other than offer repeated and respectful requests and advice through proper channels, as he did throughout his tenure in command? Lee's role model was George Washington, not Lucius Cornelius Sulla.[51] Yet, despite shortages of materiel and men brought about in great measure by the failures of his political superiors, Lee accomplished remarkable results. McKenzie's first criticism simply lacks credibility.[52]

McKenzie's second censure, which to a degree overlaps his first, is that Lee had an insufficient grasp of logistics and failed to employ an accomplished logistician on his staff. This, too, is equally lacking in supportive evidence. The general's wartime papers are replete with examples of correspondence dealing with logistical concerns, demonstrating clearly that he was fully aware of the impact supply shortages imposed on his army.[53] His supply problems were, in large part, the result of a shoddy transportation system—the crippling link in the Confederate logistical chain. There was little or nothing Lee could have done to remedy the chaotic state of Southern railroads in the middle of a war. As to McKenzie's assertion that Lee had no logistics specialist on his staff, consider the following: one member of Joe Johnston's staff, inherited by Lee when he took command of the Virginia army, was Major Robert Granderson Cole, Chief Commissary of Subsistence. Major Cole was a graduate of West Point, Class of 1850. As chief of the subsistence department, Cole was retained by Lee, promoted to lieutenant colonel, and served in that capacity for the duration of the war. Cole was also assisted by two other commissary officers at Lee headquarters. These facts seemed to have escaped McKenzie.[54]

McKenzie's third, fourth and fifth criticisms of Lee can be bundled together as calling into question Lee's battlefield generalship. Specifically, McKenzie asserts Lee "was a defensive military genius, but he preferred to use offensive strategies and tactics, areas in which he did not exhibit much expertise," and was "a poor to mediocre" commander when it came to offensive warfare.[55] To support these claims, McKenzie maintains that Lee's early successes were scored against second-rate Federal commanders at an unjustifiable price, and his offensives from the Seven Days to Second Manassas cost "more casualties than the South could afford."[56]

When Robert E. Lee took command of the Virginia army, the strategic situation facing the Confederacy was desperate. Richmond—the heart of the Confederacy's monetary and industrial base—was in immediate danger from the east, where McClellan's Army of the Potomac was almost close enough to utilize decisively its powerful siege artillery. Danger was also looming in northern Virginia, where another Federal army was gathering under John Pope. Lee had ascended to the command of a numerically inferior army pinned between two large enemy concentrations (McClellan and Pope). As a student of military history, Lee appreciated the situation called for action along the lines of Napoleon's famous "strategy of the central position." Napoleon's remedy called for bold action brought about by swift concentration, maneuver, and powerful offensive blows. According to the Corsican general, the numerically inferior force (Lee) needed to concentrate the strongest army possible, attack and drive off the most threatening enemy army (McClellan), and then turn on, maneuver against, and defeat the remaining enemy (Pope). If applied properly, Lee would throw his concentrated army against McClellan and Pope in turn, using his central position between the two enemy forces as an advantage instead of a liability.

With Richmond immediately behind him, retreat was not an option. Similarly, Lee could not play a waiting game and provide the Federals the time to effect the juncture of their armies, or a close coordination of their efforts against him. Joe

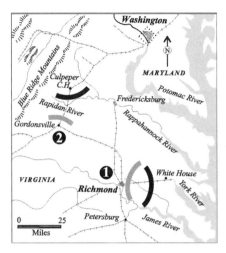

Phase One
Lee Seizes the Initiative

1. Concentration of all available Confederate troops in a central position between Federal armies under George McClellan and John Pope, with the mass facing McClellan near Richmond.

2. Secondary force observes and delays Pope.

Phase Two
Lee Strikes McClellan

1. Confederates engaged McClellan while
2. blocking Pope
3. Demonstrations fix McClellan into place while drawing attention away from the decisive flank closest to Pope.
4. McClellan's flank closest to Pope is attacked en masse in hopes of turning it away from any potential help Pope may send.

Johnston had already withdrawn the Confederate army to the very doorstep of the capital. It's loss would have doomed the new Southern Confederacy. Without any other viable options, Lee implemented Napoleon's strategy. Historian Frank E. Vandiver took an accurate measure of the general when he observed:

> Robert E. Lee was a creature of battle. When he took command of the Confederate Army near Richmond on June 1, 1862, he found another self. The terrible threat of McClellan's legions almost within cannon shot of Richmond touched a current of daring in the cool, smooth soldier. He began to plan a campaign to save the capital, which if successful, would brand him forever one of history's great captains.[57]

Lee's daring concentration of the majority of Confederate forces in the Virginia theater, followed by a less-than-perfect but nevertheless successful execution of the "strategy of the central position," not only staved off defeat by saving Richmond, but wrested the initiative from the Federals and, through the use of calculated offensives, completely changed the course of the war in the East. The operational offensive culminating in the Second Manassas Campaign—the second phase of the "strategy of the central position"—carried Lee and the Confederacy to what historian John J. Hennessy describes as "the edge of their greatest opportunity."[58] Pope's thrashing was followed with a move into Maryland which, continues Hennessy, held the "potential to force a swift and happy political solution to the war."[59] What more would McKenzie have demanded of Lee? What other soldier of his age on either side in 1862 could have conceived and executed operations on this scale with so much at stake? McKenzie's claims that Lee's offensive efforts "did not exhibit much expertise" is utterly without merit.

McKenzie's specific charge that Lee was "a poor to mediocre *commander*, in terms of offensive warfare, is also specious. The primary role of an army commander is to maneuver his force in position to be victorious, or in other words, to be an architect of battlefield victory. Many writers, including McKenzie, confuse this role with the execution of the battle plan at the corps, division, and brigade levels. Lee's record as army commander demonstrates that he understood and acted

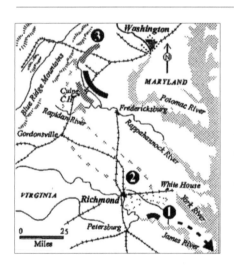

Phase Three
Lee Defeats McClellan
and then Attacks Pope

1. McClellan is defeated and driven away from Richmond;

2. Lee shifts his strength through maneuver to confront Pope;

3. Once Lee completes his concentration in front of Pope, he orders further maneuvers against Pope to create an opportunity to defeat him, which he does at the Battle of Second Manassas.

The objective of the "strategy of the central position" is to employ a central position to an advantage by boldly utilizing both concentration and maneuver to defeat your opponents in detail. This strategy can only be employed successfully by a commander possessing intelligence to appreciate his position and the moral courage to fully commit himself to such an enterprise. The results, as demonstrated here, are often impressive, and Lee's use of it in the summer of 1862 is a classic example.

upon every aspect of warfare demanded by his rank and position. His complex series of maneuvers during the Second Manassas Campaign, for example, positioned his army at exactly the right position to reap decisive victory and, combined with the patience and timing of General Longstreet's late afternoon attack against Pope's left flank, wiped the Federal Army of Virginia from the field. Complete victory eluded Lee only because of failures in tactical execution. The campaign's leading historian, John J. Hennessy, astutely points out that "it was a decisive breakdown on Jackson's part that possibly spared the Union army."[60]

Critics like McKenzie also fail to comprehend that Lee, as a commander, understood completely the nature of the men he was ordering into battle. As one 19th century writer noted, Lee realized that Southerners around the Confederacy looked to the Virginia army "as the bulwark of secession, and sent to it selected bodies of their best men to represent them." As a result, the "Army of Northern Virginia was composed of the best and the bravest men in the South, and they believed and boasted that they carried with them not only the flag, but the glory and *the very life*, of the Confederacy."[61] The majority of Lee's soldiers were descendants of people who had emigrated to America over a period of 150 years, including sons of Scottish Covenanters, French Huguenots, Irishmen and "Black" Dutchmen, many of whom had fled to America in search of religious freedom. Many Confederate soldiers had relatives who fought the English in the American Revolution and/or the War of 1812, or who had served during the Mexican War. Lee appreciated the framework of the family histories comprising the common soldiers of his command, as well as the convictions endemic in the makeup of a Southerner. Indeed, Lee recognized that the stamina and esprit de corps of the Army of Northern Virginia was drawn from the distinguished heritage of the hardy families who had forged the Southern colonies and states. Writers must understand this aspect of Lee in order to fully understand his generalship. Historian Emory Thomas, whose writings about Lee are noteworthy, recognized that these factors translated into the Confederate general's actions on the battlefield. "[Lee] remembered lessons learned with Scott in Mexico," explained Thomas, "that volunteer troops were essentially civilians, that political generals were politicians, and that bold, decisive action was likely the only way to retain the attention and energy of these civilians masquerading as soldiers."[62]

The most manifest critic of Lee's generalship, character, and motives in recent years has been Alan T. Nolan, author of the controversial *Lee Considered: Robert E. Lee and Civil War History*. In evaluating Lee's generalship, urges Nolan, "The appropriate inquiry is to ask whether the general's actions related positively or negatively to the war objectives and national policy of his government."[63] Nolan believes there was a "true" grand strategy the Confederacy should have pursued as opposed to the "official" grand strategy actually implemented. "The true grand strategy is that which, in view of the circumstances of the section, would have maximized that section's chances of achieving its war objective," Nolan writes. "The official grand strategy is that which the government of the section authorized and directed its military establishment to carry out."[64] Nolan points out that the true grand strategy of the Confederacy was defensive, but argues that Lee's grand strategy was offensive warfare. As such, Nolan maintains that his generalship contradicted the South's true grand strategy, thereby betraying the Confederacy's chance to gain independence.[65]

While there is room to question whether Nolan recognizes the difference between grand strategy and the operational direction of the Army of Northern Virginia as conducted by General Lee, there is no doubt the objective for the Southern Confederacy was achieving its independence from the United States. Thus, one must examine whether Lee's conduct of operations after he assumed control of the Virginia army increased or decreased the South's chances for winning its independence. Nolan argues that "the grand strategic defensive may at times translate into the operational or tactical offensive," but that Lee "believed that the South's grand strategic role was offensive." Nolan's conclusion is based on what he maintains was Lee's "offensive pattern." There was a "profound problem with Lee's grand strategy of the offensive: it was not feasible to defeat the North militarily as distinguished from prolonging the contest until the North gave it up."[66]

There is absolutely nothing in Robert E. Lee's writings or actions that remotely suggest he believed the Southern Confederacy was on the grand strategic offensive. If it had been, her armies would have had to invade, subjugate, and garrison the North. Instead, Lee's writings and actions reveal his complete understanding that the Confederacy was on the strategic defensive—a distinction Nolan apparently misses entirely. The issue of *how* this defensive strategy would be conducted during the summer of 1863 was the subject of the May 14-17 conference in Richmond between Lee, President Davis, and his cabinet. Nolan's confusion is complicated by his disapproval of the way Lee conducted the strategic defense of Virginia, which utilized speed and maneuver to execute operational and tactical offensives as a means of keeping the numerically superior Federals off balance. Nolan argues that Lee would have furthered the cause for Southern independence by adopting an almost totally defensive posture. Had he done so, the Confederacy would have surrendered the initiative to the powerful Federal armies, with the objective of finding a way to hang on until the Yankees got frustrated and called it quits. This line of thinking ignores virtually every immutable principle of war (as earlier discussed) that any combatant, let alone the numerically inferior one, must employ if he is to have a chance of victory.

Nolan points to the war-weariness of the North by the summer of 1864 and the significant losses U. S. Grant suffered at the hands of Lee in the Overland Campaign as evidence of Lee's failure to pursue the correct strategy earlier in the war. If he had, Nolan maintains, his army would have been larger and more capable of repulsing Grant. One might inquire why Nolan does not offer readers a single historical example in the modern era—from 1648 to the present—of a numerically inferior side winning a major war by adopting the defensive course of action he supports.

Could it be that one is hard-pressed to find such an example? Nolan's notion that the defensive would have provided the South with a better chance of victory through exhaustion seriously underestimates the desire of the Radical Republicans to not only win the war, but destroy or confiscate the South's property and obliterate its culture (slavery) and ruling class in the process. Nolan's assertion that the Confederacy could have won by adopting a "defensive policy [that] might have worn the North out," runs counter to the lessons of history.[67]

The fact that Alexander, Palmer, McKenzie, Nolan and other Lee critics cannot accept is that wars were, and are, won through some form of aggressive actions—even if the country has adopted the strategic defensive as a national policy. The American Revolution, which some critics intone as evidence that he should have waged a defensive struggle of exhaustion, is in reality an excellent example in support of Lee's offensive operational and tactical strategy. The American colonists were on the strategic defensive against England and her mercenaries, but George Washington conducted the war by repeatedly assuming the *operational and/or tactical offensive*. Even a cursory understanding of the American Revolution makes this obvious.

Following his defeat while on the defensive in the Long Island campaign, Washington audaciously switched his *modus operandi* to offensive actions—offensives that captured the imagination and attention of the citizen soldiers within the Continental Army and nurtured hope for supporters outside the army. Washington attacked or planned for attacks at Trenton, Princeton, Germantown, Monmouth, Newport, Stony Point, and Yorktown. Washington's formula for victory over a numerically superior enemy host was not lost on Robert E. Lee, who not only held a deep appreciation for the campaigns of his great-grandfather-in-law, but who also understood how Washington's generalship was consistent with the immutable principles of war as practiced by other Great Captains of history. The result, argues historian Gary Gallagher, "buoyed Southern hopes when defeat lay in all other directions, dampened spirits in the North, and impressed European leaders."[68]

*   *   *

And so it was, for all of the reasons outlined, that Lee convinced President Davis to allow him to retain the initiative, assume the operational offensive, and strike north in the summer of 1863.

Notes for Chapter 2

1. Jefferson Davis, *Robert E. Lee*, edited and with an Introduction and Notes by Colonel Harold B. Simpson (Hillsboro, 1966), pp. 8-9.

2. *The Wartime Papers of R. E. Lee*, number 827.

3. Freeman, *R. E. Lee*, vol. 1, p. 294.

4. Steven E. Woodworth, *Davis and Lee at War* (Lawrence, 1995), pp. 147-148; Jefferson Davis, *The Rise and Fall of the Confederacy Government*, 2 vols. (New York, 1959), vol. 2, p. 130. According to Lee, Abraham Lincoln, through his emissary Francis Preston Blair, had offered him command of the Federal army just over a year earlier. See J. Wm. Jones, "The Friendship Between Lee and Scott," in *Southern Historical Society Papers*, vol. 11, p. 421. In a letter dated Feb. 25, 1868, to the Hon. Reverend Johnson, United States Senate, Lee detailed his interview with Francis Preston Blair, and what happened afterwards. "After listening to his remarks, I declined the offer he made to me to take command of the army that was to be brought into the field, stating candidly and as courteously as I could, that though opposed to secession, and deprecating war, I could take no part in an invasion of the Southern States. I went directly from the interview with Mr. Blair to the office of General Scott, told him of the proposition that had been made to me, and my decision. Upon reflection after returning to my home [at Arlington], I concluded that I ought no longer to retain any commission I held in the United States Army, and on the second morning thereafter, I forwarded my resignation to General Scott."

5. Freeman, *R. E. Lee*, 1, pp. 2-10, 30-32; Mapp, *Frock Coats and Epaulets: Psychological Portraits of Confederate Military and Political Leaders*, p. 136.

6. George W. Cullum, *Biographical Register of the Officers and Graduates of the United States Military Academy* (Houghton-Mifflin, 1891); Emory Thomas, "Robert E. Lee," *Encyclopedia of the Confederacy*, p. 916; Mapp, *Frock Coats and Epaulets: Psychological Portraits of Confederate Military and Political Leaders*, p. 137. Two of Lee's fellow graduates who would also become Confederate generals included Joseph E. Johnston and Theophilus H. Holmes, who ranked, respectively, 13th and 44th in their class. Robert K. Krick, "Robert E. Lee," in William C. Davis, ed., *The Confederate General*, 6 vols. (National Historical Society, 1991), vol. 4, p. 45.

7. James L. Morrison, Jr., *The Best School in the World: West Point, the Pre-Civil War Years, 1833-1866* (Kent, 1986).

8. David J. Eicher, *Robert E. Lee: A Life Portrait* (Dallas, 1997), pp. 212-214; Freeman, *R. E. Lee*, 1, pp. 159-169.

9. Charles P. Roland, *Reflections on Lee: A Historian's Assessment* (Mechanicsburg, 1995), p.10.

10. Roland, *Reflections on Lee*, p. 10.

11. John S. D. Eisenhower, *Agent of Destiny: The Life and Times of General Winfield Scott* (New York, 1997), pp. 249-251.

12. Eisenhower, *General Winfield Scott*, p. 251; Roland, *Reflections on Lee*, p. 11.

13. Roland, *Reflections on Lee*, p. 11.

14. Freeman, *R. E. Lee*, 1, pp. 253-255.

15. Roland, *Reflections on Lee*, p. 12.

16. Mapp, *Frock Coats and Epaulets: Psychological Portraits of Confederate Military and Political Leaders*, p. 146.

17. Freeman, *R. E. Lee*, 1, p. 271.

18. Roland, *Reflections on Lee*, pp. 12-13;

19. Freeman, *R. E. Lee*, 1, p. 272.

20. Freeman, *R. E. Lee*, 1, p. 283.

21. Freeman, *R. E. Lee*, 1, p. 285.

22. J. Wm. Jones, "The Friendship Between Lee and Scott," *Southern Historical Society Papers*, 11, p. 424.

23. Jones, "The Friendship Between Lee and Scott," *Southern Historical Society Papers,* 11, p. 424.

24. General Winfield Scott, as quoted in Freeman, *R. E. Lee,* 1, p. 294.

25. Jones, "The Friendship Between Lee and Scott," *Southern Historical Society Papers*, 11, p. 424.

26. Jones, "The Friendship Between Lee and Scott," *Southern Historical Society Papers*, 11, p. 425.

27. Timothy D. Johnson, *Winfield Scott: The Quest for Military Glory* (Lawrence, 1988), p. 242.

28. Clifford Dowdey, *Lee's Last Campaign: The Story of Lee and His Men Against Grant—1864* (Lincoln, 1993 reprint of the 1960 original), p. 8.

29. Johnson, *Winfield Scott*, pp. 158-170.

30. John S. D. Eisenhower, *So Far From God: The U.S. War With Mexico 1846-1848* (New York, Anchor Book Edition, 1990), pp. 266-327; see Archer Jones, *Civil War Command and Strategy* (New York, 1992), pp. 270-272, for a discussion of how Scott's campaigns demonstrated a relation between military actions and politics. Civilians in Maryland and Pennsylvania were paid by Lee's agents in what the non-combatants considered to be worthless Confederate script, but it was a gesture rarely offered to civilians in the South when Federal troops moved through their lands.

31. Emory M. Thomas, *Robert E. Lee* (New York, 1995), p. 139.

32. Thomas, *Robert E. Lee*, p. 139.

33. Johnson, *Winfield Scott: The Quest for Military Glory*, p. 158.

34. Dowdey, *The Seven Days*, pp. 168-315; Ernest B. Furgurson, *Chancellorsville 1863: The Souls of the Brave* (New York, 1992), pp. 36-86; Augutus C. Hamlin, *The Attack of Stonewall Jackson at Chancellorsville* (reprint of 1896 edition; Fredericksburg, 1997), pp. 6-78; and John J. Hennessy, *Return to Bull Run: The Campaign and Battle of Second Manassas* (New York, 1993), pp. 22-94.

35. In addition to the many examples during the fighting on July 2 provided later in the text, other examples for the Army of Northern Virginia include the Texas Brigade at Second Manassas, William Barksdale's Brigade at Sharpsburg, and Harry Hays' Louisiana Tigers at Second Winchester. Of course, a host of variables influenced this issue to one degree or another, but the fighting at Gettysburg provides abundant evidence to support it. This theme is developed in more detail in Chapter 7 and Chapter 8.

36. Stephen W. Sears, *To the Gates of Richmond: The Peninsula Campaign* (New York, 1992), p. 151.

37. Thomas, *Robert E. Lee*, p. 158.

38. Gary W. Gallagher, "'Upon their Success Hang Momentous Interests': Generals," *Why the Confederacy Lost*, Gabor S. Boritt, ed. (New York, 1992), p. 107.

39. Stephen W. Sears, *Landscape Turned Red* (New York, 1983), p. 54.

40. John Keegan, *The Mask of Command* (New York, 1987), p. 197; Gallagher, "'Upon their Success Hang Momentous Interests': Generals," *Why the Confederacy Lost*, p. 104.

41. Gallagher, "'Upon their Success Hang Momentous Interests': Generals," *Why the Confederacy Lost*, pp. 104-105.

42. Richard M. McMurry, "The Pennsylvania Gambit and the Gettysburg Splash," *The Gettysburg Nobody Knows*, edited by Gabor S. Boritt (New York, 1997), p. 191.

43. Bevin Alexander, *Robert E. Lee's Civil War* (Holbrook, 1998), pp. 39 and xi. This criticism of Lee is somewhat tempered by Alexander's acknowledgment that the Confederate general was an excellent defensive fighter.

44. Alexander, *Robert E. Lee's Civil War*, p. 11.

45. *OR* 11, pt. 2, p. 497.

46. *OR* 19, pt. 1, p. 145; Joseph L. Harsh, *Taken at the Flood: Robert E. Lee & Confederate Strategy in the Maryland Campaign of 1862* (Kent, 1999), pp. 46-50; Joseph L. Harsh, *Sounding the Shallows: A Confederate Companion for the Maryland Campaign of 1862* (Kent, 2000), pp. 145-148. One question rarely asked is why Joe Johnston allowed the months of inactivity leading up the Peninsula Campaign to pass without ordering his generals to practice maneuvers and marches with large bodies of troops.

47. Michael A. Palmer, *Lee Moves North: Robert E. Lee on the Offensive from Antietam, to Gettysburg, to Bristow's Station* (New York, 1998), pp. 66-67.

48. Lee's decentralized style of command depended on timely and accurate information, which is why he relied so heavily on cavalryman Jeb Stuart for reliable intelligence about the enemy and their movements.

49. John D. McKenzie, *Uncertain Glory: Lee's Generalship Reexamined* (New York, 1997), p. 25.

50. McKenzie, *Uncertain Glory: Lee's Generalship Reexamined*, pp. 350-359.

51. In 88 B.C., Sulla (138-78 B.C.), a Roman consul, became fed up with the lack of political support from the Senate and put himself at the head of his army in order to lead it against Rome. By marching his six legions on the capital, Sulla violated one of Rome's most sacred laws. As might be expected, controversy over his actions continues to this day. For an authoritative account of Sulla's life, see Arthur Keaveney, *Sulla: The Last Republican* (Dover, New Hampshire, 1986 edition of 1982 original).

52. See *The Wartime Papers of R. E. Lee*, numbers 233, 257, and 358, for just a few examples supporting Lee's efforts in this regard, and his treatment of political officials.

53. Lee was constantly pressing Commissary General Lucius Northrop in Richmond for sufficient supplies. These pleadings convinced Northrop to send his agents scouring for supplies for the Virginia army as far west as Tennessee, where Northrop's subsistence agents paid higher prices than those being offered by Braxton Bragg's agents from the Army of Tennessee. These efforts netted impressive yields. Despite the fact that Bragg's Army of

Tennessee operated in the Volunteer state throughout much of 1862 and the first half of 1863, Northrop's agents succeeded in securing "thousands of bushels of wheat and barrels of flour, over 2 million pounds of bacon, thousands of heads of cattle, and almost 100,000 hogs [that] were withdrawn to the commissary depot at Atlanta" and earmarked for shipment to Virginia. Thomas Lawrence Connelly, *Autumn of Glory* (Baton Rouge, 1971), p. 17.

54. Crute, *Confederate Staff Officers*, p. 115. The other officers serving under Cole in the commissary department of the Army of Northern Virginia were Major Fred R. Scott and Major W. O. Harvie. For additional referenced to Major Cole, see: "Battle of Chancellorsville—Report of General Lee," in *Southern Historical Society Papers*, 3, p. 243; *OR* 27, pt. 2, p. 443, which is also printed in *Southern Historical Society Papers*, 10, p. 294; *Southern Historical Society Papers*, 15, pp. 2, 340-341; 19, p. 266; 30, p. 62; 35, p. 26; and 38, p. 156.

55. McKenzie, *Uncertain Glory: Lee's Generalship Reexamined*, p. 350.

56. McKenzie, *Uncertain Glory: Lee's Generalship Reexamined*, p. 352.

57. Frank E. Vandiver, *Their Tattered Flags: The Epic of the Confederacy* (College Station. 1987 reprint of the 1970 original), p. 141.

58. Hennessy, *Return to Bull Run: The Campaign and Battle of Second Manassas*, p. 456.

59. Hennessy, *Return to Bull Run: The Campaign and Battle of Second Manassas*, p. 456. McKenzie argues that Lee's Seven Day's Battles cost more casualties than the Confederacy could afford, but no plausible alternative to attacking, and attacking aggressively, existed. Thus, no price was too high to pay to drive McClellan from Richmond, the political and logistical cornerstone of the Confederacy, since losing the capital in 1862 probably meant losing the war—and everyone knew it. Under these circumstances, blaming Lee for adopting a successful strategy because that strategy incurred heavy losses is illogical. Censure is better placed on the shoulders of Joe Johnston, who maneuvered the Confederacy perilously close to defeat without waging a single major battle, or Jefferson Davis, for retaining a general whose policies were so antithetical to Southern national strategy. Successful army commanders in any age have the intuitive ability to recognize military reality, identify opportunities, and act on those opportunities whenever and wherever they present themselves. Lee's vigorous execution of Napoleon's "strategy of the central position" in the summer of 1862 provides a singular example of exceptional generalship.

60. Hennessy, *Return to Bull Run: The Campaign and Battle of Second Manassas*, p. 459. Chancellorsville offers yet another example of Lee's offensive ability as an army commander. Instead of retreating after being outflanked, Lee placed the pieces of his army in position to score a major victory. Then, while Stonewall Jackson was conducting his famous (and dangerous) flanking march, Lee launched a convincing demonstration against Joe Hooker's front that successfully distracted the Federal high command, allowing Jackson's to complete his movement.

61. Hamlin, *The Attack of Stonewall Jackson at Chancellorsville*, p. 6.

62. Emory M. Thomas, "Davis, Lee and Confederate Grand Strategy," *Jefferson Davis's Generals*, edited by Gabor S. Boritt (New York, 1999), pp. 30-31.

63. Alan T. Nolan, *Lee Considered: General Robert E. Lee and Civil War History*, (Chapel Hill, 1991), pp. 62-63.

64. Nolan, *Lee Considered: General Robert E. Lee and Civil War History*, p. 62.

65. Nolan, *Lee Considered: General Robert E. Lee and Civil War History*, p. 105.

66. Nolan, *Lee Considered: General Robert E. Lee and Civil War History*, pp. 78-79. In a correct and technical sense, the conflict was not a civil war, in which two or more sides struggle for control of the same country or central government, but rather a war for independence.

67. Nolan, *Lee Considered: General Robert E. Lee and Civil War History*, p. 101.

68. Gallagher, "'Upon their Success Hang Momentous Interests': Generals," *Why the Confederacy Lost*, p. 98.

Chapter 3

"In Either Case ... After Crossing the River,
You Must Move on & Feel the Right of Ewell's Troops"

Robert E. Lee and Jeb Stuart

"Like the rest of the army generally, nothing gave me much concern so long as I knew that Gen. Lee was in command. I am sure there can never have been an army with more supreme confidence in its commander than that army had in Gen. Lee. We looked forward to victory under him as confidently as to successive sunrises."
— Edward Porter Alexander[1]

The Battle of Brandy Station forever humiliated Jeb Stuart, but it never did satisfactorily answer the question uppermost in Joe Hooker's mind: Where was the Army of Northern Virginia?

Rumors of a new Southern offensive had been pouring into Federal headquarters for days, but a reconnaissance by the Federal Sixth Corps over the Rappahannock River at Franklin's Crossing on June 5 had failed to confirm it. Desperate for information, Hooker dispatched Brigadier General Alfred Pleasonton and his cavalry, supported by infantry and artillery, some 11,000 men, to find out what his enemy was up to. With surprising speed and—especially to the Southern eyes—unusual aggressiveness, Pleasonton's troopers splashed across the Rappahannock at a pair of fords and attacked Stuart's men early on the morning of June 9, 1863, just seven miles northeast of Culpeper, Virginia, along the Orange and Alexandria Railroad at Brandy Station. Pleasonton was looking for clues as to the

James Ewell Brown Stuart
(1833-1864)

Supremely confident in his abilities and in those of his men, Jeb Stuart was one of the Confederacy's most famous soldiers. The dashing cavalryman's qualities seemed to embody the romantic chivalric myth so dear to the South. Yet these qualities sowed many of the seeds of disaster in the Gettysburg Campaign.

Library of Congress

whereabouts of Lee's infantry. What he found instead was the largest cavalry action of the entire war.

Although initially surprised by the attack, Stuart recovered quickly by gathering together his scattered horse brigades and aggressively moving to counter Pleasonton's thrusts. Within a short time thousands of sword-wielding, pistol-shooting horsemen were involved in the chaotic and seesaw affair. Charges, counter-charges, and hand-to-hand fighting marked much of the contest. Fleetwood Hill, the site of Stuart's headquarters, witnessed especially heavy combat and changed hands several times. By the time the fighting ended late that afternoon, some 500 Confederates and twice as many Federals had been killed, wounded, or captured. Stuart and his men held the field, but by the thinnest of margins.

Aftermath of Brandy Station

Although he had not been defeated at Brandy Station, for the first time in the war Jeb Stuart had been thoroughly surprised. And for the flamboyant and famous Southern cavalier, that patently visible fact—coupled with a victory by the narrowest of margins—added up to an embarrassing setback. Two years of virtually uninterrupted and unchallenged superiority over the Federal cavalrymen had helped construct Jeb Stuart's opinion of what he could do, and when he could do it, to the

Federal horse regiments. The confident general had relished in his abilities and those of his men to really get a twist on the enemy. Brandy Station changed all that. Never mind that the careless brigadier, Beverly Robertson, had contributed significantly to Stuart's troubles at the outset by letting the Federals surprise the Southern troopers, or that his troops had inflicted almost twice as many casualties as they had suffered. Stuart discovered on June 9 that the hard-fighting and vastly improved Federal cavalry lacked only the natural ability and *élan* of the Confederate horsemen.[2]

Brandy Station did not sit well with the man in the plumed hat, who made no mention in his report that he had been caught flat-footed by Pleasonton's sudden strike. General Lee knew only too well that the Federals had penetrated Stuart's lax screen and had came close to discovering the army's infantry gathered around Culpeper. "The dispositions made by you to meet the strong attack of the enemy appear to have been judicious and well planned," Lee wrote Stuart one week after the battle, pointedly omitting any reference to the cavalryman's preparations, or lack thereof, before the action commenced. Stuart's ego had been badly bruised, but his confidence remained unshaken. The remedy to restore his injured honor was through new glories in the field, and the road north promised fresh opportunities.[3]

Milroy Gets a Shellacking: The Confederate March Down the Valley and the Battle of Second Winchester

Although large and ominous, the fighting at Brandy Station did not deter General Lee from ordering his army to resume its advance. Hill's Corps was ordered to remain behind the Rappahannock and Longstreet's to mark time around Culpeper in support while Ewell's Second Corps moved rapidly east into the Shenandoah Valley and then northward. Assuming all went according to plan, Longstreet's infantry would then shield Hill's men as they withdrew and moved west, following Ewell's route to the Potomac. "Old Pete's" men would then bring up the rear. On June 12, advance elements of Ewell's Corps entered the Valley, a natural corridor that allowed Lee to use the eastern boundary of the Blue Ridge Mountains to shield his march to the Potomac River. As Ewell's spearhead approached Winchester and its strong enemy garrison of some 7,000 effectives, Hooker received word of Lee's advance and ordered his army to march out of its Rappahannock line on June 13 and gather around Centreville. The Federals at Winchester were led by Major General Robert H. Milroy, who had suffered defeat at the hands of Stonewall Jackson at McDowell, the first battle of the 1862 Shenandoah Valley Campaign. Milroy's other distinguishing characteristic was his six months of ruthless dealings with defenseless Southern civilians, unchivalrous acts that had earned him the wrath of Jackson's Confederates, who were even now plotting his destruction.[4]

And the hapless Milroy completely misread the situation. Reports that Confederates were headed down the Valley were dismissed out of hand. Lee and his large army were still far to the south opposite Fredericksburg, reasoned Milroy.[5] The increased Southern activity was merely "the anticipated cavalry raid of General Stuart," or a small group of Confederates known to be operating in the area, rather than an invasion by the entire Army of Northern Virginia. Besides, Milroy considered his position at Winchester strong enough to hold out against anything the Confederates were likely to send against him.[6] Milroy and his division soon paid for his false sense of security.

With Albert Jenkins' cavalry trying their best to screen them,[7] Ewell's infantry approached Winchester from the south without being discovered until a clash with screening Federal cavalry on the afternoon of June 12 announced their arrival. Ewell revealed himself just south of the city late the next day.[8] By then it was too late for Milroy, whose optimism had been fed by his departmental superior, Robert C. Schenck. Instead of ordering the general to withdraw, Schenck directed him to remain in Winchester until further notice. By the time "further notice" was dispatched on June 13, the telegraph lines between Winchester and Martinsburg had been cut by Confederate cavalry.[9]

The strong works north and west of Winchester offered Milroy a false sense of security. The largest of these was Fort Milroy (Flag Fort to the Confederates), a bastion studded with 22 guns and capable of holding 2,200 men positioned less than a mile northwest of Winchester and a short distance south of the Pughtown Road. Above the road was the Star Fort, another irregular eight-sided earthwork armed with eight guns and large enough for 400 men. The smallest but most important of Milroy's bulwarks was West Fort, an open-ended fortification roughly 900 yards west of Star Fort and flanked by a small additional work. West Fort was the key to Winchester's entire defensive network since its guns commanded the more powerful Flag Fort. Milroy knew it, and packed the outer bastion with infantry and guns.[10]

Dick Ewell knew it too. Although the Federal defensive works at Winchester were formidable, and Jubal Early's Division had already marched 10 miles under excessive heat, Ewell correctly judged that the sudden approach of his corps had surprised Milroy and that an immediate and audacious attack was necessary. His reconnaissance with Early confirmed that an attack from the west off a wooded hill was the best method of capturing West Fort.[11] In order to divert attention away from the main assault, John B. Gordon's Georgia brigade and the Maryland Line would demonstrate against the south side of Winchester while Early and his three remaining brigades marched west down the Cedar Creek Turnpike before striking north cross country to get into position to launch the main assault.[12]

After another march of some eight miles, Early's brigades finally filed into position on the wooded slope of the aptly named Little North Mountain about 4:00 p.m. on June 14. Early selected his best shock troops for the attack: Harry Hays' Louisiana Tigers. The brigade deployed for the attack in two lines: the 6th, 7th and

9th Louisiana in the front line, and the 5th and 8th Louisiana in a supporting second line to protect the flanks of the leading regiments.[13] William "Extra Billy" Smith's Virginians remained behind in support, while most of Colonel Isaac Avery's North Carolinians formed the divisional reserve, the 57th North Carolina having been detached to protect the division's artillery battalion under the yet-undistinguished Lieutenant Colonel Hilary P. Jones.[14] Once the infantry was ready, Jones had his 20 pieces of ordnance rolled by hand out of the timber and into an orchard and a cornfield, from which they opened a bombardment on the startled Federals in West Fort. For the next 45 minutes, Jones' four batteries peppered the Federal position, killing over 50 horses and blowing up caissons and limbers. "So well directed was this fire," Hays reported, "that in a few minutes the enemy were forced to seek shelter behind their works, and scarcely a head was discovered above the ramparts."[15]

At about 6:00 p.m., Hays ordered his Tigers to advance. "So rapidly did this brigade push forward," the Louisianian explained, "that the enemy had time to give us but a few volleys of musketry and only four or five rounds of canister from their field pieces before the position was reached, and carried."[16] The fort's defenders—323 men of the 110th Ohio, a company of the 116th Ohio, and 99 artillerists from the 5th U. S. Artillery, Battery L, manning six 3-inch Ordnance rifles—put up a short fight before fleeing eastward toward Winchester, leaving behind them 40 men killed, wounded, and captured. The garrison in the small redoubt supporting West Fort abandoned their position as soon as the attack began, but quick thinking on the part of some of the charging Pelican State troops gobbled up a section of 3-inch rifles and their caissons.[17]

With his field glasses pressed tightly to his eyes, Dick Ewell watched as his Tigers took the West Fort and nearby redoubt. "Hurrah for the Louisiana Boys!" he yelled at the top of his voice. The swift capture of the enemy's breastworks demonstrated that quality determined troops, properly supported by their own artillery, could overrun average quality Federal infantry supported by small-caliber 3-inch Ordnance rifles. The canister discharges from these pieces were simply too small to stop onrushing élite formations. In his after-action report, Lieutenant E. D. Spooner of Battery L, 5th U. S. Artillery, reported exactly that, claiming his canister discharges "did not appear to have a particle of effect." The light casualty returns from the Confederate brigade support Spooner's observation. The Louisianians had stormed a fortified position and suffered only 12 killed and 67 wounded, and in the process killed, wounded, captured, or drove away the defending Federal infantry.[18]

Now Ewell had to decide his next move. He knew the loss of the fort was a critical defeat for Milroy, and predicted he would abandon Winchester that night by moving north on the Martinsburg Pike. Four miles north of Winchester the road forked at a place called Stephenson's Depot, one route angling northeast to Harpers Ferry, the other continuing on to Martinsburg. With a decision reminiscent of Old Jack himself, Ewell decided that Stephenson's Depot was the place to intercept the

Federal withdrawal. The corps chief immediately dispatched Edward Johnson along with most of his division to that place, keeping his other troops deployed around Winchester. If Milroy fled under cover of darkness, Johnson would be in position to intercept him. If, on the other hand, Milroy decided to keep his command around Winchester, Johnson and Early, supported by their artillery battalions and the corps reserve battalions, would be in a position to bombard and assault Milroy's troops on June 15.[19]

Milroy did indeed choose to cut and run, but it was too late to save his command. After a short but tiring march, Edward Johnson's men arrived just outside Stephenson's Depot at 3:30 a.m. on June 15, just in time to deploy parallel to the pike behind a low stone wall. When the beleaguered Milroy realized his enemy controlled the only avenue of escape, he hurriedly launched several attacks in an attempt to cut his way through to Harpers Ferry. At one point it looked as though the Federals would outflank Johnson's line, but the timely arrival of the Stonewall Brigade ended the effort. The sharp night engagement concluded thereafter with a mass Federal surrender. Nearly half of Milroy's division was captured in Ewell's brilliant gambit; only Milroy and a few hundred cavalrymen of the 13th Pennsylvania managed to slip the noose and escape.[20]

According to General Early, who was given temporary command of Winchester, 3,358 Federal prisoners were dispatched to Richmond while hundreds more, too sick or injured to be transported, remained behind. Ewell's ordnance officers rejoiced over the capture of 23 Federal pieces and their accompanying quality ammunition. Johnson's troops also bagged 300 wagons, numerous teams of horses and harnesses, thousands of small arms, and the remainder of Milroy's artillery (four 20-pounder Parrott rifles, nine 3-inch Ordnance rifles, and two 24-pounder howitzers).[21] Except for the howitzers, all the captured guns were immediately exchanged by Ewell's gunnery officers, who left their older and inferior pieces in Winchester.[22] Milroy also suffered another 95 killed and 348 wounded. At the cost of only 269 men, Ewell had annihilated Milroy's division and opened the invasion route through the Shenandoah Valley to the Potomac.[23]

Richard Ewell's aggressive and stunning victory at Second Winchester brushed away any doubts as to his readiness to take the field and Lee's choice of the one-legged general to replace the fallen Stonewall Jackson. It also fueled the confidence of the officers and men of the army. The battle was "one of the most perfect pieces of work the Army of Northern Virginia ever did," wrote Robert Stiles a gunner with the Second Corps.[24] Another artillerist, William White went a step further by claiming Ewell's masterpiece "equaled any movement made during the war."[25] Even the generally disagreeable Richmond *Examiner* waxed eloquent, if hyperbolically, about the battle: "The rapidity of its completion or the magnificence of the result will stand comparison with any chapter in the history of any leader of any country or age."[26] The action had been so reminiscent of the late great Jackson that some Federals did not believe he was really dead. "No officer in either army," wrote a captured colonel, ". . .could have executed that movement but 'Old Jack.'"[27] Jackson was indeed dead, but a suitable replacement in Ewell had apparently been found. Thus, confidence was high among the Confederates as they marched north. Perhaps their mood is best summed up by the commanding general's nephew, Fitzhugh Lee, who noted that "the heart of every Southern soldier beat with the lofty confidence of certain victory."[28]

Davis Continues to Refuse to Reinforce the Army

Even though the campaign was well underway, General Lee had not yet given up hope of reinforcing his army with his missing brigades. In a lengthy discourse with President Davis on June 10, Lee offered counsel as to the importance of strengthening the Virginia army and the political imperative attached to the present campaign. Three days later, while Ewell was orchestrating Milroy's destruction, Lee was again petitioning Richmond to reunite his army. "You can realize the difficulty of operating in any offensive movement with this army if it has to be divided to cover Richmond. It seems to me useless to attempt it with the force against it. You will have seen its effective strength by the last returns," Lee penned Secretary Seddon. "I grieve over the desolation of the country & the distress to innocent women & children occasioned by spiteful excursions of the enemy, unworthy of a civilized nation," Lee lamented, countering that such depredations "can only be prevented by local organizations & bold measures." The lack of horsemen was particularly bothersome to Lee. "I have not half as much as I require to keep back the enemy's mounted force in my front. If I weaken it I fear a heavier calamity may befall us than that we wish to avoid."[29] Even in the face of these continuous requests, President Davis refused to allow the army's missing brigades to return to Lee, keeping them instead in static garrison roles to protect Richmond and portions of southern Virginia and North Carolina.

Like General Lee, Major General George Pickett was also disgusted with Richmond's reluctance to return his absent soldiers. On June 21, he wrote to Brigadier General Robert Hall Chilton, Lee's assistant adjutant and inspector general of the Army of Northern Virginia, to inquire of their status and ask that they be returned or additional troops be added to his division. "I have the honor to report that in point of numerical strength this division has been very much weakened," wrote Pickett before explaining the circumstances of how it came about that his five-brigade division had been cleaved by two brigades:

> One brigade (Jenkins') was left on the Blackwater. Corse was left at Hanover Junction as a guard by my own order, upon the receipt of a telegram from the general commanding this army to bring up my division to Culpeper Court-House if I could leave the Junction. Being anxious to carry out his

wishes, I marched immediately with three brigades, leaving Corse with orders to follow as soon as relieved, and sent a staff officer to Richmond to report the circumstance to the Adjutant-General, and reported the fact by telegraph and letter to the commanding general.

"I have now only three brigades, not more than 4,795 men, and unless these absent troops are certainly to rejoin me, I beg that another brigade be sent to this division," the Virginia general continued. Desirous to avoid giving the wrong impression, he added, "I ask this in no spirit of complaint, but merely as an act of justice to my division and myself, for it is well known that a small division will be expected to do the same amount of hard service as a large one, and, as the army is now divided, my division will be, I think, decidedly the weakest."[30]

General Lee, of course, was painfully aware of Pickett's plight. In an attempt to repatriate Montgomery Corse's four veteran regiments to Virginian's command, Lee wrote two letters on June 23, one to Davis and the other to Adjutant and Inspector General Samuel Cooper. The 44th North Carolina, Lee pointed out to Cooper, had been sent to Hanover Junction to enable Corse's Brigade to rejoin Pickett's Division. "I think the regiment [44th North Carolina] will suffice for a guard at that point, and wish Corse's brigade to be ordered to rejoin its division under General Pickett as soon as possible . . . I wish to have every man that can be spared, and desire that Cooke's brigade may be sent forward." There is no necessity "for keeping a large number of troops at [Richmond]," he added.[31] Lee's plea of the same day to Davis considered the lack of evidence of any serious enemy activity for southern Virginia and North Carolina. The troops in those regions, he continued, "could be organized under the command of General [P. G. T.] Beauregard and pushed forward to Culpeper Court-House, threatening Washington from that direction." Such a move, he added, would "relieve us of any apprehension of an attack upon Richmond during our absence." Lee was imploring Davis to use inactive troops to capture the strategic initiative in Virginia and launch a diversion to distract the Federals and disrupt any plans they might have against the Southern capital or the coastal regions. Lee was also hoping the plan would convince the president that some of his missing brigades could be returned to the army.[32]

Lee's running rearguard action with Richmond included an important June 25 letter to Davis. The dispatch discussed a variety of matters, the most important of which was contained within it opening sentences. "So strong is my conviction of the necessity of activity on our part in military affairs," began Lee, "that . . . it seems to me that we cannot afford to keep our troops awaiting possible movements of the enemy, but our true policy is, as far as we can, so to employ our own forces as to give occupation to his at points of our selection."[33] Lee's keen insight merely demonstrated again the general's sagacious appreciation of how a numerically inferior force must be employed in order to have a chance of achieving its political and military goals.

Unable to get Richmond to forward the troops he so desperately needed, let alone respond seriously to his reasoned petitions for action, an exasperated Lee finally resolved himself to the idea that additional help would not be forthcoming. On June 29, Lee authorized Major Walter Taylor of his staff to respond to Pickett's entreaty for reinforcements. "I am directed by the commanding general to say that he has repeatedly requested that the two brigades [Corse and Jenkins] be returned, and had hoped that at least one of them (Corse) would have been sent to the division ere this."[34]

Departure: Lee's Orders to Jeb Stuart

Petty-minded departmental commanders and an uncooperative chief executive were not the only problems Lee had to deal with. His premier cavalryman, Jeb Stuart, was still seething over his surprise and near-defeat at Brandy Station. For the fame-seeking and vainglorious trooper, the lingering humiliation of June 9 was but a thorn requiring extraction. Editorials and articles in newspapers across the South offered caustic criticisms of the army's "puffed up cavalry" and the cavalier's stewardship of that mounted arm. "The more the circumstances of the late affair at Brandy Station are considered, the less pleasant do they appear," offered the *Richmond Examiner* in a scathing editorial. "If this was an isolated case, it might be excused under the convenient head of accident or chance. But this puffed up cavalry of the Army of Northern Virginia has been twice, if not three times, surprised since the battles of December, and such repeated accidents can be regarded as nothing but the necessary consequences of negligence and bad management."[35] For someone as sensitive as Stuart was to public opinion, censures such as this must have stung mightily. Still, the popular general was not without his admirers and defenders. Stuart, they predicted, would make the Yankees pay for their sortie at Brandy Station.[36]

The proud cavalier was determined to fulfill the prognostications of his supporters, while at the same time refute those who questioned his leadership and tactical abilities. The army, however, was now embarked on its most important campaign to date, and embarrassment or not, Stuart needed to keep in mind that General Lee and the entire Army of Northern Virginia relied entirely on his scouting and screening abilities to shield the marching columns from prying enemy eyes. Before the army struck out for Maryland and Pennsylvania, Lee had directed Stuart to deploy his cavalry to screen the army's movements northward, as well as to report any movements of the Federal army. The task of keeping the probing and numerically superior Federal cavalry east of the Blue Ridge Mountains so that the march of the Army of Northern Virginia remained unimpeded and undiscovered was a difficult one. Little if any glory would result from it.

For five consecutive days, June 17 through June 21, Stuart performed his operational mission well. The primary area of his operations were along a 10-mile front of the eastern edge of the Blue Ridge range, from Ashby's Gap to Sniper's (or Snicker's) Gap, extending eastward 17 miles to Aldie and Bull Run Mountain. Within this triangulated swath of Loudoun County, Federal forces under Pleasanton, David Gregg, and John Buford, did their best to penetrate Stuart's screening horsemen. The horse encounters were usually running skirmishes with small numbers of men, although three battles of note were fought at Aldie, Middleburg, and Upperville. "All that the 'butternut' Southerners possessed of courage, resourcefulness and endurance, they needed in those fights. . ." explained historian Douglas Southall Freeman. If any lasting glory was scored it belonged to Wade Hampton and his gallant horsemen. Hard-pressed at Upperville on June 21, the South Carolina planter-turned-soldier led a series of charges that forced back aggressive Federal cavalry. "General Hampton's brigade participated largely and in a brilliant manner," Stuart proudly wrote in his report of the campaign.[37]

By any standard Stuart and his lieutenants had performed brilliantly during the five days of June 17 through 21. The hard pressed and outnumbered Southerners inflicted 883 casualties on the Federals and captured several pieces of ordnance and numerous standards, suffering in return losses less than half that number.[38] If the casualties of Brandy Station are brought into the mix, the proportion of losses holds steady (approximately 900 Confederates to 1,800 Federals) over the two week period from June 9 through June 21. Thus, from strictly a casualty-ratio perspective, the dominance of Stuart's regiments over their mounted opponents seems not to have changed. Although some of the actions during this time had forced Confederate cavalrymen to retire from the field, they had done so only after accomplishing their mission of preventing Federal troopers from penetrating their screen and finding out what the Confederate infantry was up to.

For reasons not readily obvious to Stuart's subordinates, the cavalryman conducted himself differently during the cavalry operations in Loudoun and Fauquier counties. While the "old" Stuart had always been seen in the middle of the hardest fight, leading his troopers from the front, the "new" cavalier had remained largely in the rear, posting his brigades and shifting formations where they were most needed. The reason for this change was a simple one: Stuart's screening and scouting mission during the early weeks of the Gettysburg Campaign encompassed a wide and fluid front, which forced him to act as a true cavalry division commander on outpost duty. When Henry B. McClellan, Stuart's assistant adjutant general, inquired about his recent and, for him, unconventional behavior, Stuart responded by saying "he had given all necessary instructions to his brigade commanders, and he wished them to feel the responsibility resting upon them, and to gain whatever honor the field might bring."[39]

In reality, the operational circumstances provided Stuart with little choice but to direct the screening operations from a position removed from the front lines.

Otherwise, he might find himself personally involved in a combat at one place and utterly surprised and embarrassed on another sector of the expansive and constantly shifting front—and Stuart was not about provide the Southern press with another opportunity to label his leadership negligent. Thus, it must have been particularly galling to Stuart when the Southern journalistic bloodhounds dipped their writing utensils in vitriol and reported what appeared to be daily tactical reverses, when in fact his men were accomplishing the objectives General Lee had in mind.[40]

These correspondents failed to realize that every day Stuart's troopers prevented the enemy from discovering Lee's whereabouts constituted an operational victory. Stuart's mission forced him into a command straightjacket not of his choosing, an arrangement that limited his opportunities for both tactical victories and the consequent glory that followed. Coming on the heels of the Brandy Station fiasco, these press reports constituted more (and unjust) criticism than Stuart had ever experienced. Wounded by the verbal barbs of Brandy Station, Stuart's fragile egocentric mind set—which craved unequivocal victory no matter how minor the engagement—was damaged further by the continued ranting of a handful of reporters lost in a fog of military ignorance. "I . . . feel not unlike a tiger pausing before its spring," Stuart had written his brother only the previous week, "[and] that spring will not be delayed much longer."[41] The Stuart of old was more than ready to pull off some spectacular military deed to silence his critics. As far as he was concerned, it was time to burnish his tarnished star.

Jeb's window of opportunity finally arrived in the wake of the Upperville fight. By this time Ewell's Second Corps had crossed over the Potomac (he did so on June 19) and was now in Maryland. Longstreet's First Corps was moving down (north) the Shenandoah Valley behind the Blue Ridge range, and Powell Hill's Third Corps was bringing up the army's rear some miles to the south. The cavalryman put forth a proposal to Lee of how to utilize the army's five cavalry brigades (few in the Virginia army considered the two brigades of raiders under Albert Jenkins and John Imboden to be "cavalry" in the true sense of the word). Stuart suggested that he be allowed to take three brigades of horse and, while in route to the Potomac River, move across the rear of several Federal corps positioned along the eastern base of Bull Run Mountain, leaving behind the remaining two brigades in order to guard the mountain passes and cover the rear of the Southern army as it continued it march north.[42]

Stuart's opinion about the feasibility of passing around the flank of the Federals was influenced by cavalryman John Singleton Mosby, who had been moving through and scouting the areas near the Potomac crossings and in the rear of the idle Federal army. When Mosby informed Stuart of "the scattered condition of Hooker's corps, he determined, with the approval of General Lee, to pass around, or rather through, them, as the shortest route to reaching [Richard] Ewell."[43] The possibilities of what might be accomplished by such a bold move fanned Stuart's desire for fame and glory. It was early in the morning on June 22 when Stuart realized the Federals had given up trying to penetrate the Confederate cavalry screen east of the Blue Ridge. He promptly informed General Longstreet of that development and that the Yankee horsemen had retired from the Loudoun Valley to beyond the Bull Run—Catoctin mountains.[44] Longstreet dutifully passed the message on to Lee's headquarters. Unbeknownst to anyone, Stuart had set in motion a series of events that would culminate in one of the most controversial aspects of the Gettysburg Campaign.

The cavalryman's note and proposal required the commanding general address the issue of what to do with Stuart's five cavalry brigades. The two mounted brigades of raiders with the army, under Jenkins and Imboden, were operating in front and west of Ewell's advancing Second Corps columns, which were moving generally northeast toward the Susquehanna River.[45] Stuart's own five brigades, under the command of Beverly Robertson, Wade Hampton, Fitzhugh Lee, John Chambliss, and William "Grumble" Jones, were in or near the Blue Ridge providing screening and scouting services for army's eastern flank—that nearest and most exposed to the Federals. With these dispositions in mind, Lee had Major Charles Marshall set forth his wishes in a dispatch to Stuart.[46]

The order Marshall drafted comprised the first of two important directives to Stuart. In order to fully grasp what Lee expected and ordered, it is important to read and understand Marshall's dispatch in conjunction with two others sent to General Ewell during this period, along with letters sent from Longstreet to both Lee and Stuart, in their *unedited* form. The necessarily detailed review that follows develops this important series of correspondence and carefully analyzes their content as it relates to Stuart's infamous ride around the Army of the Potomac.

Charles Marshall (1830-1902)

Marshall served as part of General Lee's inner circle for three years. Educated at Warren Green Academy and at the University of Virginia, where he "bore off the highest honors of the University" with a masters degree at the age of 18, Marshall penned many of Lee's most famous directives, including the orders and parameters of operations for the Gettysburg Campaign sent to Stuart. Marshall's writings on Gettysburg rank among the most important penned by Confederate participants. *Eleanor S. Brockenbrough Library, The Museum of the Confederacy, Richmond*

Lee's initial dispatch to Stuart reads as follows:

> I have just received your note of 7:45 this morning [June 22] to Genl
> Longstreet. I judge the efforts of the enemy yesterday [fighting at Upperville]
> were to arrest our progress and ascertain our whereabouts. Perhaps he is
> satisfied. Do you know where he is and what he is doing? I fear he will steal a
> march on us and get across the Potomac before we are aware. If you find that he
> is moving northward, and that two brigades can guard the Blue Ridge & take
> care of your rear, you can move with the other three [brigades] into Maryland &
> take position on General Ewell's right, place yourself in communication with
> him, guard his flank, keep him informed of the enemy's movements, & collect
> all the supplies you can for the use of the army. One column of Genl Ewell's
> army [corps] will probably move towards the Susquehanna by the Emmitsburg
> route; another by Chambersburg. Accounts from him last night state that there
> was no enemy west of Fredericktown [Frederick, Maryland]. A cavalry force
> (about 100) guarded the Monocacy Bridge, which was barricaded. You will of
> course take charge of [Albert G.] Jenkins' brigade, and give him necessary
> instructions.
>
> All supplies taken in Maryland must be by authorized staff officers for their
> respective departments, by no one else. They will be paid for, or receipts for the
> same given to the owners. I will send you a general order on this subject [No.
> 72], which I wish you to see is strictly complied with.[47]

That same day, June 22, Lee also wrote twice to Ewell. The content of these
orders, which clearly reveal the commanding general's intent, must be considered
with the preceding order sent to Stuart. The first of the letters to Ewell reads as
follows:

> Your letter of 6 P.M. yesterday has been received. If you are ready to move, you
> can do so. I think your best course will be towards the Susquehanna, taking the
> routes by Emmitsburg, Chambersburg, McConellsburg. Your trains had better
> be, as far as possible, kept on the center route. You must get command of your
> cavalry, & use it in gathering supplies, obtaining information, & protecting
> your flanks. If necessary, send a staff officer to remain with Genl [Albert G.]
> Jenkins. It will depend upon the quantity of supplies obtained in that country
> whether the rest of the army can follow. There may be enough for your
> command, but none for the others. Every exertion should therefore be made to
> locate and secure them. Beef we can drive with us, but bread we cannot carry,
> and must secure it in the country. I send you copies of a general order [No. 72]
> on this subject, which I think is based on rectitude and sound policy, and the
> spirit of which I wish you to see enforced in your command. I am much
> gratified at the success which has attended your movements, and feel assured, if
> they are conducted with the same energy and circumspection, it will continue.
> Your progress and direction will of course depend upon development of
> circumstances. If Harrisburg comes within your means, capture it. Genl A. P.

Hill arrived yesterday in the vicinity of Berryville. I shall move him on today if possible. Saturday Longstreet withdrew from the Blue Ridge. Yesterday the enemy pressed our cavalry so hard with infantry & cavalry on the Upperville road that McLaws' division had to be sent back to hold Ashby's Gap. I have not yet heard from there this morning. Genl Stuart could not ascertain whether it was intended as a real advance towards the Valley or to ascertain our position. The pontoons will reach Martinsburg today, and will be laid at the point you suggest, four or five miles below Williamsport, if found suitable. I have not countermanded your order withdrawing the cavalry from Charlestown. I will write you again if I receive information affecting your movements. Trusting in the guidance of a merciful God, and invoking His protection for your corps.[48]

At 3:30 that afternoon Lee wrote again to Ewell:

I have just received your letter of this morning from opposite Shepherdstown. Mine of today, authorizing you to move towards the Susquehanna, I hope has reached you ere this. After dispatching my letter, learning that the enemy had not renewed his attempts of yesterday to break through the Blue Ridge, I directed Genl R. H. Anderson's division to commence its march towards Shepherdstown. It will reach there tomorrow. I also directed Genl Stuart, should the enemy have so far retired from his front as to permit of the departure of a portion of the cavalry, to march with three brigades across the Potomac, and place himself on your right, & in communication with you, keep you advised of the movements of the enemy, and assist in collecting supplies for the army. I have not heard from him since. I also directed Imboden, if opportunity offered, to cross the Potomac, and perform the same offices on your left. I shall endeavor to get Genl Early's regiments to him as soon as possible. I do not know what has become of the infantry of the Maryland Line. I had intended that to guard Winchester.[49]

At 7:00 p.m. that evening, General Longstreet sent the following letter to Jeb Stuart:

General Lee has inclosed to me this letter for you [dated June 22], to be forwarded to you, provided you can be spared from my front, and provided I think that you can move across the Potomac without disclosing our plans. He [Lee] speaks of your leaving, via Hopewell Gap, and passing by the rear of the enemy. If you can get through by that route, I think that you will be less likely to indicate what our plans are than if you should cross by passing to our rear. I forward the letter of instructions with these suggestions.

Please advise me of the condition of affairs before you leave, and order General Hampton—whom I suppose you will leave here in command—to report to me at Millwood, either by letter or in person, as may be most agreeable to him.

P. S.—I think that your passage of the Potomac by the rear at the present moment will, in a measure, disclose our plans. You had better not leave us, therefore, unless you can take the proposed route in rear of the enemy.[50]

Thirty minutes later, Longstreet sent the following to Lee: "Yours of 4 o'clock this afternoon is received. I have forwarded your letter to General Stuart, with the suggestion that he pass by the enemy's rear if he thinks that he may get through. We have nothing of the enemy today."[51]

After Lee received two messages from Stuart on June 23 and reviewed Longstreet's communiqué to Stuart, the commanding general realized that Longstreet's message failed to take into account the affirmative order that if he discovered the enemy "moving northward," Stuart was to position his troopers on Ewell's right flank. Consequently, Lee directed Marshall to send a follow up message to Stuart reiterating the orders issued the previous day. "I remember saying to the General that it could hardly be necessary to repeat the order," Marshall wrote after the war, "as General Stuart had had the matter fully explained to himself *verbally* [emphasis added] and my letter had been full and explicit." Still, Lee "felt anxious about the matter and desired to guard against the possibility of error, and desired me to repeat it."[52]

Thus Marshall penned the following to Stuart at 5:00 p.m. on June 23:

Your notes of 9 & 10 ½ A.M. today have just been received. . . . If Genl Hooker's army remains inactive you can leave two brigades to watch him & withdraw with the three others, but should he not appear to be moving northward I think you had better withdraw this side of the [Blue Ridge] mountain tomorrow night, cross at Shepherdstown next day, & move over to Frederickstown.

You will however be able to judge whether you can pass around their army without hindrance, doing them all the damage you can, & cross the river east of the mountains. In either case, after crossing the [Potomac] river, you must move on & feel the right of Ewell's troops, collecting information, provisions, &c.

Give instructions to the commander of the brigades left behind to watch the flank & rear of the army, & (in event of the enemy leaving their front) retire from the mountains west of the Shenandoah, leaving sufficient pickets to guard the passes, bringing everything clean along the Valley, closing upon the rear of the army.

As regards the movements of the two brigades of the enemy moving towards Warrenton, the commander of the brigades to be left in the mountains must do what he can to counteract them, but I think the sooner you cross into Maryland after tomorrow the better.

The movements of Ewell's corps are as stated in my former letter. Hill's first division will reach the Potomac today and Longstreet will follow tomorrow.

Be watchful & circumspect in all your movements.[53]

A careful reading of these six pieces of correspondence is necessary to understand Lee's clarity of purpose and direction with regard to what he expected of Stuart. It is important to consider these writings in light of the information Lee and Stuart possessed at the time, rather than confusing the analysis with what these men subsequently learned.

When Lee sent his June 22 letter to Stuart, he was well aware that the enemy probing around Upperville on the 21st included infantry, and that the Federal troops had pushed Stuart's cavalry back into Ashby's Gap by sundown.[54] If the Federals seized the pass the next day and poured into the Shenandoah Valley, they would threaten Longstreet's rear as his First Corps advanced down (north) the Valley. McLaws' Division was thus halted and sent back to Ashby's Gap in order to prevent such an occurrence. As it turned out, the Federals did not press their advantage but instead withdrew on June 22. Pleasonton's large and aggressive Federal cavalry force, supported by infantry (Strong Vincent's Third Brigade, Fifth Corps), strongly suggested to Lee that Hooker was not only trying to ascertain the whereabouts of his army, but might be preparing to ford the Potomac River in response to Lee's maneuvers.[55] Although screening the march of his army was important, Lee also had to determine Hooker's movements. Lee, however, did not know with any degree of certainty the precise location of the Federal army.[56]

Therefore, Lee's letter of the 22nd set forth his fear that Hooker would steal a march and move "across the Potomac before we are aware."[57] That is why Lee instructed Stuart in the same letter, "if you find that he is moving northward, and that two brigades can guard the Blue Ridge & take care of your rear, you can move with the other three [brigades] into Maryland & take position on General Ewell's right, place yourself in communication with him, guard his flank, keep him informed of the enemy's movements, & collect all the supplies you can for the use of the army."[58] Lee did not fix Stuart's precise route across the Potomac because Lee knew that Stuart, being on the scene, could judge best how to accomplish his mission. Nothing in Lee's order even intimates Stuart was to take his entire command and pass south and east of the entire Federal army, a move that would separate Jeb Stuart's three veteran Confederate brigades of cavalry from the remainder of the Army of Northern Virginia.

Lee also sent a note to Longstreet on June 22. Although the original has not been found, its contents can be reconstructed by reading Longstreet's subsequent note (reproduced above) to Stuart.[59] By this time Lee had approved Stuart's proposal that he be allowed to operate against the rear of the western-most elements of the Federal army strung out along the eastern base of Bull Run Mountain. It was a decision Lee could only have reached after carefully considering three important issues: First, were two brigades enough to properly screen the rear of his army? Second, who was to assume command of those brigades? Third, was it possible for Stuart to cross the Potomac and head for his rendezvous with Ewell without divulging the whereabouts of the rest of the Army of Northern Virginia?

Lee seems to have believed that two cavalry brigades were sufficient to cover the rear of the army, and probably suggested to Longstreet that Wade Hampton was the best man for the task. Longstreet's letter to Stuart leaves little doubt that Lee thought it best that Stuart bypass the Federal forces along their northwestern flank, passing through Hopewell Gap, before skirting the eastern edge of the Bull Run—Catoctin Mountains on the way to the Potomac River. However, Lee's command style allowed the commanders on the scene—Longstreet and Stuart—the discretion of which route would be best for Stuart to take across the Potomac.

On the next day, June 23, Lee received word from one of his scouts that elements of Slocum's Federal Twelfth Corps that had been at Leesburg, a small town south of the Potomac at the base of the Catoctin Mountain range, appeared to be moving east toward the Potomac River. Other Federal movements, coupled with the rumor that the Yankees had laid a pontoon bridge at Edwards Ferry, caused Lee to write to President Davis that he believed the enemy "is preparing to cross the Potomac" some six miles east of Leesburg.[60] After writing these words, Lee received confirmation from another scout that the enemy was indeed preparing to cross to the north side of the Potomac at Edwards Crossing. Thus Lee knew almost conclusively that not only was the Federal army preparing to cross the Potomac east of the Bull Run—Catoctin Mountains, but as a result of the movement, their long columns would be spread out for some distance southward on all roads leading to Edwards Ferry, which would block any attempt by the Confederate cavalry to pass through or get amongst the various corps of the Federal army.

However, Stuart painted a different picture with two reports to Lee on June 23, one at 9:00 a.m. and another at 10:30 a.m. The first of these explained that his cavalry had pushed enemy outposts as far east as Aldie, and that a column comprised of two brigades of Federal cavalry "was moving southward to Warrenton"; the second dispatch advised Lee that "Major [John Singleton] Mosby had gone east of the Bull Run Mountain and had found the enemy's infantry quietly waiting in his scattered camps."[61]

With conflicting information spread before him, Lee now had to weigh the validity of the reports brought to him by his scouts that the Federal army was preparing to move and cross the Potomac at Edwards Ferry, against two reports from his most trusted cavalry general that claimed the Federal army was largely stationary. Lee did so and carefully worded a new dispatch to Jeb Stuart dated 5:00 p.m., June 23, 1863. The commanding general believed that it was important enough to send the order directly to Stuart, rather than channel it through Longstreet. (Particular attention should be paid to how Lee addressed the different possible scenarios, given the conflicting reports he had received that day).

"If Genl Hooker's army remains inactive," Lee wrote Stuart, "you can leave two brigades to watch him & withdraw with the three others. . ." In other words, if the information given by Mosby was indeed accurate (it is important to add that Lee did not attempt to contradict Stuart with reports received by the other scouts), and if the

Federals remained in their present encampments, Stuart could take three brigades and *withdraw* by passing behind or along the northwestern and northern flanks of the Federal army with the intention of, in Mosby's words, taking "the shortest route to Ewell."[62]

Lee added this condition to his dispatch: ". . .But, should he not appear to be moving northward I think you had better withdraw this side of the [Blue Ridge] mountain tomorrow night, cross at Shepherdstown next day, & move over to Frederickstown [Frederick, Maryland]." This portion of Lee's message specifically addressed Stuart's report that Federals were already on the move "southward to Warrenton." As far as Lee knew, the Federals may have been moving south or southwest to create a diversion, and in that case he did not want Stuart sacrificing lives and wearing out his mounts in useless battles that did not affect the operations of the army. If the Federals were moving in any direction *other than* northward, Lee was instructing Stuart to conserve his men and horses and immediately close up on the rest of the Southern army still south of the Potomac and west of the Blue Ridge Mountains before crossing over the Potomac and resuming his primary mission of screening Lee's army.

Notice Lee's consistent use of the word "withdraw." In the first part of the message, Lee instructs Stuart in clear and certain terms that if the Federal army was *inactive*, the cavalryman could quickly *withdraw* past the Federals by moving in a northerly direction through Maryland and effect his juncture with Ewell in Pennsylvania. If, on the other hand, the Federals were moving in any direction other than northward, Lee did not want to risk having Stuart be caught in any compromising situation. So, in the second sentence, Lee used "withdraw" again to specifically direct Stuart back to the west over the Blue Ridge where he could close up with the rest of the army, cross the Potomac, and move on to link up with Ewell. In both phrases, Lee's use of "withdraw" was consistent. Stuart could "withdraw" from his current location to one further north, further to the northwest, or, if the enemy was on the move in any direction other than northward, due west across the Blue Ridge, before turning northward to the Potomac and beyond. Given Stuart's position when the letter was written and the understood relative position of the Federal army at that time, it is not reasonably possible to interpret Lee's use of the word "withdraw" to mean that Stuart had the authority to detach his command and move south or eastward away from the rest of the Southern army in what would amount to a horse-killing ride around the Federals.[63]

Lee's following two-sentence paragraph reinforces this point: "You will however be able to judge whether you can pass around their army without hindrance, doing them all the damage you can, & cross the [Potomac] river east of the mountains." Lee is simply reiterating and clarifying his letter of June 22 by telling Stuart what to do if the Federals were moving northward as Lee's two scouts had reported. Lee knew that Stuart understood the simple fact that if the Federal army was on the move and preparing to cross the Potomac at Edwards Crossing, its wagon trains and infantry columns would, in all likelihood, be so long that there would only be a slim chance that Stuart's three brigades could pass around the Federals "without hindrance." However, Lee recognized that his experienced cavalry general could find that out for himself. Therefore, Lee was correct in allowing Stuart the latitude to do what was the best course of action within the parameters of his orders, and thus act accordingly. If Stuart could move between the Federal corps "without hindrance" as Mosby had done, especially to take "the shortest route to Ewell" (to use Mosby's words), then Lee was telling him to do it. If Stuart could not accomplish this "without hindrance," then Lee had given Stuart restraining orders to "withdraw" in order get himself into Pennsylvania.[64]

Lee's use of the phrase "pass around their army" has been almost universally misunderstood.[65] The confusion is grounded in the false assumption that "pass around" means "ride around" the southern and eastern flank of the enemy before turning north in a move analogous to Stuart's famous "Ride Around McClellan" from June 12-16, 1862.[66] John Mosby, whom Lee knew to be a reliable scout, had reported to Stuart that the widely separated Federals corps bivouacked on the northern and northwestern ends of the Army of the Potomac could be cut "right through" without difficulty, and the Potomac crossed ten miles west of Rockville, Maryland, at Seneca Ford.[67] Mosby did not report that Southern cavalry should pass *around* the southern extremities of the entire expansive Federal army. Such an attempt would drive the cavalry far to the south and east just to get into a position to enable a ride around the eastern flank of the Federals, at which time the Southern horse would have to turn back to the west in order to reach Seneca Ford.

Lee's use of the words "pass around" was understood by the principals involved as meaning to bypass the various Federal corps (Henry Slocum's Twelfth, Oliver Howard's Eleventh, and John Reynolds' First) that formed the northern and northwestern flanks of the Army of the Potomac. This, after all, was the general route scouted by Mosby and reported by Stuart as being available for such a maneuver. Lee's words to Stuart, as well as his dispatches heretofore discussed regarding Stuart's mission in the campaign, leave no doubt that the phrase "pass around their army" meant move around and through the yawning gaps between the idle enemy corps.

This interpretation of the phrase "pass around their army" is supported by Lee's next sentence to Stuart, which restated in the clearest terms possible the essence of the orders Lee sent to Stuart the day before: "In either case, after crossing the [Potomac] river, you must move on & feel the right of Ewell's troops, collecting information, provisions, etc." The telling and vitally important phrase "in either case" indicates that Lee knew matters could be in a state of fluidity, and leaves absolutely no doubt as to what he intended Stuart's mission to be. There is nothing vague in the English language—either in 1863 or in the present day—concerning the words "in either case." General Lee was ordering his cavalry commander to assume his place on the right flank of the army *regardless* of the route he chose to ride his cavalry. The words "in either case" allowed Stuart, the subordinate officer on the scene, the flexibility and discretion of determining for himself the best route to take into Pennsylvania, where he was to "feel the right of Ewell's troops, collecting information, provisions, etc." and begin screening the right flank of the army while also foraging and scouting the movements of the Federals.

It is also instructive to observe that in this sentence Lee utilized the command verb "must" to clearly denote that some kind of immediacy of action on Stuart's part was demanded ("you *must* move on & feel the right of Ewell's troops, collecting information, provisions, etc."). Further, Lee's use and placement of commas, coming as they do after the command verb "must" provide an indication of the order of importance of the various tasks Stuart was to perform after crossing the Potomac: contacting Ewell's troops was the most important, followed by collecting information, and then obtaining provisions. This sentence, and indeed the entire dispatch, was penned by Charles Marshall, read and approved by Lee, and forwarded to Stuart, thus representing an exchange between three well educated men who understood the complexities of the English language.[68]

Additional specifics for Stuart were also included in the important phrase, "the sooner you cross into Maryland after tomorrow the better . . ." Time was of the essence, and Lee knew it. So did Stuart, who was enough of a veteran to know that the army would desperately need his services moving through Maryland and Pennsylvania. The phrase "the sooner you cross into Maryland after tomorrow the better" does not in any way suggest Lee was in favor of Stuart gallivanting off for days on a ride either south and/or east of the Federals—a journey that would be as far from Mosby's "shortest route to Ewell" as one might envision. It would also substantially delay the cavalry from crossing the Potomac *and* jeopardize the safety of both it and Lee's infantry. Lee's closing words to Stuart—"be watchful & circumspect in all your movements"—delivered in his consummate, genteel style, was Lee's way of admonishing the cavalier that this was no time for heroics. Audacity was not necessary for Stuart to fulfill his mission; close coordination between his troopers and the rest of the army, however, was of paramount importance.[69]

It is not unusual for historians to honestly disagree about the interpretation of events surrounding matters of great historic import, especially those dealing with something as controversial as Gettysburg. Any suggestion, however, such as the one penned by John R. Elting and the contributors of *The West Point Atlas of the American Wars*, that Lee's orders to Stuart "were so vague and allowed such latitude that [Stuart] could interpret them to suit himself," are simply not grounded in a basis of fact.[70]

These final instructions from Lee reached Stuart late on the night of June 23-24. The next morning, Major Mosby returned from his scouting mission east of the Bull Run — Catoctin mountain line. According to Mosby, he had ridden easily between the numerous and quiet Federal corps. There is no reason to doubt Mosby on this

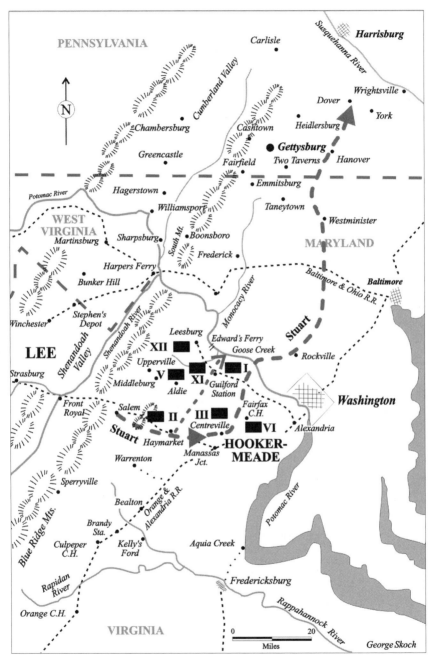

Jeb Stuart's Intended Route to the Potomac River,
and his Actual Route, June 25 - July 1, 1863

point. His route would have placed him in a position to see Howard's Eleventh Corps, which was camped at Goose Creek, some seven miles from Edwards Ferry, from the evening of June 17 until sometime on June 24, and probably elements of the Twelfth, Fifth, First, and Second Corps as well. Given Lee's orders, Stuart could not have interpreted Mosby's report to mean anything other than his cavalry was on a mission to rejoin the army by "the shortest route possible to Ewell."[71]

Jeb Stuart ordered his three best brigades, those of Fitzhugh Lee, Wade Hampton, and John R. Chambliss, to prepare for the movement east, while the brigades of William E. Jones and Beverly Robertson were directed remain behind and cover the rear of the army.[72] This parsing of his command was based upon the assumption that the Federals would not be in motion before his command had passed through their bivouacs. If the Federals were instead discovered to be moving in any direction other than northward, Stuart had orders to "withdraw." If the enemy was moving northward along Stuart's selected route, he would find "hindrance" in its miles-long tail of wagons and stragglers. Later events demonstrate that Stuart struck out on June 25 from Salem, Virginia, with the intention of obeying Lee's orders. Somewhere along the way, the great and empty caverns of his boundless ego worked against him. The gallant Stuart, upon whom Lee relied so heavily, was about to strike out on a course of action that would compromise the safety of the entire Army of Northern Virginia.

The Raid that Wasn't Ordered— Stuart's Operations from June 25 through June 30

Jeb Stuart's column consisted of 5,600 cavalry, a few ambulances, and horse artillerists accompanied by six pieces of ordnance.[73] This assemblage set out from Salem heading east at 1:00 a.m. on Thursday, June 25, using Glasscock's Gap in Bull Run Mountain to move east of that acclivity along the Warrenton Turnpike.[74] Shortly after sunrise, following a march of only 12 miles, the Confederate horsemen approached the important road hub of Haymarket, a small town about ten miles west of Centreville and a few miles east of the mountain. There, John Esten Cooke, a member of Stuart's staff and a novelist of some talent, recalled a memorable sight: "Passing rapidly toward [Gum Springs], about eight hundred yards off, were the long lines of wagons and artillery; and behind these came on the dense blue masses of infantry, the sunshine lighting up their burnished bayonets." As Stuart later noted in his report, "[Winfield] Hancock's corps was *en route* through Hay Market [and moving] for Gum Springs."[75] Stuart, who rarely passed up an opportunity to harass the foe, ordered his six guns to unlimber and open fire. "I chose a good position," he recalled, "and opened . . . on his passing columns with good effect, scattering men, wagons, and horses in wild confusion." The artillery fire also exploded one caisson.

The effort triggered a prompt response from Federal artillery, which quickly unlimbered and returned fire. When infantry advanced in an attempt to drive away the irksome guns, Stuart realized that discretion was the better part of valor and ordered his guns to limber up and move off. The horse artillerists joined their comrades as they departed the Haymarket area—heading east.[76]

Within just a few hours Stuart had discovered that Hancock's Second Corps was marching *north* toward Gum Springs, along the exact route Stuart intended to take to reach Seneca Ford.[77] It was right then and there, at Haymarket on June 25, that Stuart encountered the "hindrance" which General Lee had admonished he must avoid. And the impediment was the most serious sort—an entire Federal corps. If Stuart followed Lee's instructions, he would have immediately turned his column around and doubled back across Bull Run Mountain, following whatever protected routes would have best facilitated his speedy crossing of the Potomac.

Stuart's early movement and action at Haymarket offer the ultimate clues as to how Generals Lee, Longstreet, and Stuart worked out the plan to maneuver the three cavalry brigades northward and, ultimately, how Stuart on his own *deviated* from that plan. In order to fully understand this, we must revisit the evening of June 22, when Longstreet communicated to Stuart a possible route of march northward. At that time, the position of the various formations of the Federal army, as they related to Longstreet's position near Ashby's Gap in the Blue Ridge Mountains, was as follows: Hancock's Second Corps was in the vicinity, primarily northeast, of Thoroughfare Gap; Sykes' Fifth Corps was at Aldie; Slocum's Twelfth Corps was at Leesburg, seven miles east of Edward's Ferry; Howard's Eleventh Corps was encamped on Goose Creek, seven miles south of Edwards Ferry; Reynolds' First Corps was at Guilford Station, south of the Potomac between Edward's Ferry and Seneca Ford; Sickles' Third Corps was at Centreville; and the army's headquarters, artillery reserve, and Sedgwick's Sixth Corps were encamped around Fairfax Court House.[78]

Two portions of Longstreet's June 22 letter to Stuart help us understand his mind-set and that of Lee.[79] It is important to keep in mind that both Longstreet and Lee were west of the Blue Ridge Mountains in the Shenandoah Valley. Two questions must be raised in order to fully understand what is being referenced here: First, where was the rear of the Confederate army at this time, and second, what was the route Stuart was to have taken in the rear of the Federal army? Since Longstreet's Confederates were peering east across Loudoun Valley towards the Federals, his rear was *west* of the Blue Ridge range, or in other words, the Shenandoah Valley. Confronting Longstreet were the Federal Second, Fifth, Twelfth, and Eleventh corps at Thoroughfare Gap, Aldie, Leesburg, and Goose Creek, respectively. The answer to the second question regarding Stuart's route in the rear of the Federals is provided by John Singleton Mosby, who reconnoitered on the night of June 23-24 between the widely separated Federal corps. Hooker's army, he later wrote in his memoirs, was "scattered through three counties in Virginia, with his right resting on the Potomac.

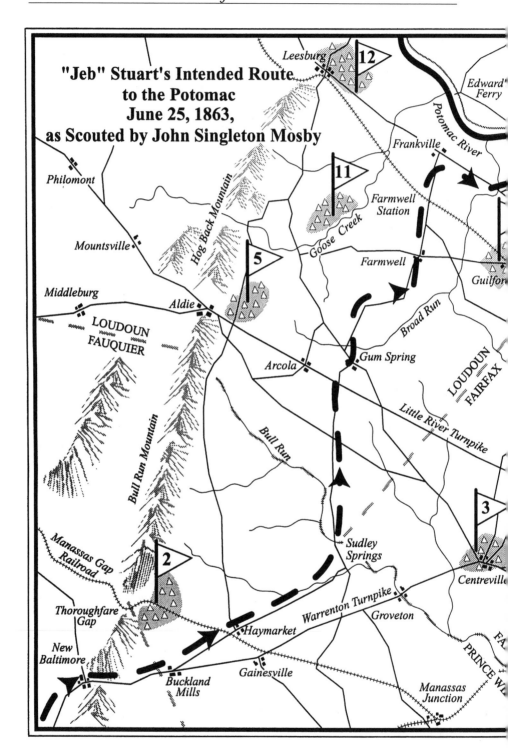

"Jeb" Stuart's Intended Route
to the Potomac
June 25, 1863,
as Scouted by John Singleton Mosby

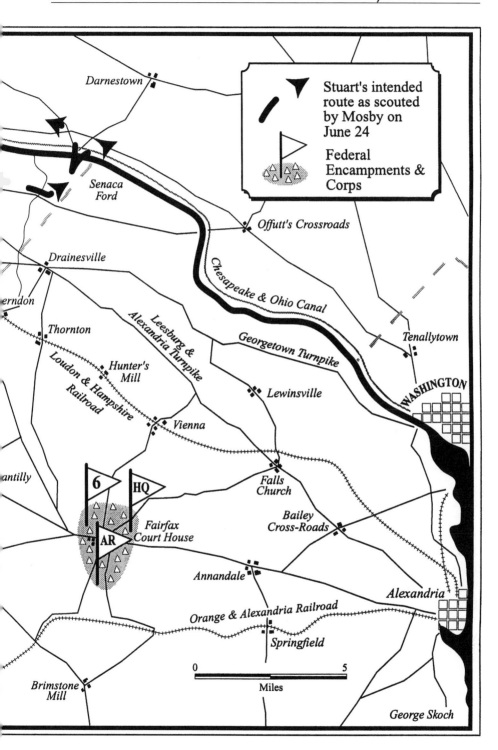

Darnestown

Stuart's intended
route as scouted
by Mosby on
June 24

Federal
Encampments &
Corps

Senaca
Ford

Offutt's Crossroads

Drainesville

Chesapeake & Ohio Canal

erndon

Leesburg & Alexandria Turnpike

Thornton

Georgetown Turnpike

Tenallytown

Loudon & Hampshire Railroad

Hunter's
Mill

WASHINGTON

Lewinsville

Vienna

antilly

6   HQ

Falls
Church

Bailey
Cross-Roads

AR

Fairfax
Court House

Annandale

Alexandria

Orange & Alexandria Railroad

Springfield

0   5

Miles

Brimstone
Mill

George Skoch

The plan for Stuart to pass *through* [emphasis added] Hooker's army was really a copy of the campaign of Marengo, when [Napoleon] Bonaparte crossed the Alps and cut the Austrian communications in Italy." According to Mosby, "it was known that the camps of the different [Federal] corps were so far apart that a column of cavalry could easily pass *between* [emphasis added] them."

"I was at headquarters when Stuart wrote his last dispatch to Lee," Mosby explained in greater detail,

> informing him of the route he would go, and sat by him when he was writing it—in fact, I dictated a large part of it. I had just returned from a scout inside the enemy's lines and brought the intelligence that induced Stuart to undertake to *pass through* [emphasis added] them. I had arrived from this scout early on the morning of June 24 and found that Stuart had just received the orders to join Ewell with three brigades and had been given discretion to *pass by the rear* [emphasis added] of the Union army.[80]

At first blush all this seems utterly confusing and contradictory. How could Stuart be "passing by the rear" of the enemy, as Longstreet's letter of June 22 states, or "pass around their army," as Lee writes, while at the same time "pass through Hooker's army," which would also "pass by the rear" of the Federal front lines, as Mosby recalls? However, they make perfect sense when the relative positions of Lee, Longstreet, the corps of the Federal army, and the route scouted by Mosby are taken into consideration. As it turns out, Stuart was to "pass around" the Federal Corps facing Longstreet, i.e., the Second, Fifth, Twelfth, and Eleventh corps, which was the same thing as "pass by the rear" of these troops. In order to do so, Stuart had to ride between the aforementioned Federal corps and the remainder of the Federal army known to be encamped many miles to the east (the First, Third, and Sixth corps). Thus, Stuart would "pass through" the Federal army, as Mosby declares, and at the same time be "passing by the rear" of the four enemy corps closest to the main body of the Confederate army beyond the Blue Ridge Mountains. Therefore, the route scouted and selected by Mosby ran as follows: Glasscock's Gap in Bull Run Mountain eastward along the Warrenton Turnpike, then north near Haymarket on the road to Gum Springs, through Loudoun County (probably following the road north to Farmwell and Farmwell Station), and then east—northeast to the Potomac crossing at Seneca Ford on the Potomac.[81] Stuart's surprise encounter with Hancock's Second Corps at Haymarket after Stuart turned north on the road leading to Gum Springs demonstrates that, as originally planned, Stuart was *attempting* to pass behind the several Federal corps opposite Longstreet and making up the front line of Hooker's army. When viewed in this logical manner, there is nothing unclear or conflicting in the descriptions of Stuart's ride.

After the encounter at Haymarket, however, Stuart deviated from the planned march route scouted by Mosby and approved by Lee. Instead of doubling back across Bull Run Mountain and heading north to effect a speedy passage over the Potomac and a juncture with Ewell, Stuart sent a message to Lee about Hancock's movement—a dispatch that never reached the commanding general—and then pushed Fitzhugh Lee's Brigade southeastward to reconnoiter towards the Manassas Gap Railroad depot of Gainesville. A halt was ordered at Buckland, where the brigades of Hampton and Chambliss camped for the remainder of June 25.[82]

Several factors support the conclusion that Stuart's actions deviated from what Lee expected him to do. First, as both Lee and Longstreet understood it, Stuart's trek was to be a rapid movement across the Potomac, where he would then contact Ewell and deploy his command on Ewell's right flank before the Federal army could react. Stuart's movement, therefore, was part of Lee's overall plan to steal a march on his enemy. Second, why would a veteran cavalry commander like Stuart ride northeast off the Warrenton Turnpike to reach Haymarket if his intention all along was to ride around the *entire* Federal host? In other words, Stuart would have never turned north to go to Haymarket, but would instead have taken a different road angling southeast in order to avoid Dan Sickles' Third Corps encamped at Centreville. Third, Mosby was not only a superb scout but an attorney, and thus certainly knew the difference between riding through—or between—different enemy corps and riding *around* the entire Federal army. According to the scout, the plan to "pass through" the idle Federals "was bold in conception and perfectly practicable in execution." It would also result in the Federal army's "transportation [being] destroyed and communications broken," which might seriously impact any attempt to pursue Lee's army into Pennsylvania. Mosby never suggested, advised, or intimated that Stuart undertake a ride around the entirety of the Federal host. In fact, Mosby was supposed to rendezvous with Stuart and his brigades where the juncture of the Haymarket to Gum Springs Road intersected the Little River Turnpike. When he arrived, however, all he found was the "head of Hancock's column . . . moving towards the Potomac." When he discovered the Yankees moving north along the same route he had scouted for Stuart, and heard Stuart's "cannon about Haymarket," Mosby realized the rendezvous would not take place. Prudently, the Confederate major retraced his "steps and went on to Pennsylvania through the Shenandoah Valley"—the very thing General Lee's restraining orders mandated Stuart do should he encounter "hindrance" or the Federals marching northward.[83]

All of this evidence considered in its totality—Lee's letters, Longstreet's correspondence, Mosby's scouting reports and memoirs, and Jeb Stuart's attempt to turn his command northward at Haymarket—presents clear and unmistakable proof that Stuart, in attempting to "pass by the rear" of the Federal troops on the eastern slopes of Bull Run Mountain, was an attempt to "pass through" the widely separated Federal corps. Thus, when Lee used the term "pass around their army," and Longstreet penned the phrase "passing by the rear," both generals were referring to the path scouted by Mosby which was to "pass through" the idle Federal corps nearest the Confederates. Neither Lee nor Longstreet implied, ordered, or gave

Stuart permission to embark on a route that would carry his command around the southern, eastern, and northeastern extremities of the entire Army of the Potomac.

Yet that is exactly what the gray cavalier proceeded to do. Stuart's confidence in himself and his men, coupled with his bruised ego, began to undermine the entire campaign. With his planned route to the Potomac blocked by Hancock's Second Corps, Stuart looked to that portion of Lee's orders instructing him to "doing them all the damage you can." In Stuart's mind, those words granted him the discretion to override all other considerations in Lee's letter and conduct a raid that would restore his glory and reputation. Lee, of course, intended this infliction of damage to take place during Stuart's planned route through the stationary enemy corps. With Hancock blocking his northward route at Haymarket, Stuart diverted his command south and east in order to fulfill his personal quest. Stuart not only ignored Lee's wishes and specific restraining orders, but also forgot or discounted the fact that there would be little or no forage available for his already weakened horses along a revised march route traversing some of the most war ravaged regions of Virginia. Stuart must have realized that his decision would lengthen his march by more than just the time needed to traverse the added distance, because precious time would be consumed stopping and searching for forage to feed his exhausted animals. Stuart's quest for glory was never more blinding.

Resuming the march early on the 26th, Stuart continued moving in a southeasterly direction below Broad Run and south of Manassas. Without observing any Federals, the cavaliers passed Brentsville and turned north before reaching Wolf Run Shoals on the Occoquan River, where Stuart stopped to graze his tired horses. By the time night fell on June 26, Stuart must have realized that his alternate and circuitous route, coupled with the weakened state of his animals, had placed him far behind where he needed to be. Had he double-backed from Haymarket and headed west across the Blue Ridge and then north down the better provisioned Shenandoah Valley, he would have been in a position to cross the Potomac at Shepherdstown on the evening of the 26th or early on the 27th. From there, he could have moved on to "feel the right of Ewell's troops." But Stuart and his horsemen were now in a far different situation. As Lieutenant Colonel William R. Carter of the 3rd Virginia Cavalry described it, the cavalry was in "miserably poor country . . . the armies having entirely consumed it," forcing Stuart to call early halts so his troopers had enough time to feed their horses. As a result, the cavalry column traversed only 35 miles in two days. And it was far removed from the rest of the Army of Northern Virginia, which was shuffling in the other direction.[84]

Stuart only compounded his problems by dispatching Fitzhugh Lee's Brigade further east on Saturday morning, June 27, to scout for the enemy, cut the telegraph, and tear up the railroad at Burke's Station. Once this was accomplished, the brigade was ordered to move north to rejoin the other two brigades beyond Hooker's old headquarters at Fairfax Station. East of that point at Annandale, Lee's troopers found the encampment Sedgwick's Sixth Corps had abandoned three days earlier on

June 24.[85] The commanding general's nephew pushed his weary men and horses beyond Fairfax Court House and Hunter's Mill to Dranesville, where locals informed him that Sedgwick's troops had passed through that morning in the direction of Edward's Ferry.[86]

While Fitzhugh Lee was toiling, Hampton and Chambliss followed Stuart northward toward the Orange and Alexandria Railroad at Fairfax Station, with Hampton's 1st North Carolina Cavalry leading the way. Perhaps overeager to see what prize awaited him, the man in the plumed hat rode ahead of his advance guard and was almost captured by an 86-man detachment consisting of Companies B and C of 11th New York Cavalry (also known as "Scott's Nine Hundred"). Galloping to Stuart's rescue, the North Carolinians killed or captured 26 of the New Yorkers and scattered the rest.[87] The column resumed its march and reaching Fairfax Court House "where, to the infinite cheer of hungry boys, several sutlers' shacks were found."[88] As the starving Southerners fell upon the abandoned Federal supplies, Stuart ordered the horses grazed in a nearby field and passed the next few hours contemplating his growing predicament.[89]

Without knowing where, exactly, the enemy was, Hampton and Chambliss resumed their march from Fairfax Court House. Stuart halted Chambliss' Brigade at Dranesville late in the afternoon of June 27, where Fitzhugh Lee rejoined them. Hampton, meanwhile, was dispatched to find a suitable ford across the mile-wide Potomac. Recent rains compounded Stuart's problems by raising the river level two feet above normal, making any crossing by horse artillery treacherous at best. After some delay, Hampton determined that Rowser's Ford was the best place to attempt a crossing.[90] The South Carolinian's regiments were the first to wade over shortly after midnight, followed by those of Fitz Lee and Chambliss. The horse artillerists took their turn next, breaking down the guns and lashing them to flat boards, and carrying the shells and powder above their heads as they waded across the strong currents. By 3:00 a.m. on June 28, Stuart's command was finally across the Potomac and standing on Maryland soil. It had taken the cavalryman four entire days to cross the Potomac, something Lee had been anxious for him to do as soon as possible after June 24.[91]

Following his belated crossing of the Potomac, Stuart let his worn and hungry animals rest and graze until late on the morning of June 28. When he resumed his march, Stuart lost more valuable time acting as though he was conducting a raid—which was *exactly* Stuart's mind set—rather than a time-sensitive mission to link up with Ewell in Pennsylvania. Instead of driving north, Stuart had his cavalrymen break a locked gate and ambush a dozen or so boats on the Chesapeake and Ohio Canal, which Stuart described as "the supplying medium of Hooker's army."[92]

Once this work was finished, Stuart claims to have "realized the importance of joining our army in Pennsylvania." Information, however, was "ascertained that Hooker was on the day previous [June 27] at Poolsville, and his army in motion for

"Secure the Crossing"

This Dale Gallon painting illustrates Southern horsemen securing a ford, just as Stuart's cavalry would have done along the Potomac River at Rowser's Ford on the night of June 27-28, 1863. *Courtesy Gallon Historical Art. Gettysburg. Pennsylvania.*

Frederick [Maryland]." Lee had informed Stuart in the letter of June 22 that "one column of Genl Ewell's army [corps] will probably move towards the Susquehanna by the Emmitsburg route; another by Chambersburg."[93] If the Federals were moving toward or already in Frederick, however, the road to Emmitsburg was blocked. That meant the only available route north towards the Susquehanna was the road to Hanover, from whence Stuart could either continue north in the direction of Harrisburg and Carlisle, or northeast to York.

The road to Hanover mandated a detour further east to Rockville, Maryland. Located on a direct line between Washington and Frederick, Rockville was squarely on the Federal army's existing line of supply. As the Confederates approached Rockville from the west, Stuart's scouts returned with word that a large Federal wagon train was moving up the road from Washington. And large it was. The eight-mile long train was a prize the hungry Confederate cavalry had never seen before, and would never see again. Yelling at the tops of their lungs, Stuart's adrenaline-charged troopers ran down the wagons, pursuing some of them for miles in the direction of the Federal capital. Most of the vehicles were stuffed with sorely needed oats and corn, some of which were immediately fed to undernourished Southern horses, while other wagons contained foodstuffs on which the lean troopers feasted; broken or overturned vehicles were torched. The captured wagons posed an immediate problem: should Stuart and his men load up with food, take along a few wagons to carry fodder for their horses and burn the balance, or drive the entire captured column of wagons with them, further slowing their rate of march? The decision came easily to Stuart, who was not about to abandon the symbol of his resurgent star, let alone something the Southern army was in great need of—more than 125 of the "best United States model wagons and splendid teams."[94]

The 400 Federal prisoners Stuart bagged with the wagons created another headache. What was he going to do with them? According to Henry McClellan, "At the urgent solicitation of [two of their] officers, Stuart consented to a parole, and the whole of the night was consumed at Brooksville and much time the next morning at Cooksville in accomplishing this business," which, as it turned out, was "a useless task." To McClellan's disgust, "the Federal authorities refused to acknowledge the parole, and returned officers and men immediately to duty." More precious hours had been frittered away.[95]

On the morning of June 29 Stuart headed his column and wagons north, lumbering 20 miles to Cookesville where a small Federal command was put to flight. The skirmish only served to further delay the column, which was additionally inconvenienced by the capture of more Federals. After slowly moving three more miles, Stuart finally reached the Baltimore and Ohio Railroad at Hood's Mill. There, he decided to pause yet again so his troopers could tear up the track while Fitzhugh Lee and his brigade made a two-mile detour to the east with orders to burn the B&O Railroad bridge at Sykesville.[96] The work further fatigued Stuart's already jaded men, who had few tools suitable for the task at hand. With the track torn up, telegraph wire cut, and the important bridge smoldering in ruins, the raiders took to their saddles and resumed their northward trek, moving without incident another 15 miles to Westminster, located on the main road from Baltimore to Gettysburg. Just outside Westminster at about 5:00 p.m., the Southerners clashed briefly with a detachment of Federal cavalry before pushing on a few miles more beyond the town, finally halting near Union Mills. The day's long hours and demanding exertions were compounded by the fact that many of Stuart's men had to stay up all night distributing food to their exhausted and enervated animals.[97]

Before dawn on the last day of June, scouts returned with word that enemy cavalry was operating northwest of Union Mills just across the Pennsylvania line at Littletown.[98] Stuart, it will be recalled, had received reports two days earlier that Hooker's army had crossed over the Potomac at Edwards Ferry and was at or near Frederick. If Pleasonton's cavalry was now around Littletown, it would have been logical for someone as experienced as Stuart to conclude the enemy horsemen were screening a northward march for Hooker's infantry columns. Littletown was less than a day's march southeast of Gettysburg.

Ironically, Stuart had a better idea of where Hooker's infantry might be than where Ewell's Corps was operating. With Chambliss' small brigade in the van, the Southern horsemen left Union Mills on the morning of June 30 and continued riding north toward Hanover, a distance of 12 miles. Stuart caught sight of Hanover at about 9:30 a.m., and the Federal cavalry guarding the town shortly thereafter. Troopers of the 2nd North Carolina Cavalry put spur to horse flesh and charged. Their sudden thrust met and threw back a portion of Elon Farnsworth's brigade. The brisk running engagement swirled through the streets of the town, where prisoners were taken and wagons and ambulances captured. Pistols and sabers were freely used in the melee. Farnsworth skillfully rallied his scattered troopers and counterattacked, driving the Southern horsemen out of Hanover. The spirited Federal thrust caught Stuart by surprise. Only the strength and nimbleness of his bay mare, Virginia, saved him the humiliation of capture when she jumped a wide ditch to carry her owner out of danger.[99] Thoroughly in his element, Stuart calmly ordered up his six artillery pieces to help stabilize the situation, largely ending the sharp affair that had cost Stuart some 117 killed, wounded, and missing. Federal losses totaled 215 for all categories. Henry McClellan later complained that Chambliss' North Carolinians were not properly supported, and he was right. Hampton's regiments were far to the rear behind Stuart's booty train—which was further encumbered by almost 400 more prisoners, about the same number he had earlier stopped to parole—while Fitz Lee's men were covering the flanks of the captured wagons to prevent an attack from the direction of Littletown. A quick and overwhelming victory might have netted Stuart enough captives to confirm where the Southern infantry had been seen or reported, which in turn would have dictated his line of march. Instead, Stuart learned only that Federal cavalry under Brigadier General Judson Kilpatrick was operating somewhere west of his position.[100]

If Stuart considered burning his captured wagons (which now totaled 200 following the skirmish at Hanover) in order to free his brigades for swift maneuver and combat, he never admitted it. Instead, he sought out the best route over which to direct his lumbering column far enough *away* from the Federal cavalry to protect it. "My numerous skirmish[es] had greatly diminished—almost exhausted—my supply of ammunition," Stuart explained in his campaign report. His situation was so desperate that he risked running out of cartridges if his enemy forced him into a major engagement.[101] Left with little choice, Stuart turned his mounts and wagons northeast toward Jefferson, about seven miles distant. At some point during June 30—whether before or after he made this decision to march to Jefferson—Stuart was handed captured Yankee newspapers claiming that Jubal Early's Division of Ewell's Second Corps had been in York, Pennsylvania, just two days earlier. But where was it now?[102]

An exceptionally dark night blanketed the triumvirate of exhausted Confederate cavalry brigades and their wheeled charges as they walked and rolled away from Hanover. The night's blackness could not have improved the troopers' glum moods, and served as an apt metaphor for how little Stuart knew about the whereabouts of the rest of the Southern army. The column reached Jefferson without incident before heading north for Dover, another dozen miles away. The spent troopers, Stuart later wrote, "slept in the saddle, their faithful animals keeping the road unguided. In some instances they fell from their horses, overcome with physical fatigue and sleepiness."[103]

This was the state of Stuart's command as midnight approached on June 30. For six days the cavalier had been out of contact with his army, even though Lee's orders on this point had been clear ("In either case, after crossing the [Potomac] river, you must move on & feel the right of Ewell's troops, collecting information, provisions, &c.") Only once during that period—the same day that he had begun his raid—had Stuart bothered to send Lee a dispatch that would never arrive. Instead of being in position to shield Lee's vulnerable columns and provide him with valuable intelligence information, Stuart had worn out the army's three finest cavalry brigades on an unauthorized raid that violated his orders. It would take days of rest to get them back in their normal fighting trim. In return, he had captured 200 wagons, 72 ambulances, 3,000 horses, 1,200 mules, and 746 officers and men (half of whom had been paroled).[104] With the enemy close at hand and the whereabouts of his own army still a mystery, one wonders when Stuart anticipated he would be able to give his command the rest it so desperately needed. The gallant cavalier, whose exploits had made him a legend in his own time—he was the very embodiment of the romantic chivalric myth the South held so dear—was failing miserably in the most important assignment Lee had ever given him. And he knew it. He could not have helped but have known it.

*   *   *

After an exhausting night ride, Jeb Stuart probably welcomed the day's first light. It was now July 1, 1863. His decision to disobey Lee's orders and embark on a ride around the entire Federal army was about to manifest repercussions that would resound to this hour.

Notes for Chapter 3

1. Edward Porter Alexander, *Fighting for the Confederacy: The Personal Recollections of General Edward Porter Alexander*, edited by Gary W. Gallagher (Chapel Hill, 1989) p. 222.

2. Stuart's report of Brandy Station is found in *OR* 27, pt. 2, pp. 679-685. There is no current or thorough book length treatment of this important cavalry battle. Th only book available is Fairfax Downey, *Clash of Cavalry: The Battle of Brandy Station, June 9, 1863* (New York, 1959), which is outdated in many respects. See also, Edward Longacre, *The Cavalry at Gettysburg* (Lincoln, 1993), which contains a substantial amount of information on this topic.

3. *OR* 27, pt. 2, p. 687, 718-719; pt. 1, p. 905.

4. *OR* vol. 21, pp. 1054, 1086 and 1102; Charles S. Grunder and Brandon H. Beck, *The Second Battle of Winchester, June 12-15, 1863* (Lynchburg, 1989), pp. 8-10.

5. *OR* 27, pt. 2, pp. 41 and 51.

6. *OR* 27, pt. 2, p. 43, 93 and 124.

7. Two of Jenkins' companies under Major Harry Gilmor were ambushed neared Middletown on June 12. Although Gilmor escaped, the majority of the two companies,

including Captain William Independence Rasin, were captured. This incident helped provide Milroy with a false sense of security and a belief that he was facing only a minor cavalry raiding party. *OR* 27, pt 2, pp. 50-51 and 69; Longacre, *The Cavalry at Gettysburg*, pp. 94-95.

8. Coddington, *The Gettysburg Campaign*, p. 88.

9. *OR* 27, pt. 2, p. 50.

10. Flag Fort was also called Main Fort. Grunder and Beck, *The Second Battle of Winchester*, pp. 15-16.

11. *OR* 27, pt. 2, p. 440; Terry L. Jones, *Lee's Tigers: The Louisiana Infantry in the Army of Northern Virginia* (Baton Rouge, 1987), p. 158.

12. *OR* 27, pt. 2, pp. 440-441; 459-464.

13. James P. Gannon, *Irish Rebels, Confederate Tigers: A History of the 6th Louisiana Volunteer Infantry, 1861-1865* (Campbell, 1997), pp. 169-18, provides an excellent account of the Second Battle of Winchester and the role of the Louisiana troops in that action. See also, Terry L. Jones, *The Civil War Memoirs of Captain William J. Seymour: Reminiscences of a Louisiana Tiger* (Baton Rouge, 1991), p. 61; Jones, *Lee's Tigers,* p. 159.

14. Robert K. Krick, *Lee's Colonels* (Dayton, 1991), p. 214. According to Stonewall Jackson's star artillerist, Stapelton Crutchfield (who lost his leg at Chancellorsville and was killed at the end of the war at Sayler's Creek), Hilary Jones was "a moderately good officer; no very strong points, nor yet any objectionable ones." Jones enjoyed his finest hour at Second Winchester.

15. *OR* 27, pt. 2, p. 61, 74, 146, 462, 477-478.

16. *OR* 27, pt. 2, pp. 477-478.

17. *OR* 27, pt. 2, p. 59, 61 and 146.

18. *OR* 27, pt. 2, p. 74; Jones, *Lee's Tigers*, p. 161.

19. *OR* 27, pt. 2, p. 441.

20. Jones, *Lee's Tigers*, p. 162, *OR* 27, pt. 2, pp. 71, 441. Major M. Kerwin, commanding the 13th Pennsylvania Cavalry, states in his report (*OR* 27, pt. 2, p. 71) that the regiment arrived in Harpers Ferry with 301 men and 20 officers, after suffering a loss of 333 officers and men—more than half the regiment. Fragments of other cavalry companies also escaped into the night.

21. *OR* 27, pt. 2, p. 456 and 464.

22. *OR* 27, pt. 2, p. 456. Five more 3-inch Ordnance rifles were captured from the Federals by General Robert Rodes at Martinsburg. These pieces were also exchanged. Therefore, even before the Second Corps crossed the Potomac River, some 26 Federal pieces had been incorporated into its artillery battalions (22 3-inch Ordnance rifles and four 20-pounder Parrotts), along with abundant quantities of ammunition. For example, the Rockbridge Virginia Artillery "abandoned two blockade-run British Blakelys" and took two of the captured 20-pounder Parrotts so that the battery had the same type and caliber pieces "for the first time in the war." Clifford Dowdey, *The Land They Fought For: The Story of the South as the Confederacy 1832-1865*, p. 267.

23. *OR* 27, pt. 2, pp. 53, 442. Milroy lists his total captured and missing at 4,000.

24. Robert Stiles, *Four Years Under Marse Robert* (New York, 1903), p. 415.

25. William S. White, *Richmond Howitzer's Battalion* (Richmond, 1880), p. 185.

26. Donald Pfanz, *Richard S. Ewell: A Soldier's Life* (Chapel Hill, 1998), p. 290.

27. Pfanz, *Richard S. Ewell*, p. 290.

28. Fitzhugh Lee, "A Review of the First Two Days' Operations at Gettysburg and a Reply to General Longstreet," *Southern Historical Society Papers,* vol. 5, p. 163.

29. *OR* 27, pt. 3, p. 886; Dowdey and Manarin, *The Wartime Papers of R. E. Lee,* number 473; *OR* 27, pt. 3, pp. 880-882. It was about this time, on June 20, that Brigadier General Micah Jenkins, officially part of George Pickett's Division but temporarily assigned to Harvey Hill's department in North Carolina, had begged Hill "as a personal and great favor that you . . . arrange with [Adjutant] General Cooper to send my brigade . . . to Lee's army." *OR* 27, pt. 3, p. 908. Also, see Jenkins' letter to Cooper of July 14 on pp. 1004-1005. Hill refused the request. It is interesting to note, however, that two weeks after Gettysburg, Robert Ransom, who had been forcibly estranged from Lee's army and had just taken command of Hill's former Department of North Carolina and Southern Virginia (in late May this department had been enlarged to include Petersburg, Virginia, and the southern approaches to Richmond), requested that Jenkins' "first-rate" troops "sent to the Army of Northern Virginia." *OR* 27, pt. 3, p. 1005.

30. *OR* 27, pt. 3, p. 910.

31. *OR* 27, pt. 3, pp. 925-926.

32. *OR* 27, pt. 3, pp. 924-925.

33. *OR* 27, pt. 3, pp. 931-932; Dowdey and Manarin, *The Wartime Papers of R. E. Lee,* numbers 496 and 497.

34. *OR* 27, pt. 3, p. 944.

35. Freeman, *Lee's Lieutenants*, 3, p. 19. A North Carolina civilian echoed the *Examiner's* sentiment. The more we hear of the battle at Brandy Station," wrote the woman, "the more disgraceful is the surprise." Peter Carmichael, "Brandy Station," in Richard N. Current, ed., *Encyclopedia of the Confederacy*, 4 vols. (New York, 1993), vol.1, p. 211.

36. *Richmond Dispatch,* June 11, 12, 13, and 18, 1863; *Richmond Whig*, June 17, 1863.

37. Freeman, *Lee's Lieutenants*, 3, p. 19; *OR* 27, pt. 2, p. 691.

38. *OR* 27, pt. 1, pp. 171-172, 193 and 922; *OR* 27, pt. 2, p. 313 Fitzhugh Lee, "A Review of the First Two Days' Operations at Gettysburg and a Reply to General Longstreet," *Southern Historical Society Papers,* vol. 5, p. 164. Confederate losses of 510 combatants, as recorded in *OR* 27, pt. 2, pp. 712-713, are for the two weeks of June 10 through 24. Therefore, the losses for the five-days running action discussed here were less than half those suffered by the Federals. Descriptions of these five days of action may be found in Longacre, *The Cavalry at Gettysburg*, pp. 103-133; and Mark Nesbitt, *Saber and Scapegoat* (Mechanicsburg, 1994), pp. 43-56. The best treatment of these actions is found in Robert O'Neill, *The Cavalry Battles of Aldie, Middleburg, and Upperville* (Lynchburg, 1993).

39. Henry B. McClellan, *I Rode with Jeb Stuart: The Life and Campaigns of Major General J.E.B. Stuart* (New York, 1994 reprint of the 1958 edition from the 1885 original), p. 314.

40. See specific entries in O'Neil, *Aldie, Middleburg and Upperville*, for more information on this topic and the running battles that took place during this period.

41. John W. Thomason, Jr., *Jeb Stuart* (New York, 1930), p. 412.

42. *OR* 27, pt. 2, p. 316 and 692; Charles Marshall, *An Aide-de-Camp of Lee*, Sir Frederick Maurice, ed. (Boston, 1927), p. 201.

43. John Mosby, "The Confederate Cavalry in the Gettysburg Campaign" *Battles and Leaders of the Civil War*, 4 vols. (New York, 1887-88), vol. 3, p. 251.

44. *OR* 27, pt. 2, p. 691; pt. 3, p. 913.

45. *OR* 27, pt. 3, pp. 905-906. Rodes' Division of Ewell's Corps crossed into Pennsylvania on the afternoon of June 22. Pfanz, *Richard S. Ewell*, p. 294.

46. Charles Marshall, *An Aide de Camp of Lee*, pp. 201-202.

47. *OR* 27, pt. 3, p. 913; Dowdey and Manarin, *The Wartime Papers of R. E. Lee,* number 488.

48. *OR* 27, pt. 3, p. 914; Dowdey and Manarin, *The Wartime Papers of R. E. Lee,* number 489.

49. *OR* 27, pt. 3, pp. 914-915; Dowdey and Manarin, *The Wartime Papers of R. E. Lee,* number 490.

50. *OR* 27, pt. 3, p. 915; James Longstreet, *From Manassas to Appomattox* (Bloomington, 1960), pp. 342-343.

51. *OR* 27, pt. 3, p. 915.

52. Charles Marshall, *An Aide-de-Camp of Lee*, pp. 206-207. Most accounts dealing with Stuart's Gettysburg orders gloss over the fact that Marshall *personally* discussed them with Stuart. General Longstreet, in *From Manassas to Appomattox*, p. 342, emphasizes that the commanders—Lee, Stuart, and himself—were on the same page when it came to what Stuart's orders required. "All of which General Stuart understood as well as I did," wrote Longstreet. "Especially did he know that *my orders were that he [Stuart] should ride on the right of my column, as originally designed*, to the Shepherdstown crossing [emphasis in the original]."

53. *OR* 27, pt. 3, p. 923; Dowdey and Manarin, *The Wartime Papers of R. E. Lee,* number 492.

54. *OR* 27, pt. 2, pp. 357 and 691.

55. *OR* 27, pt. 1, pp. 172 and 615-616.

56. *OR* 27, pt. 3, p. 913; Dowdey and Manarin, *The Wartime Papers of R. E. Lee,* number 488.

57. *OR* 27, pt. 3, p. 913; Dowdey and Manarin, *The Wartime Papers of R. E. Lee,* number 488.

58. *OR* 27, pt. 3, p. 913; Dowdey and Manarin, *The Wartime Papers of R. E. Lee,* number 488.

59. *OR* 27, pt. 3, p. 915.

60. *OR* 27, pt. 1, pp. 788, 796-797, 803; pt. 2, p. 297; Dowdey and Manarin, *The Wartime Papers of R. E. Lee,* number 495. This letter was written to President Davis.

61. Freeman, *R. E. Lee*, 3, pp. 44-45.

62. Mosby, "The Confederate Cavalry in the Gettysburg Campaign," p. 251.

63. Stuart apologists claim that this is what Lee was ordering. For an example of this strained interpretation, see Mark Nesbitt, *Saber and Scapegoat,* pp. 57-71.

64. Douglas Southall Freeman missed the point of Lee's sentence as well when he wrote that Lee had given Stuart authority to "ride around the Federal army" only if it was on the move! Freeman, *R. E. Lee*, 3, pp. 547-551.

65. Freeman, *R. E. Lee*, 3, p. 549.

66. See *Historical Times Illustrated Encyclopedia of the Civil War*, Patricia L. Faust, ed. (New York, 1986), pp. 728-729, for a general description of this operation.

67. John S. Mosby, *Mosby's War Reminiscences* (Camden, 1996), pp. 172-173.

68. It can also be posited that the way this sentence was constructed—especially when compared to Lee's letter of the 22nd to Stuart—meant that Stuart was *not* to attempt any serious "collecting [of] information, provisions, etc." until he had made contact with Ewell.

69. Some Stuart defenders point to his actions in June 1862, when he took part of his cavalry on the famous "Ride Around McClellan," as being analogous to what Lee ordered him to do in the Gettysburg Campaign. Unfortunately, these advocates overlook two crucial points. First, the June 1862 operational situation and its strategic implications were totally different from those that existed in June 1863. Second, and more important, Lee's orders to Stuart in June 1863 in no way resembled those authorizing his "Ride Around McClellan" a year earlier. For more information, compare Lee's June 11, 1862, orders to Stuart in Dowdey and Manarin, *The Wartime Papers of R. E. Lee,* number 202, against Lee's June 22 and 23, 1863, directives in numbers 488 and 492.

70. John Elting, ed., *West Point Atlas of American Wars,* 2 vols. (New York, 1959), 1, text to map 94. A recent example that embodies the argument employed by Stuart defenders is found in Mark Nesbitt, *Saber and Scapegoat*, pp. 57-71; another is Alan Nolan, "R. E. Lee and July 1 at Gettysburg," in Gary Gallagher, ed., *The First Day at Gettysburg: Essays on Confederate and Union Leadership* (Kent, 1992), pp. 14-20. Nolan is particularly hard on Lee, although his conclusions, like Nesbitt's, are based on an incomplete examination of available evidence and an imperfect appreciation of the situation that existed vis-a-vis the participants of the controversy.

71. McClellan, *I Rode with Jeb Stuart,* p. 316. *OR* 27, pt. 1, pp. 723, 788, 790, 798, 803; Mosby, *Mosby's War Reminiscences*, pp. 172-176.

72. *OR* 27, pt. 2, p. 692. When W. H. F. "Rooney" Lee was wounded at Brandy Station, the brigade's senior colonel, John Chambliss of the 13th Virginia Cavalry, assumed temporary command of the brigade.

73. The horse artillery consisted of Captain James Breathed's 1st Stuart Virginia Horse Artillery with four 3-inch Ordnance rifles, reinforced by a section of 12-pounder Napoleons from Captain William M. McGregor's 2nd Stuart Virginia Horse Artillery. Fitzhugh Lee, "A Review of the First Two Days' Operations at Gettysburg and a Reply to General Longstreet," *Southern Historical Society Papers,* vol. 5, p. 165; *OR* 27, pt. 2, p. 692; John Esten Cooke, *Wearing of the Gray* (Bloomington, 1959), pp. 235, 241, 242 and 245; McClellan, *I Rode with Jeb Stuart,* p. 337; and Gettysburg National Military Park Tablets.

74. *OR* 27, pt. 2, p. 692; Lieutenant Colonel William R. Carter, CSA, *Sabres, Saddles, and Spurs,* edited by Walbrook D. Swank, Colonel USAF (Ret.) (Shippensburg, 1998), p. 71.

75. Cooke, *Wearing of the Gray,* p. 230; *OR* 27, pt. 2, p. 692.

76. *OR* 27, pt. 2, p. 692; Cooke, *Wearing of the Gray,* pp. 230-231.

77. *OR* 27, pt. 2, p. 692.

78. *OR* 27, pt. 1, pp. 788, 790, 798 and 803; pt. 3, pp. 171, 173, 226, 266, 271, 281, 286, 289 and 307.

79. *OR* 27, pt. 3, p. 915.

80. John S. Mosby, *Mosby's Memoirs* (Nashville, 1995 reprint of the originally published work in 1917), pp. 215-216.

81. Mosby, *Mosby's War Reminiscences*, pp. 172-174.

82. *OR* 27, pt. 2, p. 692; Longacre, *The Cavalry at Gettysburg*, p. 153. Longacre states that Stuart selected "a bivouac amid a field of clover."

83. Mosby, *Mosby's War Reminiscences*, pp. 178-180. One can assume that Mosby's ride north into southern Pennsylvania was a continuation of his search for Stuart , with whom he was supposed to have formed a junction near Haymarket. If so, Mosby was searching for the cavalier in the area where Mosby believed he should have been operating. Mosby's biographer claims Mosby was seeking Lee. Kevin Siepel, *Rebel: The Life and Times of John Singleton Mosby* (New York, 1983), p. 96. General Longstreet claims in no uncertain terms that Stuart intentionally violated orders he clearly understood. "So our plans," writes Longstreet, "adopted after deep study, were suddenly given over to gratify the youthful cavalryman's wish for a nomadic ride." Longstreet, *From Manassas to Appomattox*, p. 343.

84. Carter, *Sabres, Saddles, and Spurs*, pp. 71-72.

85. *OR* 27, pt. 1, p. 692.

86. *OR* 27, pt. 2, p. 693.

87. *OR* 27, pt. 1, p. 1037. Only 18 New Yorkers made it back to friendly lines.

88. Freeman, *Lee's Lieutenants*, vol. 3, p. 64.

89. *OR* 27, pt. 2, p. 693; Longacre, *The Cavalry at Gettysburg*, p. 154.

90. McClellan, *I Rode with Jeb Stuart,* p. 323.

91. *OR* 27, pt. 2, p. 693. Lee's June 23 orders had reached Stuart during the early morning hours of June 24.

92. *OR* 27, pt. 2, p. 694.

93. *OR* 27, pt. 2, p. 694.

94. *OR* 27, pt. 2, p. 694; Cooke, *Wearing of the Gray,* p. 237, states that there were "almost 200 wagons—new, fresh-painted, drawn each by six sleek mules." According to Cooke, the Confederates found out that the wagon train was called the "Reserve Forage Train" of the Department at Washington, which was used to collect forage.

95. McClellan, *I Rode with Jeb Stuart,* pp. 325-326.

96. *OR* 27, pt. 2, p. 695; McClellan, *I Rode with Jeb Stuart,* p. 326.

97. *OR* 27, pt. 2, p. 695; McClellan, *I Rode with Jeb Stuart,* pp. 326-327.

98. *OR* 27, pt. 2, p. 695.

99. McClellan, *I Rode with Jeb Stuart,* p. 328; *OR* 27, pt. 2, p. 695; Longacre, *The Cavalry at Gettysburg*, pp. 174-178; James Ewell Brown Stuart IV, handout accompanying his speech "Jeb Stuart—The Making of the Man," at the *Confederate History Symposium: Confederate Horse,* April 1, 2000, Hill College, Hillsboro, Texas.

100. *OR* 27, pt. 2, p. 696.

101. *OR* 27, pt. 2, p. 696.

102. *OR* 27, pt. 2, p. 707. Stuart's report for the Gettysburg Campaign does not specify what date he received the newspapers. According to Freeman, *Lee's Lieutenants*, 3, p. 68, n88: "Early entered York on the 28th . . . no available newspapers that could have fallen into Stuart's hands during the forenoon of the 29th carried any report of Early's arrival at York. The *National Intelligencer* (Washington) of June 29, p. 3, col. 4, stated that Early had reached

the railroad between York and Hanover. That afternoon, the *Evening Bulletin* (Philadelphia) p. 2, col. 1, announced that Early was at Gettysburg. On the morning of the 30th, the *Philadelphia Inquirer,* p. 1, col. 3, and the *National Republican* (Washington) p. 1, col. 4, placed Early at York."

103. *OR* 27, pt. 2, p. 696; David Gregg McIntosh, "Review of the Gettysburg Campaign," *Southern Historical Society Papers*, vol. 37, p. 96.

104. *OR* 27, pt. 2, pp. 694-696; Carter, *Sabres, Saddles, and Spurs*, p. 77.

Chapter 4

"I Hope With These Advantages to Accomplish Some Signal Result and to End the War"

General Lee Concentrates the Army Around Gettysburg

"At the commencement of a campaign, to advance or not to advance is a matter for grave consideration, but when once the offensive has been assumed, it must be sustained to the last extremity." —Napoleon[1]

"An army ought only to have one line of operation. This should be preserved with care, and never abandoned but in the last extremity." —Napoleon[2]

"Roads that lead from an army's position back to the main sources of [supply] have two purposes. In the first instance they are lines of communication serving to maintain an army, and in the second they are lines of retreat."
—Major General Carl von Clausewitz[3]

"Co-equal with the security of flanks, the maintenance and full use of the line of communications to the rear are of major concern to the commander."
—Brigadier General S. L. A. Marshall[4]

hile his Second Corps comrades were planning and then reaping victory at Winchester, Robert Rodes was marching his division north toward the Potomac River. Screened by Albert Jenkins' cavalry, Rodes passed through Berryville on June 13 and tramped on to Martinsburg the next day. By June 16 his men were in Williamsport, looking across the wide river into Maryland. General Ewell and his remaining pair of divisions under Jubal Early and Edward Johnson joined Rodes there two days later. The next morning, June 19, Ewell's infantry were ordered to begin crossing over. Virtually unopposed, the Confederate column moved up the agricultural breadbasket known as the Cumberland Valley. By June 24 both Rodes and Johnson were gathered around Chambersburg, Pennsylvania; three days later they occupied Carlisle while Early's Division marched east for York.[5]

Powell Hill's and James Longstreet's men were not far behind. After passing through Hill's hometown of Culpeper on June 17, the new Third Corps leader drove his infantry under a suffocating sun over the Blue Ridge through Chester's Gap. On June 23, the commanding general himself joined Hill as his divisions marched past Berryville and Shepherdstown. Longstreet arrived the following day and the three generals discussed the campaign's progress while a steady rain beat a drumbeat on Lee's headquarter's tent. Over the next two days long gray columns of men crossed over the Potomac under a confident verbal umbrella of yelling, screaming, and song. Hill's men conquered the muddy roads around Hagerstown, Maryland, without incident. On June 26, they arrived in Chambersburg, Pennsylvania, marched east a few miles, and went into camp near Fayetteville. Longstreet reached Chambersburg the following day.[6]

General Lee was pleased with the progress of the campaign. His infantry was largely closed up, Hooker had not interfered with the movement, and supplies were being gathered in the lush Cumberland Valley. The absent trio of cavalry brigades caused him some concern since he has not yet heard from Stuart, but on June 25, his missing brigades of infantry languishing in North Carolina and elsewhere bred similar unease. Lee wrote President Davis twice that day, once from the southern side of the Potomac opposite Williamsport, and again from that town after crossing over the river. After discussing a number of other issues, Lee got to the point of his letter: "I have not sufficient troops to maintain my communications [with Virginia], and therefore have to abandon them. I think I can throw Genl Hooker's army across the Potomac and draw troops from the South, embarrassing their plan of campaign in a measure, if I can do nothing more and have to return." The implication of the general's dispatch could not have been lost on Davis: if Lee was not reinforced, he could not long remain north of Potomac. Lee reminded the president that "it is incumbent upon us to call forth all our energies," and urged him to call into the field the valuable troops Lee had long been petitioning for—formations "which Genls [Harvey] Hill & Elzey think cannot be spared." At the least, pleaded Lee, these men should be formed into an army, "even in effigy," around Culpeper Court House to help divert Federal attention from the Army of Northern Virginia, thereby taking some of the pressure off his invading Confederates.[7]

Lee's second letter of the day came as close to lecturing Davis as he could without crossing the line of propriety. "So strong is my conviction of the necessity of activity on our part in military affairs," he began, "that you will excuse my adverting to the subject again, notwithstanding what I have said in my previous letter of today." Lee then explained the principle that all great captains knew about waging war with numerically inferior forces: "It seems to me that we cannot afford to keep our troops awaiting possible movements of the enemy, but that our true policy is, as far as we can, so to employ our own forces as to give occupation to his at points of our selection."[8]

The general's longstanding concerns and pleas were being ignored in Richmond when he left Williamsport that Friday morning on June 26. His ride carried him across the narrow western stretch of Maryland to Hagerstown, where he turned north and crossed the Pennsylvania state line for the first time since the war began.[9] Female admirers gathered along his route, some asking for locks of hair from the aging general who was already a legend. Lee and his small entourage continued riding northward towards Chambersburg, where he arrived that afternoon. After a meeting with Powell Hill, Lee had his headquarters pitched on the east side of town in a small grove of trees formerly known as Shetter's Woods.[10]

Even before the commanding general crossed the Mason-Dixon Line on June 26, the first fruits of the Confederate advance were hoofing it south on the way to Dixie. Long trains composed of thousands of well fed horses and fat beef cattle procured by Lee's agents were being driven across the Potomac and up the Shenandoah Valley deep into Virginia. The supply of fresh horses especially interested Confederate quartermasters of the artillery battalions and cavalry arm. These officers lost little time exchanging their tired and malnourished animals for Pennsylvania Percherons and Conestogas. As the Southern soldiers soon learned, however, the large animals were not well suited to hauling field artillery and other mobile equipment; the guns were better served by keeping the hard-muscled little Virginia horses and increasing their food supply.[11]

The matter of feeding the army's draft animals was a serious consideration, but sustaining the half-starved and ill-clothed men in the ranks was finally less of a concern than usual. For the first time in a long time, Lee's veterans were able to eat their fill and send what they could not consume back to Virginia. Brigadier General John Brown Gordon, one of Ewell's brigade commanders, expressed the anticipation of the army's lean warriors this way: "The hungry hosts of Israel did not look across Jordan to the vine-clad hills of Canaan with more longing eyes than did Lee's braves contemplate the yellow grainfields of Pennsylvania beyond the Potomac."[12] Usually empty knapsacks were stuffed with food and the landscape picked clean of livestock. By the time Lee arrived in Chambersburg, army quartermasters had already amassed a mountain of supplies from the bountiful countryside.[13]

Full stomachs served to augment soaring Confederate morale. The Army of Northern Virginia impressed Arthur Fremantle, a foreign observer and lieutenant colonel with the Coldstream Guards. "They marched very well, and there was no attempt at straggling," he remarked, "quite a different state of things from [Joe] Johnston's men in Mississippi." The Englishman also observed that the high-stepping men of Lafayette McLaws' Division were "well shod and efficiently clothed," which only served to bolster their good humor. "All the men seem in the highest spirits, and were cheering and yelling most vociferously."[14]

Fremantle's comments were confirmed by Dorsey Pender, the longstanding veteran brigade leader now in charge of the Light Division, Powell Hill's Third Corps. Writing to his wife on June 28, the North Carolina major general noted, "Our men seem to be in the spirit and feel confident. I never saw troops march as ours do. They will go 15 or 20 miles a day without having a straggler, and whoop and yell on all occasions. I wish we could meet Hooker and have the matter settled at once."[15] First Corps division leader John Bell Hood remembered how his disciplined and excited men waded the Potomac and moved into Maryland while the bands played "Dixie." "Never before, nor since," Hood wrote, "have I witnessed such intense enthusiasm as that which prevailed throughout the entire Confederate Army."[16] This sentiment was echoed by his men. "We now have seventy five or eighty thousand as good troops as ever shouldered a musket [and] confident of victory," wrote J. Mark Smither, 5th Texas Infantry, to his mother on June 28. "I think wherever we meet the Yankees our country need not fear anything."[17]

Two Engineers Study a Map

After establishing his headquarters at Chambersburg, Lee set about assessing the relative positions of the different corps of his army. As he studied his maps, the student of military history may have recalled one of Napoleon's guiding principles: "The distances permitted between corps of an army upon the march must be governed by the localities, by circumstances, and by the object in view."[18] Circumstances, at least in this part of the campaign, called for Lee's army to gather as many supplies as possible, which was being done in several localities. His three infantry corps were deployed in an arc stretching across lower Pennsylvania. Longstreet and Hill, camped around Chambersburg, formed the southwestern corner of the crescent. Thirty miles to the northeast was Carlisle, where two of Ewell's three divisions (Rodes and Johnson) were resting. Southeast of Carlisle about 28 miles was the town of York and the remaining Second Corps formation under Jubal Early, less Gordon's Brigade, which was a short march east at Wrightsville along the Susquehanna River. With Jenkin's raiders, augmented by Lieutenant Colonel Elijah V. White's 35th Virginia Cavalry Battalion, working with Ewell and threatening Harrisburg from below, and Imboden's troopers covering the army's western flank in near South Mountain, Lee turned his attention "to the object in view": preparing the Army of Northern Virginia for a much anticipated opportunity to strike the enemy a serious blow.[19]

As the commanding general was mulling matters over in his tent that busy last Friday of June, an officer well advanced in years arrived at headquarters seeking an

Isaac Ridgeway Trimble
(1802-1888)

One of the Army of Northern Virginia's excellent combat generals, Isaac Trimble was not utilized to his full potential during the Gettysburg Campaign. Some modern historians have minimized his recollections of the invasion and assert that Lee viewed him as a pest. This view is wholly unsupported by the evidence.

Library of Congress

audience with Lee. One of the elders of the army, Isaac Ridgeway Trimble had graduated from West Point 17th in the 42-member class of 1822. Ten years as a lieutenant of artillery in the Regular Army were followed by almost three lucrative decades as a civilian building and operating railroads, mainly in Maryland. When the war broke out, Trimble was offered a lieutenant colonelcy in May 1861 and bumped up to brigadier just three months later. With a brigade of mixed regiments and the opportunity to use it, he set about earning a reputation as a fiery commander and rendered distinguished service under Stonewall Jackson during the 1862 Valley Campaign. A severe wound at Groveton on August 29, 1862 during the Second Manassas Campaign mangled his leg and kept him out of the field for much of the next year. His service was not forgotten by Old Jack, however, whose fervent recommendations earned Trimble a promotion to major general on January 17, 1863. Five months later Trimble wrote General Lee to advise that he was again ready for service, but the army had little need for an additional major general and no suitable vacancy to fill within its ranks. Lee was familiar with Trimble's engineering and leadership skills and, coupled with his knowledge of the region, believed he would make a valuable asset in whatever capacity he served. As a result, he was offered command of a handful of Southern forces operating in the Shenandoah Valley.[20]

The conversation between the two engineers in Lee's tent at Chambersburg was a resumption of their earlier discussions held over the past week at Berryville and Hagerstown. In an article written after the war, Trimble recalled his first meeting with Lee at Berryville on June 21. "We have again outmaneuvered the enemy, who even now does not know where we are or what our designs are," the commanding general enthusiastically told the Marylander. "Our whole army will be in Pennsylvania day after tomorrow, leaving the enemy far behind and obliged to follow us by forced marches. *I hope with these advantages to accomplish some signal result and to end the war, if Providence favors us* [emphasis added]." The pair of engineers met again five days later near Hagerstown and resumed their conference later that same day.[21]

Lee's plans for the ongoing campaign matured over the course of those days and between conferences with Trimble. He may have unveiled them, perhaps for the first time in detail, during the afternoon conference in Chambersburg. With Trimble at his elbow, Lee unfolded a map of Pennsylvania and queried the general about his knowledge of the topography east of South Mountain, which included Adams County and a small town at which many roads converged—Gettysburg. Satisfied with Trimble's engineer-like response that almost every square mile was suitable for maneuver and battle, Lee shared his vision of victory with Trimble, who said that he recalled and recorded "nearly verbatim" what the commanding general said:

> Our army is in good spirits, not over fatigued, and can be concentrated at any one point in twenty-four hours or less. I have not yet heard that the enemy have crossed the Potomac and am waiting to hear from General Stuart. When they hear where we are, they will make forced marches to interpose their forces between us and Baltimore and Philadelphia. They will come up, probably through Frederick, broken down with hunger and hard marching, strung out on a long line, and much demoralized when they come into Pennsylvania. I shall throw an overwhelming force on their advance, crush it, follow up the success, drive one corps back on another, and by successive repulses and surprises before they can concentrate create a panic and virtually destroy the army.
>
> Hereabout [putting his hand to the map and touching Gettysburg] we shall probably meet the enemy and fight a great battle, and if God gives us the victory, the war will be over and we shall achieve the recognition of our independence.[22]

Lee also shared a similar revelation with Henry "Harry" Heth (the only man outside the commanding general's immediate family that Lee, at least according to legend, addressed by his first name). "His intention [for the invasion]," recalled Heth, "was to strike his enemy the very first available opportunity that offered—believing he could, when such an opportunity offered—crush him."[23]

These statements offer students of military history penetrating insight into Lee's understanding of his own army, that of his adversary, Stuart's orders, and what Lee needed to accomplish to achieve the South's political imperative and how he intended to carry it off.

*   *   *

It was patently obvious to everyone associated with the Southern army—even foreign observer Arthur Fremantle, who was with Lee's legions for the first time—that its soldiers and leaders were, as Lee put it, "in good spirits [and] not over fatigued." The general's comments about a demoralized enemy were also right on the mark. Lee frequently read Yankee newspapers to keep abreast of the enemy's political situation. He knew another major defeat of the Army of the Potomac, only this time on Northern soil, could severely damage the Lincoln administration and its ability to conduct the war. While her soldiers were not dispirited, confidence of success in the Federal army was fragile at best, and another defeat would further wound their psyche. On June 13, 1863, Brigadier General Marsena Rudolph Patrick, the Army of the Potomac's provost marshal, confided to his diary, "We are likely to be outgeneraled & for ought I know, whipped out again by Lee."[24] Patrick's faith in his commanding general was at its nadir. "Hooker has declared that the enemy are over 100,000 strong," he journaled on June 19 from his headquarters at Fairfax Court House, "it is his only salvation to make it appear that the enemy's forces are larger than his own, which is all false & he knows it." Hooker, the provost general stated flatly, "knows that Lee is his master & is afraid to meet him in fair battle."[25]

General Patrick was not alone in his pessimistic outlook on the future, which Lee knew was also spreading through the general public at large. John Gibbon, the hard fighting commander of the army's Second Division, Hancock's Second Corps, was disgusted with the apparent failing of the populace to rally behind the army and defeat Lee's invaders. On June 23, Gibbon read that Pennsylvania state troops were refusing to be mustered into service for fear that they might be kept under arms for six months. "I give up in despair," Gibbon lamented.[26] This lack of enthusiasm reflected, in part, the declining popularity of the Lincoln administration. One officer, sent to organize the defenses around the Gettysburg area, was quoted as saying that he would "first fight the Rebels, but, after the war, the Administration."[27]

In addition to matters of Northern and Southern morale, Lee's words leave little doubt as to what his expectations were regarding his missing cavalry commander. As far as Lee was concerned, his written instructions of June 22 and 23 clearly ordered Stuart to cross the Potomac as soon as possible and place his cavalry on the right flank of the army. Lee's comment to Trimble on the 26th, "I am waiting to hear from General Stuart," indicates that Stuart was already expected to be in a position to communicate with the army and in position for screening and scouting duties. Stuart, however, was more than 100 miles to the south conducting a raid on the far side of the entire enemy army with Lee's three best cavalry brigades. "Every officer who conversed with General Lee for several days previous to the battle," Heth later explained, "well remembers having heard such expressions as these: 'Can you tell me where General Stuart is?' 'Where on earth is my cavalry?' 'Have you any news of the enemy's movements?'" Now that Lee had gathered his army in Pennsylvania, he was blind, or as Heth described it, "The eyes of the giant were out; he knew not where to strike; a movement in any direction might prove a disastrous blunder."[28]

Sightless or not, the odds of fighting a battle with the powerful Army of the Potomac loomed larger with each passing day. Lee's description to Trimble—"I shall throw an overwhelming force on their advance, crush it, follow up the success, drive one corps back on another, and by successive repulses and surprises before they can concentrate create a panic and virtually destroy the army"—described what he was seeking and is grounded in another of Napoleon's Maxims: "The greatest disaster that can happen is when the [different corps of an army] are attacked in detail, and before their junction."[29] Lee understood the war better than anyone else in the South, and his conversations with the pair of generals confirm his grasp of the difficult subject. A victory like the one he described to Trimble would cause incalculable political and military damage to the Yankee war effort and achieve advantages for Lee and the South that could never be accomplished on the tactical defensive behind the Rappahannock River. The life of the Confederacy's premier army could not be risked again and again in the hope of gaining another Fredericksburg or Chancellorsville—neither of which had brought the South a step closer to its political goal of independence. Lee wielded the one only instrument in the only theater of war capable of bringing about conditions that might, ultimately, realize Southern Independence.

And now, in late June 1863, one of the largest and finest armies Lee had ever fielded was coiled north of the Potomac River and ready to strike that blow for independence.

A Scout is Brought to Lee and the Confederate Army is Ordered to Concentrate

While Jeb Stuart spent the last Saturday of June skirmishing with enemy cavalry and riding north in the vicinity of Fairfax Court House, Lee's hours were consumed in his tent headquarters outside Chambersburg. Six days earlier, on June 21, he had issued strict orders outlining how his men would seize and pay for supplies while operating in enemy territory. The wanton destruction of Southern civilian property by Federals was a barbarity Lee was determined his soldiers would avoid. "I cannot hope that Heaven will prosper our cause when we are violating its laws," Lee had informed Trimble. "I shall, therefore, carry the war into Pennsylvania without offending the sanctions of a high civilization and of Christianity."[30] General Orders No. 72, promulgated on June 27, updated the Army of Northern Virginia's code of conduct. In addition to complimenting his men on their conduct, Lee admonished that they must remember "that we make war only upon armed men, and that we cannot take vengeance for the wrongs our people have suffered without lowering ourselves in the eyes of all whose abhorrence has been excited by the atrocities of our enemies, and offending against Him to whom vengeance belongth, without whose favor and support our efforts must all prove in vain." [31]

There was more behind Lee's latest orders than a display of Christian charity. While his words do indeed reflect his strong character, integrity, and sense of moral responsibility, they also demonstrate a realistic understanding of the current military and political realities he faced in Pennsylvania. Maintaining order and discipline while moving through enemy territory was absolutely vital because it kept every man in the ranks. This was especially important because Lee was already missing five valuable brigades of infantry.[32] Avoiding a repeat of the widespread straggling and desertion that had so weakened the army during the Sharpsburg Campaign in the autumn of 1862 was critical to the success of the current Pennsylvania operation. Further, outrages against the locals would only serve to galvanize support for the Lincoln administration and fuel partisan operations against the invading Southern army. Lee's latest general order was both militarily sound and politically astute.

Restrictions against foraging and looting seems not to have lowered the morale of his rank and file, who relished in such pleasures. On June 27, as Longstreet's veterans marched through the streets of Chambersburg to the tune of "Dixie," Arthur Fremantle looked on as the townspeople "point[ed] and laugh[ed] at Hood's ragged Jacks . . . . This division, well known for its fighting qualities, is composed of Texans, Alabamians, and Arkansans, and they certainly are a queer lot to look at."

The dichotomy that was Lee's army never ceased to amaze Fremantle:

> They carry less than any other troops; many of them have only got an old piece of carpet or rug as baggage; many have discarded their shoes in the mud; all are ragged and dirty, but full of good-humor and confidence in themselves and in their general, Hood. They answered the numerous taunts of the Chambersburg ladies with cheers and laughter. One female had seen fit to show her ample bosom with a huge Yankee flag, and she stood at the door of her house, her countenance expressing the greatest contempt for the barefooted Rebs; several companies passed her without taking any notice; but at length a Texan gravely remarked: 'Take care, madam, for Hood's boys are great at storming breastworks when the Yankee colors is on them.[33]

While his troops tramped through Chambersburg, Hood stopped his mount to pay his respects to the commanding general who, remembered Hood, enjoyed "the same buoyant spirits which pervaded his magnificent army." The sight of his troops marching in well-closed columns excited Lee about the prospects of coming to grips with the Federals. "Ah! general," Lee greeted his division leader, "the enemy is a long time finding us. If he does not succeed soon, we must go in search of him." The equally anxious Hood assured Lee that he "was never so well prepared or more willing" for a confrontation with the Army of the Potomac.[34] Lee felt the same way and was prepared to launch a powerful strike, should the opportunity arrive. First and Third corps were concentrated immediately west of South Mountain in the Chambersburg-Greenwood area, and Ewell—who would soon enjoy Trimble's assistance—was encamped around Carlisle and threatening Harrisburg.[35] Still, the absence of information from Jeb Stuart on his own and the enemy's whereabouts continued to plague him. How could he confidently concentrate and strike the enemy in detail if he did not know where Hooker's army was?

The early morning hours of June 28, like the several days preceding it, came and went without word from Stuart. Based on his long association with that officer, Lee had every reason to believe that Stuart would have notified him if Hooker was moving north of the Potomac. If Hooker was still in Virginia, however, the safety of the Southern capital became a real concern. Lee thus began formulating a plan to compel the Federals to quit Virginia and march into Pennsylvania. If successful, it would both guarantee the safety of Richmond and perhaps cultivate an opportunity for beating the enemy in detail. According to staffer Major Charles Marshall, Lee intended to dangle the Pennsylvania capital of Harrisburg as bait to induce the Federals to march north after him. The loss or threat of loss of the state's capital would likely prompt Republican Governor Andrew Curtin to demand immediate relief from President Lincoln. On the evening of June 28, Marshall "was directed by General Lee to order General Ewell to move directly upon Harrisburg." Longstreet would march "to his support," while Hill was "directed to move eastward to the Susquehanna, and, crossing the river, below Harrisburg, seize the railroad between Harrisburg and Philadelphia."[36] Marshall dispatched the orders about 10: 00 p.m. to Generals Ewell and Hill and had just returned to his tent when the commanding general sent for him. When the aide-de-camp arrived, he found the general seated and in deep conversation with a shadowy character known as "Edward Harrison."[37]

Harrison, General Longstreet's favorite "scout"—or more accurately, spy—had been dispatched by the First Corps commander earlier in the month with instructions to travel to Washington and pick up any important information he could discover. The "filthy and ragged" scout, reputed to be a Mississippian, returned bearing startling news: the Federal army was north of the Potomac.[38] Lee was dumbfounded. If the Federals were on the move and had crossed the Potomac, why hadn't Stuart reported it? Temporarily paralyzed, Lee confessed to Major John W. Fairfax, a member of Longstreet's staff, "I do not know what to do."[39] If Harrison's information was correct, it was the first solid intelligence Lee had received about the enemy for several days. While he had little confidence in spies, Lee knew Harrison had been recommended to Longstreet by Secretary Seddon, and that Longstreet thought him credible.

Lee questioned Harrison at length and listened to his answers with "great composure and minuteness." The scout recalled a fantastical story of traveling from Culpeper to Washington, from Frederick to Chambersburg, frequenting saloons and gossiping with Federal officers along the way. His travels included mingling with the Federal army in Frederick, where two enemy corps were camped with another

Harrison

James Longstreet's favorite scout brought information to General Lee that the Army of the Potomac was moving in his direction, and that Hooker had been replaced by George Gordon Meade. His report changed the direction of the entire campaign.

From Manassas to Appomattox

close by. The fact that the Federal army was north of the Potomac was bad enough; Harrison's additional observation that there wasn't a Confederate cavalryman to be seen only added to Lee's distress. Almost as if it was an afterthought, Harrison added that he had heard Joe Hooker had been replaced by George Gordon Meade.[40]

Harrison's detailed report manifestly impressed Lee, who related the story to Marshall when the aide arrived at army headquarters. Although he did not have corroborating intelligence from Stuart, the report's level of detail convinced Lee of its credibility. The Federals, according to Harrison, were moving west from Frederick toward the Cumberland Valley, which if true threatened Lee's line of communications. "[Our] principal need for communicating with Virginia," explained Major Marshall, "was to procure ammunition. . . . He [Lee] considered it of great importance that the enemy's army should be kept east of the mountains." While the news of the enemy's movement was troubling enough, the replacement of Hooker with Meade was true cause for distress. Lee held the 1835 graduate of West Point and former Regular Army comrade in high regard. A native of Cadiz, Spain, Meade had distinguished himself in the battles of Palo Alto and Monterey during the Mexican War and had carved out a solid, if unspectacular, Civil War career as a brigade, division, and corps leader. Lee also knew him to be a careful engineering officer who would not make any major mistakes in Pennsylvania. With few viable alternatives, Lee had little choice but to act on Harrison's news.[41]

The challenge confronting Lee was how and where to concentrate the army to facilitate the campaign's operational plan and goals. The difficult task was made more complex by the absence of Stuart and his veteran brigades and Lee's imperfect knowledge of the exact disposition of Ewell's Second Corps. With the headquarters and a large portion of the Federal army reportedly southeast of Hagerstown in the

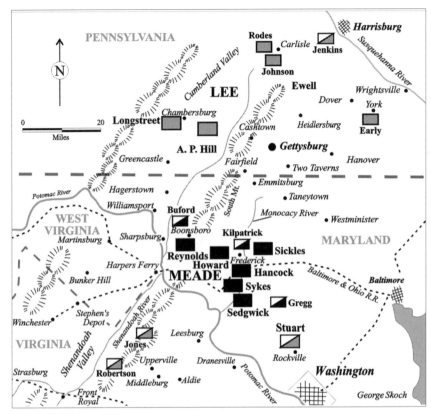

Operational Situation on June 28, 1863

valley between the South Mountain and Catoctin ranges, Lee had to find a way to maintain the freedom to maneuver and the initiative, protect his logistics lifeline with Virginia, and offer his lieutenants the opportunity to deliver a decisive blow. "Consequently," Marshall explained, "he determined to move his own army to the east side of the Blue Ridge, so as to threaten Washington and Baltimore, and detain the Federals forced on that side of the mountains to protect those cities."[42]

The entire tenor of the campaign had changed in an instant.

*   *   *

Several excellent reasons undergirded Lee's decision to pull his army together on the east side of South Mountain, which was the northern extremity of the Blue Ridge Mountain range. Meade could do the Confederate army considerable mischief if the Southerners remained idle. Once he discovered where Lee's corps were operating, his obvious move would be to attempt a Napoleonic *manœuvre sur les derrières* to get astride Southern lines of supply and communications. Meade's presence in the Cumberland Valley would sever the Confederate army from

Virginia. If that were accomplished Lee's protected route to "procure ammunition," communicate with Richmond, drive cattle and other supplies south, and evacuate his wounded would be blocked—and there was no other practical avenue Lee could utilize. Dispatching sufficient troops to garrison his lines of communication was impossible.

Replenishing the army's artillery ammunition was especially critical for Lee. According to gunner E. Porter Alexander, each artillery piece had, "including canister, about 130 to 150 [rounds]—about enough for one hour and a half of rapid firing. I am very sure that our ordnance trains did not carry into Pennsylvania a reserve supply of more than 100 rounds per gun additional, and I don't believe they had over 60 rounds to a gun." The army's total ammunition supply, including what was carried in the limbers, caissons, and the wagons of the ordnance trains, was between 190 to 250 rounds per gun. Lee knew there were only two ways he could resupply his artillery: capture what he needed or haul it up with wagon trains from Virginia. The first method was a byproduct of successful offensive action (as evidenced by the Battle of Second Winchester), but was hardly something Lee could rely upon. Confederate wagons, loaded with ammunition and bound for the army or full of wounded men returning to Virginia, would be easy pickings for Federal raiding cavalry, and would have no chance of making the long trek to or from Lee's army.[43]

With his entire offensive campaign dependent upon controlling the Cumberland Valley, Lee correctly ascertained that he could continue to use it as his line of supply only as long as the Federals were kept on the eastern side of South Mountain. Therefore, he had to concentrate east of that range. He could best accomplish this by unifying his army utilizing the road network that fed into the Cashtown-Gettysburg area before moving northeast towards York. Lee reasoned—correctly—that this move would compel Meade both politically and militarily to keep his army on the east side of South Mountain. It was also the only choice Lee could make that would maintain his own freedom of maneuver to threaten Baltimore and Washington and preserve the integrity of his line of supply with Virginia. He also appreciated the geography of the region in which he was operating, for if his army was forced to retreat, the South Mountain passes would allow him to keep at bay any pursuing forces.

On the basis of these solid military principles, Lee issued orders for his army to promptly concentrate. Although his infantry populated five southern Pennsylvania counties, gathering it together was not a difficult task. Ewell's Second Corps, which had the farthest to travel, was ordered "to march to Cashtown or Gettysburg, according to circumstances"; Jubal Early's detached division was to rejoin the corps along the way.[44] Longstreet's First Corps and Hill's Third Corps, both gathered around Chambersburg, were to move to the east side of South Mountain. Since Hill's Third Corps was already in the Fayetteville-Greenwood area, Lee ordered it to lead the march east to Cashtown, and from there "to move on [the Chambersburg Pike] in the direction of York." Longstreet would follow in Hill's wake.[45] According to Major Charles Marshall of Lee's staff, Ewell was "to march from Carlisle, so as to form a junction with Hill either at Cashtown or Gettysburg, as circumstances might direct."[46]

Dealing with the cavalry arm was more problematic. Without word from Stuart, and with the enemy now on the move, Lee immediately required more horsemen. Consequently, the brigades of Beverly Robertson and William E. "Grumble" Jones were ordered to rejoin the main body of the army. These 2,883 troopers were still south of the Potomac, where they had been ordered by Stuart to guard the passes of the Blue Ridge and cover the rear of the army as it moved north. Robertson, the senior brigadier of the pair, demonstrated yet again his incompetence by losing contact with the Confederate infantry and the Federals he was charged to observe. By the time Robertson realized that he and Jones had been left far behind in the wake of both armies and better get moving northward, Lee's courier arrived with an order to the same effect.[47]

Surgeon John Syng Dorsey Cullen, the medical director of Longstreet's First Corps, watched as couriers, quartermasters, and commissaries spurred their mounts to and from Lee's headquarters throughout the 29th of June. Lee sensed that the great opportunity for which he had waited so long was close at hand, and Cullen saw the excitement radiate within the commanding general as he stood in front of his tent. Outwardly suppressing any anxiety about the absence of Stuart, the commanding general appeared cool and confident. Dr. Cullen remembered Lee saying to those around him: "Tomorrow, gentlemen, we will not move on Harrisburg as we expected, but will go over to Gettysburg and see what General Meade is after."[48]

Ambrose Powell Hill Marches to Gettysburg

Pursuant to Lee's orders, Powell Hill directed Harry Heth's Division to promptly move out from Fayetteville and march toward Cashtown on June 29, which he reached that afternoon. Dorsey Pender's Light Division and Colonel R. Lindsay Walker and the corps' reserve artillery battalions followed Heth on the next day, and Richard Anderson's brigades brought up the rear on July 1. While waiting for elements of Third Corps to negotiate the mountain pass west of Cashtown on June 30, Heth gave Johnston Pettigrew permission to take his large 2,700-man North Carolina brigade nine miles east to Gettysburg, where it was rumored some much-needed shoes and supplies could be obtained for his men.[49]

Johnston Pettigrew—he dropped his first name for most purposes—returned that evening without any additional footwear. In fact, he never made it into Gettysburg. When he approached its western outskirts, he discovered "a large force

Ambrose Powell Hill (1825-1865)

One of Lee's most aggressive and favorite division commanders, "Little Powell"
carved out a stellar record second to none in the entire Army of Northern Virginia.
His service earned him a promotion to lieutenant general at the head of the new
Third Corps in May 1863 in the reorganization that followed Chancellorsville.
How he would perform in this role was one of the questions Lee faced as the army
coursed its way through Pennsylvania. *Eleanor S. Brockenbrough Library, The Museum of
the Confederacy. Richmond*

of [Federal] cavalry near the town." Although the prewar lawyer had no formal military training and limited combat experience, Pettigrew was shrewd enough to realize that his brigade, strung out in road column and without the benefit of mounted scouts, was vulnerable. The brigadier judiciously concluded he had no way of ascertaining the size of the enemy force in front of him, and returned to Cashtown late that afternoon.[50]

When Powell Hill arrived in Cashtown later that evening, Pettigrew and Heth met with the corps commander and explained the aborted search for shoes. The North Carolinian's story did not deter "Little Powell." The only Federal force at Gettysburg," he confidently proclaimed, "is cavalry, probably a detachment of observation. I am just from General Lee, and the information he has from his scouts corroborates that I received from mine—that is, the enemy are still in Middleburg [Maryland], and have not struck their tents."[51]

"If there is no objection," Heth answered, "I will take my division tomorrow and go to Gettysburg and get those shoes."

"None in the world," came Hill's reply.[52]

Hill's nonchalance in the face of such an important issue concerned Pettigrew enough to summon his adjutant general, Captain Louis G. Young. Young had accompanied Pettigrew to Gettysburg and had observed Federal movements around the town. The captain informed Hill that the cavalry belonged to the Army of the Potomac and was not merely local militia. Further, some of the brigade's officers had heard drums, which indicated the presence of infantry. Hill's initial reaction was disbelief. "I still cannot believe that any portion of the Army of the Potomac is up," the corps commander declared, adding, "I hope that it is, for this is the place I want it to be."[53] Hill backed up his statement with plans for Third Corps to move in force, Heth in the lead the next morning, followed by Pender's Light Division and Walker's two reserve artillery battalions.

Couriers were dispatched late on the evening of June 30. One rode west along the Chambersburg Pike in search of General Lee to advise that Hill "intended to advance the next morning and discover what was in my front."[54] Knowing that Lee had ordered Second Corps to concentrate in the same area as his own, Hill sent another rider in search of Ewell with similar information. Lee was found near Greenwood very late in the evening of June 30. The limited information did not overly concern him since Hill's movement conformed with previously issued orders and Ewell was being told of Third Corps' planned movement. The same messenger Hill sent to Lee also carried orders for Richard Anderson to start his division from Fayetteville "early" on July 1 and march to Cashtown.[55] Still queasy about his nonexistent cavalry screen, Lee prudently summoned Major Walter Taylor, his assistant adjutant general—Lee's equivalent of the chief of staff of the army—with orders to deliver to Heth "instructions" concerning the parameters for his movement to Gettysburg. Taylor found Heth in the pre-dawn darkness of July 1 and informed him he was "to ascertain what force was at Gettysburg, and, if he found the infantry opposed to him, to report the fact immediately, without forcing an engagement."[56]

While some have chided Hill for sending such a large force to Gettysburg (he appeared, at least in hindsight, too eager for a fight), he apparently pushed his corps eastward to accomplish two goals: the ordered concentration of the army and the procurement of needed supplies. Hill truly did not suspect his troops would meet serious opposition. After dispatching Heth's and Pender's divisions along with Walker's artillery, Hill remained behind at Cashtown, probably because the unhealthy commander was once again ill and confined to his cot that morning. Whatever was troubling the man many called "Little Powell" at the outset of his first battle as a corps leader was only just beginning to manifest itself. The aggressive and intrepid style of command that had marked Hill's early war record, and upon which Lee was relying, left him on Wednesday, July 1, 1863.[57]

Admonished to avoid anything that might bring about a major engagement, Harry Heth had his four brigades marching on the Chambersburg Pike to Gettysburg by 5:00 a.m.

Henry Heth (1825-1899)

It is said Henry "Harry" Heth was the only soldier Robert E. Lee addressed by his first name. He was largely inexperienced at division command and Gettysburg promised to be his first opportunity to demonstrate his capabilities at that level. Heth's advance to Gettysburg on July 1, 1863, sparked the initial fighting of the epic three-day battle. *Library of Congress*

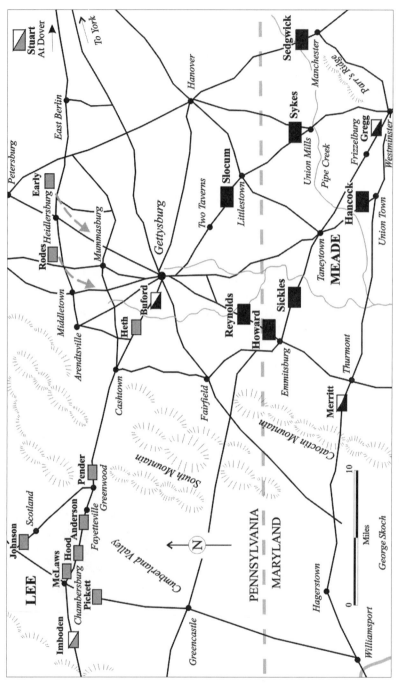

Operational Situation at Dawn, July 1, 1863

Oddly, a battalion of artillery led the column, which indicated that Heth, like Hill, did not expect serious trouble. James Archer's Brigade followed the guns, with the brigades of Joe Davis, Johnston Pettigrew, and John Brockenbrough completing the marching order. At about 7:30 a.m., a handful of enemy cavalry was discovered about three miles west of town, triggering a light skirmish that moved slowly eastward. About two miles from Gettysburg on Herr Ridge, Heth deployed his two leading brigades in line of battle, Archer south of the road and Davis north of it. Artillery unlimbered in support and the guns began lobbing shells at the Federal horsemen. Without reconnoitering, Heth ordered Archer and Davis to advance. It was about 9:30 a.m.[58]

Powell Hill, meanwhile, spent the early morning hours on his cot at the Cashtown Inn while the sound of gunfire drifted into the village from the south and east. The noise of battle had thus far not stirred him to action, but the familiar figure on a gray horse arriving from the opposite direction provided "Little Powell" with the wherewithal to get out of bed and assume his place at the front. Astride his beloved Traveller, Robert E. Lee—who had just left James Longstreet and some of his staff officers—rode towards Cashtown through Edward Johnson's Second Corps division.[59] The appearance of one-third of Ewell's scattered corps reassured a cheerful and composed Lee, but the distant rumbling of artillery that had reached his ears a short time earlier in the South Mountain pass above Cashtown troubled him.

"Serious Work Ahead"

When the sound of battle rolled across the Adams County landscape, General Lee rode down a crowded Chambersburg Pike in the direction of Gettysburg in search of answers. When he arrived in Cashtown, he found Ambrose Powell Hill, commander of Third Corps, in front of the Cashtown Inn. Artist Dale Gallon captures the moment when an anxious Lee queries Hill about what was going on up ahead. *Courtesy Gallon Historical Art, Gettysburg, Pennsylvania.*

Without Stuart available to send a courier with news of what was transpiring at the front, he had no way of knowing whether the gunfire was merely a skirmish or the beginning of a serious engagement.[60]

Recent information regarding the cavalier's whereabouts only made his absence more troubling. On the previous day James Power Smith, a staff officer with Second Corps, rejoined the army at Chambersburg after temporary duty in North Carolina. When Lee inquired whether he had seen or "heard anything of General Stuart and his movements," Smith mentioned that while crossing the Potomac at Williamsport the night before, he had ridden "through the river with two cavalrymen who stated that they were couriers from Stuart's headquarters, and that they had left Stuart the day before [the 28th] somewhere east of the Blue Ridge and south of the Potomac. They had brought dispatches for detachments in the Valley, and had orders to follow the army trains into Pennsylvania."[61]

The news of Stuart's location so astonished Lee that he asked Smith to repeat the story. A short time later Lee sent Major Taylor of his staff to question Smith yet a third time. Taylor, Smith later recalled, said "it was a great disappointment to General Lee, who expected that Stuart would have reported to him in Pennsylvania, and that Lee was troubled that his cavalry forces were not between him and the enemy, as he had expected them to be."[62]

Armed with this knowledge—and leaving Longstreet behind to help expedite the snarled mess crawling along the pike—Lee rode on a short distance and paused just west of Cashtown where, recalled artillerist William Nelson Pendleton, "the commanding general, finding the cannonade to continue and increase, moved rapidly forward"east on the crowded Chambersburg Pike. When Lee arrived at the Cashtown Inn, a noticeably pale and shaken Powell Hill greeted him with a salute. The two spoke briefly about the meaning of the artillery fire, which grew steadily louder as the minutes ticked away. Hill, of course, knew little of what was happening with Heth, but understood enough to realize that Lee's inquiries demanded answers. The ill corps leader mounted his horse and galloped as best he could to the sound of the guns.[63]

Lee remained briefly at Cashtown and summoned Major General Richard Anderson, one of Hill's division commanders, whose men were resting nearby. "I cannot think what has become of Stuart. I ought to have heard from him long before now," an obviously agitated Lee disclosed to Anderson. "He may have met with disaster, but I hope not. In the absence of reports from him, I am in ignorance as to what we have in front of us here. It may be the whole Federal army, it may be only a detachment. If it is the whole Federal force, we must fight a battle here. If we do not gain a victory, those defiles and gorges which we passed this morning will shelter us from disaster." Anderson, however, had nothing in the way of additional information for Lee, who ordered him to start his division at once for Gettysburg. If there was serious work to be found up ahead, Lee wanted every available regiment marching to the sound of the guns.[64]

Sometime after Lee finished with Anderson, Major George Campbell Brown, Ewell's stepson and aide-de-camp, "reined in his lathered mount in front of the army commander."[65] Brown brought word that Ewell, acting upon the message received from Hill earlier that morning that Third Corps was concentrating towards Gettysburg, had ordered the divisions of Robert Rodes and Jubal Early to march there as well, with the former taking the Middletown Road and the latter the Heidlersburg Road. Lee welcomed the news that Second Corps was already marching to Gettysburg, asking the young aide, "with a peculiar searching, almost querulous, impatience . . . whether General Ewell had heard anything from General Jeb Stuart, and on my reply in the negative, said that he had heard nothing from him or of him for three days—and that General Stuart had not complied with his instructions." A scout, continued Lee, "reports Meade's whole army marching this way, but that is all I know about his position. Tell General Ewell to send out his left and try to open communications with General Stuart." Lee concluded his message for Ewell by telling Brown that if the enemy proved to be "very large, he did not want a general engagement brought on till the rest of the army came up."[66] With Lee's instructions firmly in mind, the young aide spurred his horse off to find his stepfather.

*   *   *

General Lee's statements to Richard Anderson and Campbell Brown are rather revealing. First, both exchanges imply that as far as Lee was concerned, he had *not* given discretionary orders to Jeb Stuart that would have allowed him to conduct a raid instead of shielding and scouting for the army. Second, as of the morning of July 1, Lee clearly intended to avoid a general engagement if there was a "very large" Federal force in his front. If the enemy was already present in strength at Gettysburg, Lee's options would be limited. Without adequate cavalry and with his line of communications stretching eighteen miles west to Chambersburg, his ability to freely maneuver would be seriously curtailed, as would his tactical choices should he decide to commit himself in battle. Therefore, he had to find a way to advantageously continue the battle if it had already started *or* if an unforeseen opportunity suddenly presented itself.

*   *   *

With his business in and around Cashtown concluded, Lee mounted Traveller and rode east along the Chambersburg Pike toward Gettysburg. Like thunder riding a distant storm, the deep-throated rumble of artillery rolled west to greet him.

Notes for Chapter 4

1. *The Military Maxims of Napoleon*, Maxim 6.

2. *The Military Maxims of Napoleon*, Maxim 12.

3. Carl von Clausewitz, *On War*, translated by J. J. Graham (London, 1966), 3 volumes, vol. 3, p. 5.

4. S. L. A. Marshall, *Men Against Fire* (New York, 1947), p. 111.

5. Pfanz, *Richard S. Ewell*, p. 292.

6. James I. Robertson, Jr., *General A. P. Hill: The Story of a Confederate Warrior* (New York, 1987), pp. 201-203; *OR* 27, pt. 2, p. 358.

7. Dowdey and Manarin, eds., *The Wartime Papers of Robert E. Lee*, number 496. Lee knew he would not need static garrisons to maintain his lines of communication with Virginia as long as the Federal army was kept far enough away from the Confederate avenue of advance along the Cumberland Valley.

8. Dowdey and Manarin, eds., *The Wartime Papers of Robert E. Lee*, number 497.

9. Arthur J. L. Fremantle, *Three Months in the Southern States, April-June 1863* (reprinted from the 1864 edition, Lincoln, 1991), p. 236; Freeman, *R. E. Lee*, 3, p. 54; *OR* 27, pt. 2, p. 316.

10. Freeman, *R. E. Lee*, 3, p. 54. The grove was later known as Messersmith's Woods; Jacob Hoke, *The Great Invasion of 1863* (Dayton, 1887), p. 169.

11. Fremantle, *Three Months in the Southern States*, p. 226. Fremantle mentions (p. 231) that the widespread shortages of food throughout the South made it was "utterly impossible" to procure corn for his horse below the Mason-Dixon line; Stiles, *Four Years Under Marse Robert*, pp. 199-200.

12. John B. Gordon, *Reminiscences of the Civil War* (New York, 1903), p. 139.

13. *OR* 27, pt. 2, p. 443.

14. Fremantle, *Three Months in the Southern States*, p. 234.

15. William W. Hassler, ed., *One of Lee's Best Men: The Civil War Letters of General William Dorsey Pender* (Chapel Hill, 1999), p. 254.

16. Hood, *Advance and Retreat*, p. 54.

17. Eddy R. Parker, ed., *Touched by Fire: Letters from Company D, 5th Texas Infantry, Hood's Brigade, Army of Northern Virginia, 1862-1865* (Hillsboro, 2000), p. 61.

18. *The Military Maxims of Napoleon*, Maxim 13.

19. *OR* 27, pt. 2, p. 316; Fitzhugh Lee, "A Review of the First Two Days' Operations at Gettysburg and a Reply to General Longstreet," *Southern Historical Society Papers*, vol. 5, p. 164.

20. Robert K. Krick, "Isaac Ridgeway Trimble," in William C. Davis, ed., *The Confederate General*, 6, pp. 60-61; Isaac R. Trimble, "The Campaign and Battle of Gettysburg," *Confederate Veteran*, 40 vols. (Nashville, 1917), 25, p. 209.

21. Trimble, "The Campaign and Battle of Gettysburg," p. 209.

22. Trimble to John C. Bachelder, February 8, 1883, *The Bachelder Papers*, 3 volumes, edited by David L. and Audrey J. Ladd (Dayton, 1994), vol. 2, p. 925. In his letter to Bachelder, Trimble mistakenly listed the date of this meeting as June 25; Trimble, "The

Campaign and Battle of Gettysburg," *Confederate Veteran*, vol. 25, pp. 209-211; Trimble to Bachelder, February 8, 1883, *The Bachelder Papers*, 2, pp. 925-926; *Supplement to the Official Records of the Union and Confederate Armies*, 100 volumes (Wilmington, 1994), vol. 5, pp. 435-436. Hereinafter referred to as *SOR*. Unless otherwise indicated, are volumes listed are in part I.

23. Henry Heth, in a letter dated June 1877, on the topic of "Causes of Lee's Defeat at Gettysburg," *Southern Historical Society Papers*, vol. 4, p. 156.

24. Marsena Rudolph Patrick, *Inside Lincoln's Army: The Diary of Marsena Rudolph Patrick, Provost Marshal General, Army of the Potomac*, edited by David S. Sparks (New York, 1963), entry for June 13, 1863, p. 258.

25. Patrick, *Inside Lincoln's Army*, entry for June 19, 1863, p. 261.

26. John Gibbon, *Personal Recollections of the Civil War* (New York, 1928), pp. 128-129.

27. The quote is from Major Haller, as cited in Michael Jacobs, *Notes on the Rebel Invasion of Maryland and Pennsylvania and the Battle of Gettysburg* (Philadelphia, 1864), pp. 12-13.

28. Henry Heth, letter dated June 1877, on the topic of "Causes of Lee's Defeat at Gettysburg," *Southern Historical Society Papers*, vol. 4, p. 156.

29. *The Military Maxims of Napoleon*, Maxim 27. Lee's vision of the battle he intended to wage in Pennsylvania ran counter to the theory advanced after the war by First Corps leader James Longstreet, who claimed Lee planned to fight a defensive action once on Northern soil. Impressed by the tactical advantages enjoyed while on the defensive at Fredericksburg, Longstreet sought to replicate that victory in Pennsylvania. Lee, however, knew that he could never rely on an opponent to mindlessly play into his hands and duplicate the unimaginative battle plan Ambrose Burnside had undertaken at Fredericksburg. For a detailed discussion of Longstreet's theory, complete with a chronological listing of his various writings, see Freeman, *Lee's Lieutenants*, vol. 3, pp. 39-50. Longstreet mentions "the plan of defensive tactics," in Longstreet, *From Manassas to Appomattox*, p. 334. Lee's conferences with Trimble and his subsequent management of the battle at Gettysburg was, to some degree, based on his personal knowledge of George Gordon Meade, who seceded Joe Hooker in command of the Army of the Potomac on June 27, 1863. "[Meade]will commit no blunder in my front," explained Lee, who always knew how he was going to fight in Pennsylvania: he was going to employ his army's superior morale, élan, and striking power, and "with these advantages . . . accomplish some signal result and to end the war." George Cary Eggleston, *A Rebel's Recollections* (New York, 1875), pp. 145-146.

30. *Official Records*, 27, pt. 3, pp. 912-913; Isaac R. Trimble, "The Battle and Campaign of Gettysburg," *Southern Historical Society Papers*, vol. 26, p. 119.

31. See *OR* 27, pt. 3, pp. 942-943, for the complete text of Lee's order; Dowdey and Manarin, eds., *The Wartime Papers of Robert E. Lee*, number 498; Roger Long, "General Orders No. 72: 'By Command of Gen. R. E. Lee,'" *Gettysburg Magazine*, Number 7, pp. 13-22.

32. The discussion of these brigades may be found in Chapter I. Although two new brigades under Pettigrew and Davis did join the army prior to the invasion, Lee wanted and needed his tested veteran combat commands led by experienced officers.

33. Fremantle, *Three Months in the Southern States,* pp. 239-240. The Englishman mistakenly overlooked the Georgians in Hood's Division.

34. Hood, *Advance and Retreat,* p. 55. Lee's conversations with Trimble and Hood on June 27, as well as with Heth and Long on other occasions, confirm that the commanding general was eager to slip the leash on his army and pounce upon the enemy in order to, as Trimble put it, "accomplish some signal effect." Trimble, "The Campaign and Battle of Gettysburg," *Confederate Veteran,* vol. 25, p. 209. Only a few days earlier, division commander Dorsey Pender had written his wife that "The General [Lee] says he wants to meet [Hooker] as soon as possible and crush him . . ." William Dorsey Pender to his wife, June 23, 1863, *The Civil War Letters of General William Dorsey Pender,* p. 254.

35. According to Donald Pfanz, Ewell's recent biographer, Isaac Trimble was a "nuisance" to Lee, who ordered Trimble on June 26 to report to Ewell, whose forces, Lee told him, "are by this time in Harrisburg; if not, go and join him and help him take that place." Pfanz claims Lee sent the general on to Ewell as a means of getting rid of him. "Within hours," writes Pfanz, "[Trimble] was nagging Ewell to push on to Harrisburg. . . . For the next three days he pestered Ewell with chimerical proposals and gratuitous advice, just as he has pestered Lee. Pfanz, *Richard S. Ewell,* pp. 300-301. We do not subscribe to Pfanz's theory whatsoever. Trimble proved (just as we will throughout this study) that he was a reliable observer. Consider this: if Trimble was truly a nuisance and getting in the way, would Lee have sent him to bother one of his new corps commanders on an important mission? Of course not.

36. Charles Marshall, "Events Leading up to the Battle of Gettysburg," *Southern Historical Society Papers,* vol. 23, pp. 225-226.

37. Charles Marshall, "Events Leading up to the Battle of Gettysburg," *Southern Historical Society Papers,* vol. 23, p. 226; *OR* 27, pt. 2, p. 307, 358; G. Moxley Sorrel, *Recollections of a Confederate Staff Officer,* Second Edition (New York, 1917), p. 158; James Longstreet, "Lee's Invasion of Pennsylvania," in *Battles and Leaders of the Civil War,* vol. 3, p. 250; Eicher, *Robert E. Lee: A Life Portrait,* p. 91. Harrison's exact identity is a bit obscure. Even his first name is in doubt. Some cites refer to him as "Edward" and others "James" Harrison. See, for example, Faust, *Encyclopedia of the Civil War,* p. 345.

38. Longstreet, "Lee's Invasion of Pennsylvania," in *Battles and Leaders,* vol. 3, p. 244; Sorrel, *Recollections of a Confederate Staff Officer,* pp. 153, 160-161. Sorrel remembered the time as being "after 10:00 p.m." when Lee sent for Harrison, which corroborates Marshall's time frame of the events.

39. *Fairfax MSS,* in Freeman, *R. E. Lee,* 3, p.60, fn. 31; Wert, *Longstreet,* pp. 254-255.

40. Sorrel, *Recollections of a Confederate Staff Officer,* p. 161. The fact that Harrison informed Lee about Hooker being replaced by Meade is confirmed by Marshall, Long, and Sorrel. Marshall, *An Aide-de-Camp of Lee,* p. 219; Marshall, "Events Leading up to the Battle of Gettysburg," *Southern Historical Society Papers,* vol. 23, p. 226; Long, *Memoirs of Robert E. Lee,* p. 274; and Sorrel, *Recollections of a Confederate Staff Officer,* p. 161.

41. Charles Marshall, "Events Leading up to the Battle of Gettysburg," *Southern Historical Society Papers,* vol. 23, p. 226. For an interesting discussion of Meade's background and Civil War experiences leading up to Gettysburg, see Tagg, *The Generals of Gettysburg,* pp. 1-7.

42. Charles Marshall, "Events Leading up to the Battle of Gettysburg," *Southern Historical Society Papers,* vol. 23, p. 226.

43. Edward Porter Alexander, "Causes of Lee's Defeat at Gettysburg," *Southern Historical Society Papers,* vol. 4, p. 103. The tortuous supply route to Lee's army in Pennsylvania from Virginia entailed a trip by rail from Richmond to Staunton, then by wagon train down the Shenandoah Valley, across the Potomac in the Williamsport area, north to Hagerstown and Chambersburg, and then east through the South Mountain range or northeast toward Carlisle and Harrisburg.

44. Isaac R. Trimble, "The Battle and Campaign of Gettysburg," *Southern Historical Society Papers,* vol. 26, p. 121; *OR* 27, pt. 2, pp. 316-317; *OR* 27, pt. 3, pp. 943-944; Dowdey and Manarin, eds., *The Wartime Papers of R. E. Lee,* number 499. Lee's instructions to Ewell are dated 7:30 a.m., June 28, 1863. Either the date of the letter is wrong (since Lee's discussion with Harrison took place after 10:00 p.m. on June 28), or Lee was advised earlier from another source that the Federals had crossed the Potomac, as the content of this letter would indicate. Since credible and cross-referenced eyewitness accounts conclusively state that it was Harrison who informed Confederate headquarters of the whereabouts of the Federal army during his nocturnal visit late on the 28th, the time and date of this letter are almost surely incorrect.

45. *OR* 27, pt. 2, p. 606.

46. Charles Marshall, "Events Leading up to the Battle of Gettysburg," *Southern Historical Society Papers,* vol. 23, pp. 226-227. *OR* 27, pt. 2, p. 317.

47. A. L. Long, *Memoirs of Robert E. Lee,* pp. 274-275; Longacre, *The Cavalry at Gettysburg,* pp. 233-234. The 35th Virginia Battalion had been detached from Jones' Brigade and was already serving in Pennsylvania. As such, its strength is not included in the figure provided. John S. Mosby, *Philadelphia Weekly Times,* December 15, 1877, *Battles and Leaders of the Civil War,* vol. 3, pp. 251-252; Beverly H. Robertson, "The Confederate Cavalry in the Gettysburg Campaign," *Battles and Leaders of the Civil War,* vol. 3, p. 253.

48. James Longstreet, "Lee in Pennsylvania," *The Annals of the War, Written by Leading Participants North and South* (Philadelphia, 1879), p. 439.

49. *OR* 27, pt. 2, pp. 606-607, 637 and 656. For a good sketch of Pettigrew's prewar life and experience up to Gettysburg, see Tagg, *The Generals of Gettysburg,* pp. 343-346.

50. *OR* 27, pt. 2, p. 637; Heth, "Letter from Major-General Henry Heth, of A. P. Hill's Corps, A.N.V.," *Southern Historical Society Papers,* 4, p. 157. For various estimates on the strength of Pettigrew's Brigade, see John W. Busey and David G. Martin, *Regimental Strengths and Losses at Gettysburg* (Hightstown, 1994), pp. 173-174.

51. *OR* 27, pt. 2, pp. 607, 637. Middleburg was only 16 miles south of Gettysburg. It is impossible to know why Hill so completely disregarded Pettigrew's observations. One historian has postulated that it might have been a touch of "the West Pointer's disdain for civilian soldiers." Gary Gallagher, "Confederate Corps Leadership on the First Day at Gettysburg: A. P. Hill and Richard S. Ewell in a Difficult Debut," in Gallagher, ed., *The First Day At Gettysburg,* p. 42.

52. Henry Heth, letter dated June 1877, on the topic of "Causes of Lee's Defeat at Gettysburg," *Southern Historical Society Papers,* vol. 4, p. 157.

53. Henry Heth, letter dated June 1877, on the topic of "Causes of Lee's Defeat at Gettysburg," *Southern Historical Society Papers,* vol. 4, p. 157. Robertson, *A. P. Hill,* pp. 205-206, provides a good account of this critical meeting.

54. *OR* 27, pt. 2, p. 607.

55. *OR* 27, pt. 2, pp. 607, 613. Lee also sent an order to Anderson on June 30 to march to Cashtown to clear the road on the western side of South Mountain for the advance of Edward Johnson's Division and Ewell's reserve artillery. Freeman, *Lee Lieutenant's,* 3, p. 78, fn39.

56. Taylor, *Four Years With General Lee,* pp. 92-93.

57. For decades historians have argued over the nature of Powell Hill's various illnesses, with a general consensus emerging that they were probably psychosomatic in nature. James I Robertson, Jr. was the first to conclusively demonstrate that the mysterious malady plaguing Hill through much of his adult life was the result of advanced gonorrhea contracted two decades earlier. The symptoms of the disease, especially during its advanced stages, are often worsened by stress. Robertson, *A. P. Hill,* pp. 11, 12, 250. See also, Welsh, *Medical Histories of Confederate Generals,* pp. 99-100.

58. *OR* 27, pt. 2, p. 607 and 637. Lieutenant John L Mayre, "The First Gun at Gettysburg," in *Civil War Regiments: A Journal of the American Civil War,* Vol. 1, No. 1 (1991), p. 30. Heth's decision to lead his march with artillery, especially after receiving information from Johnston Pettigrew that Federals were holding Gettysburg in force, can only be described as reckless.

59. *OR* 27, pt. 2, pp. 503-504. Traveller was General Lee's favorite horse. The iron-gray house, which was originally named "Jeff Davis," "was never known to tire, was quiet and sensible, and without fear in battle." See "General Lee's Traveller," *Southern Historical Society Papers,* 41, p. 158.

60. A. L. Long, letter dated June 1877, on the topic of "Causes of Lee's Defeat at Gettysburg," *Southern Historical Society Papers,* vol. 4, p. 122; A. L. Long, *Memoirs of Robert E. Lee,* p. 275.

61. James Power Smith, "With Lee at Gettysburg," *Southern Historical Society Papers,* vol. 43, pp. 55-56. Stuart had not gotten all of his command across the Potomac until about 3:00 A.M., on 28 June.

62. James Power Smith, "With Lee at Gettysburg," *Southern Historical Society Papers,* vol. 43, p. 56.

63. *OR* 27, pt. 2, p. 348; John Esten Cooke, *A Life of Gen. Robert E. Lee* (New York, 1871), pp. 301-302; Walter Herron Taylor, *General Lee: His Campaigns in Virginia 1861-1865, with Personal Reminiscences* (Lincoln, 1994), p. 187.

64. Richard Anderson, as quoted in Longstreet, *From Manassas to Appomattox,* p. 357; Joseph C. Elliott, *Richard H. Anderson: Lee's Noble Soldier* (Dayton, 1985), p. 72; Edward Porter Alexander, *Military Memoirs of a Confederate* (New York, 1907), p. 381. According to General Anderson, his orders to resume his advance towards Gettysburg came from Hill. *OR* 27, pt. 2, p. 613.

65. Richard S. Shue, *Morning at Willoughby Run: July 1, 1863* (Gettysburg, 1995), p. 170.

66. George Campbell Brown, "Reminiscences," Tennessee State Library and Archives, Nashville, Tennessee, copy at the Confederate Research Center, Harold B. Simpson History Complex, Hill College, Hillsboro, Texas.

Chapter 5

Lee and the First Day

"War is composed of nothing but surprises. While a general should adhere to general principles, he should never lose the opportunity to profit by these surprises. It is the essence of genius. In war there is only one favorable moment. Genius seizes it."
—Napoleon[1]

Major General Henry "Harry" Heth ran into a buzz saw of Federal opposition west of Gettysburg and now seemed powerless to stop the slaughter transpiring in front of his eyes on either side of the Chambersburg Pike. As it turned out, the neophyte Pettigrew had been right after all.

Confronted by John Buford's dismounted cavalry west of Gettysburg, the new division commander decided to deploy and probe eastward. Johnston Pettigrew and John Mercer Brockenbrough (pronounced "Broke-en-bro") kept their brigades in reserve while Heth's other pair under the veteran James Jay Archer and neophyte Joseph Davis advanced with orders "to feel the enemy." After protesting that he did not know what was in his front, Archer dutifully deployed his 1,200 veteran Alabama and Tennessee troops south of the Chambersburg Pike. Once aligned, he guided them east down a gentle slope to a small creek, splashed across and continued beyond, driving enemy troopers before him. Davis, who had only three of his four regiments with him that day, about 1,700 effectives, mimicked Archer's movement on the north side of the pike. Neither brigadier knew where their marching would lead them, and both were about to suffer heavily as a result of Heth's impetuous negligence.[2]

Archer's worse fears were realized when his mixed brigade moved into an expanse of timber and head-on into Solomon Meredith's waiting Federal Iron Brigade, Major General John Reynolds' First Corps. Enjoying both the advantage of terrain and surprise, the Federals slaughtered Archer's unfortunates where they stood. A vigorous counter thrust in the face of a chaotic retreat bagged scores of Southerners and Archer himself—the first general officer of Lee's army captured in battle. Joe Davis' early success above the road turned as suddenly into disaster as had Archer's fiasco. After initially outflanking and driving back three regiments of New Yorkers and Pennsylvanians under Lysander Cutler, the president's nephew demonstrated his unfitness for command by wading his men into an unfinished railroad cut that ran roughly parallel to the Chambersburg Pike, where they found themselves trapped and unable to maneuver. Reminiscent of Archer's catastrophe one-half mile to the south, charging enemy infantry—some from the Iron Brigade—surprised and butchered them there. In little more than an hour Heth's two brigades lost some 1,200 men. Federals losses, while less, included Reynolds, who was struck down early in the action; division leader Abner Doubleday took control of First Corps.

It was the gunfire from this meeting engagement that rang in General Lee's ears as he rode Traveller eastward from Cashtown.[3]

Lee Arrives on the Field

Sometime after 1:00 p.m., the commanding general guided his mount through Dorsey Pender's Light Division, deployed astride the Chambersburg Pike at the western base of Herr Ridge.[4] He continued up the slope and crested the rise, where he turned off the main road to the left of Herr Tavern and reined in Traveller between Major Willie Pegram's 20-gun artillery battalion and a portion of Major David Gregg McIntosh's 16-gun artillery battalion.[5] The youthful, bespectacled, and "incomparable" Pegram was working his artillerists at a feverish pace, sending shot and shell flying towards the Federal lines, while McIntosh's crews trained and fired their guns at a more deliberate rate. From Herr Ridge, Lee studied the Federal troop dispositions and the nature of the ground Isaac Trimble had so accurately described several days earlier.[6]

The gently rolling timber-knotted terrain in this part of Adams County was perfectly suited for maneuver and battle. Low ridges, running generally north and south, provided excellent positions for supporting artillery fire, although the same undulating terrain also offered defenders good fields of fire. Lee's eyes took in the rich farm land that sloped downhill more than 500 yards to Willoughby Run, a shallow stream that angled across the Chambersburg Pike in a southerly direction. Whitish-gray smoke, like a morning fog, still drifted lazily in the low lying areas. A few hundred yards beyond the stream was Herbst Woods, a patch of timber crowning a gentle ridge.[7] The land beyond Willoughby Run especially interested Lee, for that was where the enemy was now known to be deployed in force. There, the ground rose to greet a double ridge that merged a mile or so northwest of town into an elevation called Oak Hill, a wooded eminence commanding all the ground south to the Chambersburg Pike. The cultivated rise closest to Lee was known locally as McPherson's Ridge, named for Edward McPherson, whose farmhouse and barn stood just south of the Chambersburg Pike. It was on McPherson's property that much of Archer's earlier misfortune had occurred. From that point east the ground gently dipped and then rose to a higher and mostly timbered elevation about 600 yards beyond McPherson's Ridge. This rise, Seminary Ridge, was named for a Lutheran Theological Seminary (whose unique edifice topped by a cupola was visible for miles around) situated amongst a grove of trees 100 yards south of the road. The portion of Seminary Ridge extending north of the Chambersburg Pike was known locally as Oak Ridge, and it ran due north into Oak Hill. From the point where the Chambersburg Pike crossed Seminary Ridge, Gettysburg's town square was 1,400 yards distant, with the edge of town just over 600 yards away. The grade over this stretch of ground fell off towards Gettysburg. Beyond the town were barely discernible heights immediately to the south and southeast.

While the terrain looked generally favorable for battle, Lee could not have been pleased by the carnage and confusion in evidence all around him. The human wreckage from Heth's earlier assault was plainly visible, as were his two considerably disordered brigades—one forming below the Grist farm at the eastern base of Herr Ridge under the protective fire of Pegram's guns (Davis), and the other trying to reform on the far right of the line among the timbers (Archer). Although someone had probably already informed him, it was readily manifest to Lee that half of Heth's Division had met with considerable difficulty. And Heth's position did not yet look fully stable. Smoke from Federal batteries and the banners representing enemy infantry were visible on McPherson's Ridge extending from the pike south into Herbst Woods. More Yankees were discernible on the distant Seminary Ridge, their lines extending north along Oak Ridge in the direction of the Mummasburg Road near Oak Hill. The strong Federal front overlapped Heth's reformed line. After learning of his division commander's rebuff (he had lost almost one-fifth of his 7,000 infantry), and seeing Federal dispositions firsthand, Lee instructed Heth to keep his men under tight rein until further orders.[8]

The information gleaned from Heth and others helped Lee understand what had happened to Archer and Davis and how the disaster might have been avoided. Heth's thrust toward Gettysburg was his first battle assignment as a major general, and he was well aware that Lee's "intention was to strike his enemy the very first available opportunity that offered—believing he could, when such an opportunity offered—

crush him."[9] Lee's words may have fueled Heth's desire to come to grips and "crush" what he and Powell Hill thought was nothing more than dismounted cavalry and perhaps state militia. The risk inherent in such an aggressive attitude was exacerbated when the division's unfortunate marching order randomly placed Archer's numerically weak veterans and Davis' large but inexperienced brigade in the vanguard of the attack. The result of this ill-planned endeavor was a sharp defeat.

Opportunity, however, had slipped through Hill's fingers. Pender's Division had marched behind Heth's brigades towards Gettysburg that morning, but had sat idly by within supporting distance while Archer and Davis fought for their lives. Pender could not act on his own accord, and Hill was not on the field to order his four veteran brigades, together with Heth's remaining pair under Pettigrew and Brockenbrough, forward into action. Lee knew these additional six brigades would have dramatically altered the fighting along Willoughby Run and on McPherson's Ridge earlier in the morning. The commanding general pondered his options. With an additional 31 pieces of ordnance in the artillery battalions of Lieutenant Colonel John Jameson Garnett and Major William Thomas Poague now arriving on the field, and Richard Anderson's Division just a handful of miles away, the entirety of Hill's Third Corps would soon be available for battle.

Lee was not about to send forward any portion of Third Corps, however, until he received further word from Ewell. Campbell Brown, Ewell's stepson, had personally informed Lee just a few hours earlier that Robert Rodes and Jubal Early were marching their divisions for Gettysburg along two different roads from, respectively, the northwest and northeast.[10] Unfortunately, Lee did not know when these troops would be arriving on the field, although he might have reasonably assumed they would be available before the end of the day. On the other hand, the commanding general knew that Ewell's third division under Edward Johnson, together with two battalions from the Second Corps artillery reserve, were marching east behind Anderson's Division across South Mountain toward Gettysburg. Given the miles-long congestion on the Chambersburg Pike, however, Johnson and the artillery were almost certainly too far away to reach the field before very late that afternoon, and after a grueling 25-miles march would render them questionable for hard service anyway. James Longstreet's First Corps was bringing up the rear of the army's eastward advance from Chambersburg. His corps, except for Pickett's Division, would be available sometime tomorrow.

Therefore, based on what he knew early on the afternoon of July 1, Lee was unwilling to risk further action until the Army of Northern Virginia was concentrated or an opportunity presented itself.[11]

Ewell's Arrival

Just as Lee was contemplating the temporary stalemate on Hill's front, Federal troops of unknown origin began shifting northward on Seminary and Oak ridges. Enemy fire during this realignment slackened along the Chambersburg Pike, allowing a closer look at the enemy's positions.[12] Lee's personal reconnaissance (in the absence of Stuart's cavalry) was interrupted by the welcome sound of Southern guns booming from Oak Hill. Riding back to his observation post on Herr Ridge, Lee listened and watched as two batteries belonging to Lieutenant Colonel Tom Carter's artillery battalion showered shells at an unseen enemy. Dick Ewell had reached the field.[13]

General Ewell, accompanied by Isaac Trimble and riding alongside Major General Robert Emmett Rodes' 8,000-man division, had left Heidlersburg early that morning. Trimble, who had been temporarily attached to Ewell by Lee only a few days earlier, recalled that "after an hour or two [of] marching, a halt was made" about 10:00 a.m. at Middletown, a village seven miles from Gettysburg. Ewell paused to read Powell Hill's note of the evening before advising that Third Corps would march toward Gettysburg the next morning. A brief discussion with Trimble followed before Ewell decided to conform to Hill's movement and order Rodes to march to Gettysburg via the Mummasburg Road.[14] This decision—reached *after* Trimble related to Ewell, Rodes, and Early that Lee's objective was "to attack the advance of the enemy, wherever found, with a superior force and turn it back in confusion"—conformed to the commanding general's intention to concentrate the two corps around Gettysburg.[15]

And it was exactly the right decision. "We heard the roar of artillery on our right" about four miles northwest of Gettysburg, recalled Trimble who, "knew the ground [and] requested to lead Rodes' Division to a good position." Ewell agreed. The situation could not have been better scripted. Ewell's advance arrived squarely on the right flank of the Federal force deployed on the western outskirts of Gettysburg. Realizing the potential opportunity unfolding before him, Ewell deployed Rodes' Division under the cover of Oak Hill. Staffers Thomas T. Turner and Ewell's stepson, George Campbell Brown (who had returned from his earlier mission to Lee), were dispatched by Ewell with orders to find Jubal Early and hurry him into position on Rodes's left, where Early was "to attack at once."[16] As Ewell would later report, "it was too late to avoid an engagement without abandoning the position [Oak Hill] already taken up, and I determined to push the attack vigorously." Ewell personally placed Thomas Carter's battalion of artillery on the nose of Oak Hill. The gunners had already begun lobbing shells into the Federal lines when Rodes received permission to deploy his brigades and assault the enemy.

Robert Emmett Rodes, whom Douglas Southall Freeman described as "a Norse God in Confederate gray," was one of the army's rising stars. His handling of a

Richard Stoddert Ewell (1817-1872)

Ewell's career within Lee's army is somewhat analogous to that of Powell Hill's. Although he served with distinction as an aggressive brigade and division commander, Ewell's record as a corps leader left much to be desired. Stonewall Jackson had recommended Ewell to lead Second Corps, and his first test at that level in the Second Battle for Winchester seemed to confirm the decision to elevate him to that important position. How he would perform in a large scale general engagement was still an open question during the middle hours of July 1, 1863. *Library of Congress*

brigade during the Seven Days' Battles impressed his superior officers, and his performance at South Mountain and Sharpsburg marked him as a man destined for higher command. At Chancellorsville, Rodes led one of Jackson's divisions in the sweeping attack that resulted in his much-deserved promotion to major general. No one expected anything but excellence from the Virginia native and graduate of VMI. As his troops tramped under a hot sun into position on Oak Hill, Rodes watched with interest as Federal infantry snaked its way out of the northern outskirts of Gettysburg and deployed into line of battle below.[17]

The formations Rodes surveyed from Oak Hill belonged to the beleaguered Federal Eleventh Corps under the command of the one-armed Major General Oliver Otis Howard. During the summer of 1863, Howard's corps, more than any other in the entire Army of the Potomac, was suffering from a lack of confidence. Known as the "German Corps" because of its high percentage of German-speaking regiments, Howard's luckless organization had endured one defeat after another and was riven with command rivalries and mistrust from the lowliest private to Howard himself. Just eight weeks earlier it had fallen prey to Stonewall Jackson's rolling flank assault at Chancellorsville, and Howard's negligence had contributed largely to the collapse that followed. Many of these same Eleventh Corps regiments had also been roughly handled at Second Manassas, and had unsuccessfully fought Jackson's troops in the Valley Campaign of 1862. Although Howard commanded an abundance of outstanding regiments led by capable officers, much of the rest of the Army of the Potomac considered the unfortunate Eleventh Corps infantry to be the least battle worthy soldiers in the entire army. As one historian noted, "Oliver Howard marched to Gettysburg at the head of an uninterrupted string of battlefield setbacks. He was a general desperately in need of a change of luck."[18] He would not find it in Pennsylvania.

The sudden appearance of Howard's Federals prompted Rodes to accelerate his preparations. "I determined to attack with my center and right," he later reported, "holding at bay still another force, then emerging from the town (apparently with the intention of turning my left)." His front line stretched about one mile from the Carlisle Road to the Mummasburg Road and consisted of the capable brigadier George Doles on the far left, or eastern flank of the division, with the brigades of Col. Edward O'Neal and Brigadier General Alfred Iverson extending the line westward. Rodes' two remaining brigades under Stephen Ramseur and Junius Daniel were held in reserve. The circumstances dictating Rodes' deployment were eerily reminiscent of Heth's earlier preparations. Rodes first strike included just three of his five available brigades (Heth had utilized two of four), and the random marching order of his division deposited his least capable leaders in two of those three positions. It was about 1:30 p.m.[19]

Problems plagued Rodes' attack from the first step off Oak Hill. O'Neal and Iverson failed to coordinate their movements with each other or the balance of the division. O'Neal advanced just three of his five regiments and remained behind with the 5th Alabama. He was, Rodes later noted with some disgust, "repulsed quickly, and with loss." Iverson's men suffered an even greater misfortune. The general remembered to tell his soldiers to "give the enemy hell" but failed to deploy skirmishers for the advance across the Forney farm fields. Like O'Neal, he tarried far to the rear, an unforgivable sin for a brigadier in Lee's army. Hundreds of his men fell to a fusillade delivered by Henry Baxter's hidden regiments from behind a low stone wall at the northern end of Oak Ridge.[20]

*   *   *

Harry Heth could see it all. From his vantage point along the Chambersburg Pike, he watched as first O'Neal and then Iverson attacked the spur of Oak Ridge and fell back in confusion. Rodes was clearly having trouble and needed help. After searching unsuccessfully for Powell Hill, Heth found General Lee on Herr Ridge, binoculars pressed to his eyes silently watching the same struggle. Heth was anxious to resume the battle and redeem himself after his earlier humiliation.

"Rodes is heavily engaged," Heth announced, stating what was already obvious to everyone. "Had I not better attack?"[21]

"No," answered Lee. "I am not prepared to bring on a general engagement today—Longstreet is not up."[22]

At least one of Ewell's divisions was now on the field locked in an intense struggle north of town, and only two Federal corps were actively opposing his troops, but Lee was unwilling to risk a full-scale battle until more of his army was present—a concentration he hoped would yield an opportunity to deliver a crippling and demoralizing blow upon his adversary.

Lee had advised Ewell that a general engagement was not desirous until the army had been concentrated, but now his Second Corps leader was attacking the enemy with great vigor.[23] Why, Lee must have wondered, was Ewell allowing Rodes to launch an attack? Ewell must know or see something Lee did not. Did he perceive an advantage that he was now trying to press? Ewell knew when and where Early's Division—which Lee had been informed through Major Brown was also marching to Gettysburg—would arrive. Would his infantry soon be joining the attack, overlapping the Federal right flank on Oak Ridge?

News reached Lee about 2:30 p.m. that Early's artillery (which he could not see) had just opened fire north of Gettysburg, and that "Old Jubilee's" division was deploying to attack an exposed Federal flank extending beyond Rodes' left.[24] Lee did not have to see what was happening on Ewell's front to appreciate the significance of Early's appearance and position relative to that of the enemy. An unexpected and incredible opportunity was presenting itself. Early was exactly at the right place at the right time. When his arrival and impending attack was announced, Lee realized what Ewell was doing, and why: the right flank of the Federal line (which Lee could not see) was completely compromised: Rodes was hammering it hard from the northwest and north, and Early would soon be flanking the enemy's right and rear from the north and northwest.

The campaign Lee had envisioned in the conference with Trimble in Chambersburg a few days earlier was unfolding before his eyes. Available evidence indicated that he was fighting two corps, which certainly represented the vanguard of the Army of the Potomac. This added credence to Harrison's June 28 intelligence that two enemy corps were bivouacked at Frederick, Maryland. Their isolation at Gettysburg invited prompt destruction—but where was the third enemy corps Harrison said was also camped nearby Frederick? If it, too, was marching to the sound of the guns like Lee's own troops, how long would it be before it arrived to assist Reynolds and Howard, and where would it appear? Lee knew for sure that the Eleventh Corps north of town was being held in place by Rodes' attacks and was about to be enveloped by Early. Reynolds' First Corps, which represented the center and left end of the Federal line, was riveted to McPherson's Ridge by Powell Hill's troops. If Reynolds could be driven back at the same time into both the retreating Eleventh Corps and the head of the approaching enemy corps Lee assumed was marching to their assistance, the Confederates would not only gain another victory, but perhaps the decisive win Lee had so diligently been seeking.

Great Captains instinctively recognize opportunity and seek to take advantage of it. "War is composed of nothing but surprises," Napoleon had written. "While a general should adhere to general principles, he should never lose the opportunity to profit by these surprises. It is the essence of genius. In war there is only one favorable moment. Genius seizes it."[25] Lee knew what had to be done. Hill's Third Corps on and around Herr Ridge would vigorously assault and envelop the southern (or left) flank of the Federal line held by Reynolds' First Corps. Hill still had Heth's two unscathed brigades (Pettigrew and Brockenbrough) plus Pender's entire fresh division for the task. Lee, who usually sought to turn his opponent's flanks whenever possible, believed that these six brigades could attack and envelop the stationary enemy infantry on McPherson's Ridge, and then move on and carry Seminary Ridge. If his conception went according to plan, part of Rodes' command and Heth's two brigades would attack the Federal center, fixing the enemy in place while Pender's Division enveloped the Federal left and Early's Division and the remainder of Rodes' outfit flanked and rolled up the Federal right.

The Army of Northern Virginia had been given a miraculous opportunity to destroy two enemy corps. All Lee's troops required to gain an important victory on Northern soil was intelligent and aggressive leadership.

Hill's Attack and the Destruction of the Federal Left Flank

Powell Hill arrived on the field at Gettysburg about the same time as Lee. Ill or not, he was anxious to prove himself at the head of his new corps. Unlike Lee, Hill had been ready to fight a general engagement from the moment his gray stallion Champ set hoof on Herr Ridge. After learning of Heth's defeat, he had ordered Pender to ready his division to renew the assault. Lee's intervention stopped it cold. Now, with Ewell's guns thundering north of town and Rodes' infantry engaged, Lee finally ordered Hill to slip the leash from Third Corps. And he was ready. Hill always seemed to be ready.[26]

Ambrose Powell Hill's career with the Army of Northern Virginia got off to a rocky start when he opened the Seven Day's offensive prematurely with a direct attack at Mechanicsburg. The bloody repulse notwithstanding, Lee appreciated Hill's willingness to come to grips with the enemy when so many general officers made excuses for inaction. The Virginia native and West Point graduate also demonstrated remarkable marching abilities. At Cedar Mountain in August 1862, Hill drove his brigades for miles under a scorching sun, deployed quickly and skillfully, and saved Stonewall Jackson from an embarrassing defeat. He duplicated the deed again the following month at Sharpsburg, where his extraordinary 17-mile march from Harpers Ferry landed him squarely on the battlefield at the last possible moment to squeeze out a defensive tactical victory. Lee wrote to President Davis that after Longstreet and Jackson, "I consider A. P. Hill the best commander with me. He fights his troops well and takes good care of them." The pugnacious general stumbled with faulty defensive dispositions at Second Manassas and Fredericksburg, but his participation at Chancellorsville cemented over his earlier mistakes and enhanced his reputation. Frail, often ailing, and looking older than his 38 years, Hill was ready to order his men forward and defeat the Federals blocking his way to Gettysburg. The only question was who would show up: the impulsive Hill of Mechanicsburg, or the skillful and prudent Hill of Cedar Mountain and Sharpsburg?[27]

The answer was not long in coming. After Lee's directive, Hill ordered Harry Heth to immediately press froward and hit the Federals south of the Chambersburg Pike on McPherson's Ridge. Johnston Pettigrew's 2,744-man brigade was deployed in the center of the line, with John Brockenbrough's 1,000 Virginians on his left just below the Chambersburg Pike; perhaps 500 men from what was left of Archer's Brigade under its senior colonel, Birkett D. Fry, deployed on Pettigrew's right. A comparable number of defenders were waiting for them on McPherson's Ridge.[28]

Having Heth attack as soon as possible was perhaps the worst choice Hill could have made. Like a horse wearing blinders, Hill seems not to have carefully considered or *prepared* for any other options. Indeed, he seems not to have absorbed the lesson of Heth's earlier catastrophe. If he had, Hill would have ordered Heth to hold back his infantry until Dorsey Pender's 6,000-man division had deployed on Heth's right flank, a short and easy march that could have been accomplished with celerity. This alignment would have extended the Confederate battle line south beyond the Hagerstown (or Fairfield) Road and compromised the left flank of the Federals on McPherson's Ridge. Heth's assault would have pinned the enemy in his front along Willoughby Run on McPherson's Ridge, while the experienced Pender and his veteran brigadiers conducted a broad and sweeping flank attack. Instead, Hill ordered Heth forward around 2:30 p.m. in an unsupported frontal attack without coordinated support from Pender. His error was compounded when he ordered Edward Thomas' Georgia brigade from Pender's Division to act as a reserve near Pegram's artillery battalion in order to support his own left flank.[29]

And so Heth's lines of infantry stepped out of the timber on Herr's Ridge below the Chambersburg Pike and steadily tramped east toward the next rise. "They marched along quietly and with confidence, but swiftly," wrote one Federal artillery officer.[30] General Doubleday's (Reynolds') command included Roy Stone's L-shaped Bucktail brigade, one leg facing north and running along the roadway (it had recently participated in driving back Daniel's Brigade of Rodes' Division), and the other facing west toward Heth. On Stone's left flank was Meredith's exhausted Iron Brigade in McPherson's Woods, with Chapman Biddle's Pennsylvania and New York regiments holding the fields between the Hagerstown Road and Meredith's left flank. Even without Pender's help, Pettigrew's large brigade slightly overlapped the enemy left flank (by "the front of two regiments," remembered a Federal colonel with some embellishment). The strong attack triggered exceptional defensive performances and the presence of Colonel William Gamble's cavalry hovering beyond the Confederate right flank prolonged the inevitable—but at a horrible price. Thousands of men were killing one another within shouting distance. For the better part of an hour, most of the action up and down the line devolved into a stand-up slug fest that could have been avoided by using Pender's brigades.[31]

As Heth's men locked it up with the enemy, a minie ball struck him in the head and knocked him unconscious for the better part of a day. Only a thick wad of paper inserted in the brim of his hat saved his life.[32] It took a while before the news reached Pettigrew that he was now in command of the division, but he was in the thick of the fight and concerned with his own regiments, so there was little he could do other than drive his own men forward. With Heth down and Pettigrew's right overlapping the Federal left, Hill had another excellent opportunity to seize control of the situation and play the part of an energetic and opportunistic corps leader. Instead, he did little but watch as his men waged their bloody action. Still, Pettigrew's modest envelopment and weight of numbers eventually crushed the left regiments of Biddle's brigade and began unraveling the Federal line. Slowly, inexorably, Pettigrew's North Carolinians turned and forced back regiment after regiment, compromising Doubleday's entire position. Pinned in front and threatened on its left and rear, the Iron Brigade slowly gave way as well, followed, finally, by Stone's Pennsylvanians, who were being hammered in front by Brockenbrough's Virginians and again from the north by Daniel's North Carolinians.[32] Without Pender's brigades blocking his retreat, Doubleday broke off the action and fell back across the 600 yards of shallow fields to Seminary Ridge. There, a defensive line was reestablished anchored with several artillery batteries straddling the Chambersburg

Pike. The position ran south along the ridge in front of the Lutheran Theological Seminary. Too confused and battered to mount a pursuit, Pettigrew wisely pulled the infantry back, ending Harry Heth's afternoon assault. The intense attack had lasted more than an hour and left hundreds of killed and wounded in its wake.[33]

*   *   *

While Heth's brigades were driving the Federals off McPherson's Ridge, Dick Ewell's divisions were enjoying success north of town. The sudden demise of Rodes' initial piecemeal effort with Iverson and O'Neal forced him to modify his plan of attack. With George Doles 1,369 Georgians holding and protecting his left flank, Rodes ordered Dodson Ramseur's 1,090 crack North Carolinians, together with Junius Daniel's largely untested 2,294 North Carolinians, to move forward. Exhibiting considerable skill, these brigadiers retrieved Confederate fortunes by hammering the Federals of John Robinson's First Corps division clinging

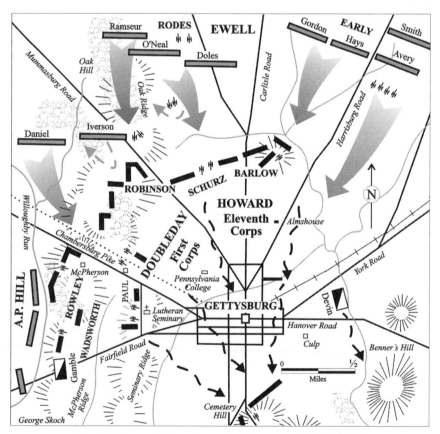

Ewell's Second Corps Attack, Afternoon, July 2, 1863

tenaciously to Oak Ridge's northern fringes. After a gallant defense, they fell back under the blows and retired south and east, with Rodes' infantry doing their best to sweep them along.[34]

Meanwhile, Jubal Anderson Early was about to have his best day of the war on July 1. The native and well-schooled Virginian graduated from West Point in 1837. After brief service he resigned to practice law and dabble in politics. When Virginia left the Union, he offered his services and was commissioned a colonel. At that rank Early conducted his brigade well at First Manassas, was promoted to brigadier soon thereafter, and led his Virginians on the Peninsula and during the Second Manassas and Sharpsburg campaigns. Early's attack at the head of a division stabilized Powell Hill's ill-deployed front at Fredericksburg, and he performed competently there again during the Chancellorsville Campaign. A hard fighter, Early was also arrogant, independent-minded, arthritic-ridden, and cantankerous. Lee jokingly called him "my bad old man."

Leaving William "Extra Billy" Smith's Brigade to watch the eastern approaches to the York Pike, Early deployed Harry Hays, John Gordon, and Isaac Avery (leading Robert Hoke's Brigade) and drove them south against Oliver Howard's hapless Eleventh Corps. Gordon's Georgians formed the spearhead of the thrust, hitting and crushing the right Federal flank on Blocher's (Barlow's) Knoll, routing that key point in the line and unraveling Howard's attempt to hold back

John Brown Gordon
(1832-1904)

Despite his lack of formal military training, John Brown Gordon was an officer of considerable talent. His rise in rank from captain to major general (in 1864) was one of the most impressive achievements in the history of Lee's army. As a brigadier general at Gettysburg, Gordon launched a crushing attack on July 1 that unhinged the right flank of Howard's Eleventh Corps line at Blocher's (now called Barlow's) Knoll.

Library of Congress

Ewell. About 4:00 p.m., Hays' 1,300 Louisianians and Avery's 1,242 North Carolinians advanced, smashing the line held by Colonel Charles Coster's small brigade that had formed on a rise between Stevens' Run and the north edge of town. Hays' screaming Tigers swept through the streets and alleys of Gettysburg, rounding up more Federal prisoners than the strength of their own brigade. Thousands of Federals were captured in the ensuing confusion as the corps' remnants fell back through Gettysburg and climbed the high ground southeast of town.[35]

Jubal Early had reached the defining moment of his career. Hays and Avery were advancing victoriously, sending prisoners by the droves to the rear, and Gordon and the division's artillery battalion under Lieutenant Colonel Hilary Pollard Jones were close behind and ready to lend support. Captain James McDowell Carrington, commanding the Charlottsville Virginia Artillery, was ordered "to advance into the town," where he unlimbered three of his four 12-pounder Napoleons in order to cover Hays' flank. Colonel John Thompson Brown, Second Corps chief of artillery, was so convinced Early would continue his advance he sought out a good road for not only Jones' guns, but also the two corps reserve battalions Brown was prepared to order forward in support. Early had more than 4,000 battle-hardened infantry at hand, 16 guns of his own division, and an additional 30 pieces from the two battalions of the Second Corps reserve ready to support his movements. The only question was how he use them.[36]

*   *   *

After Harry Heth's attack on the other side of the battlefield, the Federals used the brief lull that followed to reorganize the battered 600-yard southern flank of the First Corps line around the Lutheran Theological Seminary. As enemy artillery pieces unlimbered and officers struggled to get their men into position, the brigades of Dorsey Pender's Division slipped through Heth's spent formations and prepared to renew the assault. Hill finally ordered him forward. It was about 4:00 p.m.

The 29-year-old William Dorsey Pender was the youngest major general in the Army of Northern Virginia. His West Point education prepared him well for war, as his splendid record as a colonel and brigadier attests. Although he had assumed command of the famous Light Division after Hill was wounded at Chancellorsville, July 1 was Pender's first opportunity to march the division into battle as his own. With Edward Thomas' 1,300 Georgians held in reserve, Pender aligned his remaining three brigades, veterans all, abreast from the Chambersburg Pike south to the Hagerstown (Farifield) Road, a front of almost one mile. On the left advanced his old brigade of 1,400 North Carolinians under the command of Alfred M. Scales. In the center was Samuel McGowan's superb brigade of 1,600 South Carolinians, which fielded that day only four of its five regiments.[36] With McGowan still recovering from his Chancellorsville wound, the brigade was temporarily under the command of Colonel Abner Perrin. James Lane's brigade of 1,700 North

Carolinians finished the deployment, anchoring the division's right, or southern, flank.[37]

It was fortunate for Powell Hill that his old division was in the hands of such an accomplished officer as Dorsey Pender, for it was about to advance against some of the finest soldiers in the Army of the Potomac, deployed on excellent defensive ground and supported by several well-served batteries of artillery. All along Seminary Ridge, the Federals delivered what one South Carolinian described as "a perfectly clear, unobstructed fire upon us."[38] To the left of the South Carolinians were the Tar Heels under Alfred Scales. They moved steadily forward, holding their fire while weathering a murderous storm of shells, bullets, and finally, canister. "Their bearing was magnificent," wrote Lieutenant Colonel Rufus Dawes of the 6th Wisconsin. "They maintained their alignment with great precision. In many cases the colors of the regiments were advanced several paces in front of the line."[39] The heavy concentration of Federal ordnance and rifled small arms ripped apart Scales' regiments. "Their ranks went down like grass before the scythe from the united fire of our regiments and the battery," wrote Colonel W. W. Robinson of the 7th Wisconsin.[40] Every field officer in the brigade except one was either killed or wounded including Scales, who fell when a shell fragment ripped into his leg. With their impetus stalled, the North Carolinians halted and returned fire.[41]

On Scales' right, the Light Division's prized brigade under Perrin moved steadily up Seminary Ridge, its red battle flags marking the progress of the determined and spirited South Carolinians. As the fierce Federal fire from the remnants of Biddle's and Meredith's brigades tore into his front, Perrin noticed that his advance had outstripped Lane's North Carolinians on his right, some of whom has stopped to address the Federal cavalry firing into their exposed flank. Lane's support was important because Perrin could see a body of Federals to his oblique right front positioned to deliver an enfilade fire into his own flank, and Scales's men were melting away on his left. Perrin was determined to press home the charge. Struggling to keep the brigade's hard-pressed left half regiments—the 1st South Carolina (Provisional) and the 14th South Carolina—on course, Perrin skillfully redirected the 12th and 13th South Carolina, the right half of his command southeast toward the Hagerstown Road to assist Lane. "There was no giving back on our part," explained the brigade's historian. "[C]heering and closing up, they went, through the shells, through the Minie balls, heeding neither the dead who sank down by their sides, nor the fire from the front which killed them, until they threw themselves desperately on the line of Federals and swept them from the field."[42]

Colonel Charles Wainwright, the senior artillery officer in the Federal First Corps, watched Perrin's ranks brave the heaviest maelstrom he could deliver. "Never have I seen such a charge," Wainwright recalled. "Not a man seemed to falter."[43] After the left half of Perrin's brigade drove back Biddle's men from Seminary Ridge near the Chambersburg Pike, the victorious Confederates looked to exploit their gains by turning north and continuing their assault across the pike and

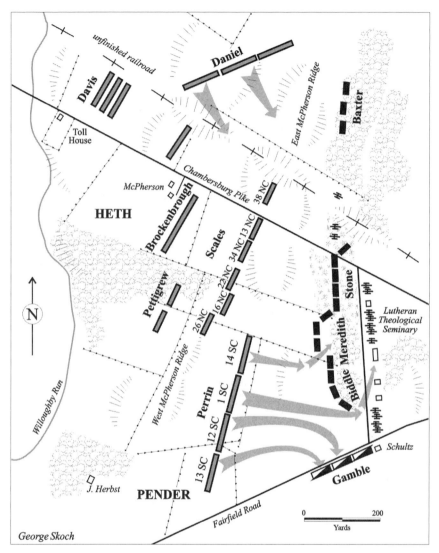

Pender's Light Division Carries Seminary Ridge, Afternoon, July 1, 1863

up the spine of the ridge. Perrin's soldiers enfiladed what was left of the Federal line there and pressed home their advantage against the Iron Brigade with fire and cold steel, inflicting greater losses upon the Midwesterners than they themselves had received during the advance. The Federals, writes one historian, were "caught in a fearful cauldron of death and maiming," and their "line unraveled."[44]

Lee must have been pleased. From his vantage point on Herr Ridge, he witnessed the heroes of Second Manassas break the strong Federal line on middle

Seminary Ridge and then roll up from south to north what was left, capturing four colors—including the First Corps' flag—one 3-inch Ordnance rifle, and scores of men.[45] Perrin's remarkable attack would have been even more successful had James Lane advanced his North Carolinians with the same determination. Lane's languid exhibition including allowing his brigade to drift south and become distracted by the demonstrations of a single regiment of Federal cavalry (the 8th Illinois), instead of sweeping in on the Federal left flank as Pender intended.[46] Nevertheless, by the time Lane reached Seminary Ridge, the enemy line had already been "broken to pieces" by Perrin's whooping South Carolinians.[47] His impressive victory notwithstanding, Perrin was angry with Lane's failure to keep pace with his men. "If we had any support [from Lane]," Perrin wrote South Carolina Governor Milledge Luke Bonham, "we could have taken every piece of artillery they had and thousands of prisoners."[48]

Colonel Perrin's observation concerning Lane's timidity should also be applied to Powell Hill. Focusing on the heroic charge of the South Carolinians, contemporaries and many historians have ignored the unnecessary casualties suffered by Hill's Third Corps on July 1. The fact that two of his three divisions had been heavily mauled attacking positions that could have easily been flanked only drives home the point that Hill ignored or did not fully explore the opportunities open to him. The location of the southern end of the Federal left flank on

Abner Monroe Perrin (1827-1864)

Described by a fellow South Carolinian as "an officer of remarkable gallantry," Abner Perrin was another of the many talented soldiers who rose to prominence from within the ranks of Maxcy Gregg's and Samuel McGowan's legendary brigade. McGowan was wounded at Chancellorsville, so Perrin directed the brigade at Gettysburg. On July 1 his skill and audacity, coupled with the valorous conduct of his South Carolinians, broke the Federal First Corps line in the area of the Lutheran Theological Seminary. *Eleanor S. Brockenbrough Library, The Museum of the Confederacy, Richmond*

both McPherson's and Seminary ridges was no mystery to anyone. Pender's full division could easily have been deployed more to the south for either Heth's second assault or for the attack on Seminary Ridge. Used like a giant gate around the flank of the Federal First Corps, Pender's brigades would have cut off its route of retreat. Had Pender been employed earlier (with Heth) or fully (with Thomas' Brigade), Hill's casualties would have been significantly lower and the results substantially more impressive.

As it was, Pender's determined assault, combined with Robert Rodes's thrust from the north shattered what was arguably the finest infantry corps in the Army of the Potomac. Pender's effort is all the more impressive because Scales and Perrin were outnumbered at the point of their attack by a foe who enjoyed a strong defensive position supported with 22 pieces of artillery and clear fields of fire.[49] Perrin's charge provided yet another example of the ferocity with which many units of the Army of Northern Virginia delivered their assaults. By 4:30 p.m., John Reynolds' proud First Corps—which had offered stubborn and heroic resistance—was an eviscerated, broken and retreating wreck. Even the famed Iron Brigade had been effectively destroyed.[50] Confederate losses, while significant, were not nearly as heavy.[51] Pender, however, could not yet stop and tabulate his losses. After taking possession of Seminary Ridge, he watched as Perrin's South Carolinians continued pursuing and rounding up prisoners on the downward slope to Gettysburg.[52] Working hard, the new division commander rallied elements of Scales' Brigade and brought up Lane in an attempt to reorganize his command. As he did so, a small group of mounted officers approached from the west on the Chambersburg Pike, including one on a gray horse looking for an opportunity to inflict further damage on the defeated and retreating enemy.

Lee Orders the High Ground Taken

General Lee had watched from afar while the Federals were pushed off the ridges west of Gettysburg. He of all people knew from past experience that the heavy losses some of his units had sustained might be in vain if the successes of the afternoon attacks were not vigorously followed up. Was another opportunity beyond the town's spires waiting to be exploited? He ascended Seminary Ridge to find out, reined in Traveller north of the Lutheran Theological Seminary, and studied the situation. One observer remembered seeing Lee eagerly "sweep the horizon with his glasses," looking across the long and gentle downhill slope towards Gettysburg and to the heights looming beyond. The general, he continued, "scanned [the high ground] with great attention."[53]

As far as Lee could see in any direction the Federal army was in retreat. Thousands of men were streaming into and out of the town in great confusion and without any visible organization. Others were moving across fields and walking up the wooded height just southeast of town. The scene was also witnessed by Powell Hill. Like Lee, Hill too was bothered by the absence of Stuart's troopers. "The want of cavalry," he noted, "had been and was again seriously felt." But, "the rout of the enemy was complete." Lee, however, knew that was not the case. As he quickly learned from prisoners, only the vanguard of the approaching Army of the Potomac had been defeated. Unless he could develop the opportunity visible before him, the Federals would soon regroup on the hills beyond Gettysburg.[54]

And there was plenty of daylight left to do something. All that was needed was one more determined assault to grasp what might well develop into the decisive victory Lee sought on Northern soil. "I shall throw an overwhelming force on their advance," he had informed General Trimble a few days earlier, "crush it, follow up the success, drive one corps back on another, and by successive repulses and surprises before they can concentrate create a panic and virtually destroy the army." The battle he had articulated was taking place. With victory within his grasp, Lee believed continued pressure in the form of artillery fire, followed up with energetic infantry assaults, would carry the day.

Powell Hill was directed to bring up his artillery and open fire on the retreating foe, including those already positioned on Cemetery Hill.[55] Lee also ordered Brigadier General William N. Pendleton, the army's nominal chief of artillery, to determine "whether positions on the right could not be found to enfilade the valley between our position and the town and the enemy's batteries next to the town."[56] The battalions of John Garnett and William Poague, which had been in reserve behind Herr Ridge, were ordered to the front. Pendleton positioned Garnett's 15 guns in a vale on the west side of the ridge just south of the seminary. Poague's 16-gun outfit was sent to the right of Garnett, south of where the Hagerstown Road crested Seminary Ridge. Pendleton decided to leave the guns "in park," until his staff could locate a good position for their use.[57] The reverend-general rode out on the Hagerstown (Fairfield) Road "to the ridge adjoining the town, intending to put there Garnett's and other guns. . . . The position was within range of the hill beyond town," he later wrote, "to which the enemy was retreating, and where he was massing his batteries." General Dodson Ramseur, however, left his brigade in Gettysburg at this time and sought out Pendleton. He "requested that our batteries might not then open, as they would draw a concentrated fire upon his men, much exposed," reported the artillerist. While Ramseur's concern for his men was laudable, Pendleton's orders from the commanding general were to find an artillery platform and smother Cemetery Hill. And a good location had been found. Instead of following his instructions, Pendleton decided that "unless as part of a combined assault, I at once saw it would be worse than useless to open fire there [Cemetery Hill]."[58]

Pendleton disobeyed Lee's order to open fire on Cemetery Hill.[59] His decision *not* to fire did nothing to advance the Confederate cause, did nothing to silence or drive away enemy batteries, and allowed Federal officers time to rally demoralized troops. As we shall also soon learn in greater detail, while Pendleton was deciding to keep his guns "in park," Generals Ewell, Early, and Rodes were busy convincing themselves that Second Corps needed assistance from Hill's Third Corps in order to attack Cemetery Hill. Since they were waiting for some show of support, it is impossible to calculate the negative impact of Pendleton's disobedience. At a minimum, 31 guns directed against Cemetery Hill would have substantially impacted enemy efforts to rally broken formations and organize an effective defense. Lee had ordered it, and Pendleton failed to deliver.

While Pendleton was frustrating the commanding general's orders, Lee was conferring with Powell Hill about the possibility of sending his infantry across the valley and delivering one final attack against the reforming enemy on Cemetery Hill. The normally aggressive Hill demurred. "My own two divisions [were] exhausted by some six hours' hard fighting,"he later reported, and "prudence led me

to be content with what had been gained, and not push forward troops exhausted and necessarily disordered, probably to encounter fresh troops of the enemy."[60] It is difficult this long after the fact to challenge what, at least initially, appears to be a judicious decision. Still, a careful examination reveals that Hill's opinion was not warranted by the day's action. In light of Perrin's successful direct charge against some of the best troops the Federals had to offer, why would Hill conclude that his fresh brigades and artillery battalions were incapable of

William Nelson Pendleton (1809-1883)

The Episcopal Reverend was the army's nominal chief of artillery and the weakest link in the chain of Lee's small staff. Pendleton owed his rank and status to Jefferson Davis—a situation General Lee recognized. Lee's reorganization of his artillery following Chancellorsville was designed, at least in part, to minimize Pendleton's impact and influence on the battlefield. *Library of Congress*

accomplishing similar feats against a disorganized enemy? It was a questionable observation offered by a general who was ill and had missed the morning fight that triggered the meeting engagement, and then had offered little if any guidance during most of the afternoon action. After what was perhaps the army's finest tactical success of the war, this same officer claimed to be "content with what had been gained" instead of realizing—as Lee and so many others did—that there was still daylight left to deliver a knockout punch.

Hill's claim that Third Corps was too exhausted to advance is simply not accurate. Heth's four-brigade division and Scales and Perrin from Pender's Division had indeed shot their bolt for the day. But Hill still had at hand two brigades from the Light Division—Edward Thomas' fresh Georgians, and James Lane's almost equally untouched North Carolinians, a total of almost 3,000 men. Substantial artillery was also available to Hill. Although the reserve battalions under Willie Pegram and David Gregg McIntosh had worked for hours and had suffered some losses, they could still be counted upon for good service. Standing idly at the western base of Seminary Ridge were the 31 guns in the battalions of Garnett and Poague; only one of their batteries had fired a shot that day. If Pendleton could not (or would not) use them, there was nothing to prevent Hill from employing them on the eastern glacis of Seminary Ridge. Also, David McIntosh's Third Corps artillery reserve battalion was in good condition and possessed the best long-range battery in Confederate service—Hardaway's Alabama Artillery with its two accurate 12-pounder Whitworth breech-loading rifles and two 3-in. Ordnance rifles. These pieces could have easily joined Garnett and Poague on the eastern side of Seminary Ridge before 5:00 p.m. Therefore, Hill had immediately available one of the army's best division commanders in Dorsey Pender and 3,000 men, all of whom could have moved forward by 5:00 p.m. supported by a minimum of 35 guns from the battalions of Garnett, Poague and McIntosh.[61]

In addition to all these troops, Hill's largest division under Richard Anderson, five fresh brigades totaling 6,925 men, was just a few miles away occupying "the position in line of battle which had earlier that day been vacated by Pender's Division [Schoolhouse Ridge]."[62] If Hill had promptly ordered Anderson to advance his division from Schoolhouse Ridge, he could have organized and launched a seven-brigade attack with some 10,000 infantry, supported by five battalions of artillery boasting more than 75 guns. His opposition consisted of a depleted Federal force totaling less than half that number that had already suffered defeat.[63] This type of Herculean effort, however, would have required imagination, enterprise, and energy—characteristics Hill had not demonstrated all day. Admittedly, under the best of circumstances it is unlikely that an attack of this magnitude could have been delivered much before 6:30 p.m. (about two hours after the completion of Pender's successful charge), which would have left more than one hour of daylight for the operation.

Warfare is an uncertain business. Given the day's events, it seems reasonable to conclude that even with Howard's single uncommitted Eleventh Corps brigade under Colonel Orland Smith (1,639 men), the remaining disorganized and previously routed Eleventh and First corps formations (and the late-arriving reinforcements from other commands), no longer possessed the military capabilities necessary to successfully repulse a large-scale Third Corps infantry assault preceded by an artillery bombardment. If the weight of Early's and Rodes' divisions were added to the attack (or any portions of them), the Federal task of holding Cemetery Ridge would have been virtually impossible.[64]

Powell Hill was willing to settle for a partial victory, but many of his officers realized the opportunity slipping through Southern fingers. Major David Gregg McIntosh observed the fleeing Federals with the eye of a trained artillerist. A veteran of many fields, McIntosh believed that concentrated artillery fire directed against Cemetery Hill would have been disastrous to the Federals and made it very difficult for them to rally their units. "A greater military blunder was never committed," he penned after the war. It would have been easy "to have placed thirty or forty guns on Seminary Ridge, south of Cashtown road, and used them precisely as they were used before Pickett's charge on the third day."[65] McIntosh's Federal counterpart, Colonel Charles Wainwright, thought the same thing. After witnessing the defeat of Reynold's First Corps, Wainwright was convinced certain doom would have befallen his army had Hill's infantry continued their pursuit. "There was not a doubt in my mind but that I should go to Richmond [as a POW]," the artillerist recalled. "There was nothing to stop the advancing [Rebel] line."[66] But it was not to be. Hill needed to reach inside himself and find the aggressive spirit he had exhibited so often in the past. But on July 1, when he needed it the most, it was no where to be found.

General Lee accepted Hill's claim that his men were not capable of continuing the attack. With Ewell and two divisions of his infantry much closer to the objective, he looked to Second Corps to seize the high ground and complete the victory before the shattered Federal formations rallied, or before Federal reinforcements arrived. Staffer Major Walter Taylor was summoned by the commanding general, who pointed in the direction of the fleeing Federals and the hills beyond and issued one of the most famous orders of the American Civil War. According to Taylor, Lee instructed him ride over to Ewell and tell him that it was "only necessary to press 'those people' in order to secure possession of the heights." The order ended with the words "if possible" or "if practicable."[67] Both phrases were interchangeable to Lee and represented the accustomed measure of respect—either in speech or in writing—he accorded his lieutenants when giving them an order.[68] Spurring his horse Fleetfoot, Taylor galloped off Seminary Ridge and followed the route of Perrin's victorious South Carolinians into Gettysburg, where he found Ewell and his staff in the town square. The corps leader, remembered Taylor, did not express any objection to the order and did not indicate that there was any impediment to obeying it. Ewell, he explained after the war, "left the impression upon my mind that it would be executed." Satisfied that Ewell understood what was expected of him, Taylor returned to Lee.[69]

*   *   *

After Taylor departed, Jubal Early and Robert Rodes met with Ewell in the square to discuss what to do next. Early, after his victorious sweep from the north, had already carefully examined the terrain and the enemy visible south and east of the town. The highest elevation in the immediate area was Culp's Hill, a heavily timbered and rocky eminence about three-quarters of a mile southeast of Gettysburg. Both Culp's Hill and a treeless hillock at its western base (now known as Stevens' Knoll) appeared to be unoccupied. These heights were especially important because they enfiladed the Federal position on East Cemetery Hill and the generals knew the Baltimore Pike, an important logistical line, ran immediately behind Meade's right.[70] Cemetery Hill appeared lightly held by the last organized body of Federal troops in sight (the 1,639 men belonging to Orland Smith's Second Brigade, supported at that time by only four 3-inch Ordnance rifles of Captain Michael Wiedrich's New York battery). Hundreds of survivors of the day's fighting were running and walking up and over Cemetery Hill. Rallying these broken formations would pose a serious challenge for the enemy.[71]

About 800 yards separated the thinly held Federal defensive line on Cemetery Hill and Jubal Early's brigades under Hays and Avery. If Early had ever studied Napoleon's Maxims, he might have recalled two that had more relevance at that

Walter Herron Taylor (1838-1916)

Walter Taylor served as assistant adjutant general on Lee's staff from the spring of 1861 to Appomattox. The young Virginian was an exceedingly capable and tireless worker with many responsibilities. Had Taylor performed the same duties while on Napoleon's staff, his functions would have been equivalent of *two* of Napoleon's most trusted and powerful lieutenants—the Grand Marshal of the Palace and Chief of Staff.

Eleanor S. Brockenbrough Library, The Museum of the Confederacy, Richmond

moment than perhaps at any other time: "Hesitation and half measures lose all in war," and "The destiny of States depend upon a moment."[72] Early, however, one of Lee's most aggressive subordinates, was not thinking of military maxims. His division was largely undamaged, his artillery ready to advance, the enemy in utter chaos. But now, with a complete victory sitting in his hand, he suddenly and inexplicably straightened his fingers instead of closing his fist. He convinced himself that pursuit was necessary—but that he needed help to do it. As Early was casting his gaze south, Gordon's Georgians caught their breath and refilled their cartridge boxes, Avery's regiments advanced to the railroad before sliding around town to the east, and Hays' Louisianians were vigorously clearing out the eastern half of Gettysburg before reforming for further action.[73] With three brigades and his artillery battalion poised for action, Early suspended his pursuit and rode to the right in search of Ewell, Rodes, or even Powell Hill, whose South Carolinians under Abner Perrin had already entered the town from the west. Early was looking for someone to help him continue the attack and support from units in other commands before the enemy "should recover from his evident dismay, in order to get possession of the hills to which he had fallen back with the remnant of his forces."[74]

Perhaps we will never know why Early, who was schooled under the tutelage of Stonewall Jackson, believed his undamaged and ably led brigades and artillery needed assistance in storming Cemetery Hill when others in the division from brigadier general to private believed they could accomplish the mission themselves. General Gordon watched the retreating Federals flooding over the heights like a torrent, large numbers of whom were throwing away their arms, while officers tried to stem the tide of their defeated countrymen. "In less than half an hour," the Georgian wrote after the war, "my troops would have swept up and over those hills, the possession of which was of such momentous consequence."[75] Another of Early's brigadiers, Harry Hays, concluded the same thing. After the war, Hays told General Longstreet that his brigade of Louisianians could have attacked unsupported up Cemetery Hill and swept away the single brigade of Eleventh Corps holding the position without losing 10 men. While Hays' boastful claim was delivered long after the fact, contemporary scribblings support that this was indeed his state of mind on the evening of July 1. Captain Seymour of Hays' command echoed a similar opinion. An attack by the five Louisiana regiments would "undoubtedly have" carried Cemetery Hill, he wrote, and the soldiers around him openly pined for the dead Jackson.[77]

North Carolinians in Avery's Brigade recognized the same opportunity. "Let's go on!" shouted Lieutenant Colonel Hamilton Chamberlain Jones, Jr. of the 57th North Carolina. "There was not an officer, not even a man, who did not expect that the war would be closed upon that hill that evening, for there was still two hours of daylight when the final charge was made, yet for reasons that have never been explained nor ever will be . . ." remembered Jones. "[S]ome one made a blunder that lost the battle of Gettysburg, and, humanly speaking, the Confederate cause."[78]

Others echoed these views. "We had possession of the town of Gettysburg, and I could not understand why we did not pursue them and drive them off the face of the earth and take possession of Cemetery Ridge, which could have been done as the enemy's troops were not all up," complained Captain Asher Waterman Garber, commander of Early's Staunton Virginia Artillery.[79] One of Early's battery commanders overheard the Second Corps generals discussing the pursuit issue. Robert Stiles' guns sat unlimbered in the outskirts of Gettysburg for "perhaps twenty minutes or half an hour" when his superior, Captain Carrington, "saw General Early ride up, and then General Gordon and several other officers, to join General [Ewell]." As Carrington remembered it: "I cannot be mistaken when I say that both General Early and General Gordon were earnestly urging an immediate and further advance. I could not hear General Ewell's language, but evidently General Ewell's manner indicated resistance to their appeal."[80] What neither Carrington nor Stiles knew was that Gordon was advocating an immediate attack with his brigade; Early was resisting him, claiming outside assistance was required. The stress of the moment, coupled with two respected generals holding diametrically opposite positions froze Ewell, who found it impossible to reach a quick or decisive decision. Ewell's procrastination rippled down the chain of command. The Confederate attack, at least for now, was on hold and a member of Early's staff ordered Captain Carrington to "limber to the rear" rather than advance in support of a continued assault. Artillerist Stiles believed that "the tide, which at the flood might have led to overwhelming victory and even to independence, had ebbed away forever."[81]

Some writers have claimed Early's failure to pursue was the result of a series of events that drained away portions of his division to deal with a supposed Federal threat on the York Pike northeast of Gettysburg. About the time Early halted Gordon and unleashed Hays and Avery against Howard's Eleventh Corps, he also called for William "Extra Billy" Smith to bring his brigade forward. While Hays and Avery were driving into town and rounding up prisoners, Early sent another request to Smith to hurry forward his 800 Virginians. Smith had still not arrived by the time Early began his search for Ewell and Rodes. Before he found either of these officers, Early crossed paths with Colonel Abner Smead, the Second Corps' inspector general. While Early was explaining his need for support, Lieutenant Frederick Smith, son and aide-de-camp of his missing brigadier, galloped up with a message from his father. On his own initiative, "Extra Billy" had moved his Virginians from their supporting position to look into a report from cavalry stragglers belonging to Albert G. Jenkins' command that Federals were advancing on the York Pike and were about to flank Early's command from the northeast. Even though Early maintained from that day until his death that he had no faith in the raiders' report, he allowed Smith to remain on the left and later ordered Gordon to take his Georgia brigade there as well, take charge of Smith's Brigade, "and stop any further alarm."[82]

Early's response to a report he admitted he did not believe merits closer scrutiny than has heretofore been given. The division commander concluded his division could not attack again that day without assistance from either Rodes or Powell Hill *before* Lieutenant Smith brought the note from "Extra Billy." Therefore, as far as Early was concerned, sending Gordon off to the left to Smith was not going to affect his division's operations during the remainder of July 1. Any attempt to explain away Early's failure to aggressively pursue the Federals by placing the blame on "Extra Billy" Smith's unilateral shift to the York Pike simply ignores Early's earlier decision. Further, if Early was hell bent on taking Cemetery Hill—as he so eloquently protested after the war—he would never have detached Gordon when, by his own admission, Smith's report was not to be believed. Jubal Early's sudden and inexplicable cessation of his division's attack was but one of many decisions that saved the Federal forces from complete defeat on July 1.

This loss of resolution also gripped Ewell. Both men seem to have forgotten the words of their old corps chief, Stonewall Jackson: "Always mystify, mislead and surprise the enemy; and when you strike and overcome him, never let up in the pursuit."[83] Dick Ewell could see the flight of the Federals through Gettysburg and across the fields towards the heights south of town even as he rode down the slopes of Oak Hill. Before reaching the town square, he was joined by Gordon, who was anxious to chase the Yankees off Cemetery Hill. The Georgian had gone straight to his corps chief to express what he saw as the immediate need to carry the heights, on which the fortune of the day depended. Apparently before Ewell could give him an answer, Major Henry Kyd Douglas, an aide from Major General Edward Johnson, appeared. Douglas advised Ewell that "Allegheny" Johnson's Division was only about an hour's march away. The men, Douglas continued, were "in prime condition" and eager to enter the battle.[84] This meeting took place before 5:00 p.m. Gordon did not wait for Ewell's answer but instead offered to join Johnson's brigades in an attack. Ewell deferred the decision to allow Gordon to attack, and sent Douglas back to Johnson with orders to advance to the front, where he would receive further orders. Ewell also dispatched Colonel Smead to find Early and discuss the approach of Johnson and his recommendations for further action.[85]

Smead found Early and the men made their way into town where they met Ewell and Gordon. The meeting, as previously noted, was the one witnessed by Captain Carrington of the Charlottsville Virginia Artillery. In answer to Ewell's question, Early suggested Johnson's approaching division occupy Culp's Hill. Early also told Ewell that his division could not resume the attack without assistance from another command—Johnson's, Rodes', or units from Hill's Third Corps. Rodes himself reached the knot of officers soon thereafter. Unlike Early, his command had suffered serious casualties earlier in the day—approximately 2,500 officers and men, or about 30% of the division. Like Early, Rodes reined in his pursuit when he reached Gettysburg. "To have attacked this line [Cemetery Hill] with my division alone . . . would have been absurd," read his after-action report.[86]

This was not the first time Stonewall Jackson's protégé displayed a lack of the killer instinct so keenly possessed by his late teacher. In his first battle as a division commander at Chancellorsville, Rodes—as well as division commander Raleigh Edward Colston—temporarily halted the sweeping flank attack that was routing Howard's Eleventh Corps without orders from Jackson to do so. The long march, slim rations, and disorder resulting from the attack over difficult terrain, Rodes explained, required a halt and reorganization. Jackson was not happy with the delay, and went in search of Powell Hill to move his division forward to jumpstart the attack. It was against Old Jack's nature to stop a successful infantry attack, regardless of the state of disorder. There was no immediate way for Jackson to visually demonstrate to his subordinates that the enemy was in a far worse state than they were. Still, Rodes' request had some merit and the careful officer wanted to be prepared for whatever was waiting for him. If Rodes and Colston had not been so eager to halt their pursuit, or if Jackson had ordered them to press on for just one more difficult mile, they would have gained possession of the open field north of the Chancellor House, which would have cut the only road over which most of the Federal Second Corps and all of the Twelfth and Third Corps could have escaped.[87]

The bushy and timbered thickets of the Wilderness prevented Rodes and others from discerning the condition of their broken enemy and the lifeline their advance was imperiling. At Gettysburg, however, there were no obstructions shielding the plight of the defeated enemy late on the afternoon of July 1. Rodes' decisions to halt and reorganize at both Chancellorsville and Gettysburg diminished the level of victory in the former action and contributed to defeat in the latter. The size of the enemy Rodes confronted in each case adds some irony to the situation. At Chancellorsville, only 1,200 to 1,500 shaken Eleventh Corps survivors rallied by Carl Schurz were available to resist Rodes' advance down Bullock Road leading to the area of the Chancellor House. (Rodes, of course, could not have known this at the time because of the thick vegetation and growing darkness.) At Gettysburg, Rodes and others could clearly see the beaten Federals fleeing for their lives. While he had no way of counting each of the 1,600 bayonets fielded by Orland Smith's Federal brigade and the four 3-inch Ordnance rifles that stood between his division and the high ground, Rodes could plainly observe that the enemy was in much worse shape than his own victorious, though bloodied, infantry. It is also interesting to note that had Rodes quickly aligned his division and pushed on, Jubal Early would have seen or learned of his advance. Early, as we know, believed he needed support to take Cemetery Hill, and Rodes' continued attack would have satisfied that requirement. Rodes had a good reason to temporarily stop and reorganize at Chancellorsville—even if he should not have—but no good excuse exists for his failure to quickly press ahead on July 1, 1863.[88]

Rodes' decision did not meet with the approval of many of his officers and men. In fact, two of his brigade leaders, Edward O'Neal and George Doles, *without orders*, passed through the town, formed their brigades below Gettysburg, and were "in the act of charging the hill" when Rodes recalled them. The inept Colonel O'Neal, who had already lost many hundreds of men that day, had somehow mustered the sagacity to realize that the assault had to continue, and had called up artillery to support the effort. According to a private in Doles' Brigade, O'Neal was so incensed by Rodes' intervention he pleaded with Doles and asked him to take charge of the division and drive the Federals away from Cemetery Hill. Doles, of course, refused.[89]

Junior officers and ordinary soldiers saw the same thing. South Carolinian Lieutenant William Calder wrote to his mother to inform her of a "great mistake . . . which lost us the advantage of so many gallant men." According to the lieutenant, "Our generals should have advanced immediately on that hill. It could have been taken then with comparatively little loss and would have deprived the enemy of that immense advantage of position which was afterward the cause of his success."[90] Seven weeks after the battle, Captain James I. Harris, 30th North Carolina (Ramseur's Brigade, Rodes' Division), explained that the army "took a great many prisoners, but halted when we got into Gettysburg. This was fatal to our interests."[91]

Ensign J. A. Stikeleather of Ramseur's 4th North Carolina was on the skirmish line in front of his regiment when the division's advance was halted. In a letter to his mother published in the August 4, 1863, edition of the Raleigh *Semi-Weekly Standard*, Stikeleather explained how vulnerable the Cemetery Hill position was and that the pursuit should have continued. "The simplest soldier in the ranks felt it," he lamented, "and we could have readily carried the position with a loss of less than 500."[92] T. M. Gorman of the 2nd North Carolina, also in Ramseur's Brigade, believed that the hesitation "was fatal to us [because] had we taken it that evening it is hardly possible to say how great our victory could have been."[93] In a postwar diary, Edward Asbury O'Neal, Jr., Colonel O'Neal's son and an aide to General Rodes, summed it up this way:

> The enemy fought long and well but could not withstand the desperate assaults of our men and commenced retiring slowly, which soon gave way to a disorderly retreat. We pursued them through the city and could easily have taken possession of the hill, which afterwards sent such havoc through our Army, but were prevented by our own division commander.[94]

With Early requesting assistance from other commands, and Rodes refusing to engage his own division, the two officers became convinced that Cemetery Hill could be taken "provided they were supported by troops on their right," i.e., Hill's Third Corps. This is why Early and Rodes suggested to Ewell that he ask General Lee for help. Ewell liked the idea of assistance from outside his corps and called for a young staff officer, James Power Smith, to carry that message to Lee. Smith had already spent some of the day with the commanding general, and had only rejoined Ewell in the town square after Eleventh Corps had been put to flight. Smith took a few moments to interview Early and Rodes and then "rode out of the town on the road leading by the seminary."[95]

Smith found Lee in the vicinity of the Lutheran Seminary. He had been joined there by Longstreet at a fence in front of a field on the east side of Seminary Ridge, possibly near McMillan's Woods.[96] The generals were standing together and studying the situation when Ewell's aide reined in his horse and dismounted. Lee had a "superb physique," recalled Smith, outlined with a simple gray uniform topped with a medium brimmed felt hat and finished off with a pair of neatly fitting boots. Despite the kaleidoscope of the noise and confusion that surrounded them, the commanding general exhibited "an unruffled calm upon his countenance" which reflected his concentration and self-control. It was, noted Smith, "probably about 5 P.M."[97] Both generals, he remembered, "greeted me courteously. I repeated to General Lee what Ewell had wished me to convey as to the wishes of Early and Rodes, to the effect that 'if General Lee would send troops to support them on their right, they could at once advance to occupy the cemetery hill in front of the town; and that it would be well for General Lee to occupy at once the higher ground in front of our right, which seemed to command the cemetery hill.'"[98]

Lee passed Smith his binoculars and pointed to Cemetery Ridge, a largely treeless rise running south from Cemetery Hill, remarking, "I suppose, Captain, this is the high ground which these gentlemen refer. You will see that some of those people are there now."[99] According to Smith's account, Lee told him that Powell Hill did not believe there were enough troops available from Third Corps to carry that position and Longstreet's First Corps would not be on the field until much later. Nevertheless, the general told him that he would direct Hill to lend what support he could. In the meantime, Lee told Smith to go return to Ewell and tell him that it was the commanding general's order for Ewell "to take Cemetery Hill if it were possible."[100] With those words, Smith spurred his mount back into town, only to discover to his surprise that Ewell had not taken any action concerning the pursuit. Smith, who had once served Stonewall Jackson in a similar capacity, lamented that rather than obeying the orders already delivered by Walter Taylor, Ewell was instead waiting for his own aide-de-camp to return from General Lee with further instructions. In Smith's eyes, the delay was critical. Ewell "was simply waiting for orders, when every moment of time could not be balanced with gold."[101]

With so many of the officers and men under his command anxious to push on and seize the heights, why did Ewell hesitate doing so—especially since he had orders from Lee to go forward? Ewell addressed the issue in his after-action report thusly:

> I had received a message from the commanding general to attack this hill, if I could do so to advantage. I could not bring artillery to bear on it, and all the troops with me were jaded by twelve hours' marching and fighting, and I was notified that General Johnson's division (the only one of my corps that had not been engaged) was close to the town.[102]

James Power Smith (1837-1923)

A seminary student before the war, James Power Smith was assigned to Jackson's staff in the fall of 1862. During the Gettysburg Campaign, Smith brought Lee information that Stuart was still south of the Potomac and east of the Blue Ridge as of June 28, and delivered to Ewell the second direct order from Lee to pursue the retreating Federals and take Cemetery Hill. Smith put the blame squarely on Ewell for not acting on this order.

Eleanor S. Brockenbrough Library, The Museum of the Confederacy, Richmond

Ewell acknowledges that he had an order "to attack" from Lee, and this is confirmed by the recollections of *both* Walter Taylor and James Power Smith. Ewell's admission is, metaphorically speaking, the smoking gun that fires the bullet through the heart of the argument that Lee merely made a suggestion to his subordinate (see the last section of this chapter for a full discussion of this issue). More important, it specifically supports the recollections offered by Taylor and Smith after the war. It is thus reasonable to presume that the messages delivered by Taylor and Smith did indeed contain the "if possible" phrase, which was translated by Ewell, at least in his after-action report, to read: "if I could do so to advantage." Ewell defenders, who quickly seize upon this phrase to brush aside the responsibility that should rightly be affixed to him, would have us believe that at the time the orders were being delivered, Ewell was looking for excuses not to press forward—which is exactly what he claims in his after-action report. Yet, the fundamental fact is that Ewell had *two* orders to *attempt* to take Cemetery Hill.

Let us examine in more detail Ewell's after-action excuses rendered to support his inactivity. He claims he "could not bring his artillery to bear on" Cemetery Hill, yet Brenner's Hill was available for his guns, as were other locations in and around Gettysburg. He maintained that "All the troops with me were jaded by twelve hours' marching and fighting," yet went on to assert that he wanted to use "Johnson's division, to take possession of [Culp's Hill] to my left, on a line with and commanding Cemetery Hill."[103] Johnson's men had been marching all day and had yet to reach the field, and had tramped longer than either Rodes' Division (which still had three reliable brigades available) or Early's Division (which was virtually undamaged). Further and as we have noted, several brigade leaders that had marched and/or fought all day (O'Neal, Gordon, Hays, and Doles, for example), were expecting and looking forward to be ordered up the heights. They did not consider themselves or their men too "jaded" to continue the action. And, from his long association with Second Corps, Ewell knew that Stonewall Jackson had often called upon these same troops to conduct forced marches before going into, and winning, battles.

Dick Ewell could not have known whether he would have carried Cemetery Hill unless he tried to do so, and it is this point that cannot be dismissed or explained away. Ewell's failure to even make the attempt on that Wednesday afternoon impeaches his after-action report. General Lee, Walter Taylor, and James Power Smith—and even Ewell himself—acknowledge that Lee's instructions were an order "to attack," which meant that Ewell was to make the attempt. If his effort was repulsed, then Ewell would have been correct in calling off the action. Everyone agreed the Federals were in various states of disorganization, but Ewell could not know the extent, and could not predict how effective their defense would be, without a determined effort to carry the hill.

As students of this remarkable battle know too well, the crux of this entire issue rests with the "if possible," or "if practicable" language both Taylor and Smith claim were in the orders they carried to Ewell. If that indeed was the case, why did Ewell later alter the phrase to read that he was to attack the hill "if I could do so to advantage?" As earlier explained, Rodes and Early had nine brigades on the field, seven of which were combat-capable. Many brigade commanders and men of all ranks were anxious to finish what had been started. Unfortunately and more importantly to Ewell, neither Rodes nor Early was in a state of mind to press home the pursuit without assistance from the other or units outside Second Corps. Lacking that assistance, Ewell had to manufacture a reason for delay and a set of excuses for not going forward unless he "could do so to advantage." Many of Ewell's defenders who rely solely on his after-action report fail to appreciate this basic and simple fact: Ewell did not know whether his troops could take the heights, with or without "advantage" unless he ordered the attempt, which Lee clearly intended he do. Ewell's failure to attempt what had been ordered is the salient point above any other rationale or excuse.

By the time James Power Smith delivered the commanding general's message (Taylor had already delivered his), it was clear to Ewell that Lee was ordering the high ground taken and that little or no help would be forthcoming from either Longstreet or Hill. That realization prompted Ewell, along with Early and Rodes, to decide to reconnoiter east of town on the York Road to confirm that "Extra Billy" Smith's warnings about Federals in that quarter were an exaggeration. Only then did Ewell refocus his attention on Cemetery Hill by asking Rodes to get into position and communicate with Hill.[104] Rodes' attempt to communicate with Hill was not successful, which might have prompted Ewell to ride around the north end of Gettysburg in a nervous exhibition of energy.

Meanwhile, Edward "Allegheny" Johnson pushed his division as fast as it could move, sometimes at the double-quick.[105] After marching a long distance, his troops were forced to negotiate wagons, artillery, and lines of Confederate wounded and

Federal prisoners on the Chambersburg Pike east of Cashtown. By the time Johnson hustled all four brigades past Gettysburg about 6:00 p.m. and deployed them on Early's left facing Culp's Hill, his men had marched about 25 miles. While there was only about one and one-half hours of daylight remaining, many important things could have been accomplished in that time (as will be seen in from the fighting on July 2).[106]

As Johnson's brigades reached the field and deployed, the men and officers of the Stonewall Brigade were "eager for the fray," while Francis Nicholl's Louisianians, under the command of Colonel Jesse Milton Williams, sensed something was amiss: they were not advancing against Culp's Hill, even though the sun was still up. Colonel David Zable of the 14th Louisiana heard the men clamoring and knew that "the troops realized there was something wanting somewhere. There was an evident feeling of dissatisfaction among our men [that] we were not doing [it] Stonewall Jackson's way."[107]

Isaac Trimble Has a Belly Full

Pennsylvania was a frustrating place for the hero of Cross Keys and captor of Manassas Junction. Long before Ed Johnson's late arrival on the battlefield, Isaac Trimble had tried his best to get the Second Corps leaders to follow up their striking victory. Another of Stonewall Jackson's proteges, Trimble remembered clearly General Lee's words—"I shall throw an overwhelming force on their advance, crush it, follow up the success, drive one corps back on another, and by successive repulses and surprises before they can concentrate create a panic and virtually destroy the army"—and having witnessed what had already transpired, believed that he had to speak up in order to help Lee realize his vision for victory. Trimble found Ewell in the town, "far from composed [and] undecided what to do next."[108]

"Well, General," we have had a grand success," Trimble declared. "Are you not going to follow it up and push our advantage?" As far as Trimble was concerned, Ewell's reply was almost beyond belief—especially considering the aggressive manner in which he had allowed Rodes and Early to attack only hours earlier:

"No," Ewell answered. " I have orders from Gen'l Lee not to bring on a general engagement."[109]

"But Gen'l," replied Trimble, "that order cannot have reference to the present situation, for we have had a general engagement and gained a great victory, and by all military rules we ought to follow up our success, and we are losing golden moments." According to Trimble, Ewell did not answer, which he took to mean that he was putting the brakes on his corps instead of accelerating the pursuit, because he "did not see clearly what course to take. His manner separated him from his staff and the approach of others."[110]

Ewell's response was also inconsistent with his actions earlier that day. After Campbell Brown had returned with Lee's order not to bring on a major engagement until the army was concentrated, Ewell saw the excellent opportunity before him and ordered Rodes to assault Oak Ridge while Early marched into position and fell upon the flank of Howard's vulnerable Eleventh Corps. Two of his three divisions had been engaged and he had suffered more than 3,000 casualties. Two enemy corps had been crushed and routed. How could Ewell possibly think a general engagement had not already begun, or that a defeated and fleeing foe should not be vigorously pursued? This is the question that so troubled Isaac Trimble, and one that Lee addressed in his order to Ewell, about to be delivered by Taylor: "it is only necessary to press 'those people.'"

Frustrated in his attempt to persuade Ewell to pursue, Trimble mounted his horse and circled around town to the northeast, where he took a closer look at East Cemetery Hill and Culp's Hill. He returned to Ewell within half an hour. Walter Taylor had arrived during his absence and delivered Lee's orders to Ewell. The firing had all but ceased on Ewell's front.[111]

"Gen'l," Trimble began where he left off, "if you have decided not to advance against the enemy and we are only to hold our ground, I want to advise that you can send a brigade with artillery to take possession of that hill [Culp's Hill]. It commands Gettysburg and Cemetery Hill."

"How do you know that?" asked Ewell.

"I have been round there and you know I am not often mistaken in judging of topography, and if we don't hold that hill, the enemy will certainly occupy it, as it is the key to the whole position about here and I beg you to send a force at once to secure it."[112] Ewell did not answer him. Trimble, never one to shy away from a sensitive subject, raised the stakes in the one-sided conversation.

"Give me a division," Trimble declared, "and I will take that hill." Ewell remained silent.

"Give me a brigade and I will do it," urged Trimble. When no response was forthcoming, the proud Trimble claims to have begged in despair, "Give me a good regiment and I will engage to take that hill!"[113]

"When I need advice from a junior officer, I generally ask it," Ewell erupted.

Isaac Trimble had had enough. Removing his sword, he threw the blade down at Ewell's feet and stormed away, leaving these prescient words ringing in Ewell's ear for the next decade until his death: "You will regret it as long as you live!"[114]

Evening, July 1

Dick Ewell was not the only corps commander upsetting his subordinates. While Trimble bent Ewell's ear and his soldiers grumbled about his failure to order them forward, Powell Hill was earning the wrath of Southern officers on the other side of the battlefield. His decision to stop the action and rest on the bloody laurels earned by Harry Heth and Dorsey Pender, coupled with his failure to bring up Richard Anderson's large division and deliver a late afternoon assault, did not sit well with Third Corps surgeon Spencer Glasgow Welch. "[We] should have been immediately reinforced by Anderson with his fresh troops," Welch wrote his wife shortly after the battle.[115]

The doctor was not alone in his assessment that Anderson's troops were wasted on July 1. Colonel Abner Perrin, whose South Carolinians had delivered such a heroic charge earlier that afternoon, agreed—although with a different twist on who was to blame. In a letter to South Carolina's governor dated July 29, 1863, Perrin averred Anderson was negligent for not getting his division forward in an aggressive manner. "His failure to us," Perrin declared, "was *the* cause of the failure of the campaign."[116] The *Richmond Enquirer* correspondent on the scene agreed with Perrin. In his July 8 dispatch from Hagerstown, the scribe blamed the division commander for moving slowly and for halting unnecessarily and for too long at Cashtown. After Lee told him to get moving to Gettysburg, claimed the reporter, Anderson did not push his troops onward and get into position as quickly as he could have when all of his brigadiers were anxious to support their Third Corps comrades in order to "get possession of the mountain range" on which the Federals were retiring. Anderson's lackadaisical performance, summed up the writer, was a "Fatal blunder!"[117]

Although anything written after the fact must be read with caution, the charges leveled against Richard Anderson ring with veracity. Anderson tried to explain away his inaction on July 1 in a postwar conversation with Louis G. Young, Pettigrew's adjutant-general during the Gettysburg Campaign and the lieutenant who had confirmed Pettigrew's report that Federals were in Gettysburg in force on June 30. Anderson claimed he halted his command and went into bivouac on General Lee's orders, and that Lee wanted his division kept in reserve in case of disaster.[118] Although many writers have accepted this claim at face value, Anderson's remarkable statement lacks verity for a host of reasons.[119]

First, his assertion is not supported by a single corroborating witness, any surviving orders, and certainly not by the actions of the commanding general or any other evidence outside the collateral circumstance of General Lee accepting Powell Hill's decision not to continue the fight with Third Corps troops.

Second, Lee's plan to defeat the enemy corps in detail on Northern soil (as related to Trimble several days before the battle) was coming to fruition on the afternoon of July 1. Two Federal corps had been shattered and the enemy was retiring in disorder before him. Why, then, would Lee order Anderson to go into bivouac just a few miles from the field with hours of daylight left and at the same time order General Pendleton to smother Cemetery Hill with artillery fire in preparation for an attack and order General Ewell "to press 'those people'"? If this scenario is to be believed, then its supporters are assigning characteristics to Lee that had never manifested themselves on the field, namely, confusion and/or doubt as to what to do once committed to action.

Third, Lee had asked Powell Hill if he could continue the battle with elements of his corps, and then ordered Hill's guns to lay down a fire on the Federal troops attempting to rally on Cemetery Hill. Fourth, Anderson's claim that Lee wanted his division as a reserve in case of disaster when the only Federal troops encountered

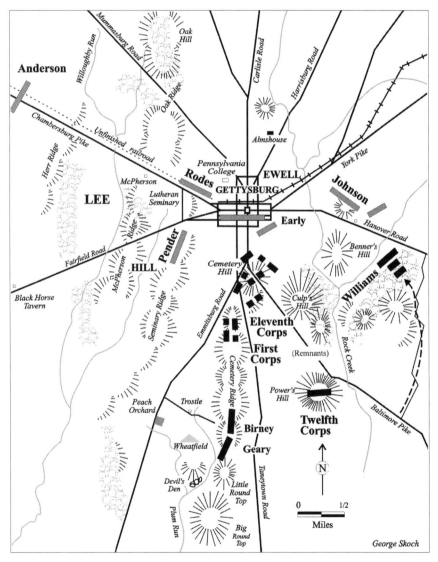

Positions of Opposing Forces, Evening, July 1, 1863

that day were either dead, wounded, captured, or retreating to Cemetery Hill strains the bounds of believability without additional supporting evidence (of which there is none). Further, if reserves were an important consideration, Lee knew that Edward Johnson's Division and the Second Corps artillery reserve were approaching and would be available before dusk—and Longstreet's First Corps was behind them. Fifth, Anderson's own battle report is silent on this important subject. His side had lost the battle and controversy over how it was conducted was already evident inside and outside the army. If Anderson had been ordered by Lee to stop west of Gettysburg, he would have mentioned it in his report. Last, Anderson's own indolent and irresponsible behavior on July 2 and July 3 (which will be discussed in detail elsewhere in this study) was consistent with his performance on July 1.

The only logical answer as to why Anderson did not come forward on July 1 lies somewhere between the failures of the minds of Powell Hill and Richard Anderson.

*   *   *

Speculation about why the attack on Cemetery Ridge and Culp's Hill was frozen in place continued to buzz through the ranks northeast of Gettysburg after Johnson's Division arrived sometime around 6:00 p.m. "Old Allegheny" deployed his four brigades along the Hanover Road facing south towards Culp's and East Cemetery hills, where they awaited orders to advance.[120] As far as his soldiers could tell, the timbered heights of Culp's Hill appeared to be unoccupied. Why, then, were they not moving at once to occupy or capture what was obviously a key terrain feature? The failure was Dick Ewell's, who in another display of timidity and ambivalence, had told Johnson to move his division to Culp's Hill and take it—*if it was unoccupied*. It took some time for Johnson to move his miles-long columns of men into position in the growing twilight, where they deployed in line of battle and rested on their arms. In the Stonewall Brigade eager men and officers alike asked the same questions: "What is the delay?" "What are we doing *here* [below Culp's Hill]?" "Why not keep going, as we used to do when Old Jack was with us?"[121] Dispatched late that evening, Johnson's scouting party stumbled upon enemy troops on the hill. When informed that Federals held the eminence, the sun was long down and Johnson did not order his men forward. Holding Culp's Hill was critically important, and Ewell should have ordered Johnson to advance his fresh division, overwhelm any defenders (Ewell's own scouting team had already informed him it was unoccupied), and solidify Confederate control there.

It was another mistake the Second Corps commander would live to regret. Ironically, the only enemy troops on the wooded rise at that time were the 7th Indiana of Cutler's brigade and the pitifully few survivors of the Iron Brigade. "Old Allegheny's" 6,400 men slept on their arms one mile away.[122]

Lee and July 1 in Retrospect

"Any listing of the most victorious days in the tactical annals of the Army of Northern Virginia must include May 2, 1863, and several days at the end of August 1862," writes Robert K. Krick, one of today's leading historians of that army. "But July 1, 1863, taken alone, was unquestionably one of the best days Lee's army ever enjoyed."[123] Significant failings of several key subordinates notwithstanding, maneuver, surprise, unparalleled fighting by the rank and file, and—once on the field—the commanding general's direction, were the cornerstone of the Confederate victory. Two-thirds each of two separate corps—four divisions totaling some 15 Southern brigades—shattered 11 Federal brigades from the First and Eleventh Corps. Both of these veteran formations waged their final battle with the Army of the Potomac on July 1.

In light of the scout Harrison's information and without Jeb Stuart's cavalry to assist him, Lee's decision to concentrate his army in the Cashtown-Gettysburg area had proven a sound one. He had to unify his corps to both keep the Federals east of South Mountain in order to protect his lines of communication and supply, and be in a position to bring on a general engagement if the right opportunity presented itself. When he arrived at Cashtown and found Powell Hill languishing in ignorance far from the rumbling front, Lee got Hill moving, advised Anderson to march east, and rode to the field. Once there, Lee restrained his troops until he realized Ewell's Second Corps had surprised the Federals from the north. "War is composed of nothing but surprises," Napoleon wrote. "While a general should adhere to general principles, he should never lose the opportunity to profit by these surprises. It is the essence of genius. In war there is only one favorable moment. Genius seizes it." Lee was a student of Napoleon's battles and he knew from personal experience that these words were true. He seized the moment and adapted to the changing circumstances brought about by Ewell's sudden appearance and flank attack. Further, Lee tried to follow up his victory, but a combination of unfortunate circumstances and recalcitrant subordinates who were not as flexible or as aggressive as they should have been resulted in a less substantial win than Lee envisioned. Still, it was quite an achievement.

Caught in a whirlwind frontal and flanking attack on largely indefensible terrain, O. O. Howard's Eleventh Corps was met north of town, turned, and routed in less than two hours. About 1,800 of his men were killed and wounded and another 1,400 were captured or missing. These casualties represent about 53% of the approximately 6,000 officers and men in the five brigades and four artillery batteries Howard managed to deploy that day.[124]

Casualties in John Reynolds' First Corps were staggering. Approximately 8,300 men in six infantry brigades were engaged on July 1; by day's end, seven out of ten had become casualties. At least 3,587 soldiers were killed or wounded and another 2,200 were missing or taken prisoners.[125] The decimation of Meredith's Iron Brigade offers a good example of the ferocity of the fighting that took place on the gentle ridges west of Gettysburg. The 2nd Wisconsin ended the day with only 69 of its original complement of 302 men.[126] The 24th Michigan was virtually annihilated, with but 97 left standing out of 496.[127] In the 19th Indiana, only 78 stood in ranks compared to the 308 that had formed up that morning.[128] Chapman Biddle's brigade also suffered heavily. Of the 263 combatants in the 121st Pennsylvania, only 80 answered roll call on Cemetery Hill. The Pennsylvanians of the 151st regiment entered the fight with 487 men and exited with 92.[129] The 150th Pennsylvania, one of Roy Stone's Bucktail regiments, had only 85 men left when the fighting stopped; 16 of its 17 officers and 316 of the remaining 400 soldiers were left on the field.[130] The severity of the losses at the regimental level reflected the destruction of their parent brigades. The Iron Brigade lost 1,153 of its 1,829 men (63%), Biddle, 897 out of 1,287 (70%), and Stone, 852 of 1,315 (65%).[131]

All told, Federal casualties for July 1 exceeded 9,000 of the 14,200 engaged—an astounding loss of 63%. The sudden death early in the action of John Reynolds, coupled with the decimation of field grade officers, provides a vivid picture of the true state of the combat readiness of these two corps by day's end. In light of this evisceration, the argument that the handful of survivors could have withstood a determined Confederate attack in the late afternoon of July 1 simply does not hold up to reasonable scrutiny.[132]

Confederate casualties, while substantial were much lighter. Of the 24,000 infantry engaged on July 1, about 5,850, or about one in four men, were killed, wounded, captured, or missing. On the plain north of town, two of Dick Ewell's three divisions saw action. Jubal Early's three engaged brigades suffered remarkably light casualties breaking apart and driving back Eleventh Corps. John Gordon's Georgians lost between 350 to 380 from all causes, while Isaac Avery suffered about 100 and Hays' Tigers only 63 casualties. Of the slightly more than 4,000 infantry engaged from Early's Division, less than 550—about 14% of those engaged and 10% of the entire division—were killed, wounded, captured, or missing.[133] Rodes' Division, which delivered the assaults that crumbled the right wing of Reynolds' First Corps along Oak Ridge and upper Seminary Ridge, suffered far more than Early's. The luckiest of his brigades belonged to George Doles, whose 1,369 Georgians had provided the link between Rodes and Early. Doles lost 179 to all causes, or about 13% casualties.[134] The balance of the division's brigades were not so fortunate. Dodson Ramseur had 177 of his 1,090 men knocked out of action, about 16%, while Edward O'Neal's missteps killed and wounded almost 700 of his 1,794 men, about 59% of his command. Junius Daniel's unlucky debut on the battlefield cost his North Carolinians 916 casualties out of an effective force of 2,294, or about 39%. It is no coincidence that Alfred Iverson's outfit, Rodes' most ineptly-led brigade, suffered the heaviest losses of the day. Iverson's breathtaking blunder on the Forney farm cost his regiments more than 800 casualties out of 1,470 effectives—a staggering 56% casualty rate. In total, Rodes lost to all causes 2,853 of his 8,017 infantry, or about 35%—heavy losses but about *one-half* those suffered by Reynolds' First Corps.[135]

Powell Hill's Third Corps west of town also had a hard time of it. Harry Heth's eyes-shut advance had triggered the battle and his four-brigade division bore the brunt of the fighting during the morning and early afternoon. At least 1,800 of his 7,000 infantrymen—about 25% of the command—were killed, wounded, captured, or missing.[136] Given how the day unfolded, his men were lucky they did not suffer more heavily. As detailed elsewhere (see note 51), Pender's Light Division lost about 1,000 men of some 4,705 engaged, or about 21%.[137] In sum, Hill lost approximately 2,800 infantrymen, or almost 22% of his engaged strength or, if Anderson's Division is factored in, 14% of the entire infantry strength of Third Corps. In conclusion, Lee and the Army of Northern Virginia lost less than 6,000 combatants of all arms. In exchange, the Confederates had heavily damaged Eleventh Corps and effectively destroyed First Corps.[138]

Something Gained, Something Lost

Fortunately for the Federals, the sacrifices paid by First and Eleventh Corps, combined with the timidity of Generals Ewell, Early, Rodes, and Hill, bought them the time they needed to bring up reinforcements and deploy on the high ground south and southwest of Gettysburg. By the early morning hours of July 2, the now-famous "fishhook" line (named for its shape) stretched from Culp's Hill, curved west and then south through Cemetery Hill, and then ran south along the spine of Cemetery Ridge. Many historians have heaped praise on both General Meade for shuttling his army into the Gettysburg area, and General Reynolds for deciding to wage a major engagement on the ridges west of town, where cavalryman John Buford had already established a defensive line. Reynolds' decision, goes the general argument, allowed reinforcements to arrive, man the heights below town, and win the battle on July 2-3. And of course, the Army of the Potomac did indeed win the battle. But how would historians assess Meade's and Reynolds' decisions if the first day had concluded as Lee had desired? If any one of several Southern generals had continued the advance and swept the gathering Federal remnants from Cemetery Hill, or if Edward Johnson had simply walked his division forward one mile onto Culp's Hill that evening, for which he had deployed and was fully prepared to do, the Federals would have been forced to evacuate the remainder of their defensive positions. The verdict on Meade's decision to advance the Army of the Potomac into the jaws of the converging Confederate columns at Gettysburg might be viewed today as a foolhardy blunder. His mistake would have been doubly embarrassing because

Meade's cavalry was screening and scouting the advance of the Federal army—a decided advantage Lee did not enjoy in Stuart's absence.

Even with the benefit of Buford's troopers, not everyone believed Reynolds' determination to accept the fight west of town, where his corps fought its last battle, was a wise one. Brigadier General Alpheus S. Williams, commander of First Division, Henry Slocum's Twelfth Corps, wrote two days after the battle that he believed it was Reynolds who was largely responsible for the defeat on July 1 because that officer "precipitated a large action by underrating the strength of his opponents. In consequence, both the 1st and 11th Corps were badly cut up."[139] Meade, however, was spared the fate of a truly decisive defeat, thanks primarily to Ewell's reluctance to obey Lee's two directives to try and take Cemetery Hill, and the troubling listlessness of several key Confederate general officers.

But could the Confederates have taken Cemetery Hill on the late afternoon of July 1? Many key Federal officers believed they could have. Major General Abner Doubleday, who led the Third Division of First Corps before assuming the corps command after Reynolds fell, concluded that had Ewell or Hill pursued, their troops "could have easily" taken the heights, "but not so readily after an hour's delay."[140] John B. Bachelder, the battle's first serious historian, reached a similar judgment. "There is no question," he concluded, "but what a combined attack on Cemetery Hill made within one hour [by about 5:30 p.m.] would have been successful."[141]

Bachelder also expressed his opinion that the position was not secure until 6:00 p.m. and if the battle had been rejoined at or after that time, there still existed "strong probabilities in favor of Confederate success. The First Corps had been engaged in a long and severe contest, in which it was everywhere beaten and had suffered heavily. The Eleventh Corps had also suffered as much, and portions of it were badly demoralized."[142] Bachelder, who is recognized even today as one of the definitive students of the battle, realized that the rallied elements of the shattered First and Eleventh Corps, along with whatever late-arriving other Federal formations were there, would have found holding Cemetery Hill almost impossible.

Major General Winfield Scott Hancock, Meade's Second Corps commander, arrived in the afternoon and organized the broken elements of First and Eleventh Corps so that they could resist further Confederate attacks until more help arrived. The army's best corps leader, Hancock saw for himself the trouble officers of Eleventh Corps encountered just trying to rally their men, and the scant number of exhausted First Corps survivors capable of organized resistance. "In my opinion," Hancock later wrote, "if the Confederates had continued the pursuit of General [Oliver O.] Howard on the afternoon of the 1st July at Gettysburg, they would have driven him over and beyond Cemetery Hill."[143]

According to Isaac Trimble, an unnamed Federal general officer told him the same thing immediately following the battle. Wounded on July 3 and later captured, Trimble was in a Federal hospital when the officer told him that if the Confederates "had advanced and pushed us vigorously, I fear our whole army would have been dispersed by night." The Army of the Potomac, he added, was "strung out between Gettysburg and Emmitsburg, hungry, weary, and ill, and you would not have had a brigade to oppose you at any one place."[144]

Although Trimble was recalling a conversation many years after the battle, we know today that the Army of the Potomac was indeed "strung out . . .hungry [and] weary," from its forced marches. General Lee's understanding of the stresses Meade's army would face as it tramped to meet his, as related in a conversation to Trimble several days before the battle, was accurate. It is but one more reason why Lee's vision for victory stood a very real chance of being realized if the Federals had been vigorously pursued on the afternoon of July 1.[145]

If Practicable . . . If Possible

Lee's generalship, especially of late, has come under increasing assault not only for his actions at Gettysburg but throughout the war. The single most often repeated criticism of Lee on July 1 is found in Edwin Coddington's *The Gettysburg Campaign: A Study in Command*. There is general consensus that Coddington's work is the finest single volume histories of the campaign. As such, it has been highly influential in shaping what people think of the battle and the generals who waged it. However, it is our opinion that Coddington significantly errs in his argument that "responsibility for the failure of the Confederates to make an all out assault on Cemetery Hill on July 1 must rest with Lee."[146] In placing the blame on Lee, Coddington concurrently absolves Ewell of the primary responsibility for failing to attack Cemetery Hill. Coddington's thesis rests on two main pillars. Let us address each in its turn.

First, Coddington asserts that Ewell did not continue the pursuit because he "felt constrained by Lee's injunction not to open a full fledged battle."[147] This claim is so flimsy it is remarkable any historians have seized upon it as legitimate. As already demonstrated at length earlier in this study, the restraint to which Coddington refers was Lee's order to Ewell's stepson issued *hours before Ewell authorized Rodes and Early to attack the enemy north of town*. In other words, once Ewell saw the opportunity before him, he realized Lee would have authorized his full scale involvement and assaulted accordingly. Further, it is difficult to imagine that late on the afternoon of July 1, after two of his three divisions had been heavily engaged north and northwest of Gettysburg and had incurred thousands of casualties, that Ewell believed a general engagement had not already begun! If he was unwilling to launch an attack (pursuit) late in the afternoon for the reason Coddington claims, why did Ewell launch a much *larger* attack earlier in the day against a stronger enemy, and then pursue that enemy for more than a mile to and through town? Coddington's first contention is simply not credible.

Coddington's second contention absolving Ewell is grounded on his mistaken interpretation of the meaning and use of the phrase "if practicable" or "if possible," as utilized in Lee's order to Ewell. Coddington asserts that the phrase constituted a *suggestion*, and not an *order*. His observation—which mimicked something similar introduced a few years earlier by historian Kenneth P. Williams—is based upon a modern perception of what that phrase means today.[148] Other historians over the last several decades have seized upon this interpretation of "if practicable" and used it to bludgeon Lee for issuing Ewell what they now refer to as "discretionary orders." Hence, Coddington's "suggestion" interpretation triggered what is now a general belief among students of the battle that Lee—with everything on the line—issued "discretionary orders" that Ewell could accept or reject as he saw fit. As explained below in great detail, just the opposite is true.

Coddington's entire analysis rests of one piece of written evidence: Lee's after-action report of the Gettysburg Campaign dated January 20, 1864.[149] Unfortunately, Coddington failed to properly understand not only the character of Lee as a man, but also how gentlemen of the old Southern society spoke to and interacted with one another (and how the report was written). Lee embodied the very best of the code of the Old South aristocracy, which included taking another gentleman for his word and treating all others with deference. Indeed, his writings in *The Wartime Papers of Robert E. Lee* are replete with similar examples. In his first order as the commander of the Army of Northern Virginia, General Order No. 75, Lee instructed his subordinate officers to move in a certain manner, "if practicable."[150] This order stands as an excellent representation of how Lee directed his lieutenants, which in Southern gentlemen's language did not ask the subordinates to *meditate* about a certain course of action, but told them in a circumspect manner to *do* it. Lee orders, carefully worded and offered in a respectful tone, left it up to the commanders on the scene to figure out the best way to accomplish the task—which constitutes an "order with discretion." This in no way implies that the subordinates were to decide for themselves if they should attempt it or not—which would have been a "discretionary order." The difference is fundamental to the issue at hand. Other examples of communiqués to various commanders, and they to Lee, not only further illustrate this point, but leave absolutely no doubt as to the manner in which these men spoke to one another. Just a few among the many compelling examples include: Lee's orders to Ewell of April 21, 1862,[151] Jackson's letter to Lee of June 13, 1862,[152] Lee's orders to Jeb Stuart of July 18, 1862,[153] Lee's instructions to Jackson of July 27, 1862,[154] Lee's orders to Jeb Stuart of May 3, 1863,[155] Lee's instructions to Lafayette McLaws of May 3, 1863,[156] and Lee's orders to Ewell of June 19, 1863.[157]

The tone and level of discourse of this age, especially via the written word, is exemplified by the manner in which Lee, and many men of his day, signed their letters to subordinates: "your obedient servant." Today's readers gloss over this as a quaint but antiquated way of closing a letter. In fact, this phrase was considered an expression of good will between gentlemen of this time, and letters or communications to either subordinates or to members of the opposing army were often concluded in this manner.[158] This helps illustrate how gentlemen of this period—especially those from the Tidewater aristocracy—spoke or wrote to one another. Coddington's contention that Lee's order to Ewell to take the high ground was just a suggestion and not an order is based upon the modern perception and usage of the "if practicable" phrase found in the commanding general's report. The historian never understood the manner in which Robert E. Lee communicated to his subordinates and has taken that phrase out of its proper historical context.

Other writers, influenced by Coddington's "suggestion" theory, have altered it slightly by arguing Lee's instructions to Ewell were something other than a direct order, or what they term a "discretionary order." In his article "Confederate Corps Leadership on the First Day at Gettysburg; A. P. Hill and Richard S. Ewell in a Difficult Debut," historian Gary Gallagher argues that Lee should have changed his style of command in order to deal with Ewell.[159] "Lee realized that Ewell was not Jackson or Longstreet," Gallagher writes, "and should have modified his method of command accordingly. If he issued a *discretionary order* [emphasis added] when he really wanted to convey a desire that Ewell take those heights (as Taylor's testimony implies), Lee should have known that an indecisive Ewell might react as he did. "Direct instructions," claims Gallagher, "would have avoided any confusion."[160] Gallagher's assertion that Ewell had proven himself an indecisive commander before Gettysburg—"the general's old inability to function without specific orders paralyzed him" is how Gallagher phrases it[161]—has been blandly accepted as dogma when it should be raising eyebrows.

Dick Ewell had served long and well under Stonewall Jackson, who was particularly intolerant of indecisive subordinates who failed to exhibit initiative and skill in the face of the enemy. Ewell's performance during the whirlwind Shenandoah Valley Campaign was utterly splendid; he fought well at Gaines' Mill, and marched and fought skillfully during the Second Manassas Campaign at Cedar Mountain and Groveton, where he was severely wounded. His first combat at corps level was his brilliant independent victory at Second Winchester, where he bagged most of Milroy's entire Federal division—without any hesitation whatsoever. His second chance to prove himself at corps level was mid-day July 1, when Ewell immediately recognized the opportunity north of Gettysburg and committed all of his troops on the field in a general engagement that routed the enemy—contrary to Lee's earlier admonition to avoid a battle until the army was concentrated. Is this a record of indecision and paralyzation? If so, why did Jackson recommend Ewell to succeed him, knowing full well how General Lee ran his army in the field? And why did Lee select Ewell? In reality, Ewell's pre-Gettysburg record was no more indecisive than James Longstreet's or even Stonewall Jackson's—and he had demonstrated more prudence and just as much skill in handling men as had Powell

Hill. How, then, could General Lee know, as Gallagher puts it, "that an indecisive Ewell might react as he did?"[162]

Finally, Gallagher's assertion that Lee issued "a discretionary order" is simply wrong. Lee issued what can only be accurately described as an "order with discretion." In other words, Ewell had been instructed to take the heights, but was allowed the latitude to determine how best to assault the hill. If Lee's command was a "discretionary order," as Gallagher holds, then Ewell would have been able to decide for himself if he was even to go to *try* to take Cemetery Hill, which Lee recognized as being critical to the battle's outcome (witness his concurrent efforts with Pendleton and Hill, as previously described). What neither of these historians tell us is that when Lee issued true "discretionary orders," he stated as much to his subordinates in *far different language*.[163] The commanding general's directives to Ewell on the field at Gettysburg constituted a classic "order with discretion."

This issue is so important that it deserves deeper scrutiny. Those Lee critics who have accepted Coddington's modern interpretation of the phrase "if practicable" and absorbed Gallagher's "discretionary orders" thesis must discount evidence suggesting otherwise, such as Walter Taylor's testimony. Before examining it in detail, it is vital to remember the distinctions between a "discretionary order" and someone having "discretion in carrying out an order," or "an order with discretion." In other words, the English language recognizes the difference between an adjective (discretionary) and a noun (discretion). With that in mind, please read carefully Taylor's eyewitness account:

> General Lee witnessed the flight of the Federals through Gettysburg and up the hills beyond. He then directed me to go to General Ewell and to say to him that, from the position which he occupied, he could see the enemy retreating over the hills, without organization and in great confusion; that it was only necessary to press 'those people' in order to secure possession of the heights, and that, if possible, he wished him to do this. In obedience to these instructions, I proceeded immediately to General Ewell and delivered the order of General Lee; and after receiving from him some message in regard to the prisoners captured and the embarrassment of looking after them, I returned to General Lee and reported that his order had been delivered. General Ewell did not express any objection, or indicate the existence of any impediment, to the execution of the order conveyed to him, but left the impression upon my mind that it would be executed. In the exercise of that discretion, however, which General Lee was accustomed to accord to his lieutenants, and probably because of an undue regard for his admonition previously given, not to precipitate a general engagement, General Ewell deemed it unwise to make the pursuit. The troops were not moved forward, and the enemy preceded to occupy and fortify the position which it was designed that General Ewell should seize.[164]

Taylor clearly considered the message he carried from Lee to Ewell to be an *order* which Ewell gave every indication he would follow. Taylor's use of the word "discretion" as a noun unmistakably shows Lee intended that the heights be taken, had ordered Ewell to do so, and was extending Ewell the latitude, or *discretion*, to decide how best to do this as the commander on the scene, which was Lee's custom. There is nothing in Taylor's description of the event indicating Lee's instructions were "a discretionary order," which uses *discretionary* as an adjective—as do historians Williams, Coddington, and Gallagher.

Harry W. Pfanz, in his monumental and important work *Gettysburg: Culp's Hill & Cemetery Hill*, summarily dismisses select portions of Taylor's account and relies almost exclusively on Ewell's undated after-action report in which he states Lee told him "to attack this hill, if I could do so to advantage." (Ewell's use of this phrase has already been discussed earlier in this chapter.) Pfanz, as will be seen, equates Ewell's language with Lee's usage of the phrase "if practicable."[165] Lee claimed in his own after-action report that he ordered Ewell to take the heights "if practicable," but there was no "think about it and try it if you want to" aspect in either Lee's order—first communicated through Walter Taylor and then reiterated through James Power Smith—or in his campaign report. As demonstrated, Lee's use of "if practicable" has been blurred by time and social convention. And, Lee's use of the phrase is consistent with how *both* Taylor and Smith remembered the incident in their respective narratives.

The manner in which Pfanz uses or discards Taylor's words should be openly questioned. "Although the message carried by Taylor to Ewell must not have been as Taylor recalled it," writes Pfanz, "his [Taylor's] impression that Ewell wished to renew the attack probably was correct."[166] Pfanz is cherry-picking strings of words that suit his purpose that Ewell was issued discretionary orders and simply chose not to attack. He would have us believe that Taylor could not accurately remember *what* it was he told Ewell, but did accurately recall *how* Ewell wanted to react. While it is certainly possible to recall reliably one portion of an event and not another, how can a historian cavalierly dismiss an eyewitness account of the order he *personally* transmitted that has corroborating support from James Power Smith, another *eyewitness* claiming the same thing?[167]

Finally, after the war General Eppa Hunton (who was a colonel at Gettysburg) claims Ewell confessed to him, "It took a dozen blunders to lose Gettysburg, and [I] had committed a good many of them."[168] The evidence strongly suggests that one of these "blunders" to which he referred was the failure to comply with Lee's order to pursue the enemy and carry Cemetery Hill.

Dick Ewell cuts a very sympathetic figure, but his actions or inactions must be viewed within proper historical context. Both of his division commanders on the field, Robert Rodes and Jubal Early, told him they needed help to storm Cemetery Hill. Even the aggressive Stonewall Jackson had paused at Chancellorsville when his division commanders urged a temporary halt to reorganize the troops. However,

Jackson resumed his attack at Chancellorsville (even without being able to see what was in his front), whereas Ewell did not even make the attempt at Gettysburg. Ewell was not a novice with the Army of Northern Virginia, and it cannot be argued that he was ignorant of how Lee communicated with his subordinates. In the final analysis, the ultimate responsibility for the failure of Second Corps to move against Culp's Hill and Cemetery Hill on July 1 rests with Richard S. Ewell and not with Robert E. Lee.

But the ongoing war of words over Lee's orders to Ewell does not stop here. Some critics argue that Ewell was correct in not attacking Cemetery Hill on July 1 because by not attacking, he was actually *obeying* Lee's orders.[169] In order to reach this tortured conclusion, these writers rely solely on Lee's after-action report without taking into consideration the context in which the report was constructed (or any of the other evidence already presented). In his report, Lee writes that the commander of Second Corps was "to carry the hill occupied by the enemy, if he found it practicable, but to avoid a general engagement."[170] Those words were written by Charles Marshall and approved by General Lee in January 1864. In order to understand this within its proper context, readers must keep in mind three important factors: the instructions Lee had communicated to Ewell through George Campbell Brown earlier that morning to avoid a general engagement; the later set of orders Lee transmitted to Ewell through Taylor and Smith for Ewell "to press 'those people'" and "take Cemetery Hill if it were possible"; and Lee's consistent penchant of carefully crafting his after-action reports in such a manner so as to shield his subordinates from the hue and cry of Southern politicians and members of the press.

By the middle of the afternoon on July 1, four of Lee' nine infantry divisions were hotly engaged in combat with at least two enemy corps. Is it possible that any clear-thinking general on the field really believed that the army was not involved in a serious general engagement? Lee certainly understood his army was fighting a major action and issued orders during the battle to his subordinates, including Ewell, reflecting this mind set. Once Ewell committed his two divisions into action, there was never any doubt a major engagement was underway, nor was there any hesitation in Lee's desire to support Ewell by ordering Hill's troops back into action against McPherson's (and Seminary) Ridge. Once the enemy lines were broken, Lee ordered Pendleton to organize artillery fire against Cemetery Hill, and Ewell's infantry, who were right below it, to continue the battle by assaulting it. It is particularly important to appreciate that neither Taylor nor Smith *ever* mentioned that Lee couched his orders to Ewell in such a way as to "avoid a general engagement"—Lee's words in his report—because they were already in the middle of one. Instead, Lee was anxious to gather the full fruits of the day's victory by continuing the battle with a vigorous pursuit. Lee's desire to press the beaten and retreating enemy is entirely consistent with his vision for victory, his reasons for concentrating the army in the Cashtown-Gettysburg area, and his reasons for reengaging early on the afternoon of July 1.

It is important to realize that Lee scrupulously avoided any wording in his reports that would have held up the actions of his subordinates to public criticism. Too often after-action reports are swallowed in their entirety without appreciating the political and military backdrop against which they are written. Robert E. Lee never openly criticized his lieutenants in any of his reports. In fact, ever the true gentleman, he offered to personally resign after Gettysburg—a move rarely recognized for what it was: an attempt to deflect criticism away from his subordinates. Lee knew Davis was not going to accept and replace him, for there was no one to take his place. Why, then, do so many writers believe that Lee would act any differently composing an after-action report? No less an authority than Charles Marshall, the man who *penned* the Gettysburg report (and reports for many other battles), admitted Lee was covering for Ewell and others. The general's Pennsylvania report, explained Marshall,

> was not complete in many particulars which should be known to understand the campaign fully. [Lee] struck from the original draft many statements which he thought might affect others injuriously, his sense of justice frequently leading him to what many considered too great a degree of lenience. It is well known that he assumed the entire responsibility of the issue of the battle of Gettysburg and thus covered the omissions of all of his officers. He declined to embody in his report anything that might seem to cast the blame of the result upon others.[171]

With this in mind, consider carefully the notion put forth by some writers that Ewell was following the commanding general's orders in *not* pursuing the retreating Federal forces on July 1.[172] In their recent biographies of Ewell, both Samuel Martin and Donald Pfanz argue this is why Ewell did not order a pursuit and assault Cemetery Hill. This is nonsensical. Is it possible Ewell believed his committing two of his three divisions to crush a fresh Federal corps at midday was *not* bringing on a "general engagement," but utilizing these same two divisions to pursue a beaten and retreating foe would violate Lee's orders about bringing on a "general engagement?" As we have already clearly set forth, Lee's instructions to "avoid a general engagement," had been given to Ewell's stepson, Major George Campbell Brown, at or near Cashtown early on the morning of July 1.[173] This warning was delivered by Brown to Ewell while the Second Corps was in route to Gettysburg, but *before* Ewell determined to commit his divisions into action. By acting aggressively and on his own initiative, Ewell was technically in violation of Lee's restraining orders. However, he knew he was acting within the spirit of Lee's command style, which allowed subordinates the latitude and flexibility to seize upon changing circumstances offering opportunity.

Ewell's own words concerning his attack against the Federal right flank are of special importance. After describing the scene, he admitted, "It was too late to avoid an engagement without abandoning the position [on Oak Hill] already taken up, and I determined to push the attack vigorously."[174] General Ewell's report makes it clear he believed he played a major role in bringing about the general engagement by his decision to "push the attack vigorously." Until he was involved, the Hill-Reynolds action was simply a meeting engagement in the classic meaning. Indeed, when Ewell ordered Rodes to move off Oak Hill and launch his attack, he acknowledged that "only desultory artillery firing was going on on the rest of the field." This clearly indicates that General Lee had arrived west of town and had restrained Powell Hill from further aggressive action until an opportunity presented itself. Ewell himself presented the opportunity. He recognized the engagement that he was triggering could not be avoided without surrendering Oak Hill, an important terrain position offering an advantage for decisive victory. When presented with this opportunity, Ewell displayed the initiative Lee not only extended to, but expected from, his principal subordinates. Why then, at the very moment of victory, did Ewell become indecisive or hesitant at the foot of Cemetery Hill?

Perhaps the most credible explanation for Ewell's anomalous behavior is simply that he was emotionally incapacitated by the prospects of the sweeping scope of his initial victory. As strange as this may sound, this phenomenon has been on display any number of times from the beginning of recorded warfare to the present. Ewell's hesitant and indecisive action in the face of Lee's multiple orders, coupled with subordinates urging a continuation of the battle suggest an emotional inability to make timely decisions. Once he triggered the battle and watched his own and Third Corps troops sweep the enemy from the field, his soldiery instincts that had served him so well deserted him. He did not try to attack Cemetery Hill because he was unable to organize himself enough to order it done. The fault rests solely with Richard S. Ewell.[175]

Historian Brooks D. Simpson offers yet another twist on the issue of pursuit. In his article "Command Relationships at Gettysburg," part of a collection of essays entitled *Civil War Generals in Defeat*, Simpson argues that Lee demanded Ewell to do what he himself would not, namely pursue the beaten foe.[176] If Lee wanted to pursue the retreating Federals, ponders Simpson, "why did he hold back Maj. Gen. Richard Anderson's division?" Simpson's stunning hypothesis is at odds with physical reality. Anderson's fresh division was at Schoolhouse Ridge more than two miles behind Third Corps' front on Seminary Ridge and more than three miles from the Federals on Cemetery Hill. Early's Division was on the outskirts of town and Rodes' was nearby, meaning Ewell's divisions were less than one-half mile from Cemetery Hill. Lee had sent two orders to Ewell for his troops to press the enemy and take the heights (and the commanding general had to allow the passage of a reasonable amount of time for this to take place). Simpson is suggesting Ewell should have waited on Anderson's Division, which was more than *six times* the distance from Cemetery Hill than his own troops.[177] Lee understood on the field what Simpson does not, even with the benefit of hindsight: time, distance, and the realties of a battlefield have serious implications when pursuing a defeated enemy. Holding back Ewell to wait for Anderson would have extended valuable time the enemy would have put to good use. And, Anderson's men would have had to move through the flotsam of Third Corps' earlier battle, a veritable obstacle course of wagons, dead, wounded, prisoners, and hardware. Simpson's declaration that on July 1 General Lee's order to Ewell "reeks of ambivalence" because, in Simpson's opinion, Lee "had not yet sorted out in his own mind what he wanted to do," simply does not square with the historical record or an appreciation of Lee's actions that day.[178]

Another critic of Lee's generalship on July 1, and one of his most visible detractors, is Alan T. Nolan. In his article "R. E. Lee and July 1 at Gettysburg," he argues that "there were significant command failures on Lee's part that were destructive to the Confederate chances of victory at Gettysburg."[179] Nolan writes that "Lee proceeded at Gettysburg without essential control of his army in three crucial respects—reconnaissance, the onset of the battle, and the renewal of the battle on the afternoon of July 1."[180] Nolan is flatly wrong on all counts. The absence of Stuart has already been dealt with at length in Chapter 3. Indeed, Nolan's argument faults Lee for Stuart not obeying orders.

The core of Nolan's second criticism is that "Lee's attempt at control came too late because of his failure to react to Hill's June 30 communication and because of the onrush of events."[181] In essence, Nolan is asserting that when Hill notified Lee on June 30 that his corps was going to "advance the next morning and discover what was in my front,"[182] Lee lost control of his army because he did not immediately answer Hill and thus avoid Heth's meeting engagement the next morning. Nolan's contention is not only disingenuous, but he seems wholly unaware of how and when these series of events unfolded. First, Hill did not arrive in Cashtown to receive subordinate reports until the *evening* of June 30.[183] He dispatched riders to both Lee and Ewell *later that evening*, and Lee's courier did not reach him until *late in the evening* of that same date.[184] Hill's message indicated only that there was cavalry at Gettysburg, not a large force of infantry. As historian Clifford Dowdey explained, "There was nothing in the report to alarm Lee."[185] Still, Lee had the good judgment to promptly send back instructions through Major Taylor to Heth, the general leading the Third Corps' march, "to ascertain what force was at Gettysburg, and, if he found the infantry opposed to him, to report the fact immediately, without forcing an engagement."[186] Taylor reached Heth with Lee's retraining orders *before* Heth moved out of Cashtown at 5:00 a.m. on July 1. Lee's immediate reaction demonstrates a remarkable degree of control over the advance of his army. Nolan also conveniently overlooks the consequences of what he suggests Lee should have done. Powell Hill's concurrent dispatch to Ewell advised that Third Corps was moving to Gettysburg on July 1. Ewell, as we know, had already been instructed by Lee "to form a junction with Hill either at Cashtown or Gettysburg, as circumstances might direct."[187] If Lee had stopped Hill in his tracks, as Nolan suggests he should have, Ewell would have been isolated in or around Gettysburg and the commanding general's orders to concentrate the army unfulfilled. Nolan's criticism that Lee failed to control his army on June 30-July 1 is contradicted by the facts.

Nolan's third criticism is that Lee was wrong to have continued the fight that afternoon after Harry Heth's initial repulse. According to Nolan:

> [Lee permitted] the renewal of the battle in the afternoon of July 1 in spite of his lack of knowledge of the Federal army's whereabouts and the absence of his own First Corps, which meant that he did it without having reason to believe that he had sufficient manpower to deprive the Federals of the high ground south of town.[188]

Even ignoring the fact that Lee could not have known he would be fighting for Cemetery Hill later that day or thereafter, this assertion is simply astounding. Nolan is arguing that Lee erred by allowing Hill's Third Corps to reengage *knowing* Ewell's Second Corps had arrived on and behind the Federal right flank! It is difficult to imagine any Great Captain of history not pressing such an advantage. (One imagines Lee's critics would today be writing about his missed opportunity if he had not attacked that afternoon.) Lee recognized the changing circumstances and the opportunities that this meeting engagement presented him. Just as George McClellan had exposed part of his army north of the Chickahominy River at the beginning of the Seven Days Battles, Meade's pair of exposed corps invited destruction at Gettysburg on July 1. While Lee could not have known exactly how much of the enemy was before him, Mosby's report provided him with a reasonable idea where the widely scattered corps of the Army of the Potomac were bivouacked on June 24, and this information was updated by Harrison's information. With his wide experience, deep knowledge of military history, and a simple map, it would not have been difficult for Lee to roughly calculate the number of corps he would likely confront *that day.* And, he had the benefit of information gleaned from prisoners.

Lee thus determined he had more than enough troops to not only defeat the Federal forces he knew to be on the field, but to pursue and drive them from the heights south of town. Nolan's claim that Lee did not "believe that he had sufficient manpower" for the task at hand is flatly impeached by Lee's own orders to Ewell. In the final analysis, Nolan's claims simply do not hold up to close scrutiny.

*   *   *

With the possible exception of the failure to press Powell Hill to organize another attack following Pender's memorable afternoon assault and capture of Seminary Ridge, it is difficult to level any *valid* major criticism of Robert E. Lee's generalship on July 1. He had displayed a remarkable ability to adapt to a changing tactical environment, encouraged his men, issued orders to hold when he should have, issued orders to attack when he should have, and issued orders to pursue the beaten foe, including directions for his subordinates to follow. His performance is even more impressive when the crippling absence of Stuart is taken into account. (Recall that Meade had his cavalry and lost two entire corps on July 1.)

Through a combination of good fortune, tremendous human material, and Lee's sound leadership and guiding hand, the Army of Northern Virginia scored a significant triumph on July 1. The victory might not have been as substantial as Lee had hoped, but it gave him the precious initiative and opened several doors of opportunity he set about to exploit.

Notes for Chapter 5

1. *The Military Maxims of Napoleon*, Maxim 95.

2. *OR* 27, pt. 2, 637; Busey and Martin, *Regimental Strengths and Losses at Gettysburg*, p. 177; Jeffry D. Wert, "James Jay Archer," in *The Confederate General*, 1, p. 30; Robert K. Krick, "Three Confederate Disasters on Oak Ridge: Failures of Brigade Leadership at the First Day of Gettysburg," in Gallagher, ed., *The First Day at Gettysburg*, pp. 99-111. Davis' 600-man 11th Mississippi was serving as the division train guard. It rejoined the brigade later that evening.

3. *OR* 27, pt. 2, pp. 607 and 638; Robert T. Mockbee, "The 14th Tennessee Infantry Regiment," *Civil War Regiments: A Journal of the American Civil War,* vol. 5, number 1, 1996, p. 27; Shue, *Morning at Willoughby Run: July 1, 1863*, pp. 225-227; Marc Storch and Beth Storch, "What a Deadly Trap We Were In," *Gettysburg Magazine*, Number 4, pp. 26-27. Archer was eventually exchanged from captivity in the summer of 1864, but in such a weakened state that he died that October. Unfortunately, this interesting brigadier does not yet have a biography. For a discussion of Davis' losses, see David G. Martin, *Gettysburg: July 1* (Conshohocken, 1995), p. 140. Major General Abner Doubleday assumed command of the Federal First Corps after Reynolds was killed. Tagg, *The Generals of Gettysburg*, p. 12.

4. *OR* 27, pt. 2, p. 656; Caldwell, *The History of a Brigade of South Carolinians*, p. 96; John B. Bachelder, *Gettysburg, July 1, Map #7* (Dayton, 1996). Pender's Division had initially stopped along Schoolhouse Ridge, then advanced to Herr Ridge about an hour before Lee's arrival.

5. Gettysburg National Military Park Tablet. McIntosh had 10 of his pieces deployed astride the Chambersburg Pike; his remaining six guns were positioned 1,000 yards to the right on higher ground in order to support Heth's reforming and vulnerable right flank and command the Fairfield Road.

6. W. Gordon McGabe, "Address at the Annual Reunion of Pegram Battalion Association," May 21, 1886, *Southern Historical Society Papers,* 14, p. 20; *OR* 27, pt. 2, pp. 612, 674.

7. Herbst Woods is also known as McPherson's Woods.

8. By this time (early afternoon) Lee was facing much of John Reynolds' First Corps. McPherson's Ridge was held by the brigades of Solomon Meredith, Roy Stone, and Chapman Biddle, while Seminary and Oak ridges were manned with the brigades of Henry Baxter, Lysander Cutler, and Gabriel Paul.

9. Henry Heth, in a letter dated June 1877, on the topic of "Causes of Lee's Defeat at Gettysburg," *Southern Historical Society Papers,* 4, p. 156.

10. Major George Campbell Brown, "Reminiscences," Tennessee State Library and Archives, Nashville, Tennessee, copy at the Confederate Research Center, Harold B. Simpson History Complex, Hill College, Hillsboro, Texas.

11. *OR* 27, pt. 2, pp. 503-504. Pickett's three brigades were guarding the rear of the army around Greenwood on July 1.

12. Freeman, *R. E. Lee,* 3, p. 69.

13. According to Gettysburg National Military Park Tablets, Carter's Battalion had a total of 16 guns. Carter was one of Lee's many cousins. *OR* 27, pt. 2, pp. 444, 552 and 564; "Strength and Casualties of Brigades of Major-General R. E. Rodes' Division in the battle of Gettysburg," *Southern Historical Society Papers,* 2, p. 172; Busey and Martin, *Regimental Strengths and Losses at Gettysburg,* p. 307.

14. *OR* 27, pt. 2, p. 444; Isaac R. Trimble to Bachelder, February 8, 1883, *The Bachelder Papers,* 2, pp. 927-928; Isaac R. Trimble, "The Battle and Campaign of Gettysburg," *Southern Historical Society Papers,* 26, p. 122.

15. Isaac R. Trimble, "The Battle and Campaign of Gettysburg," *Southern Historical Society Papers,* 26, p. 122. After he made his decision to march to Gettysburg, Ewell had dispatched his stepson, Major George Campbell Brown, to advise General Lee and/or Powell Hill.

16. Isaac R. Trimble to Bachelder, February 8, 1883, *The Bachelder Papers,* 2, p. 928; *OR* 27, pt. 2, pp. 444 and 552. The battle raging west of Gettysburg at this time (about 10:30 a.m.) involved the brigades of James Archer and Joe Davis. After Ewell failed to receive an order from P. G. T. Beauregard during First Manassas, he habitually dispatched two separate couriers to help insure that one arrived. Major George Campbell Brown, "Reminiscences," Tennessee State Library and Archives, Nashville, Tennessee, copy at the Confederate Research Center, Harold B. Simpson History Complex, Hill College, Hillsboro, Texas.

17. Major George Campbell Brown, "Reminiscences," Tennessee State Library and Archives, Nashville, Tennessee, copy at the Confederate Research Center, Harold B. Simpson History Complex, Hill College, Hillsboro, Texas. *OR* 27, pt. 2, pp. 444, 445 and 552; Trimble to Bachelder, February 8, 1883, *The Bachelder Papers,* 2, p. 928. Historian Larry Tagg makes two interesting observations. First, in hindsight, the decision to move onto Oak Hill instead of staying on the Carlisle Road was probably a mistake, since a thrust directly south would have carried Rodes into the rear of the Union troops on Oak Ridge before they had fully deployed; second, Thomas Carter's artillery opened long before Rodes' infantry was ready to advance, which only telegraphed Ewell's presence on the Federal flank. Tagg, *The Generals of Gettysburg,* pp. 284-285.

18. Tagg, *The Generals of Gettysburg,* p. 123.

19. *OR* 27, pt. 2, pp. 552-553, 564, 583; D. Massey Griffin, "Rodes on Oak Hill: A Study of Rodes' Division on the First Day at Gettysburg," *Gettysburg Magazine* (January 1991), No. 4, p. 36.

20. Krick, "Three Confederate Disasters on Oak Ridge," pp. 92-139; *OR* 27, pt. 2, p. 553; Paul Clark Cooksey, "They Died as if on Dress Parade: The Annihilation of Iverson's Brigade at Gettysburg and the Battle of Oak Ridge," *Gettysburg Magazine,* No. 20, pp. 89-105; Griffin, "Rodes on Oak Hill," pp. 36-38.

21. Freeman, *Lee's Lieutenants*, 3, p. 86.

22. Henry Heth, letter dated June 1877, on the topic of "Causes of Lee's Defeat at Gettysburg," *Southern Historical Society Papers,* 4, p. 158.

23. *OR* 27, pt. 2, p. 444.

24. *OR* 27, pt. 2, pp. 468, 492 and 495.

25. *The Military Maxims of Napoleon*, Maxim 95.

26. *OR* 27, pt. 2, p. 317. Robertson, *A. P. Hill*, p. 211.

27. James I. Robertson, Jr., "Ambrose Powell Hill," in William C. Davis, ed., *The Confederate General*, 6 vols. (Harrisburg, 1993), 3, 1991, pp. 96-98. For a look at Hill's early years, see Robertson, *A. P. Hill*, pp. 3-18.

28. The Federal troops holding McPherson's Ridge at this time consisted of three brigades: Meredith's Iron Brigade, Stone's Pennsylvania Bucktail brigade, and Biddle's (Rowley's) brigades. These formations entered the fight on July 1 with slightly more than 4,500 officers and men, but had already suffered considerable casualties by the time Heth advanced a second time. Pettigrew's Brigade numbered 2,744, Brockenbrough's slightly less than 1,000 Virginians, and a few hundred men from Archer's command under Colonel Birkett D. Fry. For estimates of strengths, see Busey and Martin, *Regimental Strengths and Losses at Gettysburg*, pp. 23, 27, 28, 174 and 176, along with the Gettysburg National Military Park Tablets.

29. *OR* 27, pt. 2, pp. 656 and 668. An excellent article dealing with the McPherson Ridge fighting is D. Scott Hartwig, "The Attack and Defense of McPherson's Ridge," *Gettysburg Magazine* (July, 1989), 1, No. 1, pp. 15-25. Holding back Thomas to protect against a possible attack north of the Chambersburg Pike off Oak Ridge reduced Pender's strength by about twenty percent, which meant that if and when Pender attacked, his frontage would be proportionally reduced. Even a casual reconnaissance would have revealed that the Federal line did not extend beyond the Hagerstown Road area, and thus was readily susceptible to being turned from the south. The fact that Hill paid little if any attention to the exposed left flank leads to the conclusion that he had not studied it—even though several good vantage points for doing so existed. This was where Hill's true opportunity rested on the afternoon of July 1. The fact that he pilfered one of Pender's brigades only confirms that he never fully understood this. Hill's decision to hold back Thomas also indicated Hill did not have much faith that the reformed regiments of Joe Davis' Brigade could defend a reasonably strong position with artillery support. Although it had been roughly handled, Davis' Brigade was rallied by the time of Heth's assault and would have been the logical choice to support Willie Pegram's well-served battalion. *OR* 27, pt. 2, p. 649. Further, Junius Daniel's large North Carolina brigade of Rodes' Division was even then pouring off Oak Hill at an oblique in its attack against Oak Ridge, and thus closing up on Third Corps, which all but eliminated any

chance of a Federal attack west off Oak Ridge. It should have been obvious to Hill that a Federal attack against his left flank (north of Heth's reformed line) from Oak Ridge would have recklessly exposed the enemy flank and rear to Rodes' infantry and a deadly artillery crossfire. *OR* 27, pt. 2, pp. 607 and 656.

30. Allan Nevins, ed., *Diary of Battle: The Personal Journals of Charles S. Wainwright* (New York, 1962), p. 233.

31. Hartwig, "The Attack and Defense of McPherson's Ridge," pp. 23-24; *OR* 27, pt. 1, p. 317. Cutler's remnants had withdrawn and taken up position on Oak Ridge north of the Chambersburg Pike.

32. Henry Heth, *The Memoirs of Henry Heth* (Westport, 1974), pp. 174-176. According to Welsh, *Medical Histories of Confederate Generals*, p. 98, "The ball broke the outer table of [Heth's] skull, supposedly cracked the inner table, but did not penetrate the brain."

33. Busey and Martin, *Regimental Strengths and Losses at Gettysburg*, pp. 23 and 174. Glenn Tucker, *High Tide at Gettysburg,* pp. 139-152, offers an excellent description of this action, as does *Gettysburg, July 1* (Conshohocken, 1997), pp. 342-377. The intensity of the action is best highlighted by a the bloody exchange between Pettigrew's large 26th North Carolina, which fielded more than 800 combatants, against a similar number of men from the Iron Brigade's 19th Indiana and 24th Michigan. The 26th lost some 550 out of 843. One company in the 26th suffered 100% casualties: every man of the company was either killed or wounded. William H. S. Burgwyn, "Unparalleled Loss of Company F, 26th North Carolina Regiment, Pettigrew's Brigade, at Gettysburg," *Southern Historical Society Papers,* 28, pp. 199-204.

34. *OR* 27, pt. 2, p. 564; "Strength and Casualties of Brigades of Major-General R. E. Rodes' Division in the battle of Gettysburg," *Southern Historical Society Papers,* 2, p. 172; Griffin, "Rodes on Oak Hill," pp. 36-38. It was during this stage of the action that Daniel's Brigade had assisted Heth's men by striking part of Stone's Brigade along the Chambersburg Pike.

35. *OR* 27, pt. 2, pp. 479-480, 492-493. Gordon's 26th Georgia was on detached duty. In *OR* 27, pt. 1, p. 704, Howard states his line had already given away by 4:10 p.m. Jones, *Lee's Tigers*, p. 168, for Hay's actions. Stiles, *Four Years Under Marse Robert,* p. 212, for artillery information. Two of the best accounts of the Eleventh Corps at Gettysburg is A. Wilson, Greene, "From Chancellorsville to Cemetery Hill: O. O. Howard and the Eleventh Corps Leadership," in Gary Gallagher, ed., *The First Day at Gettysburg* (Kent, 1992), pp. 57-91, and D. Scott Hartwig, "The 11th Army Corps on July 1," Gettysburg Magazine (1990), No. 2, pp. 33-50. Howard's effort north of town was severely hampered by the terrain; there was simply too much indefensible ground for his corps to hold.

36. James McDowell Carrington, "First Day on Left at Gettysburg," *Southern Historical Society Papers,* 37, p. 332. For the composition of the Charlottesville Virginia Artillery (four 12-pounder Napoleons), please see the Gettysburg National Military Park Tablet. *OR* 27, pt. 2, p. 456. The number of guns and their types may be found on the Gettysburg National Military Park Tablets.

37. Perrin's (McGowan's) missing regiment, the 1st South Carolina (Orr's) Rifles, joined the brigade on the evening of July 2. *OR* 27, pt. 2, pp. 656 and 668; Caldwell, *The History of a*

Brigade of South Carolinians, pp. 96-97; Busey and Martin, *Regimental Strengths and Losses at Gettysburg*, pp. 179-182.

38. Caldwell, *The History of a Brigade of South Carolinians*, p. 98.

39. Rufus R. Dawes, *Service with the Sixth Wisconsin Volunteers* (Dayton, 1991), p. 175.

40. *OR* 27, pt. 1, p. 280.

41. *OR* 27, pt. 2, p. 670; Tagg, *The Generals of Gettysburg*, p. 339.

42. Caldwell, *The History of a Brigade of South Carolinians*, p. 97; *OR* 27, pt. 2, p. 661.

43. Wainwright, *A Dairy of Battle*, p. 236. One of the most honest assessments of the fighting qualities displayed by the Confederate infantry on the first day at Gettysburg was written that very evening by Wainwright: "Lee may well be proud of his infantry; I wish ours was equal to it."

44. *OR* 27, pt. 1, pp. 321, 323 and 328; *History of the 121st Regiment Pennsylvania Volunteers by the Survivors' Association: An Account from the Ranks* (Philadelphia, 1906), pp. 55-56; John A. Leach to Bachelder, September 12, 1882, *The Bachelder Papers*, 2, pp. 904-905; Jeffry D. Wert, *A Brotherhood of Valor: The Common Soldiers of the Stonewall Brigade, C.S.A., and the Iron Brigade, U.S.A.* (New York, 1999), p. 263.

45. Abner Perrin letter, July 29, 1863, to Governor Milledge Luke Bonham, in M. L. Bonham, *A Little More Light on Gettysburg*, pamphlet at the University of South Carolina (no date, reprinted in *Mississippi Valley Historical Review* (March, 1938). For information on the brigade's performance at Second Manassas, see Edward McCrady, Jr., "Gregg's Brigade of South Carolinians in the Second Battle of Manassas," *Southern Historical Society Papers*, 13, pp. 3-40.

46. Lane's experiences provide further proof that Powell Hill should not have removed Thomas' Brigade away from Pender. Had the Georgian's regiments participated in the attack, the division's frontage would have extended well below the Hagerstown Road. That, in turn, would have made it impossible for the 8th Illinois Cavalry to interfere with Lane's advance and would have resulted in a broad flanking of the Federal line.

47. Caldwell, *The History of a Brigade of South Carolinians*, p. 99.

48. Perrin letter, July 29, 1863, to Governor Milledge Luke Bonham.

49. Eighteen of Federal artillery pieces were "on a frontage of not over 200 yards." Wainwright, *A Diary of Battle,* July 1, 1863, p. 235.

50. Busey and Martin, *Regimental Strengths and Losses at Gettysburg*, p. 273. Reynolds' Federal First Corps fielded about 12,000 effectives on July 1. Its losses by day's end were, 666 killed, 3,231 wounded, and 2,162 missing or captured, or about 50%. Meredith's Iron Brigade lost 1,153 of its 1829 men, or 63%. Many of these losses were the result of Rodes' attack off Oak Hill.

51. Pender's losses on the afternoon of July 1 totaled almost 17% of his entire division, or 21% of the 4,705 (three brigades) engaged. Scales lost more than 400 killed and wounded out of 1,405 effectives, while Perrin suffered about 500 killed and wounded out of 1,600 effectives. Lane's losses were very slight—less than 100 of his 1,700—and Thomas's 1,300 men, sitting in reserve, were inconsequential.

52. John A. Leach to Bachelder, September 12, 1882, *The Bachelder Papers*, 2, p. 905; Caldwell, *The History of a Brigade of South Carolinians*, p. 99.

53. Randolph H. McKim, "The Gettysburg Campaign," *Southern Historical Society Papers,* 40, p. 272; *A Soldier's Recollections*, pp. 175-176.

54. *OR* 27, pt. 2, p. 607. For Lee's report of this situation see OR 27, pt. 2, p. 317.

55. Freeman, *R. E. Lee,* 3, p. 71.

56. *OR* 27, pt. 2, p. 349.

57. *OR* 27, pt. 2, pp. 349, 652 and 673

58. *OR* 27, pt. 2, p. 349.

59. It is interesting to note that Pendleton's report of the battle, penned on September 12, 1863, claims Lee only "suggested whether positions on the right" could be found to enfilade Cemetery Hill. Obviously he was directed to so place his guns, and he chose unilaterally not to do so. *OR* 27, pt. 2, p. 349.

60. *OR* 27, pt. 2, p. 607.

61. *OR* 27, pt. 2, p. 612. Willie Pegram's Battalion, which had supported Heth and Pender much of the day, had used up a considerable amount of its ammunition, but one of its batteries was still capable of further service.

62. *OR* 27, pt. 2, p. 613.

63. John B. Bachelder, *Gettysburg, July 1*, Map #14.

64. Some Gettysburg students stress that the terrain of Cemetery Hill made it virtually impregnable to attack on July 1 by any Confederate force that could have been thrown against it that evening. Terrain always plays an important role in military engagements. However, when the combat capabilities of the defending troops are carefully considered together with the successful nature of the Southern attack by Hays and Avery on July 2, the terrain of Cemetery Hill does not seem so formidable.

65. Randolph H. McKim, "The Gettysburg Campaign," *Southern Historical Society Papers,* 40, p. 274; David McIntosh, "Review of the Gettysburg Campaign," *Southern Historical Society Papers,* 37, pp. 118-119.

66. Wainwright, *A Diary of Battle*, July 1, 1863, p. 236.

67. Taylor, *General Lee*, p. 190; Taylor, *Four Years With General Lee*, p. 95; *OR* 27, pt. 2, p. 318.

68. There has been substantial confusion and error regarding what "if possible" or "if practicable" actually meant. This issue is fully explored at the end of this chapter in the "General Lee and July 1 in Retrospect" section.

69. Walter Herron Taylor, Second Paper on the topic of "Causes of Lee's Defeat at Gettysburg," *Southern Historical Society Papers,* 4, p. 127; James Power Smith, "General Lee at Gettysburg," *Southern Historical Society Papers,* 33, p. 144. See Harry Pfanz, *Gettysburg: Culp's Hill and Cemetery Hill* (Chapel Hill, 1993), p. 72-73, for his analysis of Taylor's message.

70. *OR* 27, pt. 1, p. 367. See Pfanz, *Culp's Hill and Cemetery Hill*, p. 25, for a succinct discussion of the importance of these heights.

71. *OR* 27, pt. 1, p. 724; *The Civil War Memoirs of Captain William J. Seymour: Reminiscences of a Louisiana Tiger*, p. 72; Busey and Martin, *Regimental Strengths and Losses at Gettysburg*, p. 83; *OR* 27, pt. 1, pp. 368.

72. *The Military Maxims of Napoleon*, Maxim 69 and 81.

73. *OR* 27, pt. 2, pp. 468-469, 480, 484, 493.

74. *OR* 27, pt. 2, pp. 469.

75. Gordon, *Reminiscences of the Civil War*, p. 154. Gordon's recollections are entertaining and informative, but occasionally outpace facts, and thus must be used with great care.

76. Jones, *Louisiana Tigers*, pp. 168-169.

77. *The Civil War Memoirs of Captain William J. Seymour: Reminiscences of a Louisiana Tiger*, p. 72.

78. *North Carolina Regiments*, 3, p. 414.

79. Asher Waterman Garber to John W. Daniel, February 24, 1904, John W. Daniel Papers, Manuscripts Division, Special Collections Department, University of Virginia, Charlottesville, Virginia.

80. James McDowell Carrington, "First Day on Left at Gettysburg," *Southern Historical Society Papers,* 37, pp. 332-333.

81. Stiles, *Four Years Under Marse Robert,* p. 214. Pfanz, *Culp's Hill and Cemetery Hill,* p. 25

82. *OR* 27, pt. 2, p. 469. Jubal Early, *Autobiographical Sketch and Narrative of the War Between the States* (Philadelphia, 1912), pp. 269-270.

83. *May I Quote You, Stonewall Jackson? Observations & Utterances From the South's Great Generals*, edited by Randall Bedwell (Nashville, 1997), p. 46.

84. Henry Kyd Douglas, *I Rode With Stonewall* (Chapel Hill, 1940), p. 247. Douglas' memoirs, like John B. Gordon's should be used carefully.

85. Douglas, *I Rode With Stonewall,* pp. 247-248. Douglas' explicit quote of Ewell: "I do not feel like advancing and making an attack without orders from [Lee], and he is back at Cashtown," has been rejected as inaccurate by some historians, including Douglas Southall Freeman, because Ewell's after-action report (*OR* 27, pt. 2, p. 444) claims that he received later instructions from Lee. However, a closer examination leads to the conclusion that Freeman's judgment in this respect is incorrect. Douglas could easily have been accurate in recalling this statement, because Ewell evidently thought that an advance against Cemetery Hill was a *separate* action, as evidenced by the Second Corps commander's exchange with Trimble later that afternoon.

86. *OR* 27, pt. 2, p. 555.

87. Hamlin, *The Attack of Stonewall Jackson at Chancellorsville,* pp. 79-96, has an excellent discussion of what the delay advocated by Rodes cost the Southern army in terms of additional prisoners. See also Ernest B. Furguson, *Chancellorsville: Souls of the Brave* (New York, 1992), pp. 195-199, 337.

88. Some writers attribute Rodes' mixed performance at Gettysburg to ill health. See, for example, Tagg, *Generals of Gettysburg,* p. 286. Rodes may or may not have been sick at Gettysburg, but we do know that his performance there was consistent with some aspects of his performance at Chancellorsville.

89. *OR* 27, pt. 2, p. 593; Busey and Martin, *Regimental Strengths and Losses at Gettysburg,* p. 288. C. D. Grace, "Rodes' Division at Gettysburg," Confederate Veteran (1897), 5, p. 615. Although pure speculation, if O'Neal actually asked Doles to take command of the division, it lends a thread of credence to allegations that Rodes was sick that day and

that some of his officers believed it impaired his actions on the field. Otherwise, the request would have been grounds for an arrest and courts-martial.

90. Calder quote in Martin, *Gettysburg: July 1*, pp. 515-516. His papers are in the USAMHI.

91. Michael W. Taylor, "Ramseur's Brigade in the Gettysburg Campaign: A Newly Discovered Account by Capt. James I. Harris, Co. I, 30th Regt. N.C.T.," *Gettysburg Magazine*, Number 17, p. 34.

92. *Raleigh Semi-Weekly Standard*, August 4, 1863.

93. Gorman quote in Martin, *Gettysburg: July 1*, p. 516.

94. *Supplement to the Official Records of the Union and Confederate Armies*, 5, serial no. 5, p. 402.

95. James Power Smith, "General Lee at Gettysburg," *Southern Historical Society Papers*, 33, pp. 135-

160; James Power Smith, "With Lee at Gettysburg," *Southern Historical Society Papers*, 43, pp. 55-58. Smith's rank at the end of the war was Captain; however, in *OR* 27, pt. 2, p. 452, Smith's rank at the time of Gettysburg is listed as Lieutenant. The reason that the officers such as General Lee referred to Smith as "Captain," at Gettysburg was simple: Smith explains in *Southern Historical Society Papers*, 33, p. 139, that he was "in the uniform of a Confederate captain" during the campaign.

96. James Power Smith, "With Lee at Gettysburg," *Southern Historical Society Papers*, 43, p. 57.

97. James Power Smith, "General Lee at Gettysburg," *Southern Historical Society Papers*, 33, pp. 140-141.

98. James Power Smith, "With Lee at Gettysburg," *Southern Historical Society Papers*, 43, p. 57.

99. James Power Smith, "With Lee at Gettysburg," *Southern Historical Society Papers*, 43, p. 57.

100. James Power Smith, "General Lee at Gettysburg," *Southern Historical Society Papers*, 33, p. 145.

101. James Power Smith, "General Lee at Gettysburg," *Southern Historical Society Papers*, 33, p. 144.

102. *OR* 27, pt. 2, p. 445.

103. *OR* 27, pt. 2, p. 445.

104. Major George Campbell Brown, "Reminiscences," Tennessee State Library and Archives, Nashville, Tennessee, copy at the Confederate Research Center, Harold B. Simpson History Complex, Hill College, Hillsboro, Texas.

105. McKim, *A Soldier's Recollections*, pp. 295-296.

106. Randolph H. McKim, "Steuart's Brigade at the Battle of Gettysburg," *Southern Historical Society Papers*, 5, p. 292. McKim, who served on the staff of Brigadier General George Steuart, remembered that there was plenty of light remaining to read a dispatch delivered by Major Henry Douglas from General Johnson—after the brigade had deployed.

107. *Speeches and Orations of John Warwick Daniel*, edited by Edward M. Daniel (Lynchburg, 1911), p. 82; Jones, *Lee's Tigers*, p. 169. Jones incorrectly records that Colonel Zable was with the 15th Louisiana.

108. There are many examples in military history where immediate success served to mentally unhinge commanders, who thereafter failed to reap the full fruits of their advantage.

109. Ewell was referring to the order delivered by Campbell Brown when Lee was in Cashtown early that morning.

110. Isaac R. Trimble, "The Campaign and Battle of Gettysburg," *Confederate Veteran*, 25, p. 211; Isaac R. Trimble to Bachelder, February 8, 1883, *The Bachelder Papers*, 2, p. 930

111. Isaac R. Trimble to Bachelder, February 8, 1883, *The Bachelder Papers*, 2, p. 930. Trimble's estimate of one-half hour is entirely consistent with the time a good rider would have required to make this trip.

112. Isaac R. Trimble to Bachelder, February 8, 1883, *The Bachelder Papers*, 2, pp. 930-931.

113. Randolph H. McKim, "The Gettysburg Campaign," *Southern Historical Society Papers,* 40, p. 273.

114. Isaac R. Trimble to Bachelder, February 8, 1883, *The Bachelder Papers*, 2, p. 931.

115. Spencer Glasgow Welch, *A Confederate Surgeon's Letters to His Wife* (Marietta, 1954 reprint of 1911 original), p. 66.

116. Abner Perrin, letter dated July 29, 1863, to Governor Milledge Luke Bonham, in M. L. Bonham, *A Little More Light on Gettysburg*, pamphlet at the University of South Carolina (no date), reprinted in the *Mississippi Valley Historical Review*, March, 1938.

117. *Richmond Enquirer* dispatch, dated July 8, 1863, Hagerstown.

118. Louis G. Young, "Pettigrew's Brigade at Gettysburg," *North Carolina Regiments, 5,* p. 121.

119. For just two, see: Martin, *Gettysburg: July 1*, pp. 503-504, and Gary W. Gallagher, "Confederate Corps Leadership on the First Day at Gettysburg: A. P. Hill and Richard S. Ewell in a Difficult Debut," *The First Day at Gettysburg*, p. 47.

120. *OR* 27, pt. 2, pp. 504, 509, 513, 518 and 521.

121. James I Robertson, *The Stonewall Brigade* (Baton Rouge, 1977), p. 203.

122. Pfanz, *Culp's Hill and Cemetery Hill*, pp. 79-80.

123. Krick, "Three Confederate Disasters on Oak Ridge," p. 92.

124. *OR* 27, pt. 1, pp. 182-183; Busey and Martin, *Regimental Strengths and Losses at Gettysburg*, p. 270

125. *OR* 27, pt. 1, pp. 173-174, 251; Busey and Martin, *Regimental Strengths and Losses at Gettysburg*, p. 270.

126. *OR* 27, pt. 1, p. 274.

127. *OR* 27, pt. 1, p. 269.

128. The 19th Indiana started the fight with 288 combatants in ranks, with 20 others forming part of what was called the "brigade guard," along with 20 men from every other regiment of the brigade that completed that ad-hoc command.

129. Walter L. Owens to Bachelder, 6 August 1866, *Bachelder Papers*, 1, p. 268.

130. *OR* 27, pt. 1, p. 253.

131. *OR* 27, pt. 1, pp. 173, 174, 315, 338.

132. *OR* 27, pt. 1, pp. 173-174, 182-183.

133. *OR* 27, pt. 2, pp. 340-341, 480 and 493.

134. *OR* 27, pt. 2, p. 583.

135. *OR* 27, pt. 2, pp. 342, 562; Busey and Martin, *Regimental Strengths and Losses at Gettysburg*, p. 308.

136. *OR* 27, pt. 2, p. 344. Heth's losses are more specifically discussed at the beginning of this chapter. They are difficult to ascertain exactly because his division also participated in Pickett's Charge on July 3. Losses for all three days are simply lumped together.

137. *OR* 27, pt. 2, pp. 344-345. Please refer to note 51 above for more details.

138. In addition to the infantry losses of 5,850, Lee's artillery batteries suffered fewer than 150 casualties.

139. Alpheus S. Williams, *From the Cannon's Mouth: the Civil War letters of General Alpheus S. Williams*, edited with an introduction by Milo M. Quaife (Lincoln, 1995), p. 227. For a detailed examination of Reynolds' decision to fight at Gettysburg, please consult L. Patrick Nelson, "Reynolds and the Decision to Fight," *Gettysburg Magazine,* Number 23, pp. 30-50.

140. Abner Doubleday, *Chancellorsville and Gettysburg* (New York, 1994 reprint of the 1882 original), p. 152.

141. John B. Bachelder to Fitzhugh Lee, 18 January 1875, as part of "A Review of the First Two Days' Operations at Gettysburg and a Reply to General Longstreet," *Southern Historical Society Papers,* 5, p. 172.

142. John B. Bachelder to Fitzhugh Lee, 18 January 1875, as part of "A Review of the First Two Days' Operations at Gettysburg and a Reply to General Longstreet," *Southern Historical Society Papers,* 5, p. 173.

143. Winfield Scott Hancock to Fitzhugh Lee, 17 January 1878, as part of "A Review of the First Two Days' Operations at Gettysburg and a Reply to General Longstreet," *Southern Historical Society Papers,* 5, p. 168.

144. Isaac R. Trimble to Bachelder, February 8, 1883, *The Bachelder Papers*, 2, pp. 931-932. Trimble was writing years after the battle when the Confederates were fighting amongst themselves affixing blame for the defeat. These type of recollections must be used cautiously. See also, *Supplement to the OR* 5, serial no. 5, pp. 442-443.

145. Isaac R. Trimble to Bachelder, February 8, 1883, *The Bachelder Papers*, 2, pp. 930-932.

146. Coddington, *The Gettysburg Campaign: A Study in Command*, p. 320. Coddington, pp. 317-318, argues that critics have thus far failed to adequately investigate Powell Hill's actions, or inaction, on July 1. Hopefully, the analysis offered in these pages goes some way toward filling that historical gap.

147. Coddington, *The Gettysburg Campaign: A Study in Command*, p. 315.

148. Coddington, *The Gettysburg Campaign: A Study in Command*, p. 319. This interpretation of the phrase was also propounded by noted Civil War historian Kenneth P. Williams in *Lincoln Finds a General: A Military Study of the Civil War,* 5 vols. (New York, 1949-59), 2, pp. 617-618, which predated Coddington's study. Coddington, however, has been much more influential in shaping how students view the battle than Williams, and so his words form the focus of this discussion.

149. *OR* 27, pt. 2, pp. 312-326; Dowdey and Manarin, eds., *The Wartime Papers of R. E. Lee*, number 542.

150. *OR* 11, pt. 2, p. 500; Dowdey and Manarin, eds., *The Wartime Papers of R. E. Lee,* number 210.

151. Dowdey and Manarin, eds., *The Wartime Papers of R. E. Lee,* number 153.

152. Dowdey and Manarin, eds., *The Wartime Papers of R. E. Lee,* number 203.

153. Dowdey and Manarin, eds., *The Wartime Papers of R. E. Lee,* number 236.

154. Dowdey and Manarin, eds., *The Wartime Papers of R. E. Lee,* number 245.

155. *OR* 25, pt. 2, p. 769; *The Wartime Papers of R. E. Lee,* numbers 423 and 424.

156. Dowdey and Manarin, eds., *The Wartime Papers of R. E. Lee,* number 429.

157. *OR* 27, 3, p. 905; Dowdey and Manarin, eds., *The Wartime Papers of R. E. Lee,* number 485.

158. See, for example, U.S. Grant's communiqués to Lee dated April 7 and April 8, 1865. These letters discussed the subject of the surrender of the Army of Northern Virginia, and are concluded by Grant with the phrase "your obedient servant." One of the many sources in which these letters appear is *Southern Historical Society Papers,* 15, pp. vii-viii.

159. Gallagher, "Confederate Corps Leadership on the First Day at Gettysburg: A. P. Hill and Richard S. Ewell in a Difficult Debut," *The First Day at Gettysburg,* pp. 30-56. Gallagher's article also appears in his *Lee and His Generals in War and Memory,* (Baton Rouge, 1998).

160. Gallagher, "Confederate Corps Leadership on the First Day at Gettysburg," p. 56; *Lee and His Generals in War and Memory,* p. 181.

161. Gallagher, "Confederate Corps Leadership on the First Day at Gettysburg," p. 55.

162. Gallagher, "Confederate Corps Leadership on the First Day at Gettysburg," p. 56. Jackson's actions during the Seven Days' Battles, for example, and his seeming indecision or unwillingness to go over to the offensive after John Pope's men were defeated on Jackson's front (it took two hours to get his men moving) offer two example of indecision or an inability to order his men into action at critical moments. Hennessy, *Return to Bull Run,* p. 427.

163. For just two examples of General Lee's use of true "discretionary orders," see Lee's orders to Jeb Stuart dated February 13, 1863, Dowdey and Manarin, eds., *The Wartime Papers of R. E. Lee,* number 374, and his instructions to Longstreet when that commander was on detached service operating in the Suffolk area, Dowdey and Manarin, eds., *The Wartime Papers of R. E. Lee,* number 407. Read these carefully—the difference is striking.

164. Taylor, *General Lee,* p. 190; Taylor, *Four Years With General Lee,* p. 95.

165. Pfanz, *Culp's Hill and Cemetery Hill,* p. 72.

166. Pfanz, *Culp's Hill and Cemetery Hill,* p. 72.

167. *OR* 27, pt. 2, p. 318; James Power Smith, "General Lee at Gettysburg," *Southern Historical Society Papers,* 33, p. 145. Also, Major Charles Marshall related to Isaac Trimble that General Lee "directed [Ewell] to advance against the enemy 'if he was in condition to do so,'" as cited in *The Bachelder Papers,* 2, p. 931. As related by Trimble, Marshall's recollection of this incident paints a slightly different, but wholly consistent, picture of what Taylor and Smith relate in their writings.

168. Eppa Hunton, *Autobiography* (Richmond, 1933), p. 98.

169. One example is Harry W. Pfanz's, "'Old Jack' Is Not Here," in Gabor S. Boritt, ed., *The Gettysburg Nobody Knows* (New York, 1997), pp. 56-74.

170. *OR* 27, pt. 2, pp. 318. There are several examples of writers who employ Lee's after-action report to the exclusion of other evidence. One writer who uses Lee's after-action report as the sole basis of the theory that Ewell was given confusing orders and subsequently placed in an "impossible" position by General Lee is Samuel J. Martin, *The Road to Glory: Confederate General Richard S. Ewell* (Indianapolis, 1991), pp. 219 and 409, fn38. Martin actually puts words from Lee's after-action report *into* James Power Smith's mouth in an attempt to support his theory. Another example of a writer that uses exclusively Lee's after-action report, then asks "What, exactly, did this confusing order mean?" is Larry Tagg, *The Generals of Gettysburg*, p. 198.

171. Charles Marshall, *An Aide de Camp of Lee*, pp. 180-181. Marshall gives an excellent account of how after-action reports are written and the manner in which General Lee edited them.

172. Martin, *The Road to Glory: Confederate General Richard S. Ewell*, pp. 219 and 409, fn38; Tagg, *The Generals of Gettysburg: The Leaders of America's Greatest Battle,* p. 198; Donald C. Pfanz, *Richard S. Ewell: A Soldier's Life* (Chapel Hill, 1998), p. 310.

173. George Campbell Brown, "Personal Narration," Manuscript Division, Library of Congress. For many years after the war, Brown wrote that he had met Lee in Cashtown. However, he later wrote in "Answers to queries," that the meeting might have been near Cashtown several miles from Gettysburg on what "I now think . . . was a mere crossroads."

174. *OR* 27, pt. 2, p. 444.

175. It is important to remember this central issue: every one of the four principals involved—Lee, Ewell, Taylor and Smith—all agreed that the commanding general *ordered* a pursuit by Second Corps. Just a few examples from history of this type behavior include: (1) Roman General Gnaenus Pompeius Magnus (Pompey the Great) at Dyrrhacium, spring 48 B.C. Pompey's failure to follow up his victory dramatically changed history by allowing Julius Caesar to regroup his army. Caesar crushed Pompey a few months later at the Battle of Pharsalus; (2) The failures of Napoleon's marshals Soult and Murat following the Battle of Austerlitz substantially lessened the impact of Napoleon's impressive victory and allowed the Russian army to escape complete destruction; (3) Vice-Admiral Chuichi Nagumo at Pearl Harbor failed to follow up his incredible initial success scored by the leading attack wave of Japanese aircraft; (4) Lt. General Mark W. Clark's disbelief at his own success and resulting hesitation at Anzio in January 1944 allowed the Germans time to recover; and (5) Vice-Admiral Takeo Kurita's reluctance to believe his own initial success at the Battle of Leyte Gulf in October of 1944 saved much of the American invasion fleet from ruin.

176. Brooks, D. Simpson, "Command Relationships at Gettysburg," in Steven E. Woodworth, ed., *Civil War Generals in Defeat* (Lawrence, 1999), pp. 166-169.

177. John B. Bachelder, *Gettysburg, July 1, Map #14.*

178. Simpson, "Command Relationships at Gettysburg," *Civil War Generals in Defeat*, p. 167.

179. Alan T. Nolan, "R. E. Lee and July 1 at Gettysburg,"in Gary Gallagher, ed., *The First Day at Gettysburg* (Kent, 1992), pp. 1-29.

180. Nolan, "R. E. Lee and July 1 at Gettysburg," *The First Day at Gettysburg,* p. 12.

181. Nolan ,"R. E. Lee and July 1 at Gettysburg," *The First Day at Gettysburg,* p. 21.

182. *OR* 27, pt. 2, p. 607.

183. *OR* 27, pt. 2, p. 637; Henry Heth, letter dated June 1877, on the topic of "Causes of Lee's Defeat at Gettysburg," *Southern Historical Society Papers*, 4, p. 157.

184. Douglas Southall Freeman, *R. E. Lee*, 3, p. 65; Clifford Dowdey, *Lee* (Gettysburg, 1991), p. 365, states that it was "night" when the "courier came from A. P. Hill." Hill's messenger could not have left Cashtown and reached Lee near Greenwood until sometime after 10:00 p.m.

185. Dowdey, *Lee*, p. 365.

186. Taylor, *Four Years With General Lee*, pp. 92-93.

187. Charles Marshall, "Events Leading up to the Battle of Gettysburg," *Southern Historical Society Papers,* 23, pp. 226-227. If Hill had been stopped and Ewell advanced, what actually transpired on July 1 might have been reversed, i.e., Reynolds' First Corps, supported by Howard's Eleventh Corps and screened by Buford's cavalry, could have isolated and destroyed Ewell.

188. Nolan, "R. E. Lee and July 1 at Gettysburg," *The First Day at Gettysburg*, pp. 23-24.

Chapter 6

"We Must Attack Him"

General Lee's Plans for Battle
on the Second Day

*"From the nature of the country, the absence of [our] cavalry and the
proximity of an uncrippled enemy, the flank movement referred
to [by Longstreet] was simply an absurdity."*
—Colonel Armistead Lindsay Long[1]

James Longstreet, the 42-year-old commander of Lee's First Corps and the army's second in command, guided his horse through the wake of Third Corps' battle up onto Seminary Ridge near a cupola-topped building late on the afternoon of July 1. He was a bull of a man over six feet tall and strong—"a soldier every inch"[2] was how one aide described him. Fearless and dependable, he carried none of Powell Hill's impulsiveness and not a one of Dick Ewell's quirky habits—and Lee had come to depend on him absolutely. And now he was on the field.

*   *   *

The native South Carolinian came into life in 1821 but grew up in Georgia. Attracted to the military, Longstreet graduated from West Point in the famous class of 1842 near the bottom of the academic barrel. Exciting service rendered well

James Longstreet (1821-1904)

He had always been the senior corps commander of the Army of Northern Virginia, and General Lee relied heavily on the tactical expertise and calm demeanor of the man he once called "my old war horse." Longstreet's corps-level attack at Second Manassas was the largest assault ever launched by the Virginia army. His defensive prowess was displayed at Fredericksburg, where his brigades cut down successive waves of Federal attackers. Longstreet's preference for fighting on the defensive was probably grounded in his Fredericksburg victory. *Library of Congress*

during the Mexican War (where he was wounded) was followed by years of dreary outpost duty, marriage, and ten children. Longstreet was only a post paymaster when the Civil War began, but his offer to serve the South was exchanged for a brigadier's rank and within a few weeks he was leading a brigade at First Manassas. That fall Longstreet was commanding a division under Joseph E. Johnston. His solid performance at Williamsburg during the retreat up the Virginia peninsula was followed by his miserable performance at Seven Pines. Longstreet aggravated his effort by wrongly trying to blame a fellow officer. With Johnston out of action due to his wound at the latter battle, Robert E. Lee stepped into command and tasked Longstreet with a series of difficult responsibilities during the Seven Days' onslaught. He performed better than any other subordinate—and Lee never forgot it. The army's clumsy divisional command system was replaced with two "wings" (or corps), one under Longstreet and the other under Jackson. With Stonewall as the anvil, Longstreet effortlessly hammered John Pope's army at Second Manassas in one of the largest infantry attacks of the war, routing him from the field. In the near-debacle at Sharpsburg, "Old Pete," as he was called by his men, rode up and down the line, cobbling together a defensive patchwork of units that held Lee's army together. That night Lee proudly referred to him as "my old warhorse." When Lee promoted his "wing" leaders to lieutenant general, Longstreet's name was submitted ahead of Jackson's.

The Battle of Fredericksburg closed out the fighting of 1862 and offered Longstreet the most important lesson he learned during the war: the power of the defensive. With his veterans holding Marye's Heights and supported with artillery, "Old Pete" slaughtered wave after wave of Federals sent up the hill after him. Longstreet never forgot the lesson that battle taught him. Whether he would ever find similar terrain to hold and another Federal general as one-dimensional as Burnside remained to be seen. A semi-independent stint around Suffolk in the late winter of 1862-63 followed. Although there was little military glory to be found there (and some embarrassment on a small scale level) Longstreet performed his multitude of often conflicting duties well and sent back tons of foodstuffs and other supplies for the army's use. Only when Joe Hooker moved against Lee was Longstreet recalled to the army, and thus returned after the fighting at Chancellorsville had ended. The reorganization that followed cleaved the infantry from two corps into three, but Longstreet's dependable First Corps, the foundation of the Army of Northern Virginia, remained intact. After spending much of the long road into Pennsylvania covering the army's rear, Longstreet's two vanguard divisions under John Bell Hood and Lafayette McLaws expended the daylight hours of July 1 marching the 17 miles from Greenwood to Gettysburg, while the third division under George Pickett remained behind in Chambersburg.[3]

Lee Considers his Options for July 2

With the sounds of the day's battle dying away, Longstreet dismounted not far from General Lee, who filled him in on what had transpired. The pair made their way to the east side of the ridge and intently studied the terrain across the shallow mile-long valley separating them from the disorganized Federal gathering around Cemetery Hill. Both men noted how the long and low ridge across the way ran south from Cemetery Hill to a pair of uneven but formidable heights more than two miles away. The enemy was gathering on strong terrain with clear fields of fire. "Old Pete" appreciated good defensive ground and his experience had taught him to seek it out. The pair discussed the army's next course of action. Other than in general terms, exactly what was discussed we will never know. What is certain is that Longstreet suggested the entire army should be moved immediately around the right (Meade's left) and placed in position somewhere to the south, where it would threaten Meade's lines of communication with Washington and force, as Longstreet believed, the Federal army to immediately attack.[4]

Lee considered the idea and decided against it. The proposal was an arbitrary plan of action whose success depended substantially on the enemy's cooperation. Certainly Meade would not sit quietly by and let his left be turned. With Jeb Stuart and his cavalry still missing, who would scout the move and protect the miles of exposed shifting infantry? A sweeping move around the left of the Army of the Potomac would also expose Lee's own lines of communication and resupply that ran west from Gettysburg through South Mountain and south across the Potomac and into Virginia. And Lee knew well the man he still called "Major Meade." He had already concluded that, at least on an operational level, the new commander of the Federal army would "commit no blunder in my front." Simply put, Meade would not act rashly, nor would he repeat Ambrose Burnside's offensive folly at Fredericksburg. Lee was also loath to engage in an activity that offered Meade a chance to seize the operational initiative; after all, Lee's sound reason for concentrating his army east of South Mountain in the first place was with the intent of preventing Meade from maneuvering against his lines of communication. Instead, Lee sought to retain his operational initiative and to force the Federals into battle far away from Confederate lines of resupply.

For all these reasons and others—the army had just severely mauled two of the enemy's corps, and momentum—one of the most valuable psychological weapons an army commander possessed, was with the Southern army—the commanding general declined.

"No, the enemy is there," explained Lee, "and I am going to attack him there."[5]

Longstreet's response was in line with his understanding of how battles were to be conducted, and generally spoken was as follows: "General, if the enemy is there

"Tomorrow ... We Must Attack Him"

One of the high points in the drama at Gettysburg was when Lieutenant General James Longstreet met General Robert E. Lee on the east side of Seminary Ridge. Lee rejected his corps leader's suggestion to maneuver away from Gettysburg to the south and east and informed Longstreet of his decision to renew the fighting the next day on the ground in front of them. *Courtesy Gallon Historical Art, Gettysburg, Pennsylvania*

tomorrow, it is because he wants you to attack him, which is a good reason, in my judgment, for not doing so."

A general and honest exchange of views continued between the generals for several minutes, but Lee's final response must have been along the lines of "we must attack him."

Lee's decision that the Army of Northern Virginia *must* assume the offensive on July 2 appalled Longstreet, who penned after the war that the commanding general was "under a subdued excitement, which occasionally took possession of him 'when the hunt was up' and threatened his superb equipoise."[6] Lee might well have been excited, because as far as he was concerned, the opportunity to defeat the enemy had arrived, albeit in a slightly different form than he had anticipated. If no further Confederate attacks or pursuit were made on July 1, there were only a handful of possibilities open to him on the morrow: (1) withdraw the army west; (2) maneuver to the left, or north; (3) maneuver to the right, or south; (4) remain where he was, assume the defensive, and await the next Federal move; or (5) attack the enemy deployed in front of him. Since Lee has been heavily criticized for attacking at all on July 2, each of these possibilities must be examined in detail.

Lee's first choice was to withdraw from the field. That option could not have long been considered by Lee, if he even considered it at all, and for good reason: it was a terrible option. Ordering his army to fall back westward from Gettysburg would have violated one of the most basic maxims of warfare. "When once the offensive has been assumed," wrote Napoleon, "it must be sustained to the last extremity. However skillful the maneuvers, a retreat will always weaken the morale of an army, because in losing the chances of success, these last are transferred to the enemy."[7] That maxim was never truer than in the waning daylight moments of July 1, 1863. If Lee had ordered a retreat his decision would have been wholly incomprehensible to his officers and men. The army had scored a stunning victory on the battle's first day, and was still concentrating at Gettysburg as the sun set on July 1. A withdrawal following the severe defeat of two Federal corps ran the risk, however slight, of undermining the army's confidence in its generals. It does not take much imagination to divine how the Confederate officers and men who had witnessed the day's victory would have reacted if ordered to retreat.

Further, Lee would have had to overcome the logistical difficulties of turning around the army's trains stacked up for miles along the Chambersburg Pike from South Mountain heading eastward. Another position would have to be scouted and selected *before* a withdrawal order could even be issued for the wagons to reverse course. Considering the torturously slow progress many Confederate formations experienced getting over South Mountain to Gettysburg on July 1, one can speculate with some confidence the extreme difficulties that would have been encountered withdrawing much of the army down the Chambersburg Pike as far as Cashtown in one day. Such a withdrawal would also expose the troops designated as the army's rearguard to destruction—especially without the assistance of sufficient numbers of screening cavalry. (Lee knew the Federal cavalry was present in force and capable of striking his flanks and rear, while Jeb Stuart's troopers were still absent.) Therefore, from a march-management standpoint alone, an order for a withdrawal on the evening of July 1 and morning of July 2 would have exacerbated the existing traffic jam and endangered a portion of the army. Also of importance was the fact that a withdrawal would have surrendered the operational initiative to the Federal army and broken the Confederate's momentum that had been building since the Southern victories at Fredericksburg, Chancellorsville and day one at Gettysburg.

Another important factor Lee had to consider was the recent appointment of George Meade to the command of the Army of the Potomac. He certainly did not want to accommodate Meade by allowing him the precious commodity of time to become comfortable in his new role—especially after the sharp loss Meade suffered during the first day's battle on July 1. Few if any generals were more aware of the value or importance of time to a newly appointed army commander than Lee. George McClellan, for example, had generously offered Lee weeks to consolidate his new command in front of Richmond following the wounding of Joe Johnston at the Battle of Seven Pines. Lee put the time to good use and developed a plan to turn McClellan away from the Southern capital and defeat him. This is exactly what Lee would have offered Meade if he had ordered the Confederate army to withdraw to the west after July 1.

Finally, a withdrawal would have been inconsistent with Lee's character, much of which was grounded in the study of history's Great Captains and the principles of war. Lee rarely abandoned an opportunity to control events on the field of battle, and after July 1 the initiative plainly rested with his army. He had a vision of how he would maneuver his numerically inferior army into an advantageous position and defeat his enemy. That goal had been partially realized on July 1, and he believed further possibilities existed if he continued the fight on July 2. A victory by Army of Northern Virginia on Pennsylvania soil would have a profound impact on the morale of the Northern populace and their political will to support the prosecution of the war. For all these reasons, a withdrawal was simply not a viable option.[8]

The second possible course of action Lee had available to him was to maneuver the army to the left, or north. At first blush this option seemed to have more promise than a withdrawal west. By maneuvering the army to the left, Lee could make use of the existing road network to draw off to the north and, by continuing to maneuver, threaten Harrisburg while maintaining his lines of communication through the Cumberland Valley. But these benefits would not further Confederate chances to inflict stinging reversals on the Federal army, and were offset by a variety of negative consequences. First, the Confederate commander could only hope that a move around the left would draw Meade after him and open up the Army of the Potomac to a defeat in detail. Lee, however, could not count on Meade acting in such a manner. In addition, the July 1 convergence of Confederate formations that had subsequently eviscerated two Federal corps was partially the result of luck; Lee could not count on that happening again.

Next, Jeb Stuart and the army's three élite brigades of cavalry were still missing. It would have been both difficult and dangerous to have undertaken a large scale flanking maneuver with little more than one brigade of mounted troops. These cavalry units—Albert G. Jenkins' 1,600-man brigade and Lieutenant Colonel Elijah V. White's 35th Virginia Battalion, about 200 men—were experienced foragers and raiders but were by no means front line cavalry on a par with Stuart's formations.[9] The enemy, however, possessed thousands of veteran cavalrymen. Lee recognized that maneuvering to the north with the enemy concentrating in his front would invite a possible attack against his exposed flank and precious logistical tail, which was comprised in part of his ordnance trains. These supply wagons were something that the South simply could not easily or quickly replace. On July 1, the vast majority of these logistical support vehicles were stacked up along the Chambersburg Pike trailing westward from Gettysburg. At the end of line was George Pickett's infantry division, and behind that the irregular mounted troops under John Imboden. Lee simply did not have enough mounted troops on hand to screen a wide northward turning maneuver and guard his miles of trains. Detaching infantry to do the job would have entailed an enormous drain of manpower, and foot soldiers were not well suited to the task. There was yet a third good reason for not undertaking a move north: the Federal commander could have sent one or more large detachments west across South Mountain and into the Cumberland Valley and severed Lee's lifeline to Virginia. Therefore, for these reasons a move north (to the left) posed unacceptable risks.

The third choice Lee faced was to maneuver the army to the right beyond the Round Tops and Meade's left flank (around the south), as Longstreet proposed. This wide turning movement has received so much attention in the Gettysburg literature that a detailed examination of this course of action is warranted. As is often the case in military history, if a story is repeated frequently by a legion of writers, it becomes accepted as fact by many readers. These stories acquire a life of their own and become part of the popular culture; their factual foundation is no longer questioned, much less critically evaluated. One such story in American military literature is Longstreet's proposal to march the Southern army from its position north and west of Gettysburg on the evening of July 1 around to the right and position it between Meade's army and the Federal capital at Washington. Over the years, Longstreet's proposal has evolved into a statement of what Lee should have done after July 1. Was this proposal and its subsequent near-universal repeating by many of those interested in the battle a realistic and valid alternative for the Confederate army following the fighting on July 1? As with all the possible courses of action open to Lee, the crux of the argument of moving around by the right must be examined in light of the information Lee possessed at that time.

First, was Longstreet's suggestion even possible, and if so, what difficulties would have been encountered during its execution? In other words, could Lee's army have marched west and south around the Federal army on July 2 and taken up a position that would have compelled Meade, in Longstreet's view, to rashly hurl his troops against the ready and waiting Confederates? The first problem was the absence of a good road network available for the Confederates to bypass the Federal forces along Cemetery Hill and Cemetery Ridge without imposing significant delays by first detouring far to the west. The Emmitsburg Road, which ran south from Gettysburg along the front of Meade's troops, was not a viable avenue for Southern troops. Federal infantry had been moving up the Emmitsburg Road during July 1, and John Buford's cavalry had fallen back to a position covering the road south of the Sherfy peach orchard. Perhaps Lee recalled the following Napoleon military maxim: "Nothing is so rash or so contrary to principle, as to make a flank march before an army in position, especially when this army occupies heights at the foot of which you are forced to defile."[10] Whether Lee remembered this or not, he had to have been struck by the fact that the best way to move by the right was the Emmitsburg Road, and it was commanded by the muzzles of Meade's guns and was already serving as an avenue for enemy troops moving towards Gettysburg. Lee also suspected that the entire Federal army was not yet gathered before him, and thus more enemy divisions marching north up the Emmitsburg Road was a real possibility.

There were other avenues upon which to move the army, but these options also presented serious difficulties. A move south across country out of range of Meade's ordnance before eventually filing back onto the Emmitsburg Road, or a march on the Hagerstown (Fairfield) Road southwest before turning south or east, were also extraordinarily dangerous without Jeb Stuart's cavalry. As earlier stated, the most experienced regiments of Southern horse (those cavalrymen expert in scouting and outpost duties as well as combat) were off riding with the general in the plumed hat. It would have been irresponsible for Lee to rely on the 1,800 or so irregular Confederate horsemen available to him to screen such a maneuver, and they were too few in number to do so anyway.[11]

For example, if Lee had decided to move around Meade's left via the cross country route (in other words, without withdrawing along the Hagerstown Road to Fairfield before then heading south), he would have had to pull out from Gettysburg and redirect the army southward across small overland trails that would have slowed the march rate of the army to a crawl, and infantry would have been tasked to provide protection for the long and vulnerable column. Unfortunately for Lee, the Federal position atop Cemetery Hill offered clear and unobstructed views in several directions, as did the observation point on Little Round Top. There is little doubt that Meade and his officers could have mistaken what the Confederates were up to if Lee's army—especially Richard Ewell's Second Corps, then located north of town—suddenly withdrew and moved off to the west, southwest or south. Lee fully appreciated the Federals' over-anxiety for the safety of Washington. It is thus reasonable to assume that he understood a flanking move similar to the one Longstreet suggested would invite the swiftest possible reaction.

And Meade was not unaware of the possibility of Lee moving around his left flank. After General Winfield Hancock, the Federal Second Corps leader, finished reorganizing Union forces south of town on July 1, he conducted a scout and discovered the Federal left could be turned from the south. He reported this news by messenger to Meade, who was still at Taneytown.[12] Meade evidently agreed with Hancock's assessment and even feared such a move, for he ordered his chief of staff, Major General Daniel Butterfield, to issue preliminary withdrawal orders early in the morning hours of July 2. Meade's concern for his left may have, in part, been attributed to Henry Wager Halleck, Lincoln's general-in-chief. Halleck, an ardent student of the Napoleonic wars as theorized by Baron Henri Jomini, had repeatedly warned Meade about the possibility of Lee slipping by the Federal army's left flank.[13]

Federal fears of another Confederate maneuver had been heightened by the debacle at Chancellorsville two months earlier. There, Stonewall Jackson had marched thousands of men miles around the Federal right flank, formed a double line of battle along a two-mile front, and proceeded to role up the Army of the Potomac. The march had not gone undetected, but the move was misinterpreted as a retreat by several West Point officers.[14] The humiliation of Chancellorsville was still freshly impressed upon the minds of the senior officers of the Federal army. Had Lee attempted to disengage and move off on another flanking march, it is inconceivable that the careful and competent Meade would have simply sat by and waited for something to happen.

While it is sometimes true that what an enemy fears is a sound course of action, Halleck's and Meade's anxiety about a Confederate move around the Federal left flank would have been significantly lessened had they appreciated the crippling effects of Jeb Stuart's absence from Lee's army. However, Meade could not have known of the debilitating effects the continued absence of Lee's cavalry had on Confederate designs to conduct a flanking march in any direction, although he might have received some scouting information from John Buford about the constricting road network Lee would have been forced to rely upon if he decided to move his army around the left. One only need read Major General Lafayette McLaws' narrative of the difficulties he encountered moving his Southern division from the Hagerstown Road southward to Pitzer's Schoolhouse (west of lower Seminary Ridge) in preparation for his attack on July 2 to get an rough idea of the difficulty Lee would have faced moving the entire Confederate army across country to get around Meade's forces.[15]

Perhaps the single most salient point advocates of the "move to the right" have never dealt with is what Meade and the Federal army would have been doing while Lee was undertaking this maneuver. If Confederate forces were seen moving south, an officer as competent as Meade would have employed Buford's cavalry as a blocking or delaying force while his infantry utilized the Emmitsburg Road to move faster than the Southerners in the same direction. A Confederate march around the Federal left would have provided Meade with a better road network upon which to operate, and the opportunity to put his cavalry superiority into action to respond to the threat and intercept the Confederate flanking march. Meade also could have redirected additional Federal troops, like Major General Sedgwick's Sixth Corps, for example, which was on its way to Gettysburg, to link up with other Federal troops moving down from Gettysburg. Those subscribing to the theory that Lee could have marched his army around the Army of the Potomac without the benefit of adequate screening cavalry are, in effect, arguing that George Meade was incompetent and lacked the ability to recognize what the Confederate move was and how to respond to it. From what was already known at Federal headquarters, any Southern flanking movement would have been dealt with swiftly, and there is nothing to suggest Meade would have acted inappropriately (indeed, there is significant evidence to the contrary). Yet, these are the pillars upon which the "move to the right" theory rest.

There is yet another aspect of Longstreet's flanking proposal that many students of the battle fail to take into consideration: its logistical considerations. First, such a flanking movement would have strung out the Southern army even more than it had been on July 1, when Lee was moving toward his foe. This would have placed Lee's critical logistical support trains at much greater risk and made them more vulnerable to attack. A move around the Meade's left meant the Confederates would also have had to abandon their lines of communication, which for Lee meant that his lines of resupply would no longer exist. Lee would have lost the protection of South Mountain and the Cumberland Valley that already served as his line of retreat. Therefore, a move to the right on the night of July 1 and morning of July 2 would have placed the Army of Northern Virginia in a precarious position without protected lines of communication, resupply, or retreat. Lee was aware that Federal forces were in the vicinity of Frederick, Maryland, and Harpers Ferry. Without the troops necessary to garrison his line of communication, he had no way of securing or protecting his rear areas. "An army ought only to have one line of operation," Napoleon wrote. "This should be preserved with care, and never abandoned but in the last extremity."[16] What Napoleon knew was also as apparent to Lee as it was to the noted military writer Prussian General Carl von Clausewitz, who stated the following in his book *On War*: "Roads that lead from an army's position back to the main sources of [supply] have two purposes. In the first instance they are lines of communication serving to maintain an army, and in the second they are lines of retreat."[17]

Ignoring for a moment all the problematic factors associated with moving to the right, what advantage would Lee have gained had he been able to position his army between Meade and Washington? True, the Federals were sensitive about the safety of Washington, but there were almost no realistic benefits for Lee even if he could have slipped between Meade and his capital. Proponents of this maneuver argue that, if successfully executed, it could have won the campaign. Their contention rests solely on the assumption Meade would have rashly and immediately attacked once the Southerners were in position. Meade was not prone to rash behavior, and he was operating in a friendly region in which he could be readily resupplied. If Lee had taken up a strong position, Meade could just have easily (and more plausibly) maneuvered the Confederates out of their stronghold, or confronted them there while raiding Lee's lines of communication. Indeed, it is more likely that Lee would have had to retreat—or go over on the offensive—long before Meade.

While Lee certainly had great faith and trust in Longstreet as a corps commander, it is equally true that up until this time Longstreet had yet to exhibit the ability to operate independently or to develop and undertake successful operational plans. Up until this time Longstreet's successes had occurred on the tactical level carrying out Lee's plans or directives. Longstreet, in advocating the move to the right and establishing a defensive position, presented a plan to fight a battle that offered conditions appropriate to his special talents of fighting on the defensive. The shortcomings of Longstreet's plan are that they simply failed to take into consideration operational realities that actually existed at that time. "From the nature of the country," explained Colonel Armistead Lindsay Long, Lee's military secretary, "the absence of [our] cavalry and the proximity of an uncrippled enemy, the flank movement referred to [by Longstreet] was simply an absurdity."[18]

Lee appreciated what many historians and students of the battle never have been able to understand: large scale maneuvers around a powerful enemy appear easy to achieve only in the abstract. Drawing it out as a sand table exercise or on a blackboard is one thing; pulling it off is something altogether different. In the end, despite the popular lore now attached to it, the proposed turning movement around Meade's left violated almost every applicable principle of war and had absolutely no grounding in the realities of the existing military situation. As such, it was arguably the *worst* possible choice Lee could have selected. Fortunately for him and his magnificent army, Lee did not follow the well-meaning but ill-founded advice offered by his First Corps commander.

The fourth option Lee could have chosen was to simply adjust his lines into the most favorable defensive position possible around Gettysburg and wait for Meade to attack him there. If any of Lee's options were less viable than Longstreet's proposed move around the right, it was this one. Chaining the Confederate army to a position on the west side of Gettysburg would have violated all the principles already laid down in the withdrawal option. In addition, Lee's alternatives for supplying his men and animals would have been significantly reduced the longer the two armies faced one another.[19] Concentrating the Southern army for any period of time longer than a few days would have required large amounts of forage, "and that part of the country did not afford" sufficient supplies for the thousands of animals.[20]

Perhaps even more important than finding food was Lee's concern about locating enough water for his army. The sudden descent of so many men and animals into the Gettysburg area placed an immediate strain on its modest water stocks. Wells that were running low on the evening of July 1 were failing by the next morning.[21] These concerns undercut the argument that Lee could or should have adopted a defensive stance. Lee knew his opponent did not face the same level of difficulty in supplying his forces. The Federals possessed an enormous amount of logistical support, including supply wagons and railroads, and could do what was necessary in order to bring up enough food, water, forage, and ammunition to sustain the Army of the Potomac in a prolonged stalemate. The Richmond administration could not support or reinforce Lee in like fashion.

If he had opted to assume the defensive, could Lee have reasonably expected Meade to hurl his troops against his positions—especially after the Federals had suffered such a stinging defeat on July 1? Like all good generals, Lee tried to get inside the mind of his opponents. He had served with Meade before the war and knew he had participated in the attacks against the Army of Northern Virginia at both Sharpsburg and Fredericksburg. Rather than immediately attack, it is much more likely Meade would have reacted cautiously and not moved against Lee without first receiving substantial reinforcements. Therefore, Lee probably viewed a defensive stand around Gettysburg as another prolonged stalemate like the one he just left along the Rappahannock River in Virginia. A temporary stalemate in Pennsylvania did not further Lee's vision for victory or the cause for Southern independence, and the longer it dragged on, the weaker he would become.

Confederate First Corps artillerist E. Porter Alexander, whose guns had broken up the Federal infantry attacks at Fredericksburg and who was more inclined to conduct a defensive battle, conceded that standing still was not a viable option: "It must be remembered that there were great objections to be found to [Lee's army] standing still and allowing the enemy to take the initiative."[22] Alexander (whose writings some critics have used to attack Lee's judgment during the Gettysburg Campaign), realized the futility of waiting for the Federals to attack. "It is also very certain," he observed, "that General Lee could never have *established* [emphasis added] his army in Pennsylvania with communications open so as to get supplies, even of ammunition."[23] In other words, it would have been virtually impossible for Lee to place his army in a secure position or condition and await a Federal response. Thus, retaining the initiative in Pennsylvania was imperative, and with Stuart's continued absence, Lee could only do so by attacking on July 2—which is exactly what he chose to do.

Lee was under no illusions about the difficulties confronting him. The battle had "commenced in the absence of correct intelligence"[24] that continued to hamstring the commanding general. Where, thought Lee, could Stuart be, and what information about the Federal army did he possess? Without precise knowledge of the whereabouts of the enemy's forces, Lee had little to go on except the last reported positions of the Federals made by John Mosby on June 24, information provided by the scout Harrison on the 28th, the Federal troops that were engaged on July 1, and the latest scouting reports filed by his staff officers late on the afternoon of the first day's battle. Since Lee possessed a cool, calculating mathematical mind, he had to have already considered many factors long before he told Longstreet: "If the enemy is there tomorrow, we must attack him."

By the time the Southern commander uttered those words, he knew his forces had just defeated the Federal First and Eleventh corps. According to Harrison, two Federal corps were around Frederick, Maryland, on June 28, and another nearby. John Mosby had reported the positions of the First and Eleventh Corps as of the night of June 23-24 as being at Guilford Station and at Goose Creek, respectively. What's more, the Twelfth Corps was last known to be at Leesburg on the 24th, while the remainder of the Federal army was spread out further south and southeast. Also, prisoners taken during the fighting on July 1 confirmed that the Federal army had yet to totally concentrate.[25]

To Lee, this information meant the three aforementioned corps (First, Eleventh, and Twelfth) were probably the first ones to cross the Potomac at Edwards Ferry, since they were the closest Federal formations to that point on June 24, and in all likelihood comprised the leading elements of the pursuing enemy army. Lee could thus reason that the remaining Federals were wearing out shoe leather getting to Gettysburg. This opinion was confirmed near sunset of July 1 when two fresh Federal brigades were seen marching up the Emmitsburg Road about 5:30 p.m.[26] Shortly afterward Colonel Armistead Long returned from his reconnaissance and reported that an increasing number of Federals were being posted on the reverse side of Cemetery Ridge.[27] Lee correctly reasoned Meade's army was not yet concentrated. What condition would the Federal troops be in on July 2 after conducting forced marches in hot weather to reach Gettysburg? Lee knew that as of June 24, John Sykes' Fifth Corps had been at Aldie, Winfield Hancock's Second Corps had been opposite Thoroughfare Gap, and Dan Sickles' Third Corps was in the vicinity of Centreville. These troops could, by conducting very hard marches, make it to Gettysburg and join up with what remained of First and Eleventh corps, and the Twelfth Corps. That meant that John Sedgwick's Sixth Corps and Meade's artillery reserve, both of which were in the area of Fairfax as of June 24 (further east than any other troops in the Federal army), would probably not make it to Gettysburg until late in the day on July 2 or thereafter.

Lee had correctly predicted to Isaac Trimble that the enemy would be "obliged to follow us by forced marches" into Pennsylvania. Now, by the evening of July 1, the advance guard of Meade's numerically superior Army of the Potomac had been severely mauled, and the remainder was en route but would probably not be fully present for action on July 2. In other words, Lee could reasonably estimate Meade would have available the remnants of the eviscerated First and Eleventh Corps and the late-arriving Twelfth, Fifth, Second, and Third Corps. Allowing for losses suffered on July 1 and reductions through straggling, Meade could field approximately 50,000 infantry and slightly more than 150 guns. (Lee was also aware that additional Federal troops, such as Eighth Corps in and around Harpers Ferry, as well as Fourth Corps, last known to be on the Peninsula, might also be in route to further bolster Meade's numbers, further mitigated against delaying the offensive.)

Would Meade have attacked Lee on July 2 if the Southern commander had given up his hard-won initiative and assumed the defensive? The obvious answer is no. His Sixth Corps and Artillery Reserve were on the way to the battlefield, and would have pushed the number of Federal infantry and artillerists available to more than 65,000 (after deducting their losses suffered on the battlefield on July 1 as well as losses due to straggling), while more than doubling the number of Meade's ordnance to more than 300 tubes (excluding the guns with Pleasonton's Cavalry Corps). In addition, Meade could collect his stragglers, rest his fatigued men, and decide how to employ his superior numbers against Lee on his own timetable.

All of this meant that Lee appreciated that the relative strengths of the Army of Northern Virginia and the Army of the Potomac in Pennsylvania might never be closer than they were on July 1-2. Since Lee had proven on several fields that he could win battles despite being significantly outnumbered, seeking battle when the odds were virtually equal offered tantalizing possibilities rarely offered any Confederate army anywhere. In addition, Longstreet's divisions of John Hood and Lafayette McLaws—arguably the best combat divisions in the army—would be available for action on July 2. Both division leaders were proven veterans and each possessed one of the army's finest brigades, namely Jerome Robertson's Texas Brigade (Hood) and William Barksdale's Mississippians (McLaws). Readers need to keep in mind that Lee had personally witnessed on July 1 the heroic charge of Samuel McGowan's South Carolinians under Colonel Abner Perrin. The outnumbered Palmetto State warriors had successfully attacked and driven away some of the Army of the Potomac's finest infantry from good defensive ground well supported by artillery. Skillfully led and determined infantry could still accomplish remarkable things. Indeed, Lee may well have considered Perrin's impressive charge as a precursor of a renewed Confederate attack on July 2, spearheaded by the Texas Brigade, Barksdale's Mississippians, and other excellent infantry formations.

The initial elements of Lee's vision of victory, as related to Isaac Trimble, had been fulfilled. Now Lee needed to continue the battle in order to, as he put it, "follow up the success" of the first day and "drive one corps back on another . . . before they can concentrate." Lee understood the importance of momentum, which in war has value of incalculable measure. Indeed, one of the hallmarks of Lee's generalship was his ability to seize and retain the initiative, Chancellorsville being perhaps the best example of this military virtue. The last thing Lee wanted to do in Pennsylvania was allow Meade the opportunity to fully recover from the defeat his army had suffered on July 1. In short, Lee was well aware of the military principle of reinforcing success.

Another consideration driving Lee's decision to attack on July 2 was recognized by E. Porter Alexander. Drawing upon past experiences, the artillerist reasoned, as did the commanding general, that Confederate offensive success would, in turn, "capture enough [artillery ammunition] for the next" action, without having to worry about when resupply wagons (which were already in route but at that time still in Virginia) would reach the army.[28] This point was graphically illustrated only two weeks earlier at the Battle of Second Winchester, where Confederate attacks netted 23 quality Federal artillery pieces along with their excellent ammunition, caissons, and mobile equipment. The fighting on July 1 had netted two additional Federal guns. Thus the prospects of seizing more Federal ordnance and ammunition through continued offensive action would, in effect, replace the ammunition expended accomplishing that goal—another way to make war pay for war.

The continuation of the battle would also capitalize on the other advantage General Lee and his army possessed: confidence, which was manifestly at its zenith. Lee recognized this enthusiasm and no doubt wanted to reinforce his men's eagerness to finish the job begun on July 1. He was well aware of the physical deprivations his dedicated men had endured throughout the war which had, in some part, contributed to the rationale for going north in the summer of 1863. Now, their morale and faith in Robert E. Lee was at an all-time high after his string of nearly unbroken successes scored from the time he assumed command until the evening of July 1. Simply put, the men trusted Lee implicitly, and Lee had unyielding faith in what his hard-fighting troops could accomplish when properly led—terrain disadvantages notwithstanding. Theodore Ayrault Dodge—an adjutant of the 119th New York in Howard's Eleventh Corps at Gettysburg and postwar historian—analyzed the confidence of the men in the Army of Northern Virginia and Lee's decision to take the battle to the Federals on July 2. "This was the natural outcome of [Second] Manassas, Fredericksburg, and Chancellorsville," he explained. "Lee was morally unable to decline battle. He could not imperil the high-strung confidence of his men."[29] With the fighting spirit in his army soaring, Lee saw Meade's decision to remain at Gettysburg as an opportunity for the confident Southerners to defeat the Federal army before it was up and fully concentrated, not as a liability to be avoided.

Finally, Lee had to consider another enemy—time. While the Federals were in the process of concentrating, Lee's entire army—with the exception of Stuart's cavalry, Imboden's raiders, Pickett's Division, and Evander Laws' Brigade of Hood's Division—was within nine miles of Gettysburg.[30] Law would be up by midday at the head of his brigade of Alabamians. Thus, Lee stood to gain only three brigades of infantry (Pickett's) and another three of cavalry (Stuart's) if he delayed an attack until after July 2, or a total of 5,725 infantry, however many of Stuart's fatigued troopers were still in their saddles, and 24 guns.[31] Lee therefore had some 49,000 infantry and artillerists, plus 231 guns—almost the same number of infantry and artillerists, plus about 80 more cannon than Meade would probably have available if the battle was joined before the arrival of Sedgwick's Sixth Corps and Meade's artillery reserve.[32] The last thing an experienced general like Lee would do is sit by and allow a numerically superior foe to fully concentrate his strength if he had a reasonable way of preventing it. Given the high morale of his army and the stunning victory of July 1, Lee believed that if he attacked on the morrow he would be doing so with an advantage. Indeed, the odds would never be better.[33]

When considering the multitude of options before him, Lee could well have asked himself the equivalent of, "If not here, where? If not now, when?" In his mind, there was only one realistic course of action possible for July 2, 1863, consistent with every applicable principle of war—a resumption of the offensive. That conclusion was also consistent with his combative and audacious character. Several months after the battle, Lee summed up the situation in which he found himself on the evening of July 1: "A battle had, therefore, become in a measure unavoidable, and the success already gained gave hope of a favorable issue."[34] As far as Lee was concerned, the difficult decision was not *whether* to resume the offensive, but *how* and *where* he should attack.

*   *   *

With a firm answer that the army would assume the offensive on July 2, General Longstreet remounted his horse and rode back to his infantry. Lee instructed Moxley Sorrel of Longstreet's staff to order the reserve artillery battalions of First Corps forward to Gettysburg "as far as you can without distressing" the men and animals.[35] With First Corps on the way, Lee decided it was time to pay a visit to the senior officers of Second Corps and begin formulating more specific assault plans for the new day.

Lee Visits Second Corps

Just what form of paralysis had gripped the commanders of Second Corps? Why had the victorious banners of red suddenly stopped below Cemetery Hill when it appeared that it was "only necessary to press 'those people'" in order to gain possession of the heights? These must have been only two of the many questions nagging Lee as Traveller carried him across the landscape to Dick Ewell's newly established headquarters near the Almshouse on the north edge of Gettysburg. The lieutenant general greeted Lee sometime before sunset and they repaired to the arbor in the rear of the house. Robert Rodes was already there and was asked to remain. Riders were dispatched to locate Jubal Early and hasten him to the conference. According to "Old Jubilee," by the time he arrived near the Almshouse, the sun had already set.[36]

The reason Lee conferred with Early and Rodes was obvious: their divisions had fought that day and he needed to ascertain their condition and the nature of the ground before them. Although Lee was undoubtedly frustrated by Ewell's failure to drive home the pursuit, it was not his nature to question or criticize his subordinate officers in front of others. That was something usually done in private, and with Rodes already present, it was not the place or time for reprimands. Besides, Lee had little to gain pursuing the subject at that time. The important issue now that all of Second Corps was on the field was how and where the army would resume the offensive the next day. In order to determine that, he needed to speak directly with Ewell and his division commanders. "It was evident from the first that it was Lee's intention to attack on July 2," remembered Early. That the army had to attack, he continued, "was so apparent that there was not the slightest discussion or difference of opinion upon it. It was a point taken for granted."[37]

While Early's initial observation conforms to everything we know about Lee's intent, his description of the conversation that followed strains credulity. After agreeing that a resumption of the offensive was necessary, Lee asked Ewell if he could attack the next day. According to Early, Ewell remained silent while he spoke up—a curious breech of etiquette for a division commander. Any attack to the left of town by Second Corps would be difficult and the outcome doubtful, Early explained. Even if successful, he continued, it would be a great cost. Early then supposedly went on to call "General Lee's attention to the Round Tops, the outline of which we could see, though dusk was approaching, and suggested that those heights must evidently command the enemy's position and render it untenable."[38]

There are several aspects about Early's carefully crafted recollections that raise doubt as to their accuracy. The first is his claim to have spoken up in place of Ewell. It would have been highly unusual for a division general to answer a question directed at his superior by the commanding general of the army. If true, perhaps Ewell suppressed his own opinion or Early simply dominated the conversation (as was his feisty and lawyer-like nature). Early claims he spoke out because he knew the field better than anyone else and was thus more qualified to speak up. Second, Early's claim that an attack would be difficult and the outcome doubtful flies in the face of the enemy he knew confronted Second Corps: the broken First Corps and routinely routed and undistinguished Eleventh Corps. Third, Early's postwar account claims he made this statement when Culp's Hill was reportedly still unoccupied. If he believed that and had already announced he knew the terrain well and that is why he was speaking up instead of Ewell, why wasn't Early advocating moving heaven and earth to occupy that important high ground? If it was clear to him that the distant Round Tops, barely visible in the growing darkness, "must evidently command the enemy's position and render it untenable," then surely the same thing could and should have been said of high and wooded hill staring him in the face. Fourth, Early claims he arrived at Ewell's headquarters "after sunset." If so, how could he have called Lee's attention to the Round Tops "which we could see, though dusk was approaching" at a point well after the conversation had begun?[39] In fact, there is no way Early could have pointed out the Round Tops to Lee from Ewell's headquarters because those heights are not visible from where the conference was held north of town. While Early might have seen the Round Tops earlier in the day (and even this is in doubt), the entire manner in which his story is set forth smacks of untruth.

Early continued his tale by claiming Lee asked if Second Corps could be moved around to the right side of town and attack the enemy from that direction. After all, leaving Ewell's divisions where they were not only wasted them but invited a counterattack. Once again Early maintained he answered first, this time with a clamorous denial supported by boisterous amens from his fellow Second Corps officers. "I knew what a damper it would be to [my men's] enthusiasm to be withdrawn from the position gained by fighting," was Early's supposed answer. "Moreover, there were some of my wounded not in condition to be moved . . . and there were a great many muskets stacked in the streets of Gettysburg which I did not want to lose." Ewell and Rodes joined in the argument "and urged views of their own" supporting Early. After listening to these protestations, Lee declared that he would have to attack with his right, and Longstreet's Corps would lead the assault.

Second Corps, Early assured Lee, would "follow up the success that might be gained on the right."[40]

This portion of Early's story is especially curious. Since when did Lee's generals advocate sitting still? Shifting Second Corps somewhere to the west side of Gettysburg could have been easily done and would not have entailed the abandonment of many if any seriously wounded men. Nor would it have meant the loss of the captured arms stacked in town (which, if they were so valuable to Early, should already have been ordered removed.) In essence, Early was advocating an offensive battle plan with a secondary role for one of the army's three infantry corps, when aggressive action was required in order to occupy the critical position of Culp's Hill and compromise the enemy's defensive line.[41]

Lee knew exactly what Ewell, Early, and Rodes were advocating, and he could not have been happy about it. They did not wish to attack, maneuver, or withdraw. Indeed, they seemed content to remain where they were. Although the final details are unclear, Lee evidently reached a tentative understanding with his lieutenants that the army would attack on the right the next day, and the Second Corps would support the effort on its own front by making a demonstration "to be converted into a real attack should opportunity offer," and pursue the Federals if they gave away.[42] The commanding general remounted Traveller and made his way back to his headquarters, a cluster of tents established near the crest of Seminary Ridge beside the Chambersburg Pike, across from a small stone house owned by Thaddeus Stevens and occupied by the Widow Mary Thompson.[43] His meeting with the leaders of Second Corps had been most unsatisfactory.

Contemplation

With so much riding on the outcome of the battle, Lee knew he could not afford to relegate the entire Second Corps to a secondary role. By the time his mount had carried him back to Seminary Ridge, he reached the conclusion that his original instinct was correct. He had to shorten his long exterior line by moving Second Corps around to the right (west) of Gettysburg to a position from which all three corps would attack the next day. This realignment would protect the lines of communication and resupply running westward across South Mountain and offer Lee greater flexibility in coordinating the morrow's assault. Major Charles Marshall was ordered to ride to Ewell and so direct him.

"I received orders after dark to draw my corps to the right, in case it could not be used to advantage where it was," remembered Ewell. "That the commanding general thought from the nature of the ground that the position for attack was a good one on that side."[44] Marshall confirmed the meeting, with some additional detail. He told Ewell that unless he thought that the Second Corps could carry the enemy's

Lee's Headquarters

Lee established his headquarters in a group of tents on Seminary Ridge on the south side of the Chambersburg Pike. Just across the pike was the Widow Mary Thompson House, pictured here. Throughout the battle Lee and many other Confederate officers intermittently utilized this stone dwelling.

Library of Congress

positions in his front, General Lee intended to bring the Second Corps around to the right side of Gettysburg so to attack and envelop the enemy's left, or southern, flank, with Longstreet's corps leading the assault, and with Hill's corps supporting Longstreet's left followed by the Second Corps' troops being brought into action in order to cover Hill's left.[45] Ewell, stirred by the order, recalled Rodes and Early and discussed the matter out of Marshall's earshot. Instead of acknowledging he would comply, Ewell decided to ride back with Marshall and discuss the matter in person with Lee.[46]

The exact details of what the three generals discussed is not known, but the main topic of conversation was a valuable piece of reconnaissance offered by Ewell's aide, Lieutenant Thomas T. Turner, and Jubal Early's aide and cousin, Robert D. Early. Turner recalled that it was "about 5:00 p.m." on July 1 when Ewell "ordered Lieut. [Robert D.] Early and myself to ride up to Culp's Hill and, if possible, reconnoiter the enemy's position from its summit. We reached the very summit of the knoll without meeting a Federal and there saw stretched out before us the enemy's line of battle." Both Turner and Robert Early believed that Confederate occupation of Culp's Hill would render the "enemy's position untenable." Ewell asked Rodes "what he thought of sending Gen. Johnson upon [Culp's Hill] tonight?" Rodes' reply was uncharacteristically passive. Johnson's men, he answered, were tired and footsore. Besides, added Turner, "he did not think it would result in anything one way or the other." General Early offered a different assessment. Early, remembered, Turner, "(I remember his words distinctly): 'If you do not go up there tonight, it will cost you 10,000 lives to get up there tomorrow.' The result of the conversation was that Johnson was instructed to move his command to the vicinity of Culp's Hill, and to take possession of the position if, on reconnoitering the hill he found it unoccupied."[47]

The reconnaissance mission performed by Turner and Robert Early (which was discussed briefly in the previous chapter as it related to Johnson's failure to occupy Culp's Hill), is significant for several reasons. First, they rode up Culp's Hill sometime between 5:00 and 6:00 p.m. and reported back "at once," which means Ewell, Rodes, and Jubal Early had to have known this information *before* the council of war was held with General Lee.[48] Second, this report confirms Isaac Trimble's account that he had closely observed that Culp's Hill was vacant late on the afternoon of July 1, and reported that fact to Ewell with his recommendation to seize it at once. Third, according to Turner, Ewell gave orders to Ed Johnson to move his division there "if he still found the hill to be unoccupied." Johnson, however, had not yet returned to report his findings to Ewell by the time Marshall arrived with Lee's message to prepare his corps for a move around Gettysburg. Ewell, then, did not know whether Johnson was already on Culp's Hill, about to move out, or somewhere in between.[49]

This time line differs from the one offered by historian Edwin Coddington, who asserted that Ewell "very likely received the report of the reconnaissance mission to Culp's Hill" after the arbor council, but "before Lee's withdrawal order reached him."[50] Though long accepted, this is simply not supported by the evidence. Turner specifically stated he was ordered to conduct the reconnaissance "at about 5:00 p.m." and that he returned "at once." Since Culp's Hill was but a short distance away and the meeting between Lee, Ewell, Early, and Rodes was held after sunset, it is unreasonable for Coddington to conclude the scouting ride took more than three hours to complete. Also, if Ewell received this information *after* the meeting, why did he not immediately dispatch a courier to inform Lee?[51] It is much more likely Ewell had this information before he met with Lee, but only shared it with him after Lee had decided to bring Second Corps around to the right side of Gettysburg. Why he failed to share Turner's and Early's critical scouting report with the commanding general at the council meeting will probably never be known with certainty. We do know, however, that all three Second Corps generals were at least acting consistently: Ewell remained indecisive, Rodes curiously lethargic, and Early ostensibly aggressive—as long as someone else was going to attempt the movement.[52]

As might be expected, Lee found the information that Culp's Hill was unoccupied of great import. Ewell acknowledged that the Federal position running southward from Cemetery Hill along Cemetery Ridge would be seriously compromised by the capture of Culp's Hill, and Johnson's Division had already been instructed to do so—if the heights were unoccupied. As was his custom, Lee listened attentively and with an open mind. Ewell's revelation represented a significant opportunity. What is unclear is whether Ewell informed Lee that this critical information was several hours old.

If Second Corps could be usefully employed capturing Culp's Hill and turning Meade's right flank, as Ewell implied, then the next day's action was shaping up far differently than Lee had imagined. The enemy could be squeezed to advantage from both sides, Longstreet from the right with Hill in support, and Ewell from the dominating ground on the left of the line. This would compel Meade to either retreat or shore up his threatened flanks; either could open up possibilities for further action. The apparent change in Ewell's demeanor from indecisive and cautious to calculating and aggressive must have pleased the commanding general, who was induced then and there to change his mind: the plans to shift Second Corps around to the right side of town were rescinded, and Lee "directed [Ewell] to take Culp's Hill as soon as practicable."[53]

With this new instructions in hand, Ewell returned to his headquarters sometime after midnight. Infused with fresh energy and confidence, he summoned Tom Turner and sent him back to "Allegheny" Johnson with orders to take Culp's Hill if he had not already done so (pursuant to his earlier instructions).[54] To Turner's surprise, he found Johnson's Division sleeping on its arms about one mile away from Culp's Hill. When he relayed Ewell's orders, Johnson informed him that his scouting party was already reconnoitering the hill and he was awaiting its return. It had already been gone for some time. Johnson's four brigades were deployed in line abreast about 500 yards north of and parallel to the Hanover Road. Facing Culp's Hill, the 1,323 combatants of the Stonewall Brigade under James A. Walker formed the far left flank of the division. To their right was George Steuart's 2,121 men from Maryland, North Carolina and Virginia, with John M. Jones' 1,555 Virginians next in line, and Francis Nicholl's 1,100 Louisianians under Colonel Jesse Milton Williams holding the right. The division's nearby artillery battalion, ably led by Major Joseph W. Latimer, consisted of 377 artillerists and 16 guns.[55]

Unbeknownst to Johnson, his scouting party (at least 20 men and one lieutenant of the 25th Virginia from Jones' Brigade), had crossed Rock Creek and made its way to the summit of Culp's Hill. No opposition was discovered until the men approached the crest, where they ran into the 7th Indiana Infantry dug in behind temporary breastworks.[56] The Hoosier soldiers from Reynolds' First Corps had spent the morning of July 1 guarding the trains, and so missed the day's carnage west of town. Ordered to the west side of Culp's Hill after they reached the field late that afternoon, the men extended the flank of the remnants of the Iron Brigade. Either the 7th Indiana arrived after Tom Turner and Robert Early made their ride up Culp's Hill in the afternoon of July 1, or the pair missed seeing the unit entirely. Either way, the regiment was there now and the surprised Southerners ran right into them. The lieutenant leading the patrol was captured.[57]

On the return trip, the patrol intercepted a Federal courier riding towards Gettysburg (probably along Hanover Road) carrying a dispatch from Major General George Sykes, commander of Federal Fifth Corps, to Major General Henry W. Slocum, leader of Twelfth Corps. A courier turned it over to Johnson in Turner's presence. The message was dated 12:30 a.m. and bore critical news: Sykes and two of his divisions had left Hanover at 7:00 p.m. and were encamped along Hanover Road at Bonaughtown (now Bonneville); his march would resume to the battlefield at 4:00 a.m. Sykes' remaining division was following several hours behind.[58] Johnson almost certainly did not read this dispatch before 2:00 a.m., but when he did he realized the leading elements of an entire Federal corps were only four miles away. This information precluded a nighttime movement or attack against Culp's Hill because Johnson could not risk engaging an enemy of unknown strength while concurrently exposing his left flank to Sykes' approaching three divisions, about 10,000 men.[59] "Old Allegheny" turned the dispatch over to Turner with instructions to take it to Ewell along with his own message: Johnson could not occupy Culp's Hill because it was held by the enemy and additional Federal reinforcements were close at hand which could, in turn, envelop his own left flank. Johnson, other words, was awaiting further orders from Ewell.[60]

And the news for Old Dick Ewell could scarcely have been worse. Shortly after dawn the Federal Fifth Corps, led by Ewell's old classmate at West Point George Sykes and boasting a division of old army Regulars, would be joining the remnants of Howard's and Reynolds' corps already known to be on the field.[61] Since the message from Sykes was addressed to Henry Slocum, Ewell could deduce Slocum's Twelfth Corps was either already on the field or close at hand. All of this meant the golden opportunity that had earlier existed to easily capture both Cemetery and Culp's hills and compromise the Federal defensive line had passed. It also was cause for no little embarrassment, for Lee had changed his plans for Second Corps based upon Ewell's report to him that Culp's Hill could be occupied and Johnson's Division was already moving to do so.

As the Second Corps commander pondered this sudden turn of events, another dispatch arrived from General Lee. This message, Ewell later wrote, advised me "to delay my attack until I heard General Longstreet's guns open on my right." The commanding general was doing everything he could to make sure Ewell's efforts against the Federal right flank were coordinated with the attacks he intended to deliver with his remaining pair of corps. There was little else Ewell or Lee could have done since, as Ewell noted in his report, "day was breaking, and it was too late for any change of place."[62]

Lee Matures His Battle Plan

Robert E. Lee did not get much sleep that night. Although a sweeping victory had been achieved, it was also not the decisive one he knew instinctively was, for a few hours at least, within his grasp. The general state of ambivalence that had swept over Dick Ewell, Jubal Early, Robert Rodes, and even Powell Hill, combined with the troubling absence of Jeb Stuart had stopped his offensive thrust and allowed the enemy time to rest and reorganize. Even his trusted "Old Warhorse," James Longstreet, was evidencing troubling behavior with his steady resistance to Lee's plan to resume the offensive on July 2. The lingering silence from the direction of Culp's Hill meant Ewell had not yet advanced and taken Culp's Hill, which would be critical to the day's battle plan. If Lee ever needed a larger staff to lift some of the burden from his shoulders and act as his eyes and ears, it was in the midst of the 30-hour period from 3:00 p.m. on July 1 until 9:00 p.m. on July 2.

But without such a staff and with a day looming on which the fate of the Confederacy might well hinge, Lee rose after just a couple hours sleep around 3:00 a.m. and began issuing orders. Longstreet was already bringing up First Corps and would be attacking sometime later in the day. Since Ewell was still unengaged, Lee decided to make sure the effort on both flanks was coordinated by sending him clear instructions to delay attacking until he heard Longstreet open the engagement on the right.[63] Particulars for both attacks could be determined at a later hour.

With that broad aspect of the attack plan settled, at least temporarily, Lee turned his attention to how he was going to launch a major assault from the right side of town. Knowing now that the enemy Fifth Corps was on the way and Twelfth Corps was probably already up, Lee needed to know how many Federal reinforcements had arrived during the night, and how far south from Cemetery Hill the enemy line extended in order to determine whether it could be turned or successfully assaulted. Without experienced cavalry, Lee had to employ members of his small staff for these reconnaissance roles. The commanding general was so anxious to get any information about what had become of Stuart and his accompanying brigades that he decided that if Stuart could not find the army, he would find Stuart. Earlier that night Lee called upon Major Harry Gilmor, commander of the 1st Maryland Cavalry Battalion, on temporary duty attached to Ewell's corps. Lee sent word to Gilmor to get together a quality detail of riders on good horses and have them report to army headquarters for orders. Soon, James D. Watters, who after the war was a state court judge of the Third Judicial Circuit of the State of Maryland, was at hand along with about eight other troopers of the 1st Maryland. Each man was handed sealed orders for Jeb Stuart, the contents of which directed the cavalry general to ride at once to Gettysburg. Further, each rider was instructed to be sure that he destroyed the written instructions if capture was thought to be possible. After receiving their orders, Watters and the other riders were dispatched over the Pennsylvania countryside by different roads with instructions to find Stuart at the earliest moment possible.[64]

Lee directed his chief engineering officer, Captain Samuel Richards Johnston, to explore the ground extending southward from Cemetery Ridge towards the Round Tops and determine whether the enemy held it and if so, in what strength. Johnston, who remembered Lee admonished him "that while in Mexico, he had found that he could get nearer the enemy and do more with a few men than with many," took with him only Major John J. Clarke, Longstreet's chief engineer, and two others. The small party left about 4:00 a.m.[65] Although often overlooked, Johnston's mission offers additional information on Lee's command style, which encouraged personal initiative. According to the junior officer, Lee told him "to reconnoiter along the enemy's left and return as soon as possible, he said nothing about finding a route over which troops should be moved unobserved by the enemy, but it was not necessary as that was a part of my duty as a reconnoitering officer, and would be attended to without special instructions." Johnston understood Lee, and visa versa. "Indeed," concluded the Captain, "[General Lee] said nothing about the movement of troops at all, and left me only that knowledge of what he wanted which I had obtained after long service with him, and that he wanted me to consider every contingency, which might arise."[66]

Soon after Johnston's departure, Lee summoned additional staff officers for other errands. Colonel Long was ordered to scout the ground so that artillery battalion commanders could place their pieces to best advantage. "On reaching Hill's position, about sunrise," Long recalled, "there had been considerable accession to the enemy's forces on Cemetery Hill during the night; but it was chiefly massed to his right, leaving much of his center and almost his entire left unoccupied."[67] Long reported his findings to Powell Hill's artillery chief, Colonel R. Lindsay Walker, and guided him over the ground.[68] William N. Pendleton, who had failed so miserably the previous day by failing to position his guns to fire on Cemetery Hill, arrived at this time with orders from Lee to assist Long. Pendleton returned to Lee and claimed his party scouted the southern flank of the field and found only a couple dismounted enemy cavalrymen there, which they captured. Almost certainly Pendleton and company did not explore as far south or east as Johnston's party, since he reported back to Lee long before Johnston returned. Still the prospects of an attack on that end looked promising.[69]

By the time this information began filtering into headquarters it was light enough for Lee to make out the surrounding countryside. His vantage point on Seminary Ridge provided him with a clear early morning panorama of the center of the enemy's line along Cemetery Ridge. That rise, however, coupled with the heights on both flanks prevented him from determining how many Federal troops were on the field. Immediately before him the eastern glacis of Seminary Ridge fell off about 600 yards to the western edge of Gettysburg, where elements from Rodes' Division were visible. Northwest beyond town was Benner's Hill, a distance of about one and one-half miles. Although he could not see them, Ewell's other two divisions were positioned facing Culp's and Cemetery hills in that vicinity. Early's brigades were in the depression between the town and the hill, while Johnson's troops were deployed north of Hanover Road. Although Culp's Hill was less distinct, Lee could clearly see Cemetery Hill, rising before him some 1,600 yards to his right front. The graveyard-topped eminence was bustling with Federal activity and bristling with the tubes of several artillery batteries. It is unknown whether Lee

Armistead Lindsay Long (1825-1891)

A charming and highly intelligent officer, A. L. Long was an artillerist by profession assigned to Robert E. Lee in May 1862 as his military secretary. Long served in this capacity until the fall of 1863, when he was promoted and assigned commander of the artillery of Second Corps. At Gettysburg, Lee utilized Long's artillery experience to help reconnoiter terrain and place batteries.

Library of Congress

could see the troops extending the line south from Cemetery Hill along Cemetery Ridge from Ziegler's Grove to the area now known as the Copse of Trees. Almost certainly he did not see the dust kicked up by the few late arriving troops from Sickle's Third Corps, moving up the Emmitsburg Road from the south, the last of whom arrived during the morning's middle hours. But Lee could see the Round Tops looming in the distance more than two miles away. Immediately south of his position was a portion of Pender's Division and the artillery battalions from Hill's Third Corps, running along Seminary Ridge for a distance of more than a mile. If Lee had ridden to the crest of ridge and looked west toward Cashtown, he would have seen Harry Heth's battered division, less its artillery battalion under Garnett, in deep reserve along Willoughby Run; Richard Anderson's unbloodied brigades were moving up towards the field to relieve Heth's command while Longstreet's corps was pressuring Anderson's rear.[70]

Lee could not have been happy with his line of battle. Circumstances had provided him with an extended exterior line hugging the shorter and more compact Federal fishhook position. The absence of Stuart meant that both of his own flanks (Ewell's now and Longstreet's later) were subject to turning movements. Given everything he knew, the only way to remedy the situation was to find and strike one or both of Meade's flanks and roll them up, or force his enemy to shift troops in such a way as to open up possibilities for other avenues of fruitful attack. Pendleton's report had raised some hope that an attack on the field's southern portion would be effective, but Lee had not yet heard back from Johnston's party. Could an infantry attack from both ends of the line be coordinated? And now that it was daylight, what did Ewell think of the prospects of capturing Culp's Hill and employing his divisions effectively there? Lee dispatched another of his staff officers, Major Charles S. Venable, to ride to Ewell and ask him these questions.[71]

Once Venable departed, Lee met with Longstreet and Powell Hill on Seminary Ridge at about 5:15 a.m.[72] The three men must have discussed what Pendleton had earlier reported and what Johnston had already seen but had not yet had a chance to inform the commanding general: the Federal left flank was apparently not anchored on the Round Tops, and that end of the field was apparently devoid of enemy infantry.[73] It seemed as though the bulk of the enemy was facing west on upper Cemetery Ridge, west and north on Cemetery Hill, and north on Culp's Hill. Lee reasoned that if this was the case, the Army of the Potomac could be taken in flank by moving against the southern end of the line somewhere above the Round Tops. Lee must have known that the importance of the Round Tops could not have escaped fellow engineer "Major Meade." Still, if Federal forces were not already on the Round Tops, how close did their line stretch and how long would it be before the hills were occupied? Lee was too good of a soldier to not have pondered these obvious questions. If the Round Tops were occupied, how strong was the rest of the two-mile long Federal line stretching all the way from Cemetery Hill to the Round Tops? What support, if any, could Federal troops on those far-removed heights lend to their comrades fighting on the center and right center of the Federal line along Cemetery Ridge and Cemetery Hill? How would Meade respond to a vigorous attack, especially in his debut as an army commander? He was a careful officer, but would he overreact if faced with the prospect of having one or both of his flanks turned? If so, such an overreaction might lead to an "opportunity" Lee could fully exploit.

These issues and others were crossing his mind as the artillery battalions of Longstreet's First Corps rumbled onto the field about 9:00 a.m.[74] It was about midmorning when Colonel Edward Porter Alexander, who was riding "at the tail of the column" received an order from Colonel James B. Walton, Longstreet's chief of artillery, "to report in person to General Longstreet."[75] By the time Alexander arrived on Seminary Ridge sometime after 10:00 a.m., Lee—who had recently returned from a visit with Ewell and his Second Corps officers (see below for more details)—and Longstreet were standing together on the grounds of the seminary. "[We were] told that we were to attack the enemy's left flank, and was directed to take command of my own battalion—Cabell's battalion (with McLaws' division), [16] guns; Henry's battalion (with Hood's), [19] guns—leaving the Washington Artillery [of 10 guns] in reserve, and to reconnoiter the ground and cooperate with the infantry in the attack." Alexander recalled he "was especially cautioned in moving up the guns to avoid exposing them to the view of a signal station of the enemy's on Round Top mountain."[76]

Remounting his horse Dixie, Alexander left to conduct his reconnaissance after three of John Bell Hood's brigades filed into the fields between Willoughby Run and Seminary Ridge.[77] There, Jerome B. Robertson's Texas Brigade, along with two brigades of Georgians under Henry Lewis "Rock" Benning and George T. (nicknamed "Tige," for Tiger) Anderson stacked arms and fell out to rest. Other than a two-hour break at Cashtown, these men had been marching all day. Hood's last and largest brigade under Evander McIvor Law, the division's senior brigadier, was composed of five regiments of Alabamians.[78] Hood noted that both Longstreet and Powell Hill were present with the commanding general, who—"with coat buttoned to the throat, saber-belt buckled around the waist, and field glasses pending at his side—walked up and down in the shade of large trees near us, halting now and then to observe the enemy. He seemed full of hope, yet at times, buried in deep thought."[79]

While Hood's men rested, Major General Lafayette McLaws' brigades tramped wearily past their fellow First Corps comrades toward Seminary Ridge, where its van halted about 100 yards from Lee's observation point. Lee sent for its commander, who later remembered that the army's leader "was sitting on a fallen tree with a map beside him. Longstreet's Corps, Lee informed him, would attack the left flank of the enemy.

"General," explained Lee, "I wish you to place your division across this [Emmitsburg] road . . . and I wish you to get there if possible without being seen by the enemy."[80]

McLaws answered that he could do it and then asked permission from Lee if he could reconnoiter the march route. Longstreet, who had not been watching Lee's hand movement across the map, but was walking nearby within earshot, stepped into the conversation.

"No, sir, I do not wish you to leave your division. I wish your division placed so," running his finger parallel to lower Seminary Ridge and the Emmitsburg Road, exactly opposite, or perpendicular to, the position pointed out by Lee.

General Lee corrected Longstreet. "No, General, I wish it placed just perpendicular to that,"[81] pointing to a line running across the Emmitsburg Road cresting on the high ground at the Sherfy Peach Orchard.

McLaws, who certainly must have realized something was amiss between his pair of superiors, repeated his desire to reconnoiter the ground and Longstreet again declined his request. "Old Pete" had a good reason for keeping McLaws with his division. His own head engineer, Major John J. Clarke, had accompanied Captain Johnston's scouting party and had been gone for hours; when they would return was anyone's guess. It would have been foolish to have allowed one of his major generals to ride off along an unsecured flank into no-man's land.[82]

Lee's meeting with McLaws is important for several reasons. First, it confirms Alexander's recollections that Lee had decided to deliver an attack against the Federal left flank. McLaws would lead by stealth the march of the infantry of First Corps, with Hood to follow, to a position on lower Seminary Ridge before deploying and attacking in a northeasterly direction across Emmitsburg Road. If Meade did not reposition his lines prior to the attack, the result might well be another surprise and rout on the order of Chancellorsville. If the lines were readjusted before or because of First Corps' assault, other offensive possibilities for Hill's Third Corps or Ewell's

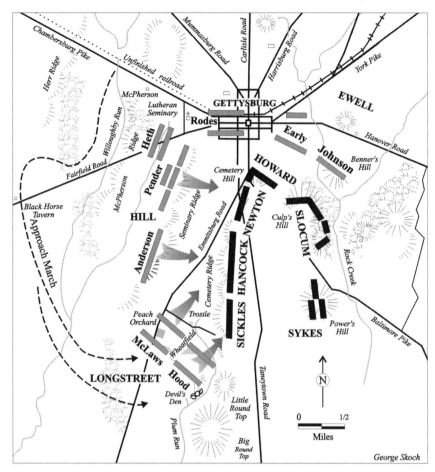

Lee's Initial Plan of Attack for July 2, 1863

Second Corps might evidence themselves. Thus, the flank march and subsequent attack against the Federal left was General Lee's design and first plan of attack. That decision would necessarily delay the fighting while march route details could be worked out to enable the Confederates to reach the southern end of the field without detection.

Second, Lee communicated precise details of his plan of attack directly to McLaws—a division commander—rather than through Longstreet. This was not the first time Lee had worked directly with McLaws, although why he did so is open to some speculation. Certainly Lee had confidence in McLaws as a division commander, but his faith had been shaken by the Georgian's fumbling at Salem Church during the Chancellorsville Campaign. Clearly Lee did not want any mix up as to where he believed the attack should be launched and how he wanted the division to go in. Speaking directly to McLaws was the best way to do this.[83]

Third and perhaps most important for our purposes is *how* Lee ordered McLaws to accomplish his deployment and attack. The division leader was instructed to march his brigades into position and "to get there *if possible* [emphasis added] without being seen by the enemy." In other words, Lee was instructing McLaws to conduct a flank march and *try* and accomplish it without being seen by the Federals. This is yet again another example of Lee's proclivity to issue "orders with discretion," but a direct order nonetheless. McLaws' subsequent action proves that he clearly understood this. This verbal order to McLaws was almost identical to the orders sent to Ewell on July 1 to carry Cemetery Hill "if practicable." Yet, no one seems to be arguing today that if McLaws did not believe he could conduct his march undetected, he would have been acting within his orders to have not even tried to do so. Richard Ewell defenders who still cling to the notion that he did not violate Lee's instructions to take Cemetery Hill "if practicable" by failing to make the attempt have only to consider McLaws' meeting with Lee the next morning to understand this point.[84]

After McLaws left to rejoin his command, Captain Johnston and his scouting party returned. Lee, Hill, and Longstreet were in conference, seated on "a fallen tree near the Seminary," recalled Johnston. The three men were holding a large map as "General Lee was talking and pointing on the map." Johnston informed the generals his group had ridden south along Willoughby Run before turning east across lower Seminary Ridge and through the fields on both sides of the Emmitsburg Road. From there, the party moved across Warfield Ridge further south and then up and down the Round Tops before returning to headquarters. Other than cavalry patrols, no Federal troops had been spotted. Lee was "was surprised at my getting so far," recalled the captain, "but showed plainly that I had given him valuable information." Lee said a few words to Hill and Longstreet and both "moved off." After additional discussion satisfied Lee of the report's accuracy, Johnston was directed to report to Longstreet and aid First Corps in its arrival and positioning.[85]

While McLaws and Hood waited for word to move out, Lee mounted Traveller and made his way to Ewell's headquarters around 9:00 a.m. Although Ewell was still out surveying Federal positions with Major Venable, the feisty Isaac Trimble was present. Within a few minutes the pair of generals were standing in the cupola of the Almshouse, which provided a panoramic view of much of the landscape facing Second Corps. To their front and 1,600 yards distant was Cemetery Hill, rising from Winebrenner's Run at the south edge of town to a height of about 100 feet. Its crest extended for almost 700 yards from the northwest to the southeast and was crowned by the Baltimore Pike and Evergreen Cemetery, its entrance marked by an arched brick gatehouse. While at first glance this position appeared nearly impregnable, Lee soon discerned it had several serious defensive flaws.

Lee had spent much of his military career scouting, designing, defending, or attacking formidable positions. Cemetery Hill, while powerful, was not formidable. It did not have the multiple lines of field works his soldiers faced at Gaines' Mill, the fortified lines of Vera Cruz, or the fields of fire of the masonry forts he had built along the Atlantic coast. In some respects Cemetery Hill even lacked the strengths of other defensive positions Lee had observed in 1847 during the Mexican War, such as Chapultepec Castle just outside Mexico City. Chapultepec had also seemed, at first look, too formidable to attack, largely because of a marsh and steep escarpments which prevented attacks from two sides. Cemetery Hill, only half as high as the hill upon which Chapultepec was constructed, could be assailed from any side. Like Chapultepec, it also offered a particularly vulnerable approach that could be exploited. Chapultepec's precipitous walls made it all but impossible for defenders to fire at attackers once they reached the base of the structure. An unusually steep grade below East Cemetery Hill offered attacking infantry similar cover from both small arms and artillery fire until just a few yards from the enemy line. Thus, Federal gunners on top of East Cemetery Hill were reduced to firing ranged shot and shell at targets hundreds of yards away, or canister when the assailants were already on top of them. Although enfilading artillery fire from Steven's Knoll posed a problem, and Federal guns stationed on the sloping ground connecting East Cemetery Hill to Stevens' Knoll had a clear field of fire against troops moving directly against them, the majority of the hill's eastern face bowed out so significantly from both its elongated military and geographical crests, that the position's imposing height was simply more a psychological benefit than a military advantage. These geographical nuances meant Federal infantry would be forced to hold the midpoint of East Cemetery Hill's forward slope along Brickyard Lane (the old trace of which can be seen today immediately below Wainwright Avenue) without the close support of their own artillery fire, all the while exposed to Confederate guns and small arms. This forward infantry line, however, was the key to the entire position for if its defenders were overrun or pushed back, they would be driven into their own guns.

Military history offers several examples of positions that appear unassailable, largely because of their geographic features, but in reality are relatively weak. Chapultepec in Mexico City is but one example. Missionary Ridge at Chattanooga epitomizes this observation. Unfortunately, many people fall into the common trap of presuming that geographic position is the most important factor in determining the outcome of a battle, thereby minimizing the importance of leadership skills and the quality of the troop involved. The Federal line at Gettysburg resembled a fishhook with Cemetery Hill forming the base between the hook and the shank. The hill was thus a juncture, and as such a weaker point than it initially appeared to be.[86]

Unlike East Cemetery Hill, however, Culp's Hill, which anchored the Federal right flank, had few if any weaknesses for an attacking force to exploit. Washed by Rock Creek on the east and with the Baltimore Pike marking its southwest boundary, Culp's Hill was in reality two peaks, the higher point of which was some 800 yards southeast of, and rising about 80 feet higher than, Cemetery Hill. The lower portion was about 400 yards south of the taller summit and 100 feet lower. Spangler's Spring and a small rivulet that drained into Rock Creek formed the southwestern end of the wooded eminence. Culp's Hill was a timbered mass of high ground strewn with numerous rock outcroppings—and unknown to either Lee or Trimble, was being strengthened even as the two Confederate generals held their private council.[87]

Neither Lee nor Trimble could have been overly excited about Confederate prospects on Second Corps' front. "The enemy have the advantage of us in a shorter and inside line and we are too much extended," Lee informed Trimble after surveying the ground. He also voiced regret that his generals "did not or . . . could not pursue our advantage of yesterday, and now the enemy are in a good position." Although Trimble did not mention it, it seems unlikely the passionate general would have passed up the opportunity to discuss with Lee his exasperating confrontation with Ewell of the previous afternoon. If it was not obvious the previous evening, it was clear to Lee now: the net effect of command mistakes on that portion of the field on July 1 had placed one-third of the Army of Northern Virginia in a position so far removed from the balance of the army it would be difficult or impossible to coordinate its movements with Longstreet's attack on the other end of the line.[88]

Lee and Trimble returned to Second Corps' headquarters sometime after 9:30 a.m., where they found Ewell had returned from his inspection tour with Venable. Ewell again reiterated that his corps should remain where it was while First and Third corps attacked on the right side of Gettysburg. None of this could have improved Lee's disposition, for there was little Ewell was going to accomplish hammering Meade's right flank unless it was performed in conjunction with Longstreet's attack. Lee so informed Ewell, who was told to pitch in Second Corps when he heard Longstreet's guns open up.[89] After explaining his general plan of attack, Lee rebuked Ewell for his decision not to continue the pursuit of July 1. According to Trimble, Lee repeated to Ewell something similar to the phrase he had used in the cupola: "we did not or we could not pursue our advantage of yesterday." While this may seem mild to modern students of the battle, for Lee to have uttered these words in public demonstrates both his state of mind and displeasure with Ewell. Coincidentally, "Early, Rodes and others" filed in at that same time, and Lee firmly repeated his reprimand to each, making "use of the same words." General Lee was dressing down the officers of Second Corps in the manner of a true Southern gentleman.[90]

* * *

Together with Armistead Lindsay Long, who had just completed his tour of artillery positions along the front where Hill's and Ewell's corps were situated, Lee rode back through town and down Seminary Ridge where part of Third Corps' artillery was already unlimbered. Both officers could see the vacant high ground between Seminary and Cemetery Ridges in and around the Sherfy Peach Orchard—the terrain Lee had earlier told McLaws to capture and use in his attack against the Federals. By the time Lee and Long returned to the general's overlook near the seminary building, it was after 10:00 a.m.[91]

Lee had already given his instructions to Alexander (previously discussed) to move First Corps' artillery battalions to the southern end of the field without being seen. This allowed Alexander the time he needed to get moving well ahead of the infantry that would follow. According to both Charles Marshall and Longstreet, General Lee ordered the infantry of First Corps to begin moving to its attack position opposite the Sherfy Peach Orchard around 11:00 a.m. McIvor Law's large Alabama brigade of Hood's Division, however, was still not up. Since George Pickett's three brigades were marching from Chambersburg with the division's artillery battalion and would probably not be available for the afternoon battle, Longstreet thought it unwise to initiate the march without the division's senior brigadier. Lee agreed with Longstreet's reasoning. The infantry of First Corps would wait for Law.[92]

At that moment McIvor Law's 2,000 Alabamians were hotfooting it towards Gettysburg. It was to be one of the longest and hardest days of the war any of them would ever experience. Their tribulations began early when they departed New Guilford just before 4:00 a.m. Marching "as rapidly as possible toward Gettysburg," Law recorded that his brigade arrived "shortly before noon" after a march of 20 miles in less than eight hours. The balance of Hood's Division was found resting either under the shade of the trees along Willoughby Run or as far west as the point where Herr's Ridge crossed Chambersburg Pike. Winded, hungry, and thirsty, Law's men fell out to catch a much-needed breather while knots of men loaded with empty canteens sought out liquid refreshment.[93]

Their respite was but a brief one. By 1:00 p.m. orders arrived for First Corps to move out.[94] According to McLaws, Lee's staff officer, Samuel Johnston, brought the news and was himself "ordered to conduct" the First Corps' infantry on the march.[95] Johnston—the same officer who had earlier scouted the southern portion of the field for Lee—later claimed that he was not the guide for the march of the two divisions, but rather had been asked by General Lee to simply "aid [Longstreet] in any way that I could."[96] As McLaws and Johnston rode ahead, eight veteran brigades snaked out behind them, McLaws' in the van with Hood's bringing up the rear.[97] Artillerist Colonel E. Porter Alexander was also on the move. Advised of the attack hours earlier and asked by Longstreet to "take command of all the artillery on the field, for the attack," Alexander had been reconnoitering the ground over which Longstreet's four artillery battalions could travel "without being seen by the enemy" before arriving "where the infantry lines were to be formed."[98] He was aided in this by General Pendleton, who claims he carefully led Alexander south and then eastward "to the advanced point of observation previously visited." This would have been the gentle rise along the Emmitsburg Road just across from the Daniel Klingle Farm, where Pendleton pointed out the high ground of the Sherfy Peach Orchard "much further to the right." Alexander parked his limbered battalions for a couple of hours while Longstreet's infantry completed its tortuous march.[99]

Alexander's successful effort unfolded as smoothly as it did because of an earlier skirmish that had taken place in Pitzer's Woods between the 10th and 11th Alabama regiments of Cadmus Wilcox's Brigade and a portion of Hiram Berdan's 1st U. S. Sharpshooters, backed up by the 3rd Maine. Dispatched by General Sickles to determine if any Confederates had wandered that far south on Seminary Ridge, Berdan's Federals advanced across the Emmitsburg Road and disappeared into Pitzer's Woods, where they discovered Richard Anderson's Division of Hill's Third Corps marching from the northwest. While Pendleton and Alexander were observing the Federal line along Cemetery Ridge from the small rise immediately northwest of the Klingle Farm, rifle fire erupted in the thick timber to their right and rear. Pendleton later reported it as a "sharp contest." Wilcox's Alabamians drove the Yankees out of the woods after a brief struggle (between 15 and 25 minutes), clearing Seminary Ridge and enabling Anderson to deploy his division there. His five brigades were deployed in "brigades abreast" stretching along Seminary Ridge from near the Bliss Farm on the north southward past the Henry Spangler Farm, a distance of almost one mile. Once deployed, Anderson's 6,925 infantry screened further Federal attempts to scout beyond the Seminary Ridge line.[100]

As Pitzer's Woods was being cleared by Wilcox, General Lee arrived "himself for a survey of the ground." There was "still a good deal of sharpshooting," remembered Pendleton, and "Lee had to examine the front with caution."[101] From a position on Seminary Ridge south and west of the Henry Spangler Farm, Lee viewed the Sherfy property and his soon-to-be-famous Peach Orchard; the hump of high ground sprinkled with fruit trees was still unoccupied. Lee continued with his reconnaissance until word reached him that Longstreet's troops "were in motion." Lee spurred Traveller after Longstreet and found him and his First Corps divisions taking a circuitous route to get into position for the upcoming fight.[102]

Unfortunately for Lee, Longstreet and his infantry, the initial route of march taken by First Corps exposed the column crossing Herr Ridge near Black Horse Tavern to the Federal signal station on Little Round Top. Captain Johnston warned Longstreet, who called a halt to the march and ordered the column to double back and take a different approach along Willoughby Run to lower Seminary Ridge. The confused and meandering march consumed precious hours that the Southerners would pine over later than night and for decades thereafter.[103]

During the final phase of the march, Lee and Longstreet rode ahead and looked over the ground where the attack would go in. Major John Cheves Haskell, a gunner in Henry's Battalion, Hood's Division, was already "on the Emmitsburg Pike" where Warfield Ridge crossed the road. Haskell, who would one day pen a fascinating account of his wartime experiences, remembered that the generals arrived ahead of the infantry and rode down the Seminary Ridge line, crossed the Emmitsburg Road and continued onto Warfield Ridge where a portion of Henry's

Battalion would later go into action. They "talked for some minutes with no apparent dissent," he remembered.[104]

When the discussion ended they temporarily parted company, Lee riding a short way back up Seminary Ridge to visit Anderson's Division, and "Old Pete" riding to rejoin the head of his infantry column as it was marching south along Willoughby Run near the Pitzer Schoolhouse. As Lafayette McLaws was tending to his brigades, Longstreet reined in and looked over the situation.

"How are you going in?" inquired the corps leader.

"That will be determined when I can see what is in my front," replied McLaws.

"There is nothing in your front; you will be entirely on the flank of the enemy."

"Then I will continue my march in columns of companies, and after arriving on the flank as far as is necessary will face to the left and march on the enemy."

"That suits me," replied Longstreet, who spurred his horse and rode away.[105]

McLaws recorded that the difficult march took about two hours and was interrupted by frequent stops and starts "owing to the rough character of the country in places." Some brigades had marched five miles and others eight, depending on where they were inserted in the marching column, when McLaws arrived near his jump off point some time after 3:00 p.m.[106] What Longstreet's major general saw when he ascended the western slope of lower Seminary Ridge and emerged on the eastern edge of the tree line must shocked him to his boots: "The enemy was massed in my front and extended to my right and left as far as I could see." It could not be so, but it was. The high ground from south of the Sherfy Peach Orchard stretching north along the Emmitsburg Road was bristling with enemy artillery and infantry. Another line jutted below the orchard eastward generally following the Wheatfield Road to a spur known as Houck's Ridge in front of the Round Tops. The line formed a giant L-shaped front with the Sherfy Peach Orchard serving as the junction of the two arms, one facing south and the other west. As McLaws calmly explained it years after the war, this "presented a state of affairs which was certainly not contemplated when the original plan or order of battle was given, and certainly was not known to General Longstreet a half hour previous." McLaws did not want to waste any time and sent instructions to his two leading brigadiers, Joe Kershaw and William Barksdale, to deploy their regiments in line of battle. Kershaw had seen the Federals and was already ordering his brigade into line behind a low stone wall along Seminary Ridge. Federal artillery in and around the Peach Orchard saw some of the movement and began lobbing shells into the woods.[107]

Longstreet and his generals were not the only officers surprised by the sudden appearance of a strong line of Federals along the Emmitsburg Road. The movement had been unilaterally undertaken by Dan Sickles, the flamboyant leader of Third Corps. Tainted by a tawdry life that included the murder of his wife's lover, the New York politician entered the Civil War determined to reclaim his prominence on the battlefield. His alliances with Joe Hooker and others catapulted him into corps command even though he was wholly lacking in military training. At

Chancellorsville, his only real combat experience, Sickles had been ordered to withdraw from a commanding piece of ground at Hazel Grove to Fairview, where Lee's artillery pounded his men mercilessly. Sickles was determined that would not happen again. Now, the randomness of the Federal marching orders had deposited his Third Corps on the southern end of the field, where Sickles was ordered by Meade to arrange his line from the left flank of Hancock's Second Corps on Cemetery Ridge south toward the Round Tops. The rocky and uneven terrain, broken up by clumps of timber, left Sickles unsure of where, exactly, he was to deploy. Worse still was the fact that he did not have enough men to stretch his line and occupy the high ground, which left his southern flank hanging without protection. When he discovered that the ground in his front along Emmitsburg Road was higher than the terrain he was defending, Sickles mounted his horse at about 11:00 a.m. and sought out Meade, who despised the New Yorker. Unable to get a satisfactory answer, Sickles made one of the most controversial decisions of the war: shortly before 3:00 p.m. he ordered his corps to advance more than half a mile to the Peach Orchard-Emmitsburg Road line and formed up as previously described. Longstreet and McLaws were shocked; Meade was outraged. As a trained engineer and experienced general, Meade saw right away that Sickles' move had left the Round Tops uncovered in his left rear and his right flank was now well in advance of Hancock's line on Cemetery Ridge.[108]

The nature of the terrain occupied by Sickles' Third Corps and the ground from that point to where Longstreet's divisions were forming was much more complex than immediately obvious and would have a significant impact on how the subsequent battle developed. As Sickles discovered, the southern extremity of Cemetery Ridge was much lower than that portion held by Hancock's Corps further to the north. The same thing was true on the opposite side of the field with Seminary Ridge, which loses elevation the further south one travels from the Lutheran Theological Seminary. A series of swales and humps dip and rise about midway between the two lower portions of these ridges. The northernmost of these gentle swells cuts across Emmitsburg Road in a southeast to northwest direction immediately around the buildings of the Klingle Farm. An entire battalion of artillery could be brought into action there only 800 yards away from Cemetery Ridge and an umbrella-shaped copse of trees that would dominate the action of July 3. More knots of ground running southward offered good fields of fire until the swell folded into a short ridge crossing Emmitsburg Road near the John Sherfy Farm complex to the southern boundary of the Peach Orchard. There, however, the ground rapidly falls off along the road and offers no cover whatsoever between Seminary Ridge to the west and the Stony Hill-Rose's Woods-Houck's Ridge line to the east.

Colonel Armistead Lindsay Long of General Lee's staff had reconnoitered this very terrain earlier in the day and, along with other Confederate officers, believed it provided a much better position for forming the Southern line of battle than did the woods along middle to lower Seminary Ridge. It was also perfectly suited as an advanced artillery position behind which Southern infantry could deploy for an attack shielded from Federal artillery fire along most of Cemetery Ridge. Long wanted to control these elevations so his artillerists could fire at the enemy along the ridge, and was apprehensive that the enemy would occupy these middle swells before Southern infantry could secure them. Long passed along this information to Lee, who looked over these rolls and dips during his reconnaissance after the Wilcox-Berdan skirmish in Pitzer's Woods. Indeed, anyone walking these shallow elevations today will immediately appreciate the accuracy of Long's observations because they are higher than the cultivated fields on Cemetery Ridge, which offered no protection for any Federal units deployed there.[109]

Dan Sickles saw it too. Meade, however, had deployed his arriving corps along Cemetery Ridge from Cemetery Hill on the north to just above Little Round Top on the south. The southern extremity of his line was initially placed behind shallow Plum Run and the trees running along its banks—all of which was overshadowed by Little Round Top. Thus Meade retained a reasonably solid line with the northern portion anchored by Ziegler's Grove and Cemetery Hill and hooking back east through East Cemetery Hill and Culp's Hill. For the Federals, the problem was the apparent weakness of middle-to-lower Cemetery Ridge, specifically that part of the line running from the position marked today by the Pennsylvania Monument southward to the northern base of Little Round Top. And that is right where Dan Sickles was standing when he looked west and was struck by the threat posed by the swells running along the Emmitsburg Road from the Klingle Farm to the Sherfy Peach Orchard. From those points Confederate artillerists could pound the Federal line along Cemetery Ridge.

And so Sickles moved his corps forward and formed the long L-shaped salient previously described. The movement, however, stretched Third Corps' frontage more than twice what it was prior to the redeployment and now neither the southern, western, or northern portions of his line possessed any natural strength. Only then did many of the officers and men realize that the new defensive line was so undesirable. Third Corps' movement to the middle ground swells rendered the Army of the Potomac's entire position significantly more vulnerable than it had been one-half mile to the east, clinging to the disappearing protection of middle-to-lower Cemetery Ridge.[110]

Winfield Hancock, Meade's excellent Second Corps commander, watched from his position on Cemetery Ridge as Sickles' men tramped forward to the new line from 800 to 1,000 yards in advance of the main Federal position. "Wait a moment," Hancock remarked to a handful of officers gathered with him, "you will see them tumbling back."[111]

Lee Modifies and Finalizes his Plan of Attack

While Kershaw and Barksdale were forming what would be his front line, Lafayette McLaws spurred rearward to get his remaining two brigades into position and order his artillery battalion under Colonel Henry Cabell to bring his guns up. Like Longstreet, McLaws was also a Georgian and graduate of the distinguished West Point Class of 1842. After a few hard years on the frontier and brief service during the Mexican conflict, Captain McLaws married and returned to army life. He was searching out Navajos when South Carolina seceded from the Union. Within a few months the captain was a brigadier general, and within a year a major general. Because of his rapid and early promotion to high rank, McLaws was the senior division commander in Lee's army in July 1863. His service thus far had been solid but not as eye-catching as Powell Hill's or John Bell Hood's. After serving on the Peninsula during the Seven Day's Battles, McLaws displayed bull dog qualities on the field similar to his corps leader. His brigades helped shatter John Sedgwick's division at Sharpsburg, and his defensive handiwork at Fredericksburg was superb. "Few of our general's equaled him in . . . the pains he took in many matters of detail," wrote the observant Porter Alexander. "He was about the best general in the army for that sort of job [Fredericksburg defense]." While Longstreet and two of his divisions foraged around Suffolk during the spring of 1863, McLaws remained with the army and raised Lee's ire with his dilatory actions during the Chancellorsville Campaign. During the fighting at Salem Church on May 3, McLaws did not speedily identify the enemy line and was slow getting his men into action—and Lee was not pleased. That performance may have tipped the scales against him and placed the new Third Corps into Powell Hill's hands. None of McLaws' brigadiers at Gettysburg were professional soldiers, but it was still one of the best on the field.[112]

His division formed in two lines 150 yards apart. The front ran along a northwest oblique away from the Emmitsburg Road from Biesecker's Woods on the right into Pitzer's Woods on the left. Kershaw's veteran South Carolina brigade, the largest of the four with 2,200 men in six regiments, manned the right front position stretching some 500 yards from end to end along lower Seminary Ridge and into the northern portion of Biesecker's Woods. The southern boundary of the Peach Orchard was visible on Kershaw's left front, with the Rose Farm, Rose Woods, and Stony Hill (today called "The Loop") dead ahead. Supporting Kershaw from behind was Paul Semmes' Georgians, four regiments numbering some 1,344 men. Three hundred yards to Kershaw's left was William Barksdale's superb 1,598-man Mississippi brigade.[113] The Mississippians' front spanned 400 yards along Pitzer's Woods opposite the Sherfy Farm and Peach Orchard behind the same type of low stone wall Kershaw's men enjoyed. Supporting them was William T. Wofford's crack brigade of Georgians, six regiments totaling approximately 1,600 men.[114] While Cabell was unlimbering his 16 guns in front of Kershaw's South Carolinians,

Lafayette McLaws (1821-1897)

Although not brilliant or especially quick on the offensive, Lafayette McLaws was a reliable division commander. James Longstreet understood his characteristics and shortcomings and regularly pulled strings to assist his fellow Georgian. At Lee's insistence, Longstreet paid special attention to how McLaws' brigades went into action on the afternoon of July 2 during the development of the *en échelon* attack. McLaws, who did not learn of Lee's involvement until long after the event, resented Longstreet's actions. The defeat helped break apart the decades-long friendship between he and Longstreet. *Eleanor S. Brockenbrough Library,* The Museum of the Confederacy. Richmond

E. Porter Alexander was bringing forward his battalion of corps reserve artillery onto the eastern side of lower Seminary Ridge and deploying it between and in front of McLaws' front line brigades.[115] Once fully deployed, McLaws' had about 6,745 infantrymen available for duty.

While McLaws' men were forming, Longstreet hurried forward John Bell Hood's Division and ordered it to take up a position on McLaws' right flank. As Hood recalled it, Longstreet directed him "to quicken the march [and] place my division across the Emmitsburg Road, form line of battle, and attack."[116] Like McLaws' division, Hood's 7,200 men deployed in two lines of battle. His first line consisted of Laws' 2,000 Alabamians on the right and Robertson's celebrated Texas Brigade, numbering about 1,800, on the left. Hood's remaining pair of brigades under Thomas Anderson and Henry Benning, Georgians all, deployed about 400 to the rear, "Tige" Anderson's 1,900 combatants supporting Robertson, and "Rock" Benning and his 1,500 supporting Law. Hood's front stretched across the Emmitsburg Road from near the P. Snyder house on his left to a position opposite Bushman's Woods and Big Round Top on his right. Two batteries of artillery unlimbered for support, with Alexander C. Latham's guns taking position in front of Robertson's men, and James Reilly's artillery in front of Law's right front. As his men were forming, Hood ordered pioneers forward to level fences in the path of the division and "picked Texas scouts to ascertain the position of the enemy's extreme left flank." They returned "soon" and provided Hood with an earful of information. It was about 3:30 p.m.[117]

Although Sickles' line was irregularly shaped, what captivated Hood's interest most was what his scouts had to say about the terrain features in his front and what lay beyond the Round Tops. Both were impressive heights. Round Top (or Big Round Top) was the southernmost of the pair, and its southern face was nearly impossible to climb. Strewn with rock outcroppings and heavily timbered, it rose to a height of about 270 feet above the valley floor. The summit of the smaller and shorter Little Round Top was about 120 feet lower and 1,000 yards north of Round Top's. Most of the timber from its western slope had been recently harvested, and other than signal corps personnel, it appeared unoccupied. Little Round Top consisted of a series of three distinct rock-faced elevations, or shelves. Its bald and rugged western face rose about 150 feet above the Plum Run valley hugging its base, and about 100 feet above Houck's Ridge immediately west and only about 500 yards away from the hill. From Round Top's summit Hood's scouts had seen the Federal army stretched out before them. As best as they could tell, the line ran south along Cemetery Ridge (Hancock's front) with another line jutted out along Emmitsburg Road (Sickles) that meandered in and out of sight in a southeasterly direction before terminating at a large clump of boulders (Devil's Den) at the northwest base of Round Top. Behind the Round Tops to the northeast was a vast ordnance and commissary train and a park of limbered guns. No large infantry formations were visible nearby.

The new Federal line angling southeast from the Peach Orchard to Houck's Ridge below Little Round Top troubled Hood. If he attacked up the Emmitsburg Road, as ordered, he would be subjecting his troops "to a destructive fire in flank and rear, as well as in front." Further, the rocky and wooded terrain strongly favored the defenders. Behind the hills, however, were Federal ordnance trains and artillery, apparently unguarded and waiting to be scooped up. Instead of attacking into the Federal strength, Hood believed the proper course was to take some or all of his division and "turn Round Top and attack the enemy in flank and rear." Hood dispatched three separate couriers with this proposal to Longstreet, one of whom was G. Moxley Sorrel, Longstreet's chief of staff. Each messenger returned with Longstreet's same answer: "Gen'l Lee's orders are to attack up the Emmitsburg Road."[118] Longstreet, who found Hood about this time behind his division and discussed the matter with him there, must have realized his recommendation was a smaller variant of the maneuver he had put forth to Lee the evening before and had repeated again earlier that day. As he later expressed it, "General Hood appealed again and again for the move . . . but, to give more confidence to his attack, he was reminded that the move to the right had been carefully considered by our chief and rejected in favor of his present orders." Longstreet may well have been sympathetic to Hood's pleas, but the day was slipping away and Hood's proposal entailed a potentially long delay and would have isolated his command and subjected it to destruction.[119]

Before Hood was fully formed for the assault, Longstreet had twice sent instructions to McLaws to open the attack. With the strong Federal line in his front and stretching far beyond his own right, the division commander appealed to

"Hood's Protest"

Just before the action of July 2 began, John Bell Hood tried one last time to persuade Longstreet to allow a part of his division to march around the Round Tops. Longstreet wisely refused and ordered Hood to attack as ordered. Hood died believing his suggestion was the great missed opportunity of the battle.

Courtesy Gallon Historical Art, Gettysburg, Pennsylvania

Longstreet to wait until Southern artillery had softened the Federal position and Hood was ready to go in. Longstreet finally ordered McLaws to hold back his assault and wait for Hood. The reason for Longstreet's change of mind was because General Lee was on the scene and had ordered a change in the method of attack. The commanding general made an appearance about this time (3:30 p.m.) opposite the Peach Orchard. Initially what he saw could not have pleased him. Not only had the situation changed from what Johnston and Pendleton had reported to him during their morning scouting missions, but it was far different from what Lee had personally observed only a couple hours earlier. Now, instead of an exposed enemy flank waiting to be rolled up, Sickles' new Third Corps position formed what at first blush looked to be a strong line supported by artillery.[120]

However, after carefully studying the enemy's new position and probably after some discussion with Longstreet, Lee realized that the new Federal front was in reality an assailable salient offering a different opportunity to crush and destroy another Federal corps—and still possibly roll up Meade's left flank. Lee thus issued new orders for an attack designed to take advantage of the Yankee redeployment and maximize the strength of his army. According to Longstreet, "General Lee at the same time gave orders for the attack to be made by my right—following up the direction of the Emmitsburg Road toward the Cemetery Ridge, holding Hood's left as well as could be toward the Emmitsburg Road, McLaws to follow the movements of Hood, attacking at the Peach Orchard the Federal Third Corps, with a part of R. H. Anderson's division following the movements of McLaws to guard his left flank." What Longstreet was describing was an attack Lee ordered on the scene and commonly referred to by three names, each of which meant the same thing: an "echelon attack," or more commonly *en échelon* (professionally trained American officers often used the French pronunciation), an "attack by progression," or an "attack in steps." This method of assault was one the Army of Northern Virginia had used several times in the preceding 13 months.[121]

Unlike a simultaneous attack, where the entire line moved forward at the same time, an attack *en échelon* was designed to begin at one end of the line and, by progression, move along the line with each successive brigade taking up the assault. Jackson's flank attack at Chancellorsville, for example, was a standard simultaneous assault dictated by his position on the flank of the enemy, the terrain, and the size of the opposing forces. After seeing Sickles' new deployment, however, Lee knew that a standard attack would not work against the left flank and left front of the Army of the Potomac, which is why he ordered an attack *en échelon* on July 2 . This offered several distinct advantages for Lee and his men.

First, an "attack by progression" was an excellent method of turning Meade's flank because the Federals were *facing* Lee's infantry and Longstreet's line overlapped Meade's left, which Lee desired to turn. Lee was on the scene at approximately 3:30 p.m. and visited with Longstreet. He knew Hood had deployed on McLaws' right below the Emmitsburg Road, and that the length of Hood's front would stretch beyond the end of the Federal line (then believed to be anchored on Houck's Ridge and the Devil's Den area). Therefore, Hood was precisely placed to begin an echelon attack. Recall that Lee's initial plan for July 2 had been to attack and turn Meade's left or southern flank. Sickles' unexpected advance to the Peach Orchard forced Lee to modify Longstreet's method of attack so that the Meade's flank could still be turned. Longstreet acknowledged the plan was General Lee's idea, and that he ordered the attack to begin with the Confederate right (i.e., Hood), to "envelop the enemy's left," which would give the Southern infantry their best chance to turn the Federal left flank.[122]

Second, an attack *en échelon* helped compensate for an army employing relatively small staffs at every level of command. The lack of instantaneous and reliable communications made the coordination of large-scale attacks on an exterior line several miles in length especially difficult. Thus, allowing subordinate commanders to visually monitor the progress of committed troops and then coordinate their attack *en échelon* offered better command control and a higher probability that reserves or supporting formations would be directed into combat at the best time and the right place. It also provided brigade, division, and corps commanders the flexibility to exploit success or respond to enemy reactions and mistakes.

Third, this method of attack fit Lee's command style perfectly, which nurtured and encouraged initiative among subordinate officers. An *en échelon* attack allowed Lee's corps and division commanders the flexibility to position their brigades and direct them into action. "It would be a bad thing," Lee once told Captain Justus Scheibert of the Prussian army, "if I could not rely on my brigade and division commanders." Thus, this method of attack was the embodiment of the best of Lee's accustomed command style of "orders with discretion." Lee placed a premium on initiative and allowed his general officers the freedom to best determine *how* to accomplish a task; the echelon method had brought out and developed the initiative and aggressive abilities of the army's subordinate commanders over the preceding 13 months, and had thus helped create the fighting power of the Army of Northern Virginia. Although it had not always been successful, Lee had employed the echelon attack on several occasions prior to Gettysburg, most notably at Gaines' Mill during the Seven Days' Battles, where his infantry carried a heavily defended position.

Fourth, *en échelon* attacks often triggered enemy mistakes, the most common of which was overreaction—especially in the area where the attack began. For example, Lee knew beforehand that if any of Hood's brigades managed to break through Sickles' line or push it back, the pressure on Meade (a new army commander) to react would be intense. Should he shore up his left and contain the breakthrough or gamble that his flank would not be turned or rolled up? Sending reinforcements from other parts of the line not yet under assault, or from his reserve, however, would unwittingly play into Lee's hand. Such a move would only weaken portions of Meade's army yet to be assailed and limit his ability to withstand the

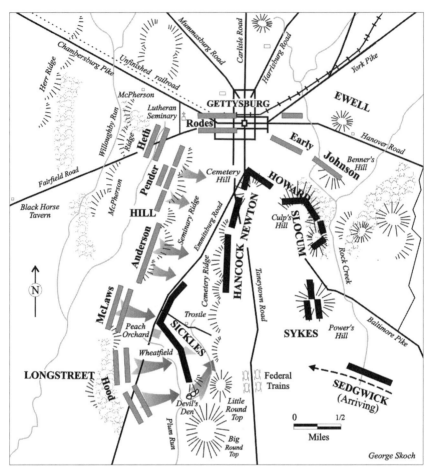

General Lee's Modified Echelon Plan of Attack for July 2, 1863

storm when it broke over that part of the line—or when his reserves were needed most. This was the manner in which Lee could impose his will upon the man he still called "Major Meade." And such an attack would place Meade on the horns of dilemma. Exactly where and what kind of "opportunity" Lee was hoping the divisions under Hood, McLaws, Anderson, and Pender would be able to exploit on July 2 would develop once the attacks were underway. [123]

Therefore, the strength of an attack *en échelon* was that it offered attacking generals with battlefield initiative and flexibility the opportunity to exploit enemy mistakes and follow up their own successes. Further, Lee was aware that the only way to stop a properly executed echelon attack was to defeat the leading elements by committing few, if any, reserves. The troops leading the assault were John Bell

Hood superb brigades, followed immediately thereafter by the equally formidable troops under Lafayette McLaws, all led by his best corps leader, James Longstreet. And First Corps' left was supported by the divisions of Richard Anderson and Dorsey Pender, nine largely fresh brigades under the command of the aggressive and experienced Powell Hill. General Lee had every reason to be confident his change of plan would exploit Sickles' folly and generate success.

In summary, Lee's overall modified plan of attack was as follows: Longstreet's First Corps would "partially envelope the enemy's left" by attacking *en échelon* from right to left (Hood and then McLaws) and "drive in" the Federal flank.[124] Meanwhile, Powell Hill's Third Corps division under Anderson and Pender were "to cooperate with [Longstreet]" and "join in with [First Corps] troops in the attack," in order "to prevent reinforcements being drawn to either wing."[125] The importance of Hill's role cannot be overlooked. In fact, it was paramount to the army's success. Hill's objective was twofold: he was to support Longstreet by having his men properly deployed and available in strength to exploit Longstreet's success and/or enemy mistakes on his front, and by doing so, would act as a triggering mechanism for Ewell's Second Corps, which was "instructed to make a simultaneous demonstration upon the enemy's right, to be converted into a real attack should opportunity offer."

The primary objective of Lee's *en échelon* attack was to partially envelop the Federal left flank and drive it in while Ewell made a simultaneous demonstration on the Federal right flank. Thus, Hill's order "to threaten the enemy's center" by attacking from Cemetery Hill southward along Cemetery Ridge and the Emmitsburg Road with the divisions of Anderson and Pender fulfilled the secondary role of the echelon attack, i.e., taking full advantage of success and/or enemy mistakes.[126] Lee intended that Hill's assault would either prevent Meade from shifting troops to beat back Longstreet and/or Ewell or, if Meade had already shifted reserves in reaction to the attacks on his flanks, break through the enemy's center on Cemetery Ridge. With battle-tested subordinate officers and men carrying out General Lee's "orders with discretion," the attack *en échelon* personified the aggressive battlefield spirit for which the Army of Northern Virginia was renowned.

* * *

For all these reasons, Robert E. Lee formulated and modified his plans for attack on July 2, 1863, with justifiable confidence that his army would emerge victorious.

Notes for Chapter 6

1. Armistead Lindsay Long, letter dated April, 1877, on the topic of "Causes of Lee's Defeat at Gettysburg," *Southern Historical Society Papers*, 4, p. 123.

2. Tagg, *The Generals of Gettysburg*, p. 203.

3. Several good summaries of Longstreet's career exist: Tagg, *The Generals of Gettysburg*, pp. 203-209; Peter S. Carmichael, "James Longstreet," *Encyclopedia of the Confederacy*, 1, pp. 944-947, and William Alan Blair, "James Longstreet," in *The Confederate General*, 4, pp. 91-95.

4. Longstreet offered details of his discussion with Lee and his proposal in his various writings after the death of Lee, but they vary by the telling. The nub of the discussion and Longstreet's subsequent behavior is that Lee, claims Longstreet, "agreed" to use defensive tactics in Pennsylvania. This seems not only contrary to Lee's nature, but contradicts virtually *everything* Lee said to others before and during the famous battle. Therefore, Longstreet's account of his proposal is probably correct only in general terms, especially in light of Lee's subsequent discussions later that evening with Early, Rodes, and Ewell. James Longstreet, "Lee's Right Wing at Gettysburg," *Battles and Leaders of the Civil War*, 3, p. 339; *Manassas to Appomattox* (Philadelphia, 1896), p. 358f, and "Lee in Pennsylvania," *Annals of the War*, pp. 421-422.

5. Longstreet, "Lee's Right Wing at Gettysburg," *Battles and Leaders of the Civil War*, 3, p. 339. A variant of Lee's answer is: "No, they are in position and I am going to whip them or they going to whip me."

6. Freeman, *Lee's Lieutenants*, 3, p. 109.

7. *The Military Maxims of Napoleon*, Maxim 6.

8. Jubal A. Early, "A Review" on the topic of "Causes of Lee's Defeat at Gettysburg," *Southern Historical Society Papers*, 4, p. 268. Other major concerns were finding sufficient food, water, and forage for the army for an indeterminable stay east of South Mountain.

9. John M. Chapman, "Comanches on the Warpath: The 35th Battalion Virginia Cavalry in the Gettysburg Campaign," *Civil War Regiments* (Mason City, 1999), 6, No. 3., pp. 2-3.

10. *The Military Maxims of Napoleon*, Maxim 30.

11. Fitzhugh Lee, "A Review of the First Two Days' Operations at Gettysburg and a Reply to General Longstreet," *Southern Historical Society Papers*, 5, pp. 165-166.

12. *OR* 27, pt. 1, pp. 115, 368.

13. *OR* 27, pt. 1, p. 71; David Homer Bates, *Lincoln in the Telegraph Office* (New York, 1907), p. 155; Stephen E. Ambrose, *Halleck: Lincoln's Chief of Staff* (Baton Rouge, 1990), pp. v, 5-6, 139.

14. Hamlin, *The Attack of Stonewall Jackson at Chancellorsville*, pp. 13, 168.

15. Lafayette McLaws, "Gettysburg," *Southern Historical Society Papers*, 7, p. 69.

16. *The Military Maxims of Napoleon*, Maxim 12.

17. Carl von Clausewitz, *On War*, 3, p. 5.

18. Armistead Lindsay Long, letter dated April, 1877, on the topic of "Causes of Lee's Defeat at Gettysburg," *Southern Historical Society Papers*, 4, p. 123.

19. *OR* 27, pt. 2, p. 318.

20. Jubal A. Early, "A Review" on the topic of "Causes of Lee's Defeat at Gettysburg," *Southern Historical Society Papers*, 4, p. 268.

21. Fitzgerald Ross, *A Visit to Cities and Camps of the Confederacy* (London, 1865), p. 52.

22. Edward Porter Alexander, letter dated 17 March 1877, on the topic of "Causes of Lee's Defeat at Gettysburg," *Southern Historical Society Papers*, 4, p. 98.

23. Edward Porter Alexander, letter dated 17 March 1877, on the topic of "Causes of Lee's Defeat at Gettysburg," *Southern Historical Society Papers*, 4, p. 99.

24. Lee, *Recollections and Letters of General Robert E. Lee*, p. 102.

25. Longstreet, "Lee in Pennsylvania," *Annals of the War*, p. 423.

26 *OR* 27, pt. 1, pp. 482, 519 and 530-531; John B. Bachelder to Fitzhugh Lee, 18 January 1875, as part of "A Review of the First Two Days' Operations at Gettysburg and a Reply to General Longstreet," *Southern Historical Society Papers*, 5, p. 173. These brigades comprised the advance elements of Dan Sickles' Federal Third Corps, which was strung out in a long road column and was not fully concentrated upon the battlefield until mid-morning July 2.

27. Jubal A. Early, letter dated 12 March 1877, on the topic of "Causes of Lee's Defeat at Gettysburg," *Southern Historical Society Papers*, 4, p. 66.

28. Edward Porter Alexander, letter dated 17 March 1877, on the topic of "Causes of Lee's Defeat at Gettysburg," *Southern Historical Society Papers*, 4, p. 99.

29. Theodore Ayrault Dodge, *A Bird's-Eye View of Our Civil War* (New York, 1998 reprint of the 1897 original), p. 137.

30. Three brigades from John Bell Hood's Division arrived at Cashtown around midnight. Hood's fourth brigade, Evander Law's Alabamians, was still well west of Gettysburg across South Mountain at New Guilford, about 20 miles from Herr Ridge.

31. Busey and Martin, *Regimental Strengths and Losses at Gettysburg*, pp. 143-147; 194-197; and the Gettysburg National Military Park Tablets. The 24 guns mentioned consist of the 18 in Dearing's Battalion of Pickett's Division and the six pieces that Stuart took with him.

32. Busey and Martin, *Regimental Strengths and Losses at Gettysburg*, pp. 129-193. This estimate includes Laws' Alabamians of Hood's division.

33. After leaving President Davis' Rappahannock line, Lee's army, through offensive action, had inflicted about 15,000 casualties from all causes (more than 7,000 prisoners and another 7,500 killed and wounded, or the equivalent of a large Federal corps) while suffering fewer than half that number. These figures include the fighting at Brandy Station, running cavalry battles from June 17 through 22, the Battle of Second Winchester, and the first day of Gettysburg 1.

34. *OR* 27, pt. 2, p. 318.

35. *OR* 51, pt. 2, p. 733; J. B. Walton, letter dated 15 October 1877, on the topic of Gettysburg, *Southern Historical Society Papers*, 5, p. 49.

36. For the location of Ewell's headquarters, see Jubal A. Early, "A Review" on the topic of "Causes of Lee's Defeat at Gettysburg," *Southern Historical Society Papers,* 4, p. 257; as well as Pfanz, *Gettysburg: Culp's Hill & Cemetery Hill*, p. 421, fn 27; Douglas Southall Freeman, *Lee's Lieutenants*, 3, p. 100; Pfanz, *Gettysburg: Culp's Hill & Cemetery Hill*, p. 81; Jubal A. Early, "A Review" on the topic of "Causes of Lee's Defeat at Gettysburg," *Southern*

Historical Society Papers, 4, p. 271. Apparently Lee did not feel it necessary to summon Ed Johnson to the conference, probably because his men had not fought that day, had just arrived, and needed to be looked after.

37. Jubal A. Early, "A Review" on the topic of "Causes of Lee's Defeat at Gettysburg," *Southern Historical Society Papers,* 4, p. 271. See Charles C. Osborne, *Jubal: The Life and Times of General Jubal A. Early, C.S.A.* (Chapel Hill, 1992), pp. 193-195, for a general discussion of this event by Early's most recent biographer.

38. Jubal A. Early, "A Review" on the topic of "Causes of Lee's Defeat at Gettysburg," *Southern Historical Society Papers,* 4, p. 271-272; Pfanz, *Richard S. Ewell,* p. 312.

39. Jubal A. Early, "A Review" on the topic of "Causes of Lee's Defeat at Gettysburg," *Southern Historical Society Papers,* 4, pp. 271-272.

40. Jubal A. Early, "A Review" on the topic of "Causes of Lee's Defeat at Gettysburg," *Southern Historical Society Papers,* 4, pp. 272-274.

41. Two brigades from Rodes' Division, Alfred Iverson's and Edward O'Neal's, were seriously damaged on July 1 and their effectiveness on July 2 was questionable.

42. *OR* 27, pt. 2, p. 319; Jubal A. Early, "A Review" on the topic of "Causes of Lee's Defeat at Gettysburg," *Southern Historical Society Papers,* 4, pp. 274-275.

43. Timothy H. Smith, *The Story of Lee's Headquarters; Gettysburg, Pennsylvania* (Gettysburg, 1995), pp. 3, 10, 40-42. Lee and a number of Confederate officers used the Widow Thompson house intermittently during the battle.

44. *OR* 27, pt. 2, p. 446.

45. *OR* 27, pt. 2, p. 446; *Southern Historical Society Papers,* 40, p. 299. Isaac Trimble claims Ewell was to be moved "behind Hill and Longstreet." *Southern Historical Society Papers,* 26, p. 125.

46. Thomas T. Turner, "Gettysburg, Captain Turner," typescript, J. A. Early Papers, College of William and Mary, Earl Gregg Swem Library, Williamsburg, Virginia.

47. Thomas T. Turner, "Gettysburg, Captain Turner," typescript, J. A. Early Papers, College of William and Mary, Earl Gregg Swem Library, Williamsburg, Virginia.

48. Thomas T. Turner, "Gettysburg, Captain Turner," typescript, J. A. Early Papers, College of William and Mary, Earl Gregg Swem Library, Williamsburg, Virginia.

49. "Allegheny" Johnson had pushed his division forward hard all day, and preparing an exhausted command for action in the darkness on unfamiliar terrain was a difficult task, especially without cavalry to screen the front. These factors are all possible explanations why Ewell's instructions were not promptly carried out once Johnson was on the field.

50. Coddington, *The Gettysburg Campaign,* p. 366; Pfanz, *Richard S. Ewell,* p. 312.

51. In his extensive writings after the war and following the deaths of Lee and Ewell, Jubal A. Early went to great lengths to advocate his belief that Culp's Hill should have been occupied on July 1, and that he so advised Ewell before the arbor council meeting with Lee. However, this claim is impeached by Early's own behavior at Gettysburg. If Early dominated the arbor conference, as he claims in his writings, and if the possession of the "unoccupied" Culp's Hill was so important, why hadn't he or Ewell mention Turner's reconnaissance during the council, rather than wait and bring it up only *after* Second Corps had been ordered to move to the right side of town? As we know, Lee changed his plan of action based on the receipt of information. Also, if Early believed Culp's Hill was so important, he could have

ordered up one or two of his own brigades to seize it until Johnson relieved him. His assertions ring hollow. Early was simply doing his best after the war to shift the blame elsewhere for what transpired east of Gettysburg on July 1.

52. Readers should pay special attention to Turner's specific and credible recollection of the order Ewell gave him and Robert Early that afternoon: ". . . ride up to Culp's Hill, *and if possible* [emphasis added], reconnoiter the enemy's positions from its summit." Turner's description of Ewell's order is identical to the "if possible" phrase included in Ewell's earlier directive from Lee, as recounted by both Walter Taylor and James Power Smith, that he take Cemetery Hill on the afternoon of July 1. Turner's account serves as yet another example of how gentlemen of the Old South communicated with one another, and also stands as a vivid and irrefutable piece of evidence that Dick Ewell understood that the term "if possible" meant Turner must to *try* and fulfill his orders, which in this instance was reconnoitering Culp's Hill. Turner's account substantiates that Ewell knew and understood Lee's order to take the heights an "order with discretion."

53. *OR* 27, pt. 2, pp. 318, 446; Freeman, *R. E. Lee,* 3, p. 83.

54. *OR* 27, pt. 2, p. 446.

55. *OR* 27, pt. 2, p. 504; Gettysburg National Military Park Tablets; Busey and Martin, *Regimental Strengths and Losses at Gettysburg*, pp. 151-156.

56. *OR* 27, pt. 1, p. 285; Busey and Martin, *Regimental Strengths and Losses at Gettysburg*, p. 24.

57. *OR* 27, pt. 1, p. 284; *OR* 27, pt. 1, pp. 284-285. The 7th Indiana garrisoned this vital position until well into July 2.

58. *OR* 27, pt. 2, p. 446; *OR* 27, pt. 3, p. 483.

59. The organization of the Fifth Corps, which was last encountered at Chancellorsville, would have been the information available to Johnson.

60. *OR* 27, pt. 2, p. 446; Thomas T. Turner, "Gettysburg, Captain Turner," typescript, J. A. Early Papers, College of William and Mary, Earl Gregg Swem Library, Williamsburg, Virginia.

61. The elements of the Federal Third Corps moving up the Emmitsburg Road from the south late on July 1 would not have been known to Ewell, unless Lee mentioned it to him during the arbor council. The vanguard of Slocum's Twelfth Corps reached the field about 6:00 p.m. or slightly thereafter. Geary's division was dispatched to cover the enemy left near the Round Tops, while Williams' was sent to the right around Wolf's Hill, just west of Culp's Hill.

62. *OR* 27, pt. 2, p. 446.

63. *OR* 27, pt. 2, p. 446.

64. David Gregg McIntosh, "Review of the Gettysburg Campaign," *Southern Historical Society Papers*, 37, p. 96.

65. Letter from S. R. Johnston to L. McLaws, June 27, 1892, S. R. Johnston MSS, Library of Congress, Douglas Southall Freeman Papers, Container 173; *Southern Historical Society Papers*, 5, p. 183; *Southern Historical Society Papers*, 7, p. 69.

66. Letter from S. R. Johnston to L. McLaws, June 27, 1892, S. R. Johnston MSS, Library of Congress, Douglas Southall Freeman Papers, Container 173.

67. Armistead Lindsay Long, letter 5 April 1876, on the topic of "Causes of Lee's Defeat at Gettysburg," *Southern Historical Society Papers*, 4, p. 67.

68. *OR* 27, pt. 2, p. 350; Armistead Lindsay Long, letter dated 5 April 1876, on the topic of "Causes of Lee's Defeat at Gettysburg," *Southern Historical Society Papers*, 4, p. 67.

69. *OR* 27, pt. 2, p. 350.

70. John B. Bachelder, *Gettysburg, July 2, Map #1.*

71. Jubal A. Early, "Supplement to General Early's Review—Reply to General Longstreet," *Southern Historical Society Papers,* 4, p. 291; *OR* 27, pt. 3, p. 876. Many writers confuse Major Charles S. Venable with Major Andrew R. Venable, who was Jeb Stuart's inspector general. *OR* 27, pt. 2, p. 710.

72. Fremantle, *Three Months in the Southern States,* p. 257; Douglas Southall Freeman, *R. E. Lee,* 3, p. 553.

73. Some writers profess amazement that neither Pendleton nor Johnston observed the several Third Corps brigades that had spent part of the night in the fields north of Little Round Top, or Hancock's marching Second Corps. Author David A. Powell, in "A Reconnaissance Gone Awry: Capt. Samuel R. Johnston's Fateful Trip to Little Round Top," *Gettysburg Magazine,* No. 23, p. 99, goes so far as to charge Johnston with "just bad scouting." We do not think these charges are warranted. The Third Corps brigades that had forced marched up the Emmitsburg Road on July 1 and into the early hours of July 2 had collapsed after their grueling journey, and their positions were covered by a low-lying fog that morning. *OR* 27, pt. 1, p. 552. While these exhausted men and horses rested, their late-arriving Third Corps comrades arrived—but not until mid-morning on July 2. Hancock's Second Corps moved up the Taneytown Road, one-half mile east of Little Round Top, and arrived about 7:00 a.m. *OR* 27, pt. 1, p. 369. Much of Little Round Top, including the eastern face, was heavily timbered and thus would have acted as a noise break while Johnston and his party were on the scene. Therefore, given the worn out condition of Sickle's command, the nature of the morning's atmospherics, terrain elements, and so forth, it is entirely believable that Johnston and Clarke carried out their duties appropriately, and yet failed to detect the enemy.

74. Longstreet's artillery formed a column miles long and had been in motion since before dawn. Captain William Parker, commanding the Richmond Virginia Battery in E. Porter Alexander's Battalion, recalled that his battery "marched at 2.30 [a.m.] for Gettysburg and arrived near there at 11." *Supplement to the OR* 5, serial no 5, p. 366, and Alexander, *Fighting for the Confederacy,* p. 235.

75. *Supplement to the OR* 5, serial no 5, p. 363; Edward Porter Alexander, letter dated 23 February 1878, *Southern Historical Society Papers*, 5, p. 201.

76. *Supplement to the OR* 5, serial no 5, p. 357. Alexander claimed he arrived on the field "about 10 a.m.," and that he was riding at the rear of the line of guns. This means he arrived soon after Lee returned from his meeting with the officers of Second Corps. See Alexander's "Supplemental report" and "Postwar letter" in *Supplement to the OR* 5, serial no 5, pp. 357-363; Edward Porter Alexander, letter dated March 17, 1877, on the topic of "Causes of Lee's Defeat at Gettysburg," *Southern Historical Society Papers*, 4, p. 101; Edward Porter Alexander, letter dated February 23, 1878, *Southern Historical Society Papers*, 5, pp. 201-202. Alexander stated Henry's Battalion had 18 guns, but the Gettysburg National Military Park Tablets list his batteries with a total of 19 guns.

77. Edward Porter Alexander, letter dated March 17, 1877, on the topic of "Causes of Lee's Defeat at Gettysburg," *Southern Historical Society Papers*, 4, p. 101. Alexander mentions that he did not see the infantry of either Lafayette McLaws or John Bell Hood, which means he met Lee before either infantry division of First Corps arrived.

78. *OR* 27, pt. 2, pp. 284-285; Busey and Martin, *Regimental Strengths and Losses at Gettysburg*, p. 132.

79. John Bell Hood, letter dated 28 June 1875, on the topic of "Causes of Lee's Defeat at Gettysburg," *Southern Historical Society Papers*, 4, p. 147.

80. Lafayette McLaws, "Gettysburg," *Southern Historical Society Papers*, 7, p. 68.

81. Lafayette McLaws, "Gettysburg," *Southern Historical Society Papers*, 7, p. 68.

82. Letter from S. R. Johnston to L. McLaws, June 27, 1892, S. R. Johnston MSS, Library of Congress, Douglas Southall Freeman Papers, Container 173. Johnston corrects McLaws' statements made in the *Southern Historical Society Papers,* 7, by advising him that he returned to headquarters to make his report to Lee *after* McLaws had met with the commanding general and then returned to his division. Therefore, since Johnston and Clarke had not yet returned when McLaws met with Lee on the morning of July 2, Longstreet was justified in refusing to allow McLaws to venture off to perform a mission that was already being undertaken by experienced officers. Longstreet also was aware that General Pendleton's group captured two Federal cavalrymen during the earlier morning reconnaissance. Based on this information alone, Longstreet knew any scouting mission McLaws' conducted ran the risk of running across enemy cavalry patrols.

83. See, for example, Krick, "Lafayette McLaws," in Davis, ed., *The Confederate General*, 4, pp. 128-131; Wert, *James Longstreet*, pp. 276-277; Tagg, *The Generals of Gettysburg*, p. 212. It is interesting to note that Lee did not praise McLaws in his Chancellorsville report, although he does mention other generals who served in the same area of fighting.

84. Lafayette McLaws, "Gettysburg," *Southern Historical Society Papers*, 7, p. 68, specifically uses this language.

85. Letter from S. R. Johnston to L. McLaws, June 27, 1892, S. R. Johnston MSS, Library of Congress, Douglas Southall Freeman Papers, Container 173. Writing years later, Johnston specifically claimed he also reconnoitered the ground for troop movements. Our investigation was "very successful, and after examining the roads over which our troops would have to move in the event of a movement on the enemy's left, I returned to Headquarters and made my report." Letter from S. R. Johnston to Fitz Lee, February 11, 1878, S. R. Johnston MSS, Library of Congress, Douglas Southall Freeman Papers, Container 173. In other words, Johnston and his escort must have left Seminary Ridge by first heading west, crossed the bridge over Willoughby Run, then turned south along the creek, and then emerged on lower Seminary Ridge, where McLaws later formed his division. Johnston believed that this was the best route over which the men of First Corps could make their march and get into attack position without being seen by the enemy.

86. Even today, a person standing where the Federal artillery was positioned on East Cemetery Hill can see and appreciate the weaknesses of this position and the restrictions it placed on the Federal artillerists. Scott Bowden presented this analysis in his address "Terrain Effects on the Battle of Gettysburg," at what was then called the North Texas Civil War Round Table, in Fort Worth, Texas, October, 1981. After studying for years the weaknesses

of the Cemetery Hill position, and after careful examination of the East Cemetery Hill approaches over which Hays' and Avery's brigades attacked, the authors consulted with artillery expert Charles Tarbox of Gettysburg, Pennsylvania, to confirm the inherent difficulties that the Federal artillery were faced with in defending East Cemetery Hill. Furthermore, Scott Bowden's two visits to Chapultepec, and the observations drawn therefrom, can be confirmed in: John S. D. Eisenhower, *So Far From God: The U.S. War With Mexico 1846-1848*, pp. 337-342; and K. Jack Bauer, *The Mexican War 1846-1848* (New York, 1974), pp. 313-318.

87. *OR* 27, pt. 1, pp. 759, 773, 778, 823, 826, 836, 847, 849, 856, 863-864, and 868.

88. Isaac R. Trimble, "The Battle and Campaign of Gettysburg," *Southern Historical Society Papers*, 26, p. 125; Long, *Memoirs of Robert E. Lee*, p. 281.

89. Long, *Memoirs of Robert E. Lee,* p. 281; Armistead Lindsay Long, letter dated April 1877, on the topic of "Causes of Lee's Defeat at Gettysburg," *Southern Historical Society Papers*, 4, p. 122; Pfanz, *Gettysburg: Culp's Hill & Cemetery Hill*, pp. 121-122.

90. Isaac R. Trimble, "The Battle and Campaign of Gettysburg," *Southern Historical Society Papers*, 26, p. 125. Lee's chastisement of Ewell is also a good indication that Lee believed his instructions to Ewell via Walter Taylor and James Power Smith constituted an "order with discretion" and not a "discretionary order." Lee's words prompted Ewell to acknowledge that his troops would be ready to cooperate with Longstreet and Hill by moving against Culp's and Cemetery hills.

91. Armistead Lindsay Long, letter dated 5 April 1876, on the topic of "Causes of Lee's Defeat at Gettysburg," *Southern Historical Society Papers*, 4, p. 68; Harry W. Pfanz, *Gettysburg: The Second Day* (Chapel Hill, 1987), p. 112. This time frame is consistent with Long's recollection of returning to Hill's gun line with General Lee "where I left Walker a few hours before" in Armistead Lindsay Long, letter dated April 5, 1876, on the topic of "Causes of Lee's Defeat at Gettysburg," *Southern Historical Society Papers*, 4, p. 68, and Long, *Memoirs of Robert E. Lee*, p. 281.

92. James Longstreet, "Account of the Campaign and Battle of Gettysburg," *Southern Historical Society Papers*, 5, p. 62; Walter Herron Taylor, "Lee and Longstreet," in the *Richmond Times*, 14 June 1898, reprinted in the *Southern Historical Society Papers*, 24, p. 76; Longstreet, *Annals of the War*, pp. 414-416; Longstreet, *Battles and Leaders of the Civil War*, 3, p. 340; Glenn Tucker, *Lee and Longstreet at Gettysburg* (Dayton, 1982), p. 44. Longstreet's decision to wait for Law has been castigated by historians as another example of his recalcitrant behavior on July 2. See, for example, Robert K. Krick, "James Longstreet and the Second Day at Gettysburg," in Gary W. Gallagher, ed., *The Second Day at Gettysburg* (Kent, 1993), pp. 70-71. Lee, however, sanctioned Longstreet's decision, so if it was a mistake, the mistake was Lee's. For a rebuttal to Krick's article, see Roger J. Greezicki, "Humbugging the Historian: A Reappraisal of Longstreet at Gettysburg," *Gettysburg Magazine* (January 1992), No. 6, pp. 62-68.

93. William C. Oates, "Gettysburg—The Battle on the Right," *Southern Historical Society Papers*, 6, p. 173. Evander Laws' command was ordered to begin the march at 3:00 a.m., but it was not begun until almost one hour later. Evander McIvor Law, "The Struggle for 'Round Top," *Battles and Leaders of the Civil War*, 3, p. 319; Evander McIvor Law to Bachelder,

February 2, 1891, *The Bachelder Papers*, 3, p. 1790. Law states that the distance his brigade covered from New Guilford to the valley of Willoughby Run was 24 miles.

94. Lafayette McLaws, "Gettysburg," *Southern Historical Society Papers*, 7, p. 69. McLaws places the order to move "about 1:00 P.M.," whereas Hood, in his letter dated 28 June 1875, on the topic of "Causes of Lee's Defeat at Gettysburg," in *Southern Historical Society Papers*, 4, p. 148, remembered the order to move as coming even later, "about three o'clock." Undoubtedly, Hood's recollection of the time that the movement order being given by Lee was far later than it really happened.

95. Lafayette McLaws, "Gettysburg," *Southern Historical Society Papers*, 7, p. 69.

96. Letter from S. R. Johnston to L. McLaws, June 27, 1892, S. R. Johnston MSS, Library of Congress, Douglas Southall Freeman Papers, Container 173. Unfortunately, no official report has been found for McLaws. His actions at Gettysburg are best set forth in the *Southern Historical Society Papers* article he penned after the war ("Gettysburg," 7, pp. 64-90). In many respects, this article serves as a worthwhile substitute.

97. John Bell Hood, letter dated 28 June 1875, on the topic of "Causes of Lee's Defeat at Gettysburg," *Southern Historical Society Papers*, 4, p. 148; *Southern Historical Society Papers*, 7, p. 69.

98. Edward Porter Alexander, "The Great Charge and Artillery Fighting at Gettysburg," in *Battles and Leaders of the Civil War*, 3, p. 359, claimed it took three hours to perform this reconnaissance. A decade earlier in the *Southern Historical Society Papers*, 4, p. 101, he had written it was "one or two hours" to finish the reconnaissance and return to the artillery battalions, all of which by then had arrived. For a good discussion of Alexander's preparations for the march and the march itself, see Alexander, *Fighting for the Confederacy*, pp. 235-237.

99. *OR* 27, pt. 2, p. 350. Klingle is sometimes spelled as "Klingel" and shown on Bachelder's Gettysburg maps as "J. Smith." The movement may also have been assisted by Sergeant Henry Wentz (Bath Virginia Artillery), a native of Gettysburg who once lived immediately north of the Sherfy Peach Orchard. All 69 pieces of ordnance under Alexander's control eventually moved to position around Pitzer's Schoolhouse without being detected by the Federals. Edward Porter Alexander, "The Great Charge and Artillery Fighting at Gettysburg," *Battles and Leaders of the Civil War*, 3, p. 359.

100. *OR* 27, pt. 1, p. 515; pt. 2, pp. 350, 613-614, 617; *Maine at Gettysburg* (Portland, 1898), p. 129; John B. Bachelder, *Gettysburg, July 2*, Map #2; Roy Marcot, Berdan's Sharpshooters at Gettysburg," *Gettysburg Magazine* (June 1989), No. 1, pp. 35-40. According to Marcot (p. 37), the Sharpshooter's lost 19 killed and wounded, while the 3rd Maine lost 48. Sickles used this encounter as an excuse to move his corps forward, believing the Confederates were attempting to flank him. In reality Lee was trying to flank him, but Berdan and company ran into Hill's Third Corps troops.

101. *OR* 27, pt. 2, p. 350.

102. Armistead Lindsay Long, letter dated 5 April 1876, on the topic of "Causes of Lee's Defeat at Gettysburg," *Southern Historical Society Papers*, 4, p. 68. Evander McIvor Law, "Gettysburg: The Second Day—The Confederate Side. The Struggle for 'Round Top,'" *The Century War Book* (New York, 1894), p. 195. Many men on the march were cheered to see Lee riding in their midst, and all indications are that he, too, was pleased to see his confident veterans marching to take up their positions.

103. Letter from S. R. Johnston to L. McLaws, June 27, 1892, S. R. Johnston MSS, Library of Congress, Douglas Southall Freeman Papers, Container 173; Lafayette McLaws, "Gettysburg," *Southern Historical Society Papers*, 7, p. 68. A detailed examination of this march is beyond the scope of this study. The literature is full of discussions on this topic. For more information, see Wert, *Longstreet*, pp. 269-270; Krick, "James Longstreet and the Second Day at Gettysburg," pp. 71-74; Greezicki, "A Reappraisal of Longstreet at Gettysburg," pp. 62-68, Pfanz, *Gettysburg: The Second Day*, pp. 119-121. It is interesting to note that after years of reflection and knowing well the controversy swirling around Longstreet's actions at Gettysburg, Walter Taylor of Lee's staff observed that "much time [had been] spent in discussing what was to be done [in scouting the route of march and coordinating the attack movements], which, perhaps, could not be avoided." Walter Herron Taylor, "Second Paper" on the topic of "Causes of Lee's Defeat at Gettysburg," *Southern Historical Society Papers*, 4, p. 131.

104. Haskell's account appears in *Supplement to the OR* 5, serial no 5, p. 352. Glenn Tucker, *Lee and Longstreet at Gettysburg*, p. 58. Haskell's published postwar, *The Haskell Memoirs: The Personal Narrative of a Confederate Officer*, edited by Gilbert E. Govan and James W. Livingood (New York, 1960), pp. 48-49, is much less detailed on this point than the *Supplement* account cited above.

105. Lafayette McLaws, "Gettysburg," *Southern Historical Society Papers*, 7, pp. 69-70. About this time Longstreet came across Joseph B. Kershaw's brigade of South Carolinians, riding at the head of McLaws' Division. He instructed the brigadier to turn left at Pitzer's Schoolhouse and march along the lane crossing lower Seminary Ridge at the Warfield house, which would lead him across the Emmitsburg Road at the Peach Orchard. Once on the high ground, Longstreet told Kershaw to deploy his brigade facing Gettysburg (generally north), using the Emmitsburg Road as a guide for his left flank. *OR* 27, pt. 2, p. 367.

106. Lafayette McLaws, "Gettysburg," *Southern Historical Society Papers*, 7, p. 69; John Bell Hood, letter dated 28 June 1875, on the topic of "Causes of Lee's Defeat at Gettysburg," *Southern Historical Society Papers*, 4, p. 148; Joseph B. Kershaw, "Kershaw's Brigade at Gettysburg," in *Battles and Leaders of the Civil War*, 3, p. 332; Pfanz, *Gettysburg: The Second Day*, pp. 122-123.

107. Lafayette McLaws, "Gettysburg," *Southern Historical Society Papers*, 7, p. 70; Pfanz, *Gettysburg: The Second Day*, pp. 150-151; *OR* 27, pt. 2, p. 367. Although McLaws did not mention it, it is quite possible Kershaw saw the enemy line first and summoned his division commander back to the ridge to see for himself. Pfanz, *Gettysburg: The Second Day*, pp. 150-1151; Kershaw, "Kershaw's Brigade at Gettysburg," p. 332.

108. The Meade-Sickles controversy continues to this day. It is beyond the purpose of the study to examine it in any detail from the perspective of those two officers. The most in-depth account is Richard Sauers, *A Caspian Sea of Ink: The Meade-Sickles Controversy* (Baltimore, 1989). Two good essays on the subject include: William Glenn Robertson, "The Peach Orchard Revisited: Daniel E. Sickles and the Third Corps on July 2, 1863," in Gary W. Gallagher, ed., *The Second Day at Gettysburg* (Kent, 1993), pp. 33-56; and David Downs, "'His Left was Worth a Glance': Meade and the Union Left on July 2, 1863, *Gettysburg Magazine* (1992), No. 7, pp. 29-40.

109. Armistead Lindsay Long, letter dated 5 April 1876, on the topic of "Causes of Lee's Defeat at Gettysburg," *Southern Historical Society Papers*, 4, p. 68; John B. Bachelder, *Gettysburg, July 2, Map #2*.

110. *OR* 27, pt. 1, pp. 523-533, 543 and 583.

111. *Pennsylvania at Gettysburg*, 2 volumes (Harrisburg, 1904), 2, p. 623.

112. Robert K. Krick, Lafayette McLaws," in Davis, ed., *The Confederate General*, pp. 129-131. Although many of his personal papers exist, a biography of McLaws has yet to be written.

113. Lafayette McLaws, "Gettysburg," *Southern Historical Society Papers*, 7, pp. 70-71; Joseph B. Kershaw to Bachelder, April 3, 1876, *The Bachelder Papers*, 1, pp. 470-471; *OR* 27, pt. 2, p. 367; Busey and Martin, *Regimental Strengths and Losses at Gettysburg*, p. 138; Benjamin G. Humphreys to Bachelder, May 1, 1876, *The Bachelder Papers*, 1, p. 481, lists 1,420 men. However, Humphreys' total appears to have been only rank and file while omitting the officers. In John Seymore McNeily, "Barksdale's Mississippi Brigade at Gettysburg. 'Most Magnificent Charge of the War.'" *Publications of the Mississippi Historical Society*, 14 (1914), p. 252, the author places the strength of the brigade at 1,590. The Gettysburg National Military Park Tablet lists the strength of the brigade at 1,598.

114. Gettysburg National Military Park Tablet shows only 1350, but this total omits the 3rd Battalion Georgia Sharpshooters that was present and engaged. Busey and Martin, *Regimental Strengths and Losses at Gettysburg*, p. 141.

115. Edward Porter Alexander, letter dated 17 March 1877, on the topic of "Causes of Lee's Defeat at Gettysburg," *Southern Historical Society Papers*, 4, p. 101; Gettysburg National Military Park Tablets; *Battles and Leaders of the Civil War*, 3, p. 359.

116. *OR* 27, pt. 2, p. 367; John Bell Hood, letter dated 28 June 1875, on the topic of "Causes of Lee's Defeat at Gettysburg," *Southern Historical Society Papers*, 4, p. 148; Lafayette McLaws, "Gettysburg," *Southern Historical Society Papers*, 7, p. 70.

117. Pfanz, *Gettysburg: The Second Day*, pp. 158-167; Busey and Martin, *Regimental Strengths and Losses at Gettysburg*, pp. 132-135; Gettysburg National Military Park Tablets; *OR* 27, pt. 2, 358; John Bell Hood, letter dated 28 June 1875, on the topic of "Causes of Lee's Defeat at Gettysburg," *Southern Historical Society Papers*, 4, p. 148. Hood, like McLaws, did not write a report for the Gettysburg Campaign.

118. John Bell Hood, letter dated 28 June 1875, on the topic of "Causes of Lee's Defeat at Gettysburg," *Southern Historical Society Papers*, 4, pp. 149-150; G. Moxley Sorrel, *Recollections of a Confederate Staff Officer* (Wilmington, 1987), pp. 159-160; Pfanz, *Gettysburg: The Second Day*, pp. 164-166.

119. Longstreet, *From Manassas to Appomattox*, p. 368; Freeman, *Lee's Lieutenants*, 3, pp. 119-121; Wert, *Longstreet*, pp. 272-273; Pfanz, *Gettysburg: The Second Day*, pp. 164-166. Until his death in 1879, Hood believed his rejected flanking plan was the lost opportunity of the battle. He died before learning his men would have run into large bodies of converging Federals—Sykes' Fifth Corps and the leading elements of Sedgwick's Sixth Corps. Isolated without screening cavalry and without the possibility of reinforcements, Hood's Division would have been severely handled—or worse. Federal general Abner Doubleday was also of the opinion that Hood's move would have brought disaster upon his division. Doubleday, *Chancellorsville and Gettysburg*, p. 162. One of Longstreet's couriers,

William Youngblood of the 15th Alabama, claimed after the war that General Lee rode up at this time and Hood pleaded directly with the commanding general on his proposal to outflank Round Top. According to Youngblood, Lee asked Longstreet for his opinion of the plan, and "Old Pete" responded, "I have great faith in General Hood's opinions and his ability to do whatever he plans to do." General Lee, claimed Youngblood, "stood with head bowed, looking upon the ground in deep thought, for, it seemed, a long time. When he raised his face to look at Generals Longstreet and Hood he said: 'Gentlemen, I cannot risk the loss of a brigade; our men are in fine spirits, and with great confidence will go into this battle. I believe that we can win upon a direct attack.'" William Youngblood, "Unwritten History of the Gettysburg Campaign," *Southern Historical Society Papers*, 38, pp. 314-315. While most writers of the Gettysburg epic ignore Youngblood's story, it is worth noting for two reasons. First, the actions of the principals as related by Youngblood seem to confirm his account. Second, Walter Taylor, who was in effect Lee's chief of staff and who survived by a number of years the publication of Youngblood's account, never challenged the veracity of his account.

120. Longstreet, "Lee's Right Wing at Gettysburg," *Battles and Leaders of the Civil War,* 3, pp. 340-341. In his memoirs, *From Manassas to Appomattox*, p. 368, Longstreet implies that Lee never showed up at the point of attack or offered assistance, which cannot be the case given his own writings and the development of the fighting that afternoon. William Youngblood, "Unwritten History of the Gettysburg Campaign," *Southern Historical Society Papers*, 38, p. 315, claims Lee was on this portion of the field at this time, as do McLaws and others. Lafayette McLaws, "Gettysburg," *Southern Historical Society Papers*, 7, p. 72. To suggest otherwise seems incredible.

121. Longstreet, "Lee's Right Wing at Gettysburg," *Battles and Leaders of the Civil War*, 3, p. 341; Longstreet, "Lee in Pennsylvania," *Annals of the War*, p. 424. Lee had ordered echelon attacks at Mechanicsville, Gaines' Mill, Frayser's Farm, and Malvern Hill. The change in orders for Longstreet to attack *en échelon* required that Hill's Third Corps have its orders amended accordingly to support Longstreet's efforts. The post-battle reports of Hill, Cadmus Wilcox, and other Third Corps generals confirm the fact that Lee issued orders to Hill to attack *en échelon*. This point is further developed in the next chapter. Since Ewell already had orders to support the assault from the right side of town, there was no reason for Lee to amend Ewell's instructions.

122. Longstreet, "Lee's Right Wing at Gettysburg," *Battles and Leaders of the Civil War*, 3, pp. 340-341; Longstreet, "Lee in Pennsylvania," *Annals of the War*, p. 424.

123. *OR* 27, pt. 2, pp. 318-319, 446 and 608.

124. 164. *OR* 27, pt. 2, p. 318; Longstreet, "Lee's Right Wing at Gettysburg," *Battles and Leaders of the Civil War*, 3, p. 341; Longstreet, "Lee in Pennsylvania," *Annals of the War*, p. 424; Edward Porter Alexander, *Military Memoirs of a Confederate* (New York, 1907), pp. 393-394.

125. *OR* 27, pt. 2, pp. 318, 608, 126. *OR* 27, pt. 2, pp. 318-319.

Chapter 7

"Half an Hour Longer and
We Would Have Carried the Enemy's Position"

Lee and the Second Day

"Battles are lost and won in a quarter of an hour."
—Napoleon[1]

*"A battle sometimes decides everything; and sometimes
the merest trifle decides a battle."*
—Napoleon[2]

No one will ever know for sure which battery fired the shell that exploded just above the head of the mounted general officer, its hot iron fragments ripping into his left arm from biceps to wrist. Perhaps the projectile was launched from one of several Federal batteries stacked along the Wheatfield Road, shooting generally south into the flanks of the advancing lines of Confederate troops. Or, it might have come from one of the Federal tubes firing from above Devil's Den on Houck's Ridge. Given the unreliable nature of Southern fixed ammunition, who can say for sure it did not come from Alexander Latham's Confederate battery, situated several hundred yards to the rear and a handful of yards north of the point of detonation.

Regardless of where it originated, the burst left the officer shocked and bleeding badly. Aides lifted him from his horse and stretcher-bearers carried him to a waiting ambulance. Within the space of a few seconds half of James Longstreet's First Corps had been effectively rendered leaderless.[3]

"Best three hours' fighting ever done by any troops on any battlefield"

The tall officer with auburn hair and flowing beard stood up in his stirrups and, with his hat in hand, waved it at the enemy and shouted out his orders: "Fix Bayonets, my brave Texans . . . Forward and take those heights!" A line officer within earshot mimicked his words of encouragement. Pointing to the regiment's flag, Lieutenant Colonel Phillip A. Work of the 1st Texas yelled as loud as he could, "Follow the Lone Star Flag to the top of the mountain!"[4] And so Hood's Division stepped off to the assault, opening General Lee's grand echelon attack to crush Meade's army. It was just after 4:00 p.m.

*   *   *

John Bell Hood uttered his famous words in front of his famous old command—the Texas Brigade. Some may have noticed he was not mounted on his familiar roan, the "spirited and fearless" Jeff Davis. Non-commissioned officers and privates of the 4th Texas Infantry had given Hood the horse on April 26, 1862, and he had ridden it through every battle thereafter unscathed. A "streak of superstition" coursed through the Texas Brigade: as long as Hood rode the lucky roan, no harm would come to him. Unable to ride his favorite horse that day as "consequence of lameness," Hood opened the action at Gettysburg on July 2 from the back of another beast.[5]

Although he is associated with Texas, Hood was born in 1831 into a prominent Kentucky family. The benefits of private tutors and local schools failed to help him academically, and he graduated from West Point in 1853 near the bottom of his class. His reward was hard service on the frontier fighting Indians with the 2nd Cavalry (Robert E. Lee's command), where he was wounded when an arrow pinned his hand to his saddle. The firing on Fort Sumter prompted his resignation and he was appointed colonel and given the 4th Texas regiment to command. Tedious combat-less months followed and in March 1862, Hood (or "Sam" as he was called by his friends) was provided with a brigade and a wreath for his collar stars. The Kentuckian and "Hood's Texas Brigade" carved out a name for themselves at the Battle of Gaines' Mill during the Seven Days. His gallant field leadership broke through the fortified enemy lines and triggered an enemy rout, giving Lee his first victory of the war and establishing Hood's men as the army's best shock troops. An ill superior allowed Hood to slip into the division's top command slot at Second

John Bell Hood (1831-1879)

A tenacious fighter whose capable tactics in coordinating infantry and artillery complimented perfectly the demeanor and confidence of his troops, John Bell Hood was at Gettysburg arguably Lee's best major general. His wounding during the opening stages of the fighting on July 2, 1863, was a heavy blow to the Confederate army, and his loss adversely affected the full contribution of his division in Lee's modified *en échelon* plan of attack.

Library of Congress

Manassas and Sharpsburg, where his skillful direction marked him as one of the best combat generals in the army. Lee recognized it as well as anyone and rewarded him with a promotion to major general in October 1862. Together with Pickett's Division, Hood moved south below Petersburg in early 1863 and participated in Longstreet's Suffolk Campaign. There, a spider web of confusion developed over just who was in charge of a particular stretch of the front; the loss of an artillery battery and scores of needless casualties resulted. As the campaign's historian described it, the performance "did not enhance Hood's reputation" as a division commander. Separation from Lee and the balance of the army caused Hood some angst, and he especially regretted missing the opportunities offered by the fighting at Chancellorsville. Suffolk notwithstanding, Lee, Longstreet, and everyone else in the army had every reason to expect great things from John Bell Hood.[6]

*   *   *

The first of Hood's four brigades to move out was Evander McIvor (pronounced "Ma-Keev-er") Law's outfit. The tired and thirsty Alabamians were still waiting for runners to return with canteens when orders came down to begin the attack. The men "sprang forward as if at a game of ball" and moved forward at the quick step remembered one witness.[7] Law's five regiments moved out almost due east across the Bushman farm in the direction of the John Slyder place. Less than a mile away loomed Round Top's wooded summit. Jerome Robertson's Texas Brigade supported Law's left flank. Similarly enthused with the prospects before them, the Texans jumped forward in a double-quick step. The nature of the terrain—fences, knots of timber, rocks, and bushy growth—hindered Law's men as much as the shower of iron fragments from the shells bursting above them. Still, they continued moving quickly east, passing south of the Bushman buildings into the largely open Slyder fields. In accordance with Lee's echelon attack plan, Law was seeking to find and turn the extreme Federal left flank, which at that time was anchored in the jumbled pile of granite boulders and ledges of Devil's Den. And from that point a Federal battery was tearing apart Law's exposed left flank. While his left three regiments continued forward, Law ordered his two right regiments to move north across the eastward line of advance into the rocky area.

Within a quarter hour the entire brigade had crossed Plum Run at the western base of Round Top, brushed away the skirmishers of the 2nd U. S. Sharpshooters, and waded into the heavily wooded terrain. The fighting here, remembered Law, "became close and severe."[8] The change in the brigade's alignment left Colonel William Calvin Oates' 15th Alabama holding Law's extreme right flank (and the right flank of the entire army). Law ordered Oates to take his 500-man regiment and find the left flank of the enemy line, "turn it if possible, and go as far as [he] could." With the other three regiments guiding on Oates' left, the bulk of Law's Brigade continued east and began climbing Round Top.[9]

* * *

Jerome Robertson's first difficult decision of the day arrived within a few minutes after his men dumped all their "knapsacks, blankets, and other cumbersome" items and advanced into action.[10] The Texans had tramped less than 200 yards when he realized that his right regiment, the 5th Texas, was losing contact with the faster-moving and eastward driving Alabamians. Hoods orders were clear: cover Law's left flank and keep your own left "on the Emmitsburg Road and in no event . . . leave it unless the exigency of the battle made it necessary or proper."[11] Robertson, however, believed that the "mountain held by the enemy in heavy force with artillery to the right of Law's center was the key to the enemy's left," and made a decision. "I abandoned the pike and closed on General Law's left," he later

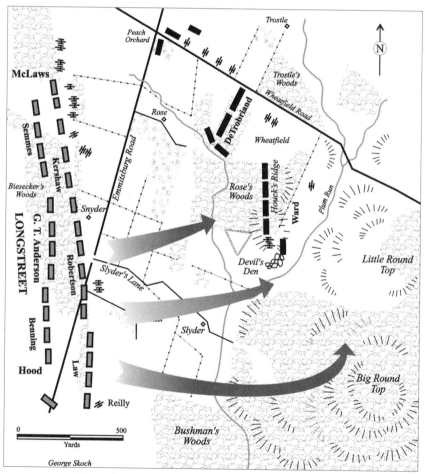

Hood Opens Lee's Echelon Attack Against Meade's
Left Flank, 4:15 p.m., July 2, 1863

reported. The order was apparently not understood by Robertson's left pair of regiments or, as Robertson later claimed, the terrain interfered with the movement. Regardless, his brigade broke into two halves, the right (4th and 5th Texas) following Law into the Devil's Den and Round Top area, and the left (1st Texas and 3rd Arkansas) moving into the southern portion of Rose Woods. As Robertson reported it, the irregular terrain and Law's movement east left "a considerable space unoccupied between [the] two wings."[12] The entire front of Hood's spearhead was on the verge of serious trouble—and Hood was nowhere to be found.

After he had stood in his stirrups directly in front of the 1st Texas and urged his men forward, Hood and his staff had ridden to an orchard, probably the small grove located on the eastern slope of Warfield Ridge just west of the Bushman barn.[13] Situated squarely in the middle and behind his divisional front, the orchard offered Hood an excellent position to observe the effects of his artillery fire and opening stages of the advance of his brigades. Thus far only Law and Robertson had moved out. As they crossed over Plum Run, the supporting brigades of Henry Benning and "Tige" Anderson waited impatiently west of the road, as did a pair of limbered batteries. The division commander could see the advancing tide of red battle flags marking the progress of Law and Robertson, but whether he could observe the effect of the cannonade from Latham's and Reilly's guns is unknown.[14]

Hood knew that attacking infantry needed close artillery support and ordered two of his four batteries to remain limbered so they could move forward at a moment's notice. That moment arrived early in the fighting when Hood called for the guns to advance. A courier reached Major Haskell, Henry's Battalion, with orders to move the guns to Hood's position on the Bushman farm. "When I reached Hood he was sitting on his horse and at once began to direct me what to do," Haskell recalled in a postwar account. It was at that moment that a shell left an artillery piece, arched overhead, and exploded near Hood, its hot iron shrapnel ripping through his left arm. "The small bone of his arm [appeared] broken," remembered Haskell. "It evidently gave him intense pain and utterly unnerved him, so I could get no orders from him, nor could his staff tell me what I was to do."[15] Just when his division needed his expert field guidance, the army's premier division commander was "borne off on a litter to the rear." Hood's participation at Gettysburg had lasted all of twenty minutes, and he would never serve with his beloved Army of Northern Virginia again.[16]

Command of Hood's Division passed to its senior brigadier, McIvor Law. How much time passed before he learned of this is unknown. A South Carolinian by birth, Law graduated from the Citadel, moved to Alabama and began the war as a captain of the 4th Alabama, one of the finest regiments in the entire Confederate service. He distinguished himself at the head of a brigade during Peninsula Campaign and Seven Days Battles, on the plains of Second Manassas, and again at Sharpsburg. Law had the combat experience to assume the reins of divisional command, but whether he could sustain the momentum of the attack and turn the Federal left remained to be seen.[17]

It is difficult to know exactly what decisions Law made as division commander, and when and why he made them. If he wrote a report for Gettysburg it has not been located, and his postwar writings are not as detailed on the subject as one would like. His concerns as a division commander were different from those of a brigadier. What, exactly, was the strength of the enemy force facing the entire division? Were the division's flanks secure? Could he still execute Hood's earlier orders to envelop the enemy's left flank? Someone of Law's experience would have realized by this time that he was facing more than a single brigade of infantry and more likely at least a division. Although he did not yet know it, his men were facing David Birney's attenuated division of Sickles' Third Corps, which stretched south and east from the Peach Orchard through Rose Woods and onto Houck's Ridge and Devil's Den. Thus, securing the tactical flanks of his advancing front had to have been one of Law's immediate concerns. However, before he could call upon the division's pair of supporting brigades, Henry Benning's four regiments of Georgians were already at the front.

Henry Lewis "Rock" Benning, a prewar lawyer and former justice of the George Supreme Court had deployed for battle several hundred yards behind Law and had been instructed by Hood to support the advance of the Alabamians. Benning, however, did not even see the ground over which he was to advance until he guided his Georgians out of the woods and across the Emmitsburg Road. "Our own first line . . .became visible advancing about 400 yards in our front. . . . I took [it] to be Law's brigade and so I followed it."[18] Unbeknownst to Benning, Law's regiments were already out of sight far to the east, and the regiments he was following belonged to Robertson's Texas Brigade. Benning's course carried his own four regiments over Plum Run into the large gap between the left wing of the Texas Brigade, which was heavily engaged in the southern portion of the Rose Woods, and its right wing, intermingled with Law's Alabamians on the northwestern spur of Big Round Top.[19]

Benning's men advanced into the action before Hood's remaining brigade under "Tige" Anderson took a step. George Thomas Anderson's military training seems to have been learned entirely from active duty. After accumulating a substantial amount of property, he volunteered and rendered good service during the Mexican War and again several years thereafter in the 1850s with the 1st United States Cavalry Regiment. Other than that, little is commonly known of his prewar endeavors. At Gettysburg, he seems to have believed his brigade was the division's reserve instead of Robertson's support. Perhaps the stumbling advance of the division's remaining pair of brigades was due to Hood's wound and the lack of an overall guiding hand. Regardless, Benning had already left by the time Anderson received an urgent message from fellow brigadier Robertson that the left of the Texas Brigade was exposed and needed his support. Anderson wasted no time driving his five regiments of Georgians northeast to a position about 250 yards behind the left wing of Texas Brigade. His own left extended far beyond Robertson's 3rd Arkansas, which meant Anderson's Brigade was now anchoring the left flank of the entire division. Every brigade in Hood's Division was now engaged and Law did his best to press the attack from the western edge of Rose Woods to Round Top, all the while seeking to envelop the enemy's left flank.[20]

As the left wing of the Texas Brigade, now supported by Benning and Anderson, surged forward, Law could see the 44th Alabama of his brigade, along with Robertson's 4th and 5th Texas, moving against Federals from Brigadier General Henry Ward's brigade immediately southeast of Devil's Den. Were the remainder of his Alabamians moving as quickly as they were supposed to? Law knew his task was to find and turn the Federal left flank as quickly as possible and he needed to know what the right half of his brigade was doing—especially Colonel Oates' 15th Alabama. To find out Law dispatched his assistant adjutant general, Captain Leigh Richmond Terrell, who picked his way around Devil's Den on horseback. Terrell would have seen the men of the 4th Alabama on the northeastern slope of Round Top, dressing ranks before resuming their advance in the direction of Little Round Top.[21]

Law's aide climbed Round Top and found Colonel Oates and the two thirsty and exhausted regiments of the 15th and 47th Alabama resting at the summit. When Terrell questioned why the regiments had stopped, Oates explained that the men needed a few minutes' rest and inquired of Law's whereabouts. Knowing the men on Round Top were the outside pivot of a line already heavily engaged, Terrell quickly explained that Hood had been wounded and Law was now in command. The order, he said, was for both Oates and Lieutenant Colonel Michael Jefferson Bulger, commanding the 47th Alabama, "to lose no time, but to press forward and drive the enemy before us as far as possible." Although Oates believed his position on Round Top was one of great importance and that the Alabamians should hold it and bring up artillery to strengthen it, he knew it was his duty to obey and did so, ordering his line to move down the "northern or northeastern portion of Round Top without encountering any opposition whatever." Oates' goal was to move his men up and occupy the smaller hill just to his north. Unfortunately for the Confederates, the ten minutes Oates lost by resting his parched men on Round Top amounted to the difference between who arrived first and secured Little Round Top. Unbeknownst to Oates or anyone else, regiments from Colonel Strong Vincent's Federal brigade (Barnes' Division, Sykes Fifth Corps) had arrived on the rocky heights just moments earlier.[22]

*   *   *

Strong Vincent's command was the first brigade of the entire Fifth Corps—eight brigades in three divisions—directed to the Federal left flank in

"Expecting a Battle"

Major General George Gordon Meade, the new commander of the Army of the Potomac, was meeting with key subordinates on July 2, 1863, when Confederate guns on the southern end of the field erupted, announcing Lee's attack against the Federal left flank. Without his own mount readily available, Meade borrowed "Slicky," Alfred Pleasonton's horse, and rode to the endangered flank. General Pleasonton is seen above holding the reins as Meade takes a salute from Winfield Scott Hancock, commander of Second Corps. *Courtesy Gallon Historical Art, Gettysburg, Pennsylvania*

response to Longstreet's attack. When the Confederate artillery fire broke over the southern end of the field announcing Lee's intention to strike that sector, Meade was holding a meeting with his corps commanders. Up until that time, he was still apparently unaware that Lee was planning to strike his left. Sickles, however, had already moved his Third Corps into an exposed position, and John Sedgwick's Sixth Corps was not yet up and was not expected to be available for battle that day.[23] Meade therefore turned to George Sykes, who recalled that he was ordered to hurry his three divisions south and hold the left flank of the army "at all hazards."[24]

The decision to commit Sykes to shore up the army's left flank was prudent, but Meade did not yet know how many men it would take to stop the determined Confederate attack against his left. The horns of Lee's echelon attack dilemma were already hoisting Meade in the air—and he did not yet know it. By committing the entire Fifth Corps to the southern end of the field before a single Confederate soldier had advanced from Warfield or Seminary ridges, Meade was in effect gambling that Sykes' divisions would not be needed elsewhere.

With Sykes' orders in hand, Meade rode south behind his line to see what kind of trouble Sickles had gotten himself into. The old engineer didn't need long to

Reacting to the pressure of the Confederate cannonade on the afternoon of July 2, Meade dispatched Brigadier General Gouverneur K. Warren, chief engineer of the Army of the Potomac, to Little Round Top to make certain that the high ground was garrisoned. As a result of Warren's subsequent efforts, the anchor position for the Federal left flank was secured. *Courtesy Gallon Historical Art, Gettysburg, Pennsylvania*

"Turning Point"

survey the new Third Corps position and realize it was a weak position and too late to change it. He also seemed to sense that Fifth Corps might not be enough to save Sickles, or that Sykes would not arrive in time to properly deploy and assist his comrades in driving back the heavy attack. After advising Sickles that Fifth Corps was en route, Meade authorized the corps leader he despised to "send for support from [Hancock's] Second Corps."[25]

Meade was concerned about his left flank being turned, but his memories of past battles against the Army of Northern Virginia had already prompted him to make contingency plans in case the Army of the Potomac was driven from the field. Earlier in the day, Daniel Butterfield, Meade's chief of staff, had instructed Sedgwick to march his Sixth Corps towards Gettysburg as far as possible and take up a strong position behind the rest of the army "in the event of the general [Meade] being compelled to withdraw."[26] At about 5:00 p.m., as Hood's men were sweeping into Rose Woods and washing around Devil's Den and over Round Top, Meade drew up additional plans: Alfred Pleasonton, the army's cavalry chief, was to mount up whatever cavalry and horse artillery he had on hand, find a position in the rear, and be prepared to cover the retreat of the Federal army.[27]

*   *   *

As Meade was making contingency plans in case of defeat and committing his ready reserves into the action, Hood's infantry continued to surge forward against the formidable defensive positions stretching from Rose Woods to Houck's Ridge to the Devil's Den. "Exposed to the artillery fire from the heights in front and on our left, as well as to the musketry of the [Federal] infantry, it required all the courage and steadiness of the veterans who composed the Army of Northern Virginia . . . to face the storm," wrote General Law after the war.[28] Closing to the attack, part of

Law's Brigade, along with the 4th and 5th Texas, swung around Devil's Den, crushed Ward's left flank regiment, the 4th Maine, and began peppering Yankee reinforcements pouring into Plum Run Valley (the ground between Houck's Ridge and the western base of Little Round Top). At the same time, the right wing of Robertson's Texas Brigade and the remainder of Law's Alabamians were picking their way down Round Top's wooded northern grade and struggling up the steep and rocky slopes of Little Round Top, where Vincent's Federal regiments were waiting for them.[29]

While Law was pounding Ward's left flank around Devil's Den, the left wing of the Texas Brigade was slugging it out with Ward's center in Rose Woods on Houck's Ridge. In many respects, this focused action characterized the entire southern end of the July 2 battlefield in miniature. Ward's Federals enjoyed the advantage of defensive tactics positioned on higher ground with supporting artillery (Smith's battery), their right flank was fairly secure, and they outnumbered the Confederates at the point of attack by a margin of about two to one. Despite these considerable advantages, the Southern infantry prevailed in this sector in a convincing fashion. Two Federal regiments assailed Robertson's left flank (Colonel Van Manning's 3rd Arkansas) in an attempt to turn it but were driven back with heavy losses. With support from a pair of Tige Anderson's Georgia regiments, Manning's Arkansans moved deeper into the southern part of Rose Woods and advanced up Houck's Ridge through a hail of bullets that tore into their front and left flank, dislodging part of Ward's brigade and capturing 25 prisoners in the process.[30]

A bit to the south on Houck's Ridge, the 1st Texas, operating with Company I of the 4th Texas, was locked in a heated struggle against two Federal regiments and several guns of Smith's 4th New York Light Battery. Fortunately for the Texans, Captain James Reilly of the Rowan North Carolina Artillery had limbered his battery from its position

"Mrs. Wigfall's Wedding Dress"

The 1st Texas Infantry advances into battle at Gettysburg against Smith's 4th New York Light Artillery on Houck's Ridge proudly displaying the "Second Wigfall Wedding Dress Flag." The new state banner replaced the original "Wigfall Wedding Dress" flag, which had been lost in the Cornfield at Sharpsburg. The silk for both flags was donated by Mrs. Louis T. Wigfall. *Courtesy Gallon Historical Art, Gettysburg, Pennsylvania*

Positioned on the far right of John Bell Hood's Division at the outset of the fighting on July 2 was the Rowan North Carolina Artillery under Captain James Reilly. Reilly later moved his guns up with the advancing infantry and helped clear enemy infantry and artillery off Houck's Ridge. *Courtesy Gallon Historical Art, Gettysburg, Pennsylvania*

"Reilly's Battery"

along Warfield Ridge and brought the pieces forward to lend them close fire support. Reilly, who was known for his audacity and called "Old Tarantula" by his men, exercised daring personal initiative by pushing his guns so close to Houck's Ridge.[31] It is likely that this is exactly the type of support Hood was preparing to order Major Haskell to perform when he was struck down on the Bushman farm. J. M. Polk of Company I, 4th Texas, was more than happy to reap the benefit of Reilly's bravery. Polk, who was reloading his rifle from behind "a big rock" on the southwestern slope of Houck's Ridge "could see Captain Reilly's Battery a little to our right and he was cleaning off the top of [Houck's Ridge]. There was a solid blaze of fire in front of his battery." Raking the Federal defenders with canister and case shot, the North Carolina gunners fired as fast as possible.[32]

With Reilly's guns blazing in support, the Confederate infantry rushed forward. In what a participant described as "one of the wildest, fiercest struggles of the war,"[33] the 1st Texas, together with Company I of the 4th Texas and supported on its right by the 15th Georgia of Benning's Brigade, raised the Rebel Yell and charged across a triangular field of ground just northwest of Devil's Den on their way up the steep slope of Houck's Ridge. At the top the gray warriors jumped over a low stone wall and planted the Lone Star flag on the heights. The charge defeated Ward's 86th and 124th New York regiments and captured three 10-pounder Parrotts of Smith's battery.[34] Within a few minutes the remainder of Benning's Georgians joined the 1st Texas and 15th Georgia atop Houck's Ridge, extending the line southward into Devil's Den. Southern rifle fire poured downhill into the flank and rear of the 40th New York, part of Col. Philippe de Trobriand's brigade that had arrived in Plum Run Valley to help stem the onslaught there. In addition to driving back the New Yorkers, the mixed units from Robertson's, Law's and Benning's brigades threw back the 4th Maine and 99th Pennsylvania, both of Ward's brigade, as well as the 6th New Jersey from Colonel George Burling's brigade. The success of the climatic charge up

Houck's Ridge killed or wounded 145 New Yorkers and probably captured, at a minimum, "between 140 to 200 prisoners." Colonel Dudley M. DuBose, colonel of the 15th Georgia, believed the catch of prisoners was even higher. My command, he later reported, "took fully as many of the enemy's prisoners as I had men in my regiment [about 375]." Considering the steep grade of Houck's Ridge, the stone wall protecting its defenders, and all the other advantages enjoyed by the Federals, the capture of the ridge and Devil's Den was no small achievement.[35]

The Texans, Georgians, and Alabamians did not have much time to savor their hard-won victory. From the top of Houck's Ridge and amidst the boulders of Devil's Den they could see other Southerners to their right front moving up a substantially more formidable position: directly before them across Plum Run Valley was the rock-strewn slope of Little Round Top, crowned with Vincent's four regiments and supported by a battery of 10-pounder Parrott rifles positioned on the summit.[36] Up the southwestern slopes of eminence struggled several regiments of Law's Alabamians and most of the 4th and 5th Texas regiments. To the left about 300-400 yards away, heavy Federal reinforcements could be seen pouring into the area. These men, two brigades from James Barnes' First Division, Sykes' Fifth Corps (Vincent's Third Brigade belonged to this same division), were heading west across the valley just north of Little Round Top to support Sickles' crumbling Third Corps line in the vicinity of the Wheatfield. Even more troops bearing the Stars and Stripes were visible behind them (Romeyn Ayres' Second Division, Sykes' Fifth Corps). Their presence meant the Confederates atop Houck's Ridge and around Devil's Den could not advance east across Plum Run Valley and join the Alabamians and Texans in the attack on Round Top without completely exposing their left flank and rear. McIvor Law and other Southern officers on the scene already knew of the fate that had befallen Federal regiments caught in the low ground between the ridge and Little Round Top, and they were not about to sacrifice their men uselessly. The carnage there was so heavy the battle's participants dubbed it the "Valley of Death." The small area due east of Devil's Den and Plum Run was known forever after as the "Slaughter Pen," while the stream itself, which ran pink from the blood of the corpses littering its banks, was called "Bloody Run."

The far right wing of the division suddenly found itself bogged down in the face of Vincent's determined defenders hugging the southwestern forward slope of Little Round Top. Unable to come to grips with the enemy, Law's assault had devolved into a bloody slug fest and the Southerners were getting the worst of it. Additional support to carry the height was desperately needed. If it would come at all, it would arrive in one of four ways: additional infantry launched directly against the western face of the hill, which would overlap Vincent's right flank and hopefully collapse resistance on Little Round Top; additional infantry directly up the face of the hill into Vincent's line in an attempt to overwhelm it; additional infantry against the south and southeastern face of the hill beyond Vincent's left flank; or additional artillery firepower to pry the defenders from the forward slope. Any additional

"Little Round Top and the Valley of Death." The capture of Houck's Ridge (foreground) by the Confederates of John Bell Hood's Division during the fighting on July 2 meant that they could bring considerable firepower to bear on Federal units in Plum Run Valley (center) and those positioned on the deforested western face of Little Round Top (background). Unfortunately, the impressive field of fire offered by the Houck's Ridge position was never fully utilized. *Courtesy Gallon Historical Art, Gettysburg, Pennsylvania*

Confederate infantry would have to come from the left flank of Hood's Division, but that portion of the line was waging a desperate fight with the Federals along Stony Hill and in Rose Woods, the western and southern boundaries, respectively, of the critical Wheatfield sector. Law, therefore, had to drive these Federals from their strong positions in order to free up troops from the division's left to support the regiments battling and dying on Little Round Top.

It was exactly for moments like this that Napoleon organized his armies so that at least one artillery specialist was on the staff of every division commander. Fifty years later, not a single division staff of any American army was either large enough or specialized along the Napoleonic model. If there had been an artillery specialist on Hood's staff that day, he could not have failed to appreciate the opportunity beckoning him. Spread out on the forward slope of Little Round Top, Vincent's four regiments (and above and slightly north on the summit, Hazlett's battery of 10-pounder Parrott rifles) were separated from Houck's Ridge by a distance of 400 to 500 yards—perfectly suited for the large-caliber 12-pounder Napoleons. The distance was too far for the infantry on Little Round Top to be particularly effective against artillery crews, but smoothbore cannons firing from Houck's Ridge and supported by sharpshooters from Devil's Den and the regiments of infantry moving against Little Round Top could punish the Federals on the higher elevation with case shot, canister, and minié balls.

Since there were no troops available to directly reinforce the attack up Little Round Top, and it was too dangerous for Rock Benning and the left wing of Robertson's Texas Brigade to expose their flank by advancing off Houck's Ridge, the assailants of Little Round Top needed Henry's artillery battalion to move forward, unlimber on the ridge, and bombard the defenders. Henry's command had 11 Napoleons. If the entire battalion could be brought to bear, the fire from these bronze field pieces, augmented by iron rifles, not only would have made Little Round Top a far more difficult proposition for the Federals to hold, but in all likelihood would have turned its rocky slopes into a charnel house of Federal dead and wounded.

Perhaps it was this point in the battle that Hood's absence was most keenly felt. His infantry had already advanced one mile, defeated the Federals on Houck's Ridge and around Devil's Den, and were poised to continue the echelon attack. Given his experience on such a wide variety of fields, it is difficult to imagine a combat officer as capable as Hood failing to see the need for Henry's guns to be brought forward to support the infantry. But the division leader was lying in an ambulance far to the rear—and McIvor Law was not John Bell Hood. Instead of remaining in the middle of the division line and riding up Houck's Ridge to ascertain what needed to be done to secure Little Round Top and turn Meade's left, Law instead "halted [the] line" because of his concern for the division's left flank. Instead of sending an aide to request help from Lafayette McLaws' Division, Law personally "hurried back to the ridge from which [he] had originally advanced" to discuss the situation. There, Law found Joe Kershaw and his brigade of South Carolinians waiting under cover of Biesecker's Woods for orders to advance. After hearing Law explain that his men were sorely needed, Kershaw evidently forwarded the request to McLaws who, with permission from Longstreet, authorized the South Carolinian to advance, triggering the second phase of Lee's echelon assault against Meade's left flank.[37]

With Law absent from the front, Hood's infantry attack stalled on a line running from the southern end of Houck's Ridge through Devil's Den and across the base of Little Round Top. The only orders for any Confederate artillery to come forward in that vicinity had already been given by Captain Reilly to his North Carolina battery. No other guns were advanced near Houck's Ridge to fire against the Federal defenders on Little Round Top. Law never mentioned this issue in any of his postwar writings, so it is logical to assume he did not recognize the opportunity and did not order Henry or Haskell to bring the other batteries forward. Further, neither officer chose to act on his own initiative. This is especially curious since Reilly had already shown the way, and the eight guns under Bachman and Garden had begun the fight limbered (ready to move to exploit opportunity), had not yet fired a shot, and could have been brought forward more easily than Reilly's own pieces, which had been relocated from the extreme right of the Confederate line near Houck's Ridge.[38]

Even without the guns, the attacking foot soldiers scored some small successes on Little Round Top's rocky slopes. Vincent's men were suffering steady casualties and Vincent himself was mortally wounded when a bullet pierced his left groin. Determined pressure from the 4th Texas struggling up the rocky slopes threw back and then broke Vincent's right regiment, the 16th Michigan, which was in the process of realigning itself. Had it not been for the timely arrival of Federal reinforcements in the form of Stephen Weed's brigade, which plugged the gap left by the 16th Michigan and then firmly secured Vincent's threatened flank, the Texas infantry might have unraveled the enemy line. The most studied aspect of the fight for Little Round Top took place on Vincent's far left, which came within a whisker of being turned by William Oates' 15th Alabama. As the exhausted and thirsty Alabamians charged up the wooded slope, an obscure school teacher named Joshua Lawrence Chamberlain and his 20th Maine threw them back with a determined bayonet attack in a hand-to-hand encounter that may well have saved the Federal position for Meade.[39]

Hood's Division was obviously in need of a overall guiding hand. While we will never know whether he would have ordered Henry's artillery to relocate to Houck's Ridge, Hood *was* in the process of bringing up the two batteries under Garden and Bachman when he was wounded. The lone artillery shell that knocked Hood from the battle, combined with Law's absence at a critical time, meant no one was available to exploit the assault to its fullest potential. Major Haskell believed Hood's wounding, combined with the inordinate amount of time that it took Law to assume command of the division, conspired to close the narrow window of opportunity to have influenced the outcome of the fighting on Little Round Top. "It was over an hour," Haskell claimed, "before [Law] got the message and got to the scene, and by that time the enemy was strongly posted [on Little Round Top] and the opportunity was lost."[40]

*   *   *

Although Hood's assault had not turned the left flank of the Army of the Potomac or captured Little Round Top, it had forced Meade to commit large numbers of troops into the fight, which was one of the primary objectives for launching an echelon assault. And now it was Lafayette McLaws' turn to strike. Joe Kershaw and his South Carolinians advanced into line on the left of "Tige" Anderson's Georgians about 5:30 p.m. Anderson had previously attacked but could not dislodge the Federals of Colonel de Trobriand's brigade from their defensive perch on Stony Hill and Rose Woods. With his left flank unsupported and compromised by de Trobriand's able tactical maneuvering, and the sudden appearance of substantial Federal reinforcements in the form of two brigades from Sykes' Fifth Corps, Anderson pulled his men back and regrouped. The newly arrived Federals, about 1,700 combatants under the direction of Colonels William Tilton and Jacob Sweitzer (Barnes' division), took up a position on Stony Hill, which had the effect of extending de Trobriand's right flank well beyond Anderson's left. Though significantly weakened by straggling, Tilton and Sweitzer combined their small numbers with remaining defenders in the Stony Hill vicinity and enjoyed the advantage of terrain. As a result, they would outnumber the Confederates moving toward them.[41]

The introduction of Tilton's and Sweitzer's reduced and fatigued brigades into the action on July 2 serves as a vivid illustration of why Lee believed it was important to take the fight to the Federals that day before Meade could concentrate his army or have time to recover his stragglers after forced marches to the battlefield. Tilton's four regiments numbered 1,175 officers and men on June 30; Sweitzer's four regiments, 1,744. The hard marching to Gettysburg took its toll on these brigades and substantially reduced their numbers. By the afternoon of July 2, Tilton could muster only 655 men for action, a loss of almost 45% of his strength. Of Sweitzer's four regiments, only three were engaged that day (the 9th Massachusetts was left on the right flank on picket duty), and these numbered but 1,010 combatants, or a reduction of 20% for those who reached the southern end of the field.[42] Or, put another way, of the 2,435 men in these seven regiments available for action on June 30, only 1,665, or 68% of them, had the stamina to remain in the ranks when the hard-marching Fifth Corps went into action late on the afternoon of July 2. In a succinct but understated observation, General Abner Doubleday noted after the war: "The Fifth and Sixth Corps would necessarily be very fatigued after making a forced march."[43] Of course General Lee had no way of knowing exactly how much fatigue and straggling Meade's army would experience chasing the Confederates in

Pennsylvania. But Lee suspected his enemy would suffer significant losses through straggling—and Meade could recover quickly if Lee had assumed a defensive posture and passed the initiative over to him.

*   *   *

The man shepherding more than 2,000 Palmetto Staters toward Tilton and Sweitzer was a prewar lawyer without formal military training. Joe Kershaw raised a militia unit while serving in the state legislature and offered it to the young Confederacy when the Civil War began. Brigade command soon followed. His talents for battlefield leadership rose to the fore at Williamsburg and Savage's Station, after which his division commander, Lafayette McLaws, warmly praised his services. The fighting at Harpers Ferry and Sharpsburg during the 1862 Maryland Campaign served to confirm McLaws' observations. The bloody fighting at the stone wall at Fredericksburg offered Kershaw an opportunity to demonstrate the capacity to command large bodies of troops. When General T. R. R. Cobb fell, Kershaw calmly assumed control of the sector and conspicuously orchestrated the defeat of several waves of attacking Federals. Wealthy, religiously devout, and intelligent, the 41-year old had distinguished himself on every field. He was about to do so again.[44]

Kershaw's half-dozen units stretched from the P. Snyder farm on the right to just below the Sherfy Peach Orchard on the left. His men crossed the Emmitsburg Road and tramped over the Rose farm heading straight for the Stony Hill position. The irregular terrain snaked the Federal line of battle from the Peach Orchard to the Rose Woods southeast of Stony hill into a large Z-shaped front. The first leg of the "Z" comprised Federal infantry and a line of batteries running east from the Peach

Joseph Brevard Kershaw (1822-1894)

Even though he did not have any formal military training, Joe Kershaw evolved into one of the Army of Northern Virginia's finest combat leaders. His brigade of South Carolinians spearheaded the attack of McLaws' Division on July 2. Kershaw led the division at Chickamauga in the fall of 1863, and served well at that level until the end of the war.

Library of Congress

Orchard along the Wheatfield Road to near Stony Hill and facing south. Sweitzer's men formed the second middle leg, facing generally west on Stony Hill from near the road stretching south into Rose Woods. The last leg of the Z-shaped line was comprised of Tilton's regiments and de Trobriand's remnants facing generally south. Sweitzer's right flank near the Wheatfield Road would have been easily flanked if Kershaw's entire brigade could have been brought to bear. William Barksdale's Brigade, Kershaw's support on the left, was not released at the same time. Thus, as Kershaw's men swept obliquely across the Rose farm, his left regiments were struck by artillery fire coming from the Peach Orchard and Wheatfield Road line, and his front was hammered by a portion of Tilton's and Sweitzer's infantry on Stony Hill. The South Carolinian split his brigade into two wings to deal with these problems. While his three left regiments, about 900 men

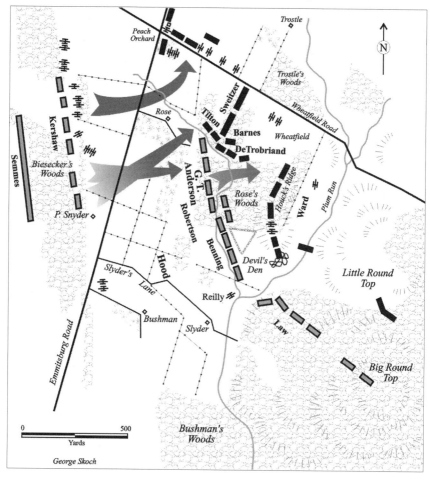

Longstreet Releases the Right Wing of McLaws' Division, July 2, 1863

from the 2nd and 8th regiments, and 3rd South Carolina Battalion, pivoted north and headed for the Federal guns along Wheatfield Road, Kershaw skillfully directed his right wing, less than 1,300 men from the 3rd, 7th and 15th South Carolina, straight for Stony Hill and Tilton's exposed right flank. General James Barnes may have seen the flanking movement and ordered Tilton's regiments to retire before the South Carolinians struck. Regardless, the result was that Tilton's brigade gave way almost without firing a shot, which left Sweitzer's three regiments without support and flooding rearward into Trostle's Woods.[45]

The pressure exerted by Kershaw's right wing, coupled with another advance by "Tige" Anderson's Georgians against de Trobriand's embattled regiments and what remained of Ward's command cleared out the remainder of the Federals from Stony Hill and Rose Woods and in turn uncovered the Wheatfield sometime after 6:00 p.m. Several regiments waged a heroic rearguard action to allow the bulk of the retreating Federals to escape the Confederate jaws snapping shut from two directions. Ward's 20th Indiana stood its ground and lost 159 of its 468 Hoosiers, and General Birney personally ordered de Trobriand's 17th Maine to charge into the Confederates to help stem the tide.[46]

By this time four Federal brigades from two different divisions (Ward and de Trobriand, Tilton and Sweitzer) had been driven to and through the Wheatfield. There was little time for the Southerners to reorganize, however, and within the space of a few minutes four fresh Federal brigades arrived from the north and swept into the trampled field of grain. The welcomed reinforcements were from Brigadier General John C. Caldwell's First Division of Hancock's Second Corps. Hancock, it will be recalled, witnessed Sickles' advance to the Peach Orchard and had calmly predicted he would not be able to hold the line for long. He could not, then, have been surprised when word arrived from Meade shortly after Longstreet opened his assault to send a division to support Third Corps. Hancock promptly complied by sending Caldwell, who was instructed to get his battle orders directly from General Sykes. Meade was steadily siphoning troops from other portions of the field to stem the assault against his far left. First all of Sykes' Fifth Corps had been dispatched, and now an entire division from the center of his line on Cemetery Ridge. Would Meade have the men to respond aggressively to heavy assaults against other portions of his line?[47]

Caldwell formed his four brigades of about 3,200 infantry in successive lines in Trostle's Woods facing south.[48] Although he could not have known it, his forthcoming attack would be the only organized division-sized thrust delivered by Meade's army at Gettysburg. Two Federal brigades under Colonels Edward Cross and John Brooke attacked first from Trostle's Wood south across the Wheatfield and into the northern fringes of Rose Woods. The assault overlapped the eastern flank of the Confederate line facing the Wheatfield and forced part of Anderson's Brigade to fall back through the timber.[49] As these men drove back the Georgians, Caldwell's other pair of brigades under Colonel Patrick Kelly and Brigadier General Samuel

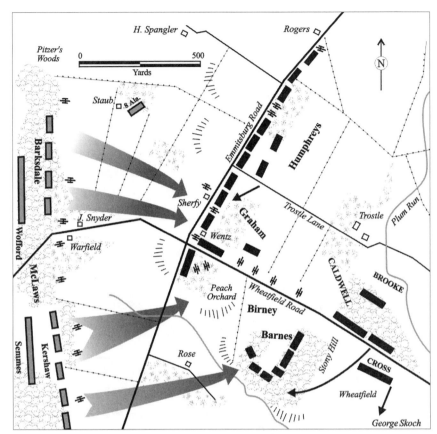

Longstreet Releases the Left Wing of McLaws' Division, July 2, 1863

Zook formed for the attack. Zook's men had some difficulty passing through Barnes' disordered infantry, which were finally ordered to lay down so the Pennsylvanians and New Yorkers could get to the front. Within a short time Kelly's Irish Brigade and Zook's four regiments struck southwest against Stony Hill, held by two of Kershaw's regiments. Like the Georgians, the South Carolinians were unable to stand their ground and fell back in the direction of the Rose Farm.[50]

Matters were beginning to look grim for Kershaw, who was working hard to re-form his 3rd and 7th South Carolina regiments. At that moment he witnessed one of the most stirring sights of the day. Tramping east and straddling the Wheatfield Road in line abreast were five Georgia regiments screened by a battalion of skirmishers, all under the command of the "very ambitious . . . and . . . most daring" William Tatum Wofford. Unbeknownst to Kershaw, while he had been fighting over Stony Hill, William Barksdale's Mississippians had attacked and crushed the Peach Orchard salient, which in turn allowed Wofford to guide his brigade up and support

"The Pride of Erin." Generals Meade and Hancock responded to the Confederate *en échelon* attack by dispatching division after division of Federal infantry to the southern end of the field. One of these, John Caldwell's from Hancock's Second Corps, was rushed to the Wheatfield, where the legendary Irish Brigade confronted Joe Kershaw's South Carolinians. All four of Caldwell's brigades were shattered on July 2, 1863. *Courtesy Gallon Historical Art, Gettysburg, Pennsylvania*

William Tatum Wofford
(1824-1884)

The Georgia lawyer-turned-soldier was another of Lafayette McLaws' brigadiers without formal military training. He led his brigade on July 2 boldly, driving it into and through the Wheatfield maelstrom. As he was herding his Georgians past First Corps batteries and into the fight, one artillerist yelled out, "Hurrah for you of the bald head!"

Library of Congress

Kershaw's left flank. (Barksdale's attack is detailed below.) Wofford was the distinguished colonel of the hard-fighting 18th Georgia when that regiment was part of the Texas Brigade prior to the army's reorganization in October 1862. When regiments from the same state began to be consolidated into homogeneous brigades, Wofford and his men joined other Georgia units under Thomas R. R. Cobb and gained lasting fame on Marye's Heights at Fredericksburg, where they decimated advancing Federals in front of the Sunken Road. After Cobb was killed Wofford assumed command of the brigade (he had temporarily led the Texas Brigade at Sharpsburg). He distinguished himself on May 4, 1863, during the fighting at Chancellorsville, and was about to do so again at Gettysburg.[51]

Wofford had deployed in support of Barksdale's Mississippians and had watched with great interest as they swept away the Federals holding the high ground around the Sherfy orchard. Moving up in Barksdale's wake and ahead of Wofford's troops was General Longstreet, who was closely monitoring the progress of his attack. Longstreet was so anxious to get to the Peach Orchard that his courier, William Youngblood, had to remind the corps leader that he was riding far in advance of Wofford's Brigade and recklessly exposing himself. Longstreet, recalled Youngblood, "checked his horse and held him until Wofford's men had gotten in front."[52] McLaws also remembered seeing Longstreet urging the Georgians onward. "General Longstreet went forward some distance with Wofford's [men]," wrote McLaws, "urging them on by voice and his personal example to the most earnest efforts. The troops needed no outside impulse, but his conduct was gallant and inspiring."[53] The image Longstreet cut that day also made an impression on Moxley Sorrel, "Old Pete's" staff officer. Longstreet, he recalled, was "personally leading the attack with splendid effect. His fine horsemanship as he rode, hat in hand, and martial figure, were most inspiring."[54] The high drama of the moment electrified Wofford's Georgians. "I saw Wofford coming in in splendid style," remembered Kershaw, who observed the heroes of Fredericksburg move past the Peach Orchard and fall in on his exposed left flank. In addition to Wofford's 1,600 men, Paul Semmes' Brigade also made an appearance, marching up behind Kershaw's right flank. The appearance of these brigades breathed new life into the exhausted Confederates south of Wheatfield Road, who surged to renew the attack against Caldwell's bloodied brigades.[55]

After clearing the Wheatfield, Caldwell's brigades had taken up positions in the woods bordering the trampled expanse of grain. The line north of the Wheatfield Road (essentially Caldwell's right flank) was held by Tilton's skittish brigade, which had rallied and taken up a new position on the western edge of Trostle's Woods. Tilton's men remained in this position while Sickles' Third Corps units in the Peach Orchard were being crushed by Barksdale's Mississippians. The retreating Federals from Charles Graham's brigade ran through Tilton's regiments as Wofford's Georgians swept down Wheatfield Road in pursuit. Tilton's brigade retreated as well and did not stop until it had crossed Plum Run and taken up a position in some woods there. A mortified Tilton later complained that Sickles' defeated troops "greatly embarrassed" and disrupted his command, and that he decided to "save my brigade from great disaster after it could no longer do any good in front" by a retreat. While this is possible, it is more likely that Tilton saw the shaken survivors of Graham's brigade running through his ranks and decided then and there that the irresistible tide of Wofford's Brigade bearing down on his command was something he wanted nothing to do with.[56]

Tilton's ignominious flight from Trostle's Woods left Caldwell's right flank completely exposed—with the Wheatfield Road acting like a giant spear pointing the way into his rear area. Like a row of dominos, Caldwell's brigades fell hard. Wofford's line overlapped and crushed Zook's front near Stony Hill and then enfiladed and rolled up the right flank of Kelly's Irish Brigade, which in turn uncovered Brooke's command on Stony Hill and in Rose Woods. Kershaw advanced at the same time with his 15th South Carolina; Georgians from Semmes' and Anderson's brigades joined in. The attack turned and routed Brooke's regiments which in turn uncovered Cross' regiments in the northern fringe of Rose Woods. Cross' men were already suffering some confusion and were almost out of ammunition. The sudden appearance of thousands of screaming Southerners on their front and flank was enough to send them tumbling back across the Wheatfield with the rest of the division streaming before them.[57]

Caldwell had called on Sweitzer for support before he fully realized the peril facing his division. When Barnes, Sweitzer's division commander, approved of the move, Sweitzer advanced his regiments out of Trostle's Woods south into the Wheatfield. Sweitzer was positioning his units when Caldwell's division unraveled and vacated the area. Caldwell's meltdown left Sweitzer's three regiments standing alone in the open, and they did not take long to attract the attention of the advancing Confederates. Protected by the timber bordering the western and southern boundaries of the grain field, Georgians and South Carolinians swept the Federal units with a murderous fire. In a matter of minutes Sweitzer's brave regiments lost more than 40% of their strength and gave way in an effort to escape the maelstrom.[58]

The confused and bloody fighting in the Wheatfield sector was not yet over. While Tilton was skedaddling from Trostle's Woods and just prior to the savaging and scattering of Caldwell's and Sweitzer's brigades, two more Federal brigades, U. S. Regulars from Romeyn Ayres' Second Division, Sykes' Fifth Corps, were committed to the fighting. One of Ayres' brigades under Stephen Weed had already been diverted to Little Round Top, where its arrival turned back the 4th Texas and secured Vincent's crumbling right flank.[59] The Regulars, meanwhile, had sloshed across Plum Run north of Little Round Top and halted in and around a small rise known today as "Day's (or Regular's) Hill." Colonel Sidney Burbank's Second Brigade was in the lead and deployed in battalions abreast, while Colonel Hannibal Day's First Brigade remained in columns of battalions behind Burbank's men. Sykes, who was watching this from the slope of Little Round Top, ordered Ayres to advance the 2,100 Regulars into the Wheatfield.[60]

Ayres had moved his battalions to the eastern edge of the Wheatfield and was conferring with Caldwell about a joint advance against the Confederates in Rose Woods when Caldwell's division came apart. Burbank's Regulars were in the process of conducting a left wheel into the Wheatfield when all hell broke loose around them. Without Caldwell's or Sweitzer's men to shield them, Burbank and Day were isolated, out of position, and outnumbered. Drawing fire from the 1st Texas and 15th Georgia on Houck's Ridge, struck by Anderson's Georgians and a portion of Kershaw's South Carolinians on their left and front, and assailed by Wofford's Georgians on their right, Burbank's men were cut to pieces in a matter of minutes. "In the midst of this inferno, whole companies evaporated," explained one writer.[61] Engulfed in a torrent of Southern lead and steel, the last Federal resistance in the Wheatfield folded up "like a jack-knife."[62] Burbank's retreating troops fled across Plum Run and made for the cover of friendly cannon on the northern shoulder of Little Round Top while Day's battalions did their best to cover the debacle unfolding before their eyes. In the space of a few minutes two brigades of Regulars had been devastated. From the Wheatfield to Plum Run, the ground was strewn with Ayres' men. Of the 80 officers and "less than 900 muskets" Burbank carried into battle, 447 remained behind. Day's men, who had deployed behind Burbank's troops, suffered less but still lost 382 casualties of about 1,200 taken into action. Neither organization inflicted many casualties in return. Thus far Longstreet's seven committed infantry brigades (Law, Robertson, Benning, Anderson, Kershaw, Semmes, and Wofford) from Little Round Top to the Sherfy Peach Orchard had met and defeated a dozen Federal brigades, shattering 10 of them.[63]

Flushed with victory, Wofford relentlessly pushed his Georgians east past the Wheatfield until he spotted Walcott's 3rd Massachusetts Battery unlimbered immediately north of Wheatfield Road east of Plum Run along J. Weikert's lane. The gunners did not have any supporting infantry to protect their six 12-pounder Napoleons. Although formidable as part of a line of battle, a battery standing alone was extremely vulnerable. Seeing nothing but six guns in their front, Wofford's Georgians pressed their advantage and drove across the west branch of Plum Run. The Federal gunners beat a hasty retreat after spiking only one of their six pieces. Hooping and hollering, Wofford's victorious infantry continued past Walcott's guns and halted at a stone wall about 60 yards east of the Weikert lane. The position was an exceptionally strong one, overlooking the muddy banks of the smaller eastern branch of Plum Run and anchored on the northern flank by Weikert's Woods. Wofford's advanced position was just in range of Weed's Federal infantry and a few artillery pieces on Little Round Top.[64]

About 300 yards southeast of where Walcott's guns had been overrun, and only about 240 yards from Wofford's right flank was another Federal battery of six

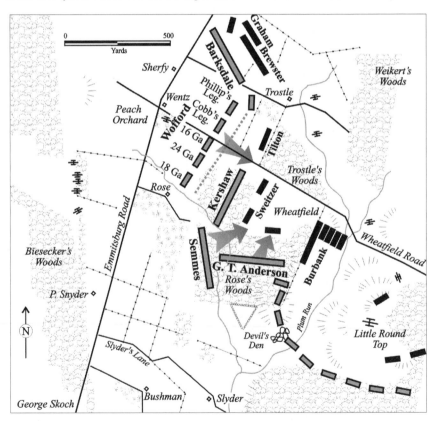

Wofford's Brigade Sweeps the Wheatfield, July 2, 1863

Napoleons belonging to Gibbs' Battery L, 1st Ohio Artillery, also of Sykes' Fifth Corps. Four of Gibbs' guns were unlimbered on the lower portion of the northern base of Little Round Top, while the remaining pair were positioned halfway up the northern shoulder of the hill. All of them were working overtime sending double charges of canister west into Rose Woods and the Wheatfield region held by Kershaw, Semmes, and Anderson. Splashing over Plum Run, disorganized fragments of Confederate infantry came face-to-face with Gibbs' death-dealing Napoleons, whose fire drove back what Gibbs described as "the irregular, yelling line."[65] Wofford could have easily taken Gibbs' battery if the guns had remained unsupported. Federal infantrymen, however, soon materialized and deployed near the four pieces south of the Wheatfield Road, the long blue line stretching to the northern slopes of Little Round Top. Another body of infantry took up a position about 150 yards to the right rear, or northeast, of Gibbs' guns along a line near present-day Sedgwick Avenue.

These reinforcements were advance elements from two different corps, all sent to keep Meade's left flank from collapsing. The infantry immediately south of Gibbs' artillery was from Brigadier General Samuel Crawford's Third Division, Ayres' Fifth Corps, while the brigade north of Gibbs' smooth bores belonged to Brigadier General Frank Wheaton's Third Division, John Sedgwick's Sixth Corps. The appearance of heavy Federal reinforcements, coupled with the approaching dusk and a shortage of cartridges convinced the Confederates who had briefly crossed to the eastern side of bloody Plum Run to retrace their steps across the Valley of Death.[66] Wofford, meanwhile, who was well north and east of Anderson, Semmes, and Kershaw, could not see any enemy in his front and thus believed his Georgians had pierced the Federal line. Without support for his flanks, however, he was reluctant to push further east. And that assistance was not going to arrive. The Federal reinforcements pouring into the area north of Little Round Top had stopped the Confederate thrust from the Wheatfield and Rose Woods, and Law's brigades (Hood's Division) had run out of steam attacking the opposite side of the rocky heights. In addition, the inordinately large number of Confederate general officers knocked out of action hampered Southern efforts to mount a coordinated effort. In addition to the early wounding of John Bell Hood, "Tige" Anderson, Paul Semmes, and Jerome Robertson had fallen, which meant Joe Kershaw was the only brigadier still standing in the Wheatfield-Stony Hill-Rose Woods area.[67]

Sam Crawford watched the Southern line stagger and recoil and decided to counterattack. By this time he had but one brigade under Colonel William McCandless available. His other, under Colonel Joseph Fisher, had been ordered to support Little Round Top, where the fighting had already ended for the day. When the Regulars finally cleared their front, McCandless' Pennsylvania Reserves left their positions on the northern slope of Little Round Top and swept across the Valley of Death. Supporting McCandless on the right was Colonel David Nevin's Sixth Corps brigade. The right end of McCandless' (and certainly Nevin's) line would have run into Wofford's Georgians had Longstreet not ordered them to retire to a shorter and more secure line. The order astonished Wofford, who had driven every enemy from his front and who now occupied a strong position. One of Wofford's regimental officers, Colonel Goode Bryan of the 16th Georgia, sought out and found Longstreet somewhere behind the brigade and protested the order. "I order you to fall back," was the corps commander's reply. Longstreet, who had two entire divisions to worry about, knew there were no other troops that could be sent to Wofford's support, and thus the brigade needed to be withdrawn to consolidate a defensive line along Sickles' old front. Infuriated that his gains could not be fully exploited, and "apprehensive that his coming back might be misconstrued," Wofford—still full of fight and on horseback with his pistol in hand—skillfully withdrew his men to the west side of Plum Run, where McLaws posted them "under the woods" and along a stone wall at the northwest corner of the blood-soaked Wheatfield.[68]

With a "Hurrah!" McCandless's Pennsylvanians charged into the valley and up toward the Wheatfield. Little more than an annoying flanking fire from the left wing of the Texas Brigade and elements of Benning's Brigade on Houck's Ridge and the Devil's Den greeted them until the line neared the stone wall on the field's eastern boundary. There, mixed Southern commands offered some hand-to-hand resistance before falling back into and through Rose Woods and onto Stony Hill. Unwilling to push his luck, Crawford ordered McCandless to halt his men in the growing darkness. The movement had done little more than adjust the lines as night fell on the field. Nevin's regiments, which had joined in the advance and were but lightly engaged, was the only Sixth Corps brigade engaged on July 2.[69]

Longstreet's assault south of the Peach Orchard had finally spent itself. The seven brigades of infantry engaged there from Hood's and McLaws' divisions had directly confronted 12 Federal brigades. Another three under McCandless, Fisher, and Nevin had been committed to the area. The lateness of their appearance, however, spared them a confrontation with Wofford's fresh Georgians and the combined strength of Anderson's, Semmes' and Kershaw's line. Therefore, of the 15 Federal brigades assigned to the Federal left flank south of the Peach Orchard, only three had not been seriously engaged. Two others under Vincent and Weed had waged a desperate fight for control of Little Round Top. The remaining 10 brigades had either been eviscerated and or so shaken as to be no longer combat worthy. The true significance of what Longstreet accomplished below the Wheatfield Road is often overlooked. The Federals enjoyed there a significant numerical superiority, superior supporting ordnance, and all the advantages of fighting on the defensive—and yet two of every three Federal brigades had been knocked apart.

The only reason Longstreet's leading elements of General Lee's echelon attack had not succeeded in turning the Federal flank was because Meade had committed large numbers of troops to the area. Therefore, Longstreet's seven Confederate brigades fulfilled the secondary purpose of the echelon attack by drawing in a disproportionally large number of enemy troops that would otherwise be available for duty elsewhere. Thus, somewhere up the Federal line running to Cemetery Hill and hooking around to Culp's Hill, Meade's defenses had been appreciably thinned. The accomplishments rendered by the Southern infantrymen under Law, Robertson, Benning, Anderson, Kershaw, Semmes, and Wofford, were enhanced (and in part made possible) by the devastating attack delivered by Longstreet's eighth brigade.

*   *   *

William Barksdale was not a patient man. He had been anxiously waiting to get into the fight for almost two hours, and the wispy white-haired brigadier was rapidly reaching the end of his patience. The 41-year old Tennessee native had moved to Mississippi after graduating from the University of Nashville. There, Barksdale practiced law, edited a pro-slavery newspaper, and dabbled in local politics. His thirst for military action led him into the 2nd Mississippi regiment during the Mexican War, and after the end of the fighting he returned home and rose to prominence as a fiery States' Rights democrat in the United States Congress. When the war began, he entered Confederate service as a colonel and led his 13th Mississippi in an important assault at First Manassas. Gallant actions during the Seven Days' fighting at the head of a brigade brought him to General Lee's attention and Barksdale was promoted to brigadier general in August 1862. He enhanced his reputation as a combat leader during the Sharpsburg Campaign and again at Fredericksburg, where his Mississippians earned lasting glory for their plucky defense of the river line. Most of his regiments had served together since early in the war. There were a number of outstanding brigades in the Army of Northern Virginia, and by the time of Gettysburg, Barksdale's Mississippians ranked among the very best in the army. William Youngblood of Longstreet's staff believed it was a combination of the quality of the men and the leadership capabilities of their brigadier that made Barksdale's outfit such an outstanding formation. "No State ever furnished braver nor better soldiers than that grand old State of Mississippi," Youngblood declared. "No troops were ever commanded by a braver man than General Barksdale."[70] As a former Congressman, Barksdale recognized the political damage that could be inflicted upon the Lincoln administration with a Southern victory on Northern soil, and the prospects for a decisive victory at Gettysburg ran like an electric current through the ranks of his regiments as they waited their turn to attack.

Under Lee's *en échelon* offensive plan, Longstreet had the discretion to decide when to feed his brigades into action. Hood's attack was kicked off shortly after 4:00 p.m., and Longstreet waited patiently along Seminary Ridge for his leading division to turn the enemy flank. The minutes ticked away as thousands of stationary infantrymen listened and watched as Hood's men battled along the Rose Woods-Houck's Ridge-Devil's Den-Round Top line. As First Corps artillery under

William Barksdale (1821-1863)

He was the commander of one of the South's finest brigades, and yet William Barksdale had no formal pre-war military training. Barksdale and his Mississippians compiled an impressive combat record before Gettysburg, but it was their crushing attack against the Peach Orchard salient on July 2, 1863, for which they are most remembered. It was, wrote one journalist, "the grandest charge of the war." Unfortunately, no wartime image of Barksdale exists.

Library of Congress

Cabell and Alexander dueled with the eight Federal batteries posted in and around the Sherfy Farm and Peach Orchard, some of Barksdale's restless soldiers volunteered to help one of the batteries handle their 24-pounder howitzers.[71] More than an hour passed without word from "Old Pete," who was giving the battle a chance to develop before allowing McLaws to slip the leash. By the time McIvor Law rode back to Pitzer's Woods seeking help from Joe Kershaw, it was becoming evident to Longstreet that the growing struggle south of the Peach Orchard was attracting large numbers of Federal troops. It was time to commit additional men. McLaws was finally authorized to release his two right wing brigades under Kershaw and Paul Semmes. Both, as we have seen, advanced to the Stony Hill-Rose Woods sector and rendered valiant service in support of Hood's left flank. To Barksdale's dismay, however, Longstreet refused to allow McLaws to commit his left wing brigades.

McLaws, too, was unhappy with this arrangement. The division commander wanted to protect Kershaw's left flank, and Barksdale was in position to do so by storming the Peach Orchard. Longstreet, of course, understood this and could have ordered McLaws' entire line to advance simultaneously. Instead, he waited to maximize the impact of the echelon attack by drawing more enemy troops below the Wheatfield Road while his artillery softened the Peach Orchard salient with hundreds of rounds of solid, canister, and case shot. Captain Osmond B. Taylor, commander of the Bath Virginia Artillery in Alexander's Battalion, remembered that his four 12-pounder Napoleons had unlimbered "within 500 yards of the enemy's batteries." The gunner was "[ordered] to dislodge them, if possible from the commanding position which they held." To accomplish this, Taylor recalled, I "opened upon the batteries with my four Napoleons, firing canister and spherical case."[72]

McLaws' concern about Kershaw's flank was understandable, but the South Carolinian quickly grasped the tactical situation developing on his left front. Left alone, the line of well-served guns would severely damage his brigade. But this line of guns had a fatal weakness: no infantry was supporting them. Recognizing this, Kershaw issued a direct challenge to the artillery crews along Wheatfield Road by offering them a choice: stand and be overrun or limber and leave; either way, the result would expose the left and rear of the line of Federal infantry facing west along the Emmitsburg Road. As the shell fragments cut through his ranks, Kershaw directed his three left units to "attack the orchard on its left rear." As these men were closing in on the artillery, an order intended for the right half of the brigade advancing against Stony Hill was overheard and through "some unauthorized person," communicated to the brigade's left wing just as they were closing in for the kill along Wheatfield Road. In obedience to orders, the left wing turned and headed east, exposing its flanks to the artillery. Surprised Federal gunners, who were already preparing to move out, returned to their pieces and poured canister and carnage through their ranks. "Hundreds of the bravest and best of Carolina fell," lamented Kershaw, "victims of this fatal blunder." As a result, Kershaw's men ended up bypassing the Wheatfield Road line near the Peach Orchard and taking Stony Hill instead. The experienced Longstreet must have realized that the enemy line stretching from the Peach Orchard northward would have to be assailed *and* turned by Barksdale's eager troops.[73]

Barksdale, meanwhile, had called together his regimental commanders for a conference. After detailing their orders, he emphasized, "The line before you must be broken—to do so let every officer and man animate his comrades by his personal presence in the front line." The officers were instructed to remain on foot in the coming fight because "the government had a great deal of difficulty replacing the horses." The general and members of his staff, however, would remain mounted. The colonels returned to their units and prepared their commands for the coming assault. The drums beat "Assembly," remembered one Mississippi soldier, and the men dropped their packs, blankets, and other unnecessary accouterments that might impede their progress and slow them down. "Every man in the brigade knew that 'our turn' had come at last."[74]

The battle had been raging for almost two hours when the "exceedingly" anxious Barksdale and his Mississippians finally received authorization to attack. Longstreet, who had closely supervised the advance of McLaws' brigades, gave the division commander the go-ahead to release his left-hand brigades shortly after 6:00 p.m. Captain Gazaway Bugg Lamar, Jr., McLaws aide-de-camp, gave Barksdale his orders. "[Barksdale's] face was radiant with joy," wrote one witness. "He was in front of his brigade, hat off, and his long white hair reminded me of the 'white plume of Navarre.'" The ebullient Barksdale rode to the front of his old regiment, the 13th Mississippi, and roared: "Attention, Mississippians! Battalions, Forward!" The commands "Dress to the colors and forward to the foe!" and "Forward, March!" echoed down the line, drums rolled, and the 1,598 officers and men of Barksdale's Brigade emerged from the woods along lower Seminary Ridge to sounds of the blood-curdling Rebel Yell.[75]

About 500 yards to the east a nervous line of Yankee infantry and artillerists stretching along the Emmitsburg Road from the Peach Orchard north beyond the Sherfy Farm waited for Barksdale to strike. The left front, from the orchard to the Trostle farm lane, was held by Brigadier General Charles Graham's 1,500-man Pennsylvania brigade, Birney's First Division, Sickles' Third Corps. Eight pieces of ordnance (six Napoleons and two 3-inch Ordnance rifles) supported Graham's front. Two brigades from Andrew Humphreys' Second Division of the same corps extended the line north beyond Graham's right flank. Colonel William Brewster's New York Excelsior Brigade, about 1,800 strong, stretched to the Klingle property, and Brigadier General Joseph Carr's brigade of similar strength extended the line north almost to the Codori farm. Five more batteries bolstered this line or were sent to strengthen the Wheatfield Road line facing south toward the Rose Farm. In short, Barksdale was being asked to attack and carry a position held by an equal number of men (Graham's front), and one that could be quickly reinforced by another 3,600 more (Brewster and Carr), all supported by dozens of pieces of ordnance.[76]

The Federals had occupied the salient along the swell crowned by the Sherfy Peach Orchard with superior numbers of infantry and excellent artillery, but the deficiencies of the position now played to the Confederates' advantage. By facing west as well as south, the Federals could not concentrate their strength against only one side. Additionally, the infantry and batteries deployed along the Emmitsburg Road had been fully exposed to the long and punishing bombardment dished out by the Confederate artillery battalions under Cabell and Alexander—a pounding that certainly affected their combat worthiness as they readied themselves for the oncoming tide of Mississippians moving across the fields and orchards at the double-quick.

Captain Lamar watched Barksdale riding in front of his fast-moving brigade "as far as the eye could follow, still ahead of his men, leading them on."[77] The Mississippians moved "at top speed," remembered one soldier, "yelling at the top of their voices, without firing a shot, the brigade sped swiftly across the field and literally rushed the goal."[78] Closing upon the enemy line, Barksdale's regiments finally leveled their muskets and delivered volley after volley while on the move. Somehow the men passed through the Federal rifle fire and canister discharges and engulfed the blue regiments and supporting artillery batteries in a storm of powder, lead, and steel. Watching the Mississippians hurl themselves against the Yankees and "slaughter . . . the 'red breeched zouaves,'" McLaws' aide-de-camp recalled that

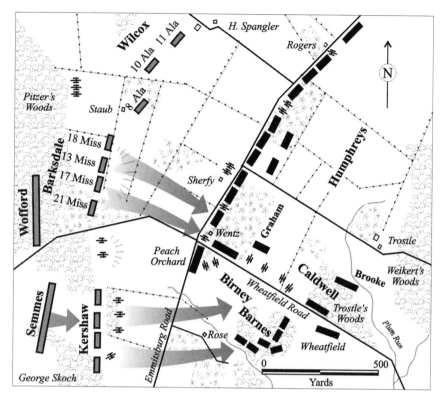

Barksdale's Charge Unhinges the Peach Orchard Salient
Shortly After 6:00 p.m., July 2, 1863

he had "witnessed many charges marked in every way by unflinching gallantry . . .
but I never saw anything to equal the heroism of the Mississippians."[79] Joseph
Hooker, the former commander of the Army of the Potomac, once noted that what
most impressed him about Lee's soldiers was the "vigorous and vehement" manner
in which they delivered an attack. The Army of Northern Virginia struck with
"blows," explained Hooker, "and the shock seemed to make the earth tremble on
which we stood."[80] If Hooker had been standing on the field that day, he could not
have painted a more appropriate portrait of Barksdale's attack.

The weakest part of the Peach Orchard line was where the western face of the
salient turned south and followed the Wheatfield Road. From that point north to the
Sherfy Farm, the center of that weak point was in and around the diminutive John
Wentz farm house, whose foundation can still be seen today close to the intersection
of the Emmitsburg and Wheatfield roads. And it was there that Barksdale directed
the center of his compact line of battle. Positioned at the southern corner, or apex, of
the salient, were several Federal regiments, including the 68th Pennsylvania, 3rd

Michigan, and 3rd Maine, supported by the 2nd New Hampshire and 7th New Jersey. These 1,364 Federals caught the full fury of one of the Confederacy's finest regiments, the 21st Mississippi, about 300 men under the command of the brigade's senior colonel, Benjamin Grubb Humphreys. The 21st was supported, at least initially, by the 440 men of Colonel William Dunbar Holder's 17th Mississippi.[81] Together the screaming demons of the two regiments charged up the gentle slope leading to the Sherfy fruit grove. The sheer force of the collision there routed Graham's 68th Pennsylvania. Displaying an incredible presence of mind, Colonel Holder redirected his 17th regiment to the left in order to conform with the direction Barksdale was pushing Colonel James W. Carter's 13th Mississippi. Humphreys, meanwhile continued to drive his 21st Mississippi straight ahead on an eastward line right down the Wheatfield Road.[82]

About the same time Barksdale's men crashed into the Federal line, William Wofford's supporting Georgia brigade stepped out of the same woods on Seminary Ridge and advanced to the attack. Wofford's right extended beyond the right flank of Barksdale's 21st Mississippi. The 3rd Maine, holding the juncture of the salient box at the southern end of the orchard, watched in horror as the Pennsylvanians to the right gave way and retreated east. As the men from Maine fought with part of the 21st Mississippi on their right, Wofford's Georgians approached and overlapped their exposed left. Discretion being the better part of valor, the 3rd Maine broke under the threat of envelopment and fled rearward.[83] When the Maine men gave way and joined the other fleeing fugitives, the 3rd Michigan offered a short but spirited resistance and then melted away as well. The rout of these two regiments left the 7th New Jersey exposed and in harm's way. Before long it, too, joined the rearward crush of retreating Federals.[84] The key to breaking open the salient was to strike hard and fast—and keep moving. After shattering the front line, it became almost impossible for other Federal regiments to engage for fear of hitting their own men. "We . . .moved forward and broke the first line," remembered Colonel Humphreys, "and drove it back on successive lines that were in turn forced to yield and retire in confusion, leaving 4 guns and some crippled caissons in the Peach Orchard." The

Benjamin Grubb Humphreys (1808-1882)

Few regiments on either side of the war could claim to have accomplished more in any one day of battle than Ben G. Humphrey's 21st Mississippi at Gettysburg on July 2, 1863. Under his able direction, the Mississippians attacked and defeated the equivalent of a large Federal infantry brigade and destroyed, captured, or drove off several batteries of artillery. Humphreys led Barksdale's Brigade with distinction until the end of the war. *Library of Congress*

colonel's description matched perfectly what Robert E. Lee had planned to do on a corps-sized scale the previous day.[85]

The domino effect continued. With the collapse of the southern portion of the salient, the 2nd New Hampshire from George Burling's brigade (which had been piecemealed all over the field wherever help was needed) stood virtually alone to oppose Humphreys' surging regiment. A murderous fire from the marksmen of the 21st blew gaping holes in the Yankee regiment until the New Hampshire men simply fell apart under the strain. Their retreat left the 141st Pennsylvania alone in the middle of the Peach Orchard, directly in the path of the 21st Mississippi.[86] Humphreys ordered his regiment to press its advantage. A desperate struggle at close range followed before the Pennsylvanians were likewise swept away like wheat before the scythe, losing 151 of the 209 men taken into action.[87] The exuberant Mississippians rounded up large numbers of prisoners including the wounded General Graham. In less than a quarter-hour, Humphreys' 21st Mississippi, with some initial help from the 17th Mississippi and the *approach* of Wofford, had broken one Federal regiment after another and completely overrun the Peach Orchard salient.

As Humphreys was clearing the fruit trees, the 13th Mississippi with Barksdale at its head, together with the 17th Mississippi, came to grips with the 114th Pennsylvania positioned between the Wentz farmhouse and the Sherfy Farm complex. Known as Collis' Zouaves, the 114th sported red pantaloons, white leggings, blue jackets, and red fez headgear. These uniforms made splendid targets for the Mississippi marksmen.[88] Scores of these pretty bright uniforms soon littered the ground and the survivors, unable to absorb the combination blows delivered by the two Mississippi regiments, broke and ran. Most tried to retreat northward past the Sherfy Farm, where they were caught by Barksdale's left regiment, the 18th Mississippi. Yankee prisoners were scooped up by the score, including the wounded Lieutenant Colonel Cavada of the 114th Pennsylvania.[89]

From his position on Barksdale's left, George Clark of Cadmus Wilcox's Alabama Brigade, Anderson's Division, Powell Hill's Third Corps, watched while the Mississippians overran the Federal front line between the Sherfy Farm and Peach Orchard. Clark, who after the war was a judge in Waco, Texas, called it "the most magnificent charge I witnessed during the war, and led by the gallant Barksdale who seemed to be fifty yards in front of his brave boys. The scene was grand beyond description."[90] Barksdale's blistering attack had not only shattered the Peach Orchard salient and turned the left flank of the remaining Third Corps Federal line deployed along the Emmitsburg Road, but had exposed the guns on the Wheatfield Road and opened up the avenue of advance east towards the Wheatfield itself (which Wofford would soon exploit) and northward up Cemetery Ridge.

The fiery Barksdale understood the importance of momentum. Ten months earlier at the Battle of Sharpsburg he had led his Mississippians into battle near the West Woods, where the brigade, supported by others, attacked and smashed John

Sedgwick's much larger Federal division. Barksdale's initial success came when he struck the flank and routed a brigade under Oliver O. Howard. He and others continued the pursuit until the entire Yankee division was wrecked.[91] A similar situation now existed along the Emmitsburg Road at Gettysburg. He had smashed through the first Federal line and, unwilling to give the Yankees a chance to reform, urged his Mississippians to keep their bayonets pressing against the enemy's backs. Spurring his mount and waving his men onward, Barksdale kept shouting, "Forward, men, forward!"[92] He pivoted the 13th, 17th and 18th regiments so their advance was generally northward up the Emmitsburg Road. This enabled the Mississippians to enfilade the Federals who were facing west when the Confederate attack began. Along this new axis of advance Barksdale relentlessly pressed his advantage with the three left-hand regiments. Captain Adolpho F. Cavada, one of Andrew A. Humphreys' staff officers, witnessed the destruction wrought by Barksdale's continued attack. The Mississippians poured in an enfilade fire that decimated one blue formation after another. They were screaming and fighting, Cavada believed, "like devils incarnate." What Cavada witnessed was the complete meltdown of the remaining regiments of Graham's brigade, and all of Brewster's Excelsior Brigade, which was either routed or shattered in turn. General Humphreys dispatched staff officers in every direction to stop the retreat, to no avail. The rout of the division, reported Cavada "was complete."[93]

The cost of delivering such enormous amounts of punishment against so many Federal regiments was high. After the breakthrough, Colonel Holder of the 17th Mississippi and Colonel Thomas M. Griffin of the 18th Mississippi wanted their brigade commander to call a temporary halt to redress the lines before pressing on. "No!" was Barksdale's immediate answer. "Crowd them—we have them on the run. Move your regiments."[94] Barksdale's decision was correct. By ruthlessly exploiting the initial breakthrough, Barksdale and the 13th, 17th, and 18th regiments were able to completely put to flight the equivalent of two infantry brigades and a pair of supporting batteries. This feat, coupled with the devastating attack of Humphreys' 21st Mississippi which routed five Yankee regiments (the equivalent of another brigade) and ruined several batteries, stands as a lasting illustration of what motivated and well led quality troops can accomplish. In about thirty minutes, Barksdale's four regiments had knocked the equivalent of an entire division of Federal infantry out of the battle. This despite the fact that the Federals had enjoyed the advantages of fighting defensively on higher ground with close supporting artillery. Perhaps the most outstanding feature of this charge was that it was initially delivered head-on; it was only after the Mississippians had broken through that they were able to maximize their tactical advantages against subsequent Federal units (much like Abner Perrin's assault in his charge the previous day on Seminary Ridge). And Barksdale's regiments were by no means finished with their work. This assault serves as yet another vivid example of why General Lee had such faith and confidence in his men.

The Mississippians were in the process of driving away Graham's brigade when Porter Alexander ordered his batteries to move forward in support. The talented Georgia artillerist was well versed in the lessons of Napoleonic warfare. As a result, he keenly understood the offensive capabilities of artillery. Alexander knew attacking infantry needed artillery to advance with them to lend supporting fire to sustain the impetus of the assault. As far as he was concerned, it looked as though the Mississippians had created an opportunity to deliver the final blow and end the war. He ordered his six batteries and more than 500 officers and men forward. Charging across the ground from Seminary Ridge to the Peach Orchard, the Confederate artillerists maneuvered their pieces over and around the debris of Sickles' wrecked units, unlimbered their guns along the Emmitsburg Road swell near the Peach Orchard, and cut loose on the retreating Federals. "An artillerist's heaven is to follow the routed enemy, after a tough resistance," Alexander later wrote, "and throw shells and canister into his disorganized and fleeing masses . . . Now we saw our heaven in front, and were already breathing the very air of victory."[95]

Alexander's elation quickly melted away when he reached the orchard. "I was very much disappointed," he wrote after the war. "It was not the enemy's main line we had broken. That loomed up near 1,000 yards before us."[96] Beyond the immediate masses of retreating blue infantry Alexander took in the natural strength of Cemetery Ridge about 900 yards to the east/northeast. There, he remembered, were "batteries in abundance . . . & troops . . . marching & fighting everywhere." Alexander saw numerous Federal formations and accompanying artillery moving from north to south as Meade continued to react to the success of the Confederate echelon attack. "There was plenty to shoot at," he noted optimistically. His gunners not only fired into the defeated Federal infantry and artillery batteries fleeing the onslaught of Barksdale's Mississippians, but also took up "a spirited duel" against the previously unengaged Federal units along "their new line" on Cemetery Ridge.[97]

As Alexander's battalion opened a supporting fire, Colonel Humphreys ordered his 21st Mississippi to resume its victorious advance eastward. Humphreys had not pivoted his infantrymen north to conform with the movement of the rest of Barksdale's Brigade because had he done so, his right flank would have been exposed to the Federal artillery along Wheatfield Road. As it now stood, the exact opposite was true: the right flank of the line of Federal artillery facing south and dealing death into Kershaw's ranks was exposed to Humphreys' Mississippians. Humphreys decided to immediately press his advantage. If he did not do so, the gunners would either limber their pieces and withdraw to a new position, or pivot their guns and blast the ranks of either Barksdale's or Wofford's men. Humphreys urged his men forward. The advance, however, further separated the 21st from Barksdale's other three regiments.[98]

Threatened by the 21st Mississippi and without their supporting infantry, the Federal battery commanders began pulling out of the Wheatfield Road line before they, too, were engulfed. There were six Federal batteries deployed abreast along the road. Two of the four batteries positioned along the western portion of the line—Watson's Battery I, 5th U.S. Artillery, and Hart's 15th New York Battery—had already made their escape while the 21st Mississippi was engaged just a handful of yards west in the orchard. Thus, the first two batteries in line to catch the undivided attention of Humphreys' men were Judson Clark's Battery B, 1st New Jersey Light Artillery, and James Thompson's Combined Batteries C and F, Independent Pennsylvania Light Artillery. Rifle fire from the 21st Mississippi wounded many of the New Jersey gunners, some of whom were later captured, and killed enough horses to force Clark to abandon one of the battery's caissons. Clark and his surviving crewmen withdrew with the rest of the equipment, including the battery's six 10-pounder Parrotts, but the damage sustained by the battery finished their participation for the rest of the battle.[99] Thompson's battery of four 3-inch Ordnance rifles wasn't as lucky. Humphreys' Mississippians shot down all of the horses of one gun team and all those of a caisson's team as well. The caisson and the 3-inch rifle, along with several crewmen, fell into the hands of the advancing Confederates.[100]

Humphreys continued to press his regiment forward in the direction of the last two batteries along Wheatfield Road. Next in line was Charles Phillips' 5th Massachusetts Battery of six 3-inch Ordnance rifles. Phillips had watched Hart's battery pull out of the line. Even before he could ascertain just how serious the danger emerging from the Peach Orchard really was, Phillips had ordered his command to prepare to move out. The precaution saved the battery. By the time hundreds of shouting Southerners were discovered heading in his direction, the guns were limbering and moving east; only the horses of the piece closest to Humphreys' men were killed. Although one limber had to be abandoned, Phillips' crew had enough time to separate it from the gun and drag it away as the remainder of the battery galloped rearward.[101]

John Bigelow's 9th Massachusetts battery, stationed along the same road just north and west of Stony Hill, was the last to leave. By the time Bigelow received orders to "limber up and get out,"[102] Humphreys' Mississippians and a handful of skirmishers from Kershaw's regiments were too close to do so. Bigelow knew that if he tried to limber his six Napoleons, the approaching Confederates would shoot down the horses and drivers and easily capture his guns. To prevent this calamity, he ordered his crews to retire by prolong, which Bigelow believed was "more properly [described] by the recoil of its guns, for the prolonges were only used to straighten the alignment and for keeping an effective front."[103] In other words, between discharges the Federal gunners would manually shift the Napoleons rearward and realign their aim, while the limbers and caissons led the retreat but remained close enough to supply ammunition. In this fashion Bigelow's battery slowly recoiled from the swell of the Wheatfield Road and Peach Orchard towards Plum Run. After using this method to retire several hundred yards, the artillerists found themselves on the Abraham Trostle Farm, where the ground to the east rose once past Plum Run.

If they were going to get the guns out, the pieces had to be limbered up. Bigelow was preparing to do so when Major Freeman McGilvery, commander of the artillery brigade, arrived and ordered him to "hold his position at all hazards for Cemetery Ridge was entirely undefended in his rear."[104] Bigelow prepared to sacrifice his command.

The Mississippians' approach to the Trostle farmyard and Bigelow's isolated battery was protected by "a slight knoll." The 21st Mississippi poured over it with rifles blazing and throats screaming the Rebel Yell. Bigelow remembered "the air was dark with smoke. a Rebel battery [from Alexander's battalion] had opened on our position and their shells were going over and among us. The enemy were yelling like demons."[105] The Southerners approached the muzzles of the guns before being driven back by the double-shotted Napoleons. When he realized the guns were without infantry support, Humphreys directed part of his regiment to envelop Bigelow's right flank. Within minutes the flanking Mississippians were rushing through the battery. The 21st's color bearer climbed up on one of Bigelow's caissons, wildly waving the battle flag while others hopped up on the limbers and caissons to shoot down Federal crewmen and horses. When it was over, Humphreys' Mississippians had inflicted the majority of the casualties suffered by Bigelow's battery that afternoon. Sixty-eight horses were down, along with more than two dozen Federal artillery officers and men killed, wounded, or captured. Four of Bigelow's Napoleons were claimed as prizes by the 21st Mississippi.[106]

After wrecking Bigelow's battery, Humphreys was reorganizing his men for a move north to join the remainder of Barksdale's Brigade when he spotted yet another undefended Federal battery unlimbering about 200 yards away on a small rise on the east side of Plum Run. The outfit was Watson's Battery I. The four 3-inch Ordnance rifles had pulled out of the Wheatfield Road line just minutes earlier to avoid the Mississippians. Humphreys was presented with the same dilemma he had faced after carrying the Peach Orchard. If he turned his regiment and moved north to conform with the rest of his brigade, his right flank would be exposed to the battery, which could not only rake his own line, but Wofford's advancing brigade as well. Left with little choice, the Mississippians "charged and captured these guns." By the time the Mississippians had claimed another Yankee battery, Humphreys realized his hard-fighting command "had advanced too far to the front for safety, though no gun was firing at us." Fresh Federal infantry was moving against the rest of Barksdale's Brigade "several hundred yards to my left." As Humphreys' latter described it, "I saw my safety was in hurried retreat."[107]

While Humphreys had been driving northeast, the other three regiments under Barksdale had continued their euphoric pursuit of the shattered Federal brigades reeling from the Emmitsburg Road line. Swinging away from the axis of the Emmitsburg Road in order to avoid becoming intermingled with Cadmus Wilcox's advancing Alabamians from Anderson's Division, Barksdale directed his tiring and diminished regiments east towards Plum Run and the low rise of southern Cemetery

Ridge beyond. Passing to the northeast of the Trostle farm complex, the 13th, 17th, and 18th Mississippi regiments approached Plum Run. This thrust, combined with Humphreys' 21st Mississippi efforts to the southeast, marked the zenith of Barksdale's advance.

It is said that a Federal colonel told a member of the 17th Mississippi that Barksdale's assault was "the grandest charge ever made by mortal man."[108] He may not be far off the mark. Barksdale's four regiments had completely wrecked or shattered 13 Federal infantry regiments—one-third of the entire infantry compliment of Sickles' Third Corps. By the time the Mississippians reached their deepest point of penetration, they had captured at least nine cannon and several caissons and limbers, and had knocked out of action the equivalent of five artillery batteries (essentially an entire Yankee artillery brigade). These accomplishments, coupled with the remarkable feats performed by other First Corps infantry and artillery units, prompted General Longstreet's proud boast that the afternoon's action had been the "best three hours' fighting ever done by any troops on any battlefield."[109] Even more important, Lee's large-scale echelon assault was drawing Federal attention and vital reinforcements away from sections of the Yankee line yet to be attacked.

Meade and Hancock Try to Stem the Confederate Tide

James Longstreet's ride into the Peach Orchard and beyond with Wofford's Georgians provided him with a clear view of his battlefield. Although his infantry had penetrated and collapsed Sickles' entire line, they had not been able to turn Meade's reformed left flank now anchored on Little Round Top. Still, the attack was drawing untold numbers of Federal troop formations from other parts of the field. The fluidity of the fighting had provided several opportunities that Wofford, Kershaw, Barksdale, Humphreys and others had exploited to their considerable tactical benefit. But now the afternoon shadows were lengthening. It must have been obvious to Lee's "Old Warhorse" that his two divisions had about spent their bolt. Fresh enemy reinforcements were pouring onto the field and Longstreet's diminishing brigades would not be able to accomplish much more. If there was more "opportunity" to be exploited, it would have to be accomplished by the heretofore unengaged troops belonging to Powell Hill and Dick Ewell further up the line. Many positions opposite these Confederate corps had either been vacated or were now appreciably weaker—and thus ripe for the supporting attacks Lee intended to deliver.

George Meade's own actions in defense of his left flank had made other parts of his line vulnerable. For more than two hours, both Meade and Winfield Hancock had rushed reinforcements to the imperiled left wing. George Sykes' entire Fifth Corps

George Meade was an unlikely choice to replace Joe Hooker as commander of the Army of the Potomac. His combat experience as a corps commander consisted of light involvement in the embarrassment at Chancellorsville. He was a thorough soldier with extensive training, however, and Lincoln realized as much. His assignment during the middle of the Pennsylvania campaign thrust him into a position of high responsibility with the weight of nations dancing on his shoulders. His active handling of the army during the fighting on July 2 at Gettysburg prevented the collapse of his left flank—but stripped reserves from his center and right, opening up a series of "opportunities" the Confederate *en échelon* attack was designed to exploit. *Library of Congress*

George Gordon Meade
(1815-1872)

had been dispatched there early in the fighting, and much of it had been decimated. John Sedgwick was ordered to bring forward whatever Sixth Corps brigades he could spare in order to assist Sickles and Sykes. Hancock's Second Corps had been bled white to prop up the crumbling left. John Caldwell's four brigades were pulled from the center of Cemetery Ridge for the slaughterhouse of the Wheat field. Meade's additional requests further diminished Hancock's corps by sending another brigade under Colonel George Willard to aid Birney's hard-pressed division, as well as two additional regiments (the 19th Massachusetts and 42nd New York of Colonel Norman Hall's brigade), to aid General Andrew A. Humphreys along the Emmitsburg Road.[110] The Second Corps began the fighting with only 10 infantry brigades. Thus, Meade's requests for reinforcements had shaved away more than half of Hancock's strength on Cemetery Ridge.

Hancock was in the process of leading Willard's brigade south down Cemetery Ridge when he "encountered General Birney, who informed me that his troops had all been driven to the rear, and had left the position to which I was moving."

Hancock also learned of Caldwell's bloody fate and was probably apprised of Fifth Corps' general meltdown. The stunning news was followed up by General Humphreys' rapid retirement from the embattled Emmitsburg Road line. John Gibbon, perhaps Hancock's best division commander, remembered that his superior "utter[ed] some expressions of discontent" of having to salvage Third Corps, "which, it was understood, had gone to pieces."[111]

The situation was desperate and Hancock knew it. Confederate artillery from Alexander's guns in and around the Peach Orchard were now dropping shells around him, Barksdale's Mississippians, along with other Southern infantry, were unraveling the Emmitsburg Road line, and fighting was still heard far to the south near Little Round Top. Worse still was the fact that additional Confederate brigades were stepping off Seminary Ridge and bearing down on thinly-held Cemetery Ridge. If the Federal battle line there was going to hold, Hancock needed more help—and fast. A staff officer was sent to Meade requesting reinforcements.[112]

Hancock propped up his defense on lower Cemetery Ridge by cobbling together whatever broken pieces of regiments he could rally. Flotsam from Humphreys' splintered division offered Hancock some immediate material with which to work. "I directed General Humphreys to form [what remained of] his command on the ground from which General Caldwell had moved to the support of the Third Corps, which was promptly done," wrote Hancock in his after-action report. "The

Winfield Scott Hancock
(1824-1886)

Hancock had fought credibly from the beginning of the war and received his promotion to head the Army of the Potomac's Second Corps before the outset of the Gettysburg Campaign. It was an excellent choice. His performance in the epic battle may well have saved Meade's army from disaster and caused one biographer to label Hancock "The Superb." He was an invaluable subordinate and Meade relied on him much as Lee relied on Longstreet. *Library of Congress*

number of his troops collected was, however, very small, *scarcely equal to an ordinary battalion* [emphasis added], but with many colors, this small command being composed of the fragments of many shattered regiments."[113] Hancock's plight aptly demonstrates just how effective Longstreet's echelon attack was that afternoon. Meade had thrown all caution to the wind. According to one Gettysburg historian, he stripped the "center and right heedlessly in the supreme emergency."[114]

Meade's problems were only just beginning. In response to Hancock's request for reinforcements to man Cemetery Ridge, Meade called upon Major General John Newton to hustle portions of First Corps' decimated remnants (which had been cut to pieces on July 1) to counter the threatened Confederate break-through.[115] Believing more help was needed, Meade also instructed Henry Slocum of Twelfth Corps to denude the all-important right flank portion of the line on Culp's Hill, which protected the army's line of retreat towards Baltimore. Twelfth Corps had but six brigades, and fortunately for the Federal army, Slocum refused to send all of them. Five were dispatched in accordance with Meade's request; one was left sitting on Culp's Hill.[116]

The new army commander was justifiably sensitive about his left wing and sent enough strength to eventually contain the sharp and sustained Confederate attacks. But in doing so, Meade dispatched more strength than he could afford *if* the remainder of his line was heavily assailed. He was, in essence, gambling that it would not be. His response to Longstreet's attacks on his left wing *validated Lee's use of the echelon attack.* Meade's reinforcement orders had reduced the rest of his long line to a thin shell of infantry and artillery. Only four and one-half brigades from Hancock's Second Corps, one brigade (George Greene's) from Slocum's Twelfth Corps, and the six undistinguished brigades of Howard's Eleventh Corps—five of which had been seriously routed the day before—remained along the entire Federal line stretching from middle Cemetery Ridge in the area just south of the Copse of Trees northward to Cemetery Hill and eastward to Culp's Hill. These 11 and one-half Federal brigades were situated opposite the Confederate divisions of Richard Anderson, Dorsey Pender, Robert Rodes, Jubal Early, and Edward Johnson—some 22 Confederate brigades. Longstreet's eight brigades, outnumbered by more than two-to-one, had devastated twice their number.

What could the remaining 22 brigades accomplish against Meade's thin line if committed aggressively to battle? That remained to be seen. The action and the "opportunity" Lee was seeking was shifting north into Powell Hill's and Dick Ewell's sectors, and there was still plenty of daylight remaining for the brigades of the Confederate Second and Third corps to strike and exploit any success they might encounter.

Breakdown: Ambrose Powell Hill and Third Corps

Powell Hill had spent much of that Thursday morning and early afternoon in the presence of General Lee. He had been with both Lee and Longstreet when John Bell Hood and Lafayette McLaws marched their divisions onto the field that morning, and was again in the company of Lee and Longstreet when Captain Johnston reported back from his reconnaissance mission to Meade's left flank. Therefore, the commander of Third Corps had firsthand knowledge of Lee's plan of attack. Indeed, Hill admitted he "was *ordered* to cooperate with [Longstreet's corps] with such of my brigades from the right as could join in with his troops in the attack." Hill's role was crucial because his troops would, as Lee later wrote, "threaten the enemy's center, to prevent reinforcements being drawn to either wing, and co-operate with his right division in Longstreet's attack."[117]

Based upon those orders, Hill (and possibly Lee) communicated them directly to Richard Anderson, one of Hill's division commanders. When the Gettysburg campaign began, Major General Richard Heron Anderson was a distinguished son of South Carolina and a graduate of West Point (Class of 1842) whose classmates included James Longstreet and Lafayette McLaws. From 1842 until 1863 Anderson had been a career soldier whose wide experiences included years on the frontier and service in the Mormon, Comanche, and Mexican wars. His reputation in the old army was a good one: intelligent, kind, and unselfish. So too was his early record of Confederate service as a brigadier on the Peninsula, which earned him a promotion to major general in the summer of 1862. Anderson also handled his division well, especially during Longstreet's counterattack at Second Manassas and at Chancellorsville, where Lee lauded him with the description "noble old soldier."

But beneath Anderson's gentle veneer was a slothful soldier lacking the discipline necessary to apply himself without the infusion of an outside influence. "He was a very brave man," wrote Moxley Sorrel of Longstreet's staff, but possessed "of a rather inert, indolent manner for commanding troops in the field, and by no means pushing or aggressive." This shortcoming was not as obvious while Anderson served under Longstreet, whose blunt firmness insured he performed as expected. When "Old Pete" was on detached duty during the Chancellorsville Campaign, Anderson took orders directly from Lee and turned in a solid, but not particularly aggressive, performance. The reorganization that followed planted Anderson and his brigades in Hill's Third Corps. Although Anderson's superior had changed, Anderson had not. Perhaps Lee hoped the more pugnacious Hill would motivate Anderson to act more aggressively on his own hook. The sick and withdrawn Hill of Gettysburg, however, was not the inspired and energetic Hill of Sharpsburg. Anderson's' lackadaisical march to the battlefield on July 1 foretold the continued requirement of close supervision. But was there a steady hand in place to insure it?[118]

His contemporaries considered him smart, cordial—and with a tendency toward laziness. They were right, and Richard Anderson's shortcomings were fully realized on July 2, 1863. With his division slated to play a key role in the *en échelon* attack, Anderson remained well to the rear and was thus unable to properly exercise his command responsibilities. To this day his negligence remains largely unexplained, and historians have routinely failed to hold him accountable for his actions.
Eleanor S. Brockenbrough Library, The Museum of the Confederacy, Richmond

Richard Heron Anderson
(1821-1879)

Anderson's five brigades stretched along Seminary Ridge from McMillian's Woods to the north south to Pitzer's Woods. His left flank butted up against Dorsey Pender's Light Division of the Third Corps, stationed near the Lutheran Seminary. On Anderson's right was Lafayette McLaws' First Corps division. Therefore, Anderson was the "right division" commander Lee mentioned in his report of the battle, and was the key link between the divisions of McLaws and Pender. Since Anderson's command was on the immediate left of Longstreet's First Corps, an understanding of Anderson's orders, and those of his five brigade commanders, is crucial in order to fully appreciate Lee's plan of attack. Anderson's report makes it plain that he understood the general plan of battle and his role therein:

> I received notice that . . . Longstreet would occupy the ground on the right . . . [and] that he would assault the extreme left of the enemy and drive him toward Gettysburg. I was at the same time *ordered* [emphasis added] to put the troops of my division into action *by brigades* [emphasis added] as soon as those of General Longstreet corps had progressed so far in their assault as to be connected with my right flank.[119]

Since Hill acknowledged that General Lee ordered him to "join in with his troops in the attack," it follows that Hill—and perhaps even Lee, who was on the scene along lower Seminary Ridge before Longstreet commenced his assault—instructed Anderson to attack *en échelon* with his division. While it was not the commanding general's usual custom to dictate how an attack was to be developed, Lee on more than one occasion had given specific instructions for his troops to conduct attacks *en échelon*. Lee gave Longstreet instructions that his First

Corps brigades were to attack *en échelon* at Gettysburg on July 2. At least one of Anderson's brigadiers, Cadmus Wilcox, was *personally* instructed by Lee prior to going into action, but whether he used the words "*en échelon*" to describe the method by which Wilcox was to deliver his attack is unknown. According to Wilcox—whose Alabama brigade was positioned at a right angle to McLaws' left flank—his orders were simply to advance when the troops on his right went forward.[120] George Clark, a member of Wilcox's Brigade, remembers it a bit differently. Wilcox, he claimed, "explain[ed] to the officers [of his brigade] the general plan of the battle . . . stating that the movement forward would be by echelon, beginning with the right of Longstreet's Corps and extending to the left as each brigade came into action."[121] One of Anderson's brigadiers, Ambrose Ransom ("Rans") Wright, specifically remembers that Anderson told him that the entire division would attack, with *brigades* taking up the action from right to left, i.e., an attack *en échelon*.[122] Both Powell Hill and Richard Anderson reported that they were to put their brigades into battle. Indeed, Hill's use of the specific phrase "into action by brigade," confirms that Lee instructed Hill as he had Longstreet: the attack would begin on the right and continue *en échelon* up the line, with each Third Corps brigade going into action as the one on its right advanced.

The instructions provided Anderson's brigadiers—and especially to Cadmus Wilcox, Anderson's right brigade leader—are especially critical because they paint an important part of the overall picture of what Lee expected from Hill's two divisions (Anderson and Pender, Heth's being held in deep reserve). The brigade was composed of five Alabama regiments numbering 1,777 officers and men. Its leader, Cadmus Marcellus Wilcox, was a West Point graduate of 1846 who had won a brevet promotion for bravery in storming Chapultepec Castle during the Mexican War. Although he had led a brigade (and even a demi-division on occasion) since the Peninsula Campaign of 1862, circumstances beyond his control limited his chances to demonstrate his field competence. Solid and steady, Wilcox's Alabama brigade served as part of Richard Anderson's Division for almost a year. His opportunity to shine finally arrived on May 3, 1863, during the height of the Chancellorsville Campaign. His brigade was picketing Banks' Ford when his keen observations determined that enemy troops were been withdrawn from the opposite bank. Disregarding his orders, Wilcox rushed his men to Fredericksburg, where his timely arrival and superb delaying tactics at Salem Church may well have saved the army from a serious disaster.[123]

Immediately after Gettysburg, Wilcox reported that his "instructions [on July 2] were to advance when the troops on my right should advance, and to report this to the division commander, *in order that the other brigades should advance in proper time* [emphasis added]."[124] Wilcox also remembered that it was so important for his brigade "to guard McLaws' flank [that] the orders were three times repeated during the day from division headquarters, [and] General Lee in person directed me what to do."[125] Lee was actively involved along Seminary Ridge prior to the battle and had

Few opportunities to shine in the field had come his way, and so by the spring of 1863 Cadmus Wilcox was one of the Army of Northern Virginia's unsung brigade commanders—solid, dependable, but not particularly noteworthy. During the Chancellorsville Campaign, however, his observant stance opposite Bank's Ford and subsequent march toward Fredericksburg without orders saved Lee's army from a serious disaster. At Gettysburg on July 2 another opportunity arose allowing Wilcox to prove himself an able tactician. His writings about Gettysburg are particularly important for understanding Confederate operations, especially as they relate to General Lee on the battle's second day. Wilcox recalled the commanding general issued personal instructions to him so that his brigade of Alabamians would properly cover the left flank of McLaws' Division during the afternoon assault. *Eleanor S. Brockenbrough Library, The Museum of the Confederacy, Richmond*

Cadmus Marcellus Wilcox
(1824-1890)

ordered Longstreet to attack with the infantry of the First Corps *en échelon.* It is thus significant that the commanding general communicated the need for Longstreet's left flank troops under McLaws to be properly protected by seeking out and speaking directly to Wilcox. What's more, Wilcox understood that the other brigades of Anderson's Division would also advance—a fact that was acknowledged by Anderson and Hill because, after all, that was Lee's plan.

On Wilcox's left was a small brigade belonging to Edward Aylesworth Perry, three regiments of Floridians totaling only 700 effectives.[126] Perry, however, had developed typhoid fever just before the opening of the campaign, and so the brigade was led at Gettysburg by Colonel David Lang of the 8th Florida. The 25-year old colonel was a Georgia native and a graduate of the Georgia Military Academy. He served long and well with Lee's army, and would again lead a brigade later in the war—still at the rank of colonel. Lang's veterans were formed in Spangler's Woods, and it was from that tree line that the colonel remembered his orders to advance came from Anderson. Only 600 yards separated the Florida Brigade from Sickles' Third Corps line along the Emmitsburg Road near the Rogers' Farm. As Lang recalled, he was ordered to "advance with General Wilcox, holding all the ground the enemy yielded." Lang reported that "as soon as [Wilcox's] left reached my right, I conformed to the movement, and advanced at double-quick."[127]

Extending the line north beyond Lang's left was Ambrose "Rans" Wright's Georgia brigade, about 1,600 men comprised of the 3rd, 22nd, and 48th Georgia and 2nd Georgia Battalion.[128] The four units of the brigade had served together since the Seven Days Battles, and had seen considerable action in all of the major engagements of the Army of Northern Virginia. Posted along the wood line on Seminary Ridge, Wright's right flank rested near the site of the present day Virginia Monument, with his left located about 300 yards north of that point.[129] In his after-action report, Wright specifically cited his battle orders as follow:

> I was informed by Major General Anderson that an attack upon the enemy's line would soon be made *by the whole division* [emphasis added], commencing on our right by Wilcox's Brigade, and that each brigade of the division would begin the attack as soon as the brigade on its immediate right commenced the movement. I was instructed to move simultaneously with Perry's [Lang's] Brigade, which was on my right, and informed that Posey's Brigade, on my left, would move forward upon my advance.[130]

On Wright's left was Carnot Posey and his brigade of four regiments of Mississippians numbering 1,322 combatants.[131] Posey had been a volunteer in Jefferson Davis' 1st Mississippi Rifles during the Mexican War, and had commanded the 16th Mississippi in Stonewall Jackson's celebrated Valley Campaign of 1862. His service at First Winchester, Cross Keys, Second Manassas, and Sharpsburg had earned honorable mention in numerous battle reports. Following the Battle of Fredericksburg, Lee removed an incompetent brigadier and named Posey in his place to lead the veteran 12th, 16th, 19th and 48th Mississippi regiments.[132] At Gettysburg, Posey held a position along Seminary Ridge opposite the Bliss Farm and orchard, about 400 yards west of the Emmitsburg Road and 600 yards from the Brian Farm on Cemetery Ridge. In his report, Posey casually referred to his orders that afternoon as follows: "I received an order to advance after Brigadier General Wright, who was posted on my right in a woods before the advance was made."[133]

Posey's left was protected by Anderson's last brigade, 1,500 men in five experienced Virginia regiments that had served together since the Battle of Seven Pines. Their leader was "an eccentric hypochondriac" named William "Billy" Mahone.[134] a Virginia Military Institute graduate, Mahone had drawn the wrath of Harvey Hill for his performance at Seven Pines where, Hill claimed, Mahone "withdrew his brigade without any order."[135] However, his performances on several other fields, including Second Manassas and Chancellorsville, were praiseworthy. At Gettysburg, Mahone's Virginians formed a line of battle in McMillan's Woods, with the left flank resting about 150 yards south of the McMillan farm buildings.

Mahone's after-action report conspicuously omits any mention of any orders he received that day. It will soon be evident why he was silent on the subject.[136]

Richard Anderson and a Missed "Opportunity"

While William Barksdale was smashing the Peach Orchard salient, and while Confederate Third Corps artillerists along Seminary Ridge were firing onto the Federals along Cemetery Ridge, Cadmus Wilcox ordered his men to move out. The Alabamians shifted and then realigned themselves for the attack about 400 or 500 yards to the left. This movement took advantage of the dead ground in and around the Henry Spangler Farm between Spangler's Woods and the Emmitsburg Road swell. This low ground was perfectly suited for staging an attack against the Federal line because the rolling terrain shielded them from Yankee fire. Wilcox's five Alabama regiments advanced east against the right front of Andrew A. Humphreys' division deployed along the Emmitsburg Road. This portion of the line was held by approximately 1,800 men in the six regiments of Joseph Carr's brigade, supported by two powerful batteries of artillery under Francis Seeley and John Turnbull, each consisting of six 12-pounder Napoleons.[137]

Wilcox's men moved forward and crested the rolling ground only 250 yards west of the road. Already threatened from the south by three of Barksdale's regiments, Carr's determined Federals engaged in "a brisk musketry fight" with the Alabamians.[138] Seeing Wilcox advance, Colonel Lang ordered his Florida Brigade into the action. The Floridians, he later reported, were met at the top of the swale "with a murderous fire of grape, canister, and musketry," but still moved "forward at the double-quick."[139] Behind but supporting Wilcox's left, Lang's regiments opened a destructive fire into the front and exposed right flank of Carr's troops north of the Rogers' Farm. The combined pressure applied by Wilcox and Lang, coupled with Barksdale's Mississippians from the south and rear, inflicted almost 50% casualties on Carr's stubborn regiments, which finally gave way and fled rearward. The last vestiges of the Federal Third Corps line had crumbled away. The sacrifices made by Carr's men impressed Lang, who later recalled that he had never "seen anywhere before, the dead lying thicker than where the Yankee infantry attempted to make a stand in our front."[140] Carr's retreat left Seeley's gunners with no option but to limber and retire to safer ground. Turnbull, however, was not as fortunate. The onrushing Alabamians wrecked his battery, shooting down men and horses and capturing four of his six pieces.[141]

According to Wilcox, the drive to the Emmitsburg Road line "impinged" his right flank elements with Barksdale's Mississippians, and he ordered his regiments to "incline slightly to the left."[142] The Alabamians resumed their advance, driving past the Klingle Farm and across the fields sloping gently down to Plum Run.

Barksdale, as we know, did not stop to redress his ranks but instead wheeled east and pushed toward the shallow Plum Run line. North of the Rogers' farm Lang's Floridians also crossed the Emmitsburg Road, "pressing on rapidly after the flying Yankees" and thus covering Wilcox's northern flank.[143] Somewhere in the vicinity of the Emmitsburg Road, the two regiments sent by Colonel Hall (19th Massachusetts and 42nd New York) to aid Humphreys' division met the advancing lines of Confederates. The Federals "delivered several volleys into the enemy in their front," reported Hall, and then were swept back "with a loss of nearly one-third of their number" by a surging gray and brown line whose "advance was irresistible, its regularity surprising, and its rapidity fearful."[144]

The staggered advance of Wilcox and Lang was the signal Rans Wright was waiting for to move out with his Georgians. Eagerly taking up the echelon attack, Wright "immediately ordered forward" his units. The 2nd Georgia Battalion, consisting of only four companies and numbering around 175 effectives, was deployed as the brigade's skirmish screen and led the advance eastward.[145] The Georgians moved out of the woods and passed "for more than a mile across an open plain," reported the brigadier. The movement was not well controlled, however. As Wright later explained it, "the impetuosity of the advance" did not allow the 2nd Georgia Battalion "to form all its companies upon the left of the brigade, some of them falling into line with other regiments," while others members of the battalion "went into action with General Perry's (Florida) Brigade, it pressing upon our right."[146]

By this time Wright was approaching the Codori farm by the Emmitsburg Road. There, along a fence line the Georgians encountered the 82nd New York and 15th Massachusetts, about 540 officers and men from William Harrow's brigade, John Gibbon's division, Hancock's Second Corps.[147] Wright could see that "just in the rear of this line of infantry were [two] advanced batteries of the enemy, posted along the Emmitsburg turnpike."[148] What the Georgian discovered next was even more troubling:

> Posey's Brigade, on my left, had not advanced, and fearing that, if I proceeded much farther with my left flank entirely unprotected, I might become involved in serious difficulties, I dispatched my aide-de-camp, Capt. R. H. Bell, with a message to Major General Anderson, informing him of my own advance and its extent, and that General Posey had not advanced with his brigade on my left. To this message I received a reply to press on: that Posey had been ordered in on my left, and that he (General Anderson) would reiterate the order.[149]

Thus reassured, Wright "immediately charged upon the enemy's line, and drove him in great confusion."[150] He accomplished this feat by enveloping both flanks of the short Yankee battle line and crushing first the New Yorkers and then the Massachusetts men. The determined action inflicted 343 casualties on both Federal regiments—a loss of more than 61%.[151] The retreat of these Federals, who had "broken and fled in great confusion," left the two nearby Federal artillery batteries under Gulian Weir and T. Fred Brown, each consisting of six 12- pounder Napoleons, unsupported and isolated.[152] Weir's guns were southeast of the Codori buildings. Already pressured from the southwest by Lang's Floridians, the battery had exhausted all of its canister rounds when Wright's Georgians charged from the

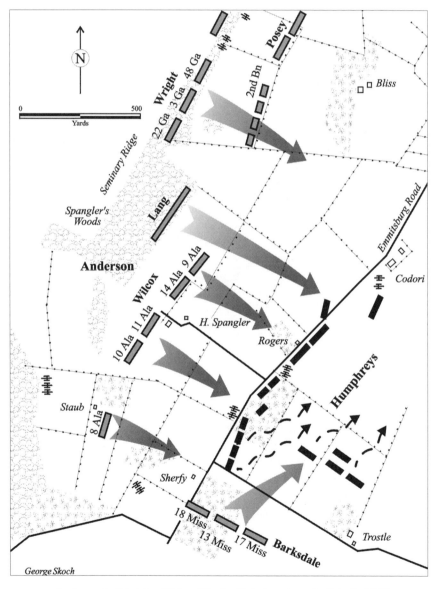

Anderson's Division Takes Up the Echelon Attack, July 2, 1863

Ambrose "Rans" Wright was another of Lee's excellent brigadiers without prewar training as a soldier. The Augusta, Georgia native enlisted as a private and rose to the rank of general by June 1862. After he recovered from his severe wounds suffered at Sharpsburg, Wright performed well at Chancellorsville and had his best day of the war on July 2, 1863, at Gettysburg. His aggressive thrust against Cemetery Ridge revealed just how weak Meade's center really was as the sun was falling that day. As he told gunner Porter Alexander the next day, the problem was not getting to the ridge but staying there. In other words, proper support was everything. *Library of Congress*

Ambrose Ransom "Rans" Wright
(1826-1872)

west. Almost before he realized it, Weir's battery was overrun by the 22nd Georgia, which captured half the guns.[153] Brown's guns, unlimbered northeast of the Codori buildings, were exposed as well. His crewmen had just enough time to limber and get away with four pieces, leaving behind two Napoleons as prizes for the hard-charging 48th Georgia.[154]

Within a short time Wright's Georgians had shattered two Federal regiments, two batteries, and had captured "several pieces of artillery"—and a nearly empty Cemetery Ridge was spread out before them.[155] Wright had advanced directly against one of the weakest sections of Meade's line, a yawning gap largely devoid of organized Federal troops south of the Copse of Trees and opposite the Codori farm. Drifting clouds of heavy powder smoke, however, coupled with the growing shadows of evening obscured much of what Wright could see in any direction. Indeed, the Federals on Cemetery Ridge were also having trouble seeing the Confederates for the same reasons. John Gibbon, one of Hancock's division commanders in the area of the Copse of Trees, remembered that "the smoke was at this time so dense that but little could be seen of the battle."[156] A line of enemy infantry held the ridge from the soon-to-be famous clump of trees south about 100 yards along Cemetery Ridge. Positioned there behind a low stone wall and formed in two lines were the remaining three regiments of Hall's depleted brigade, along with one regiment of Alexander Webb's Philadelphia Brigade, which was deployed almost in front of the trees. The balance of Webb's regiments were in column by regiment about 100 yards east of that point.[157] Artillery support for these seven regiments was deployed north of the Copse of Trees and consisted of two batteries under Alonzo Cushing and William Arnold, each with six small caliber 3-inch Ordnance rifles. These guns occupied a frontage of about 160 yards. This front was little more than a dangerously weak link between the Webb's brigade and Thomas Smyth's brigade, which was deployed to the north and extended to the Bryan farm buildings. It was the area beyond the left of his line, however, that gave Gibbon concern, for there were few if any Federal troops there for several hundred yards.

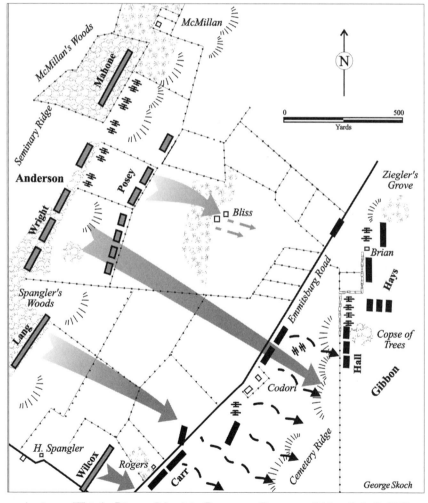

Ambrose Wright Pierces Meade's Center on Cemetery Ridge, July 2, 1863

This portion of Cemetery Ridge had been occupied earlier in the day by Caldwell's four brigades before they were diverted south to their disastrous defeat in the Wheatfield. Meade's decision to denude middle Cemetery Ridge of troops to reinforce his crumbling left flank had worked, temporarily, but now the center of his line was yawning wide open—and Rans Wright was guiding his determined troops into the gap.

Displaying gritty aggressiveness, Wright continued to push his men through the smoke and shadows up the slope of the ridge in the face of what he described as "a heavy fire from the enemy's artillery and infantry." The Georgians returned the favor and "continued to pour in a galling fire" upon the Federal line.[158] According to the unflappable Gibbon, "the enemy came on with such impetuosity that the head of his column came quite through a vacancy in our line to the left of my division, opened by detaching troops to other points."[159] Gibbon's quote offers yet another bit of evidence that General Lee's *en échelon* attack was succeeding by creating thinned positions along Meade's front. Lieutenant Frank A. Haskell, an aide-de-camp on Gibbon's staff, was impressed by the *élan* exuded by Wright's cheering warriors. "The whole slope in our front is full of [Georgians]," wrote Haskell, "and in various formations, in line, in columns, and in masses which are neither, with yells and thick volleys, they are rushing toward our crest."[160] Captain John E. Reilly's 69th Pennsylvania was deployed in front of Webb's brigade and the Copse of Trees when Wright's hellions suddenly appeared to the south. Reilly summed up the feelings of many men that day when he wrote that the Georgians "came like the fury of a whirlwind."[161]

The men holding the left side of Wright's Brigade, about 400 members of the 48th Georgia and a portion of the 2nd Georgia Battalion, shot down more of Brown's horses as the artillerists continued their hasty retreat, forcing the gunners to abandon another Napoleon a short distance in front of the stone wall.[162] These Georgians surged over the gun and continued advancing toward the stone wall, behind which waited 258 officers and men of the 69th Pennsylvania.[163] When the Georgians had approached to within 20 yards, the Pennsylvanians "met their charge with such a destroying fire that they [the Confederates] were forced back." The 48th Georgia and part of the 2nd Battalion rallied and made a second effort and their lines were thinned a second time by another well-placed round of musket fire. Unable to advance, the Southerners fell back. As they did so, the 106th Pennsylvania appeared at the crest of Cemetery Ridge on the right of the 69th Pennsylvania, moved through Cushing's battery, and began volleying into Wright's unprotected left flank.[164]

The 3rd Georgia in the middle of Wright's command, meanwhile, which had begun the battle with more than 500 combatants, was moving forward up Cemetery Ridge. Two small Federal regiments were waiting for them: the 59th New York, numbering about 110 effectives, and the 7th Michigan, about 165 men, both part of Hall's Second Corps brigade.[165] Major Sylvanus W. Curtis, commander of the 7th Michigan, remembered the Confederates advanced to "within 30 or 40 yards" of the line, where the 3rd Georgia, "partially protected by rocks and shrubs . . . . continued to pour . . . a galling fire" into the blue ranks.[166] The Confederate fire was answered with volleys from the two Federal regiments, and for a brief time the issue seemed in doubt. As men of the 3rd Georgia slugged it out a few yards to the north, the 22nd Georgia (which had begun the battle with about 465 officers and men) moved past them and into the gap south of the 7th Michigan. Their steps had carried them to the crest of Cemetery Ridge.[167]

*   *   *

While the Georgians were tramping to the hallowed high ground, the 13th Vermont appeared in the wide gap. This new regiment from George Stannard's green Second Vermont Brigade, Reynolds' First Corps, arrived at Gettysburg on the night of July 1, thus missing the disaster that had befallen the balance of the corps west of town. The untested Vermonters had been placed in reserve on Cemetery Hill behind the First and Eleventh Corps. When Longstreet's assault was unleashed the next afternoon far to the south, the 13th Vermont was ordered to advance "a little to the front and to the left of our former position, which brought us nearly in the rear of the right of the Second Corps." Matters steadily worsened and the Vermonters were hurriedly directed across the field to the threatened sector "in column by division [two company frontage]." The men were greeted by their division commander, Abner Doubleday, who informed them that the Federal center was "hard pressed" and they should seek directions from General Hancock. The regiment's colonel, Francis V. Randall, found Hancock "encouraging and rallying his [own] men to hold on to the position." Hancock was reluctant to order the raw troops into action—especially since they were not part of his corps. Still, Hancock had no one else to turn to, and thus offered Randall permission to move into the gap and restore the situation "if [Randall] thought [he] could do it."[168]

Unbeknownst to either Hancock or Colonel Randall, the reason the 13th Vermont was able to deploy and move against the 22nd Georgia was because the protection for Rans Wright's southern flank had collapsed. The disintegration of his support was the result of a domino effect that began some distance to the south. George Willard's Second Corps brigade—two regiments of which were known throughout the Army of the Potomac by the ignominious title, "The Harpers Ferry Cowards"—marched south from a position near Ziegler's Grove down Cemetery Ridge, deployed for action, and counterattacked just north of the Weikert place. Willard's 1,500 men ran right into Barksdale's three regiments along the low ground of Plum Run. a fierce exchange of musketry punctuated with artillery shells from some distant battery tore apart scores of men on both sides. Two in particular would be missed that evening. One of them was William Barksdale, who was hit in the chest and knocked from his horse. He had already suffered a wound in one leg above his knee, and a few minutes later a shell fragment had almost taken off his foot.

Somehow he had remained mounted until the final piece of metal struck his torso. The Mississippi regiments were already exhausted, in some disorder, and had suffered heavily; losing the aggressive and charismatic leadership of their beloved brigadier was more than they could stand. Firing as they fell back, the Mississippians made their way west toward the Emmitsburg Road to the cover of Alexander's flaming guns in the area of the Peach Orchard. (If Humphreys and his 21st Mississippi were not already isolated when they captured Watson's battery, the demise of Barksdale and the withdrawal of the rest of the brigade from along Plum Run decided the matter, and Humphreys ordered his men to fall back.) The second prominent officer struck down in the fight north of Weikert Woods was Federal Colonel George Williard, who lived just long enough to see his men redeem themselves and drive back the Mississippians. At the moment of his victory a large shell fragment struck him in the face and tore off part of his head, killing him instantly.[169] Barksdale's death and the retreat of his survivors left Cadmus Wilcox's right flank exposed. And the gray dominos began to tumble.

*   *   *

Once beyond the Emmitsburg Road, Wilcox, like Barksdale before him, fought his way east to Plum Run. Along the way his men captured several guns and knocked away everything in their path. The gathering dusk, heavy smoke, and general state of disorganization, however, caused Wilcox to halt his command and dress his line. The Alabamians were deep in enemy territory. Wilcox could not see much, but he saw enough to believe he could resume the attack and sweep the opposition before him if he could get some support for his exposed flanks. He had witnessed the retreat of Barksdale's Mississippians, and could no longer see the Floridians on his left. Repeated requests were sent by mounted courier to General Anderson seeking assistance, to no avail. Then, out of the smoke tramped another enemy line of battle, this one bearing down on Wilcox's left center. The troops were 262 men from Colonel William Colvill's 1st Minnesota, sent into the gaping hole on Cemetery Ridge by General Hancock himself with orders to capture the 11th Alabama's flag. The Northerners blasted a volley into the Alabama line, staggering it. A heavy exchange of fire ensued that drove back Colvill's regiment. "Three [separate] times did this last of the enemy's lines attempt to drive my men back," reported Wilcox, "and were as often repulsed." The forlorn attack, which cost the 1st Minnesota over 80% of its men, helped hold Wilcox in place and provided him with one more reason to finally decide it was time to pull back. "Without support on either my right or my left," he lamented, "my men were withdrawn to prevent their entire destruction or capture."[170] Another domino had fallen.

Wilcox's retrograde movement exposed the right flank of Lang's Floridians. Colonel Lang held his "ground until the enemy had advanced more than one hundred yards to my rear, and were about to cut off my retreat." Exactly what body of troops

Lang saw is unclear; it might have been one of Willard's regiments. Regardless, the only reason it was in his right rear was because Wilcox's Alabamians were not. This threat, plus a few rallied Third Corps remnants reformed east of the Floridians convinced Lang it was time to order his regiments to fall back.[171] Although they retreated in good order, the maneuver exposed yet another Confederate right flank—Wright's Georgia brigade.[172]

It was about 7:15 p.m. The retreat of Lang's trio of Florida regiments was bad news for Wright's Georgians. Even worse, Wright could see that Carnot Posey's Brigade on his left had, as he described it, "failed to advance." With his own ranks "seriously thinned," Wright realized that he would "not be able to hold" his ground or restart his forward momentum "unless speedily and strongly reinforced." Wright's remarkable feat now stood on the precipice of disaster—and he knew it. My brigade, he later reported, was "in a critical condition. The enemy's converging line was rapidly closing on our rear: a few moments more, and we would be completely surrounded." Without support "and with painful hearts we abandoned our captured guns, faced about, and prepared to cut our way through the closing lines in our rear. This was effected in tolerable order," he concluded, "but with immense loss."[173] The last domino was now flat on the table.

*   *   *

Where was Carnot Posey? As it turned out, he was back on Seminary Ridge. Wright's men had urged Posey's troops to move with them as they tramped past to open their attack. Posey had acknowledged his orders in his after-action report, and Wright had been reassured by Anderson's aide that the division commander would make sure Posey advanced in support of Wright's left flank. But he had not done so. The Georgian was incensed that the gallant sacrifices by his brigade had been squandered, and that the "opportunity" to permanently penetrate the enemy line had escaped him because a brigadier general had failed to follow his orders. In fact, *two* brigadier generals had failed in their duties that day.

The simple fact is that Carnot Posey lost control of his brigade just as he was to advance. A few hundred yards east of Posey's main position on Seminary Ridge were the Bliss farm buildings, infested with a few companies of men from Thomas Smyth's Federal brigade. Before the attack began, Posey had dispatched one of his regiments and part of another to the Bliss property, where a protracted skirmish fight developed. More of his men were fed into the action. From that point, some of these advanced Mississippians attached themselves to the left wing of Wright's Georgia brigade as it moved forward against Cemetery Ridge. Other Mississippi fragments moved all the way up to the Emmitsburg Road, partially shielding Wright's left until that point, where heavy fire drove them back across the wide valley. By the time Posey realized he should be advancing he discovered, certainly to his horror, that his brigade was scattered on a front a few hundred yards wide on a line running from

A Mississippi native and prewar lawyer, Carnot Posey had experience during the Mexican War in a regiment commanded by Jefferson Davis. He distinguished himself in the Shenandoah Valley in 1862 at the head of his regiment, the 16th Mississippi, as well as at Second Manassas and Sharpsburg, where he led Featherston's Brigade. His promotion to brigadier general followed. When so much was on the line, however, Posey failed in the early evening hours of July 2, 1863, when he lost control of his brigade and was unable to support Wright's penetration of Cemetery Ridge. It was a key bit of negligence. Posey was killed just a few months later at Bristoe Station. *Library of Congress*

Carnot Posey
(1818-1863)

Seminary Ridge through the Bliss Farm east to the Emmitsburg Road. Flustered, Posey sent a courier to General Anderson to determine how to handle the situation. By the time Posey reorganized his brigade it was dark and the attack was over.[174]

There is little doubt Posey knew he was culpable for failing to support Wright, and his after-action report is conspicuously evasive, contradictory, and thin. After acknowledging that he was ordered to "advance after Brigadier-General Wright, who was posted on my right," the Mississippi general added this curious sentence: "I received an order from the major-general [Anderson], through his aide-de-camp, Lieutenant [Samuel] D. Shannon, to advance but two regiments, and deploy them closely as skirmishers." He then proceeded to describe how he fed his men into the pointless but consuming skirmish on the Bliss farm. When Posey personally advanced to the barn, "I found my three regiments well up in advance. They had driven the enemy's pickets into their works and their artillerists from their guns in their front." By then it was too dark to do much of anything, the men were falling back, and eventually Anderson himself order Posey to withdraw.[175]

Posey's report is disingenuous. He implies that he understood Anderson's order to advance "but two regiments" to mean that his attack orders had been altered, but Posey fails to mention that the order carried by Shannon was delivered to Posey *before* Wright moved out. The order's obvious intent was to make sure that the brigadier's front was cleared of Federal skirmishers from the Bliss Farm in a timely manner so his brigade would enjoy an unimpeded advance. In fact, using skirmishers to clear a front was customary for a line of battle preparing to charge—and the veteran Posey had to have known this. Further, Posey's inference that the orders from Anderson had somehow sanctioned only skirmish action for his brigade (and thus did not authorize a full attack) is wholly at odds with the orders given to the other brigade commanders in the division, and differs entirely from what Anderson and Hill admitted they were themselves ordered to do by General Lee. Had Posey resolutely pushed his four regiments forward as aggressively as Wright, Lang, and Wilcox, the Federal skirmishers at the Bliss Farm would have been easily driven back. The Mississippians would have crossed the Emmitsburg Road and descended upon the weakly held Federal line immediately north of the Copse of Trees, which was defended by only two batteries of guns under Cushing and Arnold. As we have already seen on several occasions, 3-inch Ordnance rifles did not have enough firepower to stay an attack of competently led and determined infantry. The breakdown within Posey's Brigade was a significant reason for the ultimate failure of the attack on Cemetery Ridge on July 2, 1863.

Some of Posey's men at least left Seminary Ridge that afternoon and discharged their muskets. Billy Mahone's five Virginia regiments never took a step in the direction of Cemetery Ridge on July 2. Even more odd is the fact that his Gettysburg report, a mere six sentences of the most general variety, mentions nothing of the echelon attack on July 2. After Posey's diffused advance, Mahone received a plea for assistance from the Mississippian. His response, according to Posey, was that he had been "ordered to the right [and] could not comply."[176] There is no mention or corroboration from any other source that such an order had been given to Mahone, and since none of his men moved in that direction, it is safe to conclude that either Posey misconstrued Mahone's response or the Virginian was simply telling a tall tale. Thereafter, General Anderson dispatched his aide, Lieutenant Shannon, with a direct order for Mahone to move forward. In a breathtaking display of insubordination, Mahone refused to budge.

"I have orders from General Anderson to remain where I am," was the gist of Mahone's response.

"But I am just from General Anderson," stammered the incredulous aide, "and he orders you to advance!"[177] Mahone again rejected the order.

His action was eerily reminiscent of the disobedience he had displayed during the fight at Seven Pines, where his unilateral decision to yank his brigade out of line brought down Harvey Hill's wrath. Mahone violated one of the most sacred oaths of his rank by refusing to obey a direct order to advance. It was the most

A Virginia native and 1847 graduate of Virginia Military Institute, Billy Mahone dedicated his prewar years to engineering and railroading. When war broke out he joined an artillery unit as a lieutenant colonel, but his VMI diploma soon earned him a promotion to brigadier general in November 1861. At Seven Pines he withdrew his brigade without orders, raising the ire of his superior, Major General Harvey Hill. A few weeks later he had his men chopping wood at Glendale instead of pushing the enemy as General Lee intended. His eccentricities rose forth and bit the Virginia army again on July 2, 1863, when Mahone simply refused a superior's orders to advance against northern Cemetery Ridge. His recalcitrant behavior—which has never been satisfactorily explained—was a key reason Lee's echelon attack broke down. *Library of Congress*

William Mahone
(1826-1895)

unconscionable act committed by an officer on either side during any of the three days of fighting at Gettysburg. It seems almost impossible to believe that Mahone—who would develop into one of Lee's best division commanders during the last year of the war—could have witnessed or known what was going on that afternoon and done nothing. And yet this is exactly what he did. Had his 1,500 Virginians advanced across the valley as ordered, they would have faced Thomas Smyth, whose diminutive brigade of less than 1,000 held the line north of the batteries of Cushing and Arnold. Mahone squandered an excellent chance to rupture the Federal line, a key "opportunity" brought about by Lee's echelon attack and the blood of his comrades.[178]

Left of Mahone that afternoon was Dorsey Pender's Light Division. The newly-minted major general understood that his four brigades were to take up the echelon attack once Anderson's left brigades (Posey and Mahone) advanced. In order to be sure the advance of his brigades would not impeded by the enemy, Pender—in an order identical to the one issued earlier by Anderson to Posey—directed James Lane and Abner Perrin about 6:00 p.m. to send forward skirmishers and drive the Federal skirmishers beyond the Emmitsburg Road, which at this point hugged the base of Cemetery Hill. Both brigadiers responded promptly, and their skirmishers easily drove back their counterparts.[179]

With the path to Cemetery Hill clear, and anxious to unleash his Light Division against the Federals facing west on the high ground from Ziegler's Grove stretching north to where the line angled east toward Culp's Hill, Pender waited. And waited. Neither Mahone nor Posey seemed to be moving out. At this time Pender was behind the left (north) end of his battle line engaged in a conversation with Major Joseph B. Englehard, his assistant adjutant-general, and Lieutenant Colonel William G. Lewis of the 43th North Carolina. Realizing that something was wrong, Pender decided to ride south to the right flank of his command to see if he could visually ascertain why Anderson's left brigades were not moving forward. Colonel Perrin (who had led the splendid charge the day before that had broken the Federal line along Seminary Ridge) knew Pender had been ordered to participate in the attack, that the advance was imminent, and that, as he phrased it, "the best general officer in the army" was not going to be held back because someone else had dropped the ball.[180]

Federal artillery was dueling with Confederate batteries on Seminary Ridge in front of Pender's stationary division. Yankee gunners, however, were shooting long, and their shells and solid shot were falling all along Pender's line, smashing granite boulders and showering prone infantry with rock splinters. Under this iron umbrella Pender rode south, just moments away from ordering forward his four brigades. He had ridden but a short distance before fate dictated that the North Carolinian and an enemy shell would reprise John Bell Hood's early wounding. The missile exploded near him, and a ragged piece of iron about

William Dorsey Pender
(1834-1863)

He was as strict a disciplinarian as he was an aggressive and capable officer. Great things were expected of Dorsey Pender, a native of North Carolina and a rising star in the Army of Northern Virginia. His excellent combat record as a brigadier in the Light Division earned him a promotion to major general following Chancellorsville. He sustained his high reputation in his debut as commander of the Light Division on the first day's fighting at Gettysburg. His mortal wounding during the early evening hours of July 2, 1863, could not have come at a more inopportune time for General Lee's en échelon attack and the cause of Southern independence. *Library of Congress*

two inches square tore into his thigh. Although painful, the wound did not appear to be life threatening. Pender was borne from the field and his participation in the epic battle was at an end.[181]

By the time word reached Jim Lane, the division's acting senior brigadier, that he was now in command of the Light Division, it was "about sunset." According to Lane's report, "I was informed by Captain Norwood, of General Thomas' staff, that General Pender had been wounded, and that I must take command of the division, and advance, if I saw a good opportunity for doing so." Facing an immediate and serious command decision, Lane dispatched a courier to find Powell Hill to ask for instructions. By this time, he wrote, "the firing on the right was very desultory, the heavy fighting having ended." Lane was not about to advance the division on his own initiative.[182]

* * *

General Lee's echelon attack was going very well until it reached Powell Hill's Third Corps front, where the effort broke down completely. With Harry Heth's division in deep reserve, nine brigades in Hill's remaining two divisions (Anderson's and Pender's) had been slated to participate in the attack. Yet only three of these nine—those belonging to Cadmus Wilcox, David Lang, and Rans Wright—attacked with the *élan* and ferocity that typified the infantry of the Army of Northern Virginia. a fourth, under Posey, offered but a feeble attempt, and five others (Mahone, Lane, Perrin, Thomas, and Scales) did not advance into action. And yet, the three brigades of Anderson that did get into action, together with Longstreet's eight brigades under Hood and McLaws, had pushed the Federal army to the breaking point. Powell Hill knew the important role General Lee had assigned to his Third Corps. Why, then, had only one-third of the designated infantry brigades attacked?

The primary responsibility for the breakdown for the echelon attack rests on Powell Hill's shoulders. As discussed earlier, he understood what was expected of his corps and confirmed it in his report. After proudly registering the expensive accomplishments of Wilcox, Lang, and Wright, he concluded with his discussion of the day's events thusly: "The enemy threw forward heavy re-enforcements, *and no supports coming to these brigades* [emphasis added], the ground so hardly won had to be given up." Hill was not about to mention that the support could only have come from his own corps, and that neither Posey nor Mahone had moved forward as ordered; neither had the Light Division. There is no evidence that Hill ordered Anderson to personally get involved. Knowing what was on the line, Hill should have shoved Posey and Mahone forward himself. Hill's performance does not compare well when contrasted with the manner in which Longstreet handled his own brigades. Hill failed miserably on July 2.[183]

As a division commander, Richard Anderson was responsible for making sure his brigades were deployed properly and moved forward, *en échelon*, in accordance with Lee's orders. But only three of his five brigades went into action as intended, so Anderson manifestly failed to exercise his authority properly. His lapse seems even more serious in light of Wilcox's and Wright's multiple requests for support. He must have learned within just a few minutes that Mahone was disobeying his orders, transmitted via Lieutenant Shannon, to advance. Why he did not guide his horse to the left of his line and kick the tavern owner's son forward is baffling. No blame can be attached to Dorsey Pender, who knew his duties and was about to implement his orders when struck down.

One corps commander, one division commander, and two brigadiers, Third Corps generals all, were why the echelon attack failed on July 2, 1863.

Ewell (Finally) Attacks

One of the major sources for Meade's reinforcements, dispatched to the southern end of the field to stop Lee's echelon attack, had come from the Federal army's right flank around Cemetery and Culp's hills. Every brigade save one from Slocum's Twelfth Corps had been pulled from defensive positions on and around Culp's Hill, and some of these brigades had marched to the threatened Federal center. Even the battered First Corps infantry, including those units linking the defensive line from Culp's Hill to East Cemetery Hill, had been ordered to leave their positions and march south. These withdrawals to bolster the Federal left center and far left flank dangerously reduced Meade's infantry on his right, even though they were supported by powerful artillery batteries. Meade was reacting as Lee expected he might, and in so doing, provided the Southern army with another "opportunity" to exploit to advantage. And this one belonged to Dick Ewell and his Second Corps.

As previously discussed, Ewell's line ran, generally speaking, from west of Gettysburg through town and around the north side of Culp's Hill. Rodes was on Ewell's right, Early in the center opposite Cemetery Hill, and Johnson held the left facing Culp's Hill. General Lee had ordered Ewell "to make a simultaneous demonstration upon the enemy's right, to be converted into a real attack should opportunity offer." Ewell's demonstration and/or attack was to be made "as soon as [Longstreet's] guns opened."[184] Special note should be made of Lee's words "simultaneous" and "opportunity." The commanding general was giving Ewell specific instructions to demonstrate against the right wing of the enemy *at the same time* Longstreet's and Hill's troops were attacking Meade's left and center. These orders allowed Ewell the accustomed discretion to direct the troops of Second Corps as he saw fit, taking advantage of any "opportunity" the Federals presented to drive

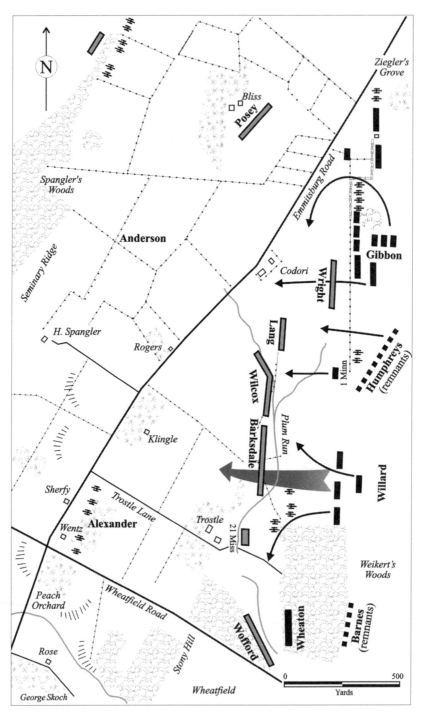

Troop Positions at the Point of the Breakdown of the Echelon Attack

home a decisive battle-winning thrust. These instructions serve as yet another example of "orders with discretion," which allowed the subordinate commander on the scene flexibility to determine *how* the orders were to be implemented (not whether they would be implemented at all). This arrangement made sound military sense, not only because of where Second Corps was positioned, but also because Lee knew when he issued those orders he was going to be closely involved in the placement, planning, and progress of the Southern troops attacking on the Confederate right side of Gettysburg.

Ewell's plans were as follows: after an artillery bombardment, Johnson's Division would move against Culp's Hill while Early's brigades supported Johnson's right (west) flank by moving against East Cemetery Hill. Early's right, in turn, would be covered by the advance of Rodes' Division, which would be covered on the right by Powell Hill's advancing Light Division under Dorsey Pender.[185] It was a sound plan considering Ewell's role, but the problems in execution rested in coordination and proper artillery support. Like Longstreet and Hill before him, the key to Ewell's success would be whether he could properly time his movement in a general sense, and then coordinate his divisions once the demonstration was underway.

Given the nature of the ground and the difficulty inherent in shifting troops in or around the outskirts of town, it is hard to understand why Ewell allowed Rodes' large division (he had five of the 13 Second Corps brigades) to remain where it was. By nightfall on July 1, his division was spread out from Seminary Ridge east into Gettysburg proper. Other than minor adjustments, this alignment remained intact until late on the afternoon of July 2. In other words, much of the town of Gettysburg was *between* Rodes' Division and the Federals on Cemetery Hill. Thus, in order to get his troops into position for an attack against Cemetery Hill, Rodes would have to first swing his brigades around the southwest corner of Gettysburg and redeploy them before he could even advance. Certainly it would have made more sense to either bring Rodes around and behind Early, to be in position to follow up that general's efforts, or further east left of Johnson's brigades, which would have extended the Confederate left and threatened to cut the Federal line of retreat along the Baltimore Pike. Whether Rodes should have remained west of town is rather beside the point; wherever he was it was incumbent upon Ewell to insure he was brought into action. With Early and Johnson deployed east of town, the only way Ewell could get Rodes into the fight and properly positioned to support Early was to have him advance and deploy ahead of Early or bring him east of town and follow Early into action. (Ironically, General Lee had urged Ewell to do something similar to this during the Almshouse arbor council and again later that night when he met with Ewell alone.)

The desire of Ewell and his division commanders to remain on the left side of Gettysburg has always been difficult to understand. The ground along both the Hanover Road and the York Pike was ill-suited for defense, and any offensive action against an enemy determined to hold the heights would be difficult to carry out successfully. Ewell's position was especially poor for employing artillery, which would be desperately needed to support any offensive infantry action. With the exception of Benner's Hill, some soil immediately north of that small rise astride the Hanover Road, and the northern portion of Seminary Ridge on the right side of town, there was nowhere for Ewell to position his guns. The open ground east of Gettysburg simply did not offer sufficient protection against the powerful Federal artillery on Cemetery and Culp's hills. Ewell had to know that any infantry attack delivered on the left side of town could only be minimally supported with his artillery. But the converse was true for the Federals. From their positions on Cemetery Hill, Sevens' Knoll, and Culp's Hill, Yankee gunners enjoyed ample room and good fields of fire. Federal artillerists would be able to bring more batteries to bear and could smother any attempt made by Southern gunners to get the upper hand on that portion of the battlefield. Even if Ewell was able to seize a portion the high ground occupied by Federal troops, the rough nature of the terrain and limited number of approaches suitable for limbered ordnance meant that a redeployment like the one E. Porter Alexander made from Seminary Ridge to the Peach Orchard would be difficult or impossible to accomplish.

Given the difficulties facing Second Corps, why did Lee order Ewell to conduct a "simultaneous demonstration upon the enemy's right, to be converted into a real attack should opportunity offer?" It would have been unrealistic for Lee to believe that an *isolated* attack by Ewell's Corps could have been successful—unless Meade stripped formations from that part of his line to shore up other areas under attack. And that, of course, is exactly what Lee believed Meade might do when faced with a heavy assault against his left and center. General Lee's orders for Ewell were simple and clear: when Longstreet attacked on the southern portion of the field, Ewell would use his men to demonstrate against Meade's lines. This tactic was designed to pin or hold in place Federal formations on Meade's right wing and thus prevent the shuttling of reinforcements from that point to other sectors. How Ewell conducted the demonstration—to be converted to a real attack should the opportunity offer itself—was left to his discretion, which was the accustomed latitude accorded by Lee to his lieutenants.[186]

Lee's intention that Ewell demonstrate just after Longstreet opened his attack was yet another effort to situate Meade on the horns of a dilemma. If, on the one hand, Meade pulled troops from his right—those opposite Ewell—and sent them elsewhere, he would weaken that flank and present an "opportunity" for Ewell to expand his demonstration into a full blown attack. The loss of either Cemetery Hill or Culp's Hill would have been devastating for the Army of the Potomac—far more so than the loss of either of the Round Tops. If, however, Ewell's "simultaneous demonstration" convinced Meade that his right flank was seriously threatened, he would not be in a position to draw troops from that sector to support other parts of his line under assault by first Longstreet, and then Hill. As we know, Meade shifted thousands of troops from the right half of his army (and from his reserve) for service on other parts of the battlefield. Without them, how else could he have stopped Longstreet and Hill? As it turned out, Meade reacted in a manner anticipated by Lee. As the sun was slowly sinking behind the Cumberland mountains on July 2, Ewell's Second Corps was presented with an incredible "opportunity" to drive in and collapse Meade's right flank. All that Dick Ewell had to do was get most or all of his brigades into the fight.

* * *

Sometime after 4:00 p.m. Longstreet's guns were heard thundering in the distance, heralding the opening of the battle. In accordance with his orders, Ewell began his demonstration by ordering the few batteries of artillery from Second Corps that could be brought to bear to open fire on the Federals occupying the high ground on a line from Cemetery Hill to Culp's Hill.[187] From the left side of Gettysburg, Major Joseph Latimer and his 16-gun battalion of Johnson's Division raced up the slope of Benner's Hill between 4:00 and 5:00 p.m. Latimer unlimbered 14 of his guns on the crest and opened fire. His two heaviest pieces—20-pounder Parrotts—were placed just north of the Hanover Road alongside four 20-pounder Parrotts of the famous 1st Rockbridge Virginia Artillery. These half-dozen guns opened a destructive fire on the Federal batteries positioned on East Cemetery Hill. Meanwhile, from Seminary Ridge on the right side of town, 12 pieces from Willis Dance's Battalion opened fire on Cemetery Hill. Their effort was supported by all but one of the battery's from David McIntosh's Battalion (12 guns) and another nine rifled pieces from John Garnett's Battalion, Hill's Third Corps.[188]

The Confederate guns from Benner's Hill and Seminary Ridge had the advantage of converging fire, but were badly outnumbered. The right side of the Federal line erupted like a volcano in response to the artillery barrage. Sending solid and percussion shot against the Confederate batteries, crews from 43 Federal guns in and near the Evergreen Cemetery, of which 33 faced Seminary Ridge and 10 were trained on Benner's Hill, responded with their own counter battery fire. Another 30 Federal pieces situated east of the Baltimore Pike facing Benner's Hill joined the action. Within a few minutes the 20 Confederate guns firing on the left (east) side of Gettysburg were exchanging rounds with twice that many Federal pieces, many of which were protected by earthworks thrown up on East Cemetery Hill, while equal numbers of Confederate and Federal pieces dueled between Cemetery Hill and a stretch of the northern end of Seminary Ridge.[189]

The gunnery duel lasted for more than one hour. Colonel Charles S. Wainwright, the intrepid Federal commander of First Corps' artillery, was observing the exchange from the cemetery. The Confederate fire, he remembered, "was the most accurate I have ever seen."[190] One 20-pounder Parrott round killed or wounded an entire Yankee artillery crew of five. Other projectiles struck and disabled two Federal guns and exploded a caisson. Federal infantry stationed on the reverse slopes were caught in the crossfire from Confederate artillery on Benner's Hill and those stationed on Seminary Ridge, and suffered accordingly.[191] Ewell's artillerists were putting the Yankee guns and superior enemy ammunition captured at the Battle of Second Winchester to good use. Good firing notwithstanding, there were simply too many Federal batteries to contend with.[192] Latimer's Battalion was smothered with iron. "Never, before or after, did I see 15 or 20 guns in such a condition of wreck and destruction as this battalion was," wrote gunner Robert Stiles. "It had been hurled backward, as it were, by the very weight and impact of metal."[193]

Latimer's Battalion was silenced and its commander mortally wounded before Ewell decided to launch his infantry against the Federal line. Evidently, Ewell initially decided to limit his demonstration to artillery fire; if he had thought otherwise, some of his infantry would have already been ordered to advance. Johnson, for example, could have aggressively pushed his skirmishers across Rock Creek to give the impression that an attack was eminent. Instead, Ewell's 13 brigades remained idle while Latimer on the left side of town and a few batteries on the right were torn to pieces.

Before the Federal batteries completely suppressed Latimer's fire, Ewell tried to ascertain the progress of the Confederate echelon attack. He and his staff picked their way through Gettysburg to Saint Francis Xavier Roman Catholic Church on High Street. Ewell remained on the street below while members of his staff climbed a ladder into the cupola to view the progress of Longstreet's and Hill's assaults. The high perch provided the officers with a view down the Emmitsburg Road to the Peach Orchard, including most of the ground over which Barksdale, Wilcox, Lang, and Wright were advancing, or preparing to advance. "Things are going splendidly!" one of the aides called down to Ewell. "We are driving them back everywhere!"[194] This encouraging news, which was possibly augmented with word from Confederate skirmishers along Rock Creek that Federal formations were quitting that portion of the line, seemed to be the tonic that prompted Ewell to convert the artillery demonstration "into a real attack," just as Lee had ordered.[195]

Messengers were soon spurring their mounts across the landscape with orders from Ewell for the infantry to attack. Ed Johnson recalled that sometime after 6:00 p.m. (and probably after 6:45 p.m.), "in obedience to an order from [Ewell], I then advanced my infantry to the assault of the enemy's strong position—a rugged and rocky mountain." By the time orders were passed down the line and final preparations completed, it must have been at least 7:00 p.m. by the time three of Johnson's four brigades (Walker's famed Stonewall Brigade was left out of this attack in order to protect the division's left flank along the Hanover Road in lieu of Stuart's missing cavalry) crossed "waist-deep" Rock Creek and reached the base of Culp's Hill about "dark."[196]

The infantrymen struggled up the rugged slopes illuminated by the light of flashing small arms fire. Although Johnson had no way of knowing it, Meade had snatched away all of the Federal Twelfth Corps from Culp's Hill except for George Greene's lone New York brigade, which was stretched from Wadsworth's First Corps sector on the left all the way to lower Culp's Hill. All of the Federal breastworks from that point to the vicinity of Spangler's Spring, about 400 yards, were empty. Johnson's attack struck Greene head-on, with John M. Jones' men on the far right, Jesse Williams' Louisianians in the middle, and George Steuart's mixed brigade of Maryland, North Carolina, and Virginia troops on the left.

The important action took place on the far left of Johnson's line on George Hume "Maryland" Steuart's front. A native of Maryland (and hence his nickname) Steuart had graduated from West Point in 1848 just above the bottom rung of the academic ladder. Thus far in the war his service had been a rather mixed bag. His resume was solid and steady at the regimental level. Stonewall Jackson, however, was not comfortable with him at the head of a brigade and transferred Steuart to the cavalry, but his service there did not please Jackson either. Steuart returned to his men only to be seriously wounded a short time later at Cross Keys during the Shenandoah Valley Campaign of 1862. His injury kept him out of the army one year. On the evening of July 2, Steuart's 2,000 soldiers found themselves scrambling up the shadowy slope of a rocky and wooded hill in Pennsylvania. Before them loomed the right front of Greene's attenuated but entrenched line. With his right regiments pinned down in front of Greene, Steuart's left regiments continued advancing and stumbled into empty trenches stretching beyond Greene's right flank. Wheeling smartly to the right, Steuart flanked the New York line and drove back at least two regiments to a traverse and summit of the hill. While the other two brigades in Johnson's attack continued holding and pressing Greene from the front, Steuart was slowly turning the New Yorker's line. His men were now within 400 yards of Meade's vital line of communication running along the Baltimore Pike.

Enemy reinforcements, however, arrived in the form of several First Corps regiments, which had been chopped up on the first day of the battle. Their appearance stalled Steuart's advance.[197] Had James Walker's splendid brigade of Virginians been included in the attack, Johnson's line would have widely overlapped Greene's and he would have had the manpower to fully exploit Steuart's gains. Instead, the division's progress was arrested through a combination of Greene's entrenched and stubborn Federals, reinforcements from Cemetery Hill, darkness, rugged terrain, and the arrival of other Yankee formations slowly making the trek back to Culp's Hill. However, more than anything else, Johnson failed to carry Culp's Hill because he did not begin his attack soon enough and could not get all of his brigades to participate.[198]

On Johnson's right, Jubal Early had been waiting about 28 hours for orders to carry Cemetery Hill. "Old Jubilee" believed that his division would need support from other commands to take the heights, and Ewell was going to provide it with

Johnson's attack on one side and Rodes on the other. As Early later reported, he was "ordered by General Ewell to advance upon Cemetery Hill with my two brigades that were in position as soon as General Johnson's division, which was on my left, should become engaged at the wooded hill on the left [Culp's], which it was about to attack." The advance, he continued "would be general, and made also by Rodes' division and Hill's divisions on my right." That suited Early just fine. "Accordingly," he concluded, "as soon as Johnson became warmly engaged, which was a little before dusk, I ordered Hays and Avery to advance and carry the heights in front."[199]

Following the fighting on July 1, the brigades of Harry Hays and Isaac Avery, approximately 2,500 effectives, had "struck camp in a deep ravine" running along a little rivulet known as Winebrenner's Run.[200] Their line, about 800 yards in length and facing generally southeast, ran from the Henry Culp farm southwest across present day East Confederate Avenue and continued to a point near the Winebrenner House at the intersection of Baltimore and Lefever streets in Gettysburg. As a result, the right flank of Hays' brigade was a mere 250 yards from the Federal infantry line on East Cemetery Hill running along and angling off of Brickyard Lane, immediately below present day Wainwright Avenue. The opposite end of the line however, consisting of Avery's left flank, was 800 yards from the enemy. Sheltered in this depression, the Confederates were protected from Federal artillery fire, but subjected to constant skirmishing and sharpshooting throughout the day.[201]

Anyone peering up at the eastern face of Cemetery Hill from Winebrenner's Run, would have viewed these heights, "crowned with strongly built fortifications and bristling with a formidable array of cannon," as imposing.[202] And indeed they were. But Cemetery Hill was not, as many writers today seem to consider, an unassailable position—especially when the quality of the attacking and defending troops are taken into consideration. While the terrain on which a battle is fought is very important, military history is full of examples that prove the *élan* and leadership qualities of the troops are even more important to a battle's outcome. Napoleon often claimed that in war, "morale is to the physical as three is to one."[203] This observation, coming from a Great Captain who fought and won more battles under dramatically varying conditions than any other general in modern history, holds up well to the scrutiny of time. Indeed, had Napoleon been alive and able to witness Longstreet's assault on July 2, he might well have repeated his well known Maxim because it describes perfectly how the Southern brigades, outnumbered by a margin of two-to-one and attacking over difficult terrain against superior ordnance, attained the success they did.

Keeping in mind the importance of morale and leadership, it can be fairly stated that while there were indeed many enemy soldiers occupying space on Cemetery Hill on July 2, their morale was fragile at best. These men were members of Howard's much-maligned and often-defeated Eleventh Corps, which had been soundly beaten and routed just the previous afternoon. Its freshest brigade, Orland

Smith's, had not been attacked on July 1 and was positioned facing west looking at Seminary Ridge (where the Taneytown and Emmitsburg roads cross). Since Smith's brigade had avoided the debacle of the previous day, three of his four regiments were assigned skirmish duty on July 2. They were heavily engaged in this capacity throughout the day on the west side of Cemetery Hill and suffered heavy casualties—close to one-third of their strength—before being driven back onto Cemetery Hill by sharpshooters from Pender's Division.[204]

The other five brigades of Eleventh Corps situated on Cemetery Hill had lost more than half of their effective strength on July 1. Colonel Andrew L. Harris of the 75th Ohio, acting commander of Adelbert Ames' brigade, recalled the pitiful remnants as they formed ranks on East Cemetery Hill on July 2. His three Ohio regiments "did not exceed 500" of the 941 men who had started the battle. The 17th Connecticut had less than 200 of the 386 who had arrived at Gettysburg.[205] Harris' estimate might even be overly-optimistic. Lieutenant Peter F. Young, adjutant of the 107th Ohio in Harris' brigade, remembered that:

> On the first day our regt. 107 Ohio went into the engagement with 434 muskets—on the evening of same day (from which I commanded regt. till I was wounded) I reported 171. Regret that I do not remember the number of killed, wounded and prisoners. The other regts. of our brigade *viz.* 25th, 75th Ohio and 17th Conn. each had I think less than 100 men left, having lost in about the same proportion.[206]

Howard's men had suffered heavy losses the day before and were saddled with the memory of their severe mauling at Chancellorsville only two months earlier. The troops of Eleventh Corps manning Cemetery Hill on July 2 were hardly analogous to the confident and rested regiments populating Meade's other Federal corps.

* * *

Jubal Early emerged from one of the side streets of Gettysburg below Cemetery Hill and rode slowly along Winebrenner's Run. Bullets from Federal sharpshooters whizzed around him, but he paid them little heed. Early was making his final inspection to make sure Hays and Avery were ready to charge. Captain William Seymour, Hays' assistant adjutant-general, looked at the battle-hardened Louisianians and remembered "the quiet, solemn mien of our men showed quietly that they fully appreciated the desperate character of the undertaking, but [on] every face was most legibly written the firm determination to do or die."[207] Early had already decided to give Hays temporary command of Avery's North Carolinians for the evening assault. Perhaps it was Hays who suggested the officers dismount for battle, for when the signal to advance was given, all the Louisiana Tigers and Tar

Heel officers, except for Colonel Avery, were on foot. The sun was already setting.[208]

The pair of Confederate brigades rose up from Winebrenner's Run and moved toward East Cemetery Hill. The North Carolinians quietly crossed a fence line close to present day East Confederate Avenue, realigned themselves, and continued on. Federal guns opened fire when the Southerners emerged from their cover, but the growing darkness made it hard to hit the moving targets.[209] Hays' Louisianians cleared a small ridge and descended into a low swell that shielded them from Federal fire. The Tigers wheeled right towards East Cemetery Hill. "The Yankee missiles are hissing," remembered Seymour, "screaming and hurtling over our heads, but doing very little damage."[210] Private Thomas E. Causby, marching on the other end of the line with the 6th North Carolina, had a similar recollection. "The enemy batteries kept up a terrific fire," he wrote, "but most of the shells and grape passed over our heads."[211]

Positioned on the left wing of the attacking line, Avery's Brigade had to march several hundred yards further than Hay's men before wheeling to the right and striking East Cemetery Hill. When the Tar Heels came out of the low bottom, the 6th's Captain Neill W. Ray recalled that every Federal gun from the cemetery gate southward to Stevens' Knoll was "brought to bear on us. The fire was terrific, but our men moved forward very rapidly, bearing to the right, having the batteries on Cemetery Hill as their objective point."[212] As the North Carolinians moved up East Cemetery Hill, their lines were enfiladed by the fire from Stevens' six Napoleons on the small knoll that connected East Cemetery to Culp's Hill. Added to this fire was that from other batteries in front of Avery's regiments.[213] The North Carolinians had made it about halfway to the Federal lines when the lone mounted officer was struck in the neck by a bullet and knocked from his horse. It was so dark by this time that few if any men were even aware that Isaac Avery's life was running out of his body. Avery's men completed their wheel and pushed onward. "Our brigade charged in good order until we were within a short distance of the stone fence," recalled Private Causby, "which did not extend all the way across the face of the hill. Here the brigade spread out across the face of the hill, part of the men making for the ends of the fence."[214]

As Avery's men were performing their wheel, the Louisianians were striking the enemy line on the north and northeastern corner of East Cemetery Hill. Andrew Harris' (Ames') brigade was positioned along a stone wall skirting the hill some 75 yards from the summit. In addition to the wall, part of Harris' line was strengthened with two rows of rocks, fence posts, boards, dirt, and rifle pits. Even though the Yankee infantry enjoyed the advantage of fighting on the defensive under cover, the position was not a strong one. The Federal batteries on East Cemetery Hill were uphill and behind the infantry. This meant that the tubes could not be depressed to fire into the infantry advancing along Brickyard Lane. As result, when Hays' Tigers charged through a field of knee-high corn and up the slope, Harris' defenders did not

Brigadier General Harry Hays (shown here without his early-war flowing beard) and Colonel Isaac Avery bravely led their brigades up East Cemetery Hill in one of the most dramatic attacks of the entire war. Their combined thrust collapsed Howard's Eleventh Corps defenders and captured the most important piece of terrain on the entire Gettysburg field. And there they waited for reinforcements that never arrived.

Author's Collection

Isaac Avery
(1828-1863)

North Carolina Regiments

Harry Hays
(1820-1876)

have the firepower to stop them. Sergeant Oscar Ladley of 75th Ohio recalled that the Louisianians came up "yelling like demons with fixed bayonets. We opened on them . . . but still they came, their officers & colors in advance."[215] The intrepid Confederate advance made a lasting impression on Colonel Harris:

> When they came into full view in Culp's meadow our artillery, on Cemetery Hill, east of the Baltimore Pike, opened on them with all the guns that could be brought to bear. But on, still on, they came, moving steadily to the assault, soon the infantry opened fire, but they never faltered. They moved forward as steadily, amid this hail of shot, shell and minnie ball, as though they were on parade far removed from danger. It was a complete surprise to us. We did not expect this assault as bravely and rapidly made.[216]

The Southerners closed quickly on Harris' line. As Seymour remembered it, "the Yankees [were] easily driven away."[217] The screaming bayonet-tipped line of veterans utterly unnerved the Ohioans and Connecticut troops, who simply came apart. Hays' men jumped the first wall and came across another line of "abatis of fallen timber, and the third line, disposed in rifle pits. This line we broke, and as before, found many of the enemy who had not fled hiding in the pits for protection. These I ordered to the rear as prisoners, and continued my progress to the crest of the hill."[218]

A few minutes later a couple hundred yards southeast down the stone wall, Leopold von Gilsa's brigade was struck by Avery's two right regiments. The shock of the elite 6th North Carolina, a regiment that had served with distinction and under notable commanders since First Manassas, smashed the 153rd Pennsylvania and 68th New York. To the left of the 6th, the 21st North Carolina passed Menchey's Spring below the stone wall and struck the Federal line. Major James Beall recalled

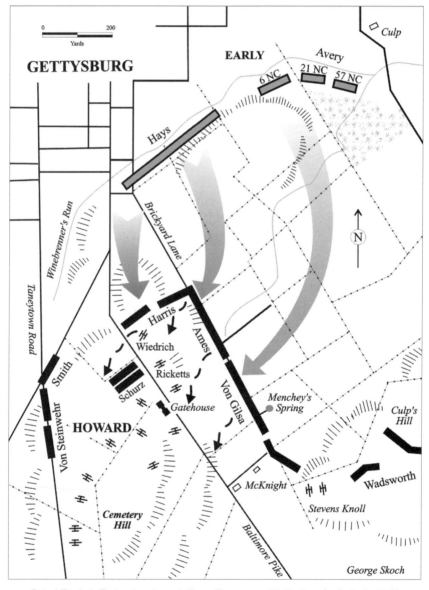

Jubal Early's Brigades Attack East Cemetery Hill, Dusk, July 2, 1863

how the Tar Heels routed the 54th New York, "killing and capturing a few of them—the greater part" having bolted up the hill towards the supporting artillery batteries in front of and in the Evergreen Cemetery.[219] The rout continued when the infantry of the 21st regiment broke seven of the nine companies of the 41st New York. The pair of companies on the far right, however, were halted and reformed by an enterprising captain. Standing fast, these half-a-hundred men protected the left flank of the 33rd Massachusetts, which had been detached from Orland Smith's brigade.[220] With their left now secure and their right covered by Stevens' powerful battery of Napoleons, the Bay Staters remained in position to confront the 57th North Carolina on the far left of the Confederate line. The solid line of infantry, supported by deadly blasts of canister from six smoothbore cannon, ripped into the North Carolina ranks and stopped their advance.[221]

Within the space of minutes the Louisianians and North Carolinians had collapsed von Gilsa's and Harris' brigades. Captain R. Bruce Ricketts watched the Confederate attack from his battery on the crest of East Cemetery Hill. "As soon as the charge commenced," wrote the artillerist, Howard's infantry, "although they had a stone-wall in their front, commenced running in the greatest confusion to the rear, hardly a shot was fired, certainly not a volley, and so panic stricken were they that

several ran into the canister fire of my guns and were knocked over."[222] Hays remembered that his men made "a simultaneous rush" in the blinding smoke, din and darkness, scooping up "four stands of colors, and a number of prisoners."[223]

The colors of the 8th Louisiana were planted on the breastworks in front of

"Night Assault"

In the growing darkness of July 2, 1863, Jubal Early launched two of his three available brigades against East Cemetery Hill. The Tigers and Tar Heels quickly overran a division of Howard's Eleventh Corps positioned on the forward slope. Men from Hay's Louisiana brigade are shown here overrunning one of the Federal batteries on the hill's summit. *Courtesy Gallon Historical Art, Gettysburg, Pennsylvania*

Captain Michael Wiedrich's Battery I, 1st New York Light Artillery. Wiedrich had six 3-inch Ordnance rifles under his command, and Wainwright later commented how ineptly the German gunners had worked their pieces during the afternoon's artillery duel and during the dusk assault. Wainwright grudgingly acknowledged that the gunners "fought splendidly, sticking to their guns" when Hays' Tigers rushed up the protruding slope of East Cemetery Hill and into their midst. The spunk displayed by Wiedrich's men, inspired by the presence of General Ames, bought them nothing but a minute or two of time and more bloodshed. Some of Hays' men spilled over the wall separating Wiedrich's guns from Ricketts' pieces and poured a destructive fire into the left section of the battery.[224] Several dozen Southerners fought the artillerists for possession of the pieces. Replaying the fight for Wiedrich's battery, Confederate small arms fire and bayonets were pitted against Federal pistols, handspikes, and rammers. Within a few minutes, those gunners who had not retreated into the darkness were dead, wounded, or prisoners. The tongues of flames discharging from their weapons illuminated the colors of the 6th North Carolina and 9th Louisiana planted on the crest of East Cemetery Hill. "At that time, every piece of artillery that had been firing on us was silenced," wrote Hays. "A quiet of several minutes now ensued."[225] The darkness that had helped shield the Confederates during their assault worked against them once they had taken the hill. Colonel Archibald Campbell Godwin of the 57th North Carolina recalled how his men "charged up the hill with heroic determination," but once the breakthrough had been achieved, "the darkness [made it] impossible to concentrate more than 40 or 50 men at any point for further advance."[226]

Jubal Early's stunning achievement on East Cemetery Hill provides yet another example of why General Lee believed his troops could "go anywhere and do anything if properly led." Now the Federals were recoiling in the darkness from the charge of "their desperate and maddened assailants." All that was needed for the Confederates to complete the capture of Cemetery Hill was for Robert Rodes to attack as Ewell had planned and as Early expected. "Gen. Hays immediately reformed his line [on top of East Cemetery Hill] and anxiously waited to hear Rodes' guns co-operating with us on the right," William Seymour recalled. "But, unfortunately, no such assistance came to us."[227]

*   *   *

Robert Rodes—Douglas Southall Freeman's "Norse God in Confederate Gray"—paid careful attention to the Federals stretched from Ziegler's Grove to Cemetery Hill when Longstreet's assault opened two miles to the south. This attack, he wrote after the battle, "produced some stir among the enemy in my immediate front, and seemed to cause there a diminution of both artillery and infantry." Rodes was right. Troops from his front were being pulled out and dispatched to shore up other sectors of Meade's line. The result was another "opportunity" to break open the enemy's position. Rodes understood completely what was expected of him that afternoon. "Orders given during the afternoon, and after the engagements had opened on the right," he later wrote, "required me to co-operate with the attacking force as soon as any opportunity of doing so with good effect was offered." While Longstreet's and Hill's brigades were battering Meade's left and center, Rodes sought out Early and the pair agreed to attack the heights in concert with their divisions. Rodes also informed "the officer commanding the troops on my right [part of Pender's Division] that, in accordance with our plan, I would attack just at dark." According to Rodes, he proceeded to make final arrangements for the planned assault. Exactly what arrangements he made are unclear.[228]

Rodes' effort was a fiasco from beginning to end. Two of his five brigades, Daniel's and O'Neal's, were on Seminary Ridge about 400 yards behind the front brigades of Ramseur, Iverson, and Doles. These formations were resting along West Middle Street in Gettysburg about 900 yards from Cemetery Hill. Ramseur was on the far right, Iverson in the middle, and Doles on the left. No one seemed to appreciate before the advance that the left side of Rodes' line would run right into the town. According to Ramseur, when it came time to move out, Rodes ordered him to "move by the right flank until Brigadier-General Doles' troops cleared the town, and then" to face left and "advance in line of battle on the enemy's position on the Cemetery Hill." If Rodes supervised the redeployment of his division before the advance, his orders to Ramseur certainly did not reflect it.

Robert Emmett Rodes
(1829-1864)

Although he is considered by many influential historians to be the best division commander in the Army of Northern Virginia after Gettysburg until his death on September 19, 1864, Robert Rodes displayed few skillful traits during the pivotal three-day Pennsylvania battle. His brigades were dripped into action on July 1, and then poorly deployed on July 2. After having eight hours to prepare for his early evening assault, Rodes was unable to get *any* of his brigades into action in time to aid Early's brigades fighting and dying on the summit of East Cemetery Hill. Gettysburg ranks as the nadir of his career. *Library of Congress*

Precious minutes ticked away and darkness crept forth as Rodes' brigades lurched to the right in an effort to find a clear field to advance across. Ramseur remembered Rodes telling him "that the remaining brigades of the division would be governed by my movements."[229] Was Rodes placing the responsibility for redeploying the entire division on the shoulders of a brigadier? It was a curious and lax arrangement that has never satisfactorily been explained and would only grow more confusing.

Once clear of the town, the three leading brigades wheeled left and crossed Long Lane. Daniel and O'Neal fell in behind them as the division slowly tramped through the long shadows toward Cemetery Hill's northwest face. Little could be seen of the enemy during the long approach. The front line reached "within 200 yards of the enemy's position" before Ramseur ordered a halt. "Two lines of infantry behind stone walls and breastworks," were seen, reported Ramseur. "The strength and position of the enemy's batteries and their supports induced me to halt and confer with General Doles, and, with him, to make representation of the character of the enemy's position, and ask further instructions."[230] George Doles reported that the front line "arrived within 100 yards of the enemy's line" before the conference between himself, Ramseur, and Iverson took place. With the moon rising and the firing on East Cemetery Hill dying down, Rodes had arrived too late to help Early. The division was ordered to quietly fall back with the front brigades taking position along Long Lane.[231] Unlike Hays and Avery, who had resolutely pushed their men up the heights to meet an opponent possessing considerably less confidence and espirit de corps than they, Rodes' generals decided that nothing could be accomplished and did not even make the effort. Not one of Rodes' five brigades fired a shot in anger that evening.

As time ticked away and the northwest side of Cemetery Hill remained quiet, Early decided against sending in additional infantry support for Hays and Avery—even though his reserve brigade was available for the effort. When Hays and Avery began their charge, John Gordon's six regiments of Georgians were brought forward to Weinbrenner's Run. They remained there throughout the attack. Once the summit was conquered, the Louisianians and North Carolinians remained in position for 15 or 20 minutes anxiously awaiting reinforcements to solidify their position and expand their breakthrough.[232] They never arrived. Without Rodes' support, Early later wrote, sending the Georgians up the hill would have been "a useless sacrifice of life."[233] At least Early was consistent. Since the previous afternoon he had maintained that help from another division was needed to capture Cemetery Hill—regardless of the condition of the defenders holding it. No one can now say with any certainty what would have happened if Gordon had been sent to reinforce Hays and Avery. Perhaps his advance and the prolonged fighting on East Cemetery Hill would have convinced Ramseur to order Rodes' Division into the fight; or maybe Early's men alone could have solidified a hold on East Cemetery Hill until more help was secured. At a minimum, had Early reinforced his success with Gordon's Georgians, it would have been far more difficult for the Federals to have recaptured the position.

An ominous silence descended over East Cemetery Hill. While the Confederates there reformed and waited, the Federals were working feverishly to direct reliable troops and snatch back the critical piece of ground. Help arrived in the form of Colonel Samuel Sprigg Carroll's "Gibraltar" brigade of Alexander Hays' division, Hancock's Second Corps. Carroll's small brigade of four veteran regiments (the 14th Indiana, 4th Ohio, 8th Ohio, and 7th West Virginia) numbered just over 900 combatants, and had been held in reserve along Cemetery Ridge.[234] The fact that Carroll was available at all illustrates the rippling effects of the breakdown of the echelon attack on Powell Hill's front. If Carnot Posey's and Billy Mahone's brigades had advanced from the west against Cemetery Ridge as ordered, the odds are they would have confronted and pushed back or routed Thomas Smyth's small brigade north of the Copse of Trees. The responsibility for plugging the resulting gap would have fallen squarely on Carroll and his under strength regiments, who in turn would not have been available for service on East Cemetery Hill. But Posey and Mahone did not advance. "It was nearly dark" when Winfield Hancock heard "a heavy engagement on General Howard's front." As the sounds of battle crept in his direction, Hancock ordered General Gibbon to send Carroll's brigade to the threatened sector.[235] It was a remarkably perceptive decision by Hancock, especially since Howard evidently had not requested assistance from anyone outside Eleventh Corps. However, Hancock knew the quality of the regiments holding that portion of the Federal line, and instinctively recognized that they were going to need help.

Facing right and moving across the Taneytown Road at the double-quick, three of Carroll's regiments (the 8th Ohio was engaged as skirmishers west of the Emmitsburg Road in the vicinity of the Bliss Farm and did not participate in this movement) hustled through the dark towards East Cemetery Hill. Carroll's infantrymen moved among the tombstones of the Evergreen Cemetery, their destination defined "entirely by [Confederate] fire."[236] The men arrived at the Baltimore Pike on the right of the cemetery gate house, where Carroll found that "it was impossible to advance by a longer front than that of a regiment." The 14th Indiana quickly deployed into line of battle and swept across the pike towards Ricketts' guns.

Harry Hays and his Louisianians, meanwhile, were waiting in the night, listening to the enemy legions forming around them. "Their heavy masses of infantry were heard and perfectly discerned through the increasing darkness, advancing in the direction of my position," Hays later reported. The Yankees "approach[ed] within 100 yards [and] a line was discovered before us, from the whole length of which a simultaneous fire was delivered." Hays, however, withheld his fire because he was "cautioned to expect friends both in front, to the right, and to the left." a second volley was launched in his direction and still Hays refused to let his men open up. "A third volley disclosed the still-advancing line to be one of the enemy," reported the intrepid brigadier, "and I then gave the order to fire." According to a Louisiana captain, "the Yankee line melt[ed] away in the darkness," when the Confederates opened on them.[237]

After the repulse of the Hoosiers, "two columns were heard advancing upon our flanks, threatening to surround and capture our little Brigade and the few men of [Avery's] Brigade who charged with us," remembered one of the Louisiana Tigers. "Gen. Hays, perceiving the imminent danger he was in and having given up all hope of a supporting force coming to his rescue, was obliged to give up his hard earned captures and marching by the right flank he led his Brigade back towards town."[238] Outnumbered and now outflanked by Carroll's clever tactics, Hays prudently withdrew his command, ending the fight for East Cemetery Hill. By 10:00 p.m., the bloodied and exhausted Louisianians and Carolinians were back in their positions along Winebrenner's Run.

Lee had done his best to get his army into position and had hammered away at Meade's forces for more than four hours. The sanguinary fighting of July 2 was over.

July 2 in Retrospect, Corps by Corps

Under the light of a July moon, James Longstreet's men lay on their arms amidst a field "black with the enemy's killed and wounded." Powell Hill's men had returned to their jump-off point on Seminary Ridge; Dick Ewell's men were scattered across the northern portion of the field; Rodes' and Early's men had returned to their pre-attack positions, but Johnson's brigades spent the night hunkered down on the slopes of Culp's Hill.[239]

The fighting prowess of Lee's outnumbered army was never more vividly illustrated than it was on July 2. The Army of the Potomac had been severely mauled—again—and had held its position by the thinnest of margins. Fourteen of the 22 Federal brigades engaged along the left wing of the army from the Copse of Trees south to Round Tops had been shattered, and three others had been roughly handled but were still intact. None of the five remaining brigades (or any of the others that had been shifted to this sector) had been subjected to direct attack or heavy fighting. On the other side of the Copse of Trees, from northern Cemetery Ridge to Cemetery Hill to Culp's Hill, only four Federal brigades had been engaged in close action defensive work.[240] Of these, three had been engaged on East Cemetery Hill, and two of those (Harris and von Gilsa) had been routed. The fourth brigade, George Greene's valiant New Yorkers, had stoically clung to its position on Culp's Hill, saving the far right flank of Meade's army. Therefore, of the 26 Federal infantry brigades heavily or moderately engaged on the second day of fighting at Gettysburg, 16 (or 61%) had been broken and were no longer combat worthy. Three others were badly damaged but remained intact, and the remaining seven were in their normal condition.

The casualties sustained by the Army of the Potomac during the first two days at Gettysburg reveals the depth of the devastation inflicted upon it by the attacking Confederates. Of the 35 Federal brigades that had experienced serious action on July 1 and 2, 25 had been shattered (71%), and two (Ames-Harris and von Gilsa) had been routed on successive days. Therefore, of the 51 infantry brigades in Meade's entire army, almost half had been so badly damaged during the first two days of fighting they were no longer reliable in combat. Even the brigades that had been fully rallied were of questionable value and certainly would not be capable of offensive action. This was clearly revealed by the performance of Howard's Eleventh Corps during the fight for East Cemetery Hill.

Officers from Dan Sickles' Third Corps admitted losing 40% of their combatants. Formations from Hancock's Second Corps also lost heavily. John Caldwell's First Division acknowledged losses comparable to Sickles', while Harrow's and Willard's brigades each suffered more than 50% casualties. The four brigades from Sykes' Fifth Corps that came to grief in the Wheatfield admitted that their ranks had been thinned by 37%. Colonel Patrick R. Guiney, whose 412 members of the 9th Massachusetts, Jacob Sweitzer's brigade, had missed the day's carnage, was shocked by what he found when he arrived that evening:

> We could scarcely be said to *join* the Brigade. It seemed to me that it would be more appropriate to say that we *constituted* the Brigade. There were flags of the regiment, & a remnant of a splendid regiment around each, & there were a few officers near their respective colors. . . . The Brigade—except ourselves—had been fought nearly to extinction.[241]

Meade's powerful artillery arm also sustained serious casualties on July 2. Lee's Confederates had overrun all or part of nine Federal batteries and had, temporarily, captured at least 41 Yankee guns. Porter Alexander was correct when he claimed that one of the reasons for continuing the offensive was that captured Federal materiel was usually the result.[242] However, the breakdown of the echelon attack, coupled with the failure of Ewell's Second Corps to hold East Cemetery Hill, resulted in the abandonment of most of the captured guns.[243] Even though they did not retain every gun they captured, the Confederates badly damaged Meade's artillery. Of the 19 Federal batteries engaged in defense of Meade's left wing south of the Copse of Trees, six had been so heavily damaged they were effectively out of action for the rest of the battle.[244] Three others involved on the left wing had been crippled and were capable of only limited action if the battle continued the next day. Several more were damaged to a lesser degree and were capable of functioning on July 3, but at a reduced level of effectiveness. Therefore, the Confederate assaults on

July 2 had completely wrecked or crippled the equivalent of at least two brigades of Federal artillery.

The morale and combat readiness of Howard's Eleventh Corps was beyond immediate repair, as indicated by its performance on East Cemetery Hill. The officers and men in Sickles' Third Corps were especially hard hit. That evening, as the pitifully few survivors of the shattered First Division were being rounded up, Regis de Trobriand, commander of the division's Third Brigade, met up with division commander David Birney. The dejected Birney knew his division had been severely mauled and believed the Confederates had won the day. As de Trobriand tried to console him, Birney remarked that his horse had been killed and wished that he had shared the same fate. Birney was evidencing a level of demoralization that, while impossible to fully measure, was widespread on the evening of July 2.[245]

After-action and casualty reports are never able to fully communicate what a battlefield at nightfall really looks like. At Gettysburg, untold thousands of men were wandering around the field or mixed in with other units. Terrorized animals (and men) inhabited the army's rear areas. Other soldiers were riding hither and yon, working to bring up ammunition and supplies for the morrow, while hundreds of stretcher bearers sought out the crying wounded spread across the field for miles in every direction. It took an incredible amount of mental toughness and physical stamina to be able to absorb such hideous experiences and still function as a soldier. That is why *élan* and esprit de corps is so valuable in war, because units with higher morale tend to better maintain their cohesion, and as a result, suffer fewer losses through combat and demoralization.

Except for a few notable exceptions, Meade's troops had fought hard and well on July 2. Like the previous day's fight, Meade was extremely fortunate that more than a dozen available Confederate brigades (about three infantry divisions) never made it into action as Lee intended. Meade and his lieutenants had been energetic and heroic in meeting the Confederate challenge, and as a result, Meade's principal lieutenants committed fewer mistakes than had Lee's generals. Still, the army could hardly survive another day like July 2. Captain Henry H. Bingham of Hancock's staff summed up the action in four words: "Our losses [were] appalling."[246]

FEDERAL FORMATIONS—
RESULT OF FIGHTING ON JULY 2, 1863

Unit	Area of Engagement	Loss	Result

SOUTH OF THE PEACH ORCHARD SALIENT
From Hancock's Second Corps—
First Division (Caldwell)

Unit	Area of Engagement	Loss	Result
1st Brig (Cross)	Wheatfield	330	Shattered
2nd Brig (Kelly)	Wheatfield	198	Shattered
3rd Brig (Zook)	Wheatfield	358	Shattered
4th Brig (Brooke)	Wheatfield	389	Shattered

From Sickle's Third Corps—
First Division(-) (Birney)

Unit	Area of Engagement	Loss	Result
2nd Brig(Ward)	Houck's Ridge / Devil's Den	781	Shattered
3rd Brig (de Trobr.)	Stony Hill / Rose's Wood	490	Shattered

From Sykes' Fifth Corps—
First Division (Barnes)

Unit	Area of Engagement	Loss	Result
1st Brig (Tilton)	Stony Hill / Trostle's Woods	125	Shattered
2nd Brig (Sweitzer)	Wheatfield	466	Shattered
3rd Brig (Vincent)	Little Round Top	352	Intact

Second Division (Ayres)

Unit	Area of Engagement	Loss	Result
1st Brig (Day)	Wheatfield	382	Shattered
2nd Brig (Burbank)	Wheatfield	447	Shattered
3rd Brig (Weed)	Little Round Top	200	Normal

Third Division (Crawford)

Unit	Area of Engagement	Loss	Result
1st Brig (McCand.)	Plum Run	100	Normal
3rd Brig (Fisher)	Plum Run / Little Round Top	50	Normal

Unit	Area of Engagement	Loss	Result

from Sedgwick's Sixth Corps—
Third Division(-) (Newton)

3rd Brig (Wheaton)	Plum Run	50	Normal

PEACH ORCHARD AND NORTH TO THE COPSE OF TREES

From Hancock's Second Corps—
Second Division (Gibbon)

1st Brig (Harrow)	Cemetery Ridge	730	Intact
2nd Brig (Webb)	Cemetery Ridge	190	Normal
3rd Brig (Hall)	Cemetery Ridge	250	Normal

Third Division(-) (Hays)

2nd Brig (Smyth)	Cemetery Ridge / Bliss Farm	250	Intact
3rd Brig (Willard)	Cemetery Ridge / Plum Run	714	Intact

From Sickle's Third Corps—
First Division(-) (Birney)

1st Brig (Graham)	Peach Orchard Salient	740	Shattered

Second Division (Humphreys)

1st Brig (Carr)	Emmitsburg Road	790	Shattered
2nd Brig (Brewster)	Peach Orchard / Emmitsburg Rd	778	Shattered
3rd Brig (Burling)	Emmitsburg Road	513	Shattered

CEMETERY, EAST CEMETERY AND CULP'S HILLS

From Hancock's Second Corps—
Third Division(-) (Hays)

Unit	Area of Engagement	Loss	Result
1st Brig (Carroll)	Bliss Farm / East Cemetery Hill	200	Normal

From Howard's Eleventh Corps—
First Division (Ames, formerly Barlow)

Unit	Area of Engagement	Loss	Result
1st Brig (von Gilsa)	East Cemetery Hill	140	Shattered
2nd Brig (Harris)	East Cemetery Hill	160	Shattered

Second Division (von Steinwehr)

Unit	Area of Engagement	Loss	Result
2nd Brig (Smith)	Cemetery Hill	348	Intact

From Slocum's Twelfth Corps—
Second Division (Geary)

Unit	Area of Engagement	Loss	Result
3rd Brig (Greene)	Culp's Hill	150	Normal
Miscellaneous, including artillery batteries and other units briefly or slightly involved and that are not included above		333	varies by unit

July 2 Federal admitted losses   11,024
(an indeterminate number of missing must be added to these losses)

July 1 Federal admitted losses (see in Chapter 5)   9,000

Admitted losses for July 1 and 2   20,024

(There were also unreported numbers of casualties, most of whom were missing.)

* * *

The cost to Lee for shattering the cohesion of more than 30% of Meade's total number of brigades on July 2 amounted to about 6,500 killed, wounded, missing, and captured. James Longstreet's two divisions, which had inflicted the majority of the casualties on that Thursday, suffered the heaviest losses. Hood and McLaws each lost about 2,000 men, but because of their high morale and esprit de corps, these units retained integrity and their morale remained largely intact. The same held true for the three brigades of Richard Anderson's Division (Cadmus Wilcox, David

Lang, and Rans Wright) that had reached and driven past the Emmitsburg Road. Their combined casualties were about 1,500.[247]

Ewell's Second Corps losses were relatively light. The brigades of Harry Hays and Isaac Avery suffered a combined loss of less than 600 from all causes, the bulk of which were suffered by Avery's North Carolinians. Given the damage they inflicted in their late evening assault, it is rather remarkable that Hays' Tigers lost but 136 men in the effort. Combined with the 45 skirmishing losses the brigade suffered earlier that day, Hays' loss for July 2 amounted to 181 of approximately 1,300 officers and men.[248] Avery's Tar Heels, who had more ground to traverse during the same attack and less dead ground to shield them from Federal artillery, lost about 345 of the brigade's 1,240 effectives.[249] Losses for Johnson's Division during its twilight confrontation with Greene's Federals on Culp's Hill are impossible to accurately represent because of the fighting that would take place a few hours later. In all likelihood, Johnson's July 2 losses numbered a few hundred men and thus were not significant.[250]

Far more serious for Lee's army were the losses suffered in its officer corps—especially in Longstreet's First Corps. John Bell Hood, arguably the finest division commander in the army (and certainly one of the most aggressive), was badly wounded and permanently lost to the army. Two of Hood's four brigadiers, "Tige" Anderson and Jerome Robertson, were also wounded. Hood's wound elevated McIvor Law to divisional command during the fighting, which left Law's Alabamians without his quality tactical leadership. Officer losses in Lafayette McLaws' Division were not quite as bad but heavy nonetheless. McLaws managed to escape Federal missiles, but two of his four brigade commanders did not. Paul Semmes ("whom I thought was the most promising major general among all the excellent brigadiers in the whole army," wrote Porter Alexander), and the irrepressible and irreplaceable William Barksdale were both dead.[251] Almost every brigade in Longstreet's two divisions lost one or more of its regimental commanders. With leadership losses such as these, the successes gained by Longstreet's attacking troops are all the more impressive and reflect the amazing offensive power of Lee's infantry. None of Richard Anderson's three brigadiers were killed or wounded, but Hill's Third Corps suffered a heavy loss in line officers; six regimental commanders, three each from Wilcox's and Wright's commands, were lost. On the other side of Gettysburg in Ewell's Corps, the only senior officer lost in the sundown charge by two of Early's brigades was the unfortunate Colonel Avery.[252]

At a cost of just some 6,500 men, Lee's army had inflicted almost twice that number of casualties on Meade's forces during the fighting on July 2. Although Lee's goal was not achieved, that statistic was, and remains, an impressive one—especially when one considers that the Confederates advanced over largely open ground against an enemy armed with superior artillery and fighting on the defensive. Total Confederate and Federals losses for both days were about 12,000 and 20,000, respectively. Expressed as a percentage, Lee's army had thus far inflicted 60% *more* casualties on the Federals that it had suffered. Or, looking at it another way, for every three casualties Lee suffered, he inflicted five on his opponent. Although seriously weakened, the Federal army still maintained a good defensive position and had not been driven from the field as Lee had hoped. Why had the success so vital to the Confederate cause alluded him?

A legion of writers have criticized Robert E. Lee for committing his army to the offensive on July 2. The reasons he did so and the options he faced on the evening of July 1 have been thoroughly examined earlier in this study. Based upon those options and what Lee knew at the time, offensive action was the correct course for him to pursue. Let us, then, examine first the method by which Lee undertook to assail Meade, i.e., a massive corps-level *en échelon* attack, which has also been the subject of much criticism. Thereafter we will examine, corps by corps, July 2 in retrospect.

The Echelon Attack

After examining the new Federal Peach Orchard salient created by Sickles' movement west in the middle of the afternoon on July 2, Lee instructed Longstreet's First Corps and Anderson's Division in Hill's Third Corps to assault *en échelon,* from right to left, with Pender's Light Division also joining in. Lee's method of attack has been criticized by almost everyone who has written about Gettysburg. The mistakes in their arguments and line of reason are perhaps best addressed by examining the arguments raised by one of the earliest critics of this decision, artillerist E. Porter Alexander. Like his corps chief, Alexander enjoyed fighting on the defensive and also wrote widely following the war. Many of his articles, letters, and books dealt with Gettysburg. He did not hold Lee's decision to attack *en échelon* in high regard. Indeed, he believed that if the offensive on July 2 was going to succeed, "our only hope was to make our attacks simultaneous."[253]

His opinion, though, seems to have been formed as a result of the battle's *outcome* rather than the plan *envisioned* by Lee. For example, Alexander acknowledged that Lee's battle plan fell short because of "faults of detail in its execution" which were the result of Hill's and Ewell's "conspicuously bad" battle management.[254] The result of this faulty execution, argued Alexander, was that the army failed "to conform to the original plan of battle, as it had been indicated by Lee." Unlike many writers, Alexander knew Lee issued his generals "orders with discretion," and not "discretionary orders" as previously discussed in several places in this study. "General instructions were given to each corps commander," Alexander wrote, "but much was left to their discretion in carrying them out. More than one fell short in performance."[255]

Thus even someone as objective and shrewd as Alexander seems to want to have it both ways. He acknowledged that remaining on the defensive would have entailed enormous logistical difficulties and would have surrendered the initiative to the Federals, but that it might have been successful if Meade had quickly attacked the Confederate army. Proof that the cautious Meade had no intention of taking the offensive is found in the fact that he had ample opportunity to do so at Gettysburg—most of July 2, all of July 3 on either side of Pickett's afternoon attack, and the entirety of July 4 passed in relative silence. Indeed, he hesitated to do so at Falling Waters more than a week later when Lee's beaten army had its back to a swollen Potomac River and a victory would have effectively ended the war in the East. Conceding all the problems inherent for the Southern army in a passive defense, Alexander still did not approve of Lee's method of attack.

But Alexander criticized the *en échelon* plan while accurately pointing out the failures of two of the three Confederate corps commanders (Hill and Ewell) in executing Lee's designs. By doing so Alexander, like many other writers, failed to recognize that it was the *manner* in which plan was executed, and not the plan itself, that contributed to its less than desired results. Alexander found nothing wrong with the way Longstreet conducted his portion of Lee's attack plan. Yet, the success enjoyed by Longstreet's troops and the manner in which they were committed to battle—and the corresponding response by the Federals—generated opportunities for decisive success up and down the Federal line from lower Cemetery Ridge all the way around to Culp's Hill, exactly as General Lee anticipated it would. The fact these tactical openings were not fully exploited (or even exploited at all, in many cases) was because of the inept leadership of Powell Hill, Dick Ewell, and Richard Anderson, among others. Hill's Corps stood to reap the major benefits of the *en échelon* attack. As the battle developed, all Hill had to do was insure that Anderson and Pender moved their men aggressively forward into action, which they had orders to do. After all, what was Powell Hill's job if it was not to get his troops into the battle within the overall parameters of General Lee's plan? With the success of Longstreet's assault, what further breathtaking possibilities might have been realized if all nine of Anderson's and Pender's brigades had vigorously joined in the assault? The thinly-spread infantry and artillery and, in some cases, gaping holes, in Meade's line late on the afternoon of July 2, all as a result of Longstreet's attack *alone*, strongly suggests that Alexander's assertion that "our only hope was to make our attacks simultaneous" was incorrect. The "only hope" was that Hill, Ewell, and Anderson would perform their duties and exploit the opportunities created by the echelon attack. They did not, and Lee's goals were not realized.

The Round Tops and Sickles' Salient: James Longstreet and First Corps

Although Alexander may not have had any unkind words about Longstreet's attack on July 2, others have criticized him mercilessly and have even claimed that his actions cost the Confederacy its chance to win at Gettysburg. One of the particular tragedies of this battle is that, of all of Lee's lieutenants, the one who performed the best that day has, through myth and misinformation, been held responsible for the defeat. Ask yourself this question: if James Longstreet had conducted the battle exactly as he did and was killed at the head of his corps on July 2 in a *winning effort* sealed in victory with aggressive action by Powell Hill and Dick Ewell, would "Old Pete" have stood tall in the legacy of the Lost Cause? Undoubtedly. Bronze statues would today be prominently displayed on several battlefields, and one depicting "Lee's Warhorse" on his horse, Hero, would have been erected in Pitzer's Woods long ago.[256]

Instead, Longstreet's reputation has been dealt severe and often unjust blows. Much of the damage is based more upon misinterpretation of his battlefield role as well as what he did *after* the war. Many former Confederate officers simply could not stomach the idea of Longstreet joining the Republican Party and criticizing Lee, and so combined their volleys against him to tarnish his reputation as a form of payback. Longstreet's own self-inflicted wounds, brought about by his political naivete and the often contradictory vistas he painted of himself as a self-defense against his energetic and spiteful accusers, alienated many who would have otherwise been sympathetic to his plight—or others who have been unable to separate truth from fiction.

The secret to Longstreet's success as a corps commander with the Army of Northern Virginia was simple: Lee understood his bulldog qualities and unflappable nature, and under his guidance and direction, Longstreet almost always employed his infantry and artillery to advantage. In other words, Longstreet was adept at skillfully bringing together the full power of his command when working within the framework of the commanding general's designs. Despite what his detractors claim to this day, Longstreet's attack on July 2 stands as an excellent example of his superb ability to effortlessly handle large numbers of men in battle. For example, once Lee saw the new Federal alignment in the Peach Orchard, he changed the plan of attack by ordering Longstreet to send in First Corps *en échelon* because that was the *best* way to drive in and turn Meade's left flank. After Hood's Division opened the action on Confederate right, Longstreet demonstrated remarkable restraint and a deep *understanding* of Lee's battle plan by patiently and judiciously allowing the Federals to overreact by siphoning away thousands of men from other parts of the line. This patience developed the battle to his (and the army's) tactical advantage. Cultivating tactical opportunities on other parts of the line *not yet under assault* is one of the primary reasons for launching an attack *en échelon*, and is often lost on students of this battle. Longstreet exploited the tactical opportunities presented in the form of shifting Federal formations by perfectly timing the advance of McLaws' four brigades—a subtlety completely lost on Lafayette McLaws (and others). These formidable brigades, led by several notable brigadiers, wrought so much havoc that *more* Federal reinforcements were required to contain their breakthrough. Longstreet sent one message (that we know of) to General Lee that Thursday afternoon after McLaws' men had been committed to battle: "We are doing well."

Well, indeed. By the time the fighting died down on the southern end of the battlefield on July 2, Longstreet's eight brigades had crushed, routed, or severely damaged all of Sickles' Third Corps except for one brigade (which was later eviscerated by Wilcox and Lang), as well as two-thirds of Sykes' Fifth Corps, and about half of Hancock's Second Corps.[257] Alexander probably put it best when he wrote:

> To express it as briefly as possible & as nearly as I can find the exact figures, our two divisions' 13,000 infantry with 62 guns took the aggressive against a strong position & captured it, fighting successfully for three hours against 40,000 infantry & 100 guns, & holding the ground gained. I think that [it was] a greater military feat than the partial success gained by Pickett's charge, where the infantry fighting was scarcely a half hour. But both events illustrate the superb capabilities of our army at Gettysburg . . .[258]

Critics also routinely overlook the effectiveness of Longstreet's artillery. The guns of First Corps opened the battle with an effective bombardment, and then continued their work in concert with the infantry. This was aptly illustrated when Alexander relocated several batteries forward to solidify the capture of the Peach Orchard salient (something he had carefully planned in advance of the assault) Unlike Jubal Early, Alexander knew how to reinforce success.

When viewed in this light, Longstreet's performance as a corps commander on July 2 demonstrated outstanding tactical ability and intelligence. Why, then, has his reputation suffered so? Although a full briefing of this issue is beyond the purview of this study, it is worth examining it in some detail in order to help understand the relationships of some key Southern officers within the Army of Northern Virginia, and how their quotes, claims, misinterpretations and oversights—as well as some by notable historians who should know better—have led to the tarnishing of Longstreet's star and have served only to cloud our understanding of the battle.

With the single exception of Lafayette McLaws—who never did understand or appreciate the manner in which Longstreet handled the advance of his division's brigades that day—the concerted assaults against Longstreet for his performance at Gettysburg did not occur until two key events took place: Longstreet's allegiance with the Republican Party in the spring of 1867, and General Lee's death three years later in 1870. To many Southerners, Republicans were the agents of radicalism and stood for the lawless and wanton destruction of private property throughout the Old South, as well as the harsh Reconstruction Acts that had been imposed upon the destitute people of the subjugated region. To align himself with these people, Longstreet was viewed by many Southerners as a traitor. Those who might have supported him against his postwar critics were largely silenced when he joined the opposition and urged his fellow Southerners to accept the Federal victory and move on with their lives. "To join the Republicans, the political instrument of conquest and defeat," explained Longstreet biographer Jeffry D. Wert, "was to betray those who had died for the cause and those who were living under an imposed rule by the conquerors."[259]

General Lee would have nothing to do with the public debate over his former lieutenant's political actions. The mere fact that the former commander of the Army of Northern Virginia was alive prevented most former Confederates from criticizing the battlefield performance of Lee's "Old Warhorse." While Lee was alive, anyone that initiated any sort of diatribe ran the risk of having his story, and thus his reputation, demolished by the icon of the South who knew the truth and could speak it. However, after Lee's death, many circles of Southern society viewed Longstreet as fair game for his perceived treachery. And his detractors began to line up, one after another, when one of the South's most controversial figures initiated one of the grossest lies to ever enter the historiography of the Civil War.

Longstreet was the most visible target against which former Confederates could vent their wrath, and Jubal Anderson Early knew it. Speaking at Washington and Lee College on the anniversary of Robert E. Lee's birthday, January 19, 1872, Early cut loose with an initial salvo that marked the beginning of a long, noisy, and intensely personal feud between several of Lee's most visible subordinates.[260] Early claimed that Lee left the arbor council meeting in the evening of July 1:

> for the purpose of ordering up Longstreet's corps in time to begin the attack at dawn next morning. That corps was not in readiness to make the attack until 4 o'clock in the afternoon of the next day. By that time Meade's whole army had arrived on the field and taken its position. Had the attack been made at daylight, as contemplated, it must have resulted in a brilliant victory. . . . The position which Longstreet attacked at four was not occupied by the enemy until late in the afternoon, and Round Top Hill, which commanded the enemy's position, could have been taken in the morning without a struggle.[261]

A careful reading of Early's words reveal that the crafty lawyer did not *directly* charge Longstreet with dereliction of duty (although the implication was unmistakable). Early was merely setting up Longstreet for the kill. Exactly one year later in another speech at Washington and Lee, General Pendleton (or "Parson

He was one of the most prominent officers in the Army of Northern Virginia from 1862 through 1864, and possessed such a forceful personality that it is said he was the only officer who regularly swore in Lee's presence. Lee, in return, called him "My bad old man." At Gettysburg, his dominating lawyer-like personality had a deleterious effect on his superior, Dick Ewell. Early also found it difficult to reinforce success with success, and thus withheld Gordon's Georgians while Hays and Avery waited on East Cemetery Hill in vain for their arrival. After the war, when answers were being sought as to why the Confederates lost at Gettysburg, Early saddled James Longstreet with the blame. *Library of Congress*

Jubal Anderson Early
(1816-1894)

Pendleton," as General Longstreet contemptuously referred to him), ripped open the debate begun by Early.[262]

Pendleton, Lee's former brigadier general and nominal chief of artillery, claimed that he had made a reconnaissance of the Federal positions on the evening of July 1, and reported to Lee that he "had found an assault was perfectly practicable and promising the best results." Then, according to Pendleton, Lee ordered Longstreet "to make an attack at daylight the next morning," and the corps commander failed to do this, "but sat on his horse until about 4:00 p.m. of that day and could plainly see the reinforcements of the enemy arriving hour after hour . . . " Pendleton then laid the loss of Gettysburg squarely on Longstreet: "the failure to assault at daylight was the cause of the loss of the Battle." And so the "sunrise attack" allegation was born.[263]

The statement was nothing short of a bald-faced lie and Pendleton knew it. His own report from Gettysburg confirmed that his reconnaissance mission was conducted early on the morning of July 2—not on the evening of July 1. Also, Lee spent the entire morning of July 2 discussing battle plans prior to the return of Johnston's scouting party from Little Round Top — all of which supports Pendleton's after-action report. When Pendleton's address first appeared in print almost two years later in the December 1874 issue of *Southern Magazine*, Colonel Charles S. Venable of Lee's staff was justifiably appalled. "I cannot but attribute his statement with regard to Gettysburg to an absolute loss of memory said to be brought on by frequent attacks resembling paralysis," wrote Venable. "His whole statement with regard to Gettysburg is full of mistakes . . . I have heard that the College faculty at Washington and Lee did not publish General Pendleton's address because they were aware of his condition. It is a pity it ever got into print."[264]

Pendleton's fiction also prompted Major Walter H. Taylor of Lee's staff to respond. In a letter to Longstreet dated April 28, 1875, Taylor wrote:

> I can only say that I never before heard of the "sunrise attack" you were to have made, as charged by General Pendleton. If such an order was given you, I never knew it, or it has strangely escaped my memory. I think it more probable that, if General Lee had had your troops available the evening previous to the day of which you speak, he would have ordered an early attack; but this does not touch the point at issue.
>
> I regard it as a great mistake on the part of those who, perhaps because of political differences, now undertake to criticize and attack your war record. Such conduct is most ungenerous . . . .[265]

Lee, of course, knew the approximate locations of Longstreet's troops before the arbor council convened on the evening of July 1. As such, he knew Longstreet's men could not have arrived until sometime the next morning. In a slight unintended, Pendleton's claim, if true, meant that General Lee exhibited a degree of recklessness by ordering an attack with troops yet to appear on the field against a front that had not been reconnoitered. Even McLaws, who had no love for Longstreet, believed that the "attack at dawn" story was "so unreasonable" that Pendleton had to be mistaken.[266] Obviously there was no order for First Corps to attack at sunrise, but Longstreet detractors were not about to let facts get in the way of their preconceived opinions. This myth, writes one prominent Gettysburg historian, was "the one most frequently advanced, tenaciously adhered to, and made the cornerstone of the Gettysburg story by" a legion of writers.[267]

Although the "attack at dawn" assertion was shot down by many of the participants soon after it was propounded, the ongoing debate surrounding Longstreet's so-called "delay" and rebellious attitude had its genesis in this myth. According to the myth, if the Confederates had somehow attacked hours earlier, a grand victory certainly would have been won. The reason they did not, so goes the story, is because Longstreet dragged his feet and did everything he could to delay the offensive ordered by Lee. The reality of the situation that confronted Lee and his generals on July 2 mitigated against this possibility. First, we know that the bulk of First Corps did not even arrive on the field until about 9:00 a.m. on July 2. At that time, Lee did not even know for certain where Meade's left flank was because Captain Johnson and his party were still absent trying to determine that fact. No responsible commander would have committed his army to offensive action without first reconnoitering the enemy line to determine a suitable point of attack. It was after 10:00 a.m. when Alexander had his important conference with Lee about moving his artillery to the right. Before then, McLaws' Division had arrived on the field and its commander also met with Lee and Longstreet. It was only after Lee's meeting with McLaws that Johnston returned and informed Lee that Meade's left was indeed vulnerable to attack, as Lee suspected it might be. We know Lee questioned Johnston closely, and it took time to fully formulate a plan, issue more specific orders, and prepare First Corps for the march. Thus, based upon what Lee and his generals *knew* that morning, they could not have prepared an attack against Meade's left (or indeed anywhere but on Ewell's front or straight across the valley from Seminary Ridge) on the morning of July 2. To assert otherwise is to argue in favor of the impossible.

Historian Bevin Alexander, who was introduced earlier in this study, has developed his own variation of the "attack at dawn" myth. "Lee himself," he asserts, "virtually foredoomed the attack when he did not insist on it going in at daybreak."[268] Alexander is arguing that Lee failed because he did not order McLaws and Hood to move into position during the night of July 1-2 for an attack the next morning. Lee, of course, did not even know where he would attack or where the Federal army was positioned when the sun went down on July 1. Bevin Alexander not only ignores the fact that Lee did not have cavalry to safely screen a nighttime march to position his men near the enemy, but seems utterly ignorant of where First Corps was in relation to the army. Longstreet's men marched all day on July 1 and the head of his column under Hood reached Cashtown, eight miles from Gettysburg, at 2:00 a.m. on the morning of July 2. Hood stopped there to rest his fatigued troops for a mere two hours before taking up the march again down the Chambersburg Pike to Gettysburg, with the Texas Brigade arriving on the battlefield one hour *after* sunrise.[269] Further, road congestion prevented any of First Corps' reserve artillery battalions from leaving Greenwood until 1:00-2:30 a.m. on July 2. They rolled through the night and arrived about one mile west of Seminary Ridge sometime about 9:00 a.m.[270] Bevin Alexander's call for a daybreak assault also ignores the importance of daylight reconnaissance (as earlier discussed). Artillerist E. Porter Alexander was correct when he observed, "I don't think Gen. Lee could have ever ordered or expected an attack by our corps at sunrise."[271] For anyone to insist otherwise is simply nonsense.

Other historians are realistic enough to appreciate that an attack could not have been launched in the morning, but chastise Longstreet for not attacking earlier than 4:00 p.m. Generally speaking, this line of argument holds that Longstreet's insistence to wait for the arrival of McIvor Law's Brigade before beginning the march to the right was nothing but a temper tantrum that threw off Lee's schedule, and that the march itself was slow and shoddily performed.[272] As noted, after Johnston returned from his scouting mission, Longstreet *asked* Lee if he could wait for Law to bring up his Alabamians. Lee was on the scene and *concurred* with Longstreet's request. That alone should end this issue, because waiting for Law delayed the march; Lee was responsible for it. However, what many writers fail to note is that every senior officer of First Corps—Longstreet, Hood and

McLaws—later acknowledged the prudence of waiting for Law, who not only led the largest brigade in the division but Hood's second in command as well.

Longstreet's movement to the right did not begin as well as it might have. Some distance into the march it was discovered that the route was visible to the Federal signal station on Little Round Top, and the divisions had to backtrack and find another route. Contrary to some writers who blame a sulking Longstreet for the botched initial effort, Captain Johnston, acting on Lee's orders, was in charge of the route and guided "every step taken," as Lafayette McLaws—no defender of Longstreet's—later wrote. Longstreet argued the same thing, as did Porter Alexander and Moxley Sorrel.[273] That delay, coupled with the earlier decision to wait for Law's Brigade certainly prevented the attack from being delivered earlier that it actually was. How long is anyone's guess, but no more than an hour or two at most. But what, if anything, was gained or lost by the delay?

Quite a bit, as it turns out. It was during this time that Sickles moved his corps forward to the Peach Orchard and Lee, as a consequence, changed the plan of assault from a simultaneous attack against Meade's left to an echelon one. Sickles' unexpected Federal advance created an "opportunity" that Lee immediately recognized: Sickles, far in advance of the main Federal line, could be destroyed. An earlier attack, between 1:00 p.m. and 2:00 p.m., would have encountered the Federal army along a more compact and arguably stronger defensive line. Many writers argue that Sickle's men served to absorb the shock of Longstreet's attack and slow down the assault in time for Meade to rescue his left; otherwise, the Round Tops would have fallen and Meade would have lost the battle. Perhaps. But it is our opinion that proponents of this theory (in addition to having been influenced to some degree by the argument that Longstreet should have attacked earlier), overemphasize the importance of the two hills and do not fully appreciate the echelon attack Lee envisioned and delivered, the opportunities it created up and down the entire Federal line, and the narrowness by which Meade escaped disaster elsewhere. Confederate chances for a decisive battlefield victory were better *because* the attack began at 4:00 p.m. than at any time previous that day.[274]

Jubal Early and William Pendleton, the purveyors of the "attack at dawn" libel, were probably the first writers to also espouse that Little Round Top was the key to winning the battle. Its capture would have turned Meade's left, they argued, and Southern artillery from that platform would have driven Meade away and given Lee the decisive victory he was seeking. As we have just seen, if you believe this, then Sickles' decision to move forward triggered a set of circumstances that ultimately saved the eminence from falling into Confederate hands. The gallant defense of Little Round Top by Joshua Chamberlain and his 20th Maine against the tenacious attack of Law's Alabamians has riveted attention to the rocky hill, promulgated scores of books and articles on the subject, and encouraged the widespread belief that two regiments, one clad in blue and the other dressed in gray, decided the battle's outcome on the shadowy south and southeastern slopes. Indeed, it is viewed as heresy to even breathe otherwise. But is it true? We do not think so.

As we have demonstrated, General Lee understood how the *en échelon* attack was supposed to progress (in steps or, to the untrained eye, in piecemeal fashion) and that it could create opportunities elsewhere up Meade's line all the way to the tip of the barbed fishhook on Culp's Hill. These opportunities, in turn, allowed Lee to bring to bear the full weight of his army rather than just a single corps on his right. If Little Round Top was the decisive geographic point on the field, as many writers enjoy arguing, why did Lee attack *en échelon*? The answer is simple: because it was not, and General Lee knew it was not. Lee had made his early career judging terrain for General Scott in Mexico, and if his intent was to carry Little Round Top he would have weighted his right accordingly and would not have ordered an echelon assault.

Regardless, the capture of Little Round Top would not have provided the Confederates with a platform from which to support the remainder of the fighting up Cemetery Ridge and around to Culp's Hill. For example, consider the less visually commanding piece of terrain of Hazel Grove at Chancellorsville. When it was captured, Southern guns were massed there in numbers large enough to support continued infantry attacks and inflict heavy casualties on Federal defenders. Little Round Top, however, was utterly incapable of supporting a similar effort. Its summit contained enough room for but a single battery. Just getting a few guns there—especially for the Confederates—could only have been accomplished by foresight (no one on that end of the field even realized the possibilities of Houck's Ridge as an artillery platform) and Herculean effort. If Southern guns could have been positioned there (the Federal pieces were hauled up by hand and only with great difficulty), Meade had at his disposal vastly superior numbers of Federal ordnance to knock them quickly out of action.

This is not to say that Little Round Top was not worth capturing, but the battle did not hang in the balance as Chamberlain and Oates struggled for its possession. A Confederate presence on Little Round Top may well have limited or denied Meade temporary use of the Taneytown Road and brought into play a whole different set of dynamics. But its wooded and rocky terrain made it wholly inappropriate for use as a staging area for an infantry attack northward. More pertinent to our discussion is whether the few Confederate guns which might have been placed on Little Round Top would have been of any value to Lee. If they were not silenced quickly, a few guns shooting onto lower Cemetery Ridge would not have driven away Meade's army. The importance of Little Round Top as an artillery position was best summed up by Meade's chief engineer, Brigadier General Gouverneur K. Warren, the man largely responsible for fortifying the hill in the first place. Warren discussed the nature of Little Round Top with Lieutenant Charles E. Hazlett, the commander of Battery D, 5th U. S. Artillery, whose guns were manhandled to its summit. Warren told the officer *during the fighting* that Little Round Top "was no place for artillery fire—both of us knew that. I told him [Hazlett] so. 'Never mind that' [Hazlett] says.

'The sounds of my guns will be encouraging to our troops and disheartening to the others, and my battery's of no use if this hill is lost.'[275]

As shocking as it is to assert, Little Round Top did not figure prominently into Lee's plans, and the proof is found in his method of attack. If Longstreet did not find and turn Meade's flank quickly—defeating the Federal army was Lee's goal, not seizing a piece of terrain of limited value to him—Lee knew that one or more opportunities would in all likelihood be created for Confederate formations far removed from Little Round Top. And indeed, as the battle of July 2 unfolded, this is exactly what happened *more than one mile away from Little Round Top*. The denuding of the Federal defensive line from north of the Copse of Trees to Cemetery Hill and around to Culp's Hill, all in response to Lee's echelon attack, brought Meade's army to the brink of defeat. Along this front Lee had available *twice* as many brigades as did Meade, and more than half of the Federals holding a large portion of this sector were Howard's beaten and demoralized Eleventh Corps troops. Thus, Meade's response to Lee's attack *en échelon* not only dangerously weakened his ability to respond to Lee's attacks elsewhere, but thinned his defenses along the weakest part of his line, the "joint" marked by Cemetery Hill.[276]

In summation, James Longstreet conducted his march and positioned his First Corps troops as effectively as anyone could have reasonably expected; he correctly refused to allow Hood to alter Lee's plan by exposing his division to destruction on the far side of Round Top, and he deployed his artillery well. He fully understood Lee's echelon attack plan and demonstrated deft abilities in handling large bodies of men by first launching Hood and then waiting patiently to send forward McLaws' brigades at precisely the right moment. Longstreet's performance created the substantial opportunities Lee was seeking elsewhere up the line, and the responsibility for exploiting those belonged to Powell Hill and Dick Ewell.

The second day of July 1863 was one of James Longstreet's finest days on any battlefield, and it is time for historians to recognize that fact.

Cemetery Ridge: Powell Hill and Third Corps

As indicated fully earlier in the text, the assault broke down on Ambrose Powell Hill's front. His first three of nine brigades (Wilcox, Lang, and Wright) went forward as ordered, and thereafter nothing went according to plan. Neither of Richard Anderson's remaining brigades contributed anything of value to the battle. Carnot Posey failed miserably to control his brigade and get it moving forward, Billy Mahone disobeyed orders to advance, and neither Anderson nor Powell Hill promptly intervened and rectified the situation. The failure on Anderson's left front prompted Dorsey Pender to ride in that direction to determine what was wrong, and his subsequent wound removed him from the battle and the resulting chaos ensured none of his four brigades would see action. The glaring failures of Anderson and Hill to perform the duties required of officers of their rank and position compromised Lee's plan of attack.[277]

Dick Anderson's slothful indifference was fully on display at Gettysburg. This is perhaps best illustrated by Cadmus Wilcox's claim that he sent three separate requests to the division commander for support. Wilcox, who stood head and shoulders above any of Anderson's other brigadiers, believed that if "the division commander [could] have seen with his own eyes" what was transpiring on Wilcox's front, he would have ordered up the support immediately and the battle may have turned out differently. The intent behind Wilcox's words was to expose Anderson's inaction for the dereliction of duty it was. After his brigade crossed the Emmitsburg Road and rushed over the Federals "like a torrent," Wilcox dispatched Captain Walter E. Winn, the brigade's assistant adjutant-general, with a message for Anderson that "with a second supporting line the heights could" be carried. Winn found Anderson and his staff in the woods on Seminary Ridge with the general's horse tied to a tree and many or all of Anderson's staff officers resting on the ground as though no battle were taking place. Exactly how Wilcox received this news is not hard to imagine. Wilcox estimated that his brigade "continued 30 minutes" in its exposed position along Plum Run before being forced to abandon his advanced line "without support on either my right or my left."[278]

Wilcox's observation about a supporting second line highlights Anderson's decision to deploy all five of his brigades in one single line of battle. Historians routinely ignore this important tactical error. If Anderson had deployed just one of his brigades in a reserve role—Mahone's Virginians would have been a logical choice given their location on the field—or had formed his division with the brigades of Wilcox, Lang and Wright in the front line and Posey and Mahone behind them, he would have had the flexibility to succor Wilcox's and Wright's penetration east of Emmitsburg Road and exploit enemy counter-moves. Both John Bell Hood and Lafayette McLaws deployed their four brigades in two lines of two brigades each, and Dorsey Pender aligned his division with three brigades in the front and one in reserve for the reasons just described. Anderson's injudicious deployment meant that all of his five brigades had to aggressively move into action in order to sustain the momentum of the echelon attack—which only emphasizes his failure as a division commander that day. His tactical alignment placed his brigadiers in the unenviable position of having to rely on each successive brigade to cover his left flank. Thus, if Wilcox advanced but Lang did not, Wilcox's uncovered left flank would be exposed and his Alabamians decimated; if Wilcox and then Lang advanced but Wright did not, Lang and eventually Wilcox would be forced to fall back, and so on.

And this is exactly what happened to Rans Wright's Georgians when Carnot Posey's Mississippians did not advance en masse and support his left flank. Anderson acknowledged that it was Hill's intention for his "entire division . . . to be employed . . . and that each brigade of the division would begin the attack as soon as the brigade on its right commenced the movement."[279] As a division commander, it was Anderson's job to place his brigades in a mutual supporting position and to be sure that they complied with orders to attack. Why he did not ride along his line as each brigade moved forward and deliver his instructions in person, if necessary, is unknown. Anderson's negligence not only doomed Wilcox, Lang, and Wright to fight their own separate battles on Cemetery Ridge, but threw a wrench in the gears of Lee's overall echelon attack plan and began the process of bringing the entire machine to a grinding halt.

Richard Anderson's failing on July 2, was predictable given what was already known of him. What was missing that afternoon was the Powell Hill of Sharpsburg, an active and energetic leader to inspire Anderson and drive him forward. Hill issued no orders that anyone is aware, nor did he coordinate Third Corps artillery movements to further support the advancing infantry (although he did ask Colonel Walker to have his artillery fire in support of Longstreet). We know Hill spent most of his time that afternoon somewhere on Seminary Ridge. His headquarters were at the Emanuel Pitzer farmhouse, several hundred yards west of Posey's Mississippians on Seminary Ridge.[280] The Pitzer farm complex is west of the crest of Seminary Ridge, so it would have been impossible for Hill to see the battle had he remained at that farm. According to Arthur Fremantle, the English military observer, Hill visited Lee at the commanding general's overlook near the Lutheran Theological Seminary soon after the cannonade began. He remained there while Longstreet's troops developed their attack, and then moved off.[281] The next time Hill's presence can be confirmed is near Pitzer's Woods, on the south end of Third Corps' line, behind McLaws' Division. After that, his movements that Thursday afternoon are an enigma.

What we do know, however, is that, like Anderson only on a larger scale, Hill failed in his duty to make sure his combat formations got into action in accordance with Lee's orders and the orders he himself had issued to his division commanders. Hill's actions stood in sharp contrast to Longstreet's comportment. "Old Pete" coordinated his divisions perfectly. Hood, his most aggressive and capable division commander was allowed to handle the tactical details along his division's front while Longstreet closely supervised the timing and coordination of the movements his other four brigades under the rather stolid and uninspiring McLaws. Hill should have done the same thing. Once Anderson's right brigades began moving forward, Hill should have been somewhere between Anderson and Pender in order to make sure his divisions moved out in a coordinated fashion. Instead, Hill allowed Anderson's attack to fall apart and was not on the scene to repair the damage; Pender went down with a mortal wound and yet Hill failed to issue the orders necessary to engage Pender's Light Division knowing full well Ewell's attack on Cemetery Hill was relying on his support. Hill's failures are even more pronounced because as a division commander, Hill had often led his troops from the front. While we are not suggesting he should have done so as a corps leader (or even as a division commander), the point is that Hill had heretofore always made sure his men were where they were supposed to be. At Gettysburg he did virtually nothing to make sure his men went into action and as a result, lost control of his corps.

Despite his inexplicable behavior, Hill is not without some notable defenders. One is Clifford Dowdey, a prominent Virginia writer of the 1950s and 1960s. In judging the fighting capabilities of Lee's lieutenants on July 2, Dowdey completely absolved him of any wrong doing with the simple pronouncement, "A.P. Hill did well in his attack straight ahead."[282] Dowdey, unfortunately, was completely taken in by the nonsense of the Early-Pendleton fictions; he was also one of the leading 20th century catalysts to fan the fires of misinformation regarding Longstreet's performance on July 2. As a result, Dowdey went to great lengths to deposit any Confederate failings of the battle's second day on Longstreet's doorstep. By doing so, Dowdey weakened his narrative by giving Powell Hill—a corps commander who got only one-third of his available brigades into action—a pass on what can only be properly described as an abominable command performance. Dowdey of course offered no evidence to support his remarkable conclusion.

Another prominent historian and Powell Hill defender is James I. Robertson, Jr. In order to place his defense of Hill's actions on July 2 into its proper context, the following lengthy passage linking Anderson, Hill, and Lee together, must be read and understood:

> Anderson did not even send in all of his brigades, as Hill desired. Mahone's Virginians never saw action, for reasons still not clear.
>
> Hill's leadership on July 2 also left something to be desired. Assigned to a cooperative role, he seemed never to get caught up in the fever of battle. Maybe it was the fact that the one division in his corps with which he was totally unfamiliar in combat was making the attack. Perhaps, in spite of the surface cordiality between Hill and Longstreet, mutual resentment still smoldered, so that neither made any attempt to clarify the responsibility for Anderson's division. In addition, Hill could have ordered Heth's division, or Pender's, to enter the action. Possibly Hill, remembering the carnage of the previous day, when he had attacked without specific instructions, decided to do nothing without directives from Lee.
>
> If Hill displayed weakness in coordination, however, so did Lee. The army commander was the only one who could have reorganized the Confederate movements once the fighting began. Had Lee wanted Hill's entire corps to cooperate fully with Longstreet, he could have ordered it forward.[283]

Robertson's contorted multifaceted defense of Hill is not persuasive, and is in some respects, incredulous.

First, the fact that Hill "desired" Anderson to commit his entire division to the attack and that Anderson did not do so in no way absolves Hill of blame, and is technically not even correct. We know from our previous discussions that Anderson had been *ordered* to attack with his entire division. Anderson was Hill's responsibility. If Anderson's attack fell apart, it was Hill's duty to do whatever he could to put it back together again. Robertson's excuses for Hill's additional shortcomings are no more persuasive. Whether Hill was "totally unfamiliar" with how Anderson and his generals acted under combat conditions or not has nothing to do with whether Hill could issue orders when the attack stalled or whether Anderson was obligated to follow them. And if Robertson's claim is true, then Hill should have glued himself to Anderson's side during the battle of July 2 to make certain Anderson went forward as ordered.

Robertson's subtle suggestion that Hill and Longstreet were confused over exactly who controlled Anderson seems to be spun from whole cloth. He substantiates this amazing claim by citing the after-action reports of Lee and Hill.[284] According to General Lee, "General Hill was instructed to threaten the center of the Federal line, in order to prevent re-enforcements being sent to either wing, and to avail himself of an opportunity that might present itself to attack." In a separate report Lee wrote: "General Hill was ordered to threaten the enemy's center, to prevent re-enforcements being drawn to either wing, and co-operate with his right division in Longstreet's attack." Hill, in fact, *specifically* stated in his report that Longstreet's corps on July 2 consisted of McLaws and Hood—"The corps of General Longstreet (McLaws' and Hood's divisions) was on my right"—and that "General Longstreet was to attack . . . and I was ordered to co-operate with him with such of my brigades from the right as could join in with him with the attack."[285]

There is nothing in these or any other reports that is confusing, misleading, or suggestive of a command-responsibility issue involving Anderson, who was *not* part of First Corps. In fact, he had not been subject to Longstreet's orders for weeks. If Anderson was Longstreet's responsibility, as Robertson implies might have been the case, Longstreet would have issued orders to Anderson just as he did to Hood and McLaws. If there was some question about who controlled Anderson, Hill would not have issued attack orders to him that afternoon, nor would Hill have had any reason to visit Pitzer's Woods behind McLaws' left and Anderson's right. Instead, he would have positioned himself a mile to the north near or alongside his old command, Pender's Light Division, which he did not do. Further, neither Longstreet nor any other officer *ever* mentioned that there was an issue about who controlled Anderson's Division.

Yet another of Robertson's excuses for Hill foists the responsibility for Pender's unengaged division onto Lee's shoulders, implying there were no specific instructions for Pender's advance. This, of course, is not true and ignores the fact that Hill already had specific orders to cooperate with Longstreet and take advantage of any "opportunity" that arose. This, again, was a classic example of how General Lee issued his orders to his generals and left it up to them to figure out how to accomplish the task. According to Lee himself, Hill was given substantial discretion to accomplish his task: "General Hill was instructed to threaten the center of the

Federal line, in order to prevent re-enforcements being sent to either wing, and to avail himself of an opportunity that might present itself to attack." The only way Hill could take advantage of any "opportunity that might present itself" was to have the tactical flexibility (i.e., discretion) to react and take advantage of the situation. And, of course, Pender himself knew he was under orders to advance. His skirmishers had already driven back their Eleventh Corps counterparts to the base of Cemetery Hill, and Pender and anxious to order his men forward when he was stricken with an artillery fragment. Robertson's justification for Hill's failing does not stand up to serious scrutiny.

The final point offered by Robertson in defense of Hill—that if Lee "wanted Hill's entire corps to cooperate fully with Longstreet, he could have ordered it forward"—is a very interesting statement. It is, of course, technically correct because Lee was the commanding general. But it is not germane to the issue at hand and is in fact nothing more than a straw man argument. As a corps commander, Hill, like Longstreet, had the authority to commit his entire corps to battle. Within the execution of the echelon attack, Hill had specific orders from Lee to accomplish a task with discretion, which is exactly what Longstreet had—specific orders from Lee to attack laced with the discretion of how best to accomplish his mission. In other words, Lee told Hill what to do, but not how to do it; Hill was the commander of Third Corps, not Lee. The "how to do it" part was Hill's responsibility. And Hill totally failed. Only three of his nine brigades in two divisions got into action on July 2. Robertson is, in effect, arguing that it was acceptable for Lee to allow Longstreet the tactical flexibility of how to accomplish his task, but not acceptable to grant the same tactical flexibility to Hill. If so, it is a damning indictment against the subject he is trying so desperately to defend.

Shortly after the battle, many Confederate officers recognized that a substantial "opportunity" had been lost along the front of Hill's Third Corps. Cadmus Wilcox believed that Cemetery Ridge could have been carried had his Alabamians been supported, which would have bolstered his drive on the Federal center and helped keep Lang's Floridians in line.[286] Rans Wright argued the same point: his Georgians could have held on to their gains along Cemetery Ridge had "a protecting force on my left, or if the brigade on my right had not been forced to retire."[287] Fifteen days after the battle, Colonel Edward J. Walker, commander of the 3rd Georgia in Wright's Brigade, ended his report with a thinly veiled indictment of both his division and corps commanders: "Had the whole line [the rest of Anderson's division, et. al.] been properly supported, there would have been no trouble about holding our position, as the enemy seemed panic-stricken, and were fleeing before us in every direction, and, in my opinion, could not have been rallied at their second line."[288] General Lee felt the same way. In a postwar conversation with Harry Heth, Lee told him that the wounding of Pender had been decisive: "I shall ever believe if General Pender had remained on his horse half an hour longer, we would have carried the enemy's position." [289]

Cemetery Hill: The Golden (Lost) Opportunity

Although Hill and Anderson fumbled their opportunity to cleave apart the Army of the Potomac on Cemetery Ridge, Lee's echelon attack developed an even greater possibility for a decisive victory late that Thursday afternoon. On the elbow of his fishhook line at Cemetery Hill, Meade had gathered together the remains of Oliver Howard's Eleventh Corps—the least reliable men in his entire army.

The Eleventh Corps contained 26 regiments at Gettysburg. Their combined history against Lee and his lieutenants is revealing, and helps explain exactly who was defending the critical ground of Cemetery Hill on July 2, 1863. Eight of these regiments had been in the field since the war's early months and experienced their first defeat at the hands of Stonewall Jackson at the Battle of Cross Keyes during the Shenandoah Valley Campaign of 1862.[290] Fifteen regiments (the original eight plus seven more enduring their first combat of the war) were roughly handled and decisively beaten at Second Manassas.[291] The remaining 11 regiments were newer formations that counted the debacle at Chancellorsville as their first battle; their regularly-beaten comrades had also been present when Jackson's sweeping flank attack routed them rearward. These were the same regiments that experienced the horror of the first day's fight north of Gettysburg just eight weeks later. There was not a single regiment in Howard's Eleventh Corps that was a stranger to ignominy and defeat. They knew it. So did Lee's veterans.

Certainly many of these men were brave and even good soldiers, just as many individual units and officers—the 26th Wisconsin and Hubert Dilger's battery jump readily to mind—worked hard to give a good account of themselves. But the contagion of defeat was in their ranks and bad luck had been their lot. These mostly Germanic descendants—often contemptuously referred to as "Flying Dutchmen" by other infantry in the army—were intensely disliked and distrusted by influential officers within that Federal army. General Hancock admitted before Congress that Eleventh Corps had never been considered part of the army and could not be depended upon to perform well. According to Second Corps historian Francis A. Walker, after Chancellorsville the officers in the army held the Germans in such low regard that Eleventh Corps was not even considered to be qualified to serve as a reserve formation. In a letter to President Abraham Lincoln on May 7, 1863, Hooker placed the loss of Chancellorsville squarely on Eleventh Corps, and several officers urged Hooker to break up the ill-fated Germans. He decided against doing so, but ill-feelings, jealousy, and intrigue percolated through the army with regard to Howard's corps. As Francis Walker summed it up, "A feeling of contempt . . . had been generally entertained by the older corps of the Army of the Potomac toward the Eleventh Corps ever since it came in the rear after Fredericksburg."[292]

In addition to its less than sterling combat record, some of the widespread feeling of hostility and contempt for Eleventh Corps can be attributed to suspicion and ignorance against foreign-born but naturalized citizens. But regardless of the reasons why the regiments of Eleventh Corps were held in contempt, one undeniable fact remains: most of the units that formed this corps never proved themselves as reliable combat outfits—for whatever reason. The collective body that comprised Eleventh Corps lacked the vital quality of confidence and conspired to leave the regiments of the corps little more than hollow organized shells filled with men. As Gettysburg historian Edwin Coddington put it, Howard's Eleventh Corps "lacked that indefinable something called morale."[293]

Following their disastrous exhibition of July 1, the remnants of Eleventh Corps, with great difficulty, had finally rallied on Cemetery Hill. As earlier noted, of the corps' six brigades, five had been shattered and put to flight. The remaining brigade under Orland Smith had not been engaged that day, but suffered unusually large skirmishing losses during the afternoon of July 2. By the time the Confederate echelon attack was rolling down the line into Anderson's Division, every one of the brigades in Eleventh Corps had suffered significant casualties since their arrival on the field. These losses, coupled with shaky morale, uneven leadership, and a checkered battlefield history rendered these Federal units almost worthless—little more than troops occupying ground without the corresponding combat value visible in Meade's other units.

These are not idle observations. The proof in found in an examination of Eleventh Corps' combat record on July 2. The corps' First Division, under the temporary command of Adelbert Ames, had coalesced on East Cemetery Hill, where its two brigades were decisively beaten by two brigades under Harry Hays and Isaac Avery. This despite the fact that the Federals had more than 24 hours to rest and fortify their position, were fighting on the defensive with supporting artillery, and had the advantage of terrain. Yet the Tigers and Tar Heels fought their way uphill over stone walls and abatis, lunettes and other earthworks, and defeated them, capturing numerous artillery pieces in the process. Meanwhile, on facing west from Cemetery Hill were several batteries of artillery along with what remained of the other four weakened brigades of Eleventh Corps, the Second and Third divisions under Adolph von Steinwehr and Carl Schurz, respectively. Howard and Schurz had tried to shift of these regiments to stem the Confederate breakthrough on East Cemetery Hill, but few responded and the burden was carried by Carroll's "Gibraltar" Brigade from Second Corps. The simple fact is that these Federal regiments—routed at Chancellorsville, seriously mauled on July 1 at Gettysburg, and on the whole looked down upon by the remainder of the Army of the Potomac—were no longer combat capable and could not even hold a position strengthened by stone walls, abatis, earthworks, and artillery.

Yet, it is these very regiments that legions of writers have asserted would have rallied and then repulsed any determined Confederate attack against Cemetery Hill on July 1. It simply does not follow that any portion of Eleventh Corps could have held Cemetery Hill in the face of continued Confederate pressure on July 1, when the pair of brigades that *were* attacked on July 2 (after 24 hours of rest and after fortifying their position) fell apart after offering but light opposition. Without exception, every time Eleventh Corps brigades came under assault at Gettysburg they were shattered.

These were the troops Meade had placed at the most vulnerable spot along his fishhook-shaped line. Formations that would have supported them were stripped away and sent elsewhere as a result of Lee's *en échelon* attack. And thus the decisive opportunity Lee was seeking was the one that arrived on Cemetery Hill on the late afternoon of July 2. We maintain this opportunity was the most important of the second day's fighting. The "joint" of Meade's line, already the weakest part of his front and held by the least reliable troops in blue uniforms, materialized for a short time only to fade away because of two events: the mortal wounding of Dorsey Pender, and the failure of several generals, including Hill, Anderson, Posey, Mahone, and Rodes) to advance their men as ordered. The failures of these officers and its effect on the echelon attack have already been discussed in detail elsewhere in this study.

Pender's fall was much more serious to Confederate fortunes than historians have realized or are willing to admit. Had he gotten his formidable division rolling, the continued attack *en échelon* would have matched up the four excellent brigades of the Light Division (about 5,500 confident veteran soldiers) against the 3,400 men in the four depleted and shaken brigades of Eleventh Corps on Cemetery Hill. "We had supreme contempt for the 11th Corps and did not look for anything from them," explained one veteran from Scales' Brigade.[294] Even a cursory examination of what happened on the other side of Cemetery Hill to Ames' division foretells what the result would have been. History also shows us that an entire division of these same survivors had not been able to handle the five regiments of Perrin's (then Maxcy Gregg's) South Carolinians at Second Manassas. Throw Rodes' Division into the equation (remember it, too was ordered to attack and almost did so) and logic dictates but one result.

Of course this is all speculation. Pender was mortally wounded, Jim Lane refused to go forward, and the assault never took place as designed. Rodes was unable to get his division into action as ordered, and Early did not reinforce his success on East Cemetery Hill with John Gordon's Georgians. As a result, the Eleventh Corps troops facing west on Cemetery Hill that Thursday evening were never pressed. Of course General Lee understood all of this. He knew the history of Pender's brigades, knew the history of Howard's Eleventh Corps, and fully appreciated what the fall of Pender and the failures of Hill, Anderson, and others meant for the army at Gettysburg.

Richard Ewell and Culp's Hill

No matter how disappointed Lee might have been by the breakdown of the Confederate echelon attack, the disjointed efforts of Third Corps might have been overcome had Dick Ewell performed as expected. Instead, he employed nothing but artillery after he heard Longstreet's guns, and then failed to see that all of his available troops got into the fight in a timely manner when he decided to convert his demonstration into an attack. As a result, the "opportunity" created by Longstreet's efforts on the far right, Anderson's three right brigades, and the successful charge by Early's two brigades under Harry Hays and Isaac Avery was wasted; Johnson's Division was sent late against Culp's Hill, where it fought gallantly, won some key ground, and bogged itself down for the night.

Unlike Little Round Top, the capture of Cemetery Hill would have completely unhinged Meade's entire line. As we know, Jubal Early committed only two of his three available brigades (Gordon was held back and the fourth brigade under "Extra Billy" Smith was posted east of town on the Yorktown Pike) and easily routed the First Division of the Eleventh Corps holding East Cemetery Hill. There they waited in vain for support. Early held back Gordon's large brigade. Robert Rodes' five brigades marched out late, stopped when they reached the northwestern face of Cemetery Hill, saw that the fighting had died out, and turned around without attacking at all. Considering the checkered history of the Federal defenders, and that quality troops would have been attacking them from at least two directions—and knowing how Early fared on the hill with just two brigades—it is reasonable to conclude that the remaining Eleventh Corps troops holding Cemetery Hill would have been routed and the position carried. But Early hesitated and Rodes did not make sure his division was ready for action in a timely fashion (and then did not apparently advance with it when it was ready). We do not know whether Early informed Ewell of his initial success on East Cemetery Hill, or whether Ewell was in a position to see it for himself. We do know that Early sought out Rodes to discover why his regiments were not attacking the heights. The excuse he was offered was that the Third Corps troops to his right (Pender's Light Division) were not attacking.[295]

Still, Early acknowledged he could have sent Gordon to the top of the hill, but chose not to do so, citing that it would have been "a useless loss of life."[296] Early's decision to withhold Gordon is consistent with his earlier behavior. The idea was firmly established in his mind that his excellent division could not take the hill, much less hold it, without help. As he had demonstrated on July 1, Early found success difficult to handle and impossible to reinforce.

Robert E. Lee and July 2

And so it was that so many opportunities for a decisive breakthrough on several points of the line had achieved so little. Perhaps Edward Porter Alexander summed it up best when he wrote after the war: "If the whole fighting force of our army could have been concentrated & brought to bear together upon that of the enemy I cannot doubt that we would have broken it to pieces . . . It would seem that after [the] long delay in beginning [the] attack that Hill & Ewell would have been thoroughly prepared. . . ."[297]

Alexander's insightful observation goes to the heart of the argument maintained within these pages: that Lee made the right decision when he ordered the Army of Northern Virginia to attack on July 2, and chose the best method for doing so with an echelon assault. Alexander, who strongly favored adopting a defensive stance, clearly articulated what would have happened had Lee's attack not miscarried. The proof is found by simply examining what was happening to Meade's army where Lee's brigades aggressively came to grips with the enemy.[298] The inability of the Confederates to achieve a significant victory on July 2 was a failure of execution rather than the pursuit of a wrong course of action.

Still, many students of the battle and Lee detractors continue to echo the tired refrain that the Confederates should have stood down on July 2, assumed the defensive, and waited for Meade to launch a direct attack against the Army of Northern Virginia. This option was discussed in some depth in the preceding chapter, but now that we have completed a detailed assessment of Lee's July 2 offensive, it is appropriate to return to this issue briefly. The fact that this argument continues to find traction at all is in itself rather curious. Its advocates ignore the logistical ramifications Lee would have faced and are in effect relying on traits Meade never manifested before the arrival of U. S. Grant and his bloody Wilderness through Petersburg fighting in the summer of 1864. The fact that Meade did not attack on July 2 proves that he was not going to attack that day. Meade was in the process of concentrating his army, which in itself validates the correctness of Lee's decision to commit his superb infantry to the offensive before the numerically superior Army of the Potomac was fully consolidated. Note also that Meade also did not attack on the morning of July 3 or anytime after Pickett's Charge was repulsed. If Lee had gone on the defensive after his victory of July 1, Meade would not have immediately thrown his army against the Southerners. Robert E. Lee knew better than to sit on the defensive on July 2 and allow Meade to rest his exhausted and beaten troops, bring up reinforcements, and gather stragglers. That decision would have violated every sound military principle. And so he assumed the offensive.[299]

One of the leading critics of assuming the offensive and Lee's handling of it was Glenn Tucker. In his influential and widely read study *Lee and Longstreet at Gettysburg*, Tucker advanced the notion that Lee lost an opportunity to defeat

Meade by not following up Longstreet's attack. According to Tucker, Lee should have had Ed Johnson's Division from Ewell's Second Corps available on his right, or George Pickett's Division, Longstreet's last remaining First Corps division, ready for attack once Pickett's troops arrived on the battlefield that afternoon. The weight of these formations, said Tucker "might have turned the scales against Meade, whose army, as McLaws expressed it, was at one point cut in twain." Tucker criticizes Lee by asking rhetorically, "was not Lee too considerate of Ewell's reluctance [to shift any troops to the right side of town] in the first instance, and too sympathetic with Pickett's jaded men in the second?"[300]

As we have already seen, Johnson's Division, and indeed the Second Corps in its entirety, remained where it ended up after the fighting of July 1 because of information provided to Lee by Richard Ewell. The corps leader convinced Lee that Culp's Hill could be, or already was, occupied by his men, and that Ewell could use his corps to advantage on the far left of the line. Tucker's assertion that Lee should have shifted Ewell or some of his troops (Johnson, for example), to Seminary Ridge is made with the knowledge that Ewell ultimately failed north of Cemetery Hill and Culp's Hill; Lee, of course, had to make the final decision without knowing what the outcome of his decision would be and with the information he had in hand at that time. Tucker's criticism also ignores the fact that two-thirds of Powell Hill's infantry brigades ordered to join in the attack did not enter the fighting at all, and that the Federals Hill would have encountered had his attack not stalled were inferior and not up to the task at hand. How could Lee have known that Longstreet would successfully handle his First Corps, but that Hill, Ewell, and several of their subordinate generals would fail to do their duty?

The second part of Tucker's criticism deals with Lee's failure to utilize Pickett's Division on July 2. Pickett's brigades were part of Longstreet's command, and Old Pete held the Virginia commander in special regard. To Hood, Longstreet had explained that he did not like attacking without Pickett, for it was like going "into battle with one boot off."[301] Pickett and his three brigades began July 2 near Chambersburg and reached Marsh Creek, about three miles west of Gettysburg, later that afternoon. Exactly when the head of Pickett's column approached Marsh Creek is unclear, for the sources vary from a few minutes before Longstreet's guns opened fire to as late as 6:00 p.m.[302] So when, exactly, did Pickett arrive and could and should he have been utilized?

Pickett's Virginians awoke about 2:00 a.m. on July 2, broke camp and marched through Chambersburg on their way to Gettysburg. The men marched about 26 miles beneath a blazing sun before arriving near Marsh Creek. Without doubt many of the men and animals were exhausted when they arrived.[303] For some, the guns served as a rejuvenating tonic. Charles T. Loehr of the 1st Virginia, James Kemper's Brigade, recalled that the men of his regiment "were in fine condition. The march from Chambersburg did not fatigue them at all [and that they] could have gone into battle . . . when they reached Gettysburg."[304] As he approached Gettysburg, Pickett sent one of his aides, Major Walter Harrison, to army headquarters with word for General Lee that the division was at hand. Harrison's message from Pickett was that the Virginians, though tired, could still be called on that day for duty. "Tell General Pickett," Lee instructed in return, "I shall not want him this evening; tell him to let his men rest and I will send word when I want them." Pickett, accompanied by another aide, Captain Edward. R. Baird, went in search of Longstreet and found him along lower Seminary Ridge. According to one account, Pickett told his superior that his men were "exhausted and must have rest." As a result of this information and with the location of the resting Virginians, Longstreet did not press Pickett to bring his division forward. Picket received a similar response when he left Longstreet and rode to find Lee, who told the division commander, "I am glad you have come. I shall have work for you tomorrow."[305]

Lee knew that history was replete with examples of exhausted troops being used in combat after forced marches to tip the scales for victory. Two of Napoleon's most famous and important victories had evolved in this manner. On June 14, 1800, French troops under General Desaix undertook a forced march before entering and helping to turn the tide at the Battle of Marengo. Five and one-half years later, Marshal Davout led elements of his corps on a forced march of 70 miles in 48 hours before going into battle and providing a key contribution to victory at Austerlitz.[306] In both these examples, however—and in many others involving the Great Captains—Napoleon's cavalry was screening his army's flanks and guiding the reinforcements into action precisely where they were needed. Further, in both cases Napoleon absolutely and unequivocally needed the exhausted troops to avoid losing the battle.

Neither of these conditions applied when Pickett arrived on July 2. Without Stuart, Lee did not know what was beyond his flanks (especially to the north and east, which forced Ewell to tie down part of his infantry in static roles of observation on the York and Hanover roads). Thus it was very reasonable for Lee to retain some sort of strategic reserve, a role Pickett played for the army on the afternoon of July 2. Further, Lee's decision to utilize an attack *en échelon* meant reinforcing his far right (Longstreet's front) early on evening of July 2 was not necessary—and might have only wasted Pickett's men by attacking *into* Meade's strength. It must be remembered that the decisive "opportunity" of the second day's fighting developed in dramatic fashion on Cemetery Hill. Lee's decision not to utilize Pickett in an offensive capacity makes good sense when these considerations are taken into account. Therefore, this criticism advanced by Tucker and repeated by others along the same line lacks merit.[307]

* * *

While the fighting of July 2 is still fresh in our minds, another recurring theme of General Lee's generalship on that day must be discussed. Both historians Edwin

Coddington and Harry Pfanz posit that Lee was "passive" in his command style because "he allowed both corps commanders [Longstreet and Hill] to conduct their assaults without interference [that] permitted problems to develop," and hence "his toleration of the shortcomings of his subordinates that day lessened the chances of Confederate success."[308] These are damning charges. One way to analyze their validity is to pose them in question form: Where did the idea that Lee was "passive" originate? Was Lee "passive" on July 2? By allowing Longstreet and Hill "to conduct their assaults without interference," was Lee somehow guilty of not doing his job? What was it about Lee's style of command that "permitted problems to develop?" and, what manner of "toleration of the shortcomings of his subordinates" do the critics claim Lee allowed?

These criticisms of Lee for July 2, as voiced by Coddington, Pfanz, and others, confuse physical activity during the battle with job performance. Their model, or benchmark for this conclusion is none other than George Gordon Meade. Once the battle was underway, Lee's counterpart rode all over the field in response to the Confederate attack, ordered formations here and there, shouted out orders, and dispatched couriers in every direction. This activity, wrote Coddington, demonstrated that Meade was "in top form."[309] Lee, meanwhile, spent much of his time in a centralized location near the vicinity of the Lutheran Seminary. Since Meade ultimately won the battle, these writers equate his frenetic activity with victory, and Lee's "passive" method of command as failure. But is this valid?

Meade was new to army command at Gettysburg, and had served as a corps commander in only one battle, Chancellorsville, where his Fifth Corps was only lightly engaged. In our opinion, at Gettysburg Meade fell back on what he knew best, and as a result assumed the role of a division or brigade commander. "Major Meade" was comfortable leading troops in person. In the crushing press of events brought about by Lee's effective echelon assaults, Meade resorted to a hands-on command style—perhaps just as Lee thought he might. In riding to and from his headquarters and up and down Cemetery Ridge, ordering subordinates to send troops from six of his seven infantry corps to the various parts of the threatened Federal line, Meade acted like a subordinate commander with authority over the entire army. In this capacity and with his focus narrowed to the emergency along his left wing, Meade utterly lost sight of just how little strength he had remaining on his right wing. The Duke of Wellington, who defeated Napoleon at Waterloo, believed that an army commander had to maintain a certain sang-froid, focus on what was transpiring along his entire front, and, as Wellington described it in his aristocratic English manner, not "run about like a wet hen."[310]

Certainly American army commanders did not look upon activity during battle quite the same way Wellington did, and Meade's energetic actions did indeed save his left flank from collapse. But the thrust of Wellington's point is clear: army commanders must remain cool and avoid snap decisions that might risk the army as a whole. And that is exactly what happened to Meade. Had Lee's subordinates carried out the orders they had been given, Meade's front on upper Cemetery Ridge and the weakly-held but all-important joint in the line at Cemetery Hill would have been irretrievably lost—because of Meade's actions. If that had happened as Lee intended (and as his troops were aligned and poised to act), Meade's harried activity would be viewed much differently by those who practice outcome-based historical analysis.

As we will also learn, even a cursory examination of Lee's general behavior on July 2 demonstrates that he was anything but "passive," as Coddington, Pfanz and others suggest. Out of bed at 3:00 a.m. after less than three hours of sleep, Lee issued orders and met with staff officers soon thereafter. He dispatched Captain Johnston and his party on their scouting mission at 4:00 a.m., and sent A. L. Long out to double check that the artillery battalions of Second and Third corps were sited as best as possible. Following this, Lee listened to General Pendleton's report of his scouting activities along the Federal left flank. As soon as there was enough sunlight, about 5:15 a.m., Lee observed the Federal lines from his overlook near the Lutheran Theological Seminary, dispatched Charles Venable on a mission to Richard Ewell, and opened a conference with Generals Longstreet and Hill (and eventually included Hood and McLaws) in which he began outlining his general plan of attack. Thereafter he mounted Traveller and rode to see Ewell on the far left of the line. It was there that Lee met with General Trimble and climbed to the cupola of the Almshouse to observe the Federal positions on East Cemetery Hill and Culp's Hill. Lee then met with and discussed the general plan of attack for the upcoming battle with Ewell, Rodes, and Early. By the time Lee rode back to his headquarters it was after 10:00 a.m.

Once Porter Alexander arrived, Lee gave the artillerist instructions to guide his guns to the Confederate right flank and how to do so without being seen. Prior to this, Lee gave specific marching and deployment instructions to McLaws, who was to lead the attack, and met with Johnston when he returned. With Alexander moving the guns of First Corps, Lee agreed to Longstreet's request to wait for Law's Brigade to arrive before moving out with the infantry. By 1:30 p.m., Lee was again on horseback, scouting the Federal left from lower Seminary Ridge. He joined First Corps infantry during their march to the designated jump off area, and later carefully examined Sickles' Federal Third Corps, which at about 3:00 p.m. advanced to a new defensive line along the Emmitsburg Road. After realizing the Federal advance offered a significant new opportunity, Lee modified his plan of attack to take advantage of the new Federal dispositions and ordered Longstreet to assault *en échelon*. The commanding general then worked his way back up Seminary Ridge, stopping to discuss his plans with Cadmus Wilcox (Anderson's Division) and the necessity that his brigade cover McLaws' left flank. Lee then told Anderson (or Powell Hill, who in turn told Anderson), that Anderson's entire division was to attack, brigade by brigade. Pender's Light Division was also ordered to attack, although whether the order came from Lee or Hill is unknown. Justus Scheibert of the Prussian Royal Engineers was at Gettysburg as an observer. He noted Lee's activity on July 2 prior to the opening of the action. Lee, he recalled, was "riding to and fro . . . making anxious inquiries here and there, and looking care worn." Once everything was ready, Lee returned to his overlook on Seminary Ridge, where he remained during the battle that followed. This summation, of course, only covers Lee's actions that have been recorded for posterity. Certainly, the general performed tasks and engaged in many additional conversations of which we know nothing.[311]

Therefore, it is fair to say that Lee had been constantly and fully involved in every facet of command that his rank and position demanded. For 13 continuous hours, the general had shown remarkable energy and duty of purpose. His tenacious and courageous determination to take the battle to the enemy, especially in the light of the difficulties stemming from the crippling absence of Stuart, was unwavering; his focus to achieve an important victory undiminished. When changing circumstances rendered his initial plan of attack obsolete, he was at the point of decision and altered his plans accordingly. Was Lee "passive" on July 2? The common definition of the word is "lacking in energy or will: lethargic," or "not active or operating," or "exhibiting no gain or control."[312] Readers will have to judge for themselves whether Coddington and Pfanz are correct in labeling Lee's performance on July 2 as "passive." We think not.

The next criticism Pfanz levels against Lee, namely that the Confederate commander allowed Longstreet and Hill "to conduct their assaults without interference," is a peculiar allegation. It implies that Lee, as the army commander, was supposed to (as Pfanz puts it), "interfere" with the execution of the battle orders at corps level. Why employ corps commanders if the army commander has to interfere? Following the Seven Days Battles, Lee reorganized the army in order to create a more efficient command structure. From that time on, it was the job of the "wing" or corps commanders to implement his orders. Lee almost always issued "orders with discretion," and the commanders who were given those orders had the latitude, or flexibility, to decide for themselves how best to carry out their mission.[313]

At Gettysburg, Lee treated his corps commanders with consideration and respect because he believed they were capable of carrying out his instructions. Longstreet accomplished his battle mission on July 2 in impressive fashion; Hill and Ewell did not. If one accepts Pfanz's argument that Lee should have interfered with Hill and Ewell when they failed (which he could not have known in advance), then Lee was also guilty of not interfering with Longstreet when he succeeded. By this same logic, Lee must therefore be censurable for not interfering with Jackson at Chancellorsville, or with Longstreet at Second Manassas, and so on. How can Lee be held culpable for following the same style of command on July 2, 1863, that had earned him in the past plaudits for boldness, audacity, and the brilliance to allow his subordinates great flexibility to achieve the army's goals?

Pfanz claims General Lee's command style "permitted problems to develop." Pfanz is maintaining that Lee as army commander made possible the problems that engulfed some of the Confederate high command on July 2.[314] At first blush this charge appears to hold some validity. Lee's command style *required* that his chief subordinates exercise discretion. It must be remembered that Lee's modified plan of attack called for an assault *en échelon* that specifically ordered his generals to take advantage of any "opportunity" that might develop on their front. In other words, his corps, division, and brigade commanders had to have the tactical flexibility to be *able* to respond to an "opportunity." And this is exactly what Lee allowed. His subordinates had the tactical flexibility—or discretion—to react to the changing circumstances of battle. Thus, for Pfanz to criticize this and frame it as he does—Lee "permitted problems to develop"—indicates, at least to us, that he does not grasp the nature of the *en échelon* attack and how it dovetailed well with Lee's established style of command.

Finally, Pfanz criticizes Lee for "his toleration of the shortcomings of his subordinates that day [which] lessened the chances of Confederate success." Like so many critiques of commanding generals, this one cannot be maintained unless Lee was aware that his subordinates had "shortcomings" *and* knew these failures would manifest themselves in the manner in which they did on that particular day. Of course Lee was aware that each of his primary subordinates had their own strengths and weaknesses; everyone does. But at some point, whether in Virginia, Maryland, or Pennsylvania, Powell Hill and Richard Ewell had to fight a major engagement at the head of their respective corps and be judged accordingly by Lee. Prior to July 2, Lee did not have enough evidence to know whether Hill and Ewell would shine in their new assignments, or fail. Some troubling indications had bubbled to the surface during July 1, but that action did not constitute a sufficient test from which Lee could draw firm conclusions. Ewell, for example, had performed his duty exceptionally well at Second Winchester, and thereafter demonstrated initiative in placing his corps north of town on July 1 and recognizing the opportunity the Federals presented to him. His failure came only at the end of a long day. Powell Hill's lackluster performance on July 1 ran counter to his entire Civil War career to that point, and Lee was probably aware Hill was sick. More action and time was required to observe Hill's basic competence at the corps level.

As we have discussed at great length, Lee's successful style of command and plan to attack *en échelon* was designed to create "opportunity" his subordinate commanders could exploit. This, as we know, required Lee— in his accustomed manner of command—to extend to his generals the tactical discretion to carry out his orders to the best of their abilities. "There was an inner compulsion to pay his corps and division commanders the compliment of trusting their modesty, their loyalty, and their ability," explained Bishop Robert R. Brown.[315] And this arrangement was an integral part of Lee's consistent and gentlemanly character and accounted for much of his success as an army commander. For Pfanz and others to assert that Lee excessively tolerated imperfections in his generals is to argue that he should have issued rigid battle plans that required little if any initiative on the part of his subordinates. That would have been the only way in which Lee could have known just what "shortcomings" were manifesting themselves amongst his lieutenants. But Lee had enough experience to know that the volatile and uncertain nature of battle *always* exposed flaws in every inflexible battle plan. This is why he always allowed his subordinates the tactical flexibility necessary to carry out their orders. And of course, an echelon attack, by definition, *precluded* a rigid battle plan. Thus, the charge that Lee tolerated "the shortcomings of his subordinates" lacks any serious foundational support. Harry Pfanz's magnificent pair of studies analyzing the battle's second day are wonderfully rich in combat detail, and add substantially to our knowledge of July 2. Unfortunately, his critique of Robert E. Lee's generalship suggests that he, like others before him, have mimicked what earlier writers have written on the subject and simply fail to grasp the general's style of command and its interplay with the essential characteristics of an echelon attack.

*   *   *

Many historians fall into the wholly human tendency of utilizing "outcome-based history" when judging a general's actions. In other words, they base their opinions and analysis upon the final result of the battle, rather than the context within which decisions were made. For example, noted historian Gary W. Gallagher says the following about the battle of the second day: "Had Southern infantry solidified the first day's victory through successful assaults on July 2, as they almost did, many of Lee's critics would have been silenced." He goes on to declare: "It is not unfair to state from the safe confines of historical perspective that Lee erred in his decision." By ordering the Confederates to attack, concludes Gallagher, Lee "bled the future offensive edge from his magnificent army."[316]

Gallagher is claiming that if the Confederates had won the day, Lee's decision to attack would be hailed today as correct; but because they did not, it was wrong. A decision cannot be both correct and incorrect at the same time, based solely upon the outcome of a future event. In other words, Lee's decision to attack was right or wrong when it was made, and that decision must be divorced from the outcome, successful or not. To argue otherwise removes the decision from its proper historical context. Put another way, a conclusion reached on the battlefield to act in a particular way must be evaluated by examining why it was made, not whether the end result was the hoped-for outcome. The same holds true for any analysis of General Lee's performance at Gettysburg. Was his decision to attack in the manner in which he did on July 2 *reasonable* based upon the military standards of the day and the information he possessed *when* he committed his forces to battle?

Gallagher's statement that Lee "bled the future offensive edge from his magnificent army" is interesting. The statement is certainly true; the Army of

Northern Virginia lost men and generals by attacking on July 2 that were not available to them later in the war. But Gallagher's observation means absolutely nothing. Any losses, whether suffered while attacking or defending, bleed the offensive edge of any army. In return for his July 2 attacks, Lee so crippled the defending Army of the Potomac that Meade was unable to undertake serious offensive operations until the following May. Many of the same Confederate troops that attacked on July 2 also assaulted and drove from the field William Rosecrans' Army of the Cumberland at the Battle of Chickamauga in September of 1863, and launched another sweeping offensive in the Wilderness eight months later. This belies the assertion that the Virginia army had suffered a loss of offensive spirit or striking power. Last, Lee—like any Great Captain—would have been guilty of squandering the sacrifices his men had made over the past year if he did not try to seize the moment presented to him at Gettysburg. What, exactly, Gallagher would have Lee save his "offensive edge" for is unclear.

History shows us that the overwhelming majority of wars brought to a successful conclusion are done so through offensive action. By attacking on July 2, Lee was not only following up his victory of the previous day and the momentum he had generated through successive victories, but was seeking the triumph on Northern soil the Confederacy so desperately needed. A protracted war was a losing one and Lee knew it. The South did not possess the resources required to wage a prolonged conflict. Its single successful army could shorten the war only by creating conditions that might bring politics and diplomacy into play. Lee was all too aware of this critical situation, which is why he carried his army north that summer. Based upon what he knew on the morning of July 2, Lee was not only correct to attack, but made the only *realistic* decision that offered his country any chance of success.

* * *

The fighting on July 2 had come as close as possible to breaking apart Meade's Army of the Potomac without actually doing so. Tired and disappointed in the outcome, Robert E. Lee maintained his determination to finish the job he had set out to do when he ordered the army north three weeks earlier.

Notes for Chapter 7

1. Napoleon's oft-repeated phrase is one of his most famous, and one that has been proved over and over again throughout military history.

2. Napoleon's letter to Barry E. O'Meara, 9 November 1816.

3. McMurry, *John Bell Hood*, p. 75; Hood, *Advance and Retreat*, p. 69; Pfanz, *Gettysburg: The Second Day*, pp. 172-173; Tagg, *The Generals of Gettysburg*, p. 226.

4. Pfanz, *Gettysburg: The Second Day*, p. 167, n72, p. 500. The Texas Brigade's new headquarters guidon was a "crimson Lone Star on a field of white." *Touched by Fire: Letters from Company D, 5th Texas Infantry, Hood's Brigade, Army of Northern Virginia, 1862-1865*, p. 58. Another witness claimed Hood's words were: "Fix bayonets! Forward, my Texans, and win this battle or die in the attempt!" According to one writer, while "the First Texas probably carried a Third Bunting Issue battle flag as its official regimental flag [at Gettysburg], but there is evidence that the First Texas unofficially retained a replacement silk Lone Star Flag made by Mrs. Louis T. Wigfall to replace the Lone Star colors lost at Sharpsburg (Antietam). The flag had special significance . . . edged in black crepe as a memorial to the many dead of the regiment." Alan K. Sumrall, *Battle Flags of Texans in the Confederacy* (Austin, 1995), p. 21. See also, F. B. Chilton, *Unveiling and Dedication of Monument to Hood's Texas Brigade* (Houston, 1911), pp. 339 and 350; Simpson, *Hood's Texas Brigade*, p. 271, fn 43. General Lee had previously issued orders forbidding units to carry specialized flags, including state flags, into action. While most regiments seemed to have modified their state colors into smaller versions that included streamers, the 1st Texas carried a true Texas state flag into action. Known as the "Second Wigfall Flag," the state color borne by the 1st Texas into battle at Gettysburg was a replacement of the state flag that had been lost at Sharpsburg. The "mountain" referred to by Work did not mean Little Round Top, but rather Houck's Ridge that was then occupied by Federal troops. General Henry L. Benning, brigade commander in Hood's Division, also referred to Houck's Ridge as "the mountain;" please see "Notes by General Benning on Battle of Gettysburg," *Southern Historical Society Papers*, 4, p. 176.

5. *OR* 27, 2, pp. 404, 407-408 and 412; Hood, *Advance and Retreat*, pp. 64-65; Harold B. Simpson, *Hood's Texas Brigade: Lee's Grenadier Guard* (Dallas, 1983), pp. 95-96, details the ceremony in which Hood was given the horse "Jeff Davis" by the NCOs and privates of the 4th Texas.

6. Richard M. McMurry, "John Bell Hood," *The Confederate General*, 2, pp. 120-127; Tagg, *The Generals of Gettysburg*, p. 223-225; Cormier, *The Suffolk Campaign*, pp. 159-160.

7. William C. Ward, "Incidents and Personal Experiences on The Battle Field of Gettysburg," *Confederate Veteran*, 8, number 8; Law, "The Struggle for 'Round Top,'" *Battles and Leaders of the Civil War*, 3, p. 323.

8. Law, "The Struggle for 'Round Top," *Battles and Leaders of the Civil War*, 3, p. 324; Law, "The Second Day at Gettysburg—The Confederate Side," *The Century War Book*, p. 195; Tagg, *The Generals of Gettysburg*, p. 228; Pfanz, *Gettysburg: The Second Day*, pp. 168-169; *OR* 27, pt. 2, p. 392. Law did not leave a Gettysburg report.

9. William C. Oates, *Gettysburg, July 2, 1863, Col. William C. Oates to Col. Homer R. Stoughton* (unpublished, 1888; William C. Oates, *The War between the Union and the Confederacy and Its Lost Opportunities* (Dayton, 1974), p. 210.

10. Simpson, *Hood's Texas Brigade*, p. 272, fn 45.

11. Jerome B. Robertson to Bachelder, May 11, 1882, *Bachelder Papers*, 2, pp. 860-861; *OR* 27, pt. 2, p. 404, 407 and 408.

12. *OR* 27, pt. 2, pp. 404, 407, 408. Robertson's postwar description of how his brigade divided into two pieces is different than what he reported immediately after the battle. See Jerome B. Robertson to Bachelder, May 11, 1882, *Bachelder Papers,* 2, p. 861. Robertson's entire advance was a confused one. In addition to what has already been described, Company I of the 4th Texas became separated from the rest of the regiment. Instead of moving around Devil's Den with its own formation and the 5th Texas, the company advanced with the right wing of the 1st Texas. J. M. Polk, *The North and South American Review* (Austin, 1912), copy in the Jenkings Garrett Special Collections, University of Texas-Arlington Library, Arlington, Texas; Simpson, *Hood's Texas Brigade,* p. 274.

13. After the war, Hood wrote in his memoirs that he was wounded "after reaching the peach orchard." Hood, *Advance and Retreat,* p. 59. The Sherfy Peach Orchard was still in Federal hands, so if his memory was correct, it was probably the grove located on the Bushman property.

14. *OR* 27, pt. 2, p. 414; George T. Anderson to Bachelder, March 15, 1876, *Bachelder Papers,* 1, p. 449; Pfanz, *Gettysburg: The Second Day,* p. 172. Major John Cheves Haskell of Henry's Battalion wrote after the war that the fire from his guns "was apparently very disastrous because the enemy's guns were placed on the crest of the mountain, which was a solid body of stone, and our artillery shots striking the stone on which their guns stood sent volleys of it almost like canister, doing them great damage." Whether he learned this later or could see it at that time is unknown. *Supplement to the OR* 5, serial no 5, p. 352.

15. *Supplement to the OR* 5, serial no 5, p. 353. Although we will never know for sure, the round was probably fired by one of the six 10-pounder Parrott rifles from Captain James E. Smith's 4th New York Light Battery, four pieces anchoring the Federal left flank on Houck's Ridge above Devil's Den. They may have been trying to hit the limbered batteries Haskell was bringing up to the Bushman orchard where Hood and his staff were watching the action. Haskell later claimed he brought forward both Garden's and Latham's batteries. However, since Garden and Bachman were the two batteries that were already limbered and waiting in reserve, Haskell probably confused the identity of Latham's and Bachman's commands. The Gettysburg National Military Park Tablet, which claims Latham's five-gun battery was already unlimbered and firing along Warfield Ridge above the Bushman Orchard, and was therefore already east of the Emmitsburg Road, seems to confirm this.

16. *Supplement to the OR* 5, serial no 5, p. 353; Harold B. Simpson, "General John Bell Hood—Southern Thunderbolt," presentation given before the Civil War Round Table of Wiesbaden, Germany, Monday, 12 March 1956, p. 34. a manuscript copy of this presentation is in the Confederate Research Center, Harold B. Simpson History Complex, Hill College, Hillsboro, Texas. Also, see John Bell Hood, letter dated 28 June 1875, on the topic of "Causes of Lee's Defeat at Gettysburg," *Southern Historical Society Papers,* 4, p. 150. According to historian Colonel Harold B. Simpson, "Although the surgeons advised against amputation of his arm, it might as well have been done for Hood was never able to use his left arm again and it remained helpless in a sling the rest of his life." Simpson, "General John Bell Hood—Southern Thunderbolt," p. 34. After he recuperated, Hood was sent west with Longstreet's First Corps and was severely wounded at Chickamauga on September 20, 1863, resulting in the amputation of his right leg just below the hip. Essentially a cripple, he was promoted to lieutenant general and given a corps in Joe Johnston's Army of Tennessee. In

July 1864, Johnston was sacked and Hood replaced him. After his bloody offensive gambit failed to hold Atlanta and his subsequent march into Tennessee wrecked his army at Franklin and Nashville, Hood resigned his command. McMurry, "John Bell Hood," pp. 121, 127.

17. J. Gary Laine and Morris M. Penny, *Law's Alabama Brigade in the War Between the Union and the Confederacy* (Shippensburg, 1996), p. 372, fn 9. Law's cousin, Tom Law, called him "Keever." See Tagg, *The Generals of Gettysburg*, pp. 227-229 for a good biographical portrait of Law.

18. *OR* 27, pt. 2, pp. 414-415.

19. *OR* 27, pt. 2, pp. 414-415, 421, 424 and 426; Pfanz, *Gettysburg: The Second Day,* pp. 174-175.

20. George T. Anderson to Bachelder, March 15, 1876, *Bachelder Papers,* 1, p. 449; Law, "Gettysburg: The Second Day—The Confederate Side. The Struggle for 'Round Top.'" *The Century War Book,* p. 195; Law, "The Struggle for 'Round Top," *Battles and Leaders of the Civil War,* 3, p. 324. For a good overview of Anderson's pre-Gettysburg experience, see Tagg, *The Generals of Gettysburg*, pp. 229-231.

21. *OR* 27, pt. 2, p. 391.

22. William C. Oates, "Gettysburg—The Battle on the Right," *Southern Historical Society Papers,* 6, pp. 174-176. Vincent's brigade consisted of the 16th Michigan, 44th New York, 83rd Pennsylvania, and 20th Maine. Tagg, *The Generals of Gettysburg*, p. 91.

23. *OR* 27, part 3, pp. 484-485, 488. Sedgwick's corps was on the road in the midst of a grueling 35-mile march from Manchester, Maryland.

24. *OR* 27, pt. 1, p. 592.

25. *OR* 27, pt. 1, p. 132.

26. *OR* 27, part 3, pp. 485.

27. George Gordon Meade, *Life and Letters of George Gordon Meade,* 2 volumes (New York, 1913), 2, p. 397.

28. Law, "Gettysburg: The Second Day—The Confederate Side. The Struggle for 'Round Top.'" *The Century War Book,* p. 195.

29. *OR* 27, pt. 2, p. 396; *Maine at Gettysburg* (Portland, 1898), pp. 163-164; Robert M. Powell, *Recollections of a Texas Colonel at Gettysburg,* edited by Gregory a. Coco (Gettysburg, 1990), p. 14. Powell was the colonel of the 5th Texas.

30. *OR* 27, pt. 2, pp. 407-408; Pfanz, *Gettysburg: The Second Day,* pp. 180, 182, 183.

31. Simpson, *Lee's Grenadier Guard,* p. 277. Simpson, whose excellent work on the Texas Brigades remains one of the best brigade histories ever published, mistakenly identifies the heights that Reilly fired on as being Little Round Top, and bases his claim on J. M. Polk's article in *The North and South American Review.* However, a careful examination of Polk's writing (pp. 27 and 28) unmistakably states that Reilly's supporting fire was directed against the Federals trying to hold onto Houck's Ridge, rather than later in the battle when the fighting spread up Little Round Top. According to Krick, *Lee's Colonels,* p. 317, Reilly's artillerists described him as "rough, gruff, grizzly, and brave." Reilly was later captured at Fort Fisher in early 1865.

32. Polk, *The North and South American Review,* copy at University of Texas-Arlington Library, Jenkings Garrett Special Collections, p. 28. One of Reilly's 3-inch Ordnance rifles

burst at this time; although Parrotts were notorious for this, it is extremely rare for a 3-inch rifle to explode in this manner. *OR* 27, pt. 2, p. 428.

33. Polley, *Hood's Texas Brigade,* p. 169.

34. *OR* 27, pt. 1, pp. 512-513 and 588-589; *OR* 27, pt. 2, pp. 409 and 422; *OR* 27, pt. 1, p. 589; *New York at Gettysburg,* 3 volumes (Albany, 1900), 2, p. 870. Smith's fourth piece had been positioned above Devil's Den but was damaged by counter battery fire—probably from Reilly's guns—and had been withdrawn before the Confederate infantry arrived.

35. *OR* 27, pt. 2, pp. 409 and 422; *Supplement to the OR* 5, serial no 5, p. 344; Busey and Martin, *Regimental Strengths and Losses at Gettysburg,* p. 134.

36. The artillery belonged to Battery D, 5th U. S. Artillery, under the command of Lieutenant Charles E. Hazlett. The battery had a total of six guns, but only four were in position at this time. For a pair of excellent accounts of how Vincent's men came to take their positions on Little Round Top and the struggle that followed, see James R. Wright, "Vincent's Brigade on Little Round Top," *Gettysburg Magazine* (July 1989), No. 1, pp. 41-44, and Kevin O'Brien, "Valley of the Shadow of Death: Col. Strong Vincent and the Eighty-Third Pennsylvania Infantry on Little Round Top," *Gettysburg Magazine* (July 1992), No. 7, pp. 41-49.

37. Law, "Gettysburg: The Second Day—The Confederate Side. The Struggle for 'Round Top.'" *The Century War Book,* p. 196; Lafayette McLaws, "Gettysburg," *Southern Historical Society Papers,* 7, p. 73.

38. Part of the paralysis problem in Hood's artillery arm might have been due to the fact that Haskell outranked Henry but was serving under him. Henry was already in command of the battalion when Haskell was ordered by Longstreet in June 1863 to report to the same battalion for duty. When Haskell arrived, he discovered that his "commission as Major was older than Henry's," and pointed it out to Longstreet, who advised Haskell "to make no point of this, but to get along as well as possible till Henry was relieved, which would be soon. Haskell "acquiesced in this view and had an understanding with Major Henry on this line." *Supplement to the OR* 5, serial no 5, p. 350.

39. *OR* 27, pt. 1, p. 617; O'Brien, "Valley of the Shadow of Death: Col. Strong Vincent and the Eighty-Third Pennsylvania Infantry on Little Round Top," p. 46, an excellent, insightful article; see also, Pfanz, *Gettysburg: The Second Day,* pp. 229-236.

40. *Supplement to the OR* 5, serial no 5, p. 353.

41. *OR* 27, pt. 2, pp. 398-399, 401 and 403. Tagg, *The Generals of Gettysburg*, pp. 86-89, offers good thumbnail descriptions of these officers and their actions at Gettysburg.

42. *OR* 27, pt. 1, p. 601; Busey and Martin, *Regimental Strengths and Losses at Gettysburg,* pp. 59-60.

43. Doubleday, *Chancellorsville and Gettysburg,* p. 156.

44. For a pair of excellent sketches of Kershaw, see: Edwin C. Bearss, "Joseph Brevard Kershaw," in William C. Davis, ed., *The Confederate General,* 4, pp. 11-13, and Larry Tagg, *The Generals of Gettysburg,* pp. 213-216.

45. *OR* 27, pt. 1, pp. 601, 607 and 610-611; *OR* 27, pt. 2, p. 368.

46. *OR* 27, pt. 1, p. 507; *OR* 27, pt. 2, pp. 407-408; Appendix D, *Bachelder Papers,* 3, p. 1982; *OR* 27, pt. 1, p. 522.

47. *OR* 27, pt. 1, pp. 369, 379; Pfanz, *Gettysburg: The Second Day,* pp. 268-272.

48. Caldwell's strength is based upon the July 4 returns, less reported battle casualties. *OR* 27, pt. 1, pp. 153 and 175. Like Tilton and Sweitzer (though not to the same degree), Caldwell also suffered a reduction in manpower because of straggling and other factors. Of the 4,006 men in Caldwell's division present on June 30, 77% reached the field. Because many casualties suffered at Gettysburg were not officially reported (this was true on both sides), it is possible that Caldwell's strength going into the fight was higher than 3,100. Even if this is true, Caldwell could not have entered the fight with more than 3,400 men, which meant that his division lost a minimum of 15% of its strength in its forced march to Gettysburg from June 30 to July 2. See also Busey and Martin, *Regimental Strengths and Losses at Gettysburg*, pp. 35-38.

49. *OR 27*, part 1 pp. 381, 384-385.

50. *Pennsylvania at Gettysburg*, 2, p. 684; Pfanz, *Gettysburg: The Second Day*, pp. 273-277. For additional information on Caldwell and his four brigade commanders, see Tagg, *The Generals of Gettysburg*, pp. 35-44. For an excellent article on Caldwell's attack, see Eric Campbell, "Caldwell Clears the Wheatfield," *Gettysburg Magazine* (July 1990), No. 3.

51. Lafayette McLaws, "McLaws' Division and the Pennsylvania Reserves." *Philadelphia Weekly Press*, 20 October 1886. Wofford is also the subject of a recent biography: Gerald Smith, *One of the Most Daring of Men: The Life of Confederate General William Tatum Wofford* (Murfreesboro, 1997).

52. William Youngblood, "Unwritten History of the Gettysburg Campaign," *Southern Historical Society Papers*, 38, p. 315.

53. Lafayette McLaws, "Gettysburg," *Southern Historical Society Papers*, 7, p. 74.

54. Sorrel, *Recollections of a Confederate Staff Officer*, p. 165.

55. *OR 27*, pt. 2, p. 369.

56. *OR 27*, pt. 1, p. 608.

57. *OR 27*, pt. 1, pp. 381-401; 27, pt. 2, pp. 369, 397, 399, 401, 403; Pfanz, *Gettysburg: The Second Day*, p. 287; *Pennsylvania at Gettysburg*, 2, p. 627; Kershaw, "Kershaw's Brigade at Gettysburg," in *Battles and Leaders of the Civil War*, 3, p. 337.

58. *OR 27*, pt. 1, pp. 611-612. Some of Sweitzer's survivors rallied east of Plum Run when the brigade's remaining and previously detached regiment, the 9th Massachusetts, was found there behind a battery. The guns probably belonged to Aaron Walcott's outfit.

59. Brian a. Bennett, "The Supreme Event in Its Existence—The 140th New York on Little Round Top," *Gettysburg Magazine*, Number 2, pp. 17-25.

60. *OR 27*, pt. 1, pp. 593, 634, 641, 643.

61. Timothy J. Reese, *Sykes' Regular Infantry Division, 1861-1864: a History of Regular United States Infantry Operations in the Civil War's Eastern Theater* (Jefferson, 1990), p. 253.

62. William H. Powell, *The Fifth Army Corps, Army of the Potomac: a Record of Operations During the Civil War* (New York, 1896), p. 535.

63. *OR 27*, pt. 1, pp. 179 and 645; Busey and Martin, *Regimental Strengths and Losses at Gettysburg*, pp. 62-63.

64. Lafayette McLaws, "McLaws' Division and the Pennsylvania Reserves." *Philadelphia Weekly Press*, 20 October 1886; John B. Bachelder, *Gettysburg, July 2, Map #2*.

65. *OR 27*, pt. 1, p. 662.

66. *OR* 27, pt. 1, p. 662; Garry Adelman, "The Third Brigade, Third Division, Sixth Corps at Gettysburg," *Gettysburg Magazine*, Number 11, pp. 91-101.

67. Paul Semmes' wound was mortal, and he died on July 10, 1863. Tagg, *The Generals of Gettysburg*, p. 217.

68. Smith, *General William Tatum Wofford*, pp. 90-91; Lafayette McLaws, "The Battle of Gettysburg." *Philadelphia Weekly Press,* 21 April 1886; Smith, *General William Tatum Wofford*, p. 91.

69. *OR* 27, pt. 1, pp. 653-654, 657, 685 and 688.

70. William Youngblood, "Unwritten History of the Gettysburg Campaign," *Southern Historical Society Papers,* 38, p. 315. Virginia artillerist Robert Stiles described Barksdale's "irrepressible" troops like this: "the finest body of men I ever saw. They were almost giants in size and power. They were healthy and hardy . . . bear hunters from the swamps and cane brakes and, naturally enough, almost without exception fine shots." Stiles, *Four Years Under Marse Robert,* p. 64.

71. Edward Porter Alexander, "Pickett's Charge and Artillery Fighting at Gettysburg," *The Century War Book* (New York, 1894), p. 203.

72. *OR* 27, pt. 2, p. 432. Taylor's choice of ammunition was perfectly suited for the range in which his Napoleons were engaged. See also, Alexander, *Fighting for the Confederacy*, pp. 240-242. McLaws was very concerned about the vulnerable left flank of Kershaw's Brigade, which was exposed to the fire from several Federal batteries in action along Wheatfield Road. Longstreet never specifically explained why he delayed Barksdale's advance. Perhaps he was waiting for Kershaw's men to strike the left rear of the Federal position behind the Peach Orchard in a sweep northeast from the Rose Farm, which would have either driven away or captured the batteries along Wheatfield Road. This, in turn, would have completely uncovered the rear of Andrew A. Humphreys' Second Division of Sickles' Third Corps. then McLaws was not aware of that reasoning. *OR* 27, pt. 2, pp. 367-368; Lafayette McLaws, "Gettysburg," *Southern Historical Society Papers,* 7, pp. 73-74.

73. Joseph B. Kershaw, "Longstreet's Attack at the Peach Orchard and Wheatfield," *The Century War Book* (New York, 1894), p. 197; *OR* 27, pt. 2, pp. 368 and 372; Tagg, *The Generals of Gettysburg*, p. 215.

74. McNeily, "Barksdale's Mississippi Brigade at Gettysburg," pp. 237-238. Dropping packs before going into action was standard practice in the Army of Northern Virginia. See also, William H. S. Burgwyn, "Unparalleled Loss of Company F, 26th North Carolina Regiment, Pettigrew's Brigade, at Gettysburg," *Southern Historical Society Papers,* 28, p. 200.

75. Lafayette McLaws, "Gettysburg," *Southern Historical Society Papers,* 7, pp. 73-74. Lamar's reference about the white plume was that of Henry II of Navarre (Henri d'Albret), a French nobleman (1503-1555); McNeily, "Barksdale's Mississippi Brigade at Gettysburg," pp. 238, 241.

76. Pfanz, *Gettysburg: The Second Day,* pp. 130-138; Busey and Martin, *Regimental Strengths and Losses at Gettysburg*, pp. 49, 53-55 and 114. The six Napoleons belonged to Bucklyn's Battery E, 1st Rhode Island Light Artillery, while the two 3-inch Ordnance rifles were a section of the newly-combined Batteries C and F of the Independent Pennsylvania Light Artillery from the Army Artillery Reserve.

77. Lafayette McLaws, "Gettysburg," *Southern Historical Society Papers,* 7, pp. 74.

78. McNeily, "Barksdale's Mississippi Brigade at Gettysburg," p. 241.

79. Lafayette McLaws, "Gettysburg," *Southern Historical Society Papers,* 7, p. 74.

80. Major General Joseph Hooker, as quoted in Coddington, *The Gettysburg Campaign,* pp. 24-25.

81. Busey and Martin, *Regimental Strengths and Losses at Gettysburg,* pp. 49, 54 and 140; McNeily, "Barksdale's Mississippi Brigade at Gettysburg," p. 252.

82. *OR* 27, pt. 1, pp. 505 and 508; Pfanz, *Gettysburg: The Second Day,* pp. 326-328.

83. *OR* 27, pt. 1, pp. 505 and 508; Pfanz, *Gettysburg: The Second Day,* pp. 326-328.

84. *OR* 27, pt. 1, pp. 505, 524 and 578; Benjamin G. Humphreys to Bachelder, May 1, 1876, *The Bachelder Papers,* 1, p. 480; Daniel G. Crotty, *Four Years Campaigning in the Army of the Potomac* (Grand Rapids, 1874), p. 91. The 63rd Pennsylvania of Graham's brigade was spared the fate shared by the rest of the brigade when it was detailed to serve as skirmishers for the brigade during the artillery bombardment. During the two hours of dueling the men used up their ammunition and were subsequently withdrawn just before Barksdale's charge. *OR* 27, pt. 1, p. 498.

85. Benjamin G. Humphreys to Bachelder, May 1, 1876, *The Bachelder Papers,* 1, p. 480. Humphreys' recollection about capturing four guns in the Peach Orchard seems to be confirmed by at least one Federal eyewitness. In *OR* 27, pt. 1, p. 887, Captain Patrick Hart, commanding the 15th New York Battery, recalled that before he was forced to limber and retire, "the batteries on my right were abandoned, with the exception of Captain Ames', which retired in good order to the rear." Ames had retired when he was all but out of ammunition, and his place in line was taken by Watson's battery.

86. *OR* 27, pt. 1, p. 574.

87. *OR* 27, pt. 1, p. 505.

88. *Echoes of Glory: Arms and Equipment of The Union,* editors of Time-Life Books (Alexandria, 1991), p. 140.

89. *OR* 27, pt. 1, p. 484.

90. George Clark, "Wilcox's Alabama Brigade at Gettysburg," *Confederate Veteran,* 17, p. 229.

91. Sears, *Landscape Turned Red,* pp. 225-226.

92. McNeily, "Barksdale's Mississippi Brigade at Gettysburg," p. 241.

93. Adolpho Fernandez de la Cabada [Cavada] Diary, 2 July 1863, The Historical Society of Pennsylvania. Philadelphia, Pennsylvania.

94. McNeily, "Barksdale's Mississippi Brigade at Gettysburg," p. 243.

95. Edward Porter Alexander, "Pickett's Charge and Artillery Fighting at Gettysburg," *The Century War Book,* p. 203; Frederick M. Colston, "Gettysburg as We Saw It," *Confederate Veteran,* 5, p. 553; Edward Porter Alexander, letter dated 17 March 1877, on the topic of "Causes of Lee's Defeat at Gettysburg," *Southern Historical Society Papers,* 4, p. 102; *Supplement to the OR* 5, serial no 5, pp. 358 and 367; Edward Porter Alexander, *Fighting for the Confederacy,* p. 240.

96. Alexander, *Fighting for the Confederacy,* p. 240.

97. Alexander, *Fighting for the Confederacy,* p. 240; *OR* 27, pt. 2, p. 430.

98. Pfanz, *Gettysburg: The Second Day,* p. 338.

99. *OR* 27, pt. 1, p. 586. ; Pfanz, *Gettysburg: The Second Day*, pp. 338-339.

100. *OR* 27, pt. 1, p. 890.

101. *OR* 27, pt. 1, p. 885.

102. John Bigelow, *The Peach Orchard, Gettysburg, July 2, 1863* (Minneapolis, 1919), p. 56.

103. John Bigelow to Bachelder, no date, *The Bachelder Papers*, 1, p. 173.

104. John Bigelow to Bachelder, no date, *The Bachelder Papers*, 1, p. 176. McGilvery held the rank of major at Gettysburg and was promoted to lieutenant colonel soon after the battle. *OR* 27, pt. 1, p. 591; Alpheus S. Williams to Bachelder, December, 1863, *The Bachelder Papers*, 1, p. 65; Henry J. Hunt to Bachelder, July 24, 1879, *The Bachelder Papers*, 1, p. 649; and Eric a. Campbell, "The Severest Fought Battle of the War: Charles Wellington Reed and the Medal of Honor," *Civil War Regiments* (Mason City, 1999), 6, number 3, p. 41.

105. John Bigelow to Bachelder, no date, *The Bachelder Papers*, 1, pp. 173-174.

106. *OR* 27, pt. 1, pp. 882 and 886; John Bigelow to Bachelder, no date, *The Bachelder Papers*, 1, p. 177; McNeily, "Barksdale's Mississippi Brigade at Gettysburg," p. 249.

107. Benjamin G. Humphreys to Bachelder, May 1, 1876, *The Bachelder Papers*, 1, p. 481. Watson's battery had escaped from the Peach Orchard and was retiring to Cemetery Ridge when Freeman McGilvery instructed him to unlimber in advance of a makeshift artillery line McGilvery was attempting to form to stem the Confederate advance. *OR* 27, pt. 1, p. 882. When Watson went down with a wound, Lieutenant MacConnell wrote in his after-action report that the crewmen of the four guns fired about 20 rounds of canister before leaving the pieces to the onrushing Mississippians. Disgusted with the performance of the battery, MacConnell noted "the conduct of officers and men throughout [the afternoon] was unexceptionable." *OR* 27, pt. 1, p. 660. This incident provides yet another example of the inability of battery of 3-inch Ordnance rifles to make an impression on determined infantry who, in turn, worked such execution, that "the battery was so cut to pieces." Henry J. Hunt to Bachelder, January 6, 1866, *The Bachelder Papers*, 1, p. 228.

108. As quoted in Tucker, *High Tide at Gettysburg*, p. 276.

109. James Longstreet, "The Mistakes of Gettysburg," *Annals of the War* (Philadelphia, 1879), p. 624.

110. *OR* 27, pt. 1, pp. 370, 417, 483, 533.

111. *OR* 27, pt. 1, p. 370; Letter from John Gibbon to Henry Hunt, May 31, 1879, Library of Congress, Hunt Papers, Box 2.

112. Kevin E. O'Brien, "'To Unflinchingly Face Danger and Death:' Carr's Brigade Defends Emmitsburg Road," *Gettysburg Magazine,* Number 12, pp. 18-19; *OR* 27, pt. 1, p. 371.

113. *OR* 27, pt. 1, p. 371. Officers during the Civil War often referred to infantry regiments "battalions." The average strength of an infantry regiment in Sickles' Third Corps on the afternoon of July 2 was only 270 officers and men. Busey and Martin, *Regimental Strengths and Losses at Gettysburg*, pp. 49-54. Thus, Hancock's claim that he could only gather together the strength of a "battalion" indicates just how badly disrupted Humphreys' division was after Barksdale's men ripped it apart. *OR* 27, pt. 1, pp. 153, 178 and 534.

114. Tucker, *High Tide at Gettysburg*, p. 281.

115. *OR* 27, pt. 1, pp. 116, 258, 290, 294 and 308.

116. Charles E. Slocum, *The Life and Times of Major General Henry Warner Slocum* (Toledo, 1913), pp. 104-105. The command situation in Twelfth Corps at Gettysburg was very confused. Slocum believed he was acting commander of the "right wing" of the army. As a result, Alpheus S. Williams, the acting commander of Twelfth Corps, and Thomas H. Ruger, acting division commander, led three First Division brigades to the threatened left flank. Meanwhile, two of the three brigades in John W. Geary's Second Division also vacated their positions on Culp's Hill but marched on the wrong road and took themselves out of the fighting. *OR* 27, pt. 1, pp. 116, 759, 764-766, 771-773, 777-778, 783, 804 and 826.

117. *OR* 27, pt. 2, pp. 318, 608.

118. Richard J. Sommers, "Richard Heron Anderson," in Davis, *The Confederate General*, 1, pp. 28-29. For information on Anderson at Chancellorsville, see Furgurson, *Chancellorsville 1863*, p. 299, and Sears, *Chancellorsville*, pp. 390, 400-402 and 414. Sorrel, *Recollections of a Confederate Staff Officer*, p. 247.

119. *OR* 27, pt. 2, p. 614.

120. Gaines' Mill and Malvern Hill provide two examples of echelon attacks previously ordered by Lee. Cadmus Marcellus Wilcox, "General C. M. Wilcox on the Battle of Gettysburg," *Southern Historical Society Papers*, 6, p. 98; Clark, "Wilcox's Alabama Brigade at Gettysburg, *Confederate Veteran*, 17, p. 229. Wilcox acknowledged speaking to Lee about the attack but denied receiving orders to deliver it *en échelon*. When Lee paid his personal visit to Wilcox, his Alabama brigade was cocked ninety degrees in relation to McLaws' Division just as the battle was beginning. This meant the Alabamians, as Wilcox later wrote, had to "move by the left flank rapidly, so as to give Barksdale's Mississippi Brigade, which would be on our immediate right, room to move forward in proper line." This may be why Lee did not order Wilcox to attack *en échelon*, because such instructions would not have been necessary.

121. Clark, "Wilcox's Alabama Brigade at Gettysburg, *Confederate Veteran,* 17, p. 229.

122. *OR* 27, pt. 2, p. 622; Ambrose Ransom Wright, "Report of Brigadier-General a. R. Wright," *Southern Historical Society Papers,* 8, p. 315.

123. Robert K. Krick, "Cadmus Marcellus Wilcox," Davis, ed., The Confederate General, 6, pp. 139-141, offers an excellent biographical sketch of this interesting officer.

124. *OR* 27, pt. 2, p. 618.

125. Cadmus Marcellus Wilcox, "General C. M. Wilcox on the Battle of Gettysburg," *Southern Historical Society Papers*, 6, p. 98.

126. Busey and Martin, *Regimental Strengths and Losses at Gettysburg*, p. 188.

127. *OR* 27, pt. 2, p. 631; Edward Aylesworth Perry, "Gettysburg," *Southern Historical Society Papers*, 27, p.195; Thomas L. Elmore, "The Florida Brigade at Gettysburg," *Gettysburg Magazine*, Number 15, pp. 45-51; Krick, *Lee's Colonels*, p. 228. It is a small mystery why Lang was never promoted to general. His service seemed to warrant the promotion.

128. [Ambrose Ransom Wright], "From Wright's Brigade," *Augusta Daily Constitutionalist,* July 23, 1863; Busey and Martin, *Regimental Strengths and Losses at Gettysburg*, p. 188.

129. John B. Bachelder, *Gettysburg, July 2, Map #3.*

130. *OR* 27, pt. 2, p. 622; Ambrose Ransom Wright, "Report of Brigadier-General a. R. Wright," *Southern Historical Society Papers*, 8, p. 315.

131. Busey and Martin, *Regimental Strengths and Losses at Gettysburg*, p. 188. The Gettysburg National Military Park Tablet lists Posey's Brigade strength at only 1,150.

132. Jeffry Wert, "Carnot Posey," in Davis, ed., *The Confederate General*, 5, p. 51. The brigade had been led by Winfield S. Featherston, who was deemed incompetent by Lee and transferred west to another command.

133. *OR* 27, pt. 2, p. 633.

134. Edwin C. Bearss, "William Mahone," in Davis, ed., *The Confederate General*, 4, p. 143.

135. *OR* 11, part 1, p. 945.

136. *OR* 27, pt. 2, p. 621.

137. *OR* 27, pt. 2, p. 618; Busey and Martin, *Regimental Strengths and Losses at Gettysburg*, p. 52; Gettysburg National Military Park Tablets.

138. *OR* 27, pt. 2, p. 618.

139. *OR* 27, pt. 2, p. 631.

140. Edward Aylesworth Perry, "Gettysburg," *Southern Historical Society Papers*, 27, p.195.

141. One of the reasons after-action reports have to carefully examined and corroborated with other known facts is illustrated by Brigadier General Joseph B. Carr's report of his brigade's action on July 2, 1863. Carr's left flank support was crumbling before Barksdale's advancing Mississippians, his right flank was being driven in by Lang's Florida Brigade, and his front was pressed by Wilcox's regiments. With that in mind, Carr wrote: "I could and would have maintained my position but for an order received direct from Major General Birney, commanding the corps [after Sickles was wounded], to fall back to the crest of the hill in my rear. At that time I have no doubt that I could have charged on the rebels and driven them in confusion, for my line was still perfect and unbroken, and my troops in the proper spirit for the performance of such a task. In retiring, I suffered a severe loss in killed and wounded." *OR* 27, pt. 1, p. 543. Carr's casualties on July 2 are listed in *OR* 27, pt. 1, p. 545. For information on Turnbull's guns, see *OR* 27, pt. 1, p. 873; *OR* 27, pt. 2, p. 618.

142. Cadmus Marcellus Wilcox, "General C. M. Wilcox on the Battle of Gettysburg," *Southern Historical Society Papers,* 6, p. 99.

143. Edward Aylesworth Perry, "Gettysburg," *Southern Historical Society Papers,* 27, p. 195.

144. *OR* 27, pt. 1, p. 436.

145. *OR* 27, pt. 2, p. 623; Busey and Martin, *Regimental Strengths and Losses at Gettysburg*, p. 190.

146. *OR* 27, pt. 2, p. 623, 630.

147. *The Bachelder Papers*, 3, p. 1988, Appendix D, Notes on the Services of Troops at the Battle of Gettysburg (ca. 1875), lists the strength of the 15th Massachusetts at 239 officers and men, while the 82nd New York is listed at 320 total combatants, for an aggregate strength of 559. In his after-action report, Harrow states that the two regiments numbered "not more than 700." See *OR* 27, pt. 1, p. 419.

148. *OR* 27, pt. 2, p. 623.

149. *OR* 27, pt. 2, p. 623.

150. *OR* 27, pt. 2, p. 623.

151. *OR* 27, pt. 1, p. 423; *The Bachelder Papers*, 3, p. 1988.

152. *OR* 27, pt. 2, p. 629.

153. *OR* 27, pt. 1, p. 880; Gulian V. Weir to Bachelder, November 25, 1885, *The Bachelder Papers*, 2, p. 1152.

154. *OR* 27, pt. 1, p. 478; John H. Rhodes, *The History of Battery B, First Regiment, Rhode Island Artillery* (Providence, 1914), p. 203.

155. *OR* 27, pt. 2, p. 623.

156. *OR* 27, pt. 1, p. 417.

157. *OR* 27, pt. 1, p. 427, 431-434, 445 and 447.

158. *OR* 27, pt. 2, p. 630; part 1, p. 447.

159. *OR* 27, pt. 1, p. 417.

160. Frank a. Haskell, *The Battle of Gettysburg*, edited by Bruce Catton (New York, 1957), p. 89.

161. *Pennsylvania at Gettysburg*, 1, p. 404.

162. Rhodes, *The History of Battery B, First Regiment, Rhode Island Artillery*, p. 203; *OR* 27, pt. 2, p. 629; Busey and Martin, *Regimental Strengths and Losses at Gettysburg*, p. 190.

163. Anthony McDermott to Bachelder, *The Bachelder Papers*, 3, p. 1414.

164. Anthony W. McDermott and John E. Reilly, *a Brief History of the 69th Regiment, Pennsylvania Veteran Volunteers* (Philadelphia, 1889), p. 28; Joseph R. Ward, *History of the One Hundred and Sixth Regiment, Pennsylvania Volunteers* (Philadelphia, 1883), pp. 191-192; William Paul, "Severe Experiences at Gettysburg," *Confederate Veteran* (1912), 19, p. 85.

165. *OR* 27, pt. 1, p. 449; Busey and Martin, *Regimental Strengths and Losses at Gettysburg*, pp. 41 and 190.

166. *OR* 27, pt. 1, p. 447.

167. Busey and Martin, *Regimental Strengths and Losses at Gettysburg*, p. 190.

168. *OR* 27, pt. 1, pp. 349-351.

169. Terry Winschel, "Their Supreme Moment: Barksdale's Brigade at Gettysburg," Gettysburg Magazine (1989), No. 1, p. 76. Barksdale was later found alone on the field by a member of the 13th Mississippi. He was carried to a Federal field hospital, where a doctor examined his chest wound and determined "it was too large to have been made by a minie ball." His leg was also fractured and displayed two additional wounds. Barksdale lost consciousness and died that night, and was buried in a temporary grave. His remains were eventually returned to Mississippi. For information on Colonel George Williard, see Tagg, *The Generals of Gettysburg*, pp. 58-59.

170. *OR* 27, pt. 2, p. 618; Pfanz, *Gettysburg: The Second Day*, pp. 410-412.

171. Edward Aylesworth Perry, "Gettysburg," *Southern Historical Society Papers*, 27, p. 195.

172. *OR* 27, pt. 1, p. 370; *OR* 27, pt. 2, p. 618 and 631; Benjamin G. Humphreys to Bachelder, *The Bachelder Papers,* 1, p. 481; McNeily, "Barksdale's Mississippi Brigade at Gettysburg," p. 239; R. L. Murray, *The Redemption of the 'Harpers Ferry Cowards': The*

Story of the 111th and 126th New York State Volunteer Regiments at Gettysburg (New York, 1994), pp. 93-110.

173. *OR* 27, pt. 2, p. 624.

174. *OR* 27, pt. 2, p. 633; see also, Tagg, *The Generals of Gettysburg*, pp. 320-321.

175. *OR* 27, pt. 2, p. 633. Shannon was only a lieutenant at the time, although Posey states he held the rank of captain. *OR* 27, pt. 2, p. 616.

176. *OR* 27, pt. 2, p. 634.

177. Cadmus Wilcox, "Gettysburg, July 2 & 3, 1863," Annotations to the official report written from Bunker Hill, Virginia, 17 July 1863, Manuscript Division, Library of Congress, Wilcox Papers, Box 1.

178. *OR* 11, pt. 1, 1, p. 945.

179. *OR* 27, pt. 2, pp. 658, 663 and 665.

180. Perrin's letter of July 29, 1863, to Bonham, in M. L. Bonham, *a Little More Light on Gettysburg*, pamphlet at the University of South Carolina, p. 522.

181. *OR* 27, pt. 2, p. 658. Lewis insisted that Pender had not yet reached the center of the division's front when he was struck down. William G. Lewis letter to D. Gilliam, 21 October 1893, as cited in *One of Lee's Best Men: The Civil War Letters of General William Dorsey Pender*, p. 260. Pender left the next day by ambulance and by the time he reached Staunton, Virginia, his wound was hemorrhaging. a second rupture of an artery necessitated the removal of the leg in an attempt to save the general's life. Within a few hours of the operation on July 18, 1863, Dorsey Pender was dead.

182. *OR* 27, pt. 2, p. 665. Lane was the division's senior brigadier that day because of a curious set of circumstances. Both he and Edward Lloyd Thomas were appointed to that rank effective November 1, 1862, but Lane's promotion to colonel was September 1861—one month earlier than Thomas'. For this reason plus some internal politics within the army, Lane assumed the reins of command when Pender fell. The division's most capable brigadier general was Sam McGowan, who was still recuperating from the wound he received at Chancellorsville. Even if he was present he would not have assumed command, since Lane ranked him.

183. OR 27, pt. 2, p. 608. Lee's report mentions Hill's instructions for July 2, but not a word of what he personally did that afternoon, while both Longstreet and Ewell were prominently mentioned. OR 27, pt. 2, pp. 308, 318-319, 608. Historian James Robertson, *a. P. Hill*, p. 218, claims Hill believed Richard Anderson's Division was under Longstreet's control that afternoon, and offers *OR* 27, pt. 2, pp. 308, 318-319, and 608 as support for Hill's confusion. In fact the reports are consistent and clear: Hill knew his orders and muffed them badly. See also the supporting text for note 284.

184. *OR* 27, pt. 2, pp. 318-319, 446.

185. *OR* 27, pt. 2, pp. 446-447, 470, 504 and 556.

186. As we have seen, many historians and writers have described Lee's orders to Ewell on the afternoon of July 1 as "discretionary," when in fact they were "orders with discretion." The same is true for July 2, although some historians have also called Lee's orders for the second day of battle "discretionary orders." Jeffry D. Wert, in *a Brotherhood of Valor*, p. 267, makes this mistake. There was absolutely nothing in Lee's instructions to Ewell on July 2 that asked the commander of Second Corps to "think about" whether or not he was to carry out the

commanding general's instructions. The only way a demonstration could "be converted into a real attack should the opportunity offer" was for Ewell and his Second Corps subordinates to make the demonstration as ordered (i.,e., simultaneously with Longstreet's assault). *How Ewell and his generals carried out their mission represents a classic case of "orders with discretion."*

187. *OR* 27, pt. 2, pp. 470, 504 and 543.

188. *OR* 27, pt. 2, pp. 604, 652 and 675.

189. *OR* 27, pt. 1, pp. 360, 748-749, 751-753, 756, 891 and 893-895.

190. Wainwright, *a Diary of Battle*, July 2, 1863, p. 243.

191. *OR* 27, pt. 1, pp. 363, 365, 752; Wainwright, *a Diary of Battle,* July 2, 1863, p. 243; Gettysburg National Military Park Tablets.

192. *OR* 27, pt. 2, pp. 543-544; Jay Jorgensen, "Joseph W. Latimer, The 'Boy Major,' at Gettysburg," *Gettysburg Magazine,* Number 10, pp. 28-35.

193. Stiles, *Four Years Under Marse Robert,* pp. 217-218.

194. Pfanz, *Richard S. Ewell: a Soldier's Life*, p. 316.

195. Federal skirmishers from Slocum's Twelfth Corps had been pushed out from Culp's Hill and were east of Rock Creek until Edward Johnson's infantry "began the advance with their line of battle." Before that time, it would have been difficult to detect Federal troop withdrawals from Meade's right flank. Nevertheless, we have included this possibility, although the observation by Ewell's staff members seem to have been the reason Ewell converted his demonstration into a real attack. For confirmation that the Federal skirmishers did not withdraw prior to Johnson's attack, see the report of Lieutenant Colonel John C. O. Redington, 60th New York, *OR* 27, pt. 1, p. 862.

196. *OR* 27, pt. 1, p. 862; *OR* 27, pt. 2, p. 504, 513, 518-519 and 532; Randolph H. McKim, "Steuart's Brigade at the Battle of Gettysburg," *Southern Historical Society Papers,* 5, p. 293; McKim, *a Soldier's Recollection,* pp. 195-199.

197. Busey and Martin, *Regimental Strengths and Losses at Gettysburg*, p. 152; *OR* 27, pt. 1, pp. 826, 856, 866-868; *OR* 27, pt. 2, p. 510; Pfanz, *Gettysburg: The Second Day,* p. 222; Wayne E. Motts, "To Gain a Second Star: The Forgotten George S. Greene," *Gettysburg Magazine*, Number 2, pp. 65-75; Thomas L. Elmore, "Courage Against the Trenches: The Attack and Repulse of Steuart's Brigade on Culp's Hill," *Gettysburg Magazine*, No. 7, pp. 86-88.

198. *OR* 27, pt. 2, pp. 504, 510, 513, 518-519 and 532.

199. *OR* 27, pt. 2, p. 470.

200. Thomas E. Causby, "Storming the Stone Fence at Gettysburg," *Southern Historical Society Papers*, 29, p. 340.

201. *OR* 27, pt. 2, pp. 480 and 484; *The Civil War Memoirs of Captain William J. Seymour: Reminiscences of a Louisiana Tiger,* p. 73; Jubal Early to Bachelder, March 23, 1876, *Bachelder Papers,* 1, p. 460; John B. Bachelder, *Gettysburg, July 2, Map #4.*

202. *The Civil War Memoirs of Captain William J. Seymour: Reminiscences of a Louisiana Tiger*, p. 73.

203. *The Military Maxims of Napoleon*, Maxim 85. The translation of Napoleon's exact words is as follows: "Morale makes up three quarters of the game; the relative balance of

manpower accounts only for the remaining quarter." Many of Napoleon's Maxims deal with the importance of morale, and its relation to different aspects of campaigning.

204. *OR* 27, pt. 1, pp. 724-725; *OR* 27, pt. 2, p. 658.

205. *OR* 27, pt. 1, pp. 164, 182, 712-713 and 716, 719; Andrew L. Harris to Bachelder, March 14, 1881, *Bachelder Papers*, 2, p. 746.

206. Peter F. Young to Bachelder, August 12, 1867, *Bachelder Papers*, 1, pp. 310-311.

207. *The Civil War Memoirs of Captain William J. Seymour: Reminiscences of a Louisiana Tiger*, p. 75.

208. *OR* 27, pt. 2, p. 480; Jones, *Lee's Tigers*, p. 172.

209. *OR* 27, pt. 2, p. 480.

210. *The Civil War Memoirs of Captain William J. Seymour: Reminiscences of a Louisiana Tiger*, p. 75.

211. Thomas E. Causby, "Storming the Stone Fence at Gettysburg," *Southern Historical Society Papers*, 29, p. 340.

212. *Histories of the Several Regiments and Battalions From North Carolina in the Great War*, edited by Walter Clark, 5 volumes (Raleigh, 1901), 1, p. 313.

213. *OR* 27, pt. 1, p. 894; R. Bruce Ricketts to Bachelder, March 2, 1866, *Bachelder Papers*, 1, p. 237.

214. *Histories of the Several Regiments and Battalions From North Carolina in the Great War*, 1, p. 416; Causby, "Storming the Stone Fence at Gettysburg," *Southern Historical Society Papers*, 29, p. 340.

215. John M. Archer, *The Hour was One of Horror: East Cemetery Hill at Gettysburg* (Gettysburg, 1997), p. 52.

216. Andrew L. Harris to Bachelder, March 14, 1881, *Bachelder Papers*, 2, p. 745.

217. *The Civil War Memoirs of Captain William J. Seymour: Reminiscences of a Louisiana Tiger*, p. 75.

218. *OR* 27, pt. 2, p. 480.

219. *Histories of the Several Regiments and Battalions From North Carolina in the Great War*, 2, p. 136.

220. *OR* 27, pt. 1, p. 714. *New York at Gettysburg*, 1, p.404.

221. *OR* 27, pt. 2, p. 484. The right portion of the 57th North Carolina was able to push up the hill with the rest of Avery's men.

222. R. Bruce Ricketts to Bachelder, March 2, 1866, *Bachelder Papers*, 1, p. 236. Colonel Wainwright saw virtually the same thing from his observation point on the hill: "So soon as the rebels began to fire, the two lines of Deutschmen in front of the batteries began to run, and nearly the whole of them cleared out . . . I pitied General Ames most heartily. His men would not stand at all, save one. I believe not a single regiment of the Eleventh Corps exposed to the attack stood fire, but ran away almost to a man." Wainwright, *A Diary of Battle*, July 2, 1863, p. 245.

223. *OR* 27, pt. 2, p. 480.

224. Peter F. Young to Bachelder, August 12, 1867, *Bachelder Papers*, 1, p. 311; Wainwright, *a Diary of Battle*, July 2, 1863, pp. 244-245.

225. Thomas E. Causby, "Storming the Stone Fence at Gettysburg," *Southern Historical Society Papers,* 29, p. 340; R. Bruce Ricketts to Bachelder, December 3, 1883, *Bachelder Papers,* 2, p. 980. Ricketts lost 20 men that evening and one of his guns was spiked.

226. *OR* 27, pt. 2, pp. 480, 484.

227. Gary Lash, *The Gibraltar Brigade on East Cemetery Hill: Twenty-Five Minutes of Fighting, Fifty Years of Controversy* (Baltimore, 1995), p. 80; *The Civil War Memoirs of Captain William J. Seymour: Reminiscences of a Louisiana Tiger,* p. 77.

228. *OR* 27, pt. 2, pp. 555-556.

229. *OR* 27, pt. 2, p. 587.

230. *OR* 27, pt. 2, p. 588.

231. *OR* 27, pt. 2, p. 582. Whether Rodes learned of Early's defeat on East Cemetery Hill before or after his division began its final advance toward Northwest Cemetery Hill is unclear. *OR* 27, pt. 2, p. 556. There is evidence that Ramseur was actually in control of the entire division during its nighttime approach to Cemetery Hill. A careful reading of Rodes' report and those filed by his brigadiers offer several clues in this regard. First, it is unclear how extensively Rodes conferred with his generals before the attack, or if he did so at all. No one mentions any details about it. Daniel and Ramseur seem to have gotten their orders directly from Rodes or through a courier. Iverson, however, claims he learned of the July 2 attack from Ramseur. "I had received no instructions" complained Iverson, who "perceived that Ramseur was acquainted with the intentions of [Rodes]" and so " I raised no question of rank." *OR* 27, pt. 2, p. 580. It seems unlikely that Iverson was the only brigadier left in the dark. Not a one of them mention or even imply that Rodes accompanied the division as it moved toward Cemetery Hill, and readers should note that it was Ramseur a*nd not Rodes* who called a halt and conferred with the other brigadiers in front of the enemy position. How often, one might ask, does a brigadier have the authority to stop an entire division in the middle of an advance? Ramseur had to send away for instructions and was later "ordered to retire quietly. . ." *OR* 27, pt. 2, p. 588. Daniel confirms this when he wrote that "I was notified by General Ramseur that he had halted, and that it was impracticable at that time to advance farther." *OR* 27, pt. 2, p. 568. The question remains: where was Rodes, and who was in charge of the division? No one seems to know.

232. *Southern Historical Society Papers,* 29, p. 340; *The Civil War Memoirs of Captain William J. Seymour: Reminiscences of a Louisiana Tiger,* p. 76.

233. *OR* 27, pt. 2, p. 470.

234. *OR* 27, pt. 1, pp. 457, 460, 462; Busey and Martin, *Regimental Strengths and Losses at Gettysburg,* p. 42. Regimental strengths for Carroll's brigade are listed in Appendix B.

235. *OR* 27, pt. 1, p. 372.

236. *OR* 27, pt. 1, p. 457; Lash, *The Gibraltar Brigade on East Cemetery Hill: Twenty-Five Minutes of Fighting, Fifty Years of Controversy,* p. 47.

237. *OR* 27, pt. 2, pp. 480-481; *The Civil War Memoirs of Captain William J. Seymour: Reminiscences of a Louisiana Tiger,* p. 76.

238. *The Civil War Memoirs of Captain William J. Seymour: Reminiscences of a Louisiana Tiger,* p. 76; Lash, *The Gibraltar Brigade on East Cemetery Hill,* p. 89; *OR* 27, pt. 1, pp. 457, 459 and 485; part 2, pp. 480-481; Thomas E. Causby, "Storming the Stone Fence at Gettysburg," *Southern Historical Society Papers,* 29, pp. 340-341. Brigadier General Adolph

von Steinwehr, one of Howard's Eleventh Corps division commanders claimed after the battle that Colonel Charles R. Coster's brigade repulsed Hays and Avery from East Cemetery Hill, with the 27th Pennsylvania bearing "a conspicuous part." *OR* 27, pt. 1, p. 722. This assertion has, at best, thin supporting evidence. Other Eleventh Corps formations also staked their claim as having been the defenders who evicted the assailants. Major Benjamin A. Willis, leader of the 119th New York reported that with General Schurz, leading, they "met the foe, and in conjunction with the gallant Fifty-eighth, drove him back." *OR* 27, pt. 1, p. 743. Captain Emil Koenig, acting commander of the 58th New York, however, admitted that the Confederate assault "was repulsed" by the time the "gallant Fifty-eighth" arrived on the scene. *OR* 27, pt. 1, p. 740. After the drubbing the Eleventh Corps took at Chancellorsville and Gettysburg on July 1, Carl Schurz claimed his men repulsed the Confederate assault, but his recollection does not coincide with a comment Oliver O. Howard's made to Colonel Wainwright *during* the fighting. First Corps chief artillery officer Charles Wainwright watched as Eleventh Corps troops failed to respond to Howard's orders at the end of the fighting and during the Confederate retreat from East Cemetery Hill. "Not an officer of rank in either regiment could be found when the order was given to advance," he recalled. "I said to General Howard, why don't you have them shot? The general answered, 'I should have to shoot all the way down; they are all alike.'" Wainwright, *a Diary of Battle,* July 2, 1863, p. 247. Perhaps some Eleventh Corps elements reformed and advanced on East Cemetery Hill, but in all likelihood they did so after Carroll's regiments had shouldered the brunt of the counterattack. Howard's reply to Wainwright lends weight to this position. Perhaps the most generous summation of the contribution made by Eleventh Corps troops that evening was written by Brevet Brigadier General Henry H. Bingham: "General Hancock dispatched Colonel Carroll and his gallant brigade to the scene of the action. General Carroll . . . led his troops forward, attacked the enemy and, assisted by some Eleventh Corps troops" reclaimed the position. *Pennsylvania at Gettysburg*, 1, p. 53.

239. J. B. Clifton Diary, as quoted in Coddington, *The Gettysburg Campaign,* p. 442.

240. Two other brigades, Thomas Smyth (Second Corps) and Orland Smith (Eleventh Corps) had been involved in skirmish action in front of Cemetery Ridge and Cemetery Hill from the Bliss Farm to the outskirts of town of Gettysburg.

241. *OR* 27, pt. 1, p. 601; Busey and Martin, *Regimental Strengths and Losses at Gettysburg,* p. 60. Colonel Patrick R. Guiney to Joshua Lawrence Chamberlain, October 26, 1865, Library of Congress, Joshua L. Chamberlain Papers. In sifting through compiled service records, many regimental historians have discovered that losses were greater than reported. For example, the 154th New York of Coster's brigade reported its losses as 22 killed and wounded, and 78 missing. Mark Dunkelman, the regiment's modern historian, claims that actual losses were 40 killed and wounded and 172 missing. Mark Dunkelman, *The Coster Avenue Mural in Gettysburg* (Providence, 1989), p. 3. Most volunteer regiments in Federal service did not receive replacements, so the result of such heavy losses was a diminished combat effectiveness.

242. Edward Porter Alexander, letter dated 17 March 1877, on the topic of "Causes of Lee's Defeat at Gettysburg," *Southern Historical Society Papers,* 4, p. 99.

243. The Confederates ended up with at least four pieces of captured Federal ordnance (along with other mobile equipment, such as limbers and caissons), as follows: three

10-pounder Parrotts from Smith's 4th New York Light Artillery (*OR* 27, pt. 2, p. 428), and one 3-inch Ordnance rifle from Thompson's C&F, Pennsylvania Light Artillery. Cadmus Wilcox claims that his brigade captured (and ultimately relinquished) eight pieces of ordnance. *OR* 27, pt. 2, p. 619. Lieutenant Young of a. a. Humphreys' Federal division remembered that the "batteries were surrounded, and one gun after another was captured by the enemy and turned against the Union forces, every horse having been killed and every man in the battery having fallen at his post." See Jesse Bowman Young, as quoted in Wheeler, *Witness to Gettysburg*, p. 207.

244. These artillery units were: Smith's 4th New York Light Battery of Third Corps, Winslow's Battery D, 1st New York Artillery of Third Corps, Hazlett's Battery D, 5th U.S. Artillery of Fifth Corps, Gibbs' Battery L, 1st Ohio Artillery of Fifth Corps, Walcott's 3rd Massachusetts Light Battery of Fifth Corps, Bigelow's 9th Massachusetts Light Battery of the 1st Volunteer Brigade from the Army Artillery Reserve, Phillips' 5th Massachusetts Light Battery of the 1st Volunteer Brigade from the Army Artillery Reserve, Clark's 2nd New Jersey Light Battery of Third Corps, Hart's 15th New York Light Battery of the 1st Volunteer Brigade from the Army Artillery Reserve, Thompson's Combined Batteries C&F, Pennsylvania Light Artillery of the 1st Volunteer Brigade from the Army Artillery Reserve, Ames' Battery G, 1st New York Artillery of the 4th Volunteer Brigade from the Army Artillery Reserve, Watson's Battery I, 5th U.S. Artillery of Fifth Corps, Dow's 6th Maine Light Battery of the 4th Volunteer Brigade from the Army Artillery Reserve, Bucklyn's Battery E, 1st Rhode Island Artillery of the Third Corps, Seeley's Battery K, 4th U.S. Artillery of Third Corps, Turnbull's Combined Batteries F&K, 3rd U.S. Artillery of the 1st Regular Brigade from the Army Artillery Reserve, Weir's Battery C, 5th U.S. Artillery, of the 1st Regular Brigade from the Army Artillery Reserve, Brown's Battery B, 1st Rhode Island Artillery of Second Corps, and Thomas' Battery C, 4th U.S. Artillery of the 1st Regular Brigade from the Army Artillery Reserve. The batteries knocked completely out of action were Smith's, Walcott's, Bigelow's, Clark's, Watson's and Bucklyn's.

245. Regis de Trobriand, *Four Years with the Army of the Potomac*, pp. 506-507.

246. Henry H. Bingham, "The Second and Third Days—July 2 and 3, 1863," *Pennsylvania at Gettysburg,* 1, p. 50. Bingham rose to the rank of Brevet Brigadier General by war's end. For Bingham's duties at Gettysburg, see *OR* 27, pt. 1, p. 376.

247. As reported, Wilcox lost 577, Lang "about 300" and Wright 688. *OR* 27, pt. 2, pp. 619, 624 and 632.

248. *OR* 27, pt. 2, pp. 480-481; Archer, *The Hour was One of Horror: East Cemetery Hill at Gettysburg*, p. 21; Busey and Martin, *Regimental Strengths and Losses at Gettysburg*, p. 287

249. *OR* 27, pt. 2, p. 340; Busey and Martin, *Regimental Strengths and Losses at Gettysburg*, p. 287, estimate the brigade's casualties for the battle at 412.

250. *OR* 27, pt. 2, pp. 504, 510, 513 and 532-533; McKim, *a Soldier's Recollection,* pp. 195-196. Several regiments in Johnson's Division absorbed substantial casualties in the fighting on July 2, but the vast majority of casualties suffered by the division would occur on July 3.

251. Alexander, *Fighting for the Confederacy*, p. 244.

252. *OR* 27, pt. 2, pp. 619 and 625.

253. Alexander, *Fighting for the Confederacy*, p. 242. One prominent Gettysburg writer who also believed this later did an about-face on the subject. When Glenn Tucker wrote *High Tide at Gettysburg* in 1958, he did so without a working grasp of the tenets behind an echelon attack. As a result, Tucker was highly critical of this method of assault as well as Longstreet's tactical handling of McLaws' Division. Tucker, *High Tide at Gettysburg*, pp. 268 and 269. However, after nine additional years of study Tucker published *Lee and Longstreet at Gettysburg* (Indianapolis, 1968), which demonstrates a keener appreciation of the "opportunity" General Lee was seeking to develop and exploit via an echelon attack. In fact, Tucker acknowledges that he should not have chastised Longstreet's for withholding McLaws as long as he did. *Lee and Longstreet at Gettysburg*, pp 64 and 262, note 15.

254. Edward Porter Alexander, letter dated 17 March 1877, on the topic of "Causes of Lee's Defeat at Gettysburg," *Southern Historical Society Papers*, 4, p. 100.

255. Alexander, *Military Memoirs of a Confederate*, pp. 393-394. Note that the word "discretion" in Alexander's quote is a noun (as opposed to an adjective), which is exactly how Walter Taylor, James Power Smith, Lafayette McLaws, and others described General Lee's battlefield directives.

256. a bronze of Longstreet was, finally, unveiled in Pitzer's Woods on July 3, 1998.

257. Longstreet's messages, as quoted in Fremantle, *Three Months in the Southern States*, p. 260. Joseph Carr's brigade of Sickles' Third Corps was routed by Wilcox and Lang, with some assistance from Barksdale's Mississippians. All of Fifth Corps, except Vincent and Weed, had been shattered, together with five of the Second Corps' ten brigades, including all four brigades in John Caldwell's division, to which must be added the severely damaged but still intact brigade under George Willard.

258. Alexander, *Fighting for the Confederacy*, pp. 242-243.

259. Wert, *General James Longstreet* (New York, 1993), p. 414.

260. Jubal a. Early, *The Campaigns of Gen. Robert E. Lee. An Address by Lieut. General Jubal a. Early, before Washington and Lee University, January 19th, 1872.* Baltimore, 1872.

261. Early, *The Campaigns of Gen. Robert E. Lee*; "Supplement to General Early's Review—Reply to General Longstreet," *Southern Historical Society Papers*, 4, pp. 284-285.

262. James Longstreet to Thomas Jewett Goree, May 12, 1875, in *The Thomas Jewett Goree Letters, Volume 1: The Civil War Correspondence,* edited and annotated by Langston James Goree, V (Bryan, 1981), p. 283.

263. Pendleton, as quoted in Tucker, *Lee and Longstreet at Gettysburg*, pp. 12-13.

264. Venable, as quoted in Tucker, *Lee and Longstreet at Gettysburg*, p. 13.

265. Taylor, *Four Years With General Lee,* p. 101.

266. Venable, as quoted in Tucker, *Lee and Longstreet at Gettysburg*, p. 20.

267. Tucker, *Lee and Longstreet at Gettysburg*, p. 2. Sadly, countless students and writers of the battle have never bothered to investigate the origin of the fictitious "attack at dawn" orders, and have instead repeated it or twisted this theme into a variety of mutations, each more unbelievable than the next. a prime example of this point is illustrated in the writings of English historian David Chandler. According to Chandler, The attacks of July 2 failed because Lee issued a "rather vaguely-worded order," and Longstreet "delayed his main effort, and allowed the Union General Sickles to extricate his men from the Peach Orchard . . . " David Chandler, *Atlas of Military Strategy* (New York, 1980), p. 181. As any beginning

student of Gettysburg knows, Sickles did not extricate his corps from the Peach Orchard salient; it was collapsed and routed from the salient by Longstreet. Additionally, there was nothing "vague" about Lee's order. Longstreet demonstrably understood it, and Powell Hill, Richard Anderson, and many other generals specifically reiterated their orders in their battle reports.

268. Bevin Alexander, *Robert E. Lee's Civil War*, p. 200.

269. Polley, *Hood's Texas Brigade,* p. 154.

270. Edward Porter Alexander, *Fighting for the Confederacy,* p. 235. Walton recalled that both battalions comprising the First Corps Reserve Artillery were on the road to Gettysburg by 2:30 a.m. on July 2. *Southern Historical Society Papers*, 5, p. 50. Captain Parker, commander of the Richmond Virginia Battery in Alexander's Battalion, remembered that his battery did not arrive near Gettysburg until 11:00 a.m. *Supplement to the OR* 5, serial no 5, p. 366.

271. Alexander, *Fighting for the Confederacy,* p. 237.

272. See, for example, Krick, "James Longstreet and the Second Day at Gettysburg," pp. 70-74. An excellent rebuttal is found in Greezicki, "a Reappraisal of Longstreet at Gettysburg."

273. Greezicki, "a Reappraisal of Longstreet at Gettysburg," p. 65, and cites for supporting contentions.

274. See, for example, Sauers, *a Caspian Sea of Ink: The Meade-Sickles Controversy*, and Robertson, "The Peach Orchard Revisited: Daniel E. Sickles and the Third Corps on July 2, 1863."

275. Emerson Gifford Taylor, *Gouverneur Kemble Warren: The Life and Letters of an American Soldier* (New York, 1932) p. 129. In order to understand the difficulties any Confederate troops on Little Round Top would have encountered directly influencing the action taking place back up the Federal defensive line, one must have a realistic appreciation for the length of the long shank of the Federal "fishhook" battle line. The best method is to simply visit the battlefield. Readers are encouraged to go to the National Cemetery on Cemetery Hill and look south toward the Rounds Tops, and then travel to Little Round Top, walk up to a high point along its northwestern face, and look north to Cemetery Hill, keeping in mind the terrain around the heights and the fact that Sykes' Fifth Corps and Sedgwick's Sixth Corps were available in the vicinity to Meade. If a visit is not possible, consult William a. Frassanito, *Gettysburg Then & Now: Touring the Battlefield With Old Photos, 1863-1889* (Gettysburg, 1996), pp. 19 and 45.

276. The discussion on why Cemetery Hill was in fact Meade's weak point is provided in Chapter 6. Without diversions sufficient to convince Meade otherwise, he could have reinforced an obvious attack directed against that point, which is why Lee's echelon attack worked so well.

277. Heth letter dated June 1877, on the topic of "Causes of Lee's Defeat at Gettysburg," *Southern Historical Society Papers*, 4, p. 154. See text accompanying note 289 for Lee's comment in this regard to Heth.

278. Cadmus Wilcox, "Gettysburg, July 2 & 3, 1863," Annotations to the official report written from Bunker Hill, Virginia, 17 July 1863, Manuscript Division, Library of Congress, Wilcox Papers, Box 1; *OR* 27, pt. 2, p. 618.

279. OR 27, pt. 2, p. 614; Ambrose Ransom Wright, "Report of Brigadier-General a. R. Wright," *Southern Historical Society Papers*, 8, p. 315.

280. John B. Bachelder, *Gettysburg, July 2, Map #3*. Hill's headquarters is indicated at the Gettysburg National Military Park on a tablet erected on an upright cannon barrel near the present North Carolina Memorial site, which overlooks the Bliss Farm.

281. Fremantle, *Three Months in the Southern States,* pp. 259-260.

282. Dowdey, *The Land They Fought For: The story of the South as the Confederacy, 1832-1865*, p. 273.

283. James I. Robertson, Jr., *General A. P. Hill: The Story of a Confederate Warrior* (New York, 1987), p. 219. 284. Robertson, *General A. P. Hill: The Story of a Confederate Warrior,* pp. 218 and 348, fn8.

285. *OR* 27, pt. 2, pp. 308, 318, 608.

286. *OR* 27, pt. 2, p. 618.

287. *OR* 27, pt. 2, p. 624.

288. *OR* 27, pt. 2, p. 628.

289. Heth letter dated June 1877, on the topic of "Causes of Lee's Defeat at Gettysburg," *Southern Historical Society Papers*, 4, p. 154. A typographical error attributes this quote by Lee to the fighting on July 3, 1863. There is no doubt, though, that Lee was describing the battle of July 2, and the error in date, or in Heth's recollection, worked its way into the finished manuscript.

290. These were the 55th Ohio, 73rd Ohio, 75th Ohio, 82nd Ohio, 41st New York, 45th New York, 73rd Pennsylvania and 75th Pennsylvania.

291. These were the 25th Ohio, 61st Ohio, 29th New York, 54th New York, 58th New York, 68th New York and the 74th Pennsylvania. At Second Manassas, Krzyzanowski's brigade was shattered, in the words of historian John J. Hennessy, "like an old pane of glass on a winter morning." Hennessy, *Return to Bull Run*, pp. 215-218. Other Germans were driven back by the famed Texas Brigade, as well as by other Confederate formations.

292. Hamlin, *The Attack of Stonewall Jackson at Chancellorsville*, pp. 22-23, 140-141.

293. Coddington, *The Gettysburg Campaign*, p. 306.

294. E. M. Hays to Bachelder, Oct. 15, 1890, *The Bachelder Papers*, vol. 3, p. 1776.

295. Early, *Narrative of the War Between the States*, pp. 273-274.

296. *OR* 27, pt. 2, p. 470.

297. Alexander, *Fighting for the Confederacy*, pp. 242-243.

298. Chapter 6 contains an in-depth discussion of Lee's options, one of which was standing on the defensive and passing the initiative to George Meade and the Army of the Potomac. Please consult that chapter for the reasons why Lee did not adopt this measure. Noted Gettysburg historian Edwin Coddington acknowledged what Lee saw on the field in real time: "The stakes were high, and they [Confederates] might never again have as good an opportunity." Coddington, *The Gettysburg Campaign*, p. 362.

299. Similarly, Lee's other choices on the evening of July 1, such as moving around the right and assuming the defensive, moving around the left, or even retreating, are discussed in depth in Chapter 6. Please consult that chapter for more information on why he did not adopt any of those measures.

300. Tucker, *Lee and Longstreet at Gettysburg*, p. 70.

301. Hood, *Advance and Retreat*, p. 57.

302. Tucker, *Lee and Longstreet at Gettysburg*, p. 68, places Pickett's arrival at 3:30 p.m. Douglas Southall Freeman, *Lee's Lieutenants*, 3, p. 136, states that the division "had reached the stone bridge on the Cashtown [Chambersburg Pike] Road during the early afternoon." George R. Stewart, *Pickett's Charge: a Microhistory of the Final Attack at Gettysburg, July 3, 1863* (Dayton, 1983), p. 3, claims his arrival was 6:00 p.m. Kathy Georg Harrison and John W. Busey, *Nothing But Glory: Pickett's Division at Gettysburg* (Gettysburg, 1987), p. 1, claims that Pickett's men were "relaxed in their encampment" as the battle was winding down.

303. *OR* 27, pt. 2, p. 388.

304. Charles T. Loehr, "The 'Old First' Virginia at Gettysburg," *Southern Historical Society Papers*, 32, p. 40.

305. H. T. Owen, *Philadelphia Times*, March 26, 1881. Lee noted in his report that Pickett arrived on the field "during the afternoon of the 2d." *OR* 27, pt. 2, p. 320.

306. Bowden, *Napoleon and Austerlitz*, p. 310.

307. Whether Pickett could have even been utilized on Longstreet's front is doubtful even if Lee had intended they be thrown into battle there. It would have taken at least two and possibly three hours for Pickett's fatigued Virginians to receive orders to join in the attack and then march from Marsh Creek to Seminary Ridge and deploy for action. Thus, even if Lee learned that Pickett was available by 4:00 p.m., the most optimistic estimate is that his division could not have been combat ready until about 7:00 p.m. (And given the condition of the army's rear at this time, this is an optimistic estimate.) Marching his men from Seminary Ridge to and beyond Emmitsburg Road and Cemetery Ridge or Little Round Top would have consumed at least another quarter-hour or more. Thus, under the best circumstances, Lee could not have counted on Pickett's participation in the First Corps area until 7:30 p.m. or later. While Pickett's three brigades would have certainly increased the pressure on the left wing of the Federal army, their advance could only have come long after the high tide of the crushing attacks delivered by William Barksdale and William Wofford. For information on the time it took for Pickett to move his division from Marsh Creek to Seminary Ridge on July 3, see Stewart, *Pickett's Charge*, p. 3, and Harrison and Busey, *Pickett's Division at Gettysburg*, pp. 13-20.

308. Coddington, *The Gettysburg Campaign*, p. 448; Pfanz, *Gettysburg: The Second Day*, pp. 415, 426-427.

309. Coddington, *The Gettysburg Campaign*, p. 448.

310. Wellington's famous quote can be found in a number of sources, including Frederick E. Smith, *Waterloo* (London, 1970), p. 116.

311. Justus Scheibert, letter dated November 21, 1877, on the topic of "Causes of Lee's Defeat at Gettysburg," *Southern Historical Society Papers*, 5, p. 92. Many writers attribute ill-health as the reason Lee remained around his overlook near the Lutheran Theological Seminary once the shooting began—and that his ability to make decisions was impaired a result. "Lee at Gettysburg was infirm," declared distinguished historian Frank E. Vandiver, "had been thrown from his horse a couple of weeks before and had sprained his hands; he may have been suffering from infectious myocarditis, did have diarrhea and stayed mainly in his tent." Frank E. Vandiver, "Lee during the War," *Confederate History Symposium, 1984*, Hill

College, Hillsboro, Texas, edited by D. B. Patterson (Hillsboro, 1984), p. 17. The primary source for the belief that Lee was suffering from diarrhea is W. W. Blackford, *War Years With Jeb Stuart* (Baton Rouge, 1993), pp. 230-231, although his description of Lee's complaint was delivered long after the Battle of Gettysburg concluded. In explaining Lee's behavior and failures at Gettysburg, James I. Robertson, Jr. speculates, "there is a good reason to believe that just before the Battle of Gettysburg [Lee] suffered a heart attack." James I. Robertson, Jr., in *Civil War Journal: The Leaders*, William C. Davis, Brian C. Pohanka, and Don Troiani, eds. (Nashville, 1997), pp. 151-152. The evidence for the litany of ailments claimed by some writers is mixed. What is clear, however, is that from 3:00 a.m. until 4:00 p.m. on July 2, General Lee was active, rode from one end of the field to the other, visited his subordinate generals, and energetically designed, and then modified, the Confederate battle plan. This level of vigorous activity is *not* indicative of a person suffering from the ailments Robertson, Vandiver, Blackford and others describe, and instead smack of excuses for why Lee attacked and failed to win a decisive victory at Gettysburg.

312. *Webster's New Collegiate Dictionary* (Springfield, 1975), p. 838. Lee spent as much of his time at or near his headquarters on Seminary Ridge as he did riding his lines and giving orders. Clearly Coddington, Pfanz and others do not fully grasp Lee's style of command, which was closely patterned on the Great Captains. Napoleon, Wellington, Frederick the Great and others habitually selected a command site for two principle reasons: it gave them the best possible view of the battlefield, and established a fixed point of reference to which subordinates could forward messengers and communiqués. Lee's command style in this regard was similar. By remaining in the vicinity of his field headquarters on July 2, Lee was not being "passive," but was instead extending his *accessibility* to his lieutenants, who might need his direction as quickly as possible. Lee understood the necessity of being available when necessary, and how crucial time was to the outcome of a battle. "Battles," wrote Napoleon, "are lost and won in a quarter of an hour." Robert E. Lee was not disengaged from what was happening on July 2, and the charge of passivity by Coddington and Pfanz against Lee is nothing more than a misreading of the Confederate general's actions.

313. Another great American general, George S. Patton, was a staunch believer in giving subordinates "orders with discretion." As Patton put it: "Never tell a subordinate exactly how to do something. Just tell him what you want done, and let him surprise you with his ingenuity."

314. *Webster's New Collegiate Dictionary*, p. 854.

315. Bishop Robert R. Brown, *The Spiritual Pilgrimage of Robert E. Lee* (Shippensburg, 1998), p. 63.

316. Gary W. Gallagher, "'If the Enemy Is There, We Must Attack Him:' Lee and the Second Day at Gettysburg," *The Second Day at Gettysburg* (Kent, 1993), p. 32; Gallagher repeats this assertion in *Lee and His Generals in War and Memory*, p. 76.

Chapter 8

"Richmond Has Nothing Left to Send Us"

Lee and the Third Day

"The attack of Pickett's division on the third has been more criticized, and is still less understood, than any other act of the Gettysburg drama."
—Colonel Armistead Lindsay Long[1]

"I have said that Lee's natural temper was combative, and to this may be ascribed his attack on the third day at Gettysburg, when the opportunity had not been seized which his genius saw was the gate to victory."
—Confederate President Jefferson Davis[2]

"In war, moral considerations account for three-quarters, the balance of actual forces only for the other quarter."
—Napoleon[3]

Where was General Lee and the Army of Northern Virginia? As June exhausted itself and July opened, the question must have weighed heavily on Jeb Stuart's mind.

The cavalry's exhausting night march from Hanover had taken the long column to Dover, a small town about six miles northwest of York, Pennsylvania.[4] Stuart's lengthening train now included 200 captured Federal wagons and teams and about 400 Yankee prisoners. The long and mind-numbing hours of continuous movement and little rest drained his men and animals, and now a lack of water and rations presented problems of crisis proportions.[5] Stuart called a halt while his men attempted to find something to eat and care for their suffering animals. It was July 1, 1863. Lee's cavalry general was just 25 miles northeast of Gettysburg. Harry Heth was preparing his men for their march east down the Chambersburg Pike.

Where was General Lee? The whereabouts of the army was now of paramount concern. Riders were dispatched.[6] Civilians were questioned. No conclusive leads could be wrangled out of the townspeople in Dover other than rumors that Lee's objective was Shippensburg (about 20 miles southwest of Carlisle), and that Jubal Early had marched his division west towards that town in the Cumberland Valley. Stuart had learned the day before that Early and his division had been in York and had advanced as far east as the Susquehanna River. Newspapers obtained at Dover convinced Stuart that Ewell's Second Corps was probably in the vicinity of Carlisle, or further southwest around Shippensburg. Since Federal cavalry at Hanover had effectively blocked any probe by Stuart's troopers in the direction of Gettysburg, Stuart decided to continue moving in the direction of Carlisle.[7]

Four hours later Stuart was again in motion. As his Confederate column lumbered northwest, the rumbling thunder of artillery overtook it. "The artillery fire of the 'first day's fight' was heard, and referring to Lloyd's map, I supposed it to be at Gettysburg, a place of which I had no knowledge," explained Captain John Esten Cooke, Stuart's divisional chief of ordnance. "How unexpected was the concentration of the great opposing forces there, will appear from General Stuart's reply, 'I reckon not,' when the firing was spoken of as 'near Gettysburg.'"[8] Stuart's response was peculiar under the circumstances and may have reflected his fatigued state of mind. Had he been thinking clearly he would have realized that Federal cavalry at Hanover and the sound of cannon fire from that direction at the very least indicated something of importance. Certainly scouting in that direction would have been prudent. Since his couriers searching for Lee had not yet returned, the sound of gunfire to the southwest offered Stuart a clarion call to move in that direction; pressing on to Carlisle would only carry his command away from whatever was transpiring near Gettysburg. His summary dismissal of these facts does not reflect favorably on his decision making abilities that day.[9]

The van of Fitzhugh Lee's Brigade pushed on to Carlisle, which was reached about midday.[10] Although they had not encountered any Federal cavalry along the way, the Confederates soon learned to their dismay that Carlisle was held by enemy militia, which meant that the place had been reoccupied after Ewell's troops pulled out. The town was of no particular importance to Stuart and he would not have sought a confrontation there except for one dire problem: he needed to feed his hungry men. Even though his column was spread out for miles, Stuart issued orders to prepare for action. "It is impossible for me to give you a correct idea of the fatigue and exhaustion of the men and beasts at this time," George W. Beale, a trooper in Chambliss' Brigade, recorded in a letter to his mother on July 13, 1863. "From great exertion, constant mental excitement, want of sleep and food, the men were overcome, and so tired and stupid as almost to be ignorant of what was transpiring around them." According to Beale,

> Even in line of battle, in momentary expectation of being made to charge, they would throw themselves upon their horses necks, and even the ground, and fall asleep. Couriers in attempting to give orders to officers would be compelled to give them a shake and a word, before they could make them understand. This was true of colonels.
>
> As soon as we reached the town, General Stuart sent an order for its surrender, which was refused. A charge was made, but repulsed by the enemy, who fired upon our men from the windows of brick buildings. After this, General Stuart put his artillery into position.[11]

It was late in the afternoon before the Confederate horse artillerists brought up their six guns and opened fire. Unfortunately, the exhausted Confederate horse artillerists were unable to operate their pieces with enough proficiency to put down an effective fire.[12] Before John Esten Cooke fell asleep "very soundly within ten feet" from one of the discharging artillery pieces of Breathed's 1st Stuart Virginia Horse Artillery, he noticed another officer lean "against a fence within a few paces of a [12-pounder Napoleon from McGregor's 2nd Stuart Virginia Horse Artillery] in process of rapid discharge, and in that upright position 'forgot his troubles.'" Stuart himself witnessed the most graphic example of what happens to a man pushed to the limit of his endurance when a trooper "put one leg over [a fence], and in that position drop[ped] asleep."[13] Even though the men were "weak and helpless," Trooper Beale observed that Stuart "seemed neither to suppose that his train was in danger, or that

his men were not in condition to fight. He could not have appeared more indifferent with fresh men and horses and no incumbrance," explained Beale.[14] The observations

"Custer at Hanover"

With a portion of his Michigan Brigade armed with 7-shot Spencer repeating rifles, George Armstrong Custer, the Federal army's youngest general officer, deploys his troopers prior to the skirmish with Jeb Stuart's Confederates at Hanover, Pennsylvania on June 30, 1863. *Courtesy Gallon Historical Art, Gettysburg, Pennsylvania*

recorded by Cooke and Beale strongly suggest Stuart was adversely affected by the fatigue of mind and body.

About dusk, Fitz Lee sent one of his staff officers to demand the surrender of the town, but the Federal commander, Brigadier General William Farrar "Baldy" Smith returned a curt refusal, "expressing his willingness to meet J. E. B. Stuart in hell before he gave up the place."[15] The Confederate shelling resumed after dark. Shortly before midnight, Fitz Lee dispatched detachments to burn Carlisle Barracks and the town's gas works and a lumber yard. The sparks from this large conflagration set off secondary fires and consumed other structures. It was during this time that Major Henry B. McClellan, Stuart's adjutant general, recalled that the dispatched riders Major Venable and Captain Lee returned with exciting news: they had found the army! What was more important, the riders brought orders from the commanding general "to move at once for Gettysburg."[16]

In reality McClellan's recollection was anti-climatic. In fact, one of the messengers sent from General Lee had already found Stuart. James D. Watters of the 1st Maryland Cavalry Battalion was part of the squad of riders dispatched by the commanding general with sealed orders for the cavalryman. Each member of the squad scattered from Gettysburg (exactly when they left is not known, but it was probably after the conclusion of the first day's fight) with the directive to "reach Stuart at any hazard and direct him to join General Lee with the least possible delay." Watters had ridden through the countryside and found the wayward Confederate cavalry general outside Carlisle. Contrary to popular belief, *Lee* found Stuart, rather than visa-versa.[17]

"Well, General Stuart, you are here at last!" Stuart Finally Rejoins the Army

Stuart canceled the Carlisle operation about 1:00 a.m. on July 2 and instructed his column to head to Gettysburg. The riders passed by the northern tip of South Mountain and, as Captain Cooke noted "went to sleep in the saddle."[18] Hunterstown, only five miles northeast of Gettysburg, was reached that afternoon. The weary riders could not have taken any pleasure in the sight of Judson Kilpatrick's approaching Federal cavalry division, with the 1st and 6th Michigan Cavalry of George Armstrong Custer's Michigan Brigade in the lead. Wade Hampton's Brigade deployed for action while the brigades under Fitzhugh Lee and John Chambliss continued moving towards Gettysburg. Tired, hungry, and mounted on horses that needed rest and nourishment as badly as their owners, Hampton's men gamely fought "a spirited affair of two hours" beginning at sundown. The see-saw covering action lasted long enough to allow the remainder of Stuart's column to move safely away.[19] Gettysburg and the extreme left flank of the Confederate army,

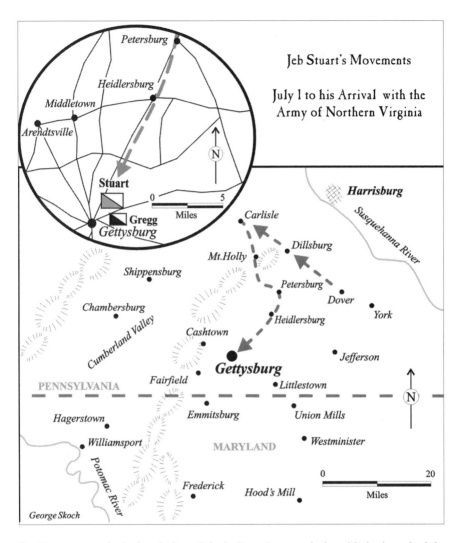

Jeb Stuart's Movements

July 1 to his Arrival with the
Army of Northern Virginia

George Skoch

finally, were reached after dark on July 2. Stuart's meandering ride had reached the end of its tether.[20]

While Hampton was occupying Kilpatrick's cavalry, Jeb Stuart rode ahead with the rest of his command. According to Cooke, "General Stuart arrived with his cavalry on the evening of the 'second day's fight' at Gettysburg." Stuart's adjutant, Henry McClellan, noted that he "reached Gettysburg on the afternoon of the 2nd, and took position on the Confederate left."[21] Regardless of exactly when Stuart arrived, the important point is that he and his three veteran brigades arrived in an utterly enervated state. Even the final ride to Gettysburg was difficult. A number of the wagons "broke down on the road," their thirsty teams unable to take another step. Lieutenant Colonel Carter of the 3rd Virginia Cavalry reported that 175 of the captured vehicles were carried into Confederate lines, along with "72 nice ambulances, 3,000 horses [and] 1,200 fine mules."[22] The horses carrying Stuart's oft-heralded troopers must have looked far different to those who had seen them before they departed Salem on June 25. The exertions of the past eight days exacted a terrible physical toll on both Stuart's men and the animals, which accounted for the "broken-down condition of his command."[23] Indeed, one writer remembered that the horses upon which Stuart's troopers rode arrived at Gettysburg "with hanging heads and trembling legs."[24] By the time trooper Beale reached the outskirts of Gettysburg, he was on his fifth horse of the campaign.[25]

After shepherding his command within Southern lines Stuart rode to see General Lee. The exact hour at which he finally made his belated arrival at army headquarters is not recorded. McClellan later told Thomas T. Munford—at that time the colonel commanding the 2nd Virginia Cavalry in Fitzhugh Lee's Brigade—that Stuart and Lee met about 11:00 p.m. on July 2. The meeting, remembered the adjutant, was "painful beyond description."[26] McClellan accompanied Stuart and Fitzhugh Lee to army headquarters, where they dismounted and found General Lee. Instead of being held in private, the encounter was conducted in the presence of McClellan, Fitzhugh Lee, and other officers from Lee's headquarters staff including Walter Taylor and Charles Marshall. If Stuart was expecting a hero's welcome, he was very disappointed. As one historian has described it, "there was not a modicum of what he loved most—glory."[27] Instead, explains Edwin Coddington, the cavalier found himself "in the position of a person who had betrayed a sacred trust."[28]

The details vary on what Lee's first words were to Stuart, but there is complete agreement that whatever they were, they constituted a strong censure. According to McClellan, Lee initially said nothing and just looked at his subordinate with a glacial stare for several moments—in itself a serious rebuke. Thereafter Lee raised his arm in a gesture of exasperation and asked, "General Stuart, where have you been?"[29] Another more popular version of the initial exchange records Lee's silent and icy stare followed with the words, "Well, General Stuart, you are here at last!"[30] Regardless of exactly what Lee uttered, his brief and terse greeting reflected a remarkable ability to maintain control of his temper, and reflected the Southern aristocracy's code of conduct.

Still, Lee's few words cut Stuart to the quick. According to McClellan, Stuart "wilted" after Lee spoke.[31] The flustered cavalryman, reported his adjutant, "attempted an explanation too long, too involved, and too vague for his superior's patience."[32] Lee was furious and there is no doubt about that. His headquarters staff personnel knew well the warning signs of his temper—according to Charles Venable, his face would flush and his temple veins would swell.[33] "Lee," recalled one witness, "cut him short with a voice that smoldered: 'I have not heard a word from you for days, and you the eyes and ears of my army!'"[34] Those within earshot had to have been embarrassed by the situation, and no one wanted to catch the attention of General Lee when his temper was up. At that point, McClellan remembered Lee's demeanor became conciliatory. "Let me ask your help now. We will not discuss this matter further. Help me fight these people."[35]

At long last General Lee's missing lieutenant had rejoined the army. In the eight days Stuart had been gone, he and his command, according to historian Emory Thomas, "had ridden at the very least 210 miles . . . traveled about twenty-six miles per day; but this travel included excursions to destroy railroad tracks and cut telegraph wires." What's more, "those eight days followed more than two weeks of combat and hard riding."[36] The misplaced exertions no doubt stressed Stuart men and animals, who needed days of rest before they would be able to recover their peak efficiency. But time was not a luxury Lee could extend to them. The exigencies of the moment would compel him to call upon Stuart and his cavalry to perform important missions the next day. Just how effective Stuart's jaded men and horses would be was just one of many diverse variables Lee had to factor in when considering the operational plans for the Army of Northern Virginia for that fateful Friday.

It was after midnight by the time the commanding general crawled onto his cot and fell asleep.

Lee Considers his Options for July 3

After but a brief slumber Lee awoke about 3:00 a.m. and began formulating his plans in the predawn darkness. In spite of the heroic assault delivered by Longstreet's First Corps and selected elements of Second and Third Corps on July 2, Lee was well aware that the results of the fighting were far less than he had envisioned they might be. What was he now to do? In spite of failures on the part of some of his subordinates, the Confederate army had attacked for two days and severely punished Meade's army. The battle, however, had not yet reached a conclusion, and Lee now had both Stuart's command and Pickett's fresh division available. Securing a major victory on Northern soil would bring new political, diplomatic, and even military variables into play—and the possibility of scoring one still existed. That, of course, was the driving reason he had taken his army north that summer.

General Lee's decision to recommit his forces to the tactical offensive on July 3 cannot be judged (although it almost always is) solely on the outcome of the day's fighting. This is especially true since the results of the July 3 fighting fell far short of Lee's goals. Rather, we must examine *why* he decided to continue attacking. His reasons are often oversimplified, misstated, or misunderstood. While we do not have a diary outlining what was going through Lee's mind that morning, there are several good indications of what he was thinking based upon his reports and later discussions with others. Also, of course, are the central military (largely logistic) principles that someone of Lee's experience and education would have taken into account before making his final plans.

First, Lee's decision to resume the offensive was grounded in the fact that he had complete confidence in the striking power of the Army of Northern Virginia. Contrary to what some writers assert, the fighting during the first two days at Gettysburg only deepened Lee's appreciation for what his army could accomplish. Even without the help of several divisions slated for use on July 2, Lee had shattered a large portion of Meade's force.[37] Three entire Federal corps (the First, Third, and Eleventh), had been virtually destroyed and several more divisions from other Federal corps had been engaged and mauled. Many of Lee's brigades had penetrated the enemy line at several points and, except for Culp's Hill and Little Round Top, wherever Southern brigades had attacked they had been successful to one degree or another. Only a breakdown in the echelon attack's *execution* had spared Meade a disastrous nighttime retreat and defeat. Taking these factors into consideration, Lee justifiably believed that if the entire army could be coordinated by his corps commanders and resolutely directed into action, the Federal line would buckle under the effort.

Lee summed up his decision to attack again on July 3, with these words:

> The result of [July 2nd's] operations induced the belief that, with proper concert of action, and with the increased support that the positions gained on the right would enable the artillery to render the assaulting columns, we should ultimately succeed, and it was accordingly determined to continue the attack.[38]

Lee's decision to resume the offensive flies in the face of conventional wisdom as offered by many Civil War writers. His most prudent choice, they argue, would have been to assume the tactical defensive and wait for Meade who, under heavy pressure to act aggressively, would attack him. This position assumes that a defensive stance was, in an unqualified sense, more powerful than an offensive one. Those subscribing to the "power of the defensive" theory universally believe that defending troops, armed with longer-ranged small arms than those carried in prior wars, inflicted more damage on attacking formations than they received in return. Most writers advancing this theory, whether they were participants during the conflict or writing after it ended, largely draw their conclusions from three Eastern theater engagements: Malvern Hill, Pickett's Charge—and an overall collective defensive performance by the Army of Northern Virginia (Fredericksburg being the most prominent of these).[39] But is this theory, which is so widely held today, valid?

The answer is yes—and no. Although attractive at first glance, the "power of the defensive" doctrine is as much myth as fact. Both Malvern Hill and Pickett's Charge, for example, were demonstrable failures from a *coordinated* offensive standpoint. Never mind that the Federals were able to concentrate their firepower and units against a limited number of piecemeal attacking formations. The same was true in reverse at Fredericksburg, where Burnside's Federals attacked in separated waves and Longstreet's infantry and Alexander's artillery shot them down by the tens of hundreds. Many defensive warfare advocates (Longstreet and Alexander, for example) were influenced by the defensive prowess of *the Army of Northern Virginia*. But the fact that Lee's men were so stellar on defense did not mean that the Army of the Potomac was going to be as equally effective trying to hold ground in the face of Southern attacks. In fact, Longstreet's July 2 hammer stroke at Gettysburg aptly demonstrates this point. The Confederate combatants who actually made it into action that day attacked over open ground and were consistently outnumbered at the point of attack at least two to one by an enemy situated on better terrain and supported by more artillery firing higher quality ammunition. Yet Lee's men inflicted almost twice as many casualties as they suffered in return. There are two possible reasons for this (and both might have been true). First, the "power of the defensive" at that time in the evolution of warfare did not provide an *unqualified* tactical advantage and has been seriously overrated. Second, the Army of Northern Virginia was a superior offensive striking force compared to other Civil War armies, and thus Lee's confidence in his battle-tested veterans was not misplaced.

Certainly fighting on the defensive offered some advantages (less likelihood of confusion, easier to keep troops in place, and so forth), but it was not the *unqualified* advantage many students advance. Consider for a moment some of the problems of fighting on the defensive. The weapons of the period, for example, produced significant amounts of smoke that choked visibility and often severely restricted engagement ranges. This, as too few people seem to appreciate, diminished significantly the effects of rifled fire. The vast majority of the engagements were waged with non-repeating weapons, which meant that the morale and quality of the troops wielding them had a direct effect on the firepower produced. Further, Confederate infantry seemed to advance and fight more often in slightly looser formations than did their counterparts, which may account to some degree for the fact that Federals tended to suffer higher casualties whether fighting on the offensive *or* defensive.

The idea that the "power of the defensive" was an unqualified advantage does not take into account the spirit of the men, the incalculable importance of quality NCOs and officers, and discounts the importance of *élan* and the ability to produce high volumes of firepower—all of which translated into offensive striking power. As Joe Hooker described it, Lee's army did not merely attack but struck with "blows," and "the shock seemed to make the earth tremble on which we stood."[40] Thus, the firepower generated by a force was a combination of the quality of the units, their morale and leadership, the actual numbers of combatants in the ranks, and any restrictions imposed by terrain. The amount of firepower a unit could deliver was (and is) an important consideration in combat. Therefore, the "power of the defensive" in an era of non-repeating infantry weapons must take into consideration the identity of both the attackers and the defenders. This is especially true because those who profess an almost universal belief in the "power of the defensive" assume that the formations from other armies would have been as equally effective as those constituting Lee's Army of Northern Virginia. That is simply not the case. Lee's army was as formidable on the defensive as it was irresistible in a properly coordinated offensive—because of its outstanding leadership and morale at the regimental level, and the consequent high volumes of firepower that resulted. Napoleon, too, understood this when he had written that "the moral considerations in war were three-quarters of the equation with the balance of forces representing the remaining quarter." This, then is one reason why Lee decided to continue the battle and try to force a decision on July 3.

Two remaining reasons driving Lee's decision on July 3 were closely linked: the battle had not yet reached a conclusion, and his primary reason for moving north was to secure a major victory on enemy soil that could open up new political, diplomatic, and military variables that would not exist with a hollow victory along the Rappahannock line in Virginia. These two inextricably related central points were still valid on the evening of July 2 and early morning of July 3.

Lee and his army also faced serious logistical concerns which would have influenced any decision he made. First, there was an immediate and increasing need for water, and local supplies were drying up. With the arrival of Stuart's three brigades and their captured teams, the number of *horses and mules* present with Lee's army around Gettysburg was approximately 33,000.[41] When his men are also taken into consideration, Lee's army required about 450,000 gallons of water every day just to sustain itself. Finding sufficient forage for the army's animals was also a major concern. As long as the army was on the move and away from war-torn middle Virginia, sufficient forage was not difficult to procure. However, the situation was far different once the Army of Northern Virginia concentrated at Gettysburg. Supply concerns were only exacerbated the longer the army remained concentrated in and around the small community.[42] Lee, of course, was well aware that this condition jeopardized the army's ability to function efficiently.[43]

All of these problems were related to the army remaining too long in one position. The artillery resupply train posed the exact opposite problem. The train, en route to his army but not expected to arrive for a few days, needed to be protected while in transit. In other words, a movement of the army deep in enemy territory ran the risk of uncovering the secured route the train was scheduled to follow, which to some degree limited Lee's movement options. He correctly gauged that he still had sufficient ammunition for a continuation of the battle. If that action was offensive in nature and successful, Lee recognized what Edward Porter Alexander explained after the war: the army often captured on the battlefield enough guns and ammunition to offset what was expended in the effort.[44] An additional logistical issue involved Lee's existing line of communications, which could also serve as an excellent line of retreat if disaster befell his army.

Perhaps the most consequential reason for striking the enemy across the valley was one of simple mathematics. Before the campaign had started Lee stressed to Jefferson Davis the importance of returning to his mobile army the missing veteran brigades detached for service elsewhere. Lee knew firsthand that the Federals were always able to replace their losses in men and material and return to the field strong and well-equipped. Even without his missing brigades, the Pennsylvania campaign offered Lee the unique opportunity to engage the Army of the Potomac with only a slight numerical disadvantage. Lee knew the chances were good that the numerical odds would never be any better than they were at Gettysburg. Breaking off the action after two largely successful days of fighting would throw away all the sacrifices of the past year without the enemy compelling him to do so. From the prisoners Lee could surmise that both "Major Sedgwick's" Sixth Corps and the Federal army's powerful artillery reserve had reached the field. Thus the last of Meade's readily available troops had arrived. What Lee did not know was whether additional reinforcements were on their way to Meade. Neither did he know the condition of Sedgwick's hard-marching divisions or how many thousands of Federal stragglers had fallen away from their commands as a result of their forced marches to Gettysburg—stragglers Meade would recover if the armies remained idle.[45]

As discussed more fully in an earlier chapter, the Eastern Theater of operations was covered thoroughly by the press and foreign diplomatic corps, thus a Southern victory in Pennsylvania would be heralded around the world as a significant event. And the combative and aggressive Lee was prepared to do everything within his power to deliver one. He knew a numerically inferior side had to take chances, and assuming the offensive was the only way to achieve a potentially decisive victory. He had but narrowly missed one on both July 1 and 2. Standing on the defensive would only weaken his odds and reduce his chances of victory. As far as he was concerned, Lee had little choice but to continue the battle before additional reinforcements and stragglers bolstered Meade's numbers and the shattered corps of his army had time to recover. As noted historian Frank E. Vandiver put it, Lee must have considered the resumption of the offensive as the "one choice [that] was open."[46] The lives of my men, Lee had written earlier that year, "are too precious to be sacrificed in the attainment of successes that inflict no loss upon the enemy beyond the actual loss in battle. Every victory should bring us nearer to the great end which it is the object of this war to reach."[47]

And that, of course, was why he was in Pennsylvania.

Lee's Attack Plans

In light of the impressive accomplishments already achieved by his men on July 1 and 2, Lee believed, as Douglas Southall Freeman phrased it, "enough troops were at hand for a supreme effort on the morning of the 3rd."[48] His army was still in good shape and ready for offensive work. Longstreet's First Corps now had available George Pickett's three brigades, as well as the division's powerful 18-gun artillery battalion under James Dearing.[49] In addition, 10 pieces served by the élite Washington Louisiana Artillery Battalion under the command of Benjamin F. Eshleman had not yet been engaged, so their employment, along with Dearing's guns, meant that First Corps now had its entire artillery compliment on the field.[50] Ewell's Second Corps was in excellent condition. Johnson's Division was intact and in place on Culp's Hill, three of Jubal Early four brigades were in solid condition, and Robert Rodes' command had been weakened by the fighting of July 1, but was now rested and available. Hill's Third Corps, too, still had several fresh brigades. In Richard Anderson's Division, Posey and Mahone had suffered only minor losses on July 2, and two of Dorsey Pender's four brigades had either not been engaged at all or had suffered light losses during the first two days of combat. Both Scales and Perrin had suffered heavily on July 1, but both outfits were rested and available for combat if called upon to serve. Harry Heth's Division had been roughly handled on July 1. Its day of rest had brought in stragglers and solidified its organization. Finally, Stuart's fatigued troopers were available for appropriate service. All things considered, Lee could roughly calculate that his army could renew the battle and face approximately the same odds that had existed the day before. While numbers were important, so was morale. And the morale of the Army of Northern Virginia was still high.[51]

Outnumbered and outgunned, the Southern regiments that had gotten into action on July 2 had once again shown their superb fighting prowess. Lee knew that Meade had channeled thousands of troops to his left in response to his echelon attack, and had only escaped a defeat by the thinnest of margins. Meade had to know this as well. The chances were good, then, that Meade would not overreact the same way to a similar attack on consecutive days. Still, Lee wanted to press Meade along as much of the line as possible so his men would be position to exploit any "opportunity" that might show itself. Lee thus formulated a "general plan [that] was unchanged."[52]

The method he would employ, however, would be far different. As already described, one of the reasons Lee ordered an echelon attack on July 2 was to drive in the Federal flank and convince Meade that unless he siphoned off troops to maintain it, it would be turned and crushed. Meade's actions, in turn, created opportunities elsewhere up the line that successive echelon waves of attack exploited. This time, Lee proposed a simultaneous attack along much of the front that would pin Federal formations into place. As Lee explained it, the main effort would consist of "Longstreet, re-enforced by Pickett's three brigades . . . to attack the next morning, and General Ewell was directed to assail the enemy's right at the same time. The latter, during the night, re-enforced General Johnson with two brigades from Rodes' and one from Early's division."[53] By attacking in this manner Lee hoped a rupture of the Federal line could be exploited at the decisive point. If so, the significant victory he was seeking in Pennsylvania would be achieved. As far as Lee was concerned, the offensive history of his army made the plan a reasonable blueprint for battle; the fighting on July 2 had only served to confirm this belief.

To prepare the way for the infantry advance and to give the assaulting columns every chance to achieve a breakthrough, Lee sought to involve as many pieces of his artillery as possible. A message was dispatched to General Pendleton ordering that "the artillery along our entire line was to be prepared for opening, as early as possible on the morning of the 3d, a concentrated and destructive fire, consequent upon which a general advance was to be made."[54] Similar orders were sent to Longstreet, who conveyed them to E. Porter Alexander during the night. "Our present position was to be held," Longstreet told his artillerist, "and the attack renewed as soon as Pickett arrived, and he was expected early. . . ."[55] Exactly what Alexander meant by "early" was detailed in a letter written on May 3, 1876: "I had orders to prepare for an assault on Cemetery Hill somewhere about 8 a.m. on the 3rd as I recollect, perhaps earlier."[56] Lee's plans for an early morning assault, with the main effort delivered from somewhere along Seminary Ridge, were confirmed with orders for Ewell and his corps to press the Federals in his front to prevent Meade from shifting Federal reserves elsewhere. Major Taylor of Lee's staff acknowledged that Ewell "had orders to cooperate with General Longstreet," and that Lee had ordered the assault to be taken up again "early the next morning."[57] Ewell confirmed the early attack. My orders, he recalled, were "to renew my attack at daylight Friday morning."[58] Powell Hill was to support Longstreet's assault "and avail himself of any success that might be gained."[59]

Jeb Stuart's tired troopers would also have a role in the fighting. His cavalry command was to ride "forward to a position to the left of General Ewell's left, and in advance of it, where a commanding ridge completely controlled a wide plain of cultivated fields stretching towards Hanover."[60] The purpose of this movement was twofold. First, Stuart's men would be in position to advance against the enemy rear, where it was hoped his appearance would divert Federal attention and reinforcements away from the decisive point the Confederates were attacking along Cemetery Ridge. Second, if the Southern infantry attack was successful and the desired dislodgment of the Federal line of battle achieved, Stuart's cavalry would be in position to maximize the enemy's psychological discomfort, not to mention inflict substantial losses against disorganized and retreating formations and supply trains.[61]

Second Corps had been kept on the left side of town because of Ewell's representations to Lee late on the evening of July 1 or in early hours of July 2 that Culp's Hill could be easily captured. That accomplishment, of course, would have comprised Meade's line and probably forced his retreat. Although Johnson's brigades had come close to reaching its summit, Culp's Hill remained, albeit tenuously, in Federal hands. Lee did not want Ewell to abandon his position on its northern slope because his strong presence hugging the Federal far right threatened the integrity of Meade's defensive position, riveted his attention there, and held large numbers of the enemy in place that might otherwise be used elsewhere. The net effect was that Ewell's position kept the Federal line stretched and threatened Meade's line of communication along the Baltimore Pike. George Steuart's Brigade in Johnson's Division, for example, was only about one-quarter of a mile from that important road.

Ewell's attack against Meade's right had barely been beaten back. The same thing was true of Longstreet's attack against Meade's opposite flank, where the Federals had finally anchored their southern wing on the high ground of Little Round Top. Like Culp's Hill, the smaller of the Round Tops also protected an important logistical avenue, the Taneytown Road. The fact that Meade had barely been able to hold each end of his line led Lee to believe that Meade had substantially reinforced both flanks. As a result, Lee decided to strike the same decisive breakthrough area that Napoleon always sought to attack and rupture when a turning movement was no longer practicable—the hinge of the enemy line connecting one wing to another. Since Meade's army was in the shape of a fishhook, the hinge between Meade's right and left wings was the area along the low ridge running south from Ziegler's Grove to the Copse of Trees to lower Cemetery Ridge. This is the area Rans Wright's Georgians had penetrated late the previous afternoon. A rupture of the Federal line in the middle of the ridge would effectively split apart the Federal host. Achieving a breakthrough could only come through a coordinated effort, complete with a large-scale artillery bombardment and sufficient supports in the form of a second wave of infantry. Such an assault, when properly led and delivered timely against the entirety of the enemy line, had never before failed to carry a Federal position.

Thus, in general terms, Lee's plan was as follows: Longstreet and Ewell would press forward and pin Meade firmly in place on both flanks to prevent the shifting of troops to his center. Meanwhile, a large artillery barrage directed against the point selected for the breakthrough would soften up the line and silence the enemy's artillery in preparation for a decisive blow, a *coup de main,* against the hinge of the enemy line, the spot considered to have "the highest promise of success."[62]

The Unexpected: Culp's Hill

Lee's plans for July 3 suffered a major setback shortly after military dawn. "At 4:30 a.m." a furious Federal cannonade opened on the Confederate left "just before the time fixed for General Johnson to advance."[63] The firing announced Meade's *localized* counterattack against Ed Johnson's brigades on Culp's Hill. This well-timed and intelligent move on the part of the Federal commander, delivered under the protection of eventually 26 pieces of artillery, was designed to secure the

Federal army's right flank, relieve the pressure on the Baltimore Pike, and "regain the works captured by Steuart the evening before."[64] Second Corps' involvement against Meade's effort would probably prevent Federal troops from that sector from being drawn off and sent elsewhere—as long as the action continued on that front. If the Southern army was going to take full advantage of this development, Lee knew that plans for the main attack, which he had already ordered, would need to be quickly completed and implemented. Thus far he had not yet heard from Longstreet concerning the progress of his preparations. It was critical that his entire army act in concert or the day's battle would not be successful. Unwilling to leave anything to chance, Lee mounted Traveller and rode to the right to find Longstreet. Apparently Lee saw nothing of Pickett's infantry during his ride, and evidence of preparations for the offensive was almost nonexistent.[65]

Dawn was about to break and Ewell was already heavily engaged. Exactly what was passing through Lee's mind at this time we will never know. Since an assault was supposed to be made "with proper concert of action," he was probably wondering why Pickett's infantry was not in position and forming up for the attack. When he reached First Corps headquarters about 4:45 a.m., Lee discovered why so few arrangements for the renewal of the offensive had been made: Longstreet had different plans.[66]

Writing less than a month after the battle in his official report, the commander of Lee's First Corps explained that on the morning of July 3 he was making "arrangements . . . for renewing the attack by my right, with a view to pass around the hill occupied by the enemy on his left [Round Top], and to gain it by flank and reverse attack."[67] Longstreet was planning some sort of attack for July 3, but the important point was that his plan to move some or all of First Corps to the south and east did not conform with Lee's attack plan, orders for which had already been issued to Ewell and Stuart. Nor did Longstreet's flanking plan comport to the tactical realities of the dispositions of the Federal forces on the southern end of the field. Longstreet's proposal referred to the ground south and east of Round Top, but the information provided to him by his scouts was inaccurate. In fact, the way to the rear of the Federal army was not open: two brigades from Sedgwick's Sixth Corps were in position on this very ground to prevent exactly the movement Longstreet was now advocating. One of these Federal brigades was deployed with its right flank "resting on Round Top Mountain" and its left on the Taneytown Road.[68]

Old Pete's flanking proposals had been rebuffed at least twice on the two preceding days by the commanding general. One was his own grand tactical plan to bypass Meade's army by moving to the right on the late afternoon of July 1, and the second was John Bell Hood's proposal to make a tactical flanking march with a portion of his division around Round Top on July 2. In fact, the maneuver Longstreet was preparing to undertake on the morning of the battle's third day was almost exactly what John B. Hood had advocated the day before. While no copies of Lee's

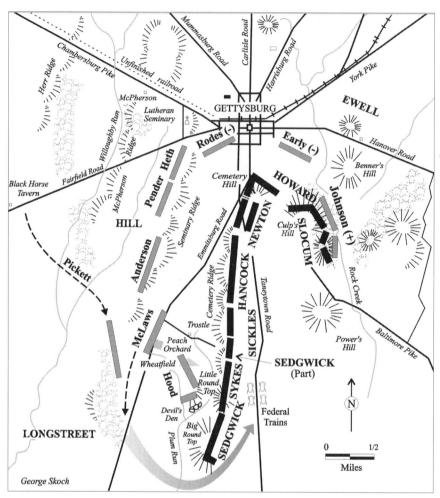

Longstreet's Proposed Flank March and Reverse Attack for July 3, 1863

exact orders to Longstreet that morning survive, a general reconstruction of what had been ordered and what was expected is possible to outline.

General Lee had already issued orders calling for the army to attack along the entire occupied front. This is substantiated by any number of Confederate officers. That fact alone seems to confirm at least three things. First, it would make no sense for the rest of the army to attack along the entire line and yet have Longstreet's corps conduct an obvious flanking maneuver within sight of the enemy. Second, Lee had rejected this flanking maneuver the previous day because it was unsound. An exposed march across the face of a deployed enemy violated every sound tactical operational precept of war. This fact alone seriously calls into question the veracity of Longstreet's postwar claim. Third, Longstreet's proposed flanking march ran counter to the orders he had already been issued and the plan of battle he had described the night before to Porter Alexander. The reliable artillerist remembered his discussion with Longstreet this way:

> During the evening I found my way to Gen. Longstreet's bivouac, a little ways to the rear, to ask the news from other quarters & orders for the morning. From elsewhere the news was indefinite, but I was told that we would renew the attack early in the morning. That Pickett's division would arrive and would assault the enemy's line. My impression is the exact point for it was not designated, but I was told it would be to our left of the Peach Orchard [i.e., against Cemetery Ridge].[69]

The only way Longstreet could have known and relayed to Alexander on the evening of July 2 that the offensive was to be resumed early in the morning "left [north] of the Peach Orchard" is if Lee had ordered it. (And of course Pickett's Charge later took place on a stretch of the line north of the Sherfy fruit grove.) Since orders for the army's other corps had already been issued, including to Stuart's cavalry, Old Pete's maneuver ran counter to the plan already underway and would have been conducted without the benefit of screening cavalry. How, exactly, Longstreet planned to pull off this daring move is something he never addressed in his various writings. Further, Longstreet's failure to act on Lee's orders and prepare for the renewed attack that morning compromised the commanding general's battle plan for that day and served to negate anything positive that might have come from Ewell's pre-dawn struggle on Culp's Hill. Longstreet's proposed flanking maneuver continued to reflect his shortcomings: he was a superb corps commander, but lacked the ability to formulate realistic battle plans independent of Lee.

During the course of this discussion between Lee and Longstreet (which was detailed and lengthy), Lee reconfirmed to his corps leader that the attack ordered would be the attack made. Since preparations had not yet gone forward to any degree, the commanding general prudently discussed the makeup of the assaulting column and conducted "a careful examination of the ground secured by Longstreet" the day before in order to determine where best to position First Corps' artillery.[70] With that understanding, Lee led the reconnaissance from Longstreet's bivouac. The generals and several staffers had not ridden far before Porter Alexander saw the mounted party arrive near his artillery battalion sometime before 8:00 a.m.—perhaps as long as three hours after Lee first arrived at Longstreet's headquarters.[71] Reining in their mounts on the long glacis that formed the eastern face of the high ground marked by the Sherfy Peach Orchard, Lee and Longstreet dismounted. The pair walked past Alexander's guns and came across a pair of skirmishers from Barksdale's (now Humphreys') Brigade along the edge of the fruit grove. The Mississippians were Adjutant Edward P. Harmon of the 13th Mississippi and W. Gart Johnson of Company C, 18th Mississippi. According to Johnson, the men were "occupying the extreme front picket line in direct range of sharpshooters," and "were hugging a pile of rubbish, anything to hide behind." Both were astonished to see "Gens. Lee and Longstreet—on foot, no aides, orderlies or couriers, fifteen or twenty steps apart, field glasses in hand—came walking past us, stopping now and then to take observations." The generals stopped a few feet from the hunkered down Mississippians when Johnson, who knew sharpshooters were plying their trade in the area, called out, "Gen. Lee, you are running a very great risk!" Just then, "the searching minnie was cutting close to him, showing that he was the mark aimed at. He went on with his observations as calm and serene as if he was viewing a landscape."[72]

Powell Hill and the wounded Harry Heth joined Lee and Longstreet at a vantage point in this general vicinity about this time.[73] According to Walter Taylor, the distinguished group studied the terrain closely and conferred about "the mode of attack and the troops to make it."[74] Looking across Plum Run, the Confederate officers viewed the long and gentle slope of Cemetery Ridge, which marked the center of Meade's line and the focus of Lee's attention. To the northeast some 2,000 yards away was a clearly defined umbrella-shaped group of trees. There, believed Lee, was the hinge of Meade's two heavily reinforced wings and the vicinity where Wright had led his Georgians the afternoon before. From that point south much of the Federal line along Cemetery Ridge was screened by the swells of the Emmitsburg Road. The rolling terrain along middle-to-lower Cemetery Ridge, coupled with the rising ground that cut across the middle of the battlefield, might serve to mask the effective range of Federal guns stationed there and shield infantry forming up and around the Spangler place and Spangler's Woods. None of this terrain would inhibit the fire from at least one Federal artillery battery: the six 10-pounder Parrotts positioned on Little Round Top. These guns could fire into the right flank of advancing infantry. Overhearing the discussion about this aspect, Colonel Long of Lee's staff, "whose judgment of artillery was usually excellent," assured the commanding general that the Confederate artillery could suppress the fire of this single Federal battery.[75]

Depending upon where the Southern infantry crossed the Emmitsburg Road, the distance from that point to Federal positions along Cemetery Ridge varied, but seemed to average about 200 to 500 yards. One significant difference between the ground covered by the Confederates at Gaines' Mill and that at Gettysburg was the formidable nature of the post and rail fencing that criss-crossed the fields and enclosed the Emmitsburg Road. The wooden structures would slow the attacking columns on their way to Cemetery Ridge. However, the fencing had not disrupted the echelon attack on July 2.

All things considered, the portion of Meade's line selected for attack at Gettysburg did not appear as strong as the Federal position at Gaines' Mill. There, the enemy lines were two, and in some places three, deep and behind Boatswain's

Creek, strengthened by abatis and supported with artillery along the front as well as on the flank. Even so, Hood's Texas Brigade spearheaded an attack that progressed up the slope between two almost imperceptible folds in the ground that protected his flanks. His thrust pierced the lines and triggered a collapse of the entire position. If the formidable Federal defensive position at Gaines' Mill could be successfully carried without significant artillery support, Lee might well have reasoned that his veteran infantry could carry Cemetery Ridge on July 3. Rans Wright's brigade, after all, had perforated the area just below the umbrella clump of trees the day before. Could not a concerted attack by infantry, led by his ablest corps commander and preceded with an unprecedented artillery bombardment duplicate that success several times over?[76] Decisions such as these are not made in a vacuum. While we will never know for certain exactly what these generals discussed, it is important to understand that armies, like individuals, developed "institutional memories." The past year had demonstrated the Army of Northern Virginia's striking power when assaults were properly led and coordinated. Lee and his generals had planned and driven their opponents from several battlefields. Why would Gettysburg be any different?

At least one other officer in addition to Longstreet (who was fervently against the attack of July 3) believed that Cemetery Ridge was a tougher position than the one carried at Gaines' Mill. Writing many years after the battle, Major Edmund Berkeley of the 8th Virginia, Richard Garnett's Brigade, Pickett's Division, recalled a visit paid to the regiment by General Cadmus Wilcox shortly before the attack that afternoon. According to Berkeley, Wilcox "told General Garnett in [earshot] of myself, my brothers, Col. Hunton & other officers, that he considered Cemetery Ridge twice as strong as Gaines' Mill."[77] Unlike Gaines' Mill, no entrenchments or abatis scarred the front of Meade's lines along Cemetery Ridge. In fact, outside of stacking up rocks or strengthening existing low stone fences, there were few defensive improvements in the area of the Copse of Trees, which was to be the focal point of the main assault.

Another of Pickett's veterans also recalls that Wilcox spoke to officers in his brigade immediately preceding the attack. Once the artillery bombardment began, remembered Captain Benjamin Lyons Farinholt, Company E, 53rd Virginia, Lewis Armistead's Brigade, General Wilcox rode up, saluted Armistead and asked him "What he thought would follow this unusually heavy fire of artillery." According to Farinholt, Armistead replied, "To charge and carry the enemy's position in front of us." Wilcox then proceeded to explain to Armistead that "There had already been heavy fighting over the fields in front of us [the day before], that our forces had been ordered to retire from the advanced positions they had taken, and that the enemy having nearly twenty-four hours in which to strengthen the stone wall behind which their infantry was massed, it would be at great sacrifice of life and very difficult to dislodge them."[78]

Wilcox never mentioned having any conversations like this in either his after-action report or his postwar articles that appeared in the *Southern Historical Society Papers*, but two independent eyewitnesses attested to their occurrence. If accurately portrayed, Wilcox seemed to be warning his comrades about the difficulty of their mission—not that it was a hopeless cause to attack Cemetery Ridge. The exchange between Wilcox and the brigadiers of Pickett's Division is consistent with Wilcox's writings in which he always maintained that the attack of July 3 failed because it lacked support to carry and hold the Federal line.[79] Wilcox's explanations are reinforced by Rans Wright's discussion with Porter Alexander shortly before the cannonade began. "General," Alexander asked Wright, "tell me exactly what *you* think of this attack." The Georgian responded: "Well, Alexander, it is mostly a question of supports. It is not as hard to get there as it looks. I was there yesterday with my brigade. The real difficulty is to stay there after you get there—for the whole infernal Yankee army is up there in a bunch."[80]

When the reconnoitering party approached Trostle's Woods, Lee and Longstreet sought out General Wofford, whose brigade of Georgians was stationed nearby. With Lee astride Traveller and Longstreet in the saddle of his horse, Hero, the two discussed the preceding day's fight and the prospects of renewing it on July 3. " I told him that the afternoon before, I nearly reached the crest," wrote Wofford. When Lee asked Wofford if he could get there that afternoon, the brigadier replied, "No, General, I think not. The enemy have had all night to entrench and reinforce. I had been pursuing a broken enemy and the situation [is] now very different."[81]

Lee was closely questioning Wofford because he was considering using McLaws' Division in the upcoming operation.[82] Probably unsatisfied with what he had just learned, Lee resumed his ride with Longstreet. The men probably moved in the direction of the Emmitsburg Road, where they were evidently rejoined by Hill, Heth, and the others. Lee reaffirmed to everyone present that Longstreet, with the entirety of First Corps and spearheaded by Pickett's brigades under the cover of massed artillery, would deliver the main blow, or *coup de main*. The effort would be supported by Hill's Third Corps—but had to be implemented while Ewell was still tying up the Federal attention on the Confederate far left. Longstreet immediately objected to the plan. The divisions of Hood and McLaws were not up to serving in the main thrust, he insisted, because of the casualties they had sustained the day before and because their use would unnecessarily expose the right flank of the army. Old Pete's protest made sense and Lee acquiesced.[83] Still, McLaws' men could be used for supporting purposes. By the time the conference ended, Lee had determined that the main effort would be delivered by a total of nine brigades, or about 12,000 to 15,000 men. Three of these brigades belonged to Pickett, and four were from Harry Heth's Division, which was under the command of Johnston Pettigrew. The last two brigades were composed of North Carolinians from Pender's Light Division. With Pender out of action, Lee tapped the fiery Isaac Trimble to lead them.[84]

Many students of the battle have come away believing that these nine brigades comprised the entire column of assault. A careful reading of reports and other writings, however, confirms that this is not so. In fact, Lee expected that other formations from First and Third Corps would also participate in supporting roles. At a minimum, at least three brigades from Richard Anderson's Division were placed under Longstreet's authority. This decision left only four Third Corps brigades—Perrin, Thomas, Posey, and Mahone—under Powell Hill's control. Still, Hill was expected to "afford General Longstreet further assistance, if required, and avail himself of any success that might be gained."[85] Because Lee's lengthy reconnaissance mission had included both Longstreet and Hill, it is reasonable to assume that both lieutenant generals received their instructions personally from the commanding general. As a result, it is unlikely that either officer was laboring under any misunderstanding of who had command of what troops or what was expected of them.

It is clear that on July 3 Lee was extending to Longstreet a level of operational command similar to what had existed in the army immediately following the Seven Days' battles. Effectively this meant that Longstreet had the authority over *every brigade of the entire First and Third Corps*. In other words, Longstreet had operational control over every Confederate infantry formation outside Ewell's Second Corps. Longstreet, of course, had demonstrated on any number of fields his ability to effectively direct large bodies of troops in battle. His sweeping counterattack at Second Manassas, the largest attack ever delivered by the Army of Northern Virginia, was but one example. Augmenting Longstreet's authority effectively reduced Powell Hill's responsibilities for the third day to that of division commander (he had but four brigades in a supporting role under his direct control). It also indicates that Lee was disappointed with Hill's performances on July 1 and July 2. Hill had proven he could handle a division in action, and so he would on July 3.[86]

In summary, Lee's tactical command structure for the attack on July 3 was similar to others that had proven successful in the past. Further, the plan was similar to the one that eventually succeeded at Gaines' Mill, where a demonstration along the entire front held the enemy in place while an assaulting column (Hood's) pierced the enemy line at a decisive point. On July 3, Lee believed that point was in the vicinity of the umbrella clump of trees—the hinge of Meade's two wings. The difficult victory at Gaines' Mill had come only after several disjointed attacks. At Gettysburg, Lee was doing everything he could to guarantee that his army would act in concert—which was why he gave Longstreet sweeping authority over so much of the army. He fully expected Longstreet to employ the troops placed at his disposal, either to demonstrate to pin the enemy in place, as part of the main assaulting effort, or in a supporting or second wave. The *coup de main* could only be successful if supports appeared in a timely manner and the troops selected to demonstrate were vigorously occupying the enemy's attention. All of this would be preceded by a massive bombardment designed to disrupt the one enemy combat arm that Lee feared the most—the Federal artillery. It is safe to assert that based upon the previous year of experience, Lee fully believed that if his infantry reached the Federal lines largely intact, his men would crack the enemy's front just as they had done on July 2.

According to Longstreet, during this combined reconnaissance-conference he told Lee he had substantial misgivings about attacking the center of Meade's army on Cemetery Ridge.[87] Captain James Risque Hutter, Company H, 11th Virginia, James Kemper's Brigade, Pickett's Division, remembered something similar. Lee, Longstreet, Pickett, and others stopped their horses under a large apple tree where Hutter and Chaplain John C. Granberry were enjoying its shade. Hutter "remember[ed] catching portions of the conversation; Gen. Longstreet saying his command would do what anybody of men on earth dared do, but no troops could dislodge the enemy from their strong position."[88] Lee, however, was undeterred. The main assault would be delivered against the broad *hinge* of the two heavy reinforced wings of Meade's army, rather than against his true center, where Meade's main strength had been concentrated. The sounds of Ewell's battle on Culp's Hill continued echoing across the landscape, no doubt reminding Lee that his plan was to have been implemented early that morning.[89] Now Ewell's men were dying and the rest of the army was unable to help them. The day's stakes were as high as they could be, and all of this could only have deepened Lee's resolve to force the battle to a favorable resolution as soon as possible.

And Pickett himself probably influenced (or at least confirmed) Lee's decision to attack. According to Captain Hutter,

> Pickett said he thought his division could drive them from his front & my recollection is that Gen. Lee on pressing Gen. Longstreet said, 'Ask the men if they can dislodge them.' One or two companies of the 11th, probably more, and I presume same numbers from other regiments were moved up to the crest of the [swell along the Emmitsburg Road], and the men were asked if they would drive the enemy from his works. I walked up with Capt. Thos. Horton when he moved his Co. B up. I was anxious to hear what the men would say. They would clasp each other by the hand and say, 'boys many a one of us will bite the dust here today but we will say to Gen. Lee if he wants them driven out, we will do it.'[90]

These words from his Virginians no doubt cheered Lee, who moved the generals' conference to another location. Exactly what Lee and Longstreet discussed immediately thereafter is unclear. In all likelihood the commanding general explained to Longstreet why Meade's position near the clump of trees was vulnerable, and Old Pete illustrated why, in his opinion, it was not. Certainly they discussed particulars of the attack. Perhaps Lee drew on his extensive knowledge of Napoleonic warfare and provided examples of how the Corsican general had triumphed on numerous battlefields with direct assaults when turning maneuvers (like the one Longstreet had been espousing) were deemed unpracticable.[91]

And so it was finalized. Lee envisioned that his plan of battle would, generally speaking, unfold along these lines: while Ewell engaged the enemy on the left flank around Culp's Hill and tied down Federal troops and Meade's attention, the rest of the Confederate line would press forward, either in the leading wave or as support for the main attack effort. Therefore, approximately 12,000 to 15,000 men would comprise the spearhead of the assault column, and would be supported by other First and Third Corps units as directed by Longstreet. Powell Hill with four brigades was instructed by General Lee to "afford General Longstreet further assistance, if required, and avail himself of any success that might be gained."[92] So too could any unengaged troops from Second Corps. Accordingly, some 25,000, and perhaps closer to 30,000 men, would be available to press the Federal lines. This supreme effort to dislodge Meade and win the battle would be preceded by a massed and prolonged artillery bombardment—"*a feu d'enfer*" or "Hell's Fire," as Napoleon had coined the phrase.[93] Lee believed concentrating his strength at the correct place through a well-coordinated use of his artillery (and later, infantry) would silence or drive away opposing enemy guns and break apart and demoralize Federal infantry on Cemetery Ridge. This was always a primary aim of the Great Captains of the past, and military history was not without precedents for this coordinated effort. Lee, of course, would have been aware of them.[94]

Many writers fail to appreciate how Lee's experience at Gaines' Mill, coupled with his complete understanding and intimate knowledge of Napoleon's victory at Wagram (1809) and the Duke of Marlborough's at Blenheim (1704) probably shaped his assault plans for July 3. The attack against Cemetery Ridge was Gaines' Mill on a larger scale, similar to Napoleon's formula for victory during the second day of fighting at Wagram, and comparable in concept to Marlborough's plan at Blenheim. Indeed, Lee's deep and abiding interest in the battles of the Great Captains was never more apparent than it was on July 3, 1863. Lee, however, wanted to do more than simply copy Napoleon's epic 1809 battle plan, which used both artillery and infantry to score a victory. Lee planned to utilize and maximize all three of his combat arms (artillery, infantry, and cavalry) in order to gain a decisive success. This is why Lee sent Stuart and his cavalry on a sweeping end run around Ewell's left flank with orders to threaten the Federal rear and act as the exploitation force he did not have in place at Gaines' Mill, and which Napoleon had lacked at the end of the second day at Wagram.[95]

Moreover, since Lee was intimate with the classic battles of history, he would have recalled Marlborough's Blenheim masterpiece, where movements against the French flanks caused Tallard to weaken his own center, which Marlborough struck and split apart. The result was a complete victory. Whether Lee actually walked through these mental exercise in military history on the morning of July 3 will never be known for sure. But we do know that he was well versed on the subject, and thus the question of how Napoleon or another Great Captain of history would have acted had he been standing on Seminary Ridge that morning could not have been far from his thoughts.

* * *

Longstreet began passing on his orders to prepare for the assault. Shortly after "General Lee came around," Alexander received word "that we were to assault Cemetery Hill [Ridge]."[96] His orders, as Alexander remembered them, was "first, to give the enemy the most effective cannonade possible. It was not meant simply to make a noise, but to try & cripple him—to tear him limbless, as it were, if possible." This was exactly what "*a feu d'enfer*" implied. Alexander recalled that Longstreet specifically instructed him to "'drive off the enemy or greatly demoralize him.' When the artillery had accomplished that, the infantry column of attack was to charge. And then, further, I was to 'advance such artillery as you can use in aiding the attack.'"[97] Lee not only wanted to cripple the Federal artillery prior to the infantry attack, but also wanted his guns to move forward and support the charging Southern foot soldiers.

Although Colonel James B. Walton was the ranking artillery officer of First Corps, Longstreet entrusted Alexander with the important task of supervising the placement and coordinating the fire of First Corps' ordnance.[98] According to Longstreet, Alexander was . . .

> an officer of unusual promptness, sagacity, and intelligence, and being more familiar with the ground to be occupied by the artillery, was directed to see that the batteries were posted to the best advantage . . . Colonel Alexander's special service, after seeing that the batteries were most advantageously posted, was to see that field artillery was ready to move with General Pickett's assault, and to give me the benefit of his judgment as to the moment the effect of the artillery combat would justify the assault.[99]

Alexander fully appreciated the daunting responsibility tossed in his direction and set out to arrange his pieces accordingly. Eight guns of Henry's Battalion were "left on our extreme right to cover our flank, and the remaining 75 were posted in an irregular line about 1,300 yards long, beginning in the Peach Orchard and ending near the northeast corner of the Spangler wood." As to the artillery of Hill's corps, continued Alexander, "Col. Walker, their chief, told me that he had 63 in action."[100] The Georgia gunner was to direct the massed artillery fire onto the Federals positioned in and around the Copse of Trees and the Angle—two landmarks below Cemetery Hill marking what Lee believed was the hinge of Meade's line. As it developed, Alexander was later instructed by Longstreet to keep a careful watch on the effectiveness of the Confederate artillery fire, and when he judged that the

Federal guns along this portion of Cemetery Ridge had been silenced or driven off, send word to Pickett for the infantry attack to commence.[101] This plan varied significantly from how Southern guns had traditionally operated since the Battle of Sharpsburg. In the past, Confederate metal was generally thrown in the direction of infantry. On July 3, however, Lee was making a deliberate attempt to concentrate fire against one particular point, and Federal ordnance in particular. Thus Lee set in motion a plan he "believed, would enable [his guns] to silence those of the enemy."[102]

Alexander began preparing for the bombardment about 9:00 a.m.[103] His work included rearranging the guns within each battalion based upon the gun's range to the target selected, as well as moving up and placing Dearing's four batteries (18 guns) along the Emmitsburg Road swell immediately west of the Klingle and Rogers farms. This position was only about 800 to 900 yards away from the Copse of Trees. Dearing's Battalion was one of the most powerful in the army. More than 400 officers and gunners served a dozen 12-pounder Napoleons, one 3-inch Ordnance rifle, three 10-pounder Parrotts, and two hard-hitting 20-pounder Parrotts.[104] The fact that the Federals allowed the Southerners to go about their business unmolested surprised Alexander. We were fully "exposed to their guns," he later wrote, "& getting ready at our leisure, & they let us do it." The enemy, Alexander concluded, "had felt the strain of the last two days, but for all that they ought to have forced our hand."[105]

The Confederate artillerists were instructed to carefully select their targets. Alexander remembered that the gunners singled out specific enemy pieces for punishment until "every gunner had his target selected."[106] According to Dearing,

Edward Porter Alexander
(1835-1910)

He was arguably the most capable Confederate artillery officer serving in the Army of Northern Virginia at Gettysburg. E. Porter Alexander's extensive writings on the battle are among the most cited accounts by any participant in Lee's army.

Library of Congress

his men targeted "the batteries immediately in my front, and which occupied the heights charged by Pickett's division."[107] In accordance with Colonel Long's promise to suppress the Federal battery on Little Round Top, "at least one two-gun section of Garden's Battery," probably two 12-pounder Napoleons, "stationed south of the Peach Orchard, was assigned to fire on the guns on Little Round Top."[108] Two 12-pounder howitzers belonging to Carlton's Georgia Troup County Light Artillery were also ordered to concentrate their efforts against the rocky heights.[109] In focusing their efforts on the area surrounding the umbrella-shaped copse of timber to be attacked by the infantry, the Confederates virtually ignored the line of 39 Federal guns along middle-to-lower Cemetery Ridge under the command of Major Freeman McGilvery.[110] The oversight would prove costly.

While preparing his gun line, Alexander was paid a visit by General Pendleton. The general offered Alexander an ad hoc group of 12-pounder howitzers. Colonel R. Lindsay Walker, Third Corps' chief of artillery, he said, "had no special use as their range was too short" to reach the Federals on Cemetery Ridge from the positions then occupied. Alexander "jumped at the idea." Major Charles Richardson of Colonel John J. Garnett's battalion was already in command of the guns, and Alexander ordered him to move the howitzers to a sheltered position from which Alexander "intended not to let them fire a shot in the preliminary cannonade, & to keep them under cover & out of view, so that with fresh men, & uninjured horses, & full chests of ammunition, these [8] light howitzers might follow Pickett's infantry in the charge."[111]

Confederate preparations for the upcoming artillery bombardment were also underway in both Second and Third Corps. The orders for these artillery battalions was to "fire, in conjunction with a large number of guns on their right, on a salient part of the enemy's line prior to the charge of infantry," or to have "their fires directed on the batteries planted on Cemetery Hill," or to attract Federal attention "in order to divert their fire from our infantry advancing from the right." The two long-ranged 12-pounder Whitworth guns belonging to Hardaway's Alabama Artillery under the command of Captain William B. Hurt were repositioned from Seminary Ridge to Oak Hill, from which they could enfilade the Federal line without fear of being subjected to any counter battery fire whatsoever.[112]

Some 135 or more pieces were thus scheduled to participate in the bombardment preceding the infantry attack.[113] In order to correctly ascertain the effect of the pieces spread along a line approximately two miles long, and to avoid wasting ammunition (which was not in abundant supply), battery personnel were ordered by Pendleton (and others) to fire with deliberation and make every shot count.[114]

Ewell's Flank Plays Out

While Alexander and others continued their preparations for the artillery bombardment and infantry assault, another important issue was already being decided on the far left end of the Confederate line. As we know, before the soldiers of Ed Johnson's Division could organize their advance to the summit of Culp's Hill and beyond to the Baltimore Pike, Federal artillery opened on them in the pre-dawn darkness with a 15-minute cannonade. The guns served as a prelude to an infantry assault whose goal, as defined by General Henry Slocum, was "to drive them out at daylight."[115] The origins of this spoiling attack came about through the collective decision made by Meade and his corps commanders to stay and fight on July 3. Deciding to commit the Federal troops in this manner was a brave, but intelligent, decision. The Army of the Potomac had suffered more than 20,000 casualties in two days, three of its corps had been shattered, and many brigades from other corps were already well used up. Water was in short supply. Alpheus S. Williams, who was in temporary command of Twelfth Corps, recalled that Meade "had but one single day's rations for the army. Many corps had not even one. We had outrun our supplies, and as all the railroad line which came near us were broken, there were no depots within reach." Still, recalled Williams, "it was thought that what with beef cattle and flour, which possibly could be got together, we could eke out a few half-fed days."[116]

With the resolution to stay at Gettysburg, the Federal high command decided to eliminate the Confederate threat to the Baltimore Pike. Because of the rocks, trees, and trenches on Culp's Hill, the opening Federal cannonade caused but few casualties. With the opening of the battle Johnson's reinforced Confederates (two of Rodes' brigades and one of Early's had joined him earlier that morning) surged forward and the fighting became general up and down the line. The confused and desperate engagement, fought one foot at a time, lasted for some six hours. During this time the Federals launched attacks of their own. Federal regiments from the First Division, Twelfth Corps splashed across the marshy ground and small stream flowing from Spangler's Spring and struck the left front and flank of Johnson's Confederates. Two other Federal brigades belonging to the Second Division, Twelfth Corps, "moved forward to recapture the line of breastworks which had been taken the night previous."[117] Brigadier General John W. Geary, commanding the Second Division, recalled that "this attack was most furious, but was stubbornly met." According to General Williams, "the defense of the Rebs on our right (opposite the 1st Division) was quite impregnable for assault." To the ready-and-waiting Southerners, "it soon became apparent from the advance of the enemy that his purpose was to turn our left flank." The Yankees, Johnson later recalled, were thrown back "with great slaughter."[118]

Some of Johnson's soldiers may have caught a glimpse, once the sun broke over the horizon, of the all-important Baltimore Pike. The sight, claims historian Glenn Tucker, "inspired Johnson to redoubled efforts."[119] Whether such a sight motivated Johnson or not is unknown, but we do know that he launched at least two more attacks. The thrusts were made "in a most gallant manner," and although Junius Daniel's Brigade "succeeded in inflicting heavy loss upon" the Federals, both attempts failed. "The enemy," explained Ed "Allegheny" Johnson, "were too securely intrenched and in too great numbers to be dislodged."[120] The fighting, much of which took place within 150 yards or less of the Federal line, was largely a musketry fight, especially as far as the Confederates were concerned. Johnson, of course, could not count on any artillery support since Southern guns could not fire without hitting their own infantry. The Federal guns incessantly belched throughout. Colonel Wainwright recalled that "such '*a feu d'enfer*,' I never heard; there was not a time during the whole four hours when there was a let-up long enough for one to draw a breath." The heavy volume wasted "at least two-thirds of this ammunition" observed Wainwright. "Such a vast expenditure speaks badly for the pluck of the men, and cannot ever be necessary with good troops; most certainly not on the part of an attacking force."[121]

One of the Federals efforts to turn Johnson's left flank was across the low ground near Spangler's Spring, where the Yankees ran into "Extra Billy" Smith's Brigade of Early's Division. These 800 Virginians—who had not yet been engaged in the battle—were situated behind a wall on advantageous ground above the spring in order to hold the Confederate left. In the opinion of Federal brigade commander Colonel Silas Colgrove, who was ordered to make the attempt to dislodge Smith's Confederates, the counterattack was doomed "to destruction." He was right. Within minutes Colgrove's outfit was cut to shreds as "it became evident to me that scarcely a man could live to gain the position of the enemy."[122]

And by 11:00 a.m. it was over. The Confederate attempt to take Culp's Hill, turn the enemy right, and draw off Federal attention and reinforcements from the area of the main attack effort, had played itself out. Every yard of trench line was firmly in Federal hands and Johnson's brigades, including the famous Stonewall Brigade, had been decisively repulsed. They withdrew and consolidated near Rock Creek.[123] Johnson's withdrawal before noon ended the infantry fighting on Ewell's front at Gettysburg. The entire Culp's Hill episode was a tragic one. It was not until half an hour *after* the attacks began that Ewell "received notice that Longstreet would not attack until 10 o'clock"—and even that assessment was wildly overly optimistic.[124] By then, however, Ewell was powerless to end the fighting on Culp's Hill because the Federals were calling the shots. The disjointed effort was far from what General Lee had wanted or ordered.

Lee Modifies his Plan of Attack

Once the action on Ewell's front died down, General Lee was faced with his most crucial command decision at Gettysburg, and perhaps one of the most important since he had taken the reins of the South's principal army. Meade's successful spoiling attack had knocked Johnson's brigades off Culp's Hill and compromised Lee's original plan. Except for some artillery units, Ewell would not be able to assist Longstreet's assault. The question Lee now had to face was whether the assault should still be delivered against Cemetery Ridge without a simultaneous threat of attack or pressure against Meade's right flank. We don't know exactly what thought process Lee employed to reach the decision that the attack could and should still go forward. Stuart's cavalry was either in position or moving toward the Federal rear as ordered, since no word to the contrary had been received, so that segment of his plan was still intact. So, too, was the most important part of his strategy—the massive artillery bombardment. Lee believed his unprecedented number of tubes, carefully positioned and properly coordinated with his infantry, would provide the support his men needed to get them onto Cemetery Ridge and break open Meade's line.

Perhaps two other factors convinced him to press ahead with the attack: the need for a victory and his peerless infantry. Lee knew it was imperative to come away with a major success on Yankee soil—regardless of the odds against him. When was there going to be a better chance for his troops to triumph north of the Mason-Dixon line? The longer the war dragged on the stronger the North became. Federal armies would only become more proficient at their task, and more materiel would be deployed against the South. Lee had always known the Confederacy could not win a war of attrition; the agrarian-based nation simply lacked the resources for an extended conflict. Abandoning the fight now, with a victorious army and after coming so close to a decisive victory, was tantamount to admitting overall defeat for the South. In addition, Lee's plan of battle demonstrated his faith in his infantry to carry the day. And that is why Lee extended to Longstreet the authority to utilize virtually all the troops stationed on the right side of Gettysburg. Even without Ewell, he must have reasoned, his infantry and artillery could carry the day.

We don't know how much thought Lee gave after Ewell's rebuff to the conservative play of calling off the attack and either assuming a defensive stand or withdrawing west to the South Mountain range. He was all too aware that if he took the defensive he could not keep his army in position for more than another day or two because of a lack of food, forage, and water. Withdrawing west would be viewed as a defeat and trumpeted around the world as such, which in turn would hearten the Federals and dampen spirits in the South. More than anyone else Lee knew that once the armies became locked in combat on July 1, the battle would have to continue until a resolution was obtained; one army or the other would leave against its will. Lee knew Meade's logistical capabilities far exceeded his own. Time, too, was his enemy since Meade's army would only grow in strength while Richmond was unwilling or unable to send Lee any more troops. In his mind, leaving the field without suffering defeat was not an option. Robert E. Lee had no intention of handing his adversary a victory in that manner—Meade had, after all, overreacted to the July 2 echelon attack and escaped defeat only because of the failure of a handful of Lee's subordinates. Perhaps Lee recalled his Mexican War experiences and remembered how Winfield Scott had defied the so-called conventional wisdom in his ultimately victorious campaign to capture Mexico City. Lee knew, and indeed had always known, that short of politics coming into play, the South would never win its war for independence with the safe play anymore than the American colonists could have beaten England by adopting a similar strategy. He might not have liked his choices, but he had to take risks to win.

Lee must have believed that an attack was a calculated risk that *had* to be taken. While this might be considered what we today would call a "Hobson's choice"—a choice apparently based upon freewill when in fact there existed no *realistic* alternative—it was indeed the only viable one open to the Confederate commander if there was going to be *any* chance for victory. In the opinion of historian Theodore Ayrault Dodge, Lee had no choice on July 3 but to attack where he did. "There was no resource for him but to break our centre," Dodge wrote.[125]

And that is what Lee proposed to do.

Final Preparations

Although none of the participants knew it at the time, the bombardment and assault about to get underway would go down as the most famous infantry charge in American military history. The attack has been popularized as "Pickett's Charge," although Pickett commanded less than half the attacking force and only three of the nine spearheading brigades. Whatever it is called, the maneuver has been the subject of extensive and exhaustive writings. Several excellent works detail this epic event. As such, only a brief recounting of the attack's major points are warranted in this study.[126]

* * *

Ed "Allegheny" Johnson's men were still struggling for possession of Culp's Hill when a separate and much smaller confrontation developed south of Gettysburg in and around the Bliss Farm and orchard. The fight was directly in the path over which the left wing of Longstreet's attack would march. Confederate sharpshooters belonging to Anderson's Division had been taking advantage of the cover of the Bliss barn and house to pick off Federal artillerists on Cemetery Ridge. The Federals

One of the most famous generals of the war, George Pickett graduated dead last in his West Point Class of 1846. Still, he displayed great bravery in the storming of Chapultepec Castle during the Mexican War and solid leadership qualities at the head of a brigade early in the war. When he was preparing his brigades for their charge on July 3, 1863, Pickett was told that supporting troops would be close behind to help him solidify his breakthrough on Cemetery Ridge. His friend and superior, James Longstreet, did not think the attack would succeed; Pickett viewed it as a grand opportunity for acquiring everlasting glory. Both men were right. *Library of Congress*

George Edward Pickett
(1825-1875)

countered by sending forward skirmishers to neutralize these bothersome Confederates. Two entire regiments were fed into the action in stages—the 12th New Jersey at about 8:30 a.m., followed by the 14th Connecticut two hours later—and by 11:00 a.m., about the time Johnson was finally driven off Culp's Hill, the Federals had captured the Bliss complex.[127] Once in this exposed position, however, they discovered they had stuck their head into a hornets' nest. The fire from swarms of Confederate skirmishers was augmented by an impromptu artillery barrage from guns belonging to Hill's Third Corps. Once these pieces opened, neither Powell Hill nor Colonel Walker, the ranking artillery officer in Third Corps, attempted to stop it. The Southern batteries firing along Seminary Ridge prompted Federal artillery crews along Cemetery Ridge to respond, until "at least 100 guns, on the two sides, got into a duel." The wise Alexander refused to allow his crews along First Corps' front to join in the affair. In his view there was nothing to be gained by expending "that much ammunition prematurely" against skirmishers. The exchange continued for "nearly a half hour" and consequently "made a great deal of noise while it lasted, & many writers have imagined it to have been a part of the cannonade to prepare the way for Pickett." The Federal skirmishers finally gave up and pulled back to Cemetery Ridge, but only after torching the Bliss buildings to deprive Confederate sharpshooters of their cover.[128]

As the fighting around the Bliss Farm died down, final preparations were being completed for the grand assault. George Pickett had already brought up his three brigadier generals and their brigades from Marsh Creek to Spangler's Woods, where they arrived around 9:00 a.m. The dark-haired and affable Pickett was one of the most popular officers in First Corps and one of Longstreet's favorites. He was not, however, one of his best. Pickett graduated last in his class in 1846 from West Point. Something of a dandy—he often carried a riding crop, always polished his boots, and enjoyed well-tailored uniforms—Pickett proved he was a brave soldier by storming the parapet at Chapultapec during the Mexican War, where he took a flag from the wounded James Longstreet and unfurled the banner over the castle. His service as a Confederate brigadier was not conspicuous, but his return to the army after a light wound was greeted with a promotion to major general. If he thanked anyone for the pay raise it was Longstreet, who had lobbied long and hard on Pickett's behalf. Unfortunately, Pickett had not yet enjoyed an opportunity to prove his worth as a division commander. His men were not seriously engaged at Fredericksburg, and he missed Chancellorsville while participating in the Suffolk expedition. According to Moxley Sorrel, Longstreet always looked after Pickett and made sure he understood his orders, perhaps because Old Pete knew George was not as reliable as he had hoped he would be.[129]

After waiting under the cover of the trees for nearly two and one-half hours, the 5,725 Virginia infantrymen deployed into lines of battle and advanced to their jump off points. The first of Pickett's three brigades was led by James Lawson Kemper, a full-bearded and fiery leader who had proven himself on several fields. Kemper's Brigade, five regiments with an effective combat force of approximately 1,775, was posted on the right of the division and in the open about 200 yards west of the Klingle House.[130] Even though Kemper's regiments were no longer under the concealment of woods, they were shielded from direct fire from most of the Federal guns because of the swell of the Emmitsburg Road.

Pickett's second brigade was led by Richard Brooke Garnett. The brave soldier had a cloud hanging over his head because of a controversy with Stonewall Jackson over his handling of a brigade at Kernstown. Lee placed him at the head of Pickett's Brigade for the Maryland Campaign (Pickett was wounded), and he did well enough to retain command of the unit when Pickett was elevated to divisional command. Garnett's five regiments of about 1,800 men also advanced out of the shade of Spangler's Woods and formed up in the low ground about 80 to 100 yards west of the Henry Spangler Farm buildings astride the lane leading from the Emmitsburg Road to the farm. As a result, Garnett's regiments were about 200 yards west of the portion of Dearing's Battalion of artillery nearest to the Rogers' farmhouse fronting the Emmitsburg Road.[131]

To the left and rear of Garnett's regiments was the largest brigade under Pickett's orders that day. Brave and tireless like Garnett, the blunt and crusty Lewis Addison Armistead actually had very little experience at the head of a brigade. He had led his men well (and into a slaughter) at Malvern Hill, but circumstances thereafter had conspired to keep him and his men out of combat. His five regiments

Richard Brooke Garnett (1817-1863)

Lewis Addison Armistead
(1817-1863)

James Lawson Kemper (1823-1895)

numbered about 2,150 officers and men. Much of his command remained in the trees along the eastern boundary of Spangler's Woods.[132]

As the officers and men of Pickett's command readied themselves for their upcoming trial by fire, many in the division seemed to suddenly grasp the responsibility resting on their shoulders. According to the ubiquitous Porter Alexander, he rode to see Pickett before the artillery bombardment began and found him "in excellent spirits . . . entirely sanguine of success in the charge, and was only congratulating himself on the opportunity."[133] Lieutenant Colonel Rawley W. Martin of the 53rd Virginia, Armistead's Brigade, felt the same way. "The *esprit de corps* could not have been better; the men were in good physical condition, self reliant and determined," Martin wrote, summing up the enthusiasm the Virginians. "They felt the gravity of the situation, for they knew well the mettle of the foe in their front; they were serious and resolute . . . I believe the general sentiment of the division was that they would succeed in driving the Federal line from what was their objective point."[134] Another member of Armistead's Brigade, James F. Crocker, the adjutant of the 9th Virginia, eloquently summed up the coming day's battle as viewed by many Southerners:

> From the teamsters to the general in chief it was known that the battle was yet undecided—that the fierce combat was to be renewed. All knew that victory won or defeat suffered, was to be at a fearful cost—that the best blood of the land was to flow copiously as a priceless oblation to the god of battle. The intelligent soldiers of the South knew and profoundly felt that the hours were potential—that on them possibly hung the success of their cause—the peace and independence of the Confederacy . . . With this end in view, all felt that victory was to be won at any cost. All were willing to die, if only their country could thereby triumph.[135]

The sentiment running through the army that one more victory could result in a favorable resolution of the war was also echoed by Eppa Hunton, colonel of the 8th Virginia in Garnett's Brigade. "All appreciated the danger and felt it was probably the last charge to most of them," wrote Hunton. "All seemed willing to die to achieve a victory there, which it was believed would be the crowning victory and the end of the war."[136] "It had been known for hours that we were to assail the enemy's lines in front," wrote a confident Captain John Holmes Smith, Company G, 11th Virginia. "We fully expected to take them."[137]

To the left and rear of the Virginians formed the six other brigades of Third Corps slated to take part in the main assault. Four of these brigades were from Harry Heth's Division. Because of the lingering effects of his July 1 wound, however, Heth's brigades were under the command of the division's senior brigadier, Johnston Pettigrew. The men formed up for the attack behind the line of Third Corps guns in one long line two ranks deep. Their order, from north to south (left to right) was as follows: Brockenbrough-Davis-Pettigrew-Archer. The division numbered perhaps 4,000 men. Two days earlier, the four brigades Heth led into action west of Gettysburg were under the leadership of James Archer, Johnston Pettigrew, Joe Davis, and John Brockenbrough. By July 3, Joe Davis was the only brigadier available to take his regiments into the field. Archer had been captured and was replaced by Colonel Birkett D. Fry; Pettigrew had replaced Heth, and was in turn replaced by Colonel James Keith Marshall; Brockenbrough was absent, and his men were led by Colonel Robert Murphy Mayo of the 47th Virginia. It is not an exaggeration to say the outfit was a wreck and had no business taking part in an offensive. Why it was involved and who determined it would participate is still not clear. Other brigades were readily at hand, including Perrin, Posey, Thomas, and Mahone. And yet none were used in any capacity.[138]

Support for Pettigrew's wounded division was provided by a pair of North Carolina brigades from Pender's Light Division. Why these brigades were selected for such an important mission is also a mystery. The first was Alfred Scales', which had been torn apart on July 1. Scales had been severely wounded and his brigade was under the command of Colonel William Lee Joshua Lowrance. The other was James Lane's outfit. Pender's wound the day before lifted Lane into his position. That vertical move, in turn, placed Lane's brigade in the hands of its senior colonel, Clarke M. Avery. According to Lane, he was directed to align his men "in rear of the right of Heth's [Pettigrew's] command." As soon as Lane marched his men into place he was relieved of divisional command and resumed control of his brigade. At the last minute a complete stranger in the form of Major General Isaac Trimble was selected to lead the North Carolina brigades into action. Unfortunately, no one seems to have realized two serious problems. First, the left of Pettigrew's (Heth's) line extended well beyond Trimble's supporting brigades, where it dangled in the air without support behind it. Second, the weakest brigade in the entire army (Brockenbrough's) anchored that exposed flank.[139]

By all accounts it was after high noon before all the arrangements for the infantry attack had been completed and all the guns designated to participate in the bombardment were in place. The infantry spearhead was in two distinct columns (Pickett's to the south and Pettigrew and Trimble further north) separated by many hundreds of yards. Whether anyone spoke in advance of how to coordinate the them is unknown. Sometime around 1:00 p.m. two guns of the Washington Artillery positioned in the Peach Orchard broke the silence and fired the signal shots for the remainder of the Confederate artillery to open fire.[140]

The Bombardment

The long line of Confederate guns erupted just as Brigadier General Henry J. Hunt, the outstanding chief of artillery of the Army of the Potomac, was finishing his inspection tour at Little Round Top. From this vantage point, Hunt witnessed:

> a furious cannonade [that] opened on our front with the heaviest artillery fire I have ever known. . . The air was filled with projectiles there being scarcely an instant but that several were seen bursting at once. No irregularity of ground offered much protection, and the plain in rear of the line of battle was soon swept of everything moveable.[141]

From his observation point along the line of his guns, Alexander "felt encouraged to believe that [the Federals] had felt very severe punishment, & that my fire had been generally well aimed & as effective as could be hoped."[142] Dearing, whose guns were just off the Emmitsburg Road and therefore the closest batteries to the Federal lines, reported the "firing on the part of my battalion was very good, and most of the shell and shrapnel burst well."[143] Unfortunately for Alexander and other Confederate gunners that day, the smoke from their guns quickly obscured their view. What they did not see was that many of their shells were passing over their intended targets along the crest of Cemetery Ridge and landing somewhere behind the main line, churning up the rear areas and scattering men and animals hither and yon.

The Federals opened a return fire, but because of what Hunt described as "our restricted position," the Yankees could not "bring more than eighty [guns] to reply effectively."[144] Major McGilvery, who commanded a line of 39 guns that had somehow avoided becoming a prime target of the Confederate bombardment, noticed from his position along middle-to-lower Cemetery Ridge that the Southern fire seemed to be "very rapid and inaccurate, most of the projectiles passing from 20 to 100 feet over our [front] lines."[145]

Lee's guns may have been overshooting McGilvery and other parts of the line, but many Federal batteries higher up Cemetery Ridge felt the full weight of Confederate iron. "Our infantry was still unshaken, and in all the cannonade suffered very little," wrote Lieutenant Frank A. Haskell, an aide-de-camp on Gibbon's staff. "The batteries had been handled much more severely [and] a great number of horses had been killed, in some batteries more than half of all." Riding down the line with General Gibbon, Haskell noted the damage wrought by the concentrated Southern gunfire:

> Guns had been dismounted. A great number of caissons, limbers and carriages had been destroyed, and usually from ten to twenty-five men at each battery had been struck, at least along part of the crest. Altogether the fire of the enemy had injured us much, both in the modes that I have stated, and also by exhausting our ammunition and fouling our guns, so as to render our batteries unfit for further immediate use.[146]

The unbroken discharges of more than 200 cannon on both sides remembered Colonel Fry of the 13th Alabama, "[was] the most terrible of the war. In it my command suffered a considerable loss."[147] George Clark in Wilcox's Brigade agreed. The cannonade, he wrote, was "terrific beyond description. Men could be seen, especially among the artillery, bleeding at both ears from concussion, and the wreck of matter and the crush of worlds seemed to be upon us."[148]

Amidst the hail of shot and shell, artillery crews on both sides battled furiously. Federal gunners were also firing too high. Their misplaced rounds, however, often landed in the vicinity of Lee's waiting infantry. Kemper's men, positioned in low ground on a line directly west of the Klingle House and Dearing's Battalion, were probably hit the hardest. Dearing's guns were the closest pieces to the Federal line and attracted the attention of enemy gunners. Thus almost every errant round dropped on or near one of Kemper's infantrymen. Colonel Waller Tazewell Patton, commander of Kemper's 7th Virginia and the great-uncle of Lieutenant General George S. Patton, Jr. of World War II fame, was appalled that his men had to sit passively by under a hot sun and be struck down by an enemy against which they could not strike back. The shells, he noticed, were hitting his men more often than Dearing's guns. Patton sought out Colonel Joseph C. Mayo of the 3rd Virginia, deployed on his left, and suggested that the infantry line be moved closer to the guns to better shelter his men. Mayo remembered that Patton called his "attention to the gallant bearing of Major Dearing, as he galloped, flag in hand, from gun to gun of his battalion and suggested that it would be safer for us to close up on the artillery." Mayo wrote long after the war that he told Patton that "he must not think of moving without orders."[149] Dearing's flag waving from the back of his large white stallion also impressed Captain Robert M. Stribling, the commander of the Fauquier Artillery. Dearing, he wrote, followed "by his staff and courier waving the battle flag rode from right to left of the battalion, backward and forward, decidedly the most conspicuous figures" along the front.[150]

The Federal artillery rounds had widely varying effects on the Confederate infantry. "Fortunately the Federal gunners [sent] most of the missiles screaming beyond us," recalled Private Randolph Shotwell of Company H, 8th Virginia, Garnett's Brigade.[151] Colonel Hunton confirmed Shotwell's observation. "When I took position behind the artillery on July 3, 1863, preparatory to the charge," Hunton explained, "I had 205 men in line. Five were killed in the greatest artillery duel the

"Old Pete"

James Longstreet sits on Hero amongst James Dearing's artillery battalion watching the progress of the cannonade preceding Pickett's attack. Dearing's were the closest pieces to the Federal lines, positioned immediately west of the Emmitsburg Road stretching from near the Daniel Klingle Farm to the vicinity of Peter Rogers' property. *Courtesy Gallon Historical Art, Gettysburg, Pennsylvania*

world ever saw. About 200 of these brave men made the charge."[152] Armistead's men, aligned behind Garnett's—exactly where behind Garnett is still of some debate—suffered even fewer casualties, largely because many were hidden in Spangler's Woods. The shells screamed through the woods, shaving limbs from the trees and showering the men below with debris. One missile struck a small hickory tree and ricocheted, severely wounding one soldier and narrowly missing General Armistead. According to Captain Farinholt of Company E, 53rd Virginia, several members of his company began shuffling their feet, as if to move a few feet in order to find a better place to wait out the bombardment. Armistead would have none of it, remembered the captain. When he saw the movement he called a halt to it, coolly reassuring the anxious soldiers, "Lie still boys, there is no safe place here."[153]

There is little agreement on how long the bombardment lasted. Porter Alexander, whom Longstreet had saddled with the responsibility of deciding when the artillery fire had had its desired effect—and thus when the infantry attack should commence—recalled that it was "exactly" 25 minutes into the bombardment when he scribbled a note and sent it to Pickett: "If you are coming at all you must come at once, or I cannot give you proper support, but the enemy's fire has not slackened at all. At least 18 guns are still firing from the cemetery itself."[154] According to Alexander:

> I began to notice signs of some of the enemy's guns ceasing to fire. At first I thought it only crippled guns; but soon, with my large glass, I discovered entire batteries limbering up & leaving their positions. Now it was a very ordinary thing with us to withdraw our guns from purely artillery duels, & save up every thing for their infantry. But the Federals had never done anything of that sort before, & I did not believe they were doing it now. Knowing what a large reserve force they always kept, I supposed that they were only relieving exhausted batteries with fresh ones, as I had relieved the Washington Art. at Marye's [Heights at Fredericksburg].[155]

The Confederate artillery fire continued for several more minutes while Alexander studied intently the activity along the enemy lines. "Some [Federal] batteries still kept up their fire, but there was not a single fresh gun replacing any that had withdrawn." Knowing "that nothing but a desperate infantry fight could ever decide the day," and believing "that we stood a good chance for the day," Alexander sent three messengers to Pickett bearing either written or verbal instructions at the 35 minute mark into the bombardment—"ten minutes after the first note [stating] 'For God's sake come quick. The 18 guns are gone. Come quick or I can't support you.'"[156]

From his position about 800 yards from the Copse of Trees, Dearing saw something similar. "Three caissons were seen by myself to blow up, and I saw several batteries of the enemy leave the field," he wrote. "At one time, just before General Pickett's division advanced, the batteries of the enemy in our front had

"Hancock's Ride"

Amidst the explosions and chaos of the incoming artillery rounds on July 3, Major General Winfield Scott Hancock rode along his lines on Cemetery Ridge. When an officer urged Hancock to stop recklessly exposing himself, he responded, "There are times when a corps commander's life does not count." Hancock's fearless demeanor inspired his troops to stand tall and repulse the Southern infantry about to step out of the woods a mile to the west. *Courtesy Gallon Historical Art, Gettysburg, Pennsylvania*

nearly all ceased firing; only a few scattering batteries here and there could be seen to fire."[157]

Similar impressions from an opposite perspective were recorded two weeks after the battle by Federal Colonel Norman J. Hall of the 7th Michigan Infantry, Gibbon's Second Division, Hancock's Corps:

> Never before during this war were so many batteries subjected to so terrible a test. Horses, men, and carriages were piled together, but the fire scarcely slackened for an instant so long as the guns were standing . . . Three of [Cushing's] limbers were blown up . . . several wheels were shot off his guns and replaced, till at last . . . [there were] but cannoneers enough to man a section.[158]

As the bombardment continued, Pickett took Alexander's *first* note to Longstreet, who, upon reading it, said nothing. "General shall I advance?" he inquired? Longstreet still made no reply, and turned his head aside. According to Longstreet, he was overcome with emotion and could not speak the order. "I could only indicate it by an affirmative bow," he later wrote. Pickett saluted and said. "I am going to move forward, Sir."[159]

As Pickett rode off, word also reached Pettigrew and Trimble that the time had come for the attack. Trimble recalled his final instructions to his two brigades of North Carolinians: "Wishing as far as I could to inspire them with confidence, I addressed them briefly, ordered that no gun should be fired until the enemy's line was broken, and that I should advance with them to the farthest point."[160] In the meantime, Lieutenant Young remembered how Pettigrew "rode up to Colonel Marshall in front of [Pettigrew's own] brigade with the bright look he always wore in the hour of danger, and said, 'Now, Colonel, for the honor of the good old North State, forward.'"[161] Colonel Joseph C. Mayo recalled how Pickett, upon returning to his division, rode "briskly" down the line, "calling to the men to get up and prepare to advance, and 'Remember Old Virginia!'"[162]

As Trimble, Pettigrew and Pickett were haranguing their troops and making preparations to move out, Alexander's second "come quick" notes were delivered to Pickett, which turned out to be "after the event [bombardment] was determined, & the orders given." Still, remembered Alexander, "they of course brought him some comfort and encouragement." During the 10 minutes it took for the infantry to dress ranks and prepare to move out, Longstreet rode up alone to see Alexander, who was sitting on his horse Dixie in the vicinity of Dearing's smoking guns. The Federal batteries in the target area had been punished and several batteries had been driven off, he told the corps chief. Others, perhaps too badly damaged to be able to withdraw, had probably been wrecked as well, and Federal fire had slackened noticeably. Despite these accomplishments, Alexander told Longstreet that he was afraid he could not give Pickett the help he would need because his ammunition was so low and the howitzers under Richardson had been removed and could not be found.

General Longstreet spoke up promptly: "Go and stop Pickett right where he is, and replenish your ammunition."[163]

That would not be possible, explained the gunner, because "the ordnance wagons had been nearly emptied replacing expenditures of the day before, and not over 20 rounds to the gun were left." Both men knew this was "too little to accomplish much." In addition, added Alexander, "the enemy would recover from the effect of the fire we were now giving him.

And then Longstreet finally said what had been on his mind all day. "I don't want to make this charge," he bluntly told his artillerist. "I don't believe it can succeed. I would stop Pickett now, but General Lee has ordered it and expects it." He also made "other remarks," remembered Alexander, "showing that he would have been easily induced, even then, to order Pickett to halt."[164]

"Remember Old Virginia!" Major General George E. Pickett rides along the line of his Virginians just prior to their ill-fated assault against the Federal lines on Cemetery Ridge on the afternoon of July 3, 1863. Men remembered Pickett haranguing the troops by calling out, "Up men, and to your posts! Don't forget today that you are from Old Virginia!" *Courtesy Gallon Historical Art, Gettysburg, Pennsylvania*

It was a just this moment that Armistead's Brigade "appeared sweeping out of the wood" on the far left of the division, and "Garnett's brigade [was] passing over us," recalled Alexander. About 45 or 50 minutes after the signal guns first fired Pickett's infantry moved through the Confederate guns "at a good fast gait," marking the beginning of one of the most famous charges in all of history.[165]

Longstreet's Assault, or "Pickett's Charge"

As his regiment approached Dearing's guns, Colonel Eppa Hunton and his 8th Virginia watched as "Major Dearing passed with his caissons to the rear at full speed." As he passed by, the gunner yelled out to Hunton, "For God's sake, wait till I get some ammunition and I will drive every Yankee from the heights!" As the colonel later noted, however, "It was too late, we were in motion."[166]

The long lines of Confederate infantry tramped forward "in splendid order" moving across the gently undulating fields. "One might have thought we were going to or were on a dress parade, so perfect was our alignment," recalled Major John Corbett Timberlake of the 53rd Virginia, Armistead's Brigade.[167] The sight of thousands of well-aligned infantry gripped the Federal soldiers, who paused in awe to view the spectacle spreading out before them. Colonel Norman Hall remembered how his troops on Cemetery Ridge reacted once the Confederate infantry were seen moving across the fields. "The perfect order and steady but rapid advance of the enemy called forth praise from our troops, but gave their line an appearance of being fearfully irresistible."[168] From his position on Cemetery Ridge, Hancock remembered that the Confederate "lines were formed with a precision and steadiness that extorted the admiration of the witnesses of that memorable scene."[169] The low stone wall running north and south in front of the Copse of Trees made a ninety degree turn to the east for some distance before making another ninety degree turn back north in the direction of Ziegler's Grove. There, in a position known as the Angle, was Pennsylvania Private William J. Burns, Alexander S. Webb's brigade, Gibbon's division. From his perspective the panorama of tramping gray and butternut infantry "was a grand sight and worth a man's while to see it."[170]

The respite enjoyed by the advancing lines of Confederates was short-lived. By the time Pettigrew's and Trimble's commands were half way across the fields, and Kemper's and Garnett's brigades had crested the swells along the Emmitsburg Road with Armistead's regiments trailing behind, the entire Federal line was ablaze. Pickett's leading brigades had a much shorter distance to traverse from their jump off points to the Federal line than either Armistead or the other half of the column under Pettigrew and Trimble. While the advance afforded Pickett some protection by the rolling terrain that included the swell of the Emmitsburg Road, no such advantages existed for Pettigrew's or Trimble's infantry. As soon as their men

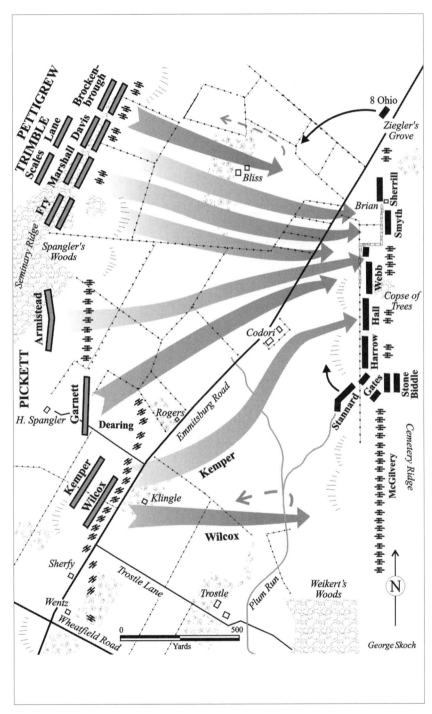

The Pickett-Pettigrew-Trimble Assault, July 3, 1863

"Pickett's Grand Assault." George Pickett's leading Virginia brigades (Kemper on the left and Garnett on the right) cross the Emmitsburg Road, pass by the Codori Farm, and press ahead to Cemetery Ridge on July 3, 1863. Major General Winfield Scott Hancock described the spectacle as a "memorable scene." Others in his command remembered the oncoming Confederate host offered "a grand sight" that gave the impression of being "fearfully irresistible."
Courtesy Gallon Historical Art, Gettysburg, Pennsylvania

appeared in the open ground east of Seminary Ridge, the fire of Federal batteries posted from Cemetery Hill south past Ziegler's Grove along upper Cemetery Ridge tore apart their ranks. Many of these batteries had not been subjected to the Confederate bombardment or were missed entirely, and had fallen silent in order to conserve ammunition and wait for the advancing infantry.

According to the indefatigable Isaac Trimble, his pair of North Carolina brigades advanced amidst "furious discharges of artillery [that] were poured on them from the line in their front, and from their left flank by the line which overlapped them near Gettysburg . . . Notwithstanding the losses as we advanced, the men marched with the deliberation and accuracy of men on drill."[171] Colonel Fry, commanding Archer's Brigade, remembered being "stormed at with shot and shell."[172] Still the men closed ranks and pushed steadily onward. Brigadier General Alexander Hays, commanding the Third Division in Hancock's Second Corps, was amazed that the troops could absorb so much punishment and continue moving in such good order. The approach of Pettigrew and Trimble, he noted, "was as steady as if impelled by machinery, unbroken by our artillery, which played upon them a storm of missiles."[173]

As the left side of the assaulting column was being heavily punished, Pickett's leading brigades several hundred yards to the south under Kemper and Garnett crested and moved beyond the Emmitsburg Road. As they did so, their banners became fully exposed to McGilvery's 39 guns unlimbered along middle-to-lower Cemetery Ridge, as well as the six guns on Little Round Top. From his previous observation position on that height, artillerist Henry J. Hunt had ridden down to McGilvery's gun line when Kemper's and Garnett's men were seen making a left oblique, which shifted the axis of advance northeast. The move was designed to drive Pickett's Virginians toward the clump of trees and (ostensibly) bring the columns together. It also opened up their right flank to McGilvery's guns. Hunt knew a good opportunity when it he saw one and ordered his artillerists "to take the enemy in flank."[174] The effect of this fire, which was delivered against the Confederates from a distance of about "700 yards," appeared to General Hancock to be "feeble . . . with no material effect."[175]

At least one of the Confederates on the receiving end of this fire disagreed. The 19th Virginia's Major Peyton remembered that McGilvery's guns tore into his ranks with "fearful effect." On occasion, he noted, "as many as 10 men [were] killed and wounded by the bursting of a single shell." But the Federal fire was not enough to stay the determined advance. As the men walked within range of the Federal infantry the enemy opened with small arms. The flying bullets buzzed through the air like angry insects and thudded into body parts, knocking more men to the ground and thinning Pickett's ranks. Still they "moved rapidly forward toward the stone wall under a galling fire both from artillery and infantry," wrote Peyton.[176] The *élan* of the Southern infantrymen so impressed Hunt that he admitted, "The enemy advanced magnificently, unshaken by the shot and shell which tore through his ranks from his front and from our left."[177]

Braving canister and small arms fire, Pickett's Virginians moved forward. By the time his front brigades were beyond the Emmitsburg Road and moving forward for the final rush, it is doubtful that much organization remained. Instead, the men probably formed a large congested mass of gray and brown that swept onward toward the umbrella-shaped trees and the Angle. The Confederate surge, directed against that portion of the line held by Webb's "Philadelphia Brigade" made a lasting impression on Captain William Davis of the 69th Pennsylvania. "Onward they came," Davis wrote, "and it would seem as if no power could hold them in check."[178] Colonel Joe Mayo in Kemper's Brigade remembered this part of the charge for the rest of his life. The troops "reserv[ed] their fire until they had approached within a hundred yards of his works," he later recalled proudly, where "our men pound into the enemy one well-directed volley and then at the command of General Kemper [started] with a cheer upon the works."[179] Once the Confederates opened fire on the Federal line, Colonel Theodore B. Gates of the 80th New York thought the contest became "especially obstinate, and for a considerable time the chances of success appeared to favor first one side and then the other."[180]

"Fire at the Angle"

Moments before he was killed and his battery overrun, Federal Lieutenant Alonzo Cushing fired a last discharge from one of his 3-inch Ordnance rifles into Pickett's onrushing masses during the fighting on July 3. Cushing's battery was positioned in the Angle just north of the Copse of Trees.

Courtesy Gallon Historical Art, Gettysburg, Pennsylvania

In this close exchange of fire General Garnett and his horse Red Eye disappeared about 25 paces from the wall. He was never seen again and was buried in an unmarked grave. Kemper also fell, seriously wounded with a shot in the groin many believed was a mortal one. Hundreds were falling within a handful of square yards of Pennsylvania soil. Still the sea of Southerners swelled forward, spilling up against the low stone wall and driving back the defenders still remaining there. General Webb watched the unwavering Virginians advance "right up to my works and fences, and shot my men with their muskets touching their breasts."[181]

Armistead had received word to bring his brigade forward in support of the weakening regiments of Kemper and Garnett. Leading his men across the Emmitsburg Road at the double quick, they passed the Codori Farm complex as Federal canister and bullets were "literally riddling the orchard."[182] While Kemper's and Garnett's men battled at the wall, Armistead paused his men in some low ground about 100 yards in front the Federal line to catch their breath and prepare for the final push. This protected undulation was out of much of the enemy's line of fire. With his

"Forward with the Colors"

At the head of a group of Virginians making a last push to the crest of Cemetery Ridge was Brigadier General Lewis Armistead. The attackers stormed over the stone wall at the Angle, overran a Federal battery, and pressed forward. With his plumed hat sliding down his blade, Armistead is about to rest his hand on one of Cushing's 3-inch rifles. Just a few moments later Armistead was struck down with a mortal wound. *Courtesy Gallon Historical Art, Gettysburg, Pennsylvania*

plumed hat struck on the end of his sword, Armistead waved his men forward with the clarion call, "Boys, give them the cold steel!"[183] With Armistead in the lead, Major John Corbett Timberlake remembered that the brigade "had nearly reached the stone fence, when there was such a rush of prisoners through our lines that I exclaimed, 'The day is ours!'"[184] With victory seemingly within their grasp the men "[I] reached the stone fence; there was a small break in the wall; General Armistead mounted the fence with his hat on the end of his sword and shouted to his men to follow him, and as he stepped off, I mounted the fence in his footsteps and cried out to the Fifty-Third, 'Look at your General! Follow him!'"[185]

Armistead and fragments of his brigade—along with men from Garnett's and Kemper's commands, swarmed into the Angle and up the muzzles of Alonzo Cushing's devastated battery. At the very moment double-canister discharges from the two remaining operational guns belched their deadly rounds into the mass of Southerners.[186] Even before the smoke had cleared Cushing's battery was engulfed in a sea of gray and butternut. With the guns in Confederate hands, the 71st Pennsylvania began to give way. Once that happened, the right flank of the 69th Pennsylvania became exposed, and Captain Davis remembered how the Virginians "literally came right on top of our men."[187]

A wild *mêlée* ensued, and many in Federal uniform thought the most serious crisis of the battle was at hand. Seeing Armistead and his men "with several battle-flags" engulfing his line, Webb believed that "the army of the Potomac was nearer being whipped that it was at any time of the battle."[188] Haskell feared that the Confederate execution against the 69th Pennsylvania was such that soon "there will be none alive for the enemy to overpower . . . The fate of Gettysburg hung upon a spider's single thread!"[189]

Hunt's take on the affair was similar if not quite as dramatic:

> this onslaught was fierce, and for a time the fate of *the battle* hung trembling in the balance, for had our line been broken here his whole army would doubtless have been upon us immediately and under circumstances which would have made it almost impossible to resist him. Had McGilvery also exhausted his ammunition before the assault, the enemy would in all probability have succeeded in carrying the position . . . As it was, the escape was a very narrow one.[190]

It was a desperate time for the participants of both armies. To the north, clumps of men from Pettigrew's and Trimble's commands hung in the face of overwhelming firepower. Pickett's Virginians battled Webb's regiments in and around the Angle and Copse of Trees. Webb tried to get one of his nearby formations, the 72nd Pennsylvania that had been held in reserve, to advance and plug the gap and relieve the pressure on the 69th Pennsylvania. Despite Webb's urging, the 72nd Pennsylvania (which consisted of firemen from Philadelphia—the so-called Fire Zouaves) refused to advance. With one of his regiments already having given way and another refusing to advance, Webb, bloodied and disgusted, returned to the 69th to share in its fate.[191]

Webb's heroism and the chaos of the moment was recalled by Captain Andrew Cowan, commanding the 1st New York Independent Battery from Sedgwick's Sixth Corps. Cowan had brought his six 3-inch Ordnance rifles "into Battery" just south of the Copse of Trees "that were soon to be stripped of their bark by the bullets of the enemy." Captain Fred Brown's Battery B, 1st Rhode Island Light Artillery in Hancock's Second Corps, had been driven from the same area as a result of the Confederate bombardment. From this proximity Cowan fired all of his rounds of canister into the charging Southerners and then ordered his guns to be manhandled, or prolonged, to the rear.[192] This was being accomplished when Cowan looked back at the fighting:

> I saw [General] Webb behind Cushing's guns surrounded by a number of officers and men and the colors of two, or perhaps three of his regiments. A great many men and officers too were running away as fast as their legs could carry them, and had been for two or three minutes before. James Plunkett, a Vermonter, attached to my battery, fought and cursed them and finally I saw him hit one fellow over the head with a coffee pot. The bottom burst in and I shall never forget seeing the fellow running away with the pot, down over his head and face.[193]

As Webb courageously struggled to hold what remained of his brigade together and keep the Confederates at bay, other Federal commanders began organizing formations to move against Pickett's regiments. The attack had clearly reached its climax, and a number of Pickett's officers and men began desperately searching for a second wave of their own troops—the all-important supports many who took part in the attack believed were supposed to follow up the leading wave. "We thought our work was done and that the day was over, for the last enemy in sight we has seen disappear over the hill in front, " remembered Captain John Holmes Smith of the 11th Virginia, who with along with "about 300 men" was fighting near the Angle on the crest of Cemetery Ridge. "I expected to see General Lee's Army marching up to take possession of the field. As I looked over the work of our advance with this expectation, I could see nothing but dead and wounded men and horses in the field behind us, and my heart never in my life sank as it did then. It was a grievous disappointment."[194]

Colonel Joseph Mayo felt the same way. "At this critical juncture," he later wrote, "when seconds seemed more precious than hours of any former time, many an anxious eye was cast back to the hill from which we came in the hope of seeing supports near at hand, and more than once I heard the despairing exclamation, 'Why don't they come!'"[195] In an article written after the war, Mayo recalled being "within a few steps the stone fence" with Private Walker, General Kemper's orderly. "As I gave one hurried glance over the field we had traversed, the thought in my mind was repeated at my side, 'Oh, colonel, why don't they support us?'"[196] Major Peyton believed (mistakenly) that the Pettigrew-Trimble column had failed to advance and support the Virginians. "We hoped for support on the left (which had started simultaneously with ourselves), but hoped in vain."[197] According to Major Timberlake, "[I] looked to my left to see what was going on there, and all that I saw were the troops to the left of us going to the rear. At the same time I looked to see if there were any supports coming to us and, to my great mortification, saw a full line of battle start, but very soon halt and go back. I mounted the stone fence and shouted with all the power I had, 'For God's sake, come on!'"[198]

The very few minutes during which Confederate supports might have made a difference quickly passed away and Federal pressure began mounting against the few hundred Virginians clinging to the rocks, trees, and fence lines around the umbrella clump of trees and Angle. "The [Confederate] line around the angle was being fast thinned out," Charles T. Loehr of the 1st Virginia recalled, "and now was the time for reinforcements to push on the victory within our grasp, but none were there to aid Pickett's men in their struggle to hold the position for which they had fought so hard."[199]

Unfortunately for the attacking infantry, the generals watching the hot action had no intention of supporting them. "Gen. A. P. Hill came and stood within my battery not ten feet from the location of my gun and was watching with us from that position the charge of Pickett's and Pender's men," wrote George L. Christian of the 2nd Richmond Virginia Howitzers, part of Dance's Battalion stationed on Seminary Ridge. Christian carefully watched Powell Hill's demeanor as he declined to support Pickett's men:

> I shall never forget his appearance on that occasion as long as I live. When he saw Pender's division falter in its advance, and afterwards break and retire, and as he watched with the most intense interest the struggling gallantry and continued advance of Pickett's men, although their lines were decimated as they went in on, Gen. Hill looked to me as if he were dazed, if not confounded at the scene before him. From where we were, we could distinctly see the Federal reinforcements under Hancock and others as they were brought up and were driving Pickett's men back after those gallant fellows had gotten within their lines, had captured some of their guns and were turning them on the Federals. As these reinforcements were being brought up, they had to cross almost immediately the line of fire of our artillery. We believed then, as I do now, that our twenty pieces [of Dance's Battalion], if allowed to reopen, could have prevented the advance of these reinforcements, and thus insure the success of Pickett's charge and consequently that of the battle of Gettysburg.
>
> Confident that we could have done this, several of our officers and men begged Gen. Hill to let us reopen with our artillery on these reinforcements; but

he declined, saying that our ammunition was too nearly exhausted to permit this. It is true that our ammunition was nearly exhausted; but we felt then, as I do now, that in saving this remnant of our ammunition, we lost the great battle of Gettysburg.[200]

During the 15 or 20 minutes the Confederates stubbornly clung to their foothold on Cemetery Ridge, many incidents permanently etched themselves into the minds of those who survived the battle. Captain Farinholt of the 53rd Virginia remembered Lewis Armistead "standing by one of the captured pieces of artillery, where the brave Federal Capt. Cushing had fallen, with his dead men and horses almost covering the ground, called on us to load and use the captured cannon on the fleeing foe."[201] In this fierce *mêlée*, Farinholt recalled how "many shots were fired at such close range as afterward to burn the clothes or flesh of the victims with powder."[202] One of them brought down General Armistead, who fell near Cushing's guns with a mortal wound. He was the last of Pickett's three brigadiers to fall.

Unable to hang on any longer in the face of growing enemy reinforcements, and with many of their officers down, the Southern tide that crested Cemetery Ridge receded. William Roane Aylett, colonel of the 53rd Virginia and great-grandson of statesman and orator Patrick Henry, summed up how many participants saw the affair when he wrote: "No supports coming up, the position was untenable, and we were compelled to retire."[203]

* * *

The Pettigrew-Trimble column fared even worse than Pickett's. As soon as the attack began Pettigrew noticed that his two left brigades under Brockenbrough (Mayo) and Davis were nowhere to be seen. They stepped out of the woods a couple minutes later and trotted to catch up with the advancing brigades on their right, but the staggered beginning of the attack did not bode well. Almost immediately Federal artillery began dropping explosive case shot up and down Pettigrew's line, pruning it with every step east. It was at this point that the mistake of anchoring the far left flank of the entire attacking column with Brockenbrough's pitiful brigade became obvious to everyone watching. According to its temporary leader, Colonel Mayo, the brigade was woefully under strength. Men were lost men at every step, some from enemy fire and others to cowardly hearts. One of the few accurate statements in Mayo's long-unpublished report was his observation that his men "were entirely unsupported"—an intentional jab at whomever approved the attack's final configuration. The ragged appearance of Pettigrew's left flank quickly attracted Federal attention, and first artillery and then rifle fire poured into the unfortunate Virginians. Thomas Osborn's 31 Federal guns from Cemetery Hill ripped into the weak Virginia flank and left front. "The havoc produced within their ranks was truly surprising," he wrote after the battle. The 8th Ohio, situated on the left front of the advancing brigade, also opened fire. Within a few minutes not a man from the brigade was in line; Mayo's command had disintegrated and was running pell-mell for the shelter of Seminary Ridge.[204]

As we have seen throughout this study, the failure of one brigade exposes the flank of the next in line. And so it was with Joe Davis' men, who received the full attention of the guns that seconds earlier had been trained on the Virginians. Lieutenant Young of Pettigrew's staff watched in horror as the Federals methodically tore to pieces the Confederate infantry. "When the left of the line approached . . . a direct, oblique and enfilade fire could be and was concentrated upon it."[205] As the three remaining brigades in Pettigrew's front line continued over the Emmitsburg Road, Davis' men surged ahead "with too much impetuosity" and were slaughtered on the slope leading up to the Abram Brian (Bryan) Farm. The concentrated fire "reduced [Davis] almost to a line of skirmishers," remembered Young, and his men eventually gave way as well.[206]

The remaining pair of front line brigades, Pettigrew's under Colonel Marshall and Archer's under Colonel Fry, continued bravely onward. Fry recalled that his men "moved steadily on, and even when grape, canister and musket balls began to rain upon it the gaps were quickly closed and the alignment preserved. Strong as was the position of the enemy, it seemed that such determination could not fail."[207] Isaac Trimble, who was following with his two brigades in support of Pettigrew's right rear, watched as the Federal maelstrom of iron and lead vaporized the lines of men ahead of him. The entire line "seemed to sink into the earth under the tempest of fire poured into them," wrote Trimble. "We passed over the remnant of their line . . . [but] the loss here was fearful, and I knew that no troops could long endure it." Somewhere near the Emmitsburg Road a bullet struck Trimble in the ankle, splintering the bone. The division was turned back over to Jim Lane and the unlucky Trimble turned his mare Jinny back toward Seminary Ridge. His Confederate service was at an end.[208]

Despite the brutal fire pouring in from three

"Imperishable Glory"

As the advancing Confederates of Davis' Brigade crossed the Emmitsburg Road and approached the Brian ("Bryan" in some accounts) Farm on the afternoon of July 3, Federal infantry opened fire. The eruption of lead and smoke, remembered one eyewitness, "disintegrated" the Confederate line.
Courtesy Gallon Historical Art, Gettysburg, Pennsylvania.

directions, several hundred gallant men from Davis', Archer's, Pettigrew's, Lane's and Scales' brigades struggled up the slope and returned fire within a handful of yards of the stone wall north of the Angle, where they were either killed, wounded, captured, or driven back. Colonel Lowrance, in command of Scales' Brigade, recalled the sickening feeling he experienced when he realized no troops were advancing to help his men along this wall. "Now all apparently had forsaken us," he lamented. With "no support in view . . . the brigade retreated."[209]

* * *

Sometime after Pickett's three brigades passed the Emmitsburg Road, Cadmus Wilcox received several orders in immediate succession to move to the Virginians' support. Colonel David Lang, who was in command of the Floridians in Anderson's Division, was ordered to conform the movements of his brigade to that of Wilcox, and "moved forward also."[210] Exactly when these orders arrived and when the order was complied with is in some dispute. Cadmus Wilcox recalled that the orders arrived "not . . . more than twenty or thirty minutes" after Kemper's men had passed through his ranks. That may indeed have been true, but according to Lang, Pickett's troops were already retiring "behind our position [when] General Wilcox began to advance."[211] By the time Wilcox's Alabamians crested the swell of the Emmitsburg Road, "not a man of the division that I was ordered to support could I see," he wrote. According to George Clark of Wilcox's Brigade, the men advanced sometime during Pickett's assault. "Just previous to our reaching Pickett's right," he wrote, "his division seemed to take somewhat of a left oblique and soon disappeared from my view."[212] Whether Wilcox just lost sight of Pickett or his men had already retired, as Lang recalled, Wilcox pressed straight ahead in an eastward direction. The movement was far too late to support anyone. Porter Alexander remembered that as Wilcox's men passed by his guns, they "looked bewildered, as if they wondered what they were expected to do, or why they were there," which is pretty good testimony that Pickett's men may indeed have already retired and that little or no fighting was taking place to the northeast around the Angle. Regardless, they were not visible to Wilcox, whose "men went down the slope [from the Emmitsburg Road]," with Lang's Brigade in tow, "until coming to the skirt of woods at the foot of the heights."[213]

The Wilcox-Lang fiasco was not only too late to assist Pickett, but doomed many of the Alabamians and Floridians to no purpose. Federal artillerists along McGilvery's gun line and serving the six 10-pounder Parrotts in Rittenhouse's battery on top of Little Round Top could not believe their good fortune and opened on the isolated regiments. The battlefield was choked with smoke that severely restricted visibility along with "the noise of artillery and small-arms so deafening that it was impossible to make the voice heard above the din." Wilcox and Lang were alone in the middle of the battlefield without any support whatsoever.[214]

While the front and right flanks were pounded by artillery fire, the left flank of the column was raked by enfilade infantry fire from a pair of Vermont regiments. The men, part of Brigadier General George Stannard's brigade, had just gotten done doing the same thing in the opposite direction to James Kemper's right flank. With no support "by either infantry or artillery, with [enemy] infantry on both flanks and front and artillery playing upon us with grape and canister," Colonel Lang decided it "was certain annihilation" to continue on. He ordered a retreat, as did Wilcox, but the retrograde movement "was not in time to save a large number of the Second Florida Infantry, together with their colors, from being cut off and captured by the flanking force on the left."[215]

From his position near Spangler's Wood in the vicinity of the present-day Virginia monument, General Lee watched intently as his troops suffered their bloody repulse and began falling back westward. The commanding general spurred Traveller down the eastern face of Seminary Ridge to meet his men. As Lee moved out to the fields across which the exhausted and bloodied survivors walked, he must have realized that his designs on achieving what he had hoped to be "some signal result and to end the war," were now in shambles. Although some of the men had reached their objective, they were too small in number and were not properly supported. First Lieutenant John Thomas James of the 11th Virginia described what many Confederates saw that afternoon: "We gained nothing but glory and lost our bravest men."[216]

General Lee knew full well what his men had accomplished and what they had suffered. He greeted the survivors with words of encouragement. An exhausted Charles T. Loehr recalled that when Lee rode up, the men:

> as was usual, wanted to know what he had to say [and] crowded around him. General Pickett broke out in tears, while General Lee rode up to him, and they shook hands. General Lee spoke to General Pickett in a slow and distinct manner . . . 'General Pickett, your men have done all that men could do; the fault is entirely my own.[217]

* * *

The assault's failure meant that Jeb Stuart and his cavalrymen would not play the role Lee had envisioned for them. It was largely irrelevant anyway, because the Southern cavalry was quickly spotted moving on the York Pike two or three miles northeast of Gettysburg. Federal cavalry was quickly shifted to prevent a movement into Meade's rear area. Pickett's men may already have been defeated by the time Stuart's troopers waged a large-scale mounted action. The bloody tactical draw resulted in nothing but casualties. Late that same afternoon on the other side of the field in the shadow of Round Top, an unsupported attack by Federal cavalry against part of Hood's Division was launched and easily beaten back, its commander killed in the effort.[218]

And so concluded the epic three-day battle at Gettysburg.

Lee and July 3 in Retrospect

The cost of the battle was exceedingly high for both combatants. Imperfect casualty figures reveal admitted losses in excess of 23,000 for Meade's Army of the Potomac, and more than 21,000 for Lee's Virginia army. Of these, Lee lost at least 8,000 men to all causes from the third day's action (including Ewell's fight on Culp's Hill), while Meade's casualties for the same day amounted to about 3,000. Without a doubt both armies lost many more men than are listed on the casualty rolls.[219]

Exact numbers, of course, are not important. The fact is that tens of thousands of men had been killed and wounded, and the suffering wrought on that battlefield—soon to be carried into thousands of homes north and south—was far reaching and everlasting. The 53rd Virginia's Captain Benjamin Lyons Farinholt had been wounded in the fighting for the Angle and taken prisoner. After "being taken to the rear we could see the terrible loss we had inflicted upon the Federal army, for every nook in the fence, every little stream of water to which they could crawl, every barn and shed, every yard and shade-tree were literally burdened with their dead, wounded, and dying." His observation was just as applicable to what captured Federals would have seen just a bit to the west.[220]

Both armies remained along their respective battle lines during the daylight hours of July 4, caring for their wounded, picking up equipment, and burying the dead. That night, as a drenching rain made the soldiers' plight even more uncomfortable, Lee began pulling his army out of Gettysburg. Several tense days followed for Lee and his veterans when they discovered that the Potomac River was swollen; the Southern army was temporarily trapped on Northern soil. Lee ordered entrenchments to protect his men and wagons and constructed a pontoon bridge to get his troops safely across. When many of the Federal army's senior officers voiced opposition to Meade's plan to attack Lee's strong position, he abandoned the idea. Light fighting followed around Williamsport, Maryland, and the Army of Northern Virginia recrossed the Potomac, bringing the campaign to anti-climactic close.[221]

* * *

The failure of the Confederate main attack on July 3 spawned a lively debate that continues to this day. Most students of the battle seem to accept the proposition that Pickett's attack on the third day at Gettysburg was a hopeless proposition from the start, generally overlooking the fact that significant errors were made by several Southern commanders that contributed to its bloody failure. There is no doubt the assault that finally materialized on July 3 bore little resemblance to the one General Lee had envisioned. Before the assault began, his plan for victory included these six major facets: 1) An effective and simultaneous demonstration by Ewell's Second Corps on the Confederate left; 2) Stuart's successful movement to threaten the Federal rear; 3) a massive Confederate artillery bombardment to cripple Federal artillery generally, and the infantry deployed at the point of attack; 4) a breaching of the Federal line by the main infantry thrust under Pickett, Pettigrew, and Trimble; 5) advanced artillery support to hold and expand that breach; and 6) a second wave of infantry supports following behind the first wave to expand the foothold, solidify gains, and dislodge the Federal line. With the exception of part of the main attacking column, all of these facets failed or stumbled badly.

The Federal army and its leaders had a lot to do with it. Meade and his subordinates performed extremely well on July 3. Meade's decision to launch a spoiling attack and the manner in which it was executed triggered the heavy engagement on Culp's Hill much earlier than Lee desired or planned. That fact, coupled with Longstreet's delay in preparing an early morning attack, threw Southern efforts completely off balance even before the sun was visible in the sky. Henry Hunt's handling of Federal artillery later in the day was excellent. Winfield Hancock showed his mettle during the Confederate bombardment, inspiring his officers and men to remain firm while actively directing the defense of his line—all of which helped save the day and earned him a painful wound in the upper thigh-groin area that never fully healed.

But once Ewell's front played out, Lee still moved forward to implement his plan—which is strong evidence that he believed his army could still achieve victory if the remaining elements of his design were realized. By the time the infantry was streaming back to Seminary Ridge, however, the only resemblance to his original strategy was that the leading attack wave had moved forward and engaged the enemy line after an artillery bombardment that was not as effective as Lee desired.

* * *

Did Robert E. Lee correctly read the altered tactical situation on the field that day once Ewell's battle for Culp's Hill had ended *and* it became obvious that Longstreet had procrastinated in his preparations to attack early that morning? Contrary to the traditional view of Gettysburg, we believe this study amply demonstrates that General Lee was in top form on July 1 and July 2. He recognized the opportunities available on the first day and crushed two Federal corps; and on the second day correctly assessed Meade's position, modified his plans as necessary, and almost broke Meade's army in several places, any of which would have driven his opponent from the field. But by 11:00 a.m. on July 3, Ewell was no longer pressuring the Federal right and Longstreet was obviously dragging his feet regarding the implementation of the morning's attack. The impending assault Lee intended to deliver was of overriding importance to both his army and his country's future. Why, then didn't General Lee assume direct tactical command over such a potentially momentous attack?

One possible reason was the commanding general's loyalty to his subordinates. Even though he was obviously delaying the attack, Longstreet had never let Lee down on any field. The commanding general maintained his trust in him just as he had in Jackson following Stonewall's lackluster performance outside Richmond in 1862. A second possible reason was that taking tactical control would not have been consistent with the command style General Lee had utilized to carry his army, in just thirteen months, to the very pinnacle of success. He had learned to trust his subordinates to perform their duties, and had adopted many aspects of leadership from the Great Captains of history. His style of command change in 1864 when he no longer had leaders capable of carrying out his orders (Longstreet was wounded on the second day at the Wilderness on May 6, 1864; Hill was chronically sick, and Ewell broke down under the stress and was relieved of command). Perhaps he realized this for the first time late on the afternoon of July 3 when he rode out to meet Pickett and his survivors. "The fault is entirely my own," he had told them. Is it possible that Lee was saying in these immortal words that it was not the *idea* of his attack that was wrong, but that he should have read the warning signs all around him and *personally* assumed tactical control of the assault? It is our opinion that Lee should have assumed direct tactical command over the attack once Ewell was defeated and evidence of Longstreet's inaction was understood. His failure to do so was one of the gravest mistakes of the entire battle.

We will never know for certain whether Lee's original plan would have been successful or not—regardless of who was in tactical command. Certainly a lack of support for the main attack, both in the form of artillery and infantry in a second sustaining wave, substantially lessened the likelihood of victory. Many surviving participants of Pickett's Division cited this as a reason for their failure. Who was responsible for the failing to implement these aspects of Lee's attack plan?

Porter Alexander, whose primary responsibility it was that day to move forward artillery to support the assault, did everything in his power to successfully do so. He had positioned the eight 12-pounder howitzers under Major Charles Richardson, on loan from Third Corps, in:

> a piece of woods & left him there with orders simply to wait until I sent for him. As I intended to take personal charge of him, when the time came, no further orders were necessary. I had with me a courier, named Catlett, whom I cautioned to note exactly where Richardson was left . . . [At the appropriate time] I told Catlett to go & bring up the major & the guns. He was gone for some time & came back & said they were not where I had left them . . . After the battle

I found that Gen. Pendleton, himself, had sent & taken four or five of the guns,
& disposed of them elsewhere without any notice to me.[222]

When he discovered his howitzers were not available to move forward with the
infantry, Alexander was left without a unified limbered command that could quickly
move out on his orders. The Georgian immediately began to improvise, riding along
his line and inspecting each individual gun to determine "if it had enough long range
projectiles left" to be eligible to advance in support of the infantry. Available horses
were also a consideration because counter battery fire had killed or wounded scores
of animals needed to haul the guns forward. All of this took valuable time that would
not have been lost had Pendleton left Richardson and the howitzers where Alexander
had posted them. Therefore when Pickett's infantry moved through the guns of First
Corps, only a few pieces were able to limber and relocate with them. Even then, they
were not close enough to enemy lines and there were not enough of them to influence
the outcome of the fighting.[223]

This is not meant to imply that the attack would have been successful if
Richardson's howitzers had advanced as intended. Their involvement under an
officer as talented as Alexander—who knew how to use guns offensively in support
of infantry—could have protected Kemper's right against the flanking maneuver
conducted by Stannard's Vermonters, made it more problematic for Webb's brigade
to stand strong around the Copse of Trees, and would have forced Federal artillery to
deal with them instead of freely concentrating on Pickett's regiments. Perhaps more
of Pickett's infantry would have reached Cemetery Ridge. We will never know. But
we do know that General Lee expected artillery batteries to move forward and
aggressively support his infantry, and that their absence was deeply felt by the men
condemned to make the unsupported attack. In this case, the blame lies squarely with
"Parson" Pendleton.

The issue of the missing supporting infantry, or second wave, is much more
involved. Many officers knew through hard experience that the July 3 attack would
require support in order to be successful. Brigadier Rans Wright knew exactly what
it took to *stay* on Cemetery Ridge because his brigade was driven from that point late
on the afternoon of July 2. Just three weeks after the battle, Wright penned a highly
critical account of the failure of the attack on the third day of the battle. As far as he
was concerned, it was not a question of whether or not the assault should have been
ordered, but the failure to properly support the leading wave that doomed the entire
enterprise. As Wright had discovered on July 2, and as he had told Alexander prior to
the attack the next day, the key to success was "mostly a question of supports."
Wright's emotionally-charged essay was published anonymously (although he was
soon discovered to have written it) in the *Augusta Daily Constitutionalist* on July 23,
1863. It read, in part: "I cannot understand why Ewell's corps and all of A. P. Hill's
were not engaged in this day's fighting. I am satisfied that if they had been, our

victory would have been complete. As it was, while we inflicted terrible loss upon the enemy—greatly larger than our [own]—we failed to carry his position."[224]

Edward Porter Alexander echoed similar sentiments in a letter to his father shortly after the battle. "Had he [Pickett] been properly supported the result would have been very different, for the charge was as gallant as ever made."[225] Colonel Armistead Lindsay Long, General Lee's military secretary, helped plan the assault for July 3. "The attack of Pickett's division on the 3d," he noted, "has been more criticized, and is still less understood, than any other act of the Gettysburg drama." Long carefully described what he believed to be the salient points of the failed effort. One of these was the absence of the second wave of infantry that had been ordered by Lee:

> General Longstreet did not enter into the spirit of it, and consequently did not support it with his wonted vigor. It has been characterized as rash and object less, on the order of 'The Charge of the Light Brigade.' Nevertheless, it was not ordered without mature consideration and on grounds that presented fair prospects of success. By extending his left wing west of the Emmitsburg road, Meade weakened his position by presenting a [relatively] weak centre, which being penetrated, his wings would be isolated and paralyzed, so far as regarded supporting each other. A glance at a correct sketch of the Federal position on the 3d will sufficiently corroborate this remark, and had Pickett's division been promptly supported when it burst through Meade's centre, a more positive proof would have been given, for his right wing would have been overwhelmed before the left could have disengaged itself from woods and mountains and come to its relief.

"The attack," continued Long,

> was not made as designed . . . there were nine divisions in the army; seven were quiet . . . A. P. Hill had orders to be prepared to assist Longstreet further if necessary. Anderson, who commanded one of Hill's divisions and was in readiness to respond to Longstreet's call, made his dispositions to advance, but Longstreet told him it was of no use—the attack had failed. Had Hood and McLaws followed or supported Pickett, and [other divisions of the Third Corps] been advanced, the design of the commanding general would have been carried out.[226]

Colonel Long was not the only officer from army headquarters who believed that other First Corps troops should have supported Pickett's Virginians. Shortly after the Pickett-Pettigrew-Trimble column was defeated, McLaws received an order from Longstreet to withdraw "to your position of yesterday." He was in the process of carrying out these instructions when Captain Samuel Richards Johnston, of General Lee's staff, "the same who had conducted my column the day before, rode up," remembered McLaws. A brief and for both officers, perplexing, conversation took place.

"General, you have your division under very fine control!" exclaimed Johnston.

"What do you mean?" asked McLaws.

"Why," answered Johnston, "your orders are obeyed so promptly."

Puzzled by the odd comment, the division commander asked, "What is strange about that?"

"Have you not been repulsed and are retreating?" asked Johnston.

"No, sir, ' replied McLaws, "I have not been engaged to-day. I am but taking up this position by order of General Longstreet."

Stunned by the revelation, Johnston apologized. "I thought you had been engaged and had been forced to retire."[227]

McLaws had never received any orders from Longstreet to support Pickett's advance. But one of Lee's staff officers (Johnston) was under the impression that McLaws had received such a directive *and* had participated in the attack! McLaws always believed Lee planned for a second wave to follow the lead attacking brigades. "It was not reasonable to suppose that Gen. Lee expected to defeat [Meade's] army, with two Divisions," he wrote after the war. "It is therefore plain that Pickett's Charge was not supported, not upheld by another force in his rear, that there was no force following to take advantage of any success he might gain . . . And no matter how we may at this day discuss the causes of our failure at Gettysburg, it remains the general opinion that if General Lee's orders had been obeyed all would have been well, and that they were not, resulted from causes beyond his control."[228]

Other members of Lee's staff understood even better than McLaws that supports for the leading wave had indeed been ordered. Major Walter Taylor, who performed duties equivalent to an army's chief of staff, had firsthand knowledge of the plan of attack. Longstreet, he alleged, had the authority to call upon all of the troops in First and Third Corps to support the assault, which "was to have been made with a column of not less than two divisions, and the remaining divisions were to have been moved forward in support of those in advance."[229] Major Charles Venable agreed, writing that he heard General Lee give the orders to support Pickett's attack by vigorous use of supports. After the attack, Venable mentioned to Lee that the supporting wave of troops had not materialized as he had ordered, to which the commanding general answered, "I know it! I know it!"[230]

William Allan, an artillery major on Ewell's staff at Gettysburg, held several postwar conversations with General Lee. According to Allan, Lee declared that "he had used every effort to insure concert of action, but had failed. As a result, wrote Allan, "Pickett's attack in the afternoon was unsupported. There was nothing foolish in Pickett's attack had it been executed as designed."[231]

Pickett himself understood and had been assured that supports would follow his brigades. In two letters to his fiancé, LaSalle Corbell, written immediately following the battle, Pickett maintained:

I was so sure of success! Early in the morning I had been assured by Alexander that General Lee had ordered that every brigade in his command was to charge Cemetery Hill; so I had no fear of not being supported . . . I was ordered to take a height, which I did, under the most withering fire I have ever known, and I have seen many battles. But alas, no support came; and my poor fellows who had gotten in were overpowered.[232]

All of this points to one inescapable conclusion: the battle as fought on July 3 was *not* the battle Lee intended or planned to wage. Arguments that "Pickett's Charge" was a rash, unwarranted, and foolhardy effort must now be viewed in this light. Certainly the attack as originally conceived was a calculated, and even desperate, risk. Yet, it must be remembered that wars are won by bold strokes and by taking risks. Given the goals at stake—a nation's existence hung in the balance—it was probably a risk commensurate with the ends sought. Who, then, was responsible for failing to conduct the battle in the manner Lee intended? As the tactical commander in charge of the enterprise, Longstreet must bear the overwhelming share of the blame for deviating from the original design.

* * *

James Longstreet's actions and words, both on July 3 and thereafter until his death, leave little doubt he wanted nothing to do with the attack that was conceived and ordered by General Lee. As with most endeavors in life, when one's heart and mind are not fully committed, success rarely follows. And so it was with Longstreet on July 3, 1863. His lack of commitment became a self-fulfilling prophesy of defeat. His efforts to shift onto Alexander the responsibility for ascertaining the effectiveness of the bombardment is understandable, but Old Pete's attempt to make a colonel of the artillery responsible for *when* the assault should go in is tantamount to abandoning his overall responsibility. When Longstreet rode up to Alexander along the gun line occupied by Dearing's Battalion, and as Pettigrew, Trimble, and Pickett were forming their men for the assault, Longstreet revealed his true state of mind. "I don't want to make this attack, and believe it will fail," he told his artillerist. "I do not see how it can succeed." He even told Alexander that he would "not make it even now, but that Gen. Lee has ordered & expects it."[233] Longstreet himself later admitted that he was "never . . . so depressed as upon that day."[234] Even Moxley Sorrel, Longstreet's staffer and admirer, acknowledged there was "apparent apathy in his [Longstreet's] movements. They lacked the fire and point of his usual bearing on the battlefield."[235] Indeed this was true; there was a vast difference between how Longstreet conducted battlefield operations on July 2, and how he conducted them on July 3.

Why was Longstreet so adamantly against renewing the offensive on July 3? Perhaps the answer rests with the fact that Longstreet had become conditioned by previous ill-planned Federal assaults against prepared Southern positions (Fredericksburg, for example); the botched Confederate attacks at Mechanicsville and Malvern Hill would have only served to reinforce his proclivity for fighting on the defensive. Regardless of how he felt about it, however, Lee was Longstreet's superior officer and had *ordered* the attack to begin on the morning of July 3. And Longstreet had not obeyed him. Thereafter and throughout the balance of the morning, Old Pete failed to fully commit himself to the task Lee had directed him to accomplish, i.e., organizing the main attack with infantry and artillery support in a second wave. Longstreet could have increased the likelihood that the second wave would not be delayed by having with him at least one aide from each supporting division and brigade. At the critical moment, they could have been dispatched with orders to move forward without delay. This method was typical in Napoleon's armies decades earlier. However, this command technique also assumes that the officer in charge of ordering forward the supports was doing his best to make sure the attack would succeed, and possessed the moral courage to commit every formation he had at his disposal to such a daring enterprise. Robert E. Lee was such a man; there is ample evidence to indicate that, on July 3, 1863, at least, James Longstreet was not.

There is even some controversy as to where Longstreet was when Pickett's men were attacking, and whether he could actually see the point of attack in order to be able to move forward reinforcements at the proper time. When Armistead's Brigade crossed over the Emmitsburg Road, Pickett sent Captain Robert A. Bright of his staff to Longstreet with an urgent appeal for reinforcements. Bright recalled that he "found General Longstreet sitting on a fence alone; the fence ran in the direction we were charging. Pickett's column had passed over the hill on our side of the Emmitsburg road, and could not then be seen." The staffer relayed Pickett's message "that the position against which he had been sent would be taken, but he could not hold it unless reinforcements be sent to him." No sooner had Bright delivered his request than Colonel Fremantle, the English observer, rode up to Longstreet and remarked that he had just come from General Lee, and wanted to get to a closer "position to see this magnificent charge. I would not have missed it for the world." "I would, Colonel Fremantle," Longstreet answered, "the charge is over. Captain Bright, ride to General Pickett, and tell him what you have heard me say to Colonel Fremantle." As Bright turned his horse and started back, Longstreet thought better of what he had just said, and yelled, "Tell General Pickett that Wilcox's Brigade is in that peach orchard [pointing], and he can order him to his assistance!" Fremantle offers a similar recollection about Longstreet's "the charge is over" response—but does not mention Bright's presence. In fact, he specifically states that "Major Walton was the only officer with him [Longstreet] when I came up." Fremantle also implies that Longstreet *did* have a view of the action from atop a fence.[236] If Bright's account is accurate, Longstreet—the officer with the authority to order troops forward—was sending word to Pickett—an officer without such authority—to order troops outside his division into action. This was not the Longstreet of Second Manassas, Sharpsburg, Fredericksburg, or July 2.

What would have resulted if the supports as originally conceived by Lee—all of Anderson's Division, part of McLaws' and Hood's divisions, plus the four brigades over which Powell Hill's exercised direct control—had all followed up the Pickett-Pettigrew-Trimble column in a timely fashion? The attack would have been substantial different, certainly, and with that difference incalculable variables would have come into play that *could* have brought General Lee the "signal result" on Northern soil he was seeking. In all of his many writings after the war, Longstreet penned one statement about the attack on the third day at Gettysburg that can be repeated forever as an absolute truth: "As we failed, I must take my share of the responsibility." It was Longstreet's responsibility to make sure the supports moved forward timely and in sufficient numbers to seize the day. He did not, and the lion's share of the failure rests with him.[237]

* * *

The next piece of the puzzle as to why the Confederate effort on July 3 failed rests with the planning and execution of the artillery bombardment preceding the main assault. In order to determine what conspired to limit the effectiveness of the Confederate barrage, one need look no further than the commanding general, his chief of artillery, and the officer in charge of the assault.

Two main issues resulted in the bombardment's ineffectiveness. First, there was an utter failure to effectively coordinate the efforts of the various artillery battalions in the three different corps to achieve an effective oblique and/or enfilade fire that would have maximized Yankee casualties. Second, the shift in tactical doctrine directing Confederate gunners to concentrate on Federal artillery rather enemy infantry.

As we have seen, Longstreet issued orders to his primary artillery officers in First Corps, Porter Alexander and James Walton—and perhaps to R. Lindsay Walker, the chief of artillery in Third Corps, as well. General Pendleton, the army's thoroughly incompetent chief of artillery, reported that detailed instructions were carefully given to the artillerists up and down the line, including Third Corps guns on Hill's front. Whatever Longstreet's (and/or Pendleton's) instructions were, they did not prevent Third Corps batteries from engaging in a senseless expenditure of ammunition in an attempt to drive away Federal skirmishers from the Bliss Farm late that morning. Nor did they take much advantage of the relative positions of the opposing lines and terrain opportunities.[238]

There is no doubt General Lee (and perhaps Longstreet as well) instructed Pendleton to help oversee the positioning of the army's guns in order to maximize the bombardment's effectiveness. Pendleton mentions as much in his report. However, his efforts do not reflect these wishes. Even though he rode up and down the Confederate lines, Pendleton never recognized the opportunity available to his gunners. The shape of the famous Federal fishhook defensive line placed Confederate batteries on an exterior line that enclosed the Yankee army on three sides. Thus, Southern artillerists had a rare opportunity to pour either an oblique and/or enfilading fire against many key enemy positions. Such a fire, if properly planned and executed, would have wrought the sort of havoc General Lee desired. However, in order to maximize this opportunity, all of Ewell's outstanding Second Corps artillery battalions needed to be employed. Instead, only some 26 to 33 rifled guns from Second Corps were brought to bear against the Yankee line. In other words, as many as 52 of Ewell's pieces remained idle on the afternoon of July 3.[239]

The failure to find a way to employ these guns *somewhere* greatly affected the usefulness of the bombardment. While Ewell did not have as many good artillery positions as either Longstreet or Hill, some of these guns could have been deployed in the area of the Hagerstown (or Fairfield) Road where it entered Gettysburg. Although at first blush this position seems undesirable, it actually afforded Confederate gunners some significant advantages. Artillery could have been unlimbered on this low ground and its teams repositioned on the far side of buildings along the northwest side of town to afford as much shelter as possible from Federal counter battery fire. Confederate guns positioned in this area could have opened fire with round shot and hit the Federal line running south along Cemetery Ridge at either an oblique or an enfilade angle, depending upon the target selected. Shots would have ricocheted down the line with deadly effect. These same guns would have been well positioned to provide a covering fire when the infantry advanced. The few Southern guns that did manage to fire from a position north or northeast of the Federal line at Cemetery Hill "enfiladed our position" recalled Major T. W. Osborn, chief of artillery in Eleventh Corps. The effect of this "fire was extremely galling." According to Osborn, the Confederate "gunners got our range at almost the first shot. . . It was admirable shooting. They raked the whole line of batteries, killed and wounded the men and horses and blew up the caissons rapidly."[240] The concept of dozens of rounds of round shot fired every minute from 12-pounder Napoleons positioned north and northeast of Gettysburg, ricocheting down the Federal line from north to south, smashing equipment, men, and animals in their path, is a vision a competent Confederate chief of artillery would have grasped as being vital to Lee's planned bombardment.

Another reason the Confederate bombardment failed is because of the change in tactical doctrine ordered by General Lee. By doing so, Lee stepped away from his previous practice of concentrating fire against enemy infantry formations rather than engaging Federal artillery in counter battery fire. Lee hoped the change would cripple Federal guns so that his infantry could arrive in front of the Yankee battle line with as few casualties as possible. Once this happened, Lee believed that a well led and coordinated effort by his troops would dislodge the enemy forces and win the day. Despite overshooting for much of the barrage, the Confederate fire succeeded in crippling or driving off several Federal batteries. The level of technology in existence at that time, however, combined with a failure to offer a widespread oblique and enfilade fire, allowed the Federals to bring up fresh batteries to replace those lost or driven away. Lee's assumption that he could knock out the enemy's guns, while understandable given the number of pieces available, was impossible unless most or all of the guns in the army could be brought to bear.

For some reason, no one seemed to realize that had Lee's gunners been instructed to direct their fire onto the enemy's infantry, which was located on the gently sloping forward side of Cemetery Ridge, every shot fired just a few feet too high would have enjoyed a good chance of striking a Federal battery positioned behind the infantry on ridge's geographic crest. Thus, Lee's actual decision *decreased* the number of Federal casualties that would have resulted if he had simply adhered to the current Confederate tactical doctrine of the day. How Webb's Federal brigade would have fared had it been the focus of several Confederate artillery battalions, for example, is interesting to ponder. If the fire had torn up Webb's men and forced them back, the surrounding batteries could not have held their positions without infantry (as we graphically illustrated time and time again during the fighting of July 2). Given all the limitations of the day, Lee—as a student of Napoleon—should have realized that it was unrealistic to expect that he could knock out a substantial number of enemy tubes with counter battery fire. Lee knew Napoleonic artillery fire was devastating against formed infantry; so was his own. His plan for July 3, however, must have been colored by technological advances in ammunition that had occurred since the Napoleonic wars, as well as the advent of rifled guns and the largest concentration of ordnance ever seen on the North American continent. But he was wrong.

Although Lee's decision to change the doctrine contributed to the failure of the attack, the fact that so many Confederates guns did not participate, and those that did were not as well positioned as they might have been, contributed more to the defeat than a decision to focus fire on enemy artillery. Thus, the responsibility for the minimal contribution made by the Confederate artillery that afternoon must fall primarily upon the shoulders of General Pendleton and James Longstreet.

* * *

"The fault is entirely my own." Nearly everyone who has read of the battle of Gettysburg is familiar with Lee's famous statement to Pickett as his defeated survivors streamed back to Seminary Ridge. But does General Lee deserve the blame as he implied for the failure of "Pickett's Charge?"

As the commanding general, Lee was ultimately responsible to his men and his civilian superiors for the success or failure of the army. And thus Lee willingly acknowledged his accountability. It is, however, equally clear that the officer vested with the tactical authority for the assault, James Longstreet, failed miserably on July

3. Lee's "Old Warhorse" was willfully disobedient that morning, and woefully negligent that afternoon in the manner in which he organized and executed the attack.

From the time the reins to the Virginia army were thrust into Lee's hands, his style of command—which heretofore had won such praise—included investing his subordinate commanders with the tactical responsibility for executing his battle plans. As result, the duo of James Longstreet and Stonewall Jackson had rarely if ever let him down. With the death of Jackson following Chancellorsville, Lee looked to Longstreet as his most trusted lieutenant. Following Old Pete's superb offensive display on July 2, it was natural for General Lee to entrust him with the tactical authority for the crucial battle the next day. And, as we have seen, Longstreet must bear the primary responsibility for the failed attack.

Perhaps the failure of each of his corps commanders at crucial moments throughout the lengthy battle caused General Lee to conclude the command style that had served him so well for so long was no longer a good fit for the lieutenants leading his army. A more active role in the tactical control of his army was necessary. The manner in which Lee led his army manifestly changed as early as the fighting in the Wilderness in May 1864—but that is another story.

What Lee knew for sure late on the afternoon of July 3, 1863, was that the decisive victory he had been earnestly seeking on Northern soil, and one which the Confederacy so desperately needed, had slipped through his grasp.

Notes for Chapter 8

1. Armistead Lindsay Long, letter dated April 1877, on the topic of "Causes of Lee's Defeat at Gettysburg," *Southern Historical Society Papers*, 4, p. 123.

2. Jefferson Davis, *Robert E. Lee*, edited and with an Introduction and Notes by Colonel Harold B. Simpson (Hillsboro, 1966), p. 11.

3. Napoleon gave this now-famous and often-repeated phrase in "Observations sur les Affaires d'Espagne," in *La Correspondance de Napoléon 1er*, 32 volumes (Paris, 1858-1870), Number 14276, 27 August 1808.

4. Please consult Chapter 3 for details of Stuart's movements up through the night of June 30.

5. H. B. McClellan, *I Rode with Jeb Stuart*, p. 330.

6. These riders were: Major Andrew R. Venable, Stuart's inspector general, and Captain Henry Lee of Fitzhugh Lee's staff.

7. *OR* 27, pt. 2, p. 696.

8. Cooke, *Wearing of the Gray*, p. 245.

9. It is interesting that Stuart's defenders apparently never question why Stuart failed to answer the call of the cannon on July 1, 1863.

10. Carter, *Sabres, Saddles, and Spurs*, edited by Walbrook D. Swank, p. 76; Stuart remembered that he arrived at Carlisle "in the afternoon" of 1 July, see *OR* 27, pt. 2, p. 696.

11. George W. Beale, "A Soldier's Account of the Gettysburg Campaign," *Southern Historical Society Papers*, 11, p. 323.

12. *OR* 27, pt. 2, p. 221. According to Brig. Gen. William F. Smith, commanding at Carlisle, his troops suffered only "12 wounded, none fatally."

13. Cooke, *Wearing of the Gray*, p. 245. Cooke's use of the word "howitzer" in reference to the artillery piece being fired is, technically speaking, accurate because the 12-pounder Napoleon was official designated as a gun-howitzer. Further, the 2nd Stuart Virginia Horse Artillery did not have any 12-pounder howitzers in the battery at this time of the war, but rather had two Napoleons and two 3-inch Ordnance rifles. Of these, the section of Napoleons made the expedition with Stuart, along with all four of the 3-inch Ordnance rifles belonging to Breathed's 1st Stuart Virginia Artillery.

14. George W. Beale, "A Soldier's Account of the Gettysburg Campaign," *Southern Historical Society Papers*, 11, p. 323.

15. Longacre, *The Cavalry at Gettysburg*, p. 197.

16. H. B. McClellan, *I Rode with Jeb Stuart*, p. 330.

17. David Gregg McIntosh, "Review of the Gettysburg Campaign," *Southern Historical Society Papers*, 37, p. 96.

18. Cooke, *Wearing of the Gray*, p. 245.

19. *OR* 27, pt. 1, pp. 992 and 999; pt. 2, pp. 697 and 724.

20. H. B. McClellan, *I Rode with Jeb Stuart*, pp. 331-332.

21. Cooke, *Wearing of the Gray*, p. 246. H. B. McClellan, *I Rode with Jeb Stuart*, p. 332.

22. Carter, *Sabres, Saddles, and Spurs*, p. 77.

23. Cooke, *Wearing of the Gray*, p. 245.

24. Thomason, *Jeb Stuart*, p. 440.

25. George W. Beale, "A Soldier's Account of the Gettysburg Campaign," *Southern Historical Society Papers*, 11, p. 325.

26. Thomas T. Munford, Manuscript letter to Mrs. Charles F. Hyde, Southern Historical Collection, University of North Carolina, Chapel Hill, North Carolina.

27. Tucker, *High Tide at Gettysburg*, p. 317.

28. Coddington, *The Gettysburg Campaign*, p. 207.

29. Longacre, *The Cavalry at Gettysburg*, p. 202.

30. Thomason, *Jeb Stuart*, New York, 1930.

31. Thomas T. Munford to Mrs. Charles F. Hyde, Southern Historical Collection, University of North Carolina, Chapel Hill, North Carolina.

32. Longacre, *The Cavalry at Gettysburg*, p. 202.

33. Charles S. Venable, "General Lee in the Wilderness Campaign," *Battles and Leaders of the Civil War*, 4, p. 240. Although Colonel (and later General) Eppa Hunton was not at army headquarters when Stuart arrived, he left a description of how Lee, on occasion, worked himself up into a "furious passion. When he got mad," explained Hunton, "he was mad all over." Eppa Hunton, *Autobiography*, p. 113.

34. Thomas T. Munford letter to Mrs. Charles F. Hyde, Southern Historical Collection, University of North Carolina, Chapel Hill, North Carolina.

35. Longacre, *The Cavalry at Gettysburg*, p. 202; E. Porter Alexander, *Military Memoirs of a Confederate* (New York, 1907), p. 377; Thomas T. Munford to Mrs. Charles F. Hyde, Southern Historical Collection, University of North Carolina, Chapel Hill, North Carolina. The traditional story of legend that Lee said only one line to Stuart—"Well, General Stuart, you are here at last!"—and nothing else of importance during this encounter is simply not believable. While Munford relayed McClellan's story many years after the battle, it is important to keep in mind that Munford's description of what transpired between Stuart and Lee is entirely consistent with Lee's character and mind set at that time.

36. Emory M. Thomas, "Eggs, Aldie, Shepherdstown, and J. E. B. Stuart," *The Gettysburg Nobody Knows*, edited by Gabor S. Boritt (New York, 1997), p. 118.

37. Long, *Memoirs of Robert E. Lee*, p. 287.

38. *OR* 27, pt. 2, p. 320.

39. Readers should keep in mind that many of the failed frontal assaults of the war had yet to occur. For example, Pickett's Charge had not yet taken place, nor had any of the Overland Campaign fighting, including the bloodshed at Cold Harbor, or the devastating attacks launched by Hood's army during the Atlanta Campaign or at Franklin—all of which are commonly utilized by writers to tout the strength of the defensive. Lee, on the other hand, had a string of offensive victories upon which to base his decision to renew the attack.

40. Major General Joseph Hooker, as quoted in Coddington, *The Gettysburg Campaign*, pp. 24-25. The importance of *élan* as related to firepower cannot be overstated in an age where most infantry units were equipped with non-repeating weapons. Men who kept their composure delivered significantly higher volumes of fire than less disciplined troops.

41. One estimate of number of horses and mules in Lee's army, and the number within each command element, may be found in Blake A. Magner, *Traveller & Company: The Horses of Gettysburg* (Gettysburg, 1995), p. 47. However, Magner does not take into consideration the additional 3,000 horses and 1,200 mules Stuart had captured and carried to Gettysburg. Although Imboden's command is not included in the 33,000 figure (because his command was not at Gettysburg proper), his unit would have raised the total to about 35,000.

42. *OR* 27, pt. 2, p. 653. The plight of the horses in one Confederate artillery battalion illustrates this problem. According to Lieutenant Colonel John J. Garnett, commander of a reserve artillery battalion in Hill's Third Corps, the horses of his command "had been but scantily supplied with forage since the 1 July, during all of which time they had not received a single feed of corn." The effect was that they were "almost totally unserviceable." John J. Garnett, "The Artillery on the Gettysburg Campaign," *Southern Historical Society Papers*, 10, p. 163. Garnett's observations were not uncommon. *OR* 27, pt. 2, pp. 457 and 655.

43. Lee, *Recollections and Letters of General Robert E. Lee*, p. 108.

44. *OR* 27, pt. 2, pp. 496 and 499; Alexander, *Southern Historical Society Papers*, 4, p. 99.

45. In fact, reinforcements were marching for the Army of the Potomac. These included William H. French's division from the Eight Corps, Middle Department, which arrived on July 7; Henry S. Briggs' brigade from the First Division, Department of North Carolina, which arrived on July 12; and two divisions of Erasmus D. Keyes' Fourth Corps, Department of Virginia, formerly garrisoned at Gloucester Point, Williamsburg and Yorktown, which reached Meade's army on July 13-14.

46. Vandiver, *Their Tattered Flags: The Epic of the Confederacy*, p. 224.

47. *The Wartime Papers of Robert E. Lee*, No. 356.

48. Freeman, *R. E. Lee*, 3, p. 105.

49. Busey and Martin, *Regimental Strengths and Losses at Gettysburg*, p. 147. Gettysburg National Military Park Tablets. Of the 18 pieces in Dearing's Battalion, a dozen were 12-pounder Napoleons, while two were 20-pounder Parrott rifles. The ordnance comprising the remainder of the battalion consisted of three 10-pounder Parrotts and one 3-inch Ordnance rifle.

50. Busey and Martin, *Regimental Strengths and Losses at Gettysburg*, p. 148; Gettysburg National Military Park Tablets.

51. A good example may be found E. M. Hays to Bachelder, October 15, 1890, *The Bachelder Papers*, 3, p. 1776.

52. *OR* 27, pt. 2, p. 320.

53. *OR* 27, pt. 2, p. 320.

54. *OR* 27, pt. 2, p. 351.

55. Alexander, "Pickett's Charge and Artillery Fighting at Gettysburg," *The Century War Book*, p. 203. Alexander, *Fighting for the Confederacy*, p. 244, states that Longstreet told him "that we would renew the attack early in the morning."

56. Alexander to Bachelder, May 3, 1876, *The Bachelder Papers*, 1, p. 484. Alexander almost certainly was referring to Cemetery *Ridge*, and not Cemetery Hill.

57. Taylor, *Four Years With General Lee*, p. 102.

58. *OR* 27, pt. 2, p. 447.

59. *OR* 27, pt. 2, pp. 320, 652, 674-675; Alexander, *Fighting for the Confederacy*, p. 247.

60. *OR* 27, pt. 2, pp. 697 and 699.

61. Longacre, *The Cavalry at Gettysburg*, p. 221.

62. Douglas Southall Freeman, *R. E. Lee*, 3, p. 108.

63. *OR* 27, pt. 1, p. 237; pt. 2, p. 447.

64. *OR* 27, pt. 1, pp. 117 and 120-121, 237. Twenty Federal guns opened fire at 4:30 a.m., and six others joined in an hour later. *OR* 27, pt. 2, p. 447

65. Freeman, *R. E. Lee*, 3, p. 107. Of all the members of Pickett's Division, there seems to be only one—Captain John Dooley of the 1st Virginia—who claims that General Lee saw the division moving up the Chambersburg Pike before dawn. If this was indeed the case, Lee was probably frustrated that Pickett's men were not already in position.

66. Richard Rollins, "Prelude to Pickett's Charge," *Columbiad: A Quarterly Review of the War Between the States*, 2, number 4, (Leesburg, 1999), p. 110; Longstreet, *From Manassas to Appomattox,* pp. 385-386, states that Lee "rode over after sunrise."

67. *OR* 27, pt. 2, p. 359. Decades later, however, Longstreet floated an entirely different version of what he was preparing to do when Lee made his appearance. "General," Longstreet supposedly said, "I have had my scouts out all night, and I find that you still have an excellent opportunity to move around to the right of Meade's army, and maneuver him into attacking us." Longstreet, "Lee in Pennsylvania," *Annals of the War*, p. 429. Why did his accounts differ so dramatically? The answer is simple: Longstreet's postwar version was an attempt to defend himself against the vitriolic attacks launched by Jubal Early, William N. Pendleton, and others, all of whom were blaming Longstreet for losing Gettysburg. Old Pete was merely trying to establish the false notion that Lee should have listened to him. This can be inferred

from the fact that none of Early's, Pendleton's, or Longstreet's pen wars took place while Robert E. Lee was alive. Lee was the one man whose word alone could demolish anything untrue any of these former Confederates advocated. Longstreet's after-action report is therefore more believable than his later account.

68. *OR* 27, pt. 2, p. 663, 674, 678.

69. Alexander, *Fighting for the Confederacy*, p. 244. According to Major Benjamin Eshleman, commander of the Washington Artillery Battalion, Alexander had ordered up the Washington Artillery about midnight so that the guns could "take position on the field before daylight" for the attack Alexander expected would take place "early in the morning." *OR* 27, pt. 2, p. 434.

70. *OR* 27, pt. 2, p. 320.

71. Alexander to Bachelder, May 3, 1876, *The Bachelder Papers*, 1, p. 484.

72. W. Gart Johnson, "Reminiscences of Lee and of Gettysburg," *Confederate Veteran*, 1, p. 246. After Gettysburg, Johnson was promoted to command Company C, 18th Mississippi.

73. Long, *Memoirs of Robert E. Lee*, p. 288. Heth had been knocked unconscious by a bullet to the head on July 1, and was not able to mount a horse until that morning. He was still unfit for command.

74. Taylor, *Four Years With General Lee*, p. 102.

75. The Federal battery on Little Round Top was Battery D, 5th United States Artillery, under the command of Lieutenant Benjamin F. Rittenhouse. Rittenhouse had taken command of the battery following the death of Hazlett. Freeman, *R. E. Lee*, 3, p. 109; Long, *Memoirs of Robert E. Lee*, p. 288.

76. While the swales of the Emmitsburg Road afforded some cover from direct fire from many of the Federal batteries along Cemetery Ridge, they would not protect the Southern infantry from Federal artillery over shots or from ricochet fire.

77. Edmund Berkeley to John W. Daniel, 26 September —, Manuscripts Department, John W. Daniel Papers, University of Virginia Library, Charlottesville, Virginia.

78. B. L. Farinholt to John W. Daniel, 15 April 1905, Manuscripts Department, John W. Daniel Papers, University of Virginia Library, Charlottesville, Virginia.

79. Cadmus Marcellus Wilcox, "Gettysburg, July 2 & 3, 1863," Annotations to the official report written from Bunker Hill, Virginia, 17 July 1863, Manuscript Division, Library of Congress, Wilcox Papers, Box 1; *OR* 27, pt. 2, p. 620; Wilcox, letter dated 26 March 1877 from General C. M. Wilcox on the topic of "Causes of Lee's Defeat at Gettysburg," *Southern Historical Society Papers*, 4, p. 117; Wilcox, "General C. M. Wilcox on the Battle of Gettysburg," *Southern Historical Society Papers*, 6, pp.117-120.

80. Alexander, *Fighting for the Confederacy*, p. 255; *OR* 27, pt. 2, p. 624.

81. Smith, *General William Tatum Wofford*, p. 93.

82. Lafayette McLaws, "Gettysburg," *Southern Historical Society Papers*, 7, p. 88. Captain Johnston of Lee's staff believed Lee intended to use McLaws in some manner in the upcoming attack (Johnston had a conversation on the subject immediately following Pickett's repulse. See note 227 below). How he came to believe this is more uncertain. His position as staff officer at army headquarters and as Lee's ranking engineering officer probably gave him access to this information. The details of Johnston's conversation with McLaws, along with General Lee's comments to others, are discussed later in this chapter.

83. It is unknown whether Lee mentioned that only a brief time earlier Longstreet himself had planned to conduct a flanking march around Round Top and launch an attack with these very same troops.

84. *OR* 27, pt. 2, pp. 320 and 361. The actual infantry strength of the brigades selected for the main assault column was closer to 12,500. See individual listings for each of these brigades in Busey and Martin, *Regimental Strengths and Losses at Gettysburg*.

85. *OR* 27, pt. 2, p. 320.

86. *OR* 27, pt. 2, pp. 320, 359, 608, 614, 620 and 632; Alexander, letter dated 17 March 1877, on the topic of "Causes of Lee's Defeat at Gettysburg," *Southern Historical Society Papers*, 4, pp. 103-106; Cadmus Marcellus Wilcox, letter dated 26 March 1877 from General C. M. Wilcox on the topic of "Causes of Lee's Defeat at Gettysburg," *Southern Historical Society Papers*, 4, 116-117; James Longstreet, "Account of the Campaign and Battle of Gettysburg," on the topic of "Causes of Lee's Defeat at Gettysburg," *Southern Historical Society Papers*, 5, pp. 68-71 and 81; Cadmus Marcellus Wilcox, "General C. M. Wilcox on the Battle of Gettysburg," *Southern Historical Society Papers*, 6, pp. 117-120; Lafayette McLaws, "Gettysburg," *Southern Historical Society Papers*, 7, pp. 79-88; Edward Aylesworth Perry, "Gettysburg," *Southern Historical Society Papers*, 27, p. 196; Randolph H. McKim, "The Gettysburg Campaign," *Southern Historical Society Papers*, 40, pp. 285-287; T. M. R. Talcott, "The Third Day at Gettysburg," *Southern Historical Society Papers*, 41, pp. 37-45; Long, *Memoirs of Robert E. Lee*, p. 288; Sorrel, *Recollections of a Confederate Staff Officer*, p. 168; Taylor, *Four Years With General Lee*, pp. 101-102.

87. Longstreet, "Lee in Pennsylvania," *Annals of the War*, p. 429.

88. J. Risque Hutter to John W. Daniel, no date, Manuscripts Department, John W. Daniel Papers, University of Virginia Library, Charlottesville, Virginia.

89. Longstreet, *From Manassas to Appomattox*, p. 387.

90. Hutter to John W. Daniel, University of Virginia Library, Charlottesville, Virginia.

91. Just a few examples of victories Napoleon won by piercing the enemy's center include Rivoli (1797), Austerlitz (1805), Wagram (1809), Borodino (1812), Lützen (1813) and Ligny (1815).

92. *OR* 27, pt. 2, p. 320.

93. Sorrel, *Recollections of a Confederate Staff Officer,* p. 168. This French phrase, which referred to an intense artillery bombardment that would be the equivalent of "Hell's Fire," was used by officers in both Confederate and Federal service who had received formal military education. For an example of a Federal officer using this term, please refer to Wainwright, *A Diary of Battle*, July 3, 1863, p. 248.

94. For example, see Napoleon's victory over the Austrians at Wagram in 1809, and the Duke of Marlborough's success at the Battle of Blenheim in 1704. In the latter battle, the Duke, while at the head of a British and allied force, triumphed over a combined French and Bavarian army under Camille de Tallard, *duc d' Hostun*.

95. A description of Napoleon's formula for victory at Wagram may be found in Scott Bowden and Charles Tarbox, *Armies on the Danube 1809* (Chicago, 1989, revised edition), pp. 168-178.

96. Alexander, "Pickett's Charge and Artillery Fighting at Gettysburg," *The Century War Book*, p. 203; Alexander, letter dated 17 March 1877, on the topic of "Causes of Lee's Defeat at Gettysburg," *Southern Historical Society Papers*, 4, pp. 102-103.

97. Alexander, *Fighting for the Confederacy*, pp. 245-246.

98. Alexander, *Fighting for the Confederacy*, p. 253; James Longstreet, letter dated 6 November 1877, *Southern Historical Society Papers*, 5, p. 52.

99. Longstreet, letter dated 6 November 1877, *Southern Historical Society Papers*, 5, p. 52.

100. Alexander, *Military Memoirs of a Confederate*, p. 418; Alexander to Bachelder, May 3, 1876, *The Bachelder Papers*, 1, p. 484; Alexander, *Fighting for the Confederacy*, p. 249. A commentary regarding the actual number of Confederate guns that participated in the bombardment is detailed later in these notes.

101. Alexander, *Fighting for the Confederacy*, pp. 254-256, offers a complete and balanced description of the exchange between Longstreet and Alexander over the issue of when Pickett should move forward.

102. *OR* 27, pt. 2, p. 320. Lee had learned through experience, especially from the battles of Malvern Hill, Sharpsburg, and Fredericksburg, that Federal ordnance was superior to his own and had to be silenced or knocked out in order to protect his infantry formations. The enemy guns posed the largest obstacle to a successful attack, and hence his decision to utilize what we call today "counter battery fire." Unfortunately, the level of technology available then, combined with the battlefield environment— equipment, fire control, ammunition, smoke, doctrine, and observation—made counter battery fire far less effective than regular fire employed against massed infantry formations. Martin van Creveld, in *Technology and War* (New York, 1988), argues that technology was more than just equipment, but instead the complete process by which the technology was integrated and employed.

103. Alexander, *Military Memoirs of a Confederate*, p. 418.

104. Gettysburg National Military Park Tablets; Busey and Martin, *Regimental Strengths and Losses at Gettysburg*, p. 147.

105. Alexander, *Fighting for the Confederacy*, p. 246.

106. Alexander, *Fighting for the Confederacy*, p. 257.

107. *OR* 27, pt. 2, pp. 388-389.

108. Rollins, "Prelude to Pickett's Charge," p. 115. Since all available rifled pieces were being positioned to fire against the portion of Cemetery Ridge assaulted by Pickett, it is reasonable to assume that the Napoleons of Garden's battery were assigned the mission to fire against Little Round Top.

109. *OR* 27, pt. 2, p. 384.

110. *OR* 27, pt. 1, p. 883. Often listed as a lieutenant colonel, McGilvery held the rank of major during the battle. *OR* 27, pt. 1, p. 591; Alpheus S. Williams to Bachelder, December, 1863, *The Bachelder Papers*, 1, p. 65; Henry J. Hunt to Bachelder, July 24, 1879, *The Bachelder Papers*, 1, p. 649.

111. Alexander, *Fighting for the Confederacy*, p. 249. In his various postwar writings Alexander mentions that he had either seven or nine howitzers on loan from Third Corps. However, a careful reading of Pendleton's and Alexander's accounts, as well as after-action reports and the Gettysburg National Military Park Tablets, leads us to conclude that neither

seven nor nine was the correct number. A total of six 12-pounder howitzers were detached from Colonel William T. Poague's Reserve Artillery Battalion of Third Corps. Of these, one howitzer was drawn from Captain George Ward's Madison Mississippi Artillery, while two were detached from Captain Joseph Graham's Charlotte North Carolina Artillery; two more were taken from the Warrington Virginia Artillery under Lieutenant Addison W. Utterback, and Captain James W. Wyatt sent one howitzer from his Albemarle "Everett" Virginia Artillery. Added to these six pieces were two 12-pounder howitzers from Colonel John J. Garnett's Battalion of Heth's Division, which came from Captain Charles R. Gandy's Norfolk Virginia Light Artillery Blues. This shifting and pilfering of guns brought the total number of loaned light howitzers from Third Corps to eight. It is noteworthy to mention that one writer believes Alexander may be mistaken in the types of guns Richardson commanded, even though Alexander never wavered from his descriptions of the pieces on loan from Third Corps. In referring to the after-action report of artillery battalion commander Lieutenant Colonel John J. Garnett (*OR* 27, pt. 2, pp. 652-653), Richard Rollins calls attention to the fact that Garnett specifically mentions Richardson as being in command of the nine *rifled* pieces of his battalion on July 2, 1863, and that Richardson "was ordered to the position held by Major-General Anderson's division, and to the right of Major Pegram's battalion. Toward the close of the day, in obedience to orders from General Longstreet, he placed his guns in position under fire at this point, but did not fire a single shot, having received orders to that effect. The remaining six guns (four Napoleons and two howitzers) bore no part in these actions [of July 2 and 3]." Rollins, "The Failure of Confederate Artillery in Pickett's Charge," *North & South Magazine*, vol. 3, number 4 (2000), p. 34. Rollins may be entirely correct in his assertion that Alexander simply made a mistake, but there is another possibility we believe is more plausible. While Richardson's rifled pieces were parked, Pendleton could have selected that officer to command the ad hoc collection of howitzers scraped together from various artillery units of Third Corps. Since the crews of the howitzers needed a commanding officer for the important action they would probably see that day, it is entirely possible to postulate that Pendleton took Richardson from his inactive command and placed him in charge of the howitzers. If that was the case, as we believe, then Alexander did indeed see howitzers with Major Richardson that morning.

112. *OR* 27, pt. 2, p. 456, 603, 675.

113. A careful reading of Alexander's accounts, together with the reports in the *OR*, etc., allows us to approximate fairly accurately the number of Confederate pieces that participated in the bombardment *against the Federal center*. The total number of guns on the field on July 3 from First Corps numbered 86, of which only 67 were available for action from the Peach Orchard to the northeast corner of Spangler's Woods, with the remaining pieces deployed to the right of the Peach Orchard or unable to be brought into action against the Federal center. Of the 67 guns mentioned above, 55 were long-range pieces, with the remaining 12 consisting of howitzers initially held in reserve. Added to the 67 available pieces were the *eight* howitzers (see note 111 above) on loan from Third Corps, giving Alexander the 75 guns he cites in his various writings. Meanwhile, at least 26 rifled guns from Second Corps and perhaps as many as 33, along with 54 or 55 pieces from Third Corps (which do not include the eight howitzers on loan to Alexander) participated in the bombardment. Therefore, the total number of guns included in the bombardment from the Peach Orchard to the left end of the

Confederate line amounted to at least 135. If the number of rifled guns from Second Corps involved in the bombardment totaled 33, then the total number of guns employed was 142. Further, if Alexander called up the 12 howitzers of First Corps initially in reserve to join in the cannonade, the number increases to 154; if the two Napoleons in Dance's Battalion in Second Corps participated, the number increases to 156. Finally, if the total number of guns from Third Corps was 55 instead of 54, then the number of guns participating in the bombardment from the Peach Orchard to the left end of the Confederate line climbs to 157. Alexander, *Military Memoirs of a Confederate*, pp. 418-419; Alexander, *Fighting for the Confederacy*, pp. 248-251; Alexander, letter dated 17 March 1877, on the topic of "Causes of Lee's Defeat at Gettysburg," *Southern Historical Society Papers*, 4, p. 103; Alexander to Bachelder, May 3, 1876, *The Bachelder Papers*, 1, p. 484; *OR* 27, pt. 2, pp. 603-605; Geo. L. Christian to John W. Daniel, 2 July 1898, Manuscripts Department, John W. Daniel Papers, University of Virginia Library, Charlottesville, Virginia, Richard Rollins, "The Failure of Confederate Artillery in Pickett's Charge," *North & South*, 3, number 4, pp. 26-42, and the Gettysburg National Military Park Tablets.

114. *OR* 27, pt. 2, p. 352.

115. Alpheus S. Williams to Bachelder, November 10, 1865, *The Bachelder Papers*, 1, p. 219.

116. Williams, *From the Cannon's Mouth: the Civil War letters of General Alpheus S. Williams*, p. 230.

117. *OR* 27, pt. 2, p. 504. Pfanz, *Culp's Hill and Cemetery Hill*, pp. 284-309. Pfanz's work is the most authoritative on the subject. As he explains it, little is understood about the fighting, especially from the Confederate perspective. Even the orders Johnson gave to his brigadiers that morning are unknown.

118. Williams, *From the Cannon's Mouth: the Civil War letters of General Alpheus S. Williams*, p. 230; *OR* 27, pt. 1, p. 806; pt. 2, pp. 504 and 521; McKim, *A Soldier's Recollections,* pp. 200-207.

119. Tucker, *High Tide at Gettysburg*, p. 323.

120. *OR* 27, pt. 2, pp. 504, 569.

121. Wainwright, *A Diary of Battle*, July 3, 1863, p. 248.

122. *OR* 27, pt. 1, p. 814.

123. *OR* 27, pt. 2, pp. 448, 511 and 526.

124. *OR* 27, pt. 2, p. 447.

125. Dodge, *A Bird's-Eye View of Our Civil War*, p. 140.

126. A few of these works are: Kathy Georg Harrison and John W. Busey, *Nothing But Glory: Pickett's Division at Gettysburg* (Gettysburg, 1987); Carol Reardon, *Pickett's Charge in History and Memory* (Chapel Hill, 1997); Richard Rollins, ed., *Pickett's Charge! Eyewitness Accounts* (Redondo Beach, 1994); and the classic, George R. Stewart, *Pickett's Charge: A Micro history of the Final Attack at Gettysburg, July 3, 1863* (Dayton, 1983). The most recent book on the subject, John Michael Priest, *Into the Fight: Pickett's Charge at Gettysburg* (Shippensburg, 1998), calls into question many of the accepted accounts of the action, but should be read with caution as many of its conclusions do not seem warranted by the research presented.

127. The 14th Connecticut was armed with breech-loading Sharps Rifles, a superior weapon when compared to muzzle-loading rifles or smooth bores that most Confederates carried.

128. Alexander, *Fighting for the Confederacy*, pp. 250-251; *OR* 27, pt. 1, p. 478. For a detailed account of the fighting at the Bliss Farm, see Elwood W. Christ, *The Struggle for the Bliss Farm at Gettysburg; July 2nd and 3rd 1863* (Baltimore, 1994), pp. 55-76.

129. For two good biographical sketches of Pickett, see Tagg, *The Generals of Gettysburg*, pp. 236-240; Peter Carmichael, "George Pickett," in Davis, ed., *The Confederate General*, 5, pp. 29-34.

130. Harrison and Busey, *Nothing But Glory: Pickett's Division at Gettysburg*, pp. 5, 15-16. The Gettysburg National Military Park Tablet lists the strength of Kemper's Brigade at 1,575, whereas Harrison and Busey's more careful study states the brigade's strength was 1,800. Busey and Martin, *Regimental Strengths and Losses at Gettysburg*, p. 144, lists Kemper's strength as 1,634. See footnote 131 for further explanation.

131. Harrison and Busey, *Nothing But Glory: Pickett's Division at Gettysburg*, pp. 5 and 18-19. Gettysburg National Military Park Tablet lists the strength of Garnett's Brigade at 1,480, whereas Harrison and Busey's study states the brigade strength at 1,800. Busey and Martin, *Regimental Strengths and Losses at Gettysburg*, p. 146, lists Garnett's strength at 1,459. See note 132 below for additional detail.

132. Harrison and Busey, *Nothing But Glory: Pickett's Division at Gettysburg*, pp. 6 and 22. Gettysburg National Military Park Tablet lists the strength of Armistead's Brigade at 1,650, whereas Harrison and Busey's study places the brigade strength at 2,100. Busey and Martin, *Regimental Strengths and Losses at Gettysburg*, p. 145, lists Armistead's strength as 1,950. While there is always an honest difference of opinion in the strengths of various commands, there seems to be considerable differences of opinions as to the strengths of Pickett's three brigades at Gettysburg. The best way to account for this is the methodology employed to determine effective strengths. Perhaps the lower estimates indicate only privates, while the higher estimates reflect all ranks, including privates, NCOs and officers. Tagg, *The Generals of Gettysburg*, pp. 240-249, offers excellent biographical sketches of Pickett's brigadiers.

133. Alexander, *Fighting for the Confederacy*, p. 255; Alexander, letter dated 17 March 1877, on the topic of "Causes of Lee's Defeat at Gettysburg," *Southern Historical Society Papers*, 4, p. 105.

134. Rawley Martin, "The Battle of Gettysburg," *Southern Historical Society Papers*, 32, p. 184.

135. James F. Crocker, "Gettysburg—Pickett's Charge," *Southern Historical Society Papers*, 33, p. 126.

136. Eppa Hunton to John W. Daniel, 15 July 1904, Manuscripts Department, John W. Daniel Papers, University of Virginia Library, Charlottesville, Virginia.

137. *Supplement to the OR* 5, serial no 5, p. 320.

138. Exactly why Brockenbrough was not with his brigade on July 3 is unknown. Perhaps it was because of his weak performance on July 1 (and elsewhere). It is more likely that the much-maligned colonel was in mourning after burying his brother, who had been killed on July 1. Brockenbrough's loss may also explain his lethargic performance later that day. He

was back in command on the retreat, although exactly when he resumed the reins is also unknown. Tagg, *The Generals of Gettysburg*, p. 348; Krick, *Lee's Colonels*, pp. 69-70.

139. *OR* 27, pt. 2, pp. 607-608, 638-639, 643-644, 646-647 and 649-651; Tagg, *The Generals of Gettysburg*, p. 335.

140. Alexander, *Fighting for the Confederacy*, p. 257; The Diary of Lieutenant Edward Owen, "In the Field and on the Town with the Washington Artillery," *Civil War Regiments: A Journal of the American Civil War*, 5, No. 1, p. 127, states that the signal guns opened fire at 1:35 p.m. No one agrees when the bombardment began or how long it lasted.

141. *OR* 27, pt. 1, p. 239; Henry J. Hunt to W. T. Sherman, February 1882, *The Bachelder Papers*, 2, p. 822.

142. Alexander, *Fighting for the Confederacy*, p. 259.

143. *OR* 27, pt. 2, p. 388.

144. *OR* 27, pt. 1, p. 239.

145. *OR* 27, pt. 1, pp. 883-884.

146. Haskell, *The Battle of Gettysburg*, p. 93.

147. Birkett Davenport Fry, "Pettigrew's Charge at Gettysburg," *Southern Historical Society Papers*, 7, p. 92.

148. Clark, "Wilcox's Alabama Brigade at Gettysburg," *Confederate Veteran*, 17, p. 230.

149. Joseph C. Mayo, "Pickett's Charge at Gettysburg," *Southern Historical Society Papers*, 34, p. 331.

150. Dearing's gallantry and the advanced placement of his guns drew the attention of large numbers of Federal ordnance, but his casualties on July 3 were surprisingly light. In Stribling's battery, for example, only three men were wounded and ten horses killed. *OR* 27, pt. 2, p. 389; Michael J. Andrus, *The Brooke, Fauquier, Loudoun and Alexandria Artillery* (Lynchburg, 1990), pp. 78-79. According to the Gettysburg National Military Park Tablet, the Fauquier Artillery had four 12-pounder Napoleons and two 20-pounder Parrotts, whereas each of the other three batteries in the battalion had four guns each. The combination of the four Napoleons and two long-range Parrotts made the battery one of the most formidable in Confederate service. Captain Miles C. Macon's Richmond "Fayette" Virginia Artillery lost three men killed, three others wounded, and eight horses; Captain William H. Caskie's Richmond "Hampden" Virginia Light Artillery suffered only three men wounded and seven horses lost; and Captain Joseph G. Blount's Lynchburg Virginia Artillery lost a total of five men killed and wounded and 12 horses. *OR* 27, pt. 2, p. 389; Robert H. Moore, II, *The Richmond Fayette, Hampden, Thomas and Blount's Lynchburg Artillery* (Lynchburg, 1991), p. 81. Of the 467 officers and men in Dearing's Battalion, only 17 men were killed or wounded—a casualty ratio of 3.6%.

151. Shotwell, as quoted in Harrison and Busey, *Nothing But Glory: Pickett's Division at Gettysburg*, p. 28.

152. *Supplement to the OR* 5, serial no 5, p. 308.

153. B. L. Farinholt to John W. Daniel, 15 April 1904, Manuscripts Department, John W. Daniel Papers, University of Virginia Library, Charlottesville, Virginia.

154. Alexander, *Fighting for the Confederacy*, p. 258.

155. Alexander, *Fighting for the Confederacy*, p. 258.

156. Alexander, *Fighting for the Confederacy*, p. 259; Alexander to Bachelder, May 3, 1876, *The Bachelder Papers*, 1, p. 489. Alexander is generally consistent about dispatching three messengers bearing the second, "come quick" appeal, although sometimes he states that one was written and two were verbal.

157. *OR* 27, pt. 2, p. 389.

158. *OR* 27, pt. 1, p. 437.

159. Longstreet, *From Manassas to Appomattox*, p. 392. There are a number of minor variations of this Pickett-Longstreet exchange. Freeman, *Lee's Lieutenants*, 3, p. 155; Stewart, *Pickett's Charge*, p. 164.

160. Isaac R. Trimble, letter dated 15 October 1875 on the topic of the "History of Lane's North Carolina Brigade," *Southern Historical Society Papers*, 9, p. 33.

161. *Supplement to the OR* 5, serial no 5, p. 429.

162. Joseph C. Mayo, "Pickett's Charge at Gettysburg," *Southern Historical Society Papers*, 34, p. 331.

163. Alexander, *Fighting for the Confederacy*, pp. 260-261.

164. Alexander to Bachelder, May 3, 1876, *The Bachelder Papers*, 1, pp. 489-490; Alexander, *Military Memoirs of a Confederate*, p. 424; Alexander, *Fighting for the Confederacy*, p. 261.

165. Alexander, *Fighting for the Confederacy*, pp. 258 and 261; Alexander to Bachelder, May 3, 1876, *The Bachelder Papers*, 1, p. 489; Alexander, letter dated 17 March 1877, on the topic of "Causes of Lee's Defeat at Gettysburg," *Southern Historical Society Papers*, 4, pp. 106-108. In his various writings, Alexander always made a point of explaining in detail that the length of time consumed for the bombardment was no longer than 50 minutes. This is supported by Wilcox's observations as detailed in *Southern Historical Society Papers*, 6, p. 118. Wilcox maintains that the cannonade "lasted on our part of the line fifty minutes." Major Charles Peyton of the 19th Virginia, who filed the after-action report for Garnett's Brigade, essentially agreed. According to that officer, the shelling "was kept up without interruption for one hour." *Southern Historical Society Papers*, 3, p. 216 and *OR* 27, pt. 2, p. 385. John Michael Priest, in his recent *Pickett's Charge at Gettysburg*, pp. 194-195, provides an extensive tabular listing of eyewitness accounts regarding the length of the bombardment, which generally supports Alexander, Wilcox and Peyton's recollections. When one factors in the amount of ammunition on hand and a reasonable rate of fire (and that several Confederate artillery officers believed the bombardment would not last long enough for them to procure additional supplies), ammunition stocks would have begun to run out about 45 or 50 minutes into the cannonade. Some contemporary accounts that claim the bombardment lasted much longer probably include the artillery duel that took place over the Bliss Farm complex as part of the great cannonade preceding the infantry assault, or mistakenly include the cannon fire from Manly's "Ellis" North Carolina Artillery, which continued providing a covering fire once the infantry was repulsed. It is our opinion that Alexander's time frame is generally accurate, and that the infantry attack began about 1:50 p.m. Sometime after 2:00 p.m. the infantry reached the Federal lines, where Pickett's men battled at the Angle and Copse of Trees for another quarter-hour before being driven back. By 3:00 p.m. the bulk of the returning survivors had returned to Confederate lines and the cannon fire ceased.

166. *Supplement to the OR* 5, serial no 5, p. 310.

167. *Supplement to the OR* 5, serial no 5, p. 335.

168. *OR* 27, pt. 1, p. 439.

169. *OR* 27, pt. 1, p. 373.

170. William J. Burns, as quoted in Reardon, *Pickett's Charge in History and Memory*, p. 19.

171. Isaac R. Trimble, letter dated 15 October 1875 on the topic of the "History of Lane's North Carolina Brigade," *Southern Historical Society Papers*, 9, pp. 31 and 33.

172. Fry, "Pettigrew's Charge at Gettysburg," *Southern Historical Society Papers*, 7, p. 92.

173. *OR* 27, pt. 1, p. 454.

174. *OR* 27, pt. 1, p. 239.

175. *OR* 27, pt. 1, p. 373.

176. *OR* 27, pt. 2, p. 386; "Garnett's Brigade at Gettysburg," *Southern Historical Society Papers*, 3, p. 216.

177. *OR* 27, pt. 1, p. 239.

178. *OR* 27, pt. 1, p. 431.

179. *Supplement to the OR* 5, serial no 5, p. 316.

180. *OR* 27, pt. 1, p. 319.

181. Webb, as quoted in Rollins, *Pickett's Charge,* p. 294.

182. Joseph C. Mayo, "Pickett's Charge at Gettysburg," *Southern Historical Society Papers*, 34, p. 332.

183. Rawley Martin, "The Battle of Gettysburg," *Southern Historical Society Papers*, 32, p. 187.

184. *Supplement to the OR* 5, serial no 5, p. 335.

185. *Supplement to the OR* 5, serial no 5, p. 336.

186. David Shultz, "*Double Canister at Ten Yards:*" *The Federal Artillery and the Repulse of Pickett's Charge* (Redondo Beach, 1995), pp. 47-55.

187. *OR* 27, pt. 1, p. 431.

188. *OR* 27, pt. 1, p. 428; Webb, as quoted in Rollins, *Pickett's Charge! Eyewitness Accounts*, p. 294.

189. Haskell, *The Battle of Gettysburg,* pp. 103 and 106.

190. Account of Brig. Gen. Henry Hunt, Chief of Artillery, Army of the Potomac, with his additions in margins, January 20, 1873, *The Bachelder Papers*, 1, p. 432.

191. *OR* 27, pt. 1, p. 428.

192. According to the 1861 edition of *Instructions for the Field Artillery,* there was no set mixture of the type ammunition rounds carried by rifled Federal batteries. Even the 1864 edition of this same work stated on page 13 that the blend of rounds *for rifled guns* was "still on experiment." Given that each ammunition chest for the 3-inch Ordnance rifle carried 50 rounds, and that each gun usually had three chests (one on the limber and two on the accompanying caisson), and assuming that each chest was packed with only six rounds of canister (which was typical), then Cowan's entire six-gun battery had only 36 total rounds of canister ammunition. He may have had even fewer rounds than that.

193. Andrew Cowan to Bachelder, November 24, 1885, *The Bachelder Papers*, 2, p. 1146; and Cowan to Bachelder, December 2, 1885, *The Bachelder Papers*, 2, pp. 1156-1157.

194. *Supplement to the OR* 5, serial no 5, p. 322.

195. *Supplement to the OR* 5, serial no 5, p. 316.

196. *Southern Historical Society Papers*, 34, pp. 333-334.

197. *OR* 27, pt. 2, p. 386; "Garnett's Brigade at Gettysburg," *Southern Historical Society Papers*, 3, p. 217.

198. *Supplement to the OR* 5, serial no 5, p. 336.

199. Charles T. Loehr, "The 'Old First' Virginia at Gettysburg," *Southern Historical Society Papers*, 32, pp. 34-35.

200. Geo. L. Christian to John W. Daniel, 2 July 1898, Manuscripts Department, John W. Daniel Papers, University of Virginia Library, Charlottesville, Virginia. Although Christian exaggerated the import of Hill's decision, his general observation was correct: the main attack was not properly supported, either by infantry or artillery.

201. B. L. Farinholt, "Battle of Gettysburg—Johnson's Island," *Confederate Veteran*, 5, p. 469.

202. Farinholt, "Battle of Gettysburg—Johnson's Island," *Confederate Veteran*, 5, p. 469.

203. *OR* 27, pt. 2, p. 1000.

204. Coddington, *Gettysburg*, p. 506; Report of R. M. Mayo, August 13, 1863, *Supplement to the OR* 5, serial no 5, p. 415; Tagg, *The Generals of Gettysburg*, p. 348. Mayo's report is disingenuous in several respects, including how far his men advanced that day. In light of his other incredible claims, Mayo's assertion that his brigade numbered but 200 men cannot be correct. Even though this brigade suffered from low morale and poor leadership, its strength was undoubtedly much higher on July 3. Bradley M. Gottfried, "To Fail Twice: Brockenbrough's Brigade at Gettysburg," *Gettysburg Magazine*, No. 23, pp. 66-75. Numerous other sources confirm the early collapse of Pettigrew's left. Isaac Trimble remembered Mayo's regiments "halt[ed] in the meadow at a deep ditch and went no further." *Supplement to the OR* 5, serial no 5, p. 444. General Edward Thomas, whose brigade was positioned in Long Lane on the southwest corner of Gettysburg, told General Lane after the attack that Brockenbrough's (Mayo's) Virginians did not even make it as far a his position before breaking for the rear. Lane to Editors, *Raleigh Observer*, September 7, 1877.

205. *Supplement to the OR* 5, serial no 5, p. 419.

206. Lane to Editors, *Raleigh Observer*, September 7, 1877; *Supplement to the OR* 5, serial no 5, p. 419.

207. Birkett Davenport Fry, "Pettigrew's Charge at Gettysburg," *Southern Historical Society Papers*, 7, pp. 92-93.

208. Isaac R. Trimble, letter dated 15 October 1875 on the topic of the "History of Lane's North Carolina Brigade," *Southern Historical Society Papers*, 9, p. 33. Trimble's lower leg was amputated and his was captured and imprisoned. He was not released until February of 1865.

209. *OR* 27, pt. 2, p. 672.

210. *OR* 27, pt. 2, p. 632.

211. *OR* 27, pt. 2, pp. 620 and 632.

212. Clark, "Wilcox's Alabama Brigade at Gettysburg," *Confederate Veteran*, 17, p. 230.

213. *Richmond Daily Dispatch,* "Gettysburg Charge," *Southern Historical Society Papers*, 23, p. 234; *OR* 27, pt. 2, pp. 620 and 632.

214. *OR* 27, pt. 2, pp. 620 and 632; Cadmus Marcellus Wilcox, letter dated 26 March 1877 from General C. M. Wilcox on the topic of "Causes of Lee's Defeat at Gettysburg," *Southern Historical Society Papers*, 4, p. 117; Wilcox, "General C. M. Wilcox on the Battle of Gettysburg," *Southern Historical Society Papers*, 6, p. 119.

215. *OR* 27, pt. 2, pp. 620 and 632.

216. Harrison and Busey, *Nothing But Glory: Pickett's Division at Gettysburg*, p. 117.

217. Charles T. Loehr, "The 'Old First' Virginia at Gettysburg," *Southern Historical Society Papers*, 32, p. 37.

218. For descriptions of these cavalry actions, please consult: Longacre, *The Cavalry at Gettysburg*, pp. 220-244; and Eric J. Wittenberg, *Gettysburg's Forgotten Cavalry Actions* (Gettysburg, 1998). For unit placements, see John B. Bachelder, *Gettysburg, East Cavalry Field, Maps #10, 11 and 12*.

219. Casualty estimates for Gettysburg vary substantially. The general numbers presented are the result of our own study of the battle. For specific tabulations, readers should consult Busey and Martin, *Regimental Strengths and Losses at Gettysburg*. Admittedly losses declared by both sides were less than actually sustained. Some historians argue that Lee's actual losses (including walking wounded, for example), approached 28,000 men. In any event, it is reasonable to assume that the actual casualties suffered by both armies amounted to 50,000 or higher. Gettysburg historian D. Scott Hartwig, in "The Gettysburg Campaign," in Current, ed., *Encyclopedia of the Confederacy*, 2, p. 683, offers generally accepted casualty estimates as follow (with the same caveats as listed above): Meade: 3,155 killed, 14,529 wounded, and 5,365 missing or captured; Lee: 4,427 killed, 12,179 wounded, and 5,592 missing or captured. According to *Pennsylvania at Gettysburg*, 1, pp. 171-172, admitted Federal losses for the entire campaign, including Second Winchester, were 32,043, while William Allen presented admitted losses for the Confederate army as about 24,000. William Allan, "Gen. Lee's Strength and Losses at Gettysburg," *Southern Historical Society Papers*, 4, pp. 34-35.

220. Farinholt, "Battle of Gettysburg—Johnson's Island, *Confederate Veteran*, 5, p. 469.

221. Only two of the army's seven corps commanders urged Meade to attack Lee: Howard (Eleventh Corps) and Wadsworth (in temporary command of First Corps). Meade's pursuit of Lee appears feeble and ineffective. *OR* 27, part 3, p. 1049, and *Southern Historical Society Papers*, 40. President Abraham Lincoln was so frustrated by Meade's lack of pursuit after Gettysburg that he said, "Trying to get him [Meade] to move, is like an old lady trying to shoo her geese across a creek." Lincoln, like many students today, was not aware of just how many formations in the Army of the Potomac had been badly damaged.

222. Alexander, *Fighting for the Confederacy*, pp. 248-249.

223. *OR* 27, pt. 2, pp. 379 and 384; Rollins, "Prelude to Pickett's Charge," p. 122.

224. [Ambrose Ransom Wright], "From Wright's Brigade," *Augusta Daily Constitutionalist*, July 23, 1863. Of course Ewell's Corps, or at least one reinforced division of it, did contribute to the fighting on July 3. Wright's point is clear, however: there were entire divisions of infantry sitting idle on July 3 that should have been utilized.

225. Alexander to Father, July 17, 1863, Marion Alexander Boggs, editor, *The Alexander Letters*, 1787-1900 (Athens, 1980).

226. Armistead Lindsay Long, letter dated April 1877, on the topic of "Causes of Lee's Defeat at Gettysburg," *Southern Historical Society Papers*, 4, p. 123; Long, *Memoirs of Robert E. Lee*, pp. 292-294.

227. Lafayette McLaws, "Gettysburg," *Southern Historical Society Papers*, 7, pp. 87-88.

228. Lafayette McLaws to Isaac R. Pennypacker, Editor, *Philadelphia Weekly Press*, [1877], copy at the Confederate Research Center, Harold B. Simpson History Complex, Hill College, Hillsboro, Texas; Lafayette McLaws, "Gettysburg," *Southern Historical Society Papers*, 7, p. 89.

229. Taylor, *Four Years with General Lee*, pp. 103-104.

230. Cadmus Marcellus Wilcox, "General C. M. Wilcox on the Battle of Gettysburg," *Southern Historical Society Papers*, 6, p. 120.

231. *OR* 27, pt. 2, p. 452; Lafayette McLaws, "Gettysburg," *Southern Historical Society Papers*, 7, p. 90.

232. George Pickett to LaSalle Corbell, July 4 and 5, 1863, in Arthur Crew Inman, editor, *Soldier of the South: General Pickett's War Letters to his Wife* (Boston, 1928), pp. 66 and 71. Pickett's letters, as presented by his wife long after his death, must be used with care, since "the weight of evidence bears decidedly toward Sallie as their true author." Reardon, *Pickett's Charge in History and Memory*, pp. 186-187. However, some of these letters are surely genuine, and it is our belief that this one is from Pickett himself. There is also the issue of Pickett's missing report. While that interesting topic is outside the scope of this book, the implication as to why Lee rejected his first draft is that Pickett castigated one or more officers for failing to support his assault as ordered. For more information, see Reardon, *Pickett's Charge in History and Memory*, pp. 159-160, 186.

233. Alexander, *Fighting for the Confederacy*, p. 261.

234. James Longstreet, "Account of the Campaign and Battle of Gettysburg," on the topic of "Causes of Lee's Defeat at Gettysburg," *Southern Historical Society Papers*, 5, p. 69; Longstreet, "Lee in Pennsylvania," *Annals of the War*, p. 430.

235. Sorrel, *Recollections of a Confederate Staff Officer*, p. 164.

236. Robert A. Bright, "Pickett's Charge: The Story of It as Told by a Member of His Staff," *Southern Historical Society Papers*, 31, pp. 231-232. Fremantle, *Three Months in the Southern States*, pp. 212-213. On the basis of Longstreet's prior movements with Alexander at Dearing's Battalion as the infantry advance was beginning, Longstreet was probably in the vicinity of the Henry Spangler Farm when Bright found him. Old Pete's heart may not have been in the assault, but Bright's assertion that he was seated on a fence and unable to see the critical point of attack strains credulity. Readers should keep in mind Bright's account was written years after the event, and by that time Longstreet was considered a pariah in the South.

237. James Longstreet, "Account of the Campaign and Battle of Gettysburg," on the topic of "Causes of Lee's Defeat at Gettysburg," *Southern Historical Society Papers*, 5, p. 55. It is interesting to note that Robert Rodes, commander of a division in Ewell's Second Corps (and thus *not* under Longstreet's command on July 3) had three of his five brigades lingering on the south side of town along Long Lane on July 3. According Rodes, he was supposed to be "on the lookout for another favorable opportunity to co-operate. When the sound of musketry was heard, it became apparent that the enemy in our front was much excited. The favorable opportunity seemed to me close at hand." However, by the time Rodes dispatched Major H. A.

Whiting of his staff to find Ewell and seek permission to move forward, the attack by Pettigrew, Trimble and Pickett "had already failed." *OR* 27, pt. 2, p. 557. Gettysburg was Rodes' worse battle as a division commander, but he was in good company: there was an utter lack of coordination up and down the line that day.

238. *OR* 27, pt. 2, pp. 351-352.

239. *OR* 27, pt. 2, p. 544.

240. *OR* 27, pt. 1, p. 750; Thomas Osborn, "The Artillery at Gettysburg," *Philadelphia Weekly Times*, May 31, 1879, reprinted in Herb S. Crum, ed. *The Eleventh Corps Artillery at Gettysburg: The Papers of Major Thomas Ward Osborn* (Hamilton, 1991), p. 72, as cited in Rollins, the "Failure of Confederate Artillery in Pickett's Charge," *North & South*, 3, number 4, pp. 39-40.

Chapter 9

"For Some Reason, Not Yet Fully Explained to Me"

Reflections

"The fact is, General Lee believed the Army of Northern Virginia, as it then existed, could accomplish anything."
— Major General Henry Heth[1]

On three successive days Robert E. Lee had positioned his Army of Northern Virginia within reach of a dramatic and potentially decisive triumph, only to see the fruits of his efforts elude him and the Confederate cause. In the early morning hours of July 4, the exhausted general sat down with cavalryman John D. Imboden and, in a unique moment, bore his soul to the officer. "I never saw troops behave more magnificently than Pickett's division of Virginians did today, in that grand charge upon the enemy," Lee declared. "And if they had been supported as they were to have been—but for some reason, not yet fully explained to me, were not—we would have held the position, & the day would have been ours."[2]

In many respects Lee's analysis of why the fighting on the third day failed, as told to Imboden, aptly describes the entire battle.

Why Lee and the Army of Northern Virginia were defeated at Gettysburg

One of the most popular explanations for Confederate defeat was penned many years after the war by E. M. Hays of Scales' Brigade, Pender's Light Division. Writing in 1890, Hays explained that "the Confederate soldier up to the close of the Gettysburg fight imagined himself invincible."[3] This comment had been uttered before by other ex-Confederates—even Lee said he believed his army was invincible—and many writers have seized upon the idea as a simple explanation for why the Confederates lost in Pennsylvania: they were overconfident and underestimated their enemy.[4] Certainly the officers and men in Army of Northern Virginia were confident in their abilities and eager to defeat their adversary on Yankee soil, and they had every reason to be sanguine and expect success.

* * *

Many more tangible and direct reasons exist that explain Lee's ultimate failure at Gettysburg. All of these have been described fully elsewhere in this study. In our opinion they number 17, and are summarized below in ascending order of importance.

17. General Lee's inadequate staff size and faulty organizational structure

General Lee was well aware of the diminutive size of his staff. The number of personnel he employed at Confederate army headquarters was roughly equivalent to the size of a staff utilized by one of Napoleon's division commanders. Not a single army commander in the American Civil War, Federal or Confederate, had ever worked in the field or trained with a complex and intricate Napoleonic-style staff. This is because professional American officers were trained at academies (West Point, for example), that emphasized engineering expertise instead of the operational art of commanding armies in the field. Too, American armies from the Revolution to the Mexican War were far smaller than those fielded during the Civil War. Because of the limited number of officers at headquarters, army commanders relied heavily on the initiative and expertise of key subordinates. The reoccurring theme in Lee's correspondence of his need for officers who have received "proper instruction" so that his men could be "properly led" bears out this point. Lee believed that his staff should be kept at a minimum in order to avoid depriving front line formations of capable officers—where the exercise of initiative was vital. The consequences of his small staff manifested themselves during the Pennsylvania campaign *when combined with* Jeb Stuart's absence. This forced Lee to utilize his few staff officers for reconnaissance missions that otherwise would have been performed more quickly and efficiently by Stuart and his troopers. This restricted the areas that could be scouted as well as the information that could be obtained and the speed with which it could be acquired—and acted upon.

One particular organizational defect of General Lee's staff was his failure to employ a general officer who was with the army but without a field command. Lee's ineffective use of Major General Isaac Trimble comes immediately to mind. Trimble was an intelligent, experienced, and aggressive officer perfectly suited for a role similar to Napoleon's Imperial aides-de-camp, a position Lee would have been familiar with because of his extensive studies of Napoleonic history. As an aide-de-camp to Lee, Trimble would have carried with him the authority of the commanding general.

16. Meade's localized counterattack at Culp's Hill early on July 3

The advance made by Edward "Allegheny" Johnson's Division late in the day of July 2 posed a serious threat to the Federal army's right flank. Once Meade and his generals agreed to stay at Gettysburg and fight out the battle, they had no realistic option other than to reestablish the defensive integrity of their right flank by eliminating the Confederate threat to the Baltimore Pike.[5] The predawn spoiling attack ultimately dislodged Johnson's reinforced division and ruined Lee's plans to use Ewell's men to draw off Federal attention and strength from the main assault against Cemetery Ridge. Meade's plan seized the tactical initiative in the sector and was a major reason why Confederate efforts on that day were not successful.

15. The collective decision by Meade and his corps commanders to stay and fight on July 3

Late on the evening of July 2, Meade held a council of war with his senior officers to determine the condition of his army and its course of action. The collective judgment of the senior officers was to "stay and fight it out."[6] It was a courageous decision. Meade's army had already suffered heavily. More than 20,000 officers and men had become casualties, and three of its seven corps had been eviscerated and another two and one-half divisions from two other corps had been roughly handled. Twenty-five of the army's 51 infantry brigades had been used up and most were no longer combat capable if faced with a determined attack.

According to Brigadier General Alpheus S. Williams of Twelfth Corps, "there were those who doubted our ability to hold where we were." Sickles' Third Corps had been so badly shattered that some of its generals believed the battle already lost. Following a discussion, Williams remembered that Meade asked for the issue to be put to a vote. The result was "unanimity for making the trial."[7] According to Abner Doubleday, Meade initially "disapproved of the battleground Hancock had selected."[8] However, after the fighting on July 2, the Federal commanding general was already disposed to stay put when the council convened. When the Federal Committee on the Conduct of the War reviewed the Gettysburg Campaign in the early months of 1864, Dan Butterfield, the army's chief of staff, and David Birney, a division commander in Third Corps, wrongly accused Meade of wanting to retreat after the fighting on July 2. This claim conflicts with the recollections of other officers attending the nocturnal meeting, none of whom ever mentioned that Meade wanted to do anything other than keep the army in place.

Given the losses he had already suffered, it would have been understandable if Meade and/or his senior officers had advised leaving the field to the Confederates. If the battle had occurred in Virginia, history tells us that the Federals would probably have withdrawn. The steady string of defeats coupled with the ramifications of losing a large scale battle north of the Mason-Dixon Line, however, kept them in place and in the end, gave them a victory.

14. The troops comprising the first wave of the Pickett-Pettigrew-Trimble assault on July 3

Once it had been decided that McLaws and Hood would not join with Pickett to lead the attack on the battle's third day, General Lee agreed that six other brigades from Hill's Third Corps would be part of the first wave. This decision was made during the long council meeting that took place, both on horseback and on foot, while Lee and his senior officers examined the Federal positions and moved over the field from the Sherfy Peach Orchard northward along the swells of the Emmitsburg Road, and finally to Seminary Ridge.

Harry Heth was the only division commander present during this meeting; his influence on the final selection of brigades, if any, remains unclear. Since one of the divisions tapped was his own (under Johnston Pettigrew), it seems likely Heth was somehow involved in the selection process. It was an unfortunate choice. Heth's brigades had been pounded on July 1. Brockenbrough's was without its regular (and inept) commander and was generally recognized as an ineffective collection of regiments. Placing it on the far left and in the front line was negligence of the highest order. Davis', too, had suffered heavily on July 1 and its commander had proven his unfitness for field duty. Archer's outfit was numerically weak, exhausted, and without the veteran leadership of its namesake, who was now a prisoner of war.

Finally, Pettigrew was leading the division, which left his large but weakened brigade in the hands of a colonel.

The length of Pettigrew's line guaranteed that the two North Carolina brigades from the Light Division selected to complete the first wave could not fully support it. Jim Lane's brigade was fresh, but Alfred Scales' had suffered serious losses on July 1. At the last moment, Isaac Trimble was put in command of these brigades, but only after they had been improperly aligned behind Pettigrew's right flank.

We hold that there are two ways to look at the selection of these troops to lead the attack on July 3. First, if Lee was selecting his best available Third Corps troops to lead the assault, he failed. Many other stronger and more battle-worthy commands were readily available, including the brigades of Posey and Mahone in Anderson's Division, as well as two of the four brigades from Pender's Light Division, namely Perrin and Thomas. The proximity of Rodes' Division should have placed his brigades in the selection mix as well, although there is no indication that Lee ever considered using any part of Second Corps to lead the attack. Why is unknown. If, on the other hand, Lee deliberately withheld quality brigades with the intention of delivering a powerful second supporting thrust to solidify and break through the gap he was confident the first wave would create, then the choice of brigades comprising the first wave looks far less suspect.

13. William Pendleton's incompetence

Brigadier General William N. Pendleton was the weakest link in the Confederate high command chain. Already on the army's staff when Robert E. Lee took command, the Episcopal rector essentially served as President Davis' spy. Lee recognized the politics involved with Pendleton's status and position. After judging Pendleton's tireless work ethic but utter lack of military ability, Lee decided to reorganize his artillery following Chancellorsville. The reorganization that eliminated the army's artillery reserve and reconfigured how the battalions were attached at divisional and corps level was designed with two important goals in mind. First and foremost, the reorganization afforded greater tactical flexibility and firepower at the corps and division levels. Second—Lee would never have publicly admitted this—it minimized Pendleton's battlefield authority. However, by eliminating the central reserve, which ostensibly had been under Pendleton's control, a large pool of guns that could have been employed to support a specific part of the line was lost. This, in turn, made such a task much more difficult to accomplish.

Despite his diminished role at Gettysburg, Pendleton's presence hurt the Confederate cause. His failure to obey General Lee's direct order to coordinate artillery fire onto the retreating Federals during the first day's fighting was exceeded only by his incompetence on the battle's third day. Pendleton's mismanagement of the Confederate artillery on July 3 included his relocation of the ordnance trains and moving Major Richardson and his howitzers without advising Alexander of that fact. He also blundered by not employing all of Second Corps' available guns. To this list may be added Pendleton's faulty management of the army artillery resupply convoy, which on July 3 was still far to the rear at Winchester, Virginia. It reached the Potomac River and was ferried across at Williamsport two days later.[9]

For all these reasons, "Parson" Pendleton can be viewed as an albatross around General Lee's neck, and one of the major contributing factors as to why the Army of Northern Virginia met with defeat at Gettysburg.

12. Winfield Hancock's excellent performance throughout the battle

The steady hand of Winfield Scott Hancock, Meade's trusted subordinate and Second Corps commander in the Army of the Potomac, brought order out of chaos and retrieved Federal fortunes on the afternoon and evening of July 1. Hancock rallied the disorganized and shattered fragments of First and Eleventh Corps and made the initial decision that evening for the army to stay and fight at Gettysburg. On July 2, despite losing effectively one and one-half of his four divisions, Hancock shifted his troops as needed and inspired his men up and down the corps line. On July 3, Hancock again displayed his leadership abilities by steadying his men and motivating them to stand strong and defeat Lee's infantry. His officers and men drew courage and strength from his actions, which earned him a painful wound that never healed and contributed to his death years later. Hancock's performance embodied what George Pickett referred to as one of the reasons the Confederates did not achieve what they hoped for at Gettysburg: "I think the Union army had something to do with it." It did, and among its generals Hancock played perhaps the largest role.[10]

11. James Longstreet's disobedience on July 3

One of the most puzzling aspects of the battle is James Longstreet's diametrically opposed performances on July 2 and 3. His tactical abilities were never more prominently displayed than on the battle's second day, as we fully explored earlier in this study. As the tactical commander for the third day's fighting, and as Robert E. Lee's most trusted subordinate, Longstreet resisted Lee's orders and displayed a petulance that dismayed many of those around him.

Longstreet had strenuously argued with Lee for a large-scale turning movement when he arrived on the field late on the afternoon of July 1. Rebuffed and visibly unhappy, he still worked hard to implement Lee's modified plan of attack the next day and fought his corps as well as anyone ever did anywhere during the war. Dismayed that Lee intended to attack again, Old Pete instead began planning his own tactical turning and "reverse attack" for July 3. General Lee only discovered this when he arrived at Longstreet's headquarters early that day, overruled him, and reiterated his orders to attack as directed. If McLaws and Hood's divisions were capable of marching around Round Top and attacking the enemy there, as Longstreet intended, his decision to keep them out entirely of the action on July 3, when Lee wanted Longstreet to call upon every formation necessary for support, smacks of bitterness.

Once it became clear to Longstreet that General Lee was going to wage an offensive battle on July 3, he organized the main wave of the attack column—and then put the responsibility for when it should attack on the shoulders of Edward Porter Alexander, a colonel of artillery. Longstreet was a professional soldier and he knew he was abandoning his responsibilities. Even if he believed that the attack was doomed to fail, it was his duty to organize and launch it to the best of his ability. Longstreet's failure to coordinate the artillery and organize the all-important second infantry wave (without which the attack had almost no chance of success) reflect poorly on the man General Lee had called his Old War Horse at Sharpsburg.

Ironically, writers castigate Longstreet for his performance on July 2—his best day—while largely ignoring or glossing over his obstreperous role on July 3, demonstrably his worst day as a corps leader. On July 2 Old Pete did everything Lee asked of him and more. He managed to get into action every available infantry brigade and artillery battalion under his command, which in and of itself is an amazing feat and one he did not even come close to approximating the next afternoon.[11]

10. General Lee's failure to assume direct tactical command on July 3

Once Lee arrived at Longstreet's headquarters early on July 3 and discovered that his planned early morning assault was not going to take place, Lee should have realized then and there something serious was amiss with Longstreet. The subsequent hours-long council conversation with Longstreet also provided Lee with ample evidence that his corps commander lacked the appetite for the attack Lee intended to deliver. Lee knew better than anyone what was riding on the outcome of the fighting, and as the commanding general should have assumed direct tactical control and not have entrusted the critical attack to a subordinate unwilling or unable to deliver it.

Lee finally realized this after watching the fiasco we know today as Pickett's Charge implode before his eyes. We believe that this is what Lee meant when he rode out to meet the remnants of Pickett's men and told them, "The fault is entirely my own." Virtually every historian has interpreted these six words as Lee's acknowledgment that the *idea* of attacking Meade on Cemetery Ridge on July 3 was wrong. This interpretation fails to take into account all of Lee's *other* statements concerning the failed attack (it was not delivered as intended, there were no supports, it failed "for reasons not yet clear to me," and so forth). When read in this context, the statement—"The fault is entirely my own"—constitutes a recognition by the best soldier in a Confederate uniform that he was at fault for not personally directing the operations on July 3 and making sure the first wave was adequately supported. No other reading of this phrase makes sense.

9. President Jefferson Davis, missing brigades, and a failure of support

By withholding from General Lee his several detached veteran brigades, President Jefferson Davis violated the cardinal military rule of reinforcing success. These experienced formations had helped make the Army of Northern Virginia successful, and partially replacing them with less experienced troops and commanders was a grave error. Davis falsely assumed that his decision would not cause any loss of efficiency within the ranks of the army, while ensuring that his one successful army commander would not have at his disposal all the support he realistically could have expected and required. A certain synergy existed between the commanding general and his regiments, and Lee's troops were never as effective *away* from him as they were *with* him. Davis sent Lee less experienced replacements, so he just as easily could have withheld those formations and returned to Lee the brigades he had requested. There are no valid military or political justifications for Davis' decision. His failure is especially pronounced in light of the deteriorating situation Mississippi and the debate about how best to employ Confederate resources for the summer campaigning season.

The subject of Confederate operations in the summer of 1863, and whether or not troops should have been dispatched from the Army of Northern Virginia and sent west to attempt to save Vicksburg, has been dealt with at length in this study. As we have argued, by the end of the first week in May (after Chancellorsville), it was too late to affect the fighting at Vicksburg with troops from Lee's army, and there was ample evidence that they would not have been employed to any good use under a general with the pitiful field record "Retreatin' Joe" Johnston had amassed. Johnston's hasty abandonment of the important rail junction of Jackson proved that point again and all but sealed the fate of John C. Pemberton's Mississippi army. Moreover, by this time in the war Vicksburg was no longer important to the Confederacy—and certainly not worth losing Pemberton's army to retain. The argument as framed and delivered by the so-called "Western Solutionists" ignores the reality and logistics of the situation faced by the Confederacy.[12]

However, politics still demanded that a relief column be dispatched for Vicksburg, even in the face of these difficulties (and one was). Lee and Davis, meanwhile, could only hope that somehow Providence would grant a favorable outcome in Mississippi. Lee was correct when he argued that the best hope for Southern forces to influence the outcome of the war existed in the area that most threatened Northern interests—and that area only existed in the Eastern Theater. Consequently, Jefferson Davis should have moved heaven and earth to see that every veteran formation of the Army of Northern Virginia (and perhaps troops from Bragg's Tennessee army) was returned to Lee for the upcoming operation.[13]

We will never know what Lee could have accomplished with the five missing veteran brigades—more than 11,000 experienced officers and men in 20 regiments and four smaller battalions. Given the presence of so many critical moments during the fighting of July 2 or July 3, it is reasonable to assume that Lee would have put them to use.[14] We do know that Lee and others always believed that these missing brigades were a significant reason the army failed in Pennsylvania. Micah Jenkins, the commander of one of Pickett's two missing brigades, was livid over being denied his chance to participate at Gettysburg.[15] After several letter writing efforts failed, he turned to Lee for help in getting President Davis to reconsider and release him.[16] Lee, too, had sensed the same frustration dealing with Davis that Jenkins was now enduring. "I regret exceedingly, the absence of yourself and your brigade from the battle of Gettysburg," wrote Lee. "There is no telling what a gallant brigade, led by an efficient commander, might have accomplished when victory trembled in the balance. I verily believe that the result would have been different if you had been present."[17]

General Lee might well have been correct. Writing after the war, Walter Harrison, Pickett's assistant adjutant general and inspector general, observed:

> With these two [missing] brigades [Corse's and Jenkins'], Pickett's Division, in its celebrated charge at Gettysburg, would have been over 8,000 instead of only 4,700 strong. Whether the presence of these two large brigades, of as good and proved fighting material as any in the army, would have materially affected the result of that terrible day—the very turning point of the war—is not for me to say.[18]

It took the Federals at least a quarter-hour to evict a few hundred exhausted officers and men from the area of the Angle and Copse of Trees on July 3. Would the presence of two more large veteran brigades (both Corse and Jenkins were part of Pickett's Division, and likely would have participated in the assault) have made a difference? What further successes would Longstreet's corps have realized if Robert Ransom's Division had been returned to the army as requested by General Lee and involved in the fighting on the southern end of the field on July 2? We don't know. But we do know Lee had desperately sought these men and was refused by Davis.

8. The sacrifice by the Federal First Corps on July 1

By standing their ground on July 1 following the death of their corps commander, John Reynolds, the officers and men of First Corps bought valuable time for the rest of the army and turned in a performance far beyond their numbers. No one knows for sure what, if any, subsequent confusion or hesitancy First Corps' heroic stand engendered in the minds of key Confederate generals like Rodes, Ewell, and Hill. By suffering a staggering casualty rate of 70% on July 1, First Corps offered more than what could have been reasonably expected from any fighting formation. General Meade was fortunate, in light of the performance of Howard's Eleventh Corps, that First Corps sacrificed itself on the ground west of Gettysburg.

7. The Failure of Second Corps' senior officers to coordinate their movements and get their commands into action on July 2

Dick Ewell had orders to demonstrate as soon as he heard Longstreet's guns on the southern end of the field, and turn it "into a real attack" when opportunity offered itself. He enjoyed about eight hours to prepare his command and officers for the job ahead of them. Once the battle was underway, Ewell developed a good general appreciation of how the attack was faring because his aides told him as much from their vantage point in the cupola of the Saint Francis Xavier Roman Catholic Church on High Street. "Things are going splendidly!" they shouted. "We are driving them back everywhere."[19] Robert Rodes reported that he could clearly see Federals shifting troops away from Cemetery Hill to help stem the collapse of Meade's left flank. For these and other reasons Ewell converted his artillery demonstration into an attack against Culp's Hill and East Cemetery Hill. He had at a minimum nine of Second Corps' 13 infantry brigades available for the task.[20]

Yet, after hours of time to prepare for just the "opportunity" General Lee hoped would show itself, Ewell's attack lacked any sense of coordination, power, or urgency. Ed Johnson's move against Culp's Hill met with partial success, largely as a result of Meade's decision to strip troops away in response to the success of Confederate troops elsewhere. Johnson's three brigades faced only one thinly-stretched Federal brigade under George Greene. However, Maryland Steuart's troops could not be reinforced or his gains exploited because daylight was fading and no one could see what was going on. On Johnson's right, opposite East Cemetery Hill, only two of Early's three available brigades were put into action because Early decided not to reinforce his initial stunning success scored by Hays and Avery. As a result, Gordon's formidable regiments of Georgians remained spectators. The most inexplicable command lapse on July 2, however, was turned in by Robert Rodes. His five brigades were improperly positioned and took too much time to align themselves for the attack. Ewell, apparently, never even realized it. While Rodes remained in the rear, his brigades marched forward, saw the fighting was dying out, and marched back again. Not a single one of Rodes' brigades entered the battle on July 2.

Ewell, Early, Rodes, and Johnson had more than ample time on July 2 to plan and execute their maneuvers to exploit any opportunities that might arise on their front. With the possible exception of Johnson, the utter inability of the senior officers of the Confederate Second Corps to undertake the necessary steps to insure the maximum employment of their troops in any attack on July 2, can only be considered a complete failure of their command responsibilities.

6. The failure of Dick Ewell to timely inform General Lee on July 1 that Culp's Hill was vulnerable and subject to capture

General Lee's decision to leave Ewell's Second Corps on the left side of Gettysburg following the first day's fighting was directly influenced by the information Ewell presented to the commanding general late on the night of July 1. Ewell's news that Culp's Hill was subject to ready capture was shared with headquarters only after Lee, through Major Charles Marshall, ordered Ewell to bring his corps around to the right side of town in preparation for the continuation of the battle the next day. In the nocturnal meeting with the commanding general that followed, Ewell shared his information and Lee extended to his corps leader the courtesy and trust to consummate the opportunity to compromise the Federal defensive line and facilitate the defeat of Meade's army. The information Ewell did not impart to Lee—that the scouting report about Culp's Hill was several hours old—profoundly impacted the operations of the Confederate army on July 2 and 3.

For reasons still unclear, Ewell failed to act with celerity when he received information from his scouts during the evening of July 1 that Culp's Hill was vacant. Isaac Trimble had personally told Ewell the same thing that same afternoon after a personal reconnaissance. Yet Ewell failed to act or notify his commanding officer. Why? It is our opinion that by late that afternoon, Dick Ewell already realized that he had bungled a golden opportunity by not pursuing the retreating Federals up Cemetery Hill as ordered. Thus, Ewell was too embarrassed to forward news to Lee that Culp's Hill was now vacant and defenseless. How would all this have looked to General Lee if Ewell, after ignoring two orders to pursue and seize the high ground south of Gettysburg, subsequently informed him that an opportunity existed for the easy capture of Culp's Hill? From Lee's perspective the news would have provoked one obvious question: why was Ewell not moving to take advantage of such an opportunity, especially in light of the two preceding pursuit orders?

Ewell missed one of the battle's greatest opportunities by not seizing Culp's Hill when he had the troops on hand and easily could have done so. He then used the scouting information knowing it would likely persuade Lee to keep his corps north of town and allow him to redeem himself in Lee's eyes. But it was too late, for by the time he ordered Johnson to move on the heights they were already occupied—and Johnson stood down. The net effect of Ewell's machinations hammered his Second Corps into an awkward position left of town, where he was unable to coordinate his attacks or employ his men to advantage. This, in turn, directly and substantially impacted the fighting during the next two days on other parts of the field. Ewell only compounded these problems when he failed to make sure his subordinates moved their available troops into action on July 2 and 3. There is *no justification* for Ewell failing to promptly forward to General Lee the vital information furnished by scouts Tom Turner and Robert Early, and his decision to withhold the news profoundly and negatively impacted the operations of the Army of Northern Virginia.

5. Powell Hill and the mishandling of Third Corps

For a reason that is still unclear, most of the scribes of Gettysburg continue to portray Ambrose Powell Hill's debut at the head of Third Corps as little more than a lackluster performance. Responsibility for the Confederate reverse rests at the feet of Longstreet or Ewell, they insist, but not Little Powell. This attitude demonstrates a lack of understanding of Lee's plans and Hill's role in the battle—especially the fighting of July 2.

The Hill of July 1 and 2 was everything Longstreet during this time frame was not: lackadaisical, lethargic, indolent, acquiescent—ill. Lee's problems with him erupted even before the guns spoke. The commanding general found his new corps commander supine in Cashtown while Heth, Hill's least experienced division commander, was miles away to the east engaged with an unknown enemy. Hill's subsequent unimaginative employment of both Heth's and Dorsey Pender's divisions that afternoon, coupled with his later belief that nothing more could be asked from his corps that day could not have sat well with Lee. Hill also failed to bring up Anderson's Division once it approached the field. Either he was incompetent at corps level or his chronic illness (recently discovered and confirmed by biographer James I. Robertson, Jr.) had advanced to the point that it impacted his ability to lead his men in the field. Hill implied the latter to the ubiquitous Englishman Arthur Fremantle on the afternoon of July 1. He was, he said, "very unwell all day." Fremantle agreed with that assessment, writing that the Third Corps leader looked "very delicate."[21] Only Hill knew whether his malady was affecting his ability to lead his divisions. If it was it was his responsibility to make that point clear to Lee and ask to be temporarily relieved of command. There is no record that he did so.

Hill's lack of a field presence directly resulted in the breakdown of the echelon attack on July 2. General Lee's modified plan of attack that afternoon required that Hill commit his troops in support of Longstreet's corps as the echelon assault rolled down the line. Hill's primary responsibility was, like Longstreet's, to ensure that his combat formations got into action. Powell Hill failed in this task. We know he understood his orders because he clearly related them in his report. As Richard Anderson was fumbling his simple assignment to move his brigades forward one after the other, Hill was no where to be found. When Carnot Posey lost control of his brigade and Billy Mahone refused to go forward, Hill was invisible. When Dorsey Pender fell with a wound while his division stood waiting to move forward, no one was there to order it done. Powell Hill did *nothing* to bring about a Confederate victory that an officer of his rank and position was expected to do. All of the evidence set forth in Chapter 7 leads to one inescapable conclusion: Powell Hill totally failed in his command responsibilities on July 2.

Perhaps by the morning of July 3 General Lee finally realized how sick Hill was; perhaps Hill told him. Or conceivably Lee was simply fed up with his indolent performance. Lee was not about to risk entrusting any part of the leading attack wave to Powell Hill that day, and consequently reduced his command responsibilities to four brigades in a supporting capacity; Hill was again, albeit unofficially, a division commander. Lee's judgment was confirmed when Hill inexplicably allowed his artillery battalions to burn up precious ammunition in a meaningless barrage around the Bliss Farm later that morning. Once the main attack got underway and Pickett, Pettigrew, and Trimble moved out, Hill took up a post of observation in an artillery battalion outside of his command authority, and then refused to allow Dance's Second Corps guns to open in support of Pickett's regiments when these artillery pieces could have raked Federal reinforcements moving against Pickett's men.

Powell Hill was certainly physically ill at Gettysburg, and he may have also been beyond his depth at the corps level. His debut left much to be desired and was a substantial reason why the Army of Northern Virginia lost at Gettysburg.

4. The Absence of Jeb Stuart and his cavalry

One of the most controversial aspects of the Gettysburg drama is the idea that General Lee gave Jeb Stuart permission to go on a raid near the beginning of the campaign. Virtually every influential writer on the subject advances the notion that Lee's written orders to Stuart were either so ambiguous that Stuart could interpret his instructions any way he saw fit, or that the commanding general's orders gave Stuart permission to perform the raid he actually undertook. *Neither view is correct.*

As detailed in Chapter 3, Stuart was given explicit instructions as to what he was to do. Stuart had the discretion *framed by certain restrictions* to choose the route he would take across the Potomac. Once across the river, Stuart's immediate and primary task was to "move on & feel the right of Ewell's troops." After Stuart linked up with the infantry, he also had instructions to collect information and provisions, all the while retaining the latitude to cause the enemy as much damage as possible *within his primary task.* Lee's parameters for Stuart's movements, including the all-important restraining orders directing Stuart to "withdraw" and retrace his steps westward before turning northward to the Potomac should the cavalry general encounter "hindrance," came out of Lee's realistic analysis of the operational situation. It is our firm conclusion that the written instructions to Stuart are easy to understand if analyzed in the historical context within which they were written (i.e., the location of the respective elements of each army, the author of each piece of correspondence, and so on). Finally, the technical construction of the orders is absolutely sound.

Still, many writers and Stuart defenders continue to wrongly insist that the cavalryman had the latitude to go off on a raid while the army was moving blindly into enemy territory, and that Lee authorized it. For support they point to the words "pass around" and "pass through." But as fully examined in Chapter 3, this interpretation is simply not supported by the evidence. Lee's smoldering words of censure when Stuart finally returned to the army on July 2 was not the greeting of a commander happy to see his cavalry general—but it was consistent with a commanding officer upset with a subordinate's willful or cavalier neglect of his orders.

A close and dispassionate examination demonstrates that Jeb Stuart, a gallant and exceptional military officer, made a critical error in judgment after he approached Haymarket on June 25 that resulted in his disobeying Lee's orders. The result was that Stuart and his three finest brigades of cavalry were not available when Lee needed them most. The ramifications of his act limited Lee's options, especially once the enemy was found and engaged. Stuart's actions seriously impacted Confederate chances for victory in Pennsylvania.

3. The loss of John Bell Hood early in the fighting on July 2

When General Lee modified the Confederate battle plan to an *en échelon* attack on the afternoon of July 2, he did so knowing that his hard-fighting division commander, John Bell Hood, would be leading the assault. Hood was an extraordinary combat leader who combined field savvy and tenacity with excellent tactical control. His troops were some of the best in the army. Hood was also one of the few division leaders who knew how to properly utilize his artillery as coordinating arm with his formidable infantry. Hood and his division were in the right place at the right time for Lee and his plan of attack on July 2.

As detailed in great length in Chapter 6, by ordering an echelon attack to begin with Hood's Division and progress up the line, Lee was seeking to place his adversary on the horns of a dilemma. Believing his right overlapped the enemy's line, Lee had every reason to conclude that Longstreet's Corps would envelop and cave in Meade's left flank. "Major Meade" could respond in one of two ways: shift troops from other portions of his line not yet under attack to support his flank, or do nothing and hope his flank remained intact. Lee knew Meade to be a careful but easily agitated engineer new to army command; he was not about to sit quietly and let Lee turn and rout his left. Thus, in all likelihood Federal troops would be moving from several parts of the field to keep Longstreet at bay, which in turn might open up what Lee often referred to as "opportunity" for subsequent attacking Confederate formations up the line. The more successful Hood (followed by McLaws) was, the greater Meade's dilemma. Any significant success on the southern end of the field would rivet Meade's attention there, which opened up possibilities on the other end of the line as more and more Confederate formations became involved in the echelon attack.

The extent of Hood's contributions to the great battle will never be known because he fell just twenty minutes after the fighting opened. But we have some inkling of what he proposed to do and how involved he intended to be. Within a short time the leading elements of his command were engaging the Federals on a line from Round Top through the Devil's Den, Houck's Ridge and Rose Woods. Hood dispatched his aide, Major William Henry Sellers, to bring up Major John Cheves Haskell and the batteries under Hugh Richardson Garden and William K. Bachman—artillery he was holding in reserve to advance with the infantry. Just as Hood began giving Haskell his orders, a shell burst above Hood's head and ended his tenure with the army he so loved. About an hour later, McIvor Law, the division's senior brigadier, "got the message [of Hood's wounding] and got to the scene."[22]

The fall of Hood had two dramatic ramifications on the second day's fighting. Without Hood's guiding hand, the division's artillery battalion was never fully employed in coordination with the attacking infantry brigades. Was Hood about to order Haskell to bring up the batteries to closely support the Texas Brigade as Reilly would do so effectively with his battery later that afternoon? There is every indication that Hood was going to do something very similar. Once the southern portion of Houck's Ridge was cleared, would Hood have ordered at least part of his artillery battalion to move onto Houck's Ridge and sweep the Valley of Death and pound Vincent's troops off Little Round Top? If anyone would have seen the possibilities offered there, Hood would have. But we will never know for sure.

Hood's fall also meant there was no single coordinating voice to control the movements of his four brigades of infantry. Each brigade commander was left to fight his own battle. Many of the units broke apart and fought regimental-sized actions, and the affair ground down to a musketry slug fest amidst the rocks and timber of that part of the field.

Even so, Hood's Division achieved remarkable success and sucked in thousands of Federal infantry reinforcements and artillery supports. It is logical to postulate that if that single errant artillery shell had not found Hood, the division would have enjoyed more success. This, in turn, would have forced Meade to dispatch even more reinforcements than he did. Since Lee was utilizing an echelon attack, the "opportunity" this would have created would have evidenced itself elsewhere—perhaps opposite Anderson or Pender. But of course we will never know this for sure because John Bell Hood fell far too early in the fighting on July 2, 1863. His loss was keenly felt.

2. Dick Ewell's failure to pursue with Second Corps on July 1

When the commander of Second Corps followed his victorious troops into Gettysburg in the middle of the afternoon on July 1, he had every reason to be pleased with himself. He had approached the field of battle with standing orders from Lee to avoid bringing on a general engagement. When he saw the opportunity to destroy a large segment of the enemy, however, he used his discretion and disregarded Lee's earlier directive, aligned his divisions in a hurry, and aggressively and skillfully dismantled Howard's Eleventh Corps and a portion of Reynolds' First Corps. To do so Ewell had utilized eight of the nine infantry brigades in his corps he had on the field. Perhaps it was the suddenness and ease of his victory, or the sheer magnitude of it all. All we know for sure is that once he rode into Gettysburg, the soldiery qualities that had served Ewell so well took flight. His dormant deportment thereafter crippled Lee's effort to decisively damage Meade's army, and was one of the primary reasons why the Army of Northern Virginia lost at Gettysburg.

Spread out before Second Corps was a sight few of its members had beheld and none would again see. Broken and routed remnants from the two Federal corps were streaming up the incline of Cemetery Hill, the area's dominant terrain feature. Some of Ewell's aggressive brigadiers urged him to pursue the visibly disorganized enemy. This belief was seconded by many lower ranking officers and men who knew they needed to deliver one final thrust to finish the day's work. Two messengers, Walter Taylor and James Power Smith, arrived with orders from General Lee to keep up the pressure against the reeling foe and take the high ground south of town. At least three soldiers (Isaac Trimble, Tom Turner, and Robert Early) provided Ewell with *firsthand* information that Culp's Hill, a short distance to the east, was unoccupied and could easily be seized. Its capture would compromise the Federals gathering on Cemetery Hill and cut the enemy's lifeline along the Baltimore Pike immediately behind it. Yet Dick Ewell, veteran of many fields and Stonewall Jackson's protégé, did nothing.

The failure of Ewell and several of his generals to act decisively during the late afternoon and evening hours of July 1 has been carefully analyzed at great length in Chapter 5, so there is no need delve deeply into the matter here beyond the presentation of a few major points. It is important to keep in mind that it was Ewell who initiated the action on that side of the field on July 1, and he did so with eight of his available nine brigades. Thus, a general engagement was *already* underway, and Ewell had brought it on (and justifiably so). Thereafter he was given "orders, with discretion," and not "discretionary orders," as some writers wrongly claim, to pursue and finish the job. (For a full accounting of these orders, how they were written and interpreted, and several other similar orders that no one found confusing, kindly refer back to the chapter in question.) Consequently Ewell's failure to follow up his grand victory cannot be explained by arguing that he had orders to avoid bringing on a "general engagement." It is our opinion that Dick Ewell, like so many other personalities throughout military history, was simply unhinged by his own initial success and confused as to what course to follow.

And Lee knew it. The commanding general's report was worded to shield Ewell and others from criticism inside and outside the army. This is not supposition but fact, and several sources support this observation. Yet there is no shortage of writers who still take Lee's after-action words out of their historical context and place them in the mouths of others—primarily to protect Ewell from the harsh criticism he so richly deserves. For example, neither messenger who delivered the pursuit orders to Ewell, Walter Taylor or James Power Smith, nor their recipient *ever* claimed that Lee's instructions that afternoon included the admonishment "not to bring on a general engagement." Why would Lee's orders have included such language? Everyone involved in the first day's fighting—including Ewell—knew that a general engagement had already taken place.

Of all human events, war is more unforgiving for the wasting of time than any other endeavor. When Dick Ewell rode into Gettysburg on the afternoon of July 1, the defeated Federals needed time more than anything; time to retreat, time to rally, time to shake off the tentacles of demoralization, pick up a rifle, and stand back in line. Time. And by failing to act as ordered Ewell gave it to them by the bucketful. It was during the few suspenseful and fleeting hours between Second Corps' triumph on the fields north and west of Gettysburg and when the final waning rays of light disappeared that a golden opportunity to achieve a decisive victory north of the Potomac River was allowed to slip away. The consequences of Ewell's negligence rippled into the battle's second and third days.

Richard Stoddert Ewell's failure to pursue the foe he and his troops had vanquished was one of the most costly errors in American military history.

1. The breakdown of the July 2 echelon attack and the wounding of Dorsey Pender

More myth and misconception enshroud the second day's fighting at Gettysburg than any other battle of the American Civil War. This is primarily because of two related reasons: the heroic Federal defense of Little Round Top, and a failure to appreciate the purpose and consequences of Lee's *en échelon* attack. Both are worth a brief concluding discussion.

Because the Federals ultimately won the battle, and Little Round Top was one of the few areas where the Confederates did not meet with localized success on July 2, substantial significance and attention has been focused on the fight for its rocky slopes. We articulated in some detail in Chapter 7 why we think the fight for Little Round Top was not as significant as some would have us believe. Certainly it did not determine either the outcome of the fighting for July 2 or the three-day battle as a whole. If the rocky heights were so critical, Meade would not have left them vacant (the summit could be seen for miles and he and his generals knew it was there), and Lee would have weighted his far right appropriately and attacked it with substantially larger numbers. Both commanding generals knew their profession well and neither was *overly* concerned about Little Round Top. The hill had some value as an anchoring position, and if the Confederates had captured it they could have threatened the southern flank of the Federal army, including the line of communications running along the Taneytown Road. But the nature of its summit, coupled with the rough and wooded terrain on and around the hill limited its usefulness as either an artillery platform or infantry staging area. Even the Federals did not believe it was of much value for artillery and recognized its limitations. If Little Round Top was not the crucial point of the battle on July 2, then where was it?

In order to fully appreciate how unimportant Little Round Top really was to the outcome of the July 2 fighting, readers must appreciate what the Confederate *en échelon* assault was designed to look like, and what Lee expected from it. The attack has either been consistently misunderstood, or simply not recognized at all for what it was—a means of delivering one or more potentially decisive points for a breakthrough and victory somewhere up the line *far away from Little Round Top.*

When Lee learned of Sickles' advance to the Peach Orchard salient, he immediately realized that a traditional assault against Meade's left flank was no longer viable. But he also realized that the Peach Orchard bulge offered a significant "opportunity" to destroy another Federal corps, possibly turn the enemy left, and pry open other opportunities up the line. He modified his plan accordingly by ordering Longstreet and Powell Hill to attack *en échelon*, which meant the assault would be taken up on the far right with Hood's Division and progress up the line in a methodical manner until all the designated Southern brigades were engaged. This method was designed to achieve two goals: envelop and crush Meade's left and/or

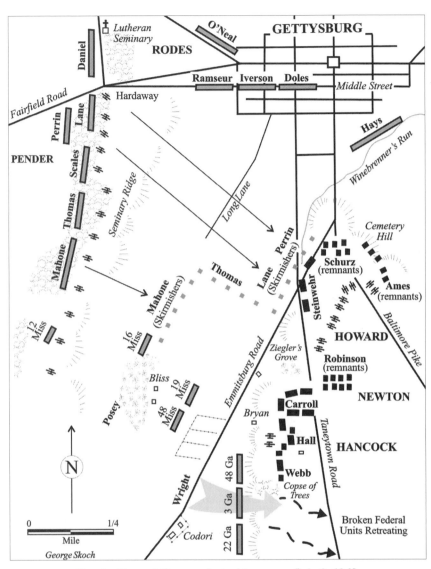

On the Cusp of Success: Late Afternoon, July 2, 1863

General Lee's careful planning and execution on the afternoon of July 2, 1863, placed his Army of Northern Virginia in a position to cut in two and wreck Meade's Army of the Potomac on Northern soil. Lee's echelon attack had crushed the Federal left and was rolling down the line. Poised to strike the Federals holding Cemetery Hill was the famed Light Division under Dorsey Pender. Pender sent skirmishers to push back their counterparts to the base of Cemetery Hill in preparation for his assault. Just minutes later, however, the skillful major general was struck down before he could order his division forward, and the chance for a decisive Confederate victory slipped away.

act as a magnet for enemy reinforcements which Meade would pull from other points of the line not yet under attack to support his collapsing left flank. In this way Lee's generals could take advantage of gaps or thin defensive fronts and shifting enemy troops, or as Lee called it, "opportunity," and develop them accordingly. The exact point where each "opportunity" would be created depended on many factors, including how Meade reacted to Longstreet's determined stroke against his left.

In other words, Lee was *not* launching either a frontal attack against Meade's left or a traditional flanking attack. A comparison of Lee's modified plan of assault at Gettysburg to Jackson's famous flank attack at Chancellorsville illustrates this point. Jackson's attack was designed and launched as a simultaneous assault several lines deep. Launching a true flank attack in any other way (i.e., *en échelon*) would only extend valuable time to the enemy to withdraw or reposition his lines to meet the attack.[23]

Lee's decision to launch an echelon attack extended the maximum flexibility possible to his corps and division leaders so they could wield their commands as they saw best, drive in the Federal left flank, and roll up the enemy line along the Emmitsburg Road and up Cemetery Ridge. Once this began, Meade had little choice but to support his endangered flank or risk its collapse. But by doing so, Meade was risking that the portions of his line from which reinforcements were drawn would not be heavily attacked. But of course, Lee did intend to attack them, and so "opportunities" surfaced as the battle evolved well up the line *away* from where the attack originated.

Lee not only gave personal instructions to Longstreet regarding how to launch the assault, but also discussed the matter directly with brigade commander Cadmus Wilcox. Wilcox's Alabamians comprised the far *right* brigade in Hill's Third Corps, and Lee wanted to impress upon Wilcox that he had to advance in a timely manner in order to cover McLaws' left flank. McLaws' Division, of course, formed the far *left* of Longstreet's First Corps. Other high ranking officers in Third Corps, including Powell Hill, Richard Anderson, Dorsey Pender, and the brigade commanders in Anderson's Division, received similar orders to move their commands into action *en échelon*, brigade by brigade, as the formations on their right advanced. This was absolutely necessary in order to both cover the neighboring brigade's flank and be in position to take advantage of any "opportunity" that arose.

Lee's deep personal involvement in deciding how his forces would attack in order to maximize their striking power, while simultaneously extending to his subordinates the tactical flexibility required to best direct the brigades into action, was essential in the conduct of an attack *en échelon*. The mental flexibility demonstrated by Lee that afternoon reflects multiple army command-level decisions that could have only been made by a Great Captain in tune with all the variables confronting him.

And yet the attack did not bring the success Lee hoped it might. Longstreet did his job perfectly, driving in Meade's left and siphoning upon himself tens of thousands of Federals from other parts of Meade's line. Hill's three right-most brigades advanced perfectly, collapsing the Federals holding the Emmitsburg Road front and driving deep into Meade's Cemetery Ridge position. The plan was working flawlessly. At that moment Anderson and Hill failed. Neither acted to thrust Anderson's remaining pair of brigades under Carnot Posey or Billy Mahone into action. The enemy front around the Angle and Copse of Trees they would have struck was but thinly held, and Wilcox, Lang, and Wright depended on their appearance to protect their vulnerable northern flank. Even more important was the fact that Posey and Mahone served as the triggering brigades for Major General Dorsey Pender, who was waiting for their movement to order his own four brigades into action. While riding to see what the hold up was, Pender was mortally wounded, and his division remained firmly in place. Robert E. Lee succinctly summed up the effect of Pender's wounding when he told Harry Heth, "Half an hour longer and we would have carried the enemy's position."[24] This observation debunks one of the most enduring myths surrounding Gettysburg: that the fighting on Little Round Top decided the battle on the second day. Lee himself never believed that, and his words and actions after the fighting prove it.

Meade had overreacted to Lee's attack and had stripped bare upper Cemetery Ridge and the line running around to Culp's Hill. Many of these troop movements—especially those relocating from Ziegler's Grove or other areas from the Federal right wing and marching south along Cemetery Ridge—were visible to the Confederates, including Robert Rodes, whose division was facing Cemetery Hill and ordered to move forward that evening. The opportunities Lee hoped the attack on the far end of the field would generate were visible and waiting to be exploited.[25] None of these openings could be realized and maximized unless each Confederate formation advanced, *en échelon,* into action.

But Posey and Mahone did not move forward, and Pender fell before he could order his division to the attack. Rodes did not aggressively advance his division in support of Early, which he had informed Pender he would do "just at dark." The Confederates significantly outnumbered the Federals on this portion of the field. Many of the defenders had been severely beaten the day before, and the all-important point of Cemetery Hill was held by the worst troops in Meade's army—Howard's Eleventh Corps. Just two brigades, those of Hays and Avery in Early's Division, Ewell's Second Corps, easily drove away Howard's men holding the high ground of East Cemetery Hill. But the fall of Pender and the negligence of Rodes withheld reinforcements from striking the heights from the west and north, and Hays and Avery were forced to fall back after cresting and remaining for some time on the battlefield's key piece of terrain.

Cemetery Hill was the decisive point for the fighting on July 2 only because of General Lee's decision to launch an echelon attack. All indications are that if Lee's subordinates had carried out the plan entrusted to them, Howard's Eleventh Corps and its few supports would have been attacked and driven off. Once that occurred,

Robert E. Lee

One of the most famous images of General Lee, captured in Julian Vannerson's studio in Richmond, Virginia, a few months after Gettysburg. *Library of Congress*

Meade's entire right wing would have collapsed. He would have then faced one of the most difficult tasks imaginable—trying to rally shattered formations in the dark while withdrawing the remainder of a beaten army. The net effect of Pender's wounding meant that his division did not go in as planned, Rodes did not follow, and Early did not reinforce his success on East Cemetery Hill. And so the echelon attack broke down completely.

This is why Robert E. Lee's "half an hour longer" observation is not only a correct and penetrating analysis of what he knew to be true, but an accurate representation of where the decisive point of the fighting on July 2 developed—and where the battle was lost.

Last Chance for Victory: Robert E. Lee in Retrospect

It is our sincere hope that if readers come away from this study with but one thing, it is that Robert E. Lee planned and waged one of his finest battles of the war at Gettysburg. The myth that Lee was a disinterested bystander who passively allowed his subordinates to do whatever they pleased and desired only to throw his legions forward in a direct attack against Meade's powerful front must be put to bed once and for all.

The heart of this myth is the notion that Lee was either disengaged from the army's operations, or did not conduct himself in the manner he exhibited on other battlefields. Lee performed well before and after Gettysburg, but his performance in Pennsylvania, so the fiction goes, represented the nadir of his career. John R. Elting, in *West Point Atlas of American Wars*, perpetuated this fable by summing up Lee's role in the Gettysburg battle this way:

> Undoubtedly, Gettysburg was the lowest point of Lee's generalship. He was careless; his orders were vague; he suggested when he should have commanded; and he sacrificed the pick of his infantry in a foredoomed attempt to win a battle he had already lost. But, on 4 July, he reasserted himself.[26]

Noted historian Gary W. Gallagher breathes life into this illusion by writing: "Lee, of course, had failed at least as much as any of his subordinates."[27] The facts simply do not bear this out. Did Robert E. Lee fail as badly as Jeb Stuart, who disobeyed orders and left the army blind in enemy territory? Did Lee fail as badly as Powell Hill who, for all practical purposes was AWOL during the three days of the battle? Did Lee fail as badly as Dick Ewell, who threw away the victory of July 1, and can be generously described as unimaginative thereafter? Did Lee fail as badly as James Longstreet on July 3, when the commander of First Corps acted like a petulant child who had not gotten his way and did not prepare the attack as ordered?

Outside of his failure to assume direct tactical control of the assault on July 3, deep dispassionate analysis reveals that General Lee exhibited at Gettysburg all of the qualities of leadership one would expect from a Great Captain.

Robert E. Lee understood that military action always influenced politics, and visa versa. It was impossible to separate the two. Given that and his realistic appreciation for how the war was progressing, Lee risked his reputation and his people's hopes for independence in Pennsylvania. Jefferson Davis, on the other hand, trapped by his own red tape and bureaucratic instincts, was unwilling to give Lee and the only successful army of the Confederacy the wholehearted support they deserved. While Lee recognized the ultimate fatal consequences of continued stalemate in central Virginia, Davis failed to grasp the possibilities that a full concentration of power would offer Lee and the Army of Northern Virginia. And so the army's missing brigades loomed large in Pennsylvania.

Lee's determination to take his army north of the Potomac was the correct one. His decisions and duties as an army commander from that point until the morning of July 3 were almost flawlessly executed. Every sound principle of military, political, and logistical reasoning supported Lee's decision to shift the defense of Richmond out of Virginia and into Pennsylvania. Lee's control over the discipline of the Confederate army was excellent, and his decision to concentrate the army where and when he did was sound. His decision on July 1 to reengage Hill's Third Corps once Dick Ewell's attack was underway against the Federal right flank provides a superb example of recognition and reaction to an incredible opportunity brought about by a rapidly changing tactical situation. With the Federal forces broken and on the run, Lee understood the full potential of what was transpiring and what it presented to the Southern cause by ordering Ewell to pursue them. Ewell's failure to comply with General Lee's two direct orders remains one of the greatest missed opportunities in American military history.

As splendid as his performance was on July 1, Lee's moral courage, decisions, and performance the following day were even more impressive. Lee's realization that he needed to take the fight to the Federal army before the numerically superior foe could fully concentrate was not only an accurate reading of the military and logistical situation, but displayed remarkable courage in the face of adversity brought about by Stuart's continued absence. One is hard pressed to name another army commander in American history, with the exception of George Washington, who would have had such fearless resolve. When the tactical situation changed because Sickles unilaterally repositioned his corps in advance of the rest of the Federal army on Cemetery Ridge, Lee was on the scene to appraise its ramifications. Recognizing his initial plan was no longer feasible, while at the same time seizing upon a different unforeseen opportunity that had suddenly presented itself, Lee modified the method by which his army would attack. His assault would be conducted *en échelon*, which was the perfect solution to the new tactical problem. By committing the Southern forces to battle in that manner, Lee exhibited his unwavering faith in the striking power of his army, while delivering to his subordinates the best means possible by which the Army of Northern Virginia could achieve the potentially decisive victory that had been so eagerly sought for such a long time.

When the failure of key subordinates conspired to derail the echelon attack on July 2, General Lee—correctly—decided to continue the battle the next day for all of the reasons we set forth in Chapter 8. However, when Longstreet did not reengage early that Friday morning on July 3 as ordered, and while Ewell was heavily engaged with Ed Johnson's reinforced division on Culp's Hill, Lee made his most serious command lapse of the campaign. Perhaps it was his loyalty to Longstreet, or maybe he was too fatigued to see it. Whatever the reason, Lee did not immediately grasp the pressing need for his personal supervision of the upcoming operation. Instead, he extended command authority to a general who had already hesitated to obey orders by handing over to Longstreet the reins for most of the Confederate forces on the south side of Gettysburg. The result of this error in judgment was first recognized by Lee himself immediately after Longstreet's inadequate efforts had resulted in the slaughter of Pickett's, Pettigrew's and Trimble's commands—a realization embodied in Lee's now-famous words, "the fault is entirely my own."[28]

Robert E. Lee's important mistake on July 3, however, does not otherwise diminish the brilliant conduct displayed by the Confederate commanding general throughout the rest of the campaign and battle. Even in defeat, Lee almost always made the right decisions, for the right reasons, at the right time. A visionary in the plan of campaign, realistic in his ability to see things for what they were, mentally flexible enough to adapt to changing circumstances, unflinching in his resolve, courageous in his difficult decisions, and fully accountable for the failings of his officers, Robert E. Lee demonstrated at Gettysburg what he had shown on other fields: he was much more than a Great Captain—he was a great man. Virtually every one of his decisions—from the time he met with President Davis and other government officials in Richmond in May until the army's return to Virginia two months later—reveal an army commander at the top of his command game, a leader who inspired devotion among his officers and men.

The Army of Northern Virginia may have fallen far short of its commander's lofty goals, but four significant accomplishments were achieved that summer of 1863 that are often overlooked. First, Lee freed Virginia from hard campaigning for almost one full year. Second, his campaign reclaimed the Shenandoah Valley and all of its advantages for the South. Third, the livestock gained during the incursion into Maryland and Pennsylvania served as the cornerstone of new herds that fed Lee's army for months. Considering the dire logistical straits in which the Army of Northern Virginia found itself in May 1863, the importance of these three achievements cannot be overstated. Fourth, the losses inflicted on the Army of the Potomac so crippled its combat effectiveness that four months would pass before the operation of maneuver known as the Mine Run Campaign took place, and no serious fighting was attempted by Meade until May of 1864—ten months after Gettysburg. Certainly Lee's own losses were also very heavy, but who can argue that the several battles he would have been forced to wage along the Rappahannock line would have cost him fewer losses and greater result?

*   *   *

Almost every Great Captain of history, even while making skillful and correct decisions while on campaign, at some inopportune time meets with disappointment and/or defeat. And so it was with Robert E. Lee at Gettysburg. Adversity is the true test of an individual's spirit and the depth of a person's genius, and the personal disappointment brought about by the failure in Pennsylvania surely plagued Lee to the end of his life. Despite the disappointing outcome, the best soldier on the North American continent demonstrated anew in 1864 why *any* hope for the Confederacy had been and always would be on the shoulders of the one man General Winfield Scott had called "the very best soldier I ever saw in the field"—Robert Edward Lee.

Notes for Postscript

1. Henry Heth, letter dated June 1877, on the topic of "Causes of Lee's Defeat at Gettysburg," *Southern Historical Society Papers*, 4, p. 160.

2. John D. Imboden, "The Confederate Retreat from Gettysburg," *Battles and Leaders of the Civil War*, 3., pp. 420-421.

3. E. M. Hays to Bachelder, Oct. 15, 1890, *The Bachelder Papers*, 3, p. 1776.

4. Only one of many such examples can be found in: "Address on the Character of General R. E. Lee," by John Hampden Chamberlayne, 19 January 1876, *Southern Historical Society Papers*, 3, pp. 34-35.

5. *OR* 27, pt. 1, p. 770; Alpheus S. Williams to Bachelder, November 10, 1865, *The Bachelder Papers*, 1, pp. 218-219.

6. Minutes of Council, July 2, [18]63, as quoted in Coddington, *The Gettysburg Campaign*, p. 453.

7. Williams to Bachelder, November 10, 1865, *The Bachelder Papers*, 1, p. 217.

8. Doubleday, *Chancellorsville and Gettysburg*, p. 157.

9. *OR* 27, pt. 2, pp. 496 and 499; Tucker, *High Tide at Gettysburg*, p. 387.

10. LaSalle Corbell Pickett, "My Soldier," *McClure's Magazine* (1908), p. 569.

11. The Washington Louisiana Artillery Battalion was deliberately held out of the action on July 2, and therefore was employed by Longstreet.

12. Consider for a moment this argument in reverse. Instead of siphoning troops from Lee, why not reinforce the only successful army commander the South had in the only theater

capable of handing over a decisive victory? How strong would Lee's army have been if it was reinforced not only with the return of its original missing brigades, but also by a quality division (perhaps John C. Breckinridge's) from the Braxton Bragg's Army of Tennessee? Virtually none of Bragg's divisions saw significant action from May through July 1863 in Tennessee, or while on detached service with Johnston in Mississippi. How different would the Pennsylvania campaign have been had they instead been sent east to serve under a resourceful, aggressive, and *successful* commander like Robert E. Lee?

13. John C. Pemberton, *Compelled to Appear in Print: The Vicksburg Manuscript of General John C. Pemberton,* edited by David M. Smith (Cincinnati, 1999), pp. 39-40 and 75-160; Terrence J. Winschel, *Triumph & Defeat*, pp. 89-112.

14. Please consult Chapter 1 for a detail listing and strengths of these brigades.

15. *OR* 27, pt. 3, p. 1005; *Southern Historical Society Papers,* 2, pp. 338-339.

16. *OR* 51, pt. 2, p. 745.

17. John Peyre Thomas, *The Career and Character of General Micah Jenkins, C.S.A.* (Columbia, 1903), p. 8.

18. Walter Harrison, *Pickett's Men: A Fragment of War History* (New York, 1870), p. 79.

19. Donald C. Pfanz, *Richard S. Ewell*, p. 316.

20. Although the brigades under Iverson and O'Neal in Rodes' Division were on the field and technically "available," they were so badly damaged from the fighting on July 1 that we have not included them in the nine brigade total listed here.

21. Fremantle, *Three Months in the Southern States,* p. 254.

22. *Supplement to the OR* 5, serial no 5, p. 353. Also, please see note 15 in Chapter 7, pp. 395.

23. Hamlin, *The Attack of Stonewall Jackson at Chancellorsville*, maps 2 and 3, are excellent references for this point.

24. Henry Heth, letter dated June 1877, on the topic of "Causes of Lee's Defeat at Gettysburg," *Southern Historical Society Papers*, 4, p. 154.

25. *OR* 27, pt. 2, p. 555.

26. *West Point Atlas of American Wars*, 1, text to map 99. According to the Introduction, page viii, "the text is the product of the collaborative efforts of John R. Elting, Thomas E. Griess, and [Vincent J. Esposito]."

27. Gallagher, *Lee and His Generals in War and Memory*, p. 83.

28. Charles T. Loehr, "The 'Old First' Virginia at Gettysburg," *Southern Historical Society Papers*, 32, p. 37.

Appendix A

General Lee's January 20, 1864, After-Action Report of the Gettysburg Campaign

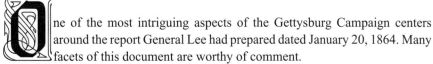ne of the most intriguing aspects of the Gettysburg Campaign centers around the report General Lee had prepared dated January 20, 1864. Many facets of this document are worthy of comment.

First, as we noted within the pages of this study, Lee's report was written to shield several of his subordinates from any blame for their actions during the campaign. Charles Marshall, Lee's staff officer, discussed at some length in his book *Lee's Aide-de-Camp* how the commanding general constructed his battle reports.[1] Marshall, who earned his Masters degree in English at the University of Virginia at age 18, garnering in the process "the highest honors of the university," was responsible for writing most of Lee's official correspondence and after-action reports. Lee knew that his report for the Pennsylvania operation would be scrutinized closely, and it took him six months to finish it.

The following excerpt from Marshall's book provides an appreciation of the intent and purpose behind what eventually appeared in General Lee's official report:

> I was a member of the staff of General R. E. Lee and wrote most of his letters to the President and War Department. Besides this it was my duty to compile his official reports of operations. The official report of the Gettysburg Campaign...was prepared by myself with every facility to make it accurate

which General Lee could give me. I had the official reports [and] opportunities of conversing with the authors of these reports. . .

When from the various sources . . . I had compiled a continuous narrative it was submitted to him for examination. He would peruse it carefully . . . weighed every sentence I wrote, frequently making minute verbal alterations, and questioned me closely as to the evidence on which I based all statements which he did not know to be correct. . .

The official [Gettysburg] report of General Lee . . . is not complete in many particulars which should be known to understand the campaign fully. He struck from the original draft many statements which he thought might affect others injuriously, his sense of justice frequently leading him to what many considered too great a degree of lenience. It is well known that he assumed the entire responsibility of the issue of the battle of Gettysburg, and thus covered the errors and omissions of all his officers. He declined to embody in his report anything that might seem to cast the blame of the result upon others, and in answer to my appeal to allow some statements which I deemed material to remain in the report, he said he disliked in such a communication to say aught to the prejudice of others. . . *But there are material facts resting upon official statements which in my opinion are necessary to a correct understanding of the campaign, and the statement of which can do injustice to no man.* [emphasis added]

Obviously much was omitted from Lee's report. Although exactly what was left out will probably never be known, students of the battle must bear in mind Marshall's explanation.

*   *   *

The following portion of Lee's report about why he undertook the campaign is often glossed over by historians:

Upon the retreat of the Federal Army commanded by Major General Hooker from Chancellorsville, it reoccupied the ground north of the Rappahannock opposite Fredericksburg, where it could not be attacked except at a disadvantage. It was determined to draw it from this position, and if practicable to transfer the scene of hostilities beyond the Potomac. The execution of this purpose also embraced the expulsion of the force under General Milroy which had invested the lower Shenandoah Valley during the preceding winter & spring. . . .[2]

Readers are urged to pay special attention to Lee's use of the words "if practicable" and his orders to Richard Ewell on the afternoon of July 1. As recited and analyzed in detail within the pages of this study (see Chapters 5 and 7), when Lee instructed someone to attempt to do something, he often couched his request in the socially polite phrases of his time and social status, i.e., "if practicable," or "if possible." In the example cited above, Lee described what he was going to attempt to do, namely, move the defense of Richmond from Virginia to somewhere "beyond [to the north of] the Potomac." Lee succeeded in that attempt. Ewell, however, did not even attempt a pursuit of the beaten enemy on July 1, despite the receipt of two orders from Lee to do so.

Lee's after-action report also provides insight into what he expected from Jeb Stuart. Lee writes:

> General Stuart was directed to hold the mountain passes with part of his command as long as the enemy remained south of the Potomac, and with the remainder to cross into Maryland and place himself on the right of General Ewell. Upon the suggestion of the former officer that he could damage the enemy and delay his passage of the river by getting in his rear, he was authorized to do so, and it was left to his discretion whether to enter Maryland east or west of the Blue Ridge, but he was instructed to lose no time in placing his command on the right of our column as soon as he should perceive the enemy moving northward.

Lee's description only reinforces our analysis of Stuart's orders contained in Chapter 3. As far as Lee was concerned, raiding was *secondary* to Stuart's primary mission, which was to meet up with and protect Ewell's infantry. Lee's words, "lose no time," are consistent with the orders that stated "in either case, after crossing the river, you must move on and feel the right of Ewell's troops."

Notes for Appendix A

1. Marshall, *Lee's Aide-de-Camp*, pp. 178-181.

2. All of the quotes utilized in this appendix from Robert E. Lee's report may be found in *OR.* 27, pt. 2, pp. 312-326; they are also available in Dowdey and Manarin, eds., *The Wartime Papers of R. E. Lee*, number 542.

Order of Battle

Army of Northern Virginia
July 1-3, 1863

Army Headquarters
General Robert Edward Lee, commanding

Headquarters Staff

Colonel Armistead Lindsay Long, Military Secretary

Major Walter Herron Taylor, Assistant Adjutant General

Major Charles Marshall, Assistant Adjutant General

Major Charles S. Venable, Assistant Adjutant General

Brigadier General William Nelson Pendleton, Chief of Artillery

Lieutenant Colonel Briscoe G. Baldwin, Chief of Ordnance

Major Thomas Mann Randolph Talcott, Engineer Officer

Captain Samuel Richards Johnston, Engineer Officer

Colonel Robert H. Chilton, Assistant Adjutant & Inspector General

Colonel George W. Lay, Assistant Adjutant & Inspector General

Major Henry E. Peyton, Assistant Adjutant & Inspector General

Lieutenant Colonel James L. Corley, Chief Quartermaster

Captain S. M. Somers, Quartermaster of Ordnance Train

Lieutenant Colonel Robert G. Cole, Chief Commissary

Major Fred R. Scott, Commissary

Surgeon Lafayette Guild, Medical Director

Attached to Army Headquarters as Escort/Couriers
39th Virginia Cavalry Battalion, Companies A & C, commanded by Major John Harvie Richardson, approximately 85 combatants

Below is an outline of the units Lee had with him in Pennsylvania. Infantry strengths are represented by two figures: the number of companies, and number of combatants in the ranks. The entry for the 5th South Carolina Regiment, for example, is followed by 10 / 450, which stands for 10 companies and 450 officers and men. Artillery batteries are also represented with two figures: the number of guns and number of men present. The entry for the Pulaski Georgia Artillery (Fraser), for example, is followed by 4 guns / 70, which means the battery had four pieces serviced by 70 officers and men.

FIRST CORPS

Lieutenant General James Longstreet
Corps headquarters staff—15 staff and field officers

McLaws' Division: Major General Lafayette McLaws
Division headquarters staff—10 other staff and field officers

Kershaw's Brigade: Brigadier General Joseph B. Kershaw
Brigade Staff—5 other staff and field officers

2nd South Carolina "Palmetto" Regiment	10 / 424
3rd South Carolina Regiment	10 / 420
7th South Carolina Regiment	12 / 400
8th South Carolina Regiment	12 / 300
15th South Carolina Regiment	10 / 450
3rd South Carolina "James'" Battalion	7 / 200

Barksdale's Brigade: Brigadier General William Barksdale
Brigade Staff—3 other staff and field officers

13th Mississippi Regiment	10 / 500
17th Mississippi Regiment	10 / 440
18th Mississippi Regiment	10 / 350
21st Mississippi Regiment	10 / 304

Semmes' Brigade: Brigadier General Paul Jones Semmes
Brigade Staff—3 other staff and field officers

10th Georgia Regiment	10 / 300
50th Georgia Regiment	10 / 300
51st Georgia Regiment	10 / 300
53rd Georgia Regiment	10 / 440

Wofford's Brigade: Brigadier General William Tatum Wofford

Brigade Staff—3 other staff and field officers

16th Georgia Regiment	10 / 300
18th Georgia Regiment	10 / 300
24th Georgia Regiment	10 / 300
Cobb's Georgia Legion	7 / 200
Phillips' Georgia Legion	9 / 300
3rd Battalion Georgia Sharpshooters	6 / 200

Divisional Artillery Battalion: Colonel Henry Coalter Cabell

Battalion Staff—3 other staff and field officers

Company A, 1st North Carolina "Ellis" Light Artillery (Manly)
consisting of two 12-pounder Napoleons and two 3-inch rifles   4 guns / 140

Troup County Georgia Light Artillery (Carlton),
consisting of two 12-pounder howitzers and two 10-pounder Parrotts   4 guns / 90

Pulaski Georgia Artillery (Fraser)consisting of two 3-inch rifles and
two 10-pounder Parrotts   4 guns / 70

1st Richmond Virginia Howitzers (McCarthy) consisting of two 12-pounder
Napoleons and two 3-inch rifles   4 guns / 100

McLaws' Division Totals:

Division headquarters staff   11

Infantry, including brigade staffs: 193 companies / 6,745
Artillerists and supporting personnel: 4 companies / 404
Total Present and Under Arms: 197 companies / 7,160 / 16 guns

Hood's Division: Major General John Bell Hood

Division headquarters staff—10 other staff and field officers

Law's Brigade: Brigadier General Evander McIvor Law

Brigade Staff—3 other staff and field officers

4th Alabama Regiment	10 / 350
15th Alabama Regiment	11 / 500
44th Alabama Regiment	10 / 375
47th Alabama Regiment	10 / 400
48th Alabama Regiment	10 / 375

Robertson's "Texas" Brigade: Brigadier General Jerome Bonaparte Robertson

Brigade Staff—4 other staff and field officers

1st Texas Regiment	12 / 450
4th Texas Regiment	10 / 425
5th Texas Regiment	10 / 425
3rd Arkansas Regiment	10 / 500

Benning's Brigade: Brigadier General Henry Lewis Benning

Brigade Staff—3 other staff and field officers

2nd Georgia Regiment	10 / 375
15th Georgia Regiment	10 / 375
17th Georgia Regiment	10 / 375
20th Georgia Regiment	10 / 375

Anderson's Brigade: Brigadier General George Thomas Anderson

Brigade Staff—9 other staff and field officers

7th Georgia Regiment	10 / 370
8th Georgia Regiment	10 / 320
9th Georgia Regiment	9 / 340
11th Georgia Regiment	10 / 320
59th Georgia Regiment	10 / 550

Divisional Artillery Battalion—Major Mathias Winston Henry,

with Major John Cheves Haskell, second in command

Battalion Staff—7 other staff and field officers

Company F, 13th North Carolina "Branch's" Battalion (Latham), consisting of
three 12-pounder Napoleons, one 12-pounder howitzer and
one 6-pounder smoothbore 5 guns   5 guns / 120

Charleston South Carolina "German" Light Artillery (Bachman),
consisting of four 12-pounder Napoleons   4 guns / 77

Palmetto South Carolina Light Artillery (Garden)
consisting of two 12-pounder Napoleons and two 10-pounder Parrotts   4 guns / 70

Company D, 1st North Carolina "Rowan" Artillery (Reilly),
consisting of two 12-pounder Napoleons, two 3-inch rifles
and two 10-pounder Parrotts   6 guns / 151

Hood's Division Totals

Division headquarters staff   11
Infantry, including brigade staffs   182 companies / 7,200
Artillerists and supporting personnel   4 companies / 427
Total Present and Under Arms   186 companies / 7,638 / 19 guns

Pickett's Division: Major General George Pickett
Division headquarters staff—9 other staff and field officers

Armistead's Brigade: Brigadier General Lewis Armistead
Brigade Staff—3 other staff and field officers

9th Virginia Regiment   8 / 250
14th Virginia Regiment   10 / 470
38th Virginia Regiment   9 / 475
53rd Virginia Regiment   10 / 450
57th Virginia Regiment   10 / 500

Kemper's Brigade: Brigadier General James L. Kemper

Brigade Staff—5 other staff and field officers

1st Virginia "Williams' Rifles" Regiment   6 / 215
3rd Virginia Regiment   10 / 350
7th Virginia Regiment   9 / 360
11th Virginia Regiment   10 / 400
24th Virginia Regiment   10 / 440

Richard Brooke Garnett's Brigade: Brigadier General Richard Brooke Garnett

Brigade Staff—3 other staff and field officers

8th Virginia Regiment   10 / 250
18th Virginia Regiment   10 / 360
19th Virginia Regiment   10 / 425
28th Virginia Regiment   9 / 375
56th Virginia Regiment   10 / 390

Corse's Brigade: Brigadier General Montgomery Dent Corse
On detached duty and not present in Pennsylvania

Jenkins' Brigade: Brigadier General Micah Jenkins
On detached duty and not present in Pennsylvania

Divisional Artillery Battalion:
The 38th Battalion of Virginia Light Artillery: Major James Dearing

Battalion Staff—8 other staff and field officers

Company A, Fauquier Virginia Artillery (Stribling), consisting of four 12-pounder Napoleons and two 20-pounder Parrotts   6 guns / 140

Company B, Richmond "Fayette" Virginia Artillery (Macon) consisting of two 12-pounder Napoleons and two 10-pounder Parrotts   4 guns / 90

Company C, Richmond "Hampden" Virginia Artillery (Caskie), consisting of two 12-pounder Napoleons, one 3-inch rifle and one 10-pounder Parrott   4 guns / 90

Company D, Lynchburg Virginia Artillery (Blount), consisting of four 12-pounder Napoleons   4 guns / 100

Pickett's Division Totals—

Division headquarters staff   10
Infantry, including brigade staffs   141 companies / 5,725
Artillerists and supporting personnel   4 companies / 429
Total Present and Under Arms   145 companies / 6,164 and 18 guns

First Corps Reserve Artillery: Colonel James B. Walton
Corps Reserve Artillery headquarters staff—3 other staff and field officers

The Washington (Louisiana) Artillery Battalion of New Orleans:
Major Benjamin Franklin Eshleman

Battalion Staff—8 other staff and field officers

1st Company, Washington Artillery (Squires), consisting of one 12-pounder Napoleon   1 gun / 80

2nd Company, Washington Artillery (Richardson), consisting of two 12-pounder Napoleons and one 12-pounder howitzer   3 guns / 85

3rd Company, Washington Artillery (Miller), consisting of three 12-pounder Napoleons   3 guns / 95

4th Company, Washington Artillery (Norcom), consisting of two 12-pounder Napoleons and one 12-pounder howitzer   3 guns / 85

Washington Artillery Battalion Totals

Artillerists and supporting personnel   4 companies / 354

Total Present and Under Arms   354 / 10 guns*

(The Washington Artillery had not yet replaced ordnance lost during the Chancellorsville Campaign.)

Alexander's Artillery Battalion: Colonel Edward Porter Alexander
Battalion Staff—8 other staff and field officers

Madison Louisiana Light Artillery (Moody),
consisting of four 24-pounder howitzers   4 guns / 130

Brooks South Carolina Light Artillery (Gilbert),
consisting of four 12-pounder howitzers   4 guns / 75

Ashland Virginia Artillery (Woolfolk), consisting of
two 12-pounder Napoleons and two 20-pounder Parrotts   4 guns / 100

Bedford Virginia Artillery (Blount),consisting
of four 3-inch rifles   4 guns / 80

Richmond "Parker's" Virginia Battery (Parker), consisting of
three 3-inch rifles and one 10-pounder Parrott   4 guns / 90

Bath Virginia Artillery (Taylor), consisting
of four 12-pounder Napoleons   4 guns / 90

Alexander's Artillery Battalion Totals

Artillerists and supporting personnel   6 companies / 574

Total Present and Under Arms   574 / 24 guns

First Corps Reserve Artillery Totals

Corps Reserve Artillery headquarters and staff   4

Artillerists and supporting personnel   10 companies / 928

Total Present and Under Arms   932 / 34 guns

First Corps Totals

Corps and division headquarters staffs   48

Infantry, including brigade staffs   516 companies / 19,670

Artillerists and supporting/staff personnel   22 companies / 2,192

Total Present and Under Arms   538 companies / 21,910 / 87 guns

SECOND CORPS

Lieutenant General Richard S. Ewell

Corps headquarters staff—16 other staff and field officers

Attached to Corps Headquarters as Escort/Couriers
39th Virginia Cavalry Battalion, Company B, commanded by
Captain William F. Randolph, numbering approximately 30 combatants

Early's Division: Major General Jubal Anderson Early
Division headquarters staff—11 other staff and field officers

Gordon's Brigade: Brigadier General John Brown Gordon
Brigade Staff—5 other staff and field officers

13th Georgia Regiment	10 / 320
26th Georgia Regiment	10 / 300
31st Georgia Regiment	10 / 250
38th Georgia Regiment	10 / 340
60th Georgia Regiment	10 / 295
61st Georgia Regiment	10 / 290

Hoke's (Avery's) Brigade: Colonel Isaac Erwin Avery
Brigade Staff—1 other officer

6th North Carolina Regiment	10 / 508
21st North Carolina Regiment	10 / 432
57th North Carolina Regiment	10 / 300

Hays' Brigade: Brigadier General Harry Thompson Hays
Brigade Staff—2 other staff and field officers

5th Louisiana Regiment	10 / 195
6th Louisiana Regiment	10 / 215
7th Louisiana Regiment	10 / 233
8th Louisiana Regiment	10 / 295
9th Louisiana Regiment	9 / 340

Smith's Brigade: Brigadier General William Smith
Brigade Staff—3 other staff and field officers

31st Virginia Regiment	10 / 270
49th Virginia Regiment	9 / 280
52nd Virginia Regiment	10 / 250

Divisional Artillery Battalion: Lieutenant Colonel Hilary Pollard Jones
Battalion Staff—8 other staff and field officers
Charlottesville Virginia Artillery (Carrington), consisting of
four 12-pounder Napoleons   4 guns / 75

Richmond "Courtney" Virginia Artillery (Tanner), consisting of
four 3-inch rifles   4 guns / 90

Louisiana Guard Artillery (Green) consisting of two 3-inch rifles
and two 10-pounder Parrotts   4 guns / 64

Staunton Virginia Artillery (Garber), consisting of
four 12-pounder Napoleons   4 guns / 64

Early's Division Totals

Division headquarters staff: 12
Infantry, including brigade staffs: 168 companies / 5,128
Artillerists and supporting personnel: 4 companies / 302
Total Present and Under Arms: 172 companies / 5,442 / 16 guns

Rodes' Division: Major General Robert Emmett Rodes
Division headquarters staff—13 other staff and field officers

Daniel's Brigade: Brigadier General Junius Daniel
Brigade Staff—3 other staff and field officers

32nd North Carolina Regiment   9 / 498
43rd North Carolina Regiment   10 / 624
45th North Carolina Regiment   8 / 488
53rd North Carolina Regiment   9 / 440
2nd North Carolina Battalion   7 / 240

Doles' Brigade: Brigadier General George Pierce Doles
Brigade Staff—3 other staff and field officers

4th Georgia Regiment   10 / 352
12th Georgia Regiment   10 / 343
21st Georgia Regiment   9 / 300
44th Georgia Regiment   10 / 370

Iverson's Brigade: Brigadier General Alfred Iverson, Jr.
Brigade Staff—3 other staff and field officers

5th North Carolina Regiment   10 / 503
12th North Carolina Regiment   10 / 232
20th North Carolina Regiment   10 / 395
23rd North Carolina Regiment   10 / 336

Ramseur's Brigade: Brigadier General Stephen Dodson Ramseur
Brigade Staff—3 other staff and field officers

2nd North Carolina Regiment   10 / 258
4th North Carolina Regiment   10 / 208
14th North Carolina Regiment   10 / 325
30th North Carolina Regiment   10 / 295

Rodes' (O'Neal's) Brigade: Colonel Edward Asbury O'Neal
Brigade Staff—2 other staff and field officers

3rd Alabama Regiment   10 / 372

5th Alabama Regiment   10 / 337

6th Alabama Regiment   12 / 406

12th Alabama Regiment   10 / 337

26th Alabama Regiment   10 / 339

Divisional Artillery Battalion: Lieutenant Colonel Thomas Henry Carter
Battalion Staff—8 other staff and field officers

Jeff Davis Alabama Artillery (Reese), consisting of
four 3-inch rifles   4 guns / 84

King William Virginia Artillery (W.P.P. Carter), consisting of
two 12-pounder Napoleons and two 10-pounder Parrotts   4 guns / 109

Louisa "Morris" Virginia Artillery (Page) consisting of
four 12-pounder Napoleons   4 guns / 121

Richmond "Orange" Virginia Artillery (Fry), consisting of
two 3-inch rifles and two 10-pounder Parrotts   4 guns / 85

Rodes' Division Totals

Division headquarters staff: 14

Infantry, including brigade staffs   215 companies / 8,017

Artillerists and supporting personnel   4 companies / 408

Total Present and Under Arms   219 companies / 8, 439 / 16 guns

Johnson's Division—Major General Edward Johnson
Division headquarters staff—8 other staff and field officers

Steuart's Brigade: Brigadier General George H. Steuart
Brigade Staff—4 other staff and field officers

1st Maryland Battalion   7 / 400
1st North Carolina Regiment   10 / 380
3rd North Carolina Regiment   10 / 545
10th Virginia Regiment   11 / 276
23rd Virginia Regiment   10 / 250
37th Virginia Regiment   9 / 265

Stonewall ("Walker's") Brigade: Brigadier General James Alexander Walker
Brigade Staff—3 other staff and field officers

2nd Virginia Regiment   10 / 330
4th Virginia Regiment   10 / 260
5th Virginia Regiment   10 / 345
27th Virginia Regiment   7 / 150
33rd Virginia Regiment   10 / 234

Jones' Brigade: Brigadier General John Marshall Jones
Brigade Staff—6 other staff and field officers

21st Virginia Regiment   8 / 195
25th Virginia Regiment   10 / 300
42nd Virginia Regiment   10 / 280
44th Virginia Regiment   9 / 235
48th Virginia Regiment   10 / 285
50th Virginia Regiment   9 / 253

Nicholls' (Williams') Brigade: Colonel Jesse Milton Williams
Brigade Staff—2 other staff and field officers

1st Louisiana Regiment   9 / 175
2nd Louisiana Regiment   10 / 230
10th Louisiana Regiment   10 / 220
14th Louisiana Regiment   10 / 280
15th Louisiana Regiment   10 / 192

Divisional Artillery Battalion: Major James W. Latimer
Battalion Staff—8 other staff and field officers

1st Maryland Battery (Dement) consisting of
four 12-pounder Napoleons   4 guns / 100

Alleghany "Rough" Virginia Artillery (J.C. Carpenter), consisting of
two 12-pounder Napoleons and two 3-inch rifles   4 guns / 97

4th "Chesapeake" Maryland Battery (W.D. Brown), consisting of
four 10-pounder Parrotts   4 guns / 81

Lynchburg "Lee" Virginia Artillery (Raine), consisting of one 3-inch rifle, one 10-pounder Parrott and two 20-pounder Parrotts   4 guns / 90

Johnson's Division Totals
Division headquarters staff: 9
Infantry, including brigade staffs: 209 companies / 6,108
Artillerists and supporting personnel: 4 companies / 377

Total Present and Under Arms: 213 companies / 6,494 / 16 guns

Second Corps Reserve Artillery: Colonel John Thompson Brown
Corps Reserve Artillery headquarters staff—3 other staff and field officers

First Virginia (Dance's) Artillery Battalion: Captain Willis Jefferson Dance
Battalion Staff—8 other staff and field officers

1st Rockbridge Virginia Artillery (Graham), consisting of four 20-pounder Parrotts   4 guns / 90

2nd Company, Richmond Virginia Artillery (Watson), consisting of four 10-pounder Parrotts   4 guns / 70

3rd Company, Richmond Virginia Artillery (B.H. Smith, Jr.), consisting of four 3-inch rifles   4 guns / 65

Powhatan Virginia Artillery (Cunningham), consisting of four 3-inch rifles 4 guns / 85

Salem Virginia "Flying Artillery" (Graham), consisting of two 12-pounder Napoleons and two 3-inch rifles   4 guns / 75

First Virginia (Dance's) Artillery Battalion Totals
Artillerists and supporting personnel: 5 companies / 394

Total Present and Under Arms: 394 and 20 guns

Nelson's Artillery Battalion: Lieutenant Colonel William Nelson
Battalion Staff—8 other staff and field officers

Amherst Virginia Artillery (Kirkpatrick), consisting of three 12-pounder Napoleons and one 3-inch rifle   4 guns / 110

Fluvanna "Consolidated" Virginia Artillery (Massie), consisting of three 12-pounder Napoleons and one 3-inch rifle   4 guns / 100

Georgia Regular Battery (Milledge), consisting of two 3-inch rifles and one 10-pounder Parrott   3 guns / 75

Nelson's Artillery Battalion Totals

Artillerists and supporting personnel: 3 companies / 294

Total Present and Under Arms: 294 / 11 guns

Second Corps Reserve Artillery Totals

Corps Reserve Artillery headquarters and staff: 4

Artillerists and supporting personnel: 8 companies / 688

Total Present and Under Arms: 692 and 31 guns

Second Corps Totals

Corps and division headquarters staffs, plus cavalry escort   1 company / 82

Infantry, including brigade staffs   592 companies / 19,253

Artillerists and supporting/staff personnel: 20 companies / 1,779

Total Present and Under Arms: 613 companies / 21,114 / 79 guns

THIRD CORPS

Lieutenant General Ambrose Powell Hill

Corps headquarters staff—14 other staff and field officers

Heth's Division: Major General Henry Heth

Division headquarters staff—7 other staff and field officers

Pettigrew's Brigade: Brig. Gen. James Johnston Pettigrew
Brigade Staff—3 other staff and field officers

11th North Carolina Regiment	10 / 650
26th North Carolina Regiment	10 / 875
47th North Carolina Regiment	10 / 600
52nd North Carolina Regiment	10 / 571

Davis' Brigade: Brigadier General Joseph Robert Davis
Brigade Staff—5 other officers

2nd Mississippi Regiment	11 / 520
11th Mississippi Regiment	10 / 624
42nd Mississippi Regiment	10 / 590
55th North Carolina Regiment	10 / 650

Brockenbrough's Brigade: Colonel John Mercer Brockenbrough
Brigade Staff—3 other staff and field officers

40th Virginia Regiment   10 / 200
47th Virginia Regiment 9 / 200
55th Virginia Regiment   11 / 200
22nd Virginia Battalion   6 / 200

Archer's Brigade: Brigadier General James Jay Archer (c)
Brigade Staff—3 other staff and field officers

13th Alabama Regiment   10 / 291
5th Alabama Battalion   4 / 131
1st Tennessee (Provisional Army) Regiment   10 / 267
7th Tennessee Regiment   10 / 276
14th Tennessee Regiment   10 / 232

Divisional Artillery Battalion—Lieutenant Colonel John Jameson Garnett
Battalion Staff—8 other staff and field officers

Norfolk Virginia Light Artillery Blues (Grandy), consisting of
two 3-inch rifles and two 12-pounder howitzers   4 guns / 111

Donaldsonville Louisiana Artillery (Maurin), consisting of
two 3-inch rifles and one 10-pounder Parrott   3 guns / 120

Pittsylvania (Lewis') Virginia Artillery (Lewis), consisting of
two 12-pounder Napoleons and two 3-inch rifles   4 guns / 95

Norfolk (Huger's) Virginia Battery (Moore), consisting of two 12-pounder
Napoleons, one 3-inch rifle and one 10-pounder Parrott   4 guns / 80

Heth's Division Totals:
Division headquarters staff   8

Infantry, including brigade staffs: 161 companies / 7,095

Artillerists and supporting personnel: 4 companies / 415

Total Present and Under Arms: 165 companies / 7,518 / 15 guns

Anderson's Division—Major General Richard Herron Anderson
Division headquarters staff—6 other staff and field officers

Wilcox's Brigade: Brigadier General Cadmus M. Wilcox
Brigade Staff—4 other staff and field officers

8th Alabama Regiment   10 / 475
9th Alabama Regiment   10 / 325
10th Alabama Regiment   10 / 327
11th Alabama Regiment   10 / 310
14th Alabama Regiment 10 / 335

Mahone's Brigade: Brigadier General William Mahone
Brigade Staff—3 other staff and field officers

6th Virginia Regiment   10 / 300
12th Virginia Regiment 10 / 360
16th Virginia Regiment   7 / 225
41st Virginia Regiment 10 / 261
61st Virginia Regiment 10 / 350

Perry's (Lang's) Brigade: Colonel David Lang
Brigade Staff—2 other staff and field officers

2nd Florida Regiment   12 / 250
5th Florida Regiment   10 / 300
8th Florida Regiment   10 / 150

Posey's Brigade: Brigadier General Carnot Posey
Brigade Staff—3 other staff and field officers

12th Mississippi Regiment   10 / 311
16th Mississippi Regiment   10 / 400
19th Mississippi Regiment   10 / 375
48th Mississippi Regiment   10 / 250

Wright's Brigade: Brigadier General Ambrose Ransom Wright
Brigade Staff—3 other staff and field officers

3rd Georgia Regiment   11 / 508
22nd Georgia Regiment   10 / 465
48th Georgia Regiment   10 / 453
2nd Georgia Battalion   4 / 175

Divisional Artillery Battalion: The 11th Georgia Artillery Battalion

"The Sumpter Artillery": Major John Lane
Battalion Staff—8 other staff and field officers

Company A (Ross), consisting of one 12-pounder Napoleon, one 12-pounder howitzer,
one 3-inch Navy rifle and three 10-pounder Parrotts   6 guns / 135

Company B (Patterson), consisting of two 12-pounder Napoleons
and four 12-pounder howitzers   6 guns / 130

Company C (Wingfield), consisting of three 3-inch Navy rifles and
two 10-pounder Parrotts   5 guns / 130

Anderson's Division Totals
Division headquarters staff   7

Infantry, including brigade staffs: 204 companies / 6,925

Artillerists and supporting personnel: 3 companies / 404

Total Present and Under Arms: 207 companies / 7,336 / 17 guns

Pender's Division ("The Light Division"):
Major General William Dorsey Pender
Division headquarters staff—10 other staff and field officers

McGowan's (Perrin's) Brigade: Colonel Abner Perrin
Brigade Staff—4 other staff and field officers

1st South Carolina "Provisional Army" Regiment   10 / 350
1st South Carolina ("Orr's") Rifles   10 / 380
12th South Carolina Regiment   10 / 385
13th South Carolina Regiment   10 / 400
14th South Carolina Regiment   10 / 450

Lane's Brigade: Brigadier General James Henry Lane
Brigade Staff—3 other staff and field officers

7th North Carolina Regiment   10 / 300
18th North Carolina Regiment   10 / 320
28th North Carolina Regiment   10 / 351
33rd North Carolina Regiment   10 / 375
37th North Carolina Regiment   10 / 350

Scales' Brigade: Brigadier General Alfred Moore Scales
Brigade Staff—3 other staff and field officers

13th North Carolina Regiment   10 / 246
16th North Carolina Regiment   10 / 335
22nd North Carolina Regiment   10 / 271
34th North Carolina Regiment   10 / 315
38th North Carolina Regiment   10 / 229

Thomas' Brigade: Brigadier General Edward Lloyd Thomas
Brigade Staff—3 other staff and field officers

14th Georgia Regiment	10 / 345
35th Georgia Regiment	10 / 325
45th Georgia Regiment	10 / 311
49th Georgia Regiment	10 / 315

Divisional Artillery Battalion—Major William Thomas Poague
Battalion Staff—8 other staff and field officers

Madison Mississippi Light Artillery (Ward), consisting of
three 12-pounder Napoleons and one 12-pounder howitzer   4 guns / 97

Albemarle "Everett" Virginia Artillery (Wyatt), consisting of two 3-inch rifles,
one 12-pounder howitzer and one 10-pounder Parrott   4 guns / 105

Company C, 1st "Charlotte" North Carolina (Graham) consisting of two 12-pounder
Napoleons and two 12-pounder howitzers   4 guns / 130

Warrenton Virginia Artillery (Brooke), consisting of consisting of two 12-pounder
Napoleons and two 12-pounder howitzers   4 guns / 62

Pender's "Light Division" Totals

Division headquarters staff: 11
Infantry, including brigade staffs:190 companies / 6,400
Artillerists and supporting personnel: 4 companies / 403
Total Present and Under Arms: 194 companies / 6,814 / 16 guns

Third Corps Reserve Artillery—Colonel Reuben Lindsay Walker
Corps Reserve Artillery headquarters staff—3 other staff and field officers

McIntosh's Artillery Battalion: Major David Gregg McIntosh
Battalion Staff—8 other staff and field officers

Hardaway Alabama Artillery (Hurt), consisting of two 12-pounder Whitworth rifles and
two 3-inch rifles   4 guns / 80

Danville Virginia Artillery (Rice), consisting of
four 12-pounder Napoleons   4 guns / 120

2nd Rockbridge Virginia Artillery (Wallace), consisting of two
12-pounder Napoleons and two 3-inch rifles   4 guns / 70

"Jackson's Flying" Richmond Virginia Artillery (Johnson), consisting of
four 3-inch rifles   4 guns / 100

McIntosh's Artillery Battalion Totals

Artillerists and supporting personnel: 4 companies / 379
Total Present and Under Arms: 379 / 16 guns

Pegram's Artillery Battalion—Major William Johnson Pegram
Battalion Staff—8 other staff and field officers

Pee Dee South Carolina Artillery (Zimmerman), consisting of
four 3-inch rifles   4 guns / 69

"Crenshaw's" Richmond Virginia Battery (Johnston), consisting of two
12-pounder Napoleons and two 12-pounder howitzers   4 guns / 80

Fredericksburg Virginia Artillery (Marye), consisting of two 12-pounder Napoleons
and two 3-inch rifles   4 guns / 75

Richmond "Letcher" Virginia Artillery (Brander), consisting of two 12-pounder
Napoleons and two 3-inch rifles   4 guns / 70

Richmond "Purcell" Virginia Artillery (McGraw), consisting of four
12-pounder Napoleons   4 guns / 95

Pegram's Artillery Battalion Totals
Artillerists and supporting personnel: 5 companies / 398
Total Present and Under Arms: 398 / 20 guns

Third Corps Reserve Artillery Totals
Corps Reserve Artillery headquarters and staff   4
Artillerists and supporting personnel: 9 companies / 777
Total Present and Under Arms: 781 / 36 guns

Third Corps Totals
Corps and division headquarters staffs: 41
Infantry, including brigade staffs: 555 companies / 20,420
Artillerists and supporting/staff personnel: 20 companies / 2,003
Total Present and Under Arms: 575 companies / 23,019 / 84 guns

Stuart's Cavalry Division: **Major General James Ewell Brown Stuart**
Division headquarters staff—19 other staff and field officers

The three brigades (Hampton's, Fitz Lee's and W. H. F. Lee's under Chambliss) riding with Stuart during the time June 25 through July 2, 1863 raid suffered heavy losses, largely as a result of straggling. The strengths shown here reflect the numbers of combatants just before the campaign began.

Hampton's Brigade: Brigadier General Wade Hampton
Brigade Staff—4 other staff and field officers

1st North Carolina Cavalry 10 / 475
1st South Carolina Cavalry 10 / 400
2nd South Carolina Cavalry 10 / 250
Cobb's Georgia Legion Cavalry 11 / 375
Jefferson Davis Mississippi Legion Cavalry 6 / 300
Phillips' Georgia Legion Cavalry 7 / 325

Fitzhugh Lee's Brigade: Brigadier General Fitzhugh Lee
Brigade Staff—3 other staff and field officers

1st Maryland Cavalry Battalion 5 / 350
1st Virginia Cavalry 10 / 550
2nd Virginia Cavalry 10 / 450
3rd Virginia Cavalry 10 / 400
4th Virginia Cavalry 9 / 625
5th Virginia Cavalry 10 / 430

William Henry Fitzhugh "Rooney" Lee's Brigade:
Colonel John Randolph Chambliss, Jr.
Brigade Staff—3 other staff and field officers

2nd North Carolina Cavalry 10 / 275
9th Virginia Cavalry 10 / 600
10th Virginia Cavalry 10 / 475
13th Virginia Cavalry 10 / 450

Jones' Brigade: Brigadier General William Edmondson Jones
Brigade Staff—3 other staff and field officers

6th Virginia Cavalry 10 / 650
7th Virginia Cavalry 10 / 550
11th Virginia Cavalry 10 / 500
35th Virginia Cavalry Battalion 6 / 200

Robertson's Brigade: Brigadier General Beverly Holcombe Robertson
Brigade Staff—3 other staff and field officers

4th North Carolina Cavalry 8 / 500
5th North Carolina Cavalry 10 / 475

Divisional Artillery Battalion—Major Robert Franklin Beckham
Battalion Staff—8 other staff and field officers

1st Stuart Virginia Horse Artillery (Breathed), four 3-inch guns 4 guns / 105

2nd Stuart Virginia Horse Artillery (McGregor), consisting of two
12-pounder Napoleons and two 3-inch rifles 4 guns / 110

Washington South Carolina Horse Artillery (Hart), consisting of three 12-pounder Blakely rifles (the battery's fourth Blakely was lost at Upperville on June 21)   3 guns / 107

2nd Baltimore Maryland Horse Artillery (Griffin), consisting of four 10-pounder Parrotts   4 guns / 105

Ashby Virginia Horse Artillery (Chew), consisting of four guns, of which one was a 3-inch rifle and one a 12-pdr. Howitzer   4 guns / 100

Lynchburg "Beauregard Rifles" Virginia Horse Artillery (Moorman), consisting of one 12-pounder Napoleon and three 3-inch rifles   4 guns / 110

Stuart's Cavalry Division Totals

Division headquarters staff: 20
Cavalry, including brigade staffs: 202 companies / 9,626
Artillerists and supporting personnel: 6 companies / 646
Total Present and Under Arms: 208 companies / 10,292 / 23 guns

Attached Mounted Commands

Jenkins' Brigade: Brigadier General Albert G. Jenkins
Brigade Staff—3 other staff and field officers

14th Virginia Cavalry   11 / 375
16th Virginia Cavalry   11 / 375
17th Virginia Cavalry   10 / 300
34th Virginia Cavalry Battalion   7 / 250
36th Virginia Cavalry Battalion   5 / 200

Charlottesville "Kanawha" Virginia Horse Artillery (Jackson), consisting of two 12-pounder howitzers and two 3-inch rifles   4 guns / 100

Imboden's Command: Brigadier General John Daniel Imboden
Brigade Staff—3 other staff and field officers

18th Virginia Cavalry   10 / 900
62nd Virginia Mounted Infantry   12 / 1025
McNeill's Virginia Partisan Rangers   1 / 75

Staunton Virginia Horse Artillery (McClanahan), consisting of four 12-pounder howitzers and two 3-inch rifle   6 guns / 100

Attached Mounted Commands Totals—

Mounted commands, including staffs: 67 companies / 3,500
Artillerists and supporting personnel: 2 companies / 200
Total Present and Under Arms: 69 companies / 3,700 / 10 guns

**Recapitulation
of the
Army of Northern Virginia
in the Gettysburg Campaign**

Formation	Inf./Cav./Art. Companies	Guns	Infantry	Cavalry	Artill.	Total Present— All Arms*
ARMY HQ	2	-0-	-0-	85	-0-	102
FIRST CORPS						
HQ (Longstreet)	-0-	-0-	-0-	-0-	-0-	16
McLaws' Division	197	16	6,745	-0-	400	7,156
Hood's Division	186	19	7,200	-0-	427	7,638
Pickett's Division (-)	145	18	5,725	-0-	429	6,164
Corps Reserve Artillery	10	34	-0-	-0-	932	932
First Corps Totals—	538	87	19,670	-0-	2,192	21,910
SECOND CORPS						
HQ (Ewell)	1	-0-	-0-	30	-0-	47
Early's Division	172	16	5,128	-0-	302	5,442
Rodes' Division	219	16	8,017	-0-	408	8,439
Johnson's Division	213	16	6,108	-0-	377	6,494
Corps Reserve Artillery	8	31	-0-	-0-	692	692
Second Corps Totals—	613	79	19,253	30	1,779	21,114
THIRD CORPS						
HQ (Hill)	-0-	-0-	-0-	-0-	-0-	15
Heth's Division	165	15	7,095	-0-	415	7,518
Anderson's Division	207	17	7,625	-0-	404	7,336
Pender's Division	194	16	6,814	-0-	403	6,400
Corps Reserve Artillery	9	36	-0-	-0-	781	781
Third Corps Totals—	575	84	20,420	-0-	2,003	23,019
CAVALRY DIVISION						
HQ (Stuart)	-0-	-0-	-0-	-0-	-0-	20
Cavalry Brigades & Art.	208	23	-0-	9,626	646	10,272
OTHER MOUNTED TROOPS	64	10	-0-	3,500	200	3,700
*Including staffs, Totals for the Army	2,000	283	59,343	13,241	6,820	80,137
*Including staffs, Totals for the Army at Gettysburg	1,920	269	59,343	8,602**	6,510	75,188**

** These totals are based upon the three brigades riding with
Stuart being at full strength, which they clearly were
not by the time they arrived at Gettysburg. Allowing
for the reduction in Stuart's command due to
strategic consumption, the total for the cavalry was
probably no more than 5,000, and the total strength
for the army at Gettysburg being less than 72,000.
Of course, allowing for casualties suffered on the
different days of the battle, General Lee never had
the army's entire compliment on the field.

Appendix C

Order of Battle

Army of the Potomac
July 1-3, 1863

Army Headquarters
Major General George Gordon Meade, commanding

Headquarters Staff
49 other staff and field officers

Attached to Army Headquarters as Escort/Couriers
Oneida New York Cavalry numbering approximately 50 combatants

Other Units at Army Headquarters
Provost Guard (General Marsena Patrick),
consisting of 32 companies of infantry and cavalry
numbering about 1,100 combatants

Below is an outline of the units Meade had with him in Pennsylvania. Infantry strengths are represented by two figures: the number of companies, and number of combatants in the ranks. The entry for the 19th Indiana Regiment , for example, is followed by 10 / 308, which stands for 10 companies and 308 officers and men. Artillery batteries are also represented with two figures: the number of guns and number of combatants present. The entry for the 5th Maine Light Battery (Stevens), for example, is followed by a description of guns followed by: 6 guns / 136, which means the battery had six pieces serviced by 136 officers and men.

FIRST CORPS

Major General John Fulton Reynolds
Corps headquarters staff—13 other staff and field officers

First Division: Brigadier General James Samuel Wadsworth
Division headquarters staff—10 other staff and field officers

First Brigade ("The Iron Brigade"): Brig.Gen. S. Meredith
Brigade Staff and Band—14 other officers and other ranks

19th Indiana Regiment	10 / 308
24th Michigan Regiment	10 / 496
2nd Wisconsin Regiment	10 / 302
6th Wisconsin Regiment	10 / 340
7th Wisconsin Regiment	10 / 339

Second Brigade: Brigadier General Lysander Cutler
Brigade Staff and Band—16 other officers and other ranks

7th Indiana Regiment (arrived after battle on July 1)	10 / 420
76th New York Regiment	10 / 375
84th New York Regiment	10 / 195
95th New York Regiment	10 / 180
147th New York Regiment	10 / 380
56th Pennsylvania Regiment	9 / 252

First Division, First Corps, Totals

Division headquarters staff: 11
Infantry, including brigade staffs, engaged on July 1:   99 companies / 3,199
Total Present and Under Arms in the battle on July 1   99 companies / 3,210

Second Division: Brigadier General John Cleveland Robinson
Division headquarters staff—7 other staff and field officers

First Brigade: Brigadier General Gabriel Rene Paul (w)
Brigade Staff—2 other staff and field officers

16th Maine Regiment	10 / 275
13th Massachusetts Regiment	10 / 280
94th New York Regiment	10 / 338
104th New York Regiment	10 / 220
107th Pennsylvania Regiment	10 / 255

Second Brigade: Brigadier General Henry Baxter
Brigade Staff—3 other staff and field officers

12th Massachusetts Regiment	10 / 200
83rd New York Regiment	10 / 140
97th New York Regiment	10 / 180
11th Pennsylvania Regiment	10 / 205
88th Pennsylvania Regiment	10 / 210
90th Pennsylvania Regiment	10 / 191

Second Division, First Corps, Totals

Division headquarters staff: 8
Infantry, including brigade staffs, engaged on July 1: 110 companies / 2,500
Total Present and Under Arms in the battle on July 1:   110 companies / 2,508

Third Division: Major General Abner Doubleday

Division headquarters staff—12 other staff and field officers
Provost Guard: Company D, 149th Pennsylvania—60 officers and other ranks

First Brigade: (BrigadierGeneral Thomas A. Rowley): Colonel Chapman Biddle
Brigade Staff—7 other staff and field officers

80th New York Regiment	10 / 287
121st Pennsylvania Regiment	10 / 263
142nd Pennsylvania Regiment	10 / 242
151st Pennsylvania Regiment	10 / 487

Second Brigade: Colonel Roy Stone
Brigade Staff—1 other staff officer

143rd Pennsylvania Regiment	10 / 471
149th Pennsylvania Regiment	9 / 425
150th Pennsylvania Regiment	9 / 417

Third Brigade: Brigadier General George Jerrison Stannard
(three regiments of the brigade arrived after the conclusion of the fighting on July 1)
Brigade Staff—5 other staff and field officers

12th Vermont Regiment (guarding army trains–not present)	(10 / 500)
13th Vermont Regiment	10 / 480
14th Vermont Regiment	10 / 475
15th Vermont Regiment (guarding army trains–not present)	(10 / 500)
16th Vermont Regiment	10 / 475

Third Division, First Corps, Totals—(excluding Third Brigade)

Division headquarters staff and Provost Guard   1 company / 73

Infantry, including brigade staffs, engaged on July 1: 68 companies / 2,602

Total Present and Under Arms in the battle on July 1:   69 companies / 2,675

First Corps Artillery Brigade: Colonel Charles Shiels Wainwright

Brigade Staff—6 other staff and field officers

2nd Maine Light Battery (J. Hall), consisting of six 3-inch rifles   6 guns / 117

5th Maine Light Battery (Stevens), consisting of six 12-pounder
Napoleons—total of 6 guns / 136

Battery L, 1st New York Light Artillery (G. Reynolds) consisting of six
3-inch rifles   6 guns / 125

Battery B, 1st Pennsylvania Light Artillery (Cooper), consisting of four
3-inch rifles   4 guns / 105

Battery B, 4th U.S. Artillery (Stewart), consisting of six
12-pounder Napoleons   6 guns / 129

First Corps Artillery Totals

Corps Artillery headquarters and staff: 7

Artillerists and supporting personnel: 5 companies / 612

Total Present and Under Arms: 619 / 28 guns

First Corps Totals July 1, 1863

Corps and division headquarters staffs: 1 / 106

Infantry, including brigade staffs: 277 companies / 8,301

Artillerists and supporting/staff personnel: 5 companies / 619

Total Present and Under Arms: 283 companis / 9,026 / 28 guns

First Corps Total: all troops on the field or on detached duty

Corps and division headquarters staffs: 1 companies / 106

Infantry, including brigade staffs: 327 companies / 10,737

Artillerists and supporting/staff personnel: 5 companies / 619

Total Present and Under Arms: 333 companies / 11,462 / 28 guns

SECOND CORPS

Major General Winfield Scott Hancock

Corps headquarters staff—5 other staff and field officers

Attached to Corps Headquarters as Escort/Couriers

6th New York Cavalry Regiment, Companies D and K,
commanded by Captain Riley Johnson, numbering approximately 82 combatants

First Division: Brigadier General John C. Caldwell

Division headquarters staff—6 other staff and field officers

Provost Guard: Companies A, B and K, 53rd Pennsylvania—63 officers and other ranks
Provost Guard: Company B, 116th Pennsylvania—29 officers and other ranks

First Brigade: Colonel Edward E. Cross (k)

Brigade Staff—2 other staff and field officers

5th New Hampshire Regiment	10 / 179
61st New York Regiment	10 / 104
81st Pennsylvania Regiment	10 / 175
148th Pennsylvania Regiment	10 / 388

Second Brigade—"The Irish Brigade": Colonel Patrick Kelly (k)

Brigade Staff—1 other officer

28th Massachusetts Regiment	10 / 224
63rd New York Regiment	2 / 75
69th New York Regiment	2 / 75
88th New York Regiment	2 / 90
116th Pennsylvania Regiment	3 / 64

Third Brigade: Brigadier General Samuel Kosciuszko Zook (k)

Brigade Staff—3 other staff and field officers

52nd New York Regiment	10 / 134
57th New York Regiment	10 / 175
66th New York Regiment	10 / 147
140th Pennsylvania Regiment	10 / 515

Fourth Brigade: Colonel John Rutter Brooke
Brigade Staff—no others

27th Connecticut Regiment   3 / 74
2nd Delaware Regiment   10 / 230
64th New York Regiment   10 / 204
53rd Pennsylvania Regiment   7 / 135
145th Pennsylvania Regiment   10 / 202

First Division, Second Corps, Totals

Division headquarters staff and provost guard: 4 companies / 99
Infantry, including brigade staffs: 139 companies / 3,200
Total Present and Under Arms: 143 companies / 3,299

Second Division: Brigadier General John Gibbon
Division headquarters staff—5 other staff and field officers

Provost Guard: Company C, 1st Minnesota—approximately 40 officers and other ranks
Attached: Company C, 1st Massachusetts Sharpshooters—approximately 40
officers and other ranks

First Brigade: Brigadier General William F. Harrow
Brigade Staff—2 other staff and field officers

19th Maine Regiment   10 / 439
15th Massachusetts Regiment   10 / 239
1st Minnesota Regiment   10 / 269
82nd New York Regiment   10 / 305

Second Brigade ("The Philadelphia Brigade"):
Brigadier General Alexander Stewart Webb
Brigade Staff and Band—18 officers and other ranks

69th Pennsylvania Regiment   10 / 258
71st Pennsylvania Regiment   10 / 287
72nd Pennsylvania Regiment   10 / 380
106th Pennsylvania Regiment   10 / 279

Third Brigade: Colonel Norman Jonathan Hall
Brigade Staff—1 other officer

19th Massachusetts Regiment   10 / 160
20th Massachusetts Regiment   10 / 230
7th Michigan Regiment   10 / 165
42nd New York Regiment   10 / 130
59th New York Regiment   4 / 110

Second Division, Second Corps, Totals

Division headquarters staff, provost guard and attached   2 companies / 86
Infantry, including brigade staffs: 124 companies / 3,275
Total Present and Under Arms: 126 companies / 3,361

Third Division—Brigadier General Alexander Hays
Division headquarters staff—7 other staff and field officers
Provost Guard: 10th New York Infantry Battalion—80 officers and other ranks

First Brigade ("Gibraltar" Brigade): Col. Samuel S. Carroll
Brigade Staff—6 other staff and field officers
Provost Guard—36 combatants

14th Indiana Regiment   10 / 160
4th Ohio Regiment   10 / 299
8th Ohio Regiment   10 / 209
7th West Virginia Regiment   10 / 210

Second Brigade: Colonel Thomas Alfred Smyth
Brigade Staff—1 other staff officer

14th Connecticut Regiment   10 / 175
1st Delaware Regiment   10 / 240
12th New Jersey Regiment   10 / 345
108th New York Regiment   10 / 200

Third Brigade: Colonel George Lamb Willard (k)
Brigade Staff—1 other staff officer

39th New York Regiment   4 / 265
111th New York Regiment   10 / 390
125th New York Regiment   10 / 375
126th New York Regiment   10 / 400

Third Division, Second Corps, Totals—

Division headquarters staff and provost guard: 1 company / 88

Infantry, including brigade staffs: 114 companies / 3,315

Total Present and Under Arms: 115 companies / 3,403

Second Corps Artillery Brigade: Captain John G. Hazzard
Brigade Staff—3 other staff and field officers

Battery B, 1st New York Light Artillery, with the 14th New York Battery
attached (Sheldon), consisting of four 10-pounder Parrotts   4 guns / 117

Battery A, 1st Rhode Island Artillery (Arnold), consisting of
six 3-inch rifles   6 guns / 120

Battery B, 1st Rhode Island Artillery (Brown)
consisting of six 12-pounder Napoleons   6 guns / 124

Battery I, 1st U.S. Artillery (Woodruff), consisting of six
12-pounder Napoleons   6 guns / 110

Battery A, 4th U.S. Artillery (Cushing), consisting of six
3-inch rifles   6 guns /125

Second Corps Artillery Totals—

Corps Artillery headquarters and staff: 4

Artillerists and supporting personnel: 5 companies / 596

Total Present and Under Arms: 600 / 28 guns

Second Corps Totals

Corps and division headquarters staffs and attached personnel: 9 companies / 361
Infantry, including brigade staffs: 377 companies / 9,790
Artillerists and supporting/staff personnel: 5 companies / 600
Total Present and Under Arms: 391companies / 10,751 / 28 guns

THIRD CORPS
Major General Daniel Edgar Sickles
Corps headquarters staff—8 other staff and field officers

Attached to Corps Headquarters as Escort/Couriers
6th New York Cavalry Regiment, Company A,
commanded by Major William Elliott Beardsley, approximately 50 combatants

First Division—Major General David Bell Birney
Division headquarters staff—3 other staff and field officers

First Brigade: Brigadier General Charles K. Graham
Brigade Staff—no others

57th Pennsylvania Regiment	8 / 205
63rd Pennsylvania Regiment	10 / 240
68th Pennsylvania Regiment	10 / 320
105th Pennsylvania Regiment	10 / 274
114th Pennsylvania Regiment	10 / 250
141st Pennsylvania Regiment	10 / 209

Second Brigade: Brigadier General John Henry Hobart Ward

Brigade Staff—5 other staff and field officers

The two regiments of U. S. Sharpshooters, plus the 3rd Maine, were detached from the brigade prior to the beginning of the action on July 2. Following these detachments, Ward claimed his effective force of remaining regiments "was not 1,500."

20th Indiana Regiment	10 / 468
3rd Maine Regiment	10 / 210
4th Maine Regiment	10 / 202
86th New York Regiment	10 / 268
124th New York Regiment	10 / 240
99th Pennsylvania Regiment	10 / 300
1st U. S. Sharpshooters Regiment	10 / 250
2nd U. S. Sharpshooters Regiment	8 / 200

Third Brigade: Colonel Philippe Régis de Trobriand
Brigade Staff—no others

17th Maine Regiment	10 / 350
3rd Michigan Regiment	10 / 280
5th Michigan Regiment	10 / 230
40th New York Regiment	10 / 431
110th Pennsylvania Regiment	6 / 152

First Division, Third Corps, Totals

Division headquarters staff:	4
Infantry, including brigade staffs:	182 companies / 5,087
Total Present and Under Arms:	182 companies / 5,091

Second Division—Brigadier General Andrew Atkinson Humphreys
Division headquarters staff—3 other staff and field officers

First Brigade: Brigadier General Joseph Bradford Carr
Brigade Staff—1 other officer

1st Massachusetts Regiment   10 / 394
11th Massachusetts Regiment   10 / 239
16th Massachusetts Regiment   10 / 205
12th New Hampshire Regiment   10 / 224
11th New Jersey Regiment   10 / 275

26th Pennsylvania Regiment   10 / 385
84th Pennsylvania Regt (guarding army trains)   (10 / 240)

Second Brigade ("The Excelsior Brigade"): Colonel William R. Brewster
Brigade Staff—2 other staff and field officers

70th New York Regiment   10 / 288

71st New York Regiment   10 / 243
72nd New York Regiment   10 / 305
73rd New York Regiment   10 / 349
74rd New York Regiment   10 / 266
120th New York Regiment   10 / 383

Third Brigade ("The New Jersey Brigade"): Colonel George Childs Burling
Brigade Staff—1 other officer

2nd New Hampshire Regiment   10 / 354
5th New Jersey Regiment   10 / 206
6th New Jersey Regiment   10 / 207
7th New Jersey Regiment   10 / 200
8th New Jersey Regiment   10 / 170
115th Pennsylvania Regiment   9 / 150

Second Division, Third Corps, Totals

Division headquarters staff: 4

Infantry, including brigade staffs: 179 companies / 4,850

Total Present and Under Arms: 179 companies / 4,854

Third Corps Artillery Brigade: Captain George E. Randolph
Brigade Staff—1 other officer

2nd New Jersey Light Artillery (Clarke), consisting of six
10-pounder Parrotts   6 guns / 120

Battery D, 1st New York Light Artillery (Winslow), consisting of
six 12-pounder Napoleons   6 guns / 116

4th New York Light Artillery (Smith), consisting of six
10-pounder Parrotts   6 guns / 120

Battery E, 1st Rhode Island Light Artillery (Bucklyn), consisting
of six 12-pounder Napoleons   6 guns / 100

Battery K, 4th U.S. Artillery (Seeley), consisting of six
12-pounder Napoleons   6 guns / 105

Third Corps Artillery Totals

Corps Artillery headquarters and staff: 2
Artillerists and supporting personnel: 5 companies / 561
Total Present and Under Arms: 563 / 30 guns

Third Corps Totals

Corps and division headquarters staffs and attached personnel: 1 company / 67

Infantry, including brigade staffs: 361 companies / 9,937

Artillerists and supporting/staff personnel: 5 companies / 563

Total Present and Under Arms: 367 companies / 10,567 / 30 guns

FIFTH CORPS

Major General George Sykes
Corps headquarters staff—6 other staff and field officers

Attached to Corps Headquarters as Escort/Couriers
6th New York Cavalry Regiment, Companies D and H,
numbering approximately 65 combatants

Provost Guard: 12th New York Infantry, Companies D and E,
commanded by Captain Henry Wines Rider, approximately 95 combatants

First Division—Major General James Barnes
Division headquarters staff—3 other staff and field officers

First Brigade: Colonel William Stowell Tilton
Brigade Staff—no others

18th Massachusetts Regiment   10 / 139
22nd Massachusetts Regiment   11 / 137
1st Michigan Regiment   10 / 145
118th Pennsylvania Regiment   10 / 233

Second Brigade: Colonel Jacob Bowman Sweitzer
Brigade Staff—no others

9th Massachusetts Regiment (not present)   (10 / 300)
32nd Massachusetts Regiment   9 / 242
4th Michigan Regiment   10 / 342
62nd Pennsylvania Regiment   12 / 426

Third Brigade: Colonel Strong Vincent
Brigade Staff—no others

20th Maine Regiment   10 / 386
16th Michigan Regiment   11 / 198
44th New York Regiment   10 / 313
83rd Pennsylvania Regiment   10 / 188

First Division, Fifth Corps, Totals

Division headquarters staff: 4

Infantry, including brigade staffs: 13 companies / 2,752

Total Present and Under Arms: 113 companies / 2,756

Second Division ("The U. S. Regulars"): Brigadier General Romeyn Beck Ayres
Division headquarters staff—4 other staff and field officers

First Brigade: Colonel Hannibal Day
Brigade Staff—1 other officer

3rd U. S. Regiment   6 / 209
4th U. S. Regiment   4 / 120
6th U. S. Regiment   5 / 150
12th U. S. Regiment   8 / 330
14th U. S. Regiment   8 / 390

Second Brigade: Colonel Sidney Burbank
Brigade Staff—1 other officer

2nd U. S. Regiment   6 / 197
7th U. S. Regiment   4 / 116
10th U. S. Regiment   3 / 93
11th U. S. Regiment   6 / 286
17th U. S. Regiment   7 / 260

Third Brigade: Brigadier General Stephen Hinsdale Weed
Brigade Staff—3 other staff and field officers

140th New York Regiment   10 / 360
146th New York Regiment   10 / 365
91st Pennsylvania Regiment   10 / 175
155th Pennsylvania Regiment   10 / 288

Second Division, Fifth Corps, Totals

Division headquarters staff: 5
Infantry, including brigade staffs: 97 companies / 3,346
Total Present and Under Arms: 97 companies / 3,351

Third Division ("The Pennsylvania Reserves"): Brigadier General Samuel Wylie Crawford

Division headquarters staff—4 other staff and field officers

First Brigade: Colonel William McCandless
Brigade Staff—no others
Band—13 officers and other ranks

1st Pennsylvania Reserves Regiment   10 / 300
2nd Pennsylvania Reserves Regiment   9 / 190
6th Pennsylvania Reserves Regiment   10 / 265
13th Pennsylvania Reserves Regiment   10 / 245

Third Brigade: Colonel Joseph W. Fisher
Brigade Staff—no others

5th Pennsylvania Reserves Regiment   10 / 235
9th Pennsylvania Reserves Regiment   10 / 265
10th Pennsylvania Reserves Regiment   10 / 295
11th Pennsylvania Reserves Regiment   10 / 265
12th Pennsylvania Reserves Regiment   9 / 220

Third Division, Fifth Corps, Totals

Division headquarters staff: 5
Infantry, including brigade staffs and band: 88 companies / 2,295
Total Present and Under Arms: 88 companies / 2,300

Fifth Corps Artillery Brigade—Captain George E. Randolph
Brigade Staff—1 other officer

3rd Battery, Massachusetts Light Artillery (Walcott), consisting of
six 12-pounder Napoleons   6 guns / 95

Battery C, 1st New York Light Artillery (Barnes),
consisting of four 3-inch rifles—total of 4 guns / 62

Battery L, 1st Ohio Light Artillery (Gibbs), consisting of six
12-pounder Napoleons—total of 6 guns / 85

Battery D, 5th U. S. Artillery (Hazlett), consisting of six
10-pounder Parrotts—total of 6 guns / 68

Battery I, 5th U.S. Artillery (Watson), consisting of
four 3-inch rifles—total of 4 guns / 60

Fifth Corps Artillery Totals

Corps Artillery headquarters and staff: 2

Artillerists and supporting personnel: 5 companies / 372

Total Present and Under Arms: 374 / 26 guns

Fifth Corps Totals

Corps and division headquarters staffs and attached personnel: 4 companies / 181

Infantry, including brigade staffs: 298 companies / 8,393

Artillerists and supporting/staff personnel: 5 companies / 374

Total Present and Under Arms: 307 companies / 8,948 / 26 guns

SIXTH CORPS

Major General John Sedgwick

Corps headquarters staff—12 other staff and field officers

Attached to Corps Headquarters as Escort/Couriers

1st New Jersey Cavalry Regiment, Company L, numbering approximately 35 combatants;
and 1st Pennsylvania Cavalry Regiment, Company H, both commanded
by Captain William S. Craft, 55 combatants; and

First Division: Brigadier General Horatio Gouverneur Wright
Division headquarters staff—5 other staff and field officers
Provost Guard—4th New Jersey, Companies A, C and H,
totalling 80 officers and other ranks

First Brigade: Brigadier General Alfred T. A. Torbert
Brigade Staff—1 other officer
Band—16 officers and other ranks

1st New Jersey Regiment   10 / 286
2nd New Jersey Regiment   10 / 404
3rd New Jersey Regiment   10 / 314
15th New Jersey Regiment   10 / 437

Second Brigade: Brigadier General Joseph Jackson Bartlett
Brigade Staff—3 other staff and field officers

5th Maine Regiment   10 / 275
121st New York Regiment   10 / 400
95th Pennsylvania Regiment   10 / 300
96th Pennsylvania Regiment   10 / 300

Third Brigade: Brigadier General David Allen Russell
Brigade Staff—5 other staff and field officers

6th Maine Regiment   10 / 375
49th Pennsylvania Regiment   4 / 250
119th Pennsylvania Regiment   10 / 206
5th Wisconsin Regiment   10 / 400

First Division, Sixth Corps, Totals

Division headquarters staff and provost guard: 3 companies / 86
Infantry, including brigade staffs: 114 companies / 3,957
Total Present and Under Arms: 117 companies / 4,043

Second Division—Brigadier General Albion Parris Howe

Division headquarters staff—2 other staff and field officers

Second Brigade: Colonel Lewis Addison Grant
Brigade Staff—5 other staff and field officers
Band—10 officers and other ranks

2nd Vermont Regiment   10 / 475

3rd Vermont Regiment   10 / 395
4th Vermont Regiment   10 / 390
5th Vermont Regiment   10 / 364
6th Vermont Regiment   10 / 375

Third Brigade: Brigadier General Thomas Hewson Neill
Brigade Staff—3 other staff and field officers
Band—12 officers and other ranks

7th Maine Regiment   6216
33rd New York Regiment   — / 60
43rd New York Regiment   10 / 370
49th New York Regiment   10 / 300
77th New York Regiment   10 / 305
61st Pennsylvania Regiment   10 / 386

Second Division, Sixth Corps, Totals—

Division headquarters staff   3

Infantry, including brigade staffs and attached troops: 96 companies / 3,668

Total Present and Under Arms: 96 companies / 3,671

Third Division—Major General John Newton

Division headquarters staff—5 other staff and field officers

First Brigade: Brigadier General Alexander Shaler
Brigade Staff—2 other staff and field officers

65th New York Regiment   10 / 275
67th New York Regiment   10 / 356
122nd New York Regiment   10 / 375
23rd Pennsylvania Regiment   10 / 450
82nd Pennsylvania Regiment   10 / 250

Second Brigade: Colonel Henry Lawrence Eustis
Brigade Staff—no others

7th Massachusetts Regiment   10 / 300
10th Massachusetts Regiment   10 / 325
37th Massachusetts Regiment   10 / 662
2nd Rhode Island Regiment   10 / 300

Third Brigade: Brigadier General Frank Wheaton
Brigade Staff—no others

62nd New York Regiment   10 / 237
93rd Pennsylvania Regiment   10 / 230
98th Pennsylvania Regiment   10 / 325
102nd Pennsylvania Regt (guarding army trains)   (12 / 300)*
139th Pennsylvania Regiment   10 / 400

* The 102nd Pennsylvania was guarding part of the army's trains at Westminster. A detachment numbering 103 officers and other ranks from the regiment accompanied some wagons to the battlefield on July 3, and were then put in line of battle. This detachment is not included in the summary totals.

Third Division, Sixth Corps, Totals

Division headquarters staff: 6
Infantry, including brigade staffs: 130 companies / 4,490
Total Present and Under Arms: 130 companies / 4,496

Sixth Corps Artillery Brigade: Colonel Charles H. Tompkins
Brigade Staff—2 other staff and field officers

1st Battery, Massachusetts Light Artillery (McCartney), consisting of
six 12-pounder Napoleons   6 guns / 135

1st New York Independent Battery (Cowan), consisting
of six 3-inch rifles   6 guns / 100

3rd New York Independent Battery (Gibbs), consisting of six
10-pounder Parrotts   6 guns / 105

Battery C, 1st Rhode Island Light Artillery (Waterman), consisting of
six 3-inch rifles   6 guns / 110

Battery G, 1st Rhode Island Light Artillery (Adams), consisting of
six 10-pounder Parrotts   6 guns / 115

Battery D, 2nd U. S. Artillery (Williston), consisting of six 12-pounder
Napoleons   6 guns / 120

Battery G, 2nd U.S. Artillery (Butler), consisting of six
12-pounder Napoleons   6 guns / 100

Battery F, 5th U.S. Artillery (L. Martin), consisting of six
10-pounder Parrotts   6 guns / 115

Sixth Corps Artillery Totals

Corps Artillery headquarters and staff: 3
Artillerists and supporting personnel: 8 companies / 900
Total Present and Under Arms: 903 / 48 guns

Sixth Corps Totals for July 3*

Corps and division headquarters staffs and attached personnel: 5 companies / 198

Infantry, including brigade staffs: 340 companies / 12,115

Artillerists and supporting/staff personnel: 8 companies / 903

Total Present and Under Arms: 353 companies / 13,216 / 48 guns

* This corps numbered approximately 12,500 on the evening of July 2; the arrival of stragglers bolstered this number by July 3.

ELEVENTH CORPS

Major General Oliver Otis Howard
Corps headquarters staff—10 other staff and field officers

Attached to Corps Headquarters as Escort/Couriers/Guard
1st Indiana Cavalry Regiment, Companies I and K, approximately 50 combatants, 17th Pennsylvania Cavalry Regiment, Company K, approximately 35 combatants; and 8th New York Infantry, Independent Company, approximately 40 combatants

First Division—Brigadier General Francis Channing Barlow
Division headquarters staff—3 other staff and field officers

First Brigade: Colonel Leopold von Gilsa
Brigade Staff—1 other officer

41st New York Regiment   9 / 218
54th New York Regiment   10 / 185
68th New York Regiment   10 / 225
153rd Pennsylvania Regiment   10 / 375

Second Brigade: Brigadier General Aldelbert Ames
Brigade Staff—3 other staff and field officers

17th Connecticut Regiment   10 / 386
25th Ohio Regiment   10 / 220
75th Ohio Regiment   10 / 205*
107th Ohio Regiment   10 / 455

*A detachment of 104 combatants arrived on the field after the fighting on July 1 had concluded, and is not included in the totals shown here.

First Division, Eleventh Corps, Totals

Division headquarters staff: 4

Infantry, including brigade staffs: 79 companies / 2,275

Total Present and Under Arms: 79 companies / 2,279

Second Division: Brigadier General Adolph Wilhelm August Frederick Baron von Steinwehr

Division headquarters staff—4 other staff and field officers

First Brigade: Colonel Charles Robert Coster

Brigade Staff—4 other staff and field officers

134th New York Regiment   10 / 400

154th New York Regiment   10 / 190

27th Pennsylvania Regiment   9 / 215

73rd Pennsylvania Regiment   10 / 220

Second Brigade: Colonel Orland Smith

Brigade Staff—no others

33rd Massachusetts Regiment   10 / 450

136th New York Regiment   10 / 410

55th Ohio Regiment   10 / 315

73rd Ohio Regiment   10 / 338

Second Division, Eleventh Corps, Totals

Division headquarters staff: 5

Infantry, including brigade staffs: 79 companies / 2,543

Total Present and Under Arms: 79 companies / 2,548

Third Division—Major General Carl Schurz

Division headquarters staff—5 other staff and field officers

First Brigade: Brigadier General Alex. von Schimmelfennig

Brigade Staff—2 other staff and field officers

82nd Illinois Regiment   10 / 240

45th New York Regiment   10 / 375

157th New York Regiment   10 / 409

61st Ohio Regiment   10 / 247

74th Pennsylvania Regiment   9 / 250

Second Brigade: Colonel Wladimir Krzyzanowski
Brigade Staff—no others

58th New York Regiment   10 / 150
119th New York Regiment   10 / 210
82nd Ohio Regiment   10 / 312
75th Pennsylvania Regiment   9 / 206
26th Wisconsin Regiment   10 / 335

Third Division, Eleventh Corps, Totals

Division headquarters staff: 6

Infantry, including brigade staffs: 98 companies / 2,738

Total Present and Under Arms: 98 companies / 2,744

Eleventh Corps Artillery Brigade: Major Thomas W. Osborn
Brigade Staff—no others

13th Battery, New York Light Artillery (Wheeler), consisting of
four 3-inch rifles   4 guns / 105

Battery I, 1st New York Light Artillery (Wiedrich), consisting of
six 3-inch rifles   6 guns / 141

Battery I, 1st Ohio Light Artillery (Dilger), consisting of
six 12-pounder Napoleons   6 guns / 125

Battery K, 1st Ohio Light Artillery (Heckman), consisting of
four 12-pounder Napoleons   4 guns / 105

Battery G, 4th U. S. Artillery (Wilkeson), consisting of six
12-pounder Napoleons   6 guns / 110

Eleventh Corps Artillery Totals

Corps Artillery headquarters and staff: 1

Artillerists and supporting personnel: 5 companies / 586

Total Present and Under Arms: 587 / 26 guns

Eleventh Corps Totals

Corps and division headquarters staffs and attached personnel: 4 companies / 151
Infantry, including brigade staffs: 256 companies / 7,556
Artillerists and supporting/staff personnel: 5 companies / 587
Total Present and Under Arms: 265 companies / 8,294 / 26 guns

TWELFTH CORPS
Major General Henry Warner Slocum
Corps headquarters staff—7 other staff and field officers

Attached to Corps Headquarters as Provost Guard
10th Maine Infantry, Companies A, B and D, numbering 170 combatants

First Division—Brigadier General Alpheus Starkey Williams
Division headquarters staff—4 other staff and field officers

First Brigade: Colonel Archibald L. McDougall
Brigade Staff—no others

5th Connecticut Regiment   10 / 221
20th Connecticut Regiment   10 / 321
3rd Maryland Regiment   10 / 290
123rd New York Regiment   10 / 495
145th New York Regiment   10 / 245
46th Pennsylvania Regiment   10 / 262

Lockwood's Brigade (designated Second Brigade after the battle):
Brigadier General Henry Hayes Lockwood
Brigade Staff—2 other staff and field officers

1st Maryland Eastern Shore Regiment   10 / 490
1st Maryland Potomac Home Brigade   10 / 598
150th New York Regiment   10 / 609

Third Brigade: Colonel Silas Colgrove
Brigade Staff—no others
Band—16 officers and other ranks

27th Indiana Regiment   10 / 344
2nd Massachusetts Regiment   10 / 316
13th New Jersey Regiment   10 / 318
107th New York Regiment   10 / 319
3rd Wisconsin Regiment   10 / 260

First Division, Twelfth Corps, Totals
Division headquarters staff: 5

Infantry, including brigade staffs: 140 companies / 5,109

Total Present and Under Arms: 140 companies / 5,114

Second Division: Brigadier General John White Geary
Division headquarters staff—4 other staff and field officers
Provost Guard—28th Pennsylvania Infantry, Company B, approximately 40 combatants

First Brigade: Colonel Charles Candy
Brigade Staff—1 other officer

5th Ohio Regiment	10 / 300
7th Ohio Regiment	10 / 280
29th Ohio Regiment	10 / 310
66th Ohio Regiment	10 / 305
28th Pennsylvania Regiment	9 / 303
147th Pennsylvania Regiment	8 / 298

Second Brigade: Brigadier General Thomas L. Kane
Brigade Staff—2 other staff and field officers

29th Pennsylvania Regiment	10 / 357
109th Pennsylvania Regiment	10 / 149
111th Pennsylvania Regiment	10 / 191

Third Brigade: Brigadier General George Sears Greene
Brigade Staff—2 other staff and field officers

60th New York Regiment	10 / 273
78th New York Regiment	10 / 198
102nd New York Regiment	10 / 215
137th New York Regiment	10 / 384
149th New York Regiment	10 / 277

Second Division, Twelfth Corps, Totals

Division headquarters staff:	1 company / 45
Infantry, including brigade staffs:	137 companies / 3,848
Total Present and Under Arms:	138 companies / 3,893

Twelfth Corps Artillery Brigade: First Lieutenant Edward D. Muhlenberg
Brigade Staff—no others

Battery M, 1st New York Light Artillery (Winegar), consisting of
four 10-pounder Parrotts   4 guns / 90

Battery E (Knap's Independent), Pennsylvania Light Artillery (Atwell), consisting
of six 10-pounder Parrotts   6 guns / 139

Battery F, 4th U. S. Artillery (Rugg), consisting of six 12-pounder Napoleons—total of 6 guns / 90

Battery K, 5th U. S. Artillery (Kinzie), consisting of four 12-pounder Napoleons—total of 4 guns / 70

Twelfth Corps Artillery Totals

Corps Artillery headquarters and staff: 1
Artillerists and supporting personnel: 4 companies / 389
Total Present and Under Arms: 390 / 20 guns

Twelfth Corps Totals

Corps and division headquarters staffs and attached personnel: 4 companies / 228
Infantry, including brigade staffs: 277 companies / 8,957
Artillerists and supporting/staff personnel: 4 companies / 390
Total Present and Under Arms: 285 companies / 9,575 / 260 guns

CAVALRY CORPS

Major General Alfred A. Pleasonton
Corps headquarters staff—26 other staff and field officers

Attached to Corps Headquarters as Escorts/Couriers
6th U. S. Cavalry, 12 companies, approximately 471 combatants

First Cavalry Division—Brigadier General John Buford
Division headquarters staff—3 other staff and field officers

First Brigade: Colonel William Gamble
Brigade Staff—3 other staff and field officers

8th Illinois Cavalry   12 / 465
12th Illinois Cavalry   4 / 235
3rd Indiana Cavalry   6 / 310
8th New York Cavalry   12 / 586

Second Brigade: Colonel Thomas C. Devin
Brigade Staff—4 other staff and field officers
Escort: 6th New York Cavalry, Company L, numbering 35 combatants

6th New York Cavalry   6 / 215

9th New York Cavalry　12 / 365

17th Pennsylvania Cavalry　9 / 465

3rd West Virginia Cavalry　2 / 55

Reserve Cavalry Brigade: Brigadier General Wesley Merritt
Brigade Staff—3 other staff and field officers

6th Pennsylvania Cavalry　10 / 242

1st U. S. Cavalry　10 / 362

2nd U. S. Cavalry　12 / 407

5th U. S. Cavalry　12 / 306

First Cavalry Division Totals

Division headquarters staff:　4

Cavalry, including brigade staffs:　108 companies / 4,061

Total Present and Under Arms:　108 companies / 4,065

Second Cavalry Division—Brigadier General David McMurtrie Gregg
Division headquarters staff—2 other staff and field officers
Escort—1st Ohio Cavalry, Company A, numbering approximately 35 combatants

First Brigade: Colonel John B. McIntosh
Brigade Staff—6 other staff and field officers
Band—12 officers and other ranks

1st Maryland Cavalry　11 / 275

Purnell Maryland Legion Cavalry　1 / 65

1st New Jersey Cavalry　9 / 200

1st Pennsylvania Cavalry　11 / 350

3rd Pennsylvania Cavalry　12 / 335

3rd Pennsylvania Heavy Artillery (Rank), consisting of two
3-inch rifles　2 guns / 52

Second Brigade: Colonel Pennock Huey
(entire command at Westminster—not present at Gettysburg)
Brigade Staff—no others

2nd New York Cavalry　12 / 225

4th New York Cavalry　12 / 250

6th Ohio Cavalry　10 / 400

8th Pennsylvania Cavalry　12 / 350

Third Brigade: Colonel J. Irvin Gregg
Brigade Staff—7 other staff and field officers

1st Maine Cavalry   10 / 310
10th New York Cavalry   12 / 325
4th Pennsylvania Cavalry   12 / 250
16th Pennsylvania Cavalry   12 / 330

Second Cavalry Division Totals

Division headquarters staff: 1 company / 38
Cavalry, including brigade staffs, at Gettysburg: 90 companies / 2,467
Artillerists and supporting personnel: 1 company / 52
Total Present and Under Arms, at Gettysburg: 92 companies / 2,557 / 2 guns

Third Cavalry Division—Brigadier General Judson Kilpatrick

Division headquarters staff—2 other staff and field officers
Escort—1st Ohio Cavalry, Company C, numbering approximately 40 combatants

First Brigade: Brigadier General Elon John Farnsworth
Brigade Staff—no others

5th New York Cavalry   12 / 420
18th Pennsylvania Cavalry   12 / 500
1st Vermont Cavalry   12 / 600
1st West Virginia Cavalry   10 / 395

Second Brigade ("The Michigan Brigade"):

Brigadier General George Armstrong Custer
Brigade Staff—no others

1st Michigan Cavalry   12 / 425
5th Michigan Cavalry   12 / 640
6th Michigan Cavalry   12 / 475
7th Michigan Cavalry   10 / 385

Third Cavalry Division Totals

Division headquarters staff: 1 company / 43
Cavalry, including brigade staffs: 92 companies / 3,842
Total Present and Under Arms: 93 companies / 3,885

Cavalry Corps—First Horse Artillery Brigade—Captain James M. Robertson
Brigade Staff—1 other officer

9th Michigan Horse Artillery Battery (Daniels), consisting of six
3-inch guns   6 guns / 110

6th New York Horse Artillery Battery (Martin), consisting of
six 3-inch rifles   6 guns / 100

Combined Batteries B&L, 2nd U. S. Horse Artillery (Heaton), consisting of
six 3-inch rifles   6 guns / 95

Battery M, 2nd U. S. Horse Artillery (Pennington), consisting of
six 3-inch rifles   6 guns / 115

Battery E, 4th U. S. Horse Artillery (Elder), consisting of four
3-inch rifles—total of 4 guns / 60

Cavalry Corps—Second Horse Artillery Brigade—Captain John C. Tidball
Brigade Staff—1 other officer

Combined Batteries E & G, 1st U. S. Horse Artillery (Randol), consisting of
four 3-inch guns   4 guns / 85

Battery K, 1st U. S. Horse Artillery (Graham), consisting of
six 3-inch rifles   6 guns / 110

Battery A, 2nd U. S. Horse Artillery (Calef), consisting of
six 3-inch rifles   6 guns / 75

Battery C (Fuller) , 3rd U. S. Horse Artillery (detached with Huey's Brigade—not at
Gettysburg) consisting of six 3-inch rifles   6 guns

Cavalry Corps Artillery Brigade Totals—at Gettysburg

Corps Artillery Brigade headquarters and staff: 2
Artillerists and supporting personnel: 8 companies / 750
Total Present and Under Arms, at Gettysburg: 8 companies / 752 / 44 guns

Cavalry Corps Totals—at Gettysburg

Corps and division headquarters staffs and attached personnel: 14 companies / 583
Cavalry, including brigade staffs: 290 companies / 10,370
Artillerists and supporting/staff personnel: 9 companies / 804
Total Present and Under Arms, at Gettysburg: 313 companies / 11,757 / 46 guns

ARTILLERY RESERVE

Brigadier General Robert O. Tyler
Artillery Reserve headquarters staff—45 other staff and field officers

Attached to the Artillery Reserve as Guards
Headquarters Provost Guard—32nd Massachusetts Infantry, Company C,
numbering approximately 45 combatants
Ammunition Train Guard—4th New Jersey Infantry, 7 companies,
numbering about 260 combatants and Ordnance Detachment—11 combatants

First Regular Artillery Brigade—Captain Dunbar R. Ransom
Brigade Staff—1 other officer

Battery H, 1st U. S. Artillery (Eakin), consisting of six
12-pounder Napoleons   6 guns / 130

Combined Batteries F & K, 3rd U. S. Artillery (Turnbull), consisting of six
12-pounder Napoleons   6 guns / 110

Battery C, 4th U. S. Artillery (Thomas), consisting of six
12-pounder Napoleons   6 guns / 90

Battery C, 5th U. S. Artillery (Weir), consisting of
six 12-pounder Napoleons   6 guns / 100

First Volunteer Artillery Brigade—Major Freeman McGilvery
Brigade Staff—1 other officer

5th Battery, Massachusetts Light Artillery (Phillips), with the 10th New York Battery
attached, consisting of six 3-inch rifles   6 guns / 104

9th Battery, Massachusetts Light Artillery (Bigelow), consisting of six
12-pounder Napoleons   6 guns / 104

15th Battery, New York Light Artillery (Hart), consisting of four
12-pounder Napoleons   4 guns / 70

Combined Batteries C & F, Penn. Independent Light Artillery (Thompson),
consisting of six 3-inch rifles—total of 6 guns / 105

Second Volunteer Artillery Brigade—Captain Elijah D. Taft
Brigade Staff—1 other officer

Battery B (Brooker), 1st Connecticut Heavy Artillery (at Westminster—not at Gettysburg)
consisting of four 4 and one-half inch rifles   4 guns

Battery M (Pratt), 1st Connecticut Heavy Artillery (at Westminster—not at Gettysburg) consisting of four 4 and one-half inch rifles   4 guns

2nd Battery, Connecticut Light Artillery (Sterling), consisting of four James rifles and two 12-pounder howitzers   6 guns / 90

5th Battery, New York Light Artillery (Taft), consisting of six 20-pounder Parrotts   6 guns / 146

Third Volunteer Artillery Brigade—Captain James F. Huntington
Brigade Staff—1 other officer

1st Battery, New Hampshire Light Artillery (Edgell), consisting of four 3-inch rifles   4 guns / 85

Battery H, 1st Ohio Light Artillery (Norton), consisting of six 3-inch rifles   6 guns /100

Combined Batteries F & G, 1st Pennsylvania Light Artillery (Ricketts), consisting of six 3-inch rifles   6 guns / 144

Battery C, West Virginia Light Artillery (Hill), consisting of four 10-pounder Parrotts—total of 4 guns / 100

Fourth Volunteer Artillery Brigade—Captain Robert H. Fitzhugh
Brigade Staff—1 other officer

6th Maine Light Battery (Dow), consisting of four 12-pounder Napoleons   4 guns / 85

1st Maryland Battery (Rigby), consisting of six 3-inch rifles   6 guns / 106

1st Battery, New Jersey Light Artillery (Parsons), consisting of six 3-inch rifles   6 guns / 100

Battery G, 1st New York Light Artillery (N. Ames), consisting of six 12-pounder Napoleons   6 guns / 84

Battery K, 1st New York Light Artillery (N. Ames), with the 11th New York Battery attached, consisting of six 3-inch rifles   6 guns / 125

Artillery Reserve Totals—at Gettysburg

Artillery Reserve headquarters and staff: 8 companies / 362
Artillerists and supporting personnel: 19 companies / 1,988
Total Present and Under Arms, at Gettysburg: 27 companies / 2,350 / 106 guns

**Recapitulation
of the
Army of the Potomac
at the Battle of Gettysburg**

Formation	Inf./Cav./Art. Companies	Guns	Infantry	Cavalry	Artill.	Total Present— All Arms*
ARMY HQ	33	-0-	see total	see total	-0-	1,199
FIRST CORPS						
HQ (Reynolds)	-0-	-0-	-0-	-0-	-0-	14
First Division	99	-0-	3,210	-0-	-0-	3,210
Second Division	110	-0-	2,508	-0-	-0-	2,508
Third Division	69	-0-	2,675	-0-	-0-	2,675
Corps Artillery Brigade	5	28	-0-	-0-	619	619
First Corps Totals—	283	28	8,393	-0-	619	9,026 *
SECOND CORPS						
HQ (Hancock)	2	-0-	-0-	82	-0-	88
First Division	143	-0-	3,299	-0-	-0-	3,299
Second Division	126	-0-	3,361	-0-	-0-	3,361
Third Division	115	-0-	3,403	-0-	-0-	3,403
Corps Artillery Brigade	5	28	-0-	-0-	600	600
Second Corps Totals—	391	28	10,063	82	600	10,751
THIRD CORPS						
HQ (Sickles)	1	-0-	-0-	50	-0-	59
First Division	182	-0-	5,091	-0-	-0-	5,091
Second Division	179	-0-	4,854	-0-	-0-	4,854
Corps Artillery Brigade	5	30	-0-	-0-	563	563
Third Corps Totals—	367	30	9,945	50	563	10,567
FIFTH CORPS						
HQ (Sykes)	4	-0-	95	65	-0-	167
First Division	113	-0-	2,756	-0-	-0-	2,756
Second Division	97	-0-	3,351	-0-	-0-	3,351
Third Division	88	-0-	2,300	-0-	-0-	2,300
Corps Artillery Brigade	5	26	-0-	-0-	374	374
Fifth Corps Totals—	307	26	8,502	65	374	8,948
SIXTH CORPS						
HQ (Sedgwick)	2	-0-	55	35	-0-	103
First Division	117	-0-	4,043	-0-	-0-	4,043
Second Division	96	-0-	3,671	-0-	-0-	3,671
Third Division	130	-0-	4,496	-0-	-0-	4,496
Corps Artillery Brigade	8	48	-0-	-0-	903	903
Sixth Corps Totals—	353	48	12,265	35	903	13,216
ELEVENTH CORPS						
HQ (Howard)	4	-0-	40	85	-0-	136
First Division	79	-0-	2,279	-0-	-0-	2,279
Second Division	79	-0-	2,548	-0-	-0-	2,548
Third Division	98	-0-	2,744	-0-	-0-	2,744
Corps Artillery Brigade	5	26	-0-	-0-	587	587
Eleventh Corps Totals—	265	26	7,611	85	587	8,294

TWELFTH CORPS

HQ (Slocum)	3	-0-	170	-0-	-0-	178
First Division	140	-0-	5,114	-0-	-0-	5,114
Second Division	138	-0-	3,893	-0-	-0-	3,893
Corps Artillery Brigade	4	20	-0-	-0-	390	390
Twelfth Corps Totals—	285	20	9,177	-0-	390	9,575

CAVALRY CORPS

HQ (Pleasonton)	12	-0-	-0-	471	-0-	498
First Division	108	-0-	-0-	4,065	-0-	4,065
Second Division	92	2	-0-	2,505	52	2,557
Third Division	93	-0-	-0-	3,885	-0-	3,885
Horse Artillery	8	44	-0-	-0-	752	752
Cavalry Corps Totals—	313	46	-0-	10,926	804	11,757

ARTILLERY RESERVE

HQ (Tyler)	8	-0-	305	-0-	11	362
First Regular Brigade	4	·24	-0-	-0-	432	432
First Volunteer Brigade	4	22	-0-	-0-	385	385
Second Volunteer Brigade	2	12	-0-	-0-	238	238
Third Volunteer Brigade	4	20	-0-	-0-	431	431
Fourth Volunteer Brig.	5	28	-0-	-0-	502	502
Artillery Reserve Totals—	27	106	305	-0-	1,999	2,350

Including staffs—						
Totals for the Army						
at Gettysburg	2,624	358	66,261	11,243	6,839	85,683***

* The First Corps totals shown here are for those formations in the battle on July 1. The 420 members of the 7th Indiana (not shown in this total) arrived on the evening of July 1, and were engaged thereafter.

** Excludes formations detached and therefore not present at Gettysburg.

*** The totals for the Federal troop formations present at Gettysburg were substantially less than the "parade states" totals, also known as "present and under arms," taken on June 30, 1863 (see *Official Records*, vol. 27, part 1, p. 151). The dramatic difference in the numbers of troops in ranks on June 30 as compared to when the Federals appeared at Gettysburg graphically illustrates the different rates of "strategic consumption" that were shrinking the Army of the Potomac formations as they forced-marched to the battlefield.

Bibliography

Manuscripts, Papers and Special Collections

Archives du Service historique de l'état-major de l'armée at the Château de Vincennes (S.H.A.T.), France

    cartons: C^2 470, 472, 474, 475, 476, 477, 479, 481, 482, 483, 484, 485 and 724

College of William and Mary, Earl Gregg Swem Library, Williamsburg, Virginia

    J. A. Early Papers

Hill College, Harold B. Simpson History Complex, Confederate Research Center, Hillsboro, Texas

    D. H. Hamilton Manuscript
    John Hay letters and diary
    Harold B. Simpson Papers
    George T. Todd Manuscript
    Watson D. Williams letters
    Library of Congress, Washington, D. C.
    George Campbell Brown Papers
    Jefferson Davis Papers
    Douglas Southall Freeman Papers
    Jedediah Hotchkiss Papers
    Cadmus Wilcox Papers
    Louis T. Wigfall Papers
    Campbell Brown Papers. "Personal Narration."
    ——. "Answers to queries."
    Wilcox Papers, Box 1. Wilcox, Cadmus Marcellus. "Gettysburg, July 2 & 3, 1863,"
    Annotations to the official report written from Bunker Hill, Virginia, July 17, 1863,

Tennessee State Library and Archives, Nashville, Tennessee

    Brown, George Campbell. "Reminiscences."

University of North Carolina, Southern Historical Collection

    E. P. Alexander Papers

Longstreet Papers
Lafayette McLaws Papers

University of Texas at Arlington, Jenkings Garrett Special Collections, Arlington, Texas
North and South American Review, Austin, 1912.

University of Virginia, Special Collections, Charlottesville, Virginia
John W. Daniel Papers

U. S. Army Military History Institute, U. S. Army History Collection, Carlisle Barracks, Pennsylvania
John S. Mosby Papers

Official Publications

The War of the Rebellion: A Compilation of the Official Records of the Union and Confederate Armies, 130 volumes, Washington, D.C., 1880-1901, proved to be the principal source of information for *Last Chance for Victory: Lee and Gettysburg.* Equally important, especially with respect to the views of the Southerners that are the focus of this work, were the extensive writings contained in the *Southern Historical Society Papers,* 52 volumes, Richmond, 1876-1957.

Supplement to the Official Records of the Union and Confederate Armies, 100 volumes (Wilmington, 1994).

Maps

Bachelder, John B. *Gettysburg, July 1. Map # 1 through 14.* Dayton, 1996.
——. *Gettysburg, July 2. Map # 1 through 5.* Dayton, 1996.
——. *Gettysburg, July 3. Map # 6 through 9.* Dayton, 1996.
——. *Gettysburg, East Cavalry Field. Map # 4a; 10, 11 and 12.* Dayton, 1996.

Newspapers and Magazines

Augusta Daily Constitutionalist
Evening Bulletin
Frank Leslie's Illustrated Newspaper
Harper's Weekly
McClure's Magazine
National Intelligencer
National Republican
Philadelphia Inquirer

Philadelphia Weekly Times
Raleigh Semi-Weekly Standard
Richmond Daily Dispatch
Richmond Enquirer
Richmond Times
Richmond Whig and Public Advertiser
The Southern Illustrated News

Correspondence, Diaries, Journals, Letters, Memoirs & Speeches

Alexander, Edward Porter. Letter dated 17 March 1877, on the topic of "Causes of Lee's Defeat at Gettysburg," *Southern Historical Society Papers.* Volume 4. Richmond, 1877.

——. Letter dated 23 February 1878. *Southern Historical Society Papers.* Volume 5. Richmond, 1878.

——. "The Great Charge and Artillery Fighting at Gettysburg." *Battles and Leaders of the Civil War.* Volume 3. New York, 1888.

——. "Pickett's Charge and Artillery Fighting at Gettysburg." *The Century War Book.* New York, 1894.

——. *Military Memoirs of a Confederate.* New York, 1907.

——. *Fighting for the Confederacy: The Personal Recollections of General Edward Porter Alexander.* Edited by Gary W. Gallagher. Chapel Hill, 1989.

The Alexander Letters, 1787-1900. Edited by Marion Alexander Boggs. Athens, 1980.

Allan, William. "Gen Lee's Strength and Losses at Gettysburg." *Southern Historical Society Papers.* Volume 4. Richmond, 1877.

The Annals of the War, Written by Leading Participants North and South. Philadelphia, 1879.

Bachelder, John B. Letter to Fitzhugh Lee. 18 January 1875. Part of: "A Review of the First Two Days' Operations at Gettysburg and a Reply to General Longstreet." *Southern Historical Society Papers.* Volume 5. Richmond, 1878.

Barclay, Ted. *Letters From the Stonewall Brigade (1861-1864).* Edited by Charles W. Turner. Berryville, 1992.

Battles and Leaders of the Civil War. 4 volumes. New York, 1887-88.

Beale, George W. "A Soldier's Account of the Gettysburg Campaign." *Southern Historical Society Papers.* Volume 11. Richmond, 1883.

——. *A Lieutenant of Cavalry in Lee's Army.* Boston, 1918.

Benning, Henry L. "Notes by General Benning on Battle of Gettysburg." *Southern Historical Society Papers.* Volume 4. 1877.

Blackford, W. W. *War Years With Jeb Stuart.* Baton Rouge, 1993 reprint of the 1945 edition.

Bingham, Henry H. "The Second and Third Days—July 2 and 3, 1863," *Pennsylvania at Gettysburg,* volume 1. Harrisburg, 1904.

von Borke, Heros. *Memoirs of the Confederate War for Independence.* 2 volumes. New York, 1938.

Bourcet, Pierre-Joseph. *Mémories Historiques su la Guerre que les François Ont Soutenue en Allemagne 1757 Jusqu'en 1762.* Paris, 1792.

Bright, Robert A. "Pickett's Charge: The Story of It as Told by a Member of His Staff." *Southern Historical Society Papers*. Volume 31. Richmond, 1903.

Burgwyn, William H. S. "Unparalleled Loss of Company F, 26th North Carolina Regiment, Pettigrew's Brigade, at Gettysburg." *Southern Historical Society Papers*. Volume 28. Richmond, 1900.

Carrington, James McDowell. "First Day on Left at Gettysburg." *Southern Historical Society Papers*. Volume 37. Richmond, 1909.

Carter, William R. *Sabres, Saddles, and Spurs*. Edited by Walbrook D. Swank. Shippensburg, 1998.

de la Cabada [Cavada], Adolpho Fernandez. Adolpho Fernandez de la Cabada [Cavada] Diary. 2 July 1863. The Historical Society of Pennsylvania. Philadelphia, Pennsylvania.

Causby, Thomas E. "Storming the Stone Fence at Gettysburg." *Southern Historical Society Papers*. Volume 29. Richmond, 1901.

Chamberlayne, John Hampden "Address on the Character of General R. E. Lee." 19 January 1876. *Southern Historical Society Papers*. Volume 3. Richmond, 1877.

Chesnut, Mary Boykin. *A Diary from Dixie*. Edited by Ben Ames Williams. New York, 1905.

———. *Mary Chesnut's Civil War*. Edited by Vann Woodward. New Haven, 1981.

Clark, George. "Wilcox's Alabama Brigade at Gettysburg." *Confederate Veteran*. Volume 17. 1909.

Colston, Frederick M. "Gettysburg as We Saw It." *Confederate Veteran*. Volume 5. 1897.

Conolly, Thomas. *An Irishman in Dixie: Thomas Conolly's Diary of the Fall of the Confederacy*. Edited by Nelson D. Lankford. Columbia, 1988.

Cooke, John Esten. *Wearing of the Gray*. Bloomington, 1959 reprint f the 1867 original.

Crocker, James F. "Gettysburg—Pickett's Charge." *Southern Historical Society Papers*. Volume 33. Richmond, 1905.

Crotty, Daniel G. *Four Years Campaigning in the Army of the Potomac*. Grand Rapids, 1874.

DeLeon, Thomas C. *Four Years in Rebel Capitals: An Inside View of Life in the Southern Confederacy from Birth to Death*. New York, 1962.

Davis, Jefferson Finis. *The Rise and Fall of the Confederate Government*. 2 volumes. New York, 1881.

———. *Robert E. Lee*. Edited and with an Introduction and Notes by Harold B. Simpson. Hillsboro, 1966.

Dawes, Rufus R. *Service with the Sixth Wisconsin Volunteers*. Dayton, 1991 reprint of the 1890 original.

DeLeon, Thomas C. *Four Years in Rebel Capitals*. New York, 1962.

Douglas, Henry Kyd. *I Rode With Stonewall*. Chapel Hill, 1940.

The Wartime Papers of R. E. Lee, Clifford Dowdey, editor, and Louis H. Manarin, associate editor. New York, 1961.

Duke, J. W. "Mississippians at Gettysburg." *Confederate Veteran*. Volume 14. 1906.

Early, Jubal Anderson. *The Campaigns of Gen. Robert E. Lee. An Address by Lieu. General Jubal A. Early, before Washington and Lee University, January 19th, 1872*. Baltimore, 1872.

———. Letter on the topic of "Causes of Lee's Defeat at Gettysburg." *Southern Historical Society Papers*. Volume 4. Richmond, 1877.

———. "Supplement to General Early's Review—Reply to General Longstreet," *Southern Historical Society Papers*. Volume 4. Richmond, 1877.

——. "A Review" on the topic of "Causes of Lee's Defeat at Gettysburg." *Southern Historical Society Papers.* Volume 4. Richmond, 1877.

——. *Narrative of the War Between the States.* New York, 1989 reprint of the 1912 edition entitled *Autobiographical Sketch and Narrative of the War Between the States.*

Eggleston, George Cary. *A Rebel's Recollections.* New York, 1875).

Evans, Clement A., editor. *Confederate Military History: A Library of Confederate States History . . . Written by Distinguished Men of the South.* 12 volumes. Atlanta, 1889.

Farinholt, B. L. "Battle of Gettysburg—Johnson's Island." *Confederate Veteran.* Volume 5. 1897.

Frederick the Great on the Art of War. Translated and edited by Jay Luvaas. New York, 1966.

——. *Instructions to His Generals, 1747.* Edited by T. R. Phillips. Harrisburg, 1985.

Freeman, Douglas Southall, ed. *Lee's Dispatches: Unpublished Letters of General Robert E. Lee, C.S.A., to Jefferson Davis and the War Department of the Confederate States of America 1862-65.* New York, 1957.

Fremantle, Arthur J. L. *Three Months in the Southern States, April-June 1863.* Lincoln, 1991 reprint of the 1864 edition.

Fry, Birkett Davenport. "Pettigrew's Charge at Gettysburg." *Southern Historical Society Papers.* Volume 7. Richmond, 1879.

Garnett, John J. "The Artillery on the Gettysburg Campaign." *Southern Historical Society Papers.* Volume 10. Richmond, 1882.

"Garnett's Brigade at Gettysburg." *Southern Historical Society Papers.* Volume 3. Richmond, 1877.

"Gettysburg Charge." *Southern Historical Society Papers.* Volume 23. Richmond, 1895.

Gibbons, John. *The Artillerist's Manual, Compiled from Various Sources, and Adapted to the Service of the United States.* New York, 1863 edition.

——. *Personal Recollections of the Civil War.* New York, 1928.

Goree, Thomas Jewett. *The Thomas Jewett Goree Letters, Volume 1: The Civil War Correspondence.* Edited and annotated by Langston James Goree, V. Bryan, 1981.

Gordon, John B. *Reminiscences of the Civil War.* New York, 1903.

Govan, Gilbert E., and Livingood, James W., eds. *The Haskell Memoirs: The Personal Narrative of a Confederate Officer.* New York, 1960.

Hancock, Winfield S. Letter to Fitzhugh Lee, 17 January 1878. Part of "A Review of the First Two Days' Operations at Gettysburg and a Reply to General Longstreet." *Southern Historical Society Papers.* Volume 5. Richmond, 1878.

Haskell, Frank A. *The Battle of Gettysburg.* Edited by Bruce Catton. New York, 1957.

Hassler, William W., editor. *One of Lee's Best Men: The Civil War Letters of General William Dorsey Pender.* With a new Foreword by Brian Wills. Chapel Hill, 1999 reprint of the 1965 original.

Heth, Henry. Letter on the topic of "Causes of Lee's Defeat at Gettysburg," *Southern Historical Society Papers.* Volume 4. Richmond, 1877.

——. *The Memoirs of Henry Heth.* Edited by James L. Morrison, Jr. Westport, 1974.

Histories of the Several Regiments and Battalions From North Carolina in the Great War. Edited by Walter Clark. 5 volumes. Raleigh, 1901).

History of the 121st Regiment Pennsylvania Volunteers by the Survivors' Association: An Account from the Ranks. Philadelphia, 1906.

Hood, John Bell. Letter dated 28 June 1875, on the topic of "Causes of Lee's Defeat at Gettysburg." *Southern Historical Society Papers.* Volume 4. Richmond, 1877. ——. *Advance and Retreat.* New Orleans, 1880.

Hotchkiss, Jedediah. *Make Me a Map of the Valley: The Civil War Journal of Stonewall Jackson's Topographer.* Edited by Archie P. McDonald. Dallas, 1973.

——. *Confederate Military History.* Volume 3, *Virginia.* Atlanta, 1899.

Howard, Oliver Otis. *Autobiography of Oliver Otis Howard.* New York, 1908.

Hunton, Eppa. *Autobiography.* Richmond, 1933.

Imboden, John D. "The Confederate Retreat from Gettysburg." *Battles and Leaders of the Civil War.* Volume 3. New York, 1888.

Jefferson Davis: Constitutionalist; His Letters, Papers and Speeches. Collected and edited by Dunbar Rowland, LL.D. 5 volumes. Jackson, 1923.

Jones, John Beauchamp. *A Rebel War Clerk's Diary.* Edited by Earl Schenck Miers. New York, 1958 reprint of 1866 original: *A Rebel War Clerk's Diary at the Confederate States Capital.*

Johnson, W. Gart. "Reminiscences of Lee and of Gettysburg." *Confederate Veteran.* Volume 1. 1892.

Kean, Robert Garlick Hill. *Inside the Confederate Government.* Edited by Edward Younger. New York, 1957.

Kershaw, Joseph B. "Kershaw's Brigade at Gettysburg." *Battles and Leaders of the Civil War.* Volume 3. New York, 1888.

——. "Longstreet's Attack at the Peach Orchard and Wheatfield." *The Century War Book.* New York, 1894.

Ladd, David L. And Audrey J., eds. *The Bachelder Papers.* 3 volumes. Dayton, 1994.

Law, Evander McIvor. *"The Struggle for 'Round Top."* Battles and Leaders of the Civil War. Volume 3. New York, 1888.

——. "Gettysburg: The Second Day—The Confederate Side. The Struggle for 'Round Top.'" *The Century War Book.* New York, 1894.

Lee, Fitzhugh. "A Review of the First Two Days' Operations at Gettysburg and a Reply to General Longstreet." *Southern Historical Society Papers.* Volume 5. Richmond, 1878.

——. *Great Commanders: General Lee.* New York, 1898.

Lee, Robert E. *The Wartime Papers of R. E. Lee.* Edited by Clifford Dowdey and Louis H. Manarin. Boston, 1961.

Lee, Robert E., Jr. *Recollections and Letters of General Robert E. Lee.* New York, 1904.

Loehr, Charles T. "The 'Old First' Virginia at Gettysburg." *Southern Historical Society Papers.* Volume 32. Richmond, 1904.

Long, Armistead Lindsay. Letter dated 5 April 1876, on the topic of the "Causes of Lee's Defeat at Gettysburg." *Southern Historical Society Papers.* Volume 4. Richmond, 1877.

——. Letter dated April 1877, on the topic of the "Causes of Lee's Defeat at Gettysburg." *Southern Historical Society Papers.* Volume 4. Richmond, 1877.

——. *Memoirs of Robert E. Lee: His Military and Personal History, Embracing a Large Amount of Information Hitherto Unpublished.* New York, 1886.

Longstreet, Helen. *Lee and Longstreet at High Tide: Gettysburg in the Light of the Official Records.* Gainesville, 1904.

Longstreet, James. Letter dated 6 November 1877. *Southern Historical Society Papers.* Volume 5. Richmond, 1878.

——. "Account of the Campaign and Battle of Gettysburg." *Southern Historical Society Papers.* Volume 5. Richmond, 1878.

——. "Lee in Pennsylvania." *The Annals of the War, Written by Leading Participants North and South.* Philadelphia, 1879.

——. "The Mistakes of Gettysburg." *The Annals of the War, Written by Leading Participants North and South.* Philadelphia, 1879.

——. "Lee's Invasion of Pennsylvania," *Battles and Leaders of the Civil War.* Volume 3. New York, 1888.

——. Manassas to Appomattox. Philadelphia, 1896.

McGabe, W. Gordon. "Address at the Annual Reunion of Pegram Battalion Association." May 21, 1886. *Southern Historical Society Papers.* Volume 14. Richmond, 1886.

McClellan, Henry B. *I Rode with Jeb Stuart: The Life and Campaigns of Major General J.E.B. Stuart.* New York, 1994 reprint of the 1958 edition from the 1885 original.

McCrady, Edward, Jr. "Gregg's Brigade of South Carolinians in the Second Battle of Manassas." *Southern Historical Society Papers.* Volume 13. Richmond, 1885.

McIntosh, David Gregg. "Review of the Gettysburg Campaign." *Southern Historical Society Papers.* Volume 37. Richmond, 1909.

McKim, Randolph H. "Steuart's Brigade at the Battle of Gettysburg," *Southern Historical Society Papers.* Volume 5. Richmond, 1878.

——. "The Gettysburg Campaign." *Southern Historical Society Papers.* Volume 40. Richmond, 1915.

——. *A Soldier's Recollections.* New York, 1910.

McLaws, Lafayette. "Gettysburg." *Southern Historical Society Papers.* Volume 7. Richmond, 1879.

——. "The Battle of Gettysburg." *Philadelphia Weekly Press,* 21 April 1886.

——. "The Federal Disaster on the Left." *Philadelphia Weekly Press,* 4 August 1886.

——. "McLaws' Division and the Pennsylvania Reserves." *Philadelphia Weekly Press,* 20 October 1886.

Marshall, Charles. *An Aide-de-Camp of Lee, Being the Papers of Colonel Charles Marshall, Sometime Aide-de-Camp, Military Secretary, and Assistant Adjutant General on the Staff of Robert E. Lee, 1862-1865.* Edited by Sir Frederick Maurice. Boston, 1927.

——. "Events Leading up to the Battle of Gettysburg," *Southern Historical Society Papers.* Volume 23. Richmond, 1895.

Martin, Rawley. "The Battle of Gettysburg." *Southern Historical Society Papers.* Volume 32. Richmond, 1904.

Mayo, Joseph C. "Pickett's Charge at Gettysburg." *Southern Historical Society Papers.* Volume 34. Richmond, 1906.

Meade, George Gordon [Jr.], editor. *Life and Letters of George Gordon Meade.* 2 volumes. New York, 1913.

——. *With Meade at Gettysburg.* Philadelphia, 1930.

Mockbee, Robert T. "The 14th Tennessee Infantry Regiment." *Civil War Regiments: A Journal of the American Civil War.* Volume 5, number 1. 1996.

Mosby, John Singleton. Article entitled "The Confederate Cavalry in the Gettysburg Campaign." December 15, 1877. Republished in volume 3 of *Battles and Leaders of the Civil War.* 4 volumes. New York, 1887.

———. "Longstreet and Stuart." *Southern Historical Society Papers.* Volume 28. Richmond, 1895.

———. *Stuart's Cavalry in the Gettysburg Campaign.* New York, 1908.

———. "Heth Intended to Cover His Error." *Southern Historical Society Papers.* Volume 37. Richmond, 1909.

———. *Mosby's Memoirs.* Nashville, 1995 reprint of the 1917.

———. *Mosby's War Reminiscences.* Camden, 1996.

Napoleon I, Emperor. *Correspondance de Napoléon 1er.* 32 volumes. Paris, 1858-1870.

———. *The Military Maxims of Napoleon.* London, 1901.

———. *Supplément à la Correspondance de Napoléon, Lettres Curieuses Omises par le Comité de Publication, Rectifications.* Edited by Albert DuCasse. Paris, 1887.

Northrop, Lucius Bellinger. "Report of Commissary General Northrop." *Southern Historical Society Papers.* Volume 2. Richmond, 1876.

Oates, William C. "Gettysburg—The Battle on the Right." *Southern Historical Society Papers.* Volume 6. Richmond, 1878.

———. *Col. William C. Oates to Col. Homer R. Stoughton.* Not published. 1888.

———. *The War between the Union and the Confederacy and Its Lost Opportunities with a History of the 15th Alabama Regiment and Forty-Eight Battles in which It was Engaged.* Dayton, 1974 reprint of the 1905 original.

Ordnance Bureau, Richmond. *The Field Manual for the Use of the Officer on Ordnance Duty.* Richmond, 1862.

Owen, Edward. "In the Field and on the Town with the Washington Artillery." *Civil War Regiments: A Journal of the American Civil War.* Volume 5. Number 1.

Patrick, Marsena Rudolph. *Inside Lincoln's Army: The Diary of Marsena Rudolph Patrick, Provost Marshal General, Army of the Potomac.* Edited by David S. Sparks. New York, 1963.

Paul, William. "Severe Experiences at Gettysburg." *Confederate Veteran.* Volume 19. 1912.

Perrin, Abner. Letter of July 29, 1863, to Governor Milledge Luke Bonham, in Milledge L. Bonham, *A Little More Light on Gettysburg.* Pamphlet at the University of South Carolina. No date; reprinted in the *Mississippi Valley Historical Review,* March, 1938.

Perry, Edward Aylesworth. "Gettysburg." *Southern Historical Society Papers.* Volume 27. Richmond, 1899.

Pickett's Charge! Eyewitness Accounts. Edited by Richard Rollins. Redondo Beach, 1994.

Pickett, LaSalle Corbell. "My Soldier." *McClure's Magazine.* 1908.

Powell, Robert M. *Recollections of a Texas Colonel at Gettysburg.* Edited by Gregory A. Coco. Gettysburg, 1990.

Reagan, John H. *Memoirs: With Special Reference to Secession and the Civil War.* New York, 1906.

Robertson, Beverly H. "The Confederate Cavalry in the Gettysburg Campaign." *Battles and Leaders of the Civil War.* Volume 3. New York, 1888.

Ross, Fitzgerald. *A Visit to Cities and Camps of the Confederacy.* London, 1865.

Scheibert, Justus. Letter dated 21 November 1877, on the topic of "Causes of Lee's Defeat at Gettysburg." *Southern Historical Society Papers.* Volume 5. Richmond, 1878.

Scott, Winfield. *Memoirs: Written by Himself.* 2 volumes. New York, 1867.

Sherman, John, and Sherman, William Tecumseh. *The Sherman Letters: Correspondence between General and Senator Sherman from 1837 to 1891.* Edited by Rachel Sherman Thorndike. New York, 1894.

Shumate, W. T. "With Kershaw at Gettysburg." *Philadelphia Weekly Press,* 6 May 1882.

Smith, James Power. "General Lee at Gettysburg." *Southern Historical Society Papers.* Volume 33. Richmond, 1905.

——. "With Lee at Gettysburg." *Southern Historical Society Papers.* Volume 43. Richmond, 1920.

Soldier of the South: General Pickett's War Letters to his Wife. Edited by Arthur Crew Inman. Boston, 1928.

Sorrel, G. Moxley. *Recollections of a Confederate Staff Officer.* Second Edition. New York, 1917.

Speeches and Orations of John Warwick Daniel. Edited by Edward M. Daniel. Lynchburg, 1911.

Stevens, George T. *Three Years in the Sixth Corps.* Albany, 1866.

Stiles, Robert. *Four Years Under Marse Robert.* Marietta, 1995.

Talcott, T. M. R. "Stuart's Cavalry in the Gettysburg Campaign." A Review of John S. Mosby's book. *Southern Historical Society Papers.* Volume 37. Richmond, 1909.

——. "The Third Day at Gettysburg." *Southern Historical Society Papers.* Volume 41. Richmond, 1916.

Taylor, Michael W. "Ramseur's Brigade in the Gettysburg Campaign: A Newly Discovered Account by Capt. James I. Harris, Co. I, 30th Regt. N.C.T." *Gettysburg Magazine.* Number 17.

Taylor, Walter Herron. Memorandum on the topic of "Causes of Lee's Defeat at Gettysburg." *Southern Historical Society Papers.* Volume 4. Richmond, 1877.

——. Second Paper on the topic of "Causes of Lee's Defeat at Gettysburg." *Southern Historical Society Papers.* Volume 4. Richmond, 1877.

——. *Four Years With General Lee.* Edited and with a New Introduction by James I. Robertson, Jr. Bloomington, 1996 reprint of the 1877 original.

——. "Numerical Strength of the Armies at Gettysburg." *Southern Historical Society Papers.* Volume 5. Richmond, 1878.

——. "Reply to the Count of Paris." Letter dated March 8, 1878. *Southern Historical Society Papers.* Volume 5. Richmond, 1878.

——. "Lee and Longstreet." The *Richmond Times,* 14 June 1898. Reprinted in the *Southern Historical Society Papers.* Volume 24. Richmond, 1896.

——. *General Lee: His Campaigns in Virginia 1861-1865, with Personal Reminiscences.* Lincoln, 1994 reprint of the 1906 original.

——. *Lee's Adjutant: The Wartime Letters of Colonel Walter Herron Taylor, 1862-1865.* Edited by R. Lockwood Tower. Columbia, 1995.

The Civil War Memoirs of Captain William J. Seymour: Reminiscences of a Louisiana Tiger. Edited by Terry L. Jones. Baton Rouge, 1991.

Thomas, Henry W. *History of the Doles-Cook Brigade.* Atlanta, 1903.

"The Correspondence of Gen. Robt. E. Lee: Chancellorsville to Gettysburg—March to August, 1863." *Southern Historical Society Papers.* Volume 28. Richmond, 1900.

Todd, George T. *Sketch of History: The First Texas Regiment, Hood's Brigade, A. N. Va.* Waco, 1963 reprint of believed original 1909 publication.

Touched by Fire: Letters from Company D, 5th Texas Infantry, Hood's Brigade, Army of Northern Virginia, 1862-1865. Edited by Eddy R. Parker. Hillsboro, 2000.

Trimble, Isaac R. Letter dated 15 October 1875 on the topic of the "History of Lane's North Carolina Brigade." *Southern Historical Society Papers.* Volume 9. Richmond, 1881.

——. "The Battle and Campaign of Gettysburg." *Southern Historical Society Papers.* Volume 26. Richmond, 1898.

——. "The Campaign and Battle of Gettysburg." *Confederate Veteran.* Volume 25. 1917.

——. Letter to John C. Bachelder, February 8, 1883, in Volume 2. *The Bachelder Papers.* 3 volumes. Edited by David L. and Audrey J. Ladd. Dayton, 1994.

de Trobriand, Philip Régis. *Four Years With the Army of the Potomac.* Translated by George K. Dauchy. Boston, 1889.

Turner, Thomas T. "Gettysburg, Captain Turner." Typescript, J. A. Early Papers. College of William and Mary. Earl Gregg Swem Library. Williamsburg, Virginia.

Venable, Charles S. "General Lee in the Wilderness Campaign." *Battles and Leaders of the Civil War.* Volume 4. New York, 1888.

Walton, J. B. Letter on the topic of Gettysburg dated 15 October 1877. *Southern Historical Society Papers.* Volume 5. Richmond, 1878.

War Department, Richmond. *Regulations for the Army of the Confederate States, 1863.* Richmond, 1863.

Ward, William C. "Incidents and Personal Experiences on The Battle Field of Gettysburg," *Confederate Veteran.* Volume 8. 1900.

Welch, Spencer Glasgow. *A Confederate Surgeon's Letters to His Wife.* Marietta, 1954 reprint of 1911 original.

Wainwright, Charles S. *A Dairy of Battle: The Personal Journals of Colonel Charles S. Wainwright.* Edited by Allan Nevins. New York, 1998 reprint of the 1962 original.

Wilcox, Cadmus M. Letter dated 26 March 1877 from General C. M. Wilcox," on the topic of "Causes of Lee's Defeat at Gettysburg." *Southern Historical Society Papers.* Volume 4. 1877.

——. "General C. M. Wilcox on the Battle of Gettysburg," *Southern Historical Society Papers.* Volume 6. Richmond, 1878.

Williams, Alpheus S. *From the Cannon's Mouth: the Civil War letters of General Alpheus S. Williams.* Edited with an Introduction by Milo M. Quaife. Lincoln, 1995.

[Ambrose Wright]. "From Wright's Brigade." *Augusta Daily Constitutionalist.* July 23, 1863.

Young, Jesse Bowman. *The Battle of Gettysburg.* New York, 1913.

Young, Louis G. "Pettigrew's Brigade at Gettysburg." *North Carolina Regiments.* Volume 5.

Youngblood, William. "Unwritten History of the Gettysburg Campaign." *Southern Historical Society Papers.* Volume 38. Richmond, 1910.

Secondary Works

Adams, Michael C. C. *Our Masters the Rebels: A Speculation on Union Military Failure in the East, 1861-1865.* Cambridge, 1978. Retitled and reprinted as *Fighting for Defeat: Union Military Failure in the East.* Lincoln, 1992.

Adelman, Garry. "The Third Brigade, Third Division, Sixth Corps at Gettysburg." *Gettysburg Magazine.* Number 11.

——. "Benning's Georgia Brigade at Gettysburg." *Gettysburg Magazine.* Number 18.

Alexander, Bevin. *Robert E. Lee's Civil War.* Holbrook, 1998.

Allen, William. *Stonewall Jackson, Robert E. Lee, and the Army of Northern Virginia, 1862.* New York, 1995. This is a retitled work, combining the *History of the Campaign of Gen. T.J. (Stonewall) Jackson in the Shenandoah Valley of Virginia* (1880) and *The Army of Northern Virginia in 1862* (1882).

Ambrose, Stephen E. *Halleck: Lincoln's Chief of Staff.* Baton Rouge, 1990 reprint.

——. *Americans at War.* New York, 1997.

Andrews, J. Culter. *The South Reports the Civil War.* Princeton, 1970.

Andrus, Michael J. *The Brooke, Fauquier, Loudoun and Alexandria Artillery.* Lynchburg, 1990.

Archer, John M. *The Hour was One of Horror: East Cemetery Hill at Gettysburg.* Gettysburg, 1997.

Bachelder, John B. *Repulse of Longstreet's Assault.* New York, 1870.

Baldwin, James J., III. *The Struck Eagle: A Biography of Brigadier General Micah Jenkins and a History of the Fifth South Carolina Volunteers and the Palmetto Sharpshooters.* Shippensburg. 1996.

Banes, Charles H. *History of the Philadelphia Brigade.* Philadelphia, 1876.

Bates, David Homer. *Lincoln in the Telegraph Office.* New York, 1907.

Bennett, Brian A. "The Supreme Event in Its Existence—The 140th New York on Little Round Top." *Gettysburg Magazine.* Number 2.

Black, Robert C. *The Railroads of the Confederacy.* Chapel Hill, 1952.

Bigelow, John. *The Campaign of Chancellorsville: A Strategic and Tactical Study.* Dayton, 1991 reprint of the 1910 original.

——. *The Peach Orchard, Gettysburg, July 2, 1863.* Minneapolis, 1919.

Boritt, Gabor S., editor. *Why the Confederacy Lost.* New York, 1992.

——., editor. *Jefferson Davis's Generals.* New York, 1999.

Bowden, Scott, and Charles Tarbox. *Armies on the Danube 1809.* Revised and expanded edition. Chicago, 1989.

Bowden, Scott. *Armies at Waterloo.* Arlington, 1983.

——. *Napoleon's Grande Armée of 1813.* Chicago, 1990.

——. *Napoleon and Austerlitz.* Chicago, 1997.

Bradford, Gamaliel. *Lee the American.* New York, 1998 reprint of the 1927 revised edition, originally published in 1912.

Brock, Robert A., editor. *Gen. Robert Edward Lee: Soldier, Citizen, and Christian Patriot.* Richmond, 1897.

Brown, Bishop Robert R. *The Spiritual Pilgrimage of Robert E. Lee.* Shippensburg, 1998.

Busey, John W., and Martin, David G. *Regimental Strengths and Losses at Gettysburg,* Hightstown, 1994 corrected version to the 1982 original.

Caldwell, J.F.J. *The History of a Brigade of South Carolinians Known First as Gregg's and Subsequently as McGowan's Brigade.* Philadelphia, 1866.

Catton, Bruce. *Glory Road.* New York, 1964.

Chandler, David G. *Atlas of Military Strategy.* New York, 1980.

Campbell, Eric A. "The Severest Fought Battle of the War: Charles Wellington Reed and the Medal of Honor." *Civil War Regiments.* Volume 6. Number 3. Mason City, 1999.

Carmichael, Peter S. "'Every Map of the Field Cries Out about It:' The Failure of Confederate Artillery at Pickett's Charge." *Three Days at Gettysburg.* Edited by Gary W. Gallagher. Kent, 1999.

Chilton, F. B. *Unveiling and Dedication of Monument to Hood's Texas Brigade.* Houston, 1911.

Christ, Elwood W. *The Struggle for the Bliss Farm at Gettysburg; July 2nd and 3rd 1863.* Baltimore, 1994 second edition.

Clark, Walter, editor. *Histories of the Several Regiments and Battalions from North Carolina, in the Great War 1861-'65.* 5 volumes. Raleigh, 1901.

von Clausewitz, Carl. *On War.* Translated by J. J. Graham. 3 volumes. London, 1966.

Cleaves, Freeman. *Meade of Gettysburg.* Norman, 1960.

Coco, Gregory A. *A Concise Guide to the Artillery at Gettysburg.* Gettysburg, 1998.

Coddington, Edwin B. *The Gettysburg Campaign: A Study in Command.* New York, 1968.

Coggins, Jack. *Arms and Equipment of the Civil War.* New York, 1983.

Coker, James Lide. *History of Company G, 9th S.C. Regiment, Infantry, and of Company E, 6th Regiment, Infantry, S.C. Army.* Greenwood, 1979.

Collier, Calvin L. *"They'll Do to Tie To!" The Story of the Third Regiment, Arkansas Infantry, C.S.A.* Little Rock, 1959.

Connelly, Thomas Lawrence. *Autumn of Glory.* Baton Rouge, 1971.

Cooke, John Esten. *A Life of Gen. Robert E. Lee.* New York, 1871.

——. *Stonewall Jackson.* New York, 1899.

Cooksey, Paul Clark. "They Died as if on Dress Parade: The Annihilation of Iverson's Brigade at Gettysburg and the Battle of Oak Ridge." *Gettysburg Magazine.* Number 20.

van Creveld, Martin. *Technology and War.* New York, 1988.

Crute, Joseph H., Jr. *Confederate Staff Officers, 1861-1865.* Powhatan, 1982.

Current, Richard N. *Encyclopedia of the Confederacy.* 4 vols. New York, 1993.

Davis, Jefferson. *Robert E. Lee.* Edited and with an Introduction and Notes by Colonel Harold B. Simpson. Waco, 1966.

Davis, William C. *Jefferson Davis: The Man and His Hour.* Baton Rouge, 1991.

——. *The Cause Lost: Myths and Realities of the Confederacy.* Lawrence, 1996.

Davis, William C., Brian C. Pohanka,, and Don Troiani, editors. *Civil War Journal: The Leaders.* Nashville, 1997.

Davis, William C., and Julie Hoffman, editors. *The Confederate General.* 6 volumes. Harrisburg, 1991.

Deaderick, Barron. *Strategy in the Civil War.* Harrisburg, 1946.

DePalo, William A., Jr. *The Mexican National Army, 1822-1852.* College Station, 1997.

Dickert, D. Augustus. *History of Kershaw's Brigade.* Newberry, 1899.

Dodge, Theodore Ayrault. *Hannibal.* 2 volumes. New York, 1891.

——. *A Bird's-Eye View of Our Civil War.* New York, 1998 reprint of the 1897 original.

——. *Napoleon: A History of the Art of War from the Beginning of the French Revolution to the End of the 18th Century. With a Detailed Account of the Wars of the French Revolution.* 4 volumes. New York, 1904-1907.

Doubleday, Abner. *Chancellorsville and Gettysburg.* New York, 1994 reprint of the 1882 original.

Dowdey, Clifford. *Death of a Nation: The Story of Lee and His Men at Gettysburg.* New York, 1958.

——. *The Land They Fought For: The story of the South as the Confederacy, 1832-1865.* Garden City, 1955. Retitled and republished in 1992 as: *The History of the Confederacy 1832-1865.*

——. *Lee's Last Campaign: The Story of Lee and His Men Against Grant—1864.* Lincoln, 1993 reprint of the 1960 original.

——. *The Seven Days: The Emergence of Lee.* Boston, 1964.

——. *Lee.* Gettysburg, 1991.

Downey, Fairfax. *The Guns at Gettysburg.* New York, 1958.

Eaton, Clement. *A History of the Southern Confederacy.* New York, 1954.

Echoes of Glory: Arms and Equipment of The Union. Editors of Time-Life Books. Alexandria, 1991.

Eckenrode, H. J., and Bryan Conrad. *James Longstreet: Lee's War Horse.* Chapel Hill, 1986 reprint of the 1936 original.

Eicher, David J. *Robert E. Lee: A Life Portrait.* Dallas, 1997.

Eisenhower, John S. D. *So Far From God: The U.S. War with Mexico 1846-1848.* New York, 1990.

——. *Agent of Destiny: The Life and Times of General Winfield Scott.* New York, 1997.

Elliott, Charles Winslow. *Winfield Scott: The Soldier and the Man.* New York, 1937.

Elmore, Thomas L. "The Effects of Artillery Fire on Infantry at Gettysburg." *Gettysburg Magazine.* Number 5.

——. "Courage Against the Trenches: The Attack and Repulse of Steuart's Brigade on Culp's Hill." *Gettysburg Magazine.* Number 7.

——. "The Florida Brigade at Gettysburg." *Gettysburg Magazine.* Number 15.

——. "The Grand Cannonade: A Confederate Perspective." *Gettysburg Magazine.* Number 19.

Epstein, Robert M. "The Creation and Evolution of the Army Corps in the American Civil War." *Journal of Military History.* Volume 55. January 1991.

Esposito, Vincent J., editor. *The West Point Atlas of American Wars.* 2 volumes. New York, 1959.

Foertsch, Hermann. *The Art of Modern Warfare.* New York, 1940.

Frassanito, William A. *Gettysburg: A Journey in Time.* New York, 1975.

——. *Gettysburg: Then and Now. Touring the Battlefield with Old Photos 1863-1889.* Gettysburg, 1996.

——. *The Gettysburg Then and Now Companion.* Gettysburg, 1997.

Freeman, Douglas Southall. *R. E. Lee.* 4 volumes. New York, 1935.

——. *Lee's Lieutenants,* 3 volumes. New York, 1942-1944.

French, Steve. "Imboden's Advance to Gettysburg." *Gettysburg Magazine.* Number 20.

Furgurson, Ernest B. *Chancellorsville 1863: The Souls of the Brave.* New York, 1992.

Gallagher, Gary W. "Confederate Corps Leadership on the First Day at Gettysburg: A. P. Hill and Richard S. Ewell in a Difficult Debut." *The First Day at Gettysburg.* Kent, 1992.

——. "'Upon their Success Hang Momentous Interests': Generals," *Why the Confederacy Lost.* Edited by Gabor S. Boritt. New York, 1992.

——. "'If the Enemy Is There, We Must Attack Him:' Lee and the Second Day at Gettysburg." *The Second Day at Gettysburg.* Kent, 1993.

——., editor. *Lee the Soldier.* Lincoln, 1996.

——. *Lee and His Generals in War and Memory.* Baton Rouge, 1998.

Gannon, James P. *Irish Rebels, Confederate Tigers: A History of the 6th Louisiana Volunteer Infantry, 1861-1865.* Campbell, 1998.

——. The 6th Louisiana Infantry at Gettysburg." *Gettysburg Magazine.* Number 21.

"General E. M. Law at Gettysburg." *Confederate Veteran.* Volume 30. 1922.

Gettysburg. Film directed by Ronald F. Maxwell. 1993.

Goff, Richard D. *Confederate Supply.* Durham, 1969.

Gottfried, Bradley M. "Wright's Charge on July 2, 1863: Piercing the Union Line or Inflated Glory?" *Gettysburg Magazine.* Number 17.

——. "Mahone's Brigade: Insubordination or Miscommunication?" *Gettysburg Magazine.* Number 18.

——. "To Fail Twice: Brockenbrough's Brigade at Gettysburg. *Gettysburg Magazine.* Number 23.

Greene, A. Wilson. "From Chancellorsville to Cemetery Hill: O. O. Howard and Eleventh Corps Leadership." *The First Day at Gettysburg.* Kent, 1992.

Greezicki, Roger J. "Humbugging the Historian: A Reappraisal of Longstreet at Gettysburg." *Gettysburg Magazine.* Number 6.

Griffin, Massy. "Rodes On Oak Hill: A Study of Rodes' Division on the First Day of Gettysburg." *Gettysburg Magazine.* Number 4.

Grunder, Charles S., and Beck, Brandon H. *The Second Battle of Winchester, June 12-15, 1863.* Lynchburg, 1989.

Haines, Douglas Craig. "A. P. Hill's Advance to Gettysburg." *Gettysburg Magazine.* Number 5.

——. "R. S. Ewell's Command June 29-July 1, 1863." *Gettysburg Magazine.* Number 9.

Hamlin, Augutus C. *The Attack of Stonewall Jackson at Chancellorsville.* Fredericksburg, 1997 reprint of the 1896 original.

Harrison, Kathy Georg., and Busey, John W. *Nothing But Glory: Pickett's Division at Gettysburg.* Gettysburg, 1987.

Harrison, Kathy Georg. "Our Principal Loss was in this Place:" Action at the Slaughter Pen and at South end of Houck's Ridge, Gettysburg, Pennsylvania, 2 July 1863." *Gettysburg Magazine.* Number 1.

Harrison, Walter. *Pickett's Men: A Fragment of War History.* New York, 1870.

Harsh, Joseph L. "Battlesword and Rapier: Clausewitz, Jomini and the American Civil War." *Military Affairs 38.* 1974.

——. *Confederate Tide Rising: Robert E. Lee and the Making of Southern Strategy, 1861-1862.* Kent, 1998.

——. *Taken at the Flood: Robert E. Lee & Confederate Strategy in the Maryland Campaign of 1862.* Kent, 1999.

——. *Sounding the Shallows: A Confederate Companion for the Maryland Campaign of 1862.* Kent, 2000.

Hartwig, D. Scott. "The Defense of McPherson's Ridge." *Gettysburg Magazine.* Number 1.

——. "The 11th Army Corps on July 1, 1863—'The Unlucky 11th.'" *Gettysburg Magazine.* Number 2.

——. "It Struck Horror To Us All." *Gettysburg Magazine.* Number 4.

——. "'No Troops on the Field Had Done Better:' John C. Caldwell's Division in the Wheatfield, July 2, 1863." *The Second Day at Gettysburg.* Kent, 1993.

Heiser, John. "Action on the Emmitsburg Road, Gettysburg, Pennsylvania, July 2, 1863." *Gettysburg Magazine.* Number 1.

Hennessy, John J. *Return to Bull Run: The Campaign and Battle of Second Manassas.* New York, 1993.

Historical Times Illustrated Encyclopedia of the Civil War. Edited by Patricia L. Faust. New York, 1986.

Hoke, Jacob. *The Great Invasion of 1863.* Dayton, 1887.

Jacobs, Michael. *Notes on the Rebel Invasion of Maryland and Pennsylvania and the Battle of Gettysburg.* Philadelphia, 1864.

Jones, Archer. *Civil War Command and Strategy.* New York, 1992.

Jones, Terry L. *Lee's Tigers: The Louisiana Infantry in the Army of Northern Virginia.* Baton Rouge, 1987.

Johnson, Timothy D. *Winfield Scott: The Quest for Military Glory.* Lawrence, 1988.

Johnston, Angus J. *Virginia Railroads in the Civil War.* Chapel Hill, 1961.

Jorgensen, Jay. "Joseph W. Latimer, the 'Boy Major,' at Gettysburg." *Gettysburg Magazine.* Number 10.

——. "['Tige'] Anderson Attacks the Wheatfield." *Gettysburg Magazine.* Number 14.

Joslyn, Mauriel P. "'For Ninety Nine Years of the War:' The Story of the 3rd Arkansas at Gettysburg." *Gettysburg Magazine.* Number 14.

Keaveney, Arthur. *Sulla: The Last Republican.* Dover, New Hampshire, 1986 edition of 1982 original.

Keegan, John. *The Mask of Command.* New York, 1987.

Kegel, James A. *North with Lee and Jackson: The Lost Story of Gettysburg.* Mechanicsburg, 1996.

Krick, Robert K. *Parker's Virginia Battery, C.S.A.* Berryville, 1975.

——. *Lee's Colonels: A Biographical Register of the Field Officers of the Army of Northern Virginia.* 4th Edition, Revised. Dayton, 1992.

——. "Three Confederate Disasters on Oak Ridge: Failures of Brigade Leadership on the First Day at Gettysburg." *The First Day at Gettysburg.* Edited by Gary W. Gallagher. Kent, 1992.

Kross, Gary M. "'I Do Not Believe That Pickett's Division Would Have Reached Our Line:' Henry J. Hunt and the Union Artillery on July 3, 1863." *Three Days at Gettysburg.* Edited by Gary W. Gallagher. Kent, 1998.

Laine, J. Gary, and Morris M. Penny. *Law's Alabama Brigade in the War Between the Union and the Confederacy.* Shippensburg, 1996.

Laney, Daniel M. "Wasted Gallantry: Hood's Texas Brigade at Gettysburg." *Gettysburg Magazine.* Number 16.

Lash, Gary. "The Philadelphia Brigade at Gettysburg." *Gettysburg Magazine.* Number 7.

——. "'A Pathetic Story:' The 141st Pennsylvania (Graham's Brigade) at Gettysburg." *Gettysburg Magazine.* Number 14.

——. *The Gibraltar Brigade on East Cemetery Hill: Twenty-Five Minutes of Fighting, Fifty Years of Controversy.* Baltimore, 1995.

Lee, Fitzhugh. *General Lee: A Biography of Robert E. Lee.* New York, 1994 reprint of the 1894 original.

Linderman, Gerald F. *Embattled Courage: The Experience of Combat in the American Civil War.* New York, 1987.

Livermore, Thomas Leonard. *Numbers and Losses in the Civil War in America, 1861-1865.* Boston, 1909.

Long, E. B. *The Civil War Day by Day: An Almanac.* Garden City, 1971.

Long, Roger. "General Orders No. 72: "By Command of Gen. R. E. Lee." *Gettysburg Magazine.* Number 7.

——. "Over the Wall." *Gettysburg Magazine.* Number 13.

Longacre, Edward G. *The Cavalry at Gettysburg.* Lincoln, 1993.

Love, William. "Mississippi at Gettysburg." *Publications of the Mississippi Historical Society.* Volume 9. 1906.

Lyman, Theodore. *Meade's Headquarters, 1863-1865.* Boston, 1922.

McDermott, Anthony W., and Reilly, John E. *A Brief History of the 69th Regiment, Pennsylvania Veteran Volunteers.* Philadelphia, 1889.

McMurry, Richard M. *Two Great Rebel Armies: An Essay in Confederate Military History.* Chapel Hill, 1989.

——. "The Pennsylvania Gambit and the Gettysburg Splash." *The Gettysburg Nobody Knows.* Edited by Gabor S. Boritt. New York, 1997.

McNeily, John Seymore. "Barksdale's Mississippi Brigade at Gettysburg. 'Most Magnificent Charge of the War.'" *Publications of the Mississippi Historical Society.* Volume 14. 1914.

McPherson, James M. *What They Fought For: 1861-1865.* Baton Rouge, 1994.

Magner, Blake A. *Traveller & Company: The Horses of Gettysburg.* Gettysburg, 1995.

Mapp, Alf J., Jr. *Frock Coats and Epaulets: Psychological Portraits of Confederate Military and Political Leaders.* Landham, 1990.

Marcot, Roy. "Berdan's Sharpshooters at Gettysburg." *Gettysburg Magazine.* Number 1.

Marshall, S. L. A. *Men Against Fire.* New York, 1947.

May I Quote You, Stonewall Jackson? Observations & Utterances From the South's Great Generals. Edited by Randall Bedwell. Nashville, 1997.

Martin, David G. *Gettysburg: July 1.* Conshohocken, 1995.

Martin, Samuel J. *The Road to Glory: Confederate General Richard S. Ewell.* Indianapolis, 1991.

Miller, J. Michael. "Perrin's Brigade on July 1, 1863." *Gettysburg Magazine.* Number 13.

Moore, Jerrold Northrop. *Confederate Commissary General: Lucius Bellinger Northrop and the Subsistence Bureau of the Southern Army.* Shippensburg, 1996.

Moore, Robert H., II. *The Richmond Fayette, Hampden, Thomas and Blount's Lynchburg Artillery.* Lynchburg, 1991.

Morrison, James L., Jr. *The Best School in the World: West Point, the Pre-Civil War Years, 1833-1856.* Kent, 1986.

Motts, Wayne E. "To Gain a Second Star: The Forgotten George S. Greene." *Gettysburg Magazine.* Number 2.

Murray, R. L. *The Redemption of the 'Harpers Ferry Cowards': The Story of the 111th and 126th New York State Volunteer Regiments at Gettysburg.* New York, 1994.

Nelson, L. Patrick. "Reynolds and the Decision to Fight." *Gettysburg Magazine.* Number 23.

Nesbitt, Mark. *Saber and Scapegoat.* Mechanicsburg, 1994.

Nolan, Alan T. *Lee Considered: General Robert E. Lee and Civil War History.* Chapel Hill, 1991.

——. "R. E. Lee and July 1 at Gettysburg." *The First Day at Gettysburg.* Edited by Gary W. Gallagher. Kent, 1992.

O'Brien, Kevin E. "'To Unflinchingly Face Danger and Death:' Carr's Brigade Defends Emmitsburg Road." *Gettysburg Magazine.* Number 12.

O'Neil, Robert F., Jr. *The Cavalry Battles of Aldie, Middleburg and Upperville: June 10-27, 1863.* Lynchburg, 1993.

Palmer, Michael A. *Lee Moves North: Robert E. Lee on the Offensive from Antietam, to Gettysburg, to Bristow's Station.* New York, 1998.

Pemberton, John C. *Compelled to Appear in Print: The Vicksburg Manuscript of General John C. Pemberton.* Edited by David M. Smith. Cincinnati. 1999.

Pfanz, Donald C. *Richard S. Ewell: A Soldier's Life.* Chapel Hill, 1998.

Pfanz, Harry. *Gettysburg: The Second Day.* Chapel Hill, 1987.

——. *Gettysburg: Culp's Hill and Cemetery Hill.* Chapel Hill, 1993.

——. "'Old Jack' Is Not Here." *The Gettysburg Nobody Knows.* Edited by Gabor S. Boritt. New York, 1997.

Piston, William Garrett. *Lee's Tarnished Lieutenant: James Longstreet and His Place in Southern History.* Athens, 1987.

——. "Longstreet, Lee, and Confederate Attack Plan for July 3 at Gettysburg." *The Third Day at Gettysburg & Beyond.* Edited by Gary W. Gallagher. Chapel Hill, 1994.

Polley, Joseph Benjamin. *Hood's Texas Brigade: Its Marches, Its Battles, Its Achievements.* Dayton, 1976 reprint of the 1910 original.

Powell, David A. "A Reconnaissance Gone Awry: Capt. Samuel R. Johnston's Fateful Trip to Little Round Top." *Gettysburg Magazine.* Number 23.

Powell, William H. *The Fifth Army Corps, Army of the Potomac: A Record of Operations During the Civil War.* New York, 1896.

Priest, John Michael. *Into the Fight: Pickett's Charge at Gettysburg.* Shippensburg, 1998.

Raus, Edmund J. *A Generation on the March—The Union Army at Gettysburg.* Lynchburg, 1987.

Reardon, Carol. *Pickett's Charge in History and Memory.* Chapel Hill, 1997.

Reese, Timothy J. *Sykes' Regular Infantry Division, 1861-1864: A History of Regular United States Infantry Operations in the Civil War's Eastern Theater.* Jefferson, 1990.

Rhodes, Charles D. *Robert E. Lee, West Pointer.* Richmond, 1932.

Rhodes, John H. *The History of Battery B, First Regiment, Rhode Island Artillery.* Providence, 1914.

Robertson, James I., Jr. *The Stonewall Brigade.* Baton Rouge, 1977 reprint of 1963 original.

——. *General A. P. Hill: The Story of a Confederate Warrior.* New York, 1987.

Robertson, William Glenn. "The Peach Orchard Revisited: Daniel E. Sickles and the Third Corps on July 2, 1863." *The Second Day at Gettysburg.* Kent, 1993.

Roland, Charles P. "The Generalship of Robert E. Lee." *Grant, Lee, Lincoln and the Radicals: Essays on Civil War Leadership.* Evanston, 1964.

——. *Reflections on Lee: A Historian's Assessment.* Mechanicsburg, 1995.

Rollins, Richard. "Black Confederates at Gettysburg—1863." *Gettysburg Magazine.* Number 6.

——. "The Second Wave of Pickett's Charge." *Gettysburg Magazine*. Number 18.

——. *"The Damned Red Flags of the Rebellion:" The Confederate Battle Flag at Gettysburg*. Redondo Beach, 1997.

——. "Prelude to Pickett's Charge." *Columbiad: A Quarterly Review of the War Between the States*. Volume 2. Number 4. Leesburg, 1999.

——. "The Failure of Confederate Artillery in Pickett's Charge." *North & South*. Volume 3. Number 4. Tollhouse. 2000.

Sauers, Richard. *A Caspian Sea of Ink: The Meade-Sickles Controversy*. Baltimore, 1989.

Sears, Stephen W. *Landscape Turned Red*. New York, 1983.

——. *To the Gates of Richmond: The Peninsula Campaign*. New York, 1992.

——. *Chancellorsville*. New York, 1996.

Shue, Richard S. *Morning at Willoughby Run: July 1, 1863*. Gettysburg, 1995.

Shultz, David. *"Double Canister at Ten Yards:" The Federal Artillery and the Repulse of Pickett's Charge*. Redondo Beach, 1995.

Sibley, F. Ray, Jr. *The Confederate Order of Battle: The Army of Northern Virginia*. Shippensburg, 1996.

Simpson, Harold B. "General John Bell Hood—Southern Thunderbolt." Presentation given before the Civil War Round Table of Wiesbaden, Germany. Monday, 12 March 1956. Harold B. Simpson Papers. Hill College, Harold B. Simpson History Complex. Confederate Research Center. Hillsboro, Texas.

——. *Gaines Mill to Appomattox, Waco and McClennan County in Hood's Texas Brigade. A History of Co. B, 4th Texas Regiment*. Waco, 1963.

——. *Hood's Texas Brigade: Lee's Grenadier Guard*. Dallas, 1983 reprint of the 1970 edition.

Simpson, Brooks, D. "Command Relationships at Gettysburg." *Civil War Generals in Defeat*. Edited by Steven E. Woodworth. Lawrence, 1999.

Slocum, Charles E. *The Life and Times of Major General Henry Warner Slocum*. Toledo, 1913.

Smith, Frederick E. *Waterloo*. London, 1970.

Smith, Gerald J. *"One of the Most Daring of Men," The Life of Confederate General William Tatum Wofford*. Journal of Confederate History Series. Volume XVI. John McGlone, Series Editor. Murfreesboro, 1997.

Smith, Timothy H. *The Story of Lee's Headquarters; Gettysburg, Pennsylvania*. Gettysburg, 1995.

Stephens, Alexander H. *A Constitutional View of the Late War Between the States; its Causes, Character, Conduct and Results*. 2 volumes. Philadelphia, 1870.

Stewart, George R. *Pickett's Charge: A Microhistory of the Final Attack at Gettysburg, July 3, 1863*. Dayton, 1983.

Strode, Hudson. *Jefferson Davis: Confederate President*. New York, 1959.

Storch, Marc, and Beth Storch. "What a Deadly Trap We Were In." *Gettysburg Magazine*. Number 4.

Stuart, James Ewell Brown, IV. "Jeb Stuart—The Making of the Man." *Confederate History Symposium: Confederate Horse*. April 1, 2000. Hill College. Hillsboro, Texas.

Sumrall, Alan K. *Battle Flags of Texans in the Confederacy*. Austin, 1995.

Swanberg, W. A. *Sickles the Incredible*. New York, 1956.

Swinton, William. *Campaigns of the Army of the Potomac*. New York, 1882.

Tagg, Larry. *The Generals of Gettysburg: The Leaders of America's Greatest Battle.* Campbell, 1998.

Tanner, Robert G. *Stonewall in the Valley.* New York, 1976.

Taylor, Emerson Gifford. *Gouverneur Kemble Warren: The Life and Letters of an American Soldier.* New York, 1932.

Taylor, Michael W. "North Carolina in the Pickett-Pettigrew-Trimble Charge at Gettysburg." *Gettysburg Magazine.* Number 8.

Thomas, Emory M. *The Confederate Nation 1861-1865.* New York, 1979.

——. *Bold Dragoon: The Life of J.E.B. Stuart.* New York, 1986.

——. *Robert E. Lee: A Biography.* New York, 1995.

——. "Eggs, Aldie, Shepherdstown, and J. E. B. Stuart." *The Gettysburg Nobody Knows.* Edited by Gabor S. Boritt. New York, 1997.

——. "Davis, Lee and Confederate Grand Strategy." *Jefferson Davis's Generals.* Edited by Gabor S. Boritt. New York, 1999.

——. *Robert E. Lee: An Album.* New York, 2000.

Thomas, John Peyre. *The Career and Character of General Micah Jenkins, C.S.A.* Columbia, 1903.

Thomason, John W., Jr. *Jeb Stuart.* New York, 1930.

Trinque, Bruce A. "Confederate Battle Flags in the July 3rd Charge." *Gettysburg Magazine.* Number 21.

Tucker, Glenn. *High Tide at Gettysburg.* Dayton, 1973 revised edition of the 1958 original.

——. *Hancock the Superb.* Indianapolis, 1960.

——. *Lee and Longstreet at Gettysburg.* Dayton, 1982 reprint of the 1968 original.

Turner, George Edgar. *Victory Rode the Rails.* Indianapolis, 1953.

Vandiver, Frank Everson. *Rebel Brass: The Confederate Command System.* Baton Rouge, 1956.

——. "Jefferson Davis and Confederate Strategy." *The American Tragedy.* Edited by Bernard Mayo. Hampden-Sydney, 1959.

——. *Their Tattered Flags: The Epic of the Confederacy.* College Station, 1987 reprint of the 1970 original.

——. "Lee during the War." *1984 Confederate History Symposium.* Hill College. Hillsboro, Texas. Edited by D. B. Patterson. Hillsboro, 1984.

——. *Ploughshares into Swords: Josiah Gorgas and Confederate Ordnance.* College Station, 1994 edition of the 1952 original publication.

Ward, Joseph R. *History of the One Hundred and Sixth Regiment, Pennsylvania Volunteers.* Philadelphia, 1883.

Welsh, Jack D., M.D. *Medical Histories of Confederate Generals.* Kent, 1995.

Wert, Jeffry D. *General James Longstreet: The Confederacy's Most Controversial Soldier.* New York, 1993.

——. *A Brotherhood of Valor: The Common Soldiers of the Stonewall Brigade, C.S.A., and the Iron Brigade, U.S.A.* New York, 1999.

Wheeler, Richard. *Witness to Gettysburg.* New York, 1987.

White, W. S. *Richmond Howitzers Battalion.* Richmond, 1880.

Williams, Kenneth. *Lincoln Finds a General: A Military Study of the Civil War.* 5 volumes. New York, 1949-59.

Williamson, James J. *Mosby's Rangers.* New York, 1896.

Winschel, Terrence J. "Their Supreme Moment: Barksdale's Brigade at Gettysburg." *Gettysburg Magazine*. Number 1.

——. "Heavy Was Their Loss: Joe Davis' Brigade at Gettysburg." *Gettysburg Magazine*. Numbers 2 and 3.

——. "Posey's Brigade at Gettysburg." *Gettysburg Magazine*. Numbers 4 and 5.

——. *Triumph & Defeat: The Vicksburg Campaign*. Mason City. 1999.

Wise, Jennings C. *The Long Arm of Lee: The History of the Artillery of the Army of Northern Virginia, with a Brief Account of the Confederate Bureau of Ordnance*. 2 volumes. Lynchburg, 1915.

——. "The Boy Gunners of Lee." *Southern Historical Society Papers*. Volume 42. Richmond, 1917.

Wittenberg, Eric J. *Gettysburg's Forgotten Cavalry Actions*. Gettysburg, 1998.

Woodworth, Steven E. *Jefferson Davis and His Generals: The Failure of Confederate Command in the West*. Lawrence, 1990.

——. *Davis and Lee at War*. Lawrence, 1995.

Wright, Marcus J. *Great Commanders: General Scott*. New York, 1894.

Wyckoff, Mac. "Kershaw's Brigade at Gettysburg." *Gettysburg Magazine*. Number 5.

——. *A History of the 2nd South Carolina Infantry: 1861-65*. Fredericksburg, 1994.

Young, Kevin R. *To the Tyrants Never Yield: A Texas Civil War Sampler*. Plano, 1992.

Miscellaneous

Gettysburg National Military Park Tablets

INDEX